Lecture Notes in Business Information Processing 102

Runtong Zhang Juliang Zhang
Zhenji Zhang Joaquim Filipe
José Cordeiro (Eds.)

Enterprise Information Systems

13th International Conference, ICEIS 2011
Beijing, China, June 8-11, 2011
Revised Selected Papers

Springer

Volume Editors

Runtong Zhang
Beijing Jiaotong University, China
E-mail: rtzhang@bjtu.edu.cn

Juliang Zhang
Beijing Jiaotong University, China
E-mail: zhangjl@bjtu.edu.cn

Zhenji Zhang
Beijing Jiaotong University, China
E-mail: zhjzhang@bjtu.edu.cn

Joaquim Filipe
Institute for Systems and Technologies of Information,
Control and Communication (INSTICC)
and Instituto Politécnico de Setúbal (IPS), Portugal
E-mail: joaquim.filipe@estsetubal.ips.pt

José Cordeiro
Institute for Systems and Technologies of Information,
Control and Communication (INSTICC)
and Instituto Politécnico de Setúbal (IPS), Portugal
E-mail: jcordeir@est.ips.pt

ISSN 1865-1348 e-ISSN 1865-1356
ISBN 978-3-642-29957-5 e-ISBN 978-3-642-29958-2
DOI 10.1007/978-3-642-29958-2
Springer Heidelberg Dordrecht London New York

Library of Congress Control Number: 2012936240

ACM Computing Classification (1998): J.1, H.3, H.4, D.2, H.5

Typesetting: Camera-ready by author, data conversion by Scientific Publishing Services, Chennai, India

Printed on acid-free paper

Springer is part of Springer Science+Business Media (www.springer.com)

Preface

The present book includes extended and revised versions of a set of selected papers from the 13th International Conference on Enterprise Information Systems (ICEIS 2011), held in Beijing, China, during June 8–11, 2011, and hosted by Beijing Jiaotong University. The conference was sponsored by the Institute for Systems and Technologies of Information, Control and Communication (INSTICC), the Chinese Academy of Engineering, the National Natural Science Foundation of China (NSFC), K.C. Wong Education Foundation (Hong Kong), University of Reading, UFIDA Software Co., Ltd, and the Publishing House of Electronics Industry (PHEI). It was also held in cooperation with the Association for Advancement of Artificial Intelligence (AAAI), the Association for Computation Machinery (ACM) Special Interest Group on Artificial Intelligence (SIGART), the ACM Special Interest Group on Management Information Systems (SIGMIS), and the Institute of Electronics Information and Communication Engineers (IEICE) Special Interest Group on Software Interprise Modelling (SWIM).

The conference was organized in six simultaneous tracks: *Databases and Information Systems Integration, Artificial Intelligence and Decision Support Systems, Information Systems Analysis and Specification, Software Agents and Internet Computing, Human–Computer Interaction* and *E*nterprise Architecture. The book is based on the same structure.

ICEIS 2011 received 402 paper submissions, from 53 countries and districts on all continents. After a blind review process, only 57 were accepted as full papers, of which 27 were selected for inclusion in this book, based on the classifications provided by the Program Committee. The selected papers reflect state-of-the-art research work that is often oriented toward real-world applications and highlight the benefits of information systems and technology for industry and services, thus making a bridge between the academic and enterprise worlds. These high-quality standards will be maintained and reinforced at ICEIS 2012, to be held in Wroclaw, Poland, and in future editions of this conference.

Furthermore, ICEIS 2011 included eight plenary keynote lectures given by Harold Krikke (Tilburg University, The Netherlands), Xuewei Li (Beijing Jiaotong University, China), Kecheng Liu (University of Reading, UK), Leszek A. Maciaszek (Macquarie University, Australia / University of Economics, Poland), Yannis A. Phillis (Technical University of Crete, Greece), Shoubo Xu (Chinese Academy of Engineering / Beijing Jiaotong University, China), Yulin Zheng (UFIDA, China) and Lida Xu (Old Dominion University, USA). We would like to express our appreciation to all of them and in particular to those who took the time to contribute with a paper to this book.

On behalf of the conference Organizing Committee, we would like to thank all participants. First of all the authors, whose quality work is the essence of the conference, and the members of the Program Committee, who helped us with their expertise and diligence in reviewing the papers. As we all know, organizing a conference requires the effort of many individuals. We wish to thank also all the members of our Organizing Committee, whose work and commitment were invaluable.

January 2012

Juliang Zhang
Zhenji Zhang
Joaquim Filipe
José Cordeiro

Organization

General Co-chairs

Xuewei Li	Beijing Jiaotong University, China
Kecheng Liu	University of Reading, UK
Joaquim Filipe	Polytechnic Institute of Setúbal / INSTICC, Portugal
Runtong Zhang	Beijing Jiaotong University, China

Program Co-chairs

Zhenji Zhang	Beijing Jiaotong University, China
Juliang Zhang	Beijing Jiaotong University, China
José Cordeiro	Polytechnic Institute of Setúbal / INSTICC, Portugal
Shifeng Liu	Beijing Jiaotong University, China
Yisheng Liu	Beijing Jiaotong University, China

Organizing Committee

Patrícia Alves	INSTICC, Portugal
Sérgio Brissos	INSTICC, Portugal
Dan Chang	Beijing Jiaotong University, China
Helder Coelhas	INSTICC, Portugal
Vera Coelho	INSTICC, Portugal
Andreia Costa	INSTICC, Portugal
Hui Du	Beijing Jiaotong University, China
Patrícia Duarte	INSTICC, Portugal
Bruno Encarnação	INSTICC, Portugal
Juanqiong Gou	Beijing Jiaotong University, China
Hongjie Lan	Beijing Jiaotong University, China
Jing Li	Beijing Jiaotong University, China
Yisong Li	Beijing Jiaotong University, China
Zikui Lin	Beijing Jiaotong University, China
Xiyan Lv	Beijing Jiaotong University, China
Liliana Medina	INSTICC, Portugal
Carla Mota	INSTICC, Portugal
Raquel Pedrosa	INSTICC, Portugal
Vitor Pedrosa	INSTICC, Portugal
Daniel Pereira	INSTICC, Portugal
Cláudia Pinto	INSTICC, Portugal

Xu Ren	Beijing Jiaotong University, China
José Varela	INSTICC, Portugal
Pedro Varela	INSTICC, Portugal
Jiayi Yao	Beijing Jiaotong University, China
Bing Zhu	Beijing Jiaotong University, China
Xiaomin Zhu	Beijing Jiaotong University, China

Senior Program Committee

Enrique Bonsón, Spain
Albert Cheng, USA
Bernard Coulette, France
Jan Dietz, The Netherlands
Schahram Dustdar, Austria
Nuno Guimarães, Portugal
Pericles Loucopoulos, UK
Andrea de Lucia, Italy
Mirko Malekovic, Croatia
José Legatheaux Martins, Portugal
Masao Johannes Matsumoto, Japan
Marcin Paprzycki, Poland
Alain Pirotte, Belgium
Klaus Pohl, Germany
José Ragot, France
Colette Rolland, France
Narcyz Roztocki, USA
Abdel-badeeh Salem, Egypt
Alexander Smirnov, Russian Federation
Ronald Stamper, UK
François Vernadat, France
Merrill Warkentin, USA

Program Committee

Miguel Angel Martinez Aguilar, Spain
Patrick Albers, France
Abdullah Alnajim, Saudi Arabia
Andreas Andreou, Cyprus
Wudhichai Assawinchaichote, Thailand
Anjali Awasthi, Canada
Cecilia Baranauskas, Brazil
Steve Barker, UK
Reza Barkhi, USA
Remi Bastide, France
Bernhard Bauer, Germany
Lamia Hadrich Belguith, Tunisia
Noureddine Belkhatir, France
Nadia Bellalem, France
Orlando Belo, Portugal
Jorge Bernardino, Portugal
Felix Biscarri, Spain
Juan A. Botía Blaya, Spain
Danielle Boulanger, France
Graça Bressan, Brazil
David Buttler, USA
Miguel Calejo, Portugal
Coral Calero, Spain
Luis M. Camarinha-Matos, Portugal
Olivier Camp, France
Roy Campbell, USA
Gerardo Canfora, Italy
Angélica Caro, Chile
Nunzio Casalino, Italy
Jose Jesus Castro-schez, Spain
Luca Cernuzzi, Paraguay
Dan Chang, China
David Chen, France
Jinjun Chen, Australia
Ming-Puu Chen, Taiwan
Shiping Chen, Australia
Shu-Ching Chen, USA
Zhixiong Chen, USA
Max Chevalier, France

William Cheng-Chung Chu, Taiwan
Daniela Barreiro Claro, Brazil
Francesco Colace, Italy
Cesar Collazos, Colombia
Jose Eduardo Corcoles, Spain
José Cordeiro, Portugal
Antonio Corral, Spain
Karl Cox, UK
Sharon Cox, UK
Alfredo Cuzzocrea, Italy
Jacob Cybulski, Australia
Mengrou Dai, China
Maria Damiani, Italy
Ding Dan, China
Vincenzo Deufemia, Italy
Anind K. Dey, USA
Kamil Dimililer, Cyprus
José Javier Dolado, Spain
Dulce Domingos, Portugal
César Domínguez, Spain
Ming Dong, China
Hui Du, China
Juan C. Dueñas, Spain
Hans-Dieter Ehrich, Germany
João Faria, Portugal
Antonio Fariña, Spain
Antonio Fernández-Caballero, Spain
Edilson Ferneda, Brazil
Paulo Ferreira, Portugal
Maria João Silva Costa Ferreira, Portugal
Rita Francese, Italy
Ana Fred, Portugal
Lixin Fu, USA
Mariagrazia Fugini, Italy
Matjaz Gams, Slovenia
Juan Garbajosa, Spain
Mouzhi Ge, Germany
Marcela Genero, Spain
Joseph Giampapa, USA
Paolo Giorgini, Italy
Raúl Giráldez, Spain
Xiaoquan Gong, China
Pascual Gonzalez, Spain
Robert Goodwin, Australia
Juanqiong Gou, China
Luis Borges Gouveia, Portugal
Feliz Gouveia, Portugal
Janis Grabis, Latvia
Maria Carmen Penadés Gramaje, Spain
Sven Groppe, Germany
Chunfang Guo, China
Sami Habib, Kuwait
Maki K. Habib, Egypt
Yaakov Hacohen-Kerner, Israel
Abdelwahab Hamou-lhadj, Canada
Shanmugasundaram Hariharan, India
Sven Hartmann, Germany
Paul Hawking, Australia
Christian Heinlein, Germany
Markus Helfert, Ireland
Francisco Herrera, Spain
Wladyslaw Homenda, Poland
Jun Hong, UK
Wei-Chiang Hong, Taiwan
Guowei Hua, China
Kai-I Huang, Taiwan
Akram Idani, France
Joshua Ignatius, Malaysia
Alexander Ivannikov, Russian Federation
Arturo Jaime, Spain
Wassim Jaziri, Tunisia
Ivan Jelinek, Czech Republic
Sabina Jeschke, Germany
Paul Johannesson, Sweden
Michail Kalogiannakis, Greece
Kim Kap-Hwan, Korea, Republic of
Nikos Karacapilidis, Greece
Nikitas Karanikolas, Greece
Stamatis Karnouskos, Germany
Hiroyuki Kawano, Japan
MariteKirikova, Latvia
Alexander Knapp, Germany
John Krogstie, Norway
Rob Kusters, The Netherlands
Hongjie Lan, China
Alain Leger, France
Kauko Leiviskä, Finland

Daniel Lemire, Canada
Joerg Leukel, Germany
Hareton Leung, China
Chao Li, China
Jing Li, China
Xiaojing Li, China
Yisong Li, China
Da-Yin Liao, USA
Therese Libourel, France
Zikui Lin, China
Luis Jiménez Linares, Spain
Matti Linna, Finland
Kecheng Liu, UK
Shifeng Liu, China
Yisheng Liu, China
Stephane Loiseau, France
Maria Filomena Cerqueira de Castro Lopes, Portugal
Víctor López-Jaquero, Spain
María Dolores Lozano, Spain
Xiaochun Lu, China
Miguel R. Luaces, Spain
Vicente Luque-Centeno, Spain
Christof Lutteroth, New Zealand
Xiyan Lv, China
Cristiano Maciel, Brazil
Rita Suzana Pitangueira Maciel, Brazil
S. Kami Makki, USA
Nuno Mamede, Portugal
Hervé Martin, France
Maria João Marques Martins, Portugal
Katsuhisa Maruyama, Japan
Viviana Mascardi, Italy
David Martins de Matos, Portugal
Javier Medina, Spain
Jerzy Michnik, Poland
Luo Ming, Singapore
Michele Missikoff, Italy
Vladimír Modrák, Slovak Republic
Ghodrat Moghadampour, Finland
Lars Mönch, Germany
Valérie Monfort, France
Paula Morais, Portugal
Fernando Moreira, Portugal
Haralambos Mouratidis, UK
Pietro Murano, UK
Tomoharu Nakashima, Japan
Paolo Napoletano, Italy
Matthias Nickles, UK
Andreas Ninck, Switzerland
Ann Nosseir, Egypt
Jose Angel Olivas, Spain
Rocco Oliveto, Italy
David L. Olson, USA
Guadalupe Ortiz, Spain
Samia Oussena, UK
Sietse Overbeek, The Netherlands
Tansel Ozyer, Turkey
Claus Pahl, Ireland
José R. Paramá, Spain
Eric Pardede, Australia
Rodrigo Paredes, Chile
Massimiliano Di Penta, Italy
Laurent Péridy, France
Dana Petcu, Romania
Paolo Petta, Austria
Josef Pieprzyk, Australia
Selwyn Piramuthu, USA
Luís Ferreira Pires, The Netherlands
José Pires, Portugal
Geert Poels, Belgium
Ramalingam Ponnusamy, India
Daniele Radicioni, Italy
Jolita Ralyte, Switzerland
T. Ramayah, Malaysia
Pedro Ramos, Portugal
Natallia Rasadka, Italy
Marek Reformat, Canada
Francisco Regateiro, Portugal
Hajo A. Reijers, The Netherlands
Michele Risi, Italy
Alfonso Rodriguez, Chile
Daniel Rodriguez, Spain
Pilar Rodriguez, Spain
Jose Raul Romero, Spain
Agostinho Rosa, Portugal
David G. Rosado, Spain
Gustavo Rossi, Argentina
Francisco Ruiz, Spain
Ozgur Koray Sahingoz, Turkey

Auxiliary Reviewers

Oscar Pedreira, Spain
Hércules Antonio do Prado, Brazil
Edie Correia Santana, Brazil
Federica Sarro, Italy
Diego Seco, Spain
Jaspaljeet Singh, New Zealand
Rosalvo Ermes Streit, Brazil
Jinhui Yao, Australia
Clemens Zeidler, New Zealand

Invited Speakers

Harold Krikke	Tilburg University, The Netherlands
Xuewei Li	Beijing Jiaotong University, China
Kecheng Liu	University of Reading, UK
Leszek Maciaszek	Macquarie University / University of Economics, Australia / Poland
Yannis A. Phillis	Technical University of Crete, Greece
Shoubo Xu	Chinese Academy of Engineering / Beijing Jiaotong University, China
Yulin Zheng	UFIDA, China
Lida Xu	Old Dominion University, USA

Table of Contents

Invited Paper

Part I: Databases and Information Systems Integration

Part II: Artificial Intelligence and Decision Support Systems

Part III: Information Systems Analysis and Specification

Invited Paper

A System-of-Systems Approach to the Analysis and Conservation of Biodiversity

Yannis A. Phillis and Vassilis S. Kouikoglou

Technical University of Crete, 73100 Chania, Greece
{phillis,kouik}@dpem.tuc.gr
http://www.sustainability.tuc.gr

Abstract. Sustainability involves ecological and human aspects whose elements are themselves complex and heterogeneous systems. System-of-Systems (SoS) models provide a unified view of such systems. This paper presents a SoS model of biodiversity and describes its lowest level in detail. The goal is to devise strategies that improve biodiversity for a given region or country subject to certain constraints such as limited budget.

Keywords: Sustainability, Biodiversity, System-of-Systems, Optimal control.

1 Introduction

In the last decades the questions of defining and monitoring sustainability on a national or global scale and problems of sustainable decision-making have received growing attention among policy-makers and scientists. Sustainability models assess the sustainability of countries or regions by aggregating measurable indicators about environmental, economic, and social conditions. These models can provide guidelines for governments and policy-makers in formulating efficient policies for sustainable development. For a review of such methods see [1].

One model that examines sustainability globally, i.e., from the social and the environmental points of view is the SAFE (Sustainability Assessment by Fuzzy Evaluation) model ([2]–[6]). Figure 1 illustrates the basic structure of the model. The state of biodiversity, water, air, and land are elements of the ecological dimension of sustainability whereas health, education, economy, and policies are elements of the human dimension. Each of these eight components of sustainability is assessed using time series of basic indicators.

In the sequel biodiversity, one of the eight constituents of the SAFE model, will be modeled as SoS.

2 System of Systems

2.1 Description

System of Systems models provide a perspective of understanding that differs from traditional systems thinking in that the components of a SoS are themselves autonomous, heterogeneous, and complex systems. More specifically, SoS:

R. Zhang et al. (Eds.): ICEIS 2011, LNBIP 102, pp. 3–15, 2012.

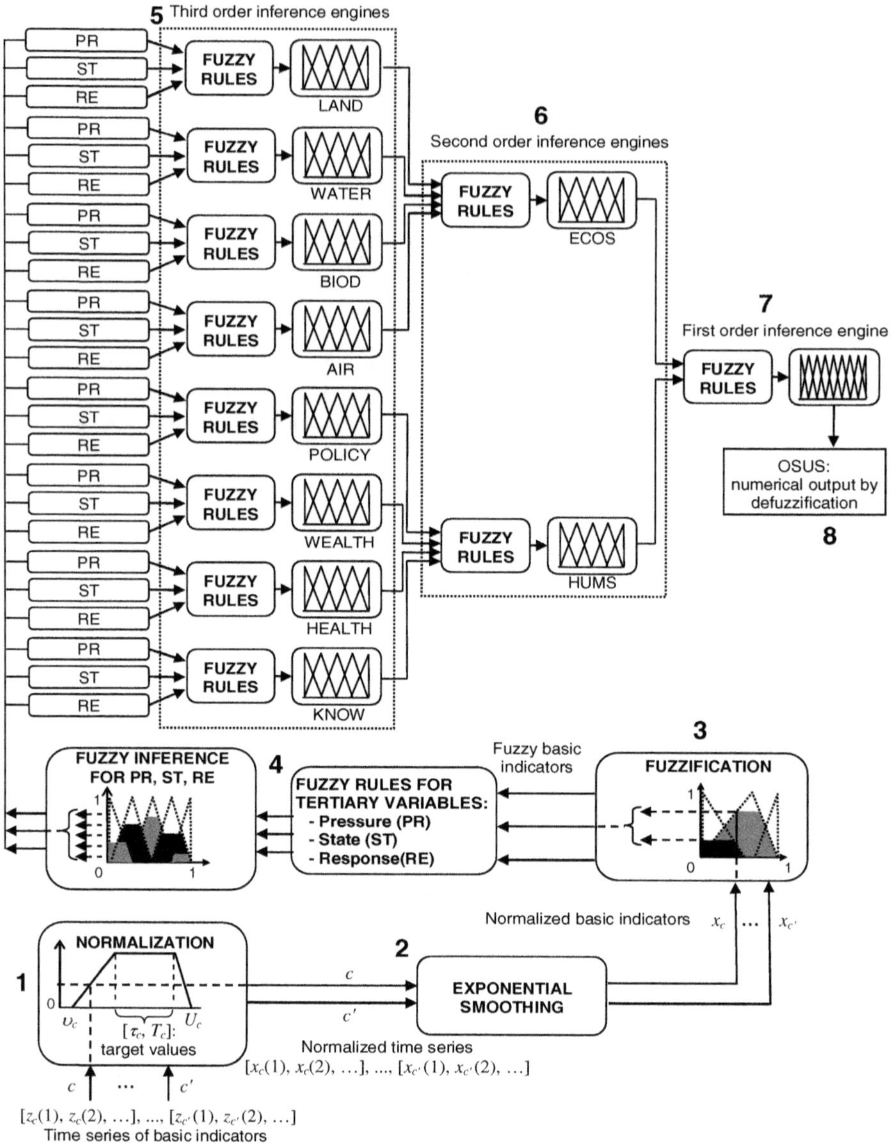

Fig. 1. Steps of the hierarchical assessment of sustainability ([4], Figure 1. ©2009 by IEEE. Used with permission)

1. Are complex assemblages of systems linked together in a functional way that does not affect individual functionalities. They comprise humans, other organisms, and processes that satisfy a set of goals.
2. Can maintain their operational features even if some of the component systems are removed or new ones are connected in the overall SoS.

3. Consist of component systems that operate for their own goals and do not necessarily function under the strict policies of the SoS.
4. Are not amenable to prediction in the way lumped parameter systems described by differential equations are.

The purpose of a SoS is to understand a very complex system by paying attention to components as well as the whole (trees and forest). We then investigate possible outcomes if certain actions are adopted. Possible sample paths are examined and those that have the highest probability of achieving the SoS goals are chosen adaptively. Phrased differently, a SoS model identifies those policies towards a goal that view the system holistically and individually at the same time. The purpose is to identify policies that should not be adopted and pick those with the best chance of success.

A SoS has the following attributes [7]:

- operational independence of the component systems;
- managerial independence of the component systems;
- geographical distribution;
- emergent behavior;
- evolutionary development;
- self-organization;
- adaptation.

A SoS in principle has a hierarchy of goals and capabilities or functionalities. This hierarchy is shown in Fig. 2.

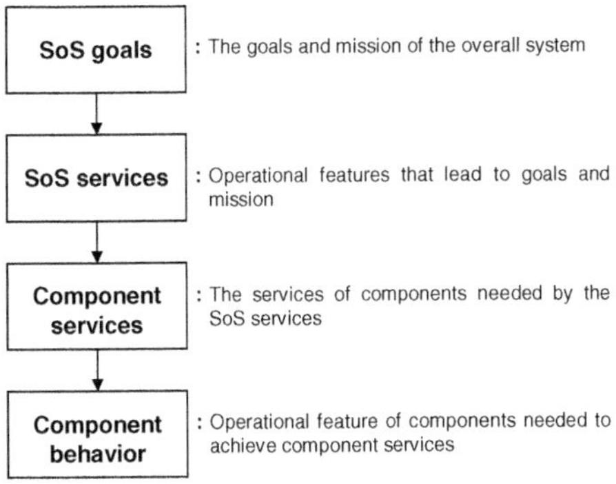

Fig. 2. SoS hierarchy

A SoS also has a set of structural hierarchical levels (see [8] and [9]) denoted by the Greek symbols alpha (α), beta (β), gamma (γ), delta (δ), and so on. These will be discussed in the next section.

2.2 Adaptive Policies

In the context of sustainability, an adaptive procedure to formulate policies for sustainable development is outlined below:

1. Set goals for 2050.
2. Simulate.
3. If targets are not met, say by 2030, examine what adjustments have to be made to correct policies by 2050.

In this paper we shall show all the steps of α-level simulation for biodiversity.

3 Biodiversity

3.1 Biodiversity as SoS

In the context of biodiversity the levels of the structural SoS hierarchy are defined in Fig. 3

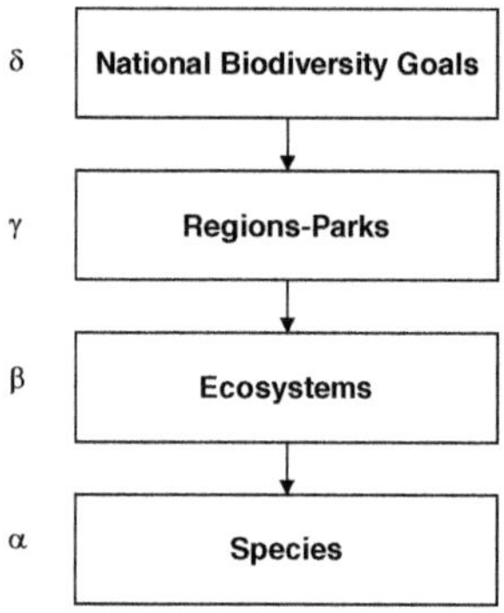

Fig. 3. Hierarchical levels of biodiversity

The functional levels of biodiversity are defined in Table 1.

Table 1. Functional levels of biodiversity

Level	Resources	Dynamics-Valuation-Economics	Policies
α	Number of species, taxa. Types of species, taxa	Dynamics of species, taxa	Threats to species (expansion of humans, habitat destruction, pollution, overharvesting, invasive species). Conservation of targeted species. Strategies
β	Identification of ecosystems (wetlands, marine, land, etc.)	Dynamics of species extinction in ecosystems	Biodiversity surveys. Conservation of targeted ecosystems. Strategies
γ	Relevant areas, regions, parks	Valuation of ecosystems	Purchase land, create parks, zoning, legislation, enforcement, policing. Strategies
δ	National biodiversity goals	Economic repercussions, development	Laws, regulations, long-term planning of fisheries, agriculture, tourism biodiversity protection. Long-term strategies

Table 2. System variables of biodiversity

Level	Variable
α	1. Captive breeding, seed banks 2. Pollution prevention • Control N, P depositions and pesticide use in agriculture • Control hazardous and toxic releases in water bodies and land 3. Fishing/hunting/collecting restrictions
β	1. Biodiversity conservation in • Agriculture • Forestry • Fresh waters • Coastal areas • Marine sectors 2. Protection of hotspots 3. Compensation of local communities 4. Prevent/repair habitat fragmentation (over/under passes, alternative road/rail/canal designs)
γ	1. Habitat protection • Set up protected areas nature reserves • Land purchases • Zoning • Law enforcement
δ	1. Reduce population 2. Climate change amelioration 3. National/regional trade • Abolish fuel subsidies for fishing • Abolish farming subsidies (overproduction of citrus, cotton, sugar cane) 4. Make agreements with third countries to prevent exhaustion of their fisheries, forests, resources by developed countries

3.2 α-Level Simulation

The number of species in an area is very well approximated by the Species-Area Relation (SAR) [10]:

$$S = cA^z \tag{1}$$

where A is the area size, c is a constant, and $z \in [0.1, 1]$ depending on the ecosystem and the species.

Species are threatened by extinction because of a number of reasons, chiefly:

- Habitat loss/fragmentation
- Introduction of invasive species
- Pollution (N, P, toxic pesticides, etc)
- Overpopulation of humans
- Overharvesting (fishing, hunting, collecting, forest cutting)
- Climate change

Strategies for the conservation of species and taxa are summarized below.

1. Habitat protection, including prevention of habitat fragmentation
2. Harvesting control (collecting, fishing, hunting)
3. Pollution prevention
4. Identification and protection of hotspots
5. Captive breeding, seed banks
6. Land purchases
7. Compensation to local communities
8. Nature reserves
9. Biodiversity conservation in
    - agriculture
    - forestry
    - fresh waters
    - coastal areas
    - marine sectors

To perform valuations of services the following services will be taken into account [11]:

1. Provisioning: food, timber, medicines, fibers, etc.
2. Regulating: climate, floods, erosion, etc.
3. Supporting of other services: pollination, pest control, etc.
4. Cultural: recreation, inspiration, esthetics.

It should be stressed that despite the importance of charismatic species such as tigers and birds, life primarily depends on microbes and invertebrates that comprise about 95% of all species [12]. These species together with plants are the ones that mainly drive forestry, agriculture, and fisheries.

Example 1 (Simulation of number of species for an island). Let

$S_0 =$ number of species in a base year (here 2000)
$S =$ number of species in 2050 (a target year)
$A_0 =$ forest area in 2000
$A =$ forest area in 2050.

In (1), $z \in 0.25$ is a good choice for islands [13]. From SAR we obtain

$$\frac{S}{S_0} = \left(\frac{A}{A_0}\right)^{0.25} \tag{2}$$

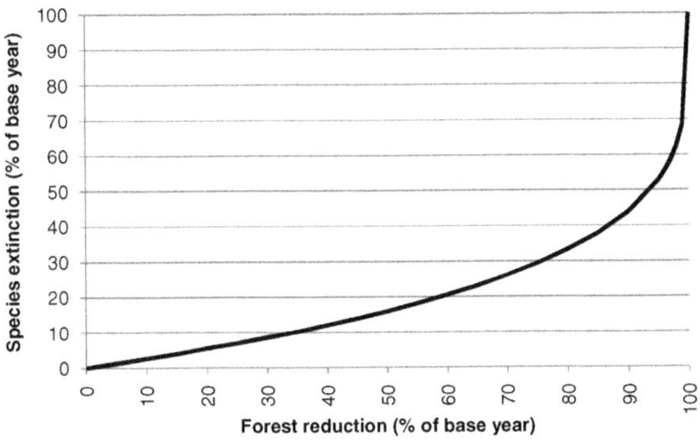

Fig. 4. Species reduction as a function of habitat destruction for an island ecosystem

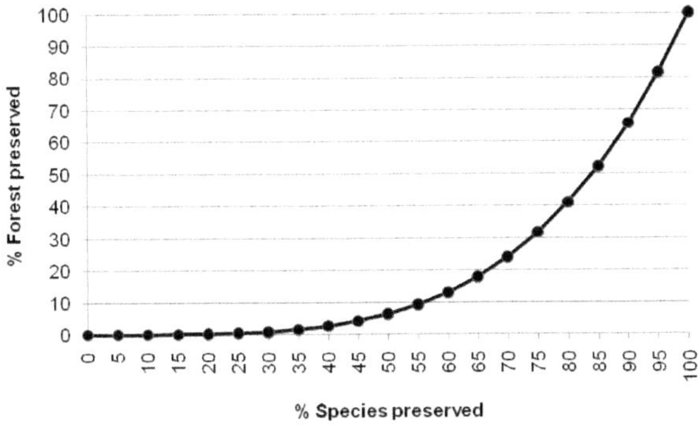

Fig. 5. Forest-to-species preservation

Equation (2) is depicted in Fig. 4, where the species extinction is given by

$$\frac{\Delta S}{S_0}100\% \triangleq \frac{S_0 - S}{S_0}100\% = \left[1 - \left(\frac{A}{A_0}\right)^{0.25}\right] 100\%$$

Conversely, if one wants to preserve a given percentage of species in a future year relative to a base year, equation (2) yields the graph shown in Fig. 5.

Table 3 gives the relative species loss for various ecosystems (biomes) using estimates of area losses from [14].

3.3 Dynamic Allocation of Conservation Funding between Two Regions

An important problem of biodiversity conservation is to dynamically allocate funding available for acquisition and maintenance of protected areas among distinct regions. The objective is to maximize the overall biodiversity at the end of a planning period.

We consider a two-region example. At time zero, in each region i, $i = 1, 2$, there is a pristine area of known size $R_i(0)$ reserved for protection and a pristine but unprotected

Table 3. Estimated eventual extinctions based on area converted 1990–2050

Index	Biome	Area in 1990 (fraction of original area), A_0	Area in 2050 (fraction of original area), A	Percentage of species lost, $(\Delta S/S_0)\,100\%$
1	Mediterranean forests, woodlands, and scrub	0.300	0.294	0.50
2	Temperate forest, steppe, and woodland	0.270	0.310	-3.51
3	Temperate broadleaf and mixed forest	0.430	0.400	1.79
4a	Tropical and sub-tropical dry broadleaf forests	0.450	0.310	8.90
4b	Tropical and sub-tropical moist broadleaf forests	0.750	0.580	6.22
5a	Flooded grasslands and savannas	0.470	0.370	5.81
5b	Montane grasslands and shrublands	0.740	0.590	5.51
6	Tropical and sub-tropical grasslands, savannas, and grasslands	0.490	0.310	10.82
7	Tropical and sub-tropical coniferous forests	0.600	0.330	13.88
8	Deserts	0.700	0.680	0.72
9	Temperate coniferous forests	0.800	0.720	2.60
10	Boreal forests	0.970	0.968	0.05
11	Tundra	1.000	0.980	0.50

area $A_i(0), i = 1, \ldots, n$. Unprotected area is being gradually lost due to urban, agricultural, industrial or other uses. Loss is assumed to occur at a constant annual rate δ_i per km^2, i.e., $A_i(t) = A_i(0)\exp(-\delta_i t)$ or $\dot{A}_i = -\delta_i A_i$. The parameter δ_i is estimated from historical area-use data.

Suppose that the annual funding available for acquisition and maintenance is B and also that 1 dollar buys $1/a_i$ square kilometers of area available for conservation in region i or maintains $1/b_i$ square kilometers of protected area for one year in this region. We assume that a_i and b_i are positive, and $B > b_1R_1(0) + b_2R_2(0)$, otherwise there will be no funding available for acquisition. Conservation planning problems without maintenance costs have been studied in [15] and [16].

At time t, the funding rate $X(t)$ left for acquisition is $X(t) = B - b_1R_1(t) - b_2R_2(t)$. Let $u_i(t)dt$ be the fraction of $A_i(t)$ purchased in the infinitesimal interval $[t, t+dt)$. The total area of region i set aside for protection in this interval is $A_i(t)u_i(t)dt$ and the corresponding acquisition cost equals $a_iA_i(t)u_i(t)dt$. This quantity is bounded from above by the maximum available funding, $X(t)dt$.

The following equations describe the evolution of the system:
the protected area of region i increases at rate

$$\dot{R}_i(t) = A_i(t)u_i(t); \tag{3}$$

the available area decreases by the same amount plus a decrease due to area loss, thus

$$\dot{A}_i(t) = -A_i(t)\left[u_i(t) + \delta_i\right]; \tag{4}$$

the funding rate available for acquisition satisfies the equation

$$\dot{X}(t) = \dot{B} - b_1\dot{R}_1(t) - b_2\dot{R}_2(t) = -b_1A_1(t)u_1(t) - b_2A_2(t)u_2(t); \tag{5}$$

state and control variables are constrained by

$$A_i(t)u_i(t) \geq 0, i = 1, 2; \tag{6}$$

and the acquisition cost rate must not exceed the corresponding funding rate $X(t)$, i.e.,

$$X(t) - a_1R_1(t) - a_2R_2(t) \geq 0; \tag{7}$$

The problem is to determine the fractions $u_i(t)dt$ of $A_i(t)$ to be purchased in each interval $[t, t+dt)$ so as to maximize the total number of species at the end of a planning period of T years. This is given by

$$S = \sum_{i=1}^{2} c_i\left[R_i(T) + A_i(T)\right]^{z_i} \tag{8}$$

where c_i and z_i are the biodiversity parameters of equation (1) corresponding to region i.

The above problem is an optimal control problem with control variables $u_i(t)$, state variables $R_i(t)$, $A_i(t)$, and $X(t)$, state equations (3)-(5), and control and state variable constraints (6) and (7). Necessary conditions for the maximization of S are given by the maximum principle. Below we use a particular formulation of the maximum principle for systems with state and control variable constraints, as stated in Informal Theorem 4.1 of [17].

The state equations (3)-(5) are adjoined to the Hamiltonian function using the multipliers $\Lambda_i(t)$, $\lambda_i(t)$, and $\lambda(t)$, respectively. Constraints (6) and (7) are adjoined to the Lagrangian function using multipliers $\mu_i(t) \geq 0$ and $\mu(t) \geq 0$. Dropping t for simplicity in the notation, we form the Hamiltonian function

$$\begin{aligned} H &= \sum_i \Lambda_iA_iu_i - \sum_i \lambda_i\left(u_i + \delta_i\right)A_i - \lambda\sum_i b_iA_iu_i \\ &= \sum_i \sigma_ia_iA_iu_i - \sum_i \lambda_i\delta_iA_i, \end{aligned} \tag{9}$$

where

$$\sigma_i \triangleq \frac{\Lambda_i - \lambda_i - \lambda b_i}{a_i}, \tag{10}$$

and the Lagrangian

$$L = H + \sum_i \mu_i A_i u_i + \mu \left(X - \sum_i a_i A_i u_i \right) \tag{11}$$

The Lagrange multipliers satisfy the complementary slackness conditions
$\mu_i \geq 0$ at each time instant and $\mu_i = 0$ whenever $A_i u_i > 0$;
$\mu \geq 0$ at each time instant and $\mu = 0$ whenever $X > \sum_i a_i A_i u_i$.

The optimal control maximizes the Hamiltonian (9) at each time instant subject to constraints (6) and (7). All these functions are linear in $a_i A_i u_i$. It then follows that H is maximized by choosing $a_i A_i u_i = X$ for the region i which has the maximum value of σ_i among all those regions j for which $A_j > 0$ and $\sigma_j > 0$. Thus, the optimal control is bang-bang, i.e.,

$$u_i = \begin{cases} \frac{X}{a_i A_i}, & \sigma_i = \sigma, \ A_i > 0 \\ 0, & \text{otherwise}, \end{cases} \tag{12}$$

where

$$\sigma \triangleq \max_{j:\, \sigma_j, A_j > 0} \sigma_j$$

The second necessary condition of the maximum principle is that the partial derivative of the Lagrangian (11) with respect to each control variable be zero. Suppose that region k is given priority in the interval $[t_1, t_2)$. It follows from the second necessary condition that

$$\mu(t) = \sigma_k(t) = \sigma(t),\ \mu_k(t) = 0, \text{ and } \mu_j(t) = [\sigma(t) - \sigma_j(t)]a_j, \quad j \neq k, \text{ for all } t \in [t_1, t_2). \tag{13}$$

To determine the functions σ_i, $i = 1, 2$ from (10) we use the adjoint differential equations and their boundary (transversality) conditions provided by the maximum principle:

$$\dot{\Lambda}_i = -\frac{\partial L}{\partial R_i} = 0 \text{ and } \Lambda_i(T) = \frac{\partial S}{\partial R_i} = c_i z_i \left[R_i(T) + A_i(T)\right]^{z_i - 1} \tag{14}$$

$$\dot{\lambda}_i = -\frac{\partial L}{\partial A_i} = -\sigma_i a_i u_i + \lambda_i \delta_i - \mu_i u_i + \mu a_i u_i \text{ and } \lambda_i(T) = \frac{\partial S}{\partial A_i} = \Lambda_i(T) \tag{15}$$

$$\dot{\lambda} = -\frac{\partial L}{\partial X} = -\mu \text{ and } \lambda(T) = \frac{\partial S}{\partial X} = 0. \tag{16}$$

Using (13) the differential equation in (15) is reduced to

$$\dot{\lambda}_i = \lambda_i \delta_i \text{ or, equivalently, } \lambda_i(t) = \lambda_i(0) e^{\delta_i t},\ i = 1, 2. \tag{17}$$

Finally, taking time derivatives in (10) and using (13)–(17), it follows that the functions $\sigma_i(t)$ satisfy the following differential equation

$$\dot{\sigma}_i(t) = -\frac{b_i}{a_i}\sigma(t) - \frac{\delta_i}{a_i}\lambda_i(t),\ i = 1, 2, \tag{18}$$

where $\sigma(t) = \sigma_k(t)$.

The method of variation of extremals can be employed to approximate the optimal conservation plan:

Algorithm for Optimal Conservation Planning

```
1. Guess the values of the adjoint variables at time zero.
2. Compute σ_i(0) from (10) and the initial optimal control from
   (12).
3. Integrate the differential equations (3)-(5) and (13)-(18) to
   compute the state and adjoint variables in the interval [0,T];
   use (12) to find the optimal funding rule at each time
   instant.
4. Calculate deviations of the adjoint variables at time T from
   the values specified by the boundary conditions in (14)-(16).
5. Perform sensitivity analysis with respect to the initial
   values of the adjoint variables to extract gradient
   information about these deviations.
6. Use the results of steps 4 and 5 to adjust the initial values
   of the adjoint variables. One technique to systematically
   improve the initial adjoint values is Newton's method for
   finding roots of systems of nonlinear equations.
7. Repeat steps 2-6 until the deviations become small enough.
```

Example 2 (Conservation planning for two regions*)*. A constant annual budget of 1.43 million USD is available for conservation of two regions over a planning period of 40 years. Table 4 gives the available data for each region.

Table 4. Data

Parameter	Region 1	Region 2
R_i Protected (reserved) areas at time 0 (km^2)	85,000	175,000
A_i Areas available for conservation at time 0 (km^2)	165,000	425,000
δ_i Annual loss rate of unprotected areas	165,000	425,000
a_i Acquisition cost (USD/km^2)	95	110
b_i Running cost of protected areas (USD/km^2/yr)	3	1
S_i Number of species (species-area relations)	$0.805\,(R_1 + A_1)^{0.25}$	$1.042\,(R_2 + A_2)^{0.25}$

Figure 6 shows the trajectories of protected areas in the two regions until year $T = 40$. The optimal policy involves two switches: in the interval [0, 5.6) region 2 is given priority; at time 5.6 the policy switches to region 1 until time 21.1 when there is no more area available for protection in that region, and finally all budget left for acquisition goes to region 2 again. The total number of species in year 40 is 43.44 and the total protected area is $\sum_{i=1}^{2} [R_i(40) + A_i(40)] = 524,773\,\text{km}^2$.

3.4 Higher-Level Simulations

Projections of species extinction rates within biomes are obtained from β-level simulations, which take into account two major causes: alteration of habitats and global

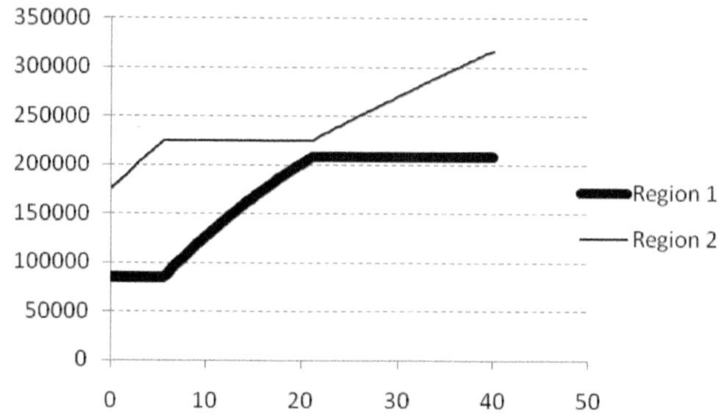

Fig. 6. Optimal acquisition plan of protected areas

warming. Next follows the γ-level simulation which involves the valuation of ecosystem services and the estimation of economic costs associated with the loss of biodiversity.

After the basic simulation and budget allocation, specific biodiversity actions should be designed and their expected benefits appraised. An example of such strategies is given in Table 5 for Greece.

Table 5. Strategies of biodiversity conservation for Greece

Level	Strategy	Range
α	1. Seed banks	0–100% of plant species
	2. Fishing/hunting/collecting restrictions	0–100% of threatened species
β	1. Biodiversity conservation in • Agriculture • Forestry • Fresh waters • Coastal areas • Marine sectors	0–100% of threatened species
	2. Protection of hotspots	0–100% of hotspots
γ	1. Habitat protection	
	• Set up protected areas - nature reserves	0–20% of existing land
	• Zoning	0–100% of towns
	• Law enforcement for land protection	0–1 (0 means no enforcement; 1 full enforcement)
δ	1. Climate change amelioration	2–2.5 °C temperature
Goal:	Reduce present extinction rates by 2050, ideally to background extinction rates.	

Long term goals about the state of biodiversity should be set and the system trajectory towards these goals observed. If the system deviates from its targets, corrective action should be taken. This is a project with a time horizon of decades. Close monitoring and measuring are important.

4 Conclusions

The SoS formulation of biodiversity allows for the unfolding of its complex dynamics and provides a better understanding of its various facets. This paper we described in detail the lowest level α of the model. β and γ-level simulations will give a sense of extinctions within biomes and species valuations respectively. Finally δ-level simulation records the effectiveness of current policies and provides ideas for adaptation so that the system goals, e.g., number of species at a certain future year, will be met. All these are subjects for future research.

References

1. Phillis, Y.A., Kouikoglou, V.S., Manousiouthakis, V.: A Review of Sustainability Models as System of Systems. IEEE Syst. J. 4(1), 19–25 (2010)
2. Phillis, Y.A., Andriantiatsaholiniaina, L.A.: Sustainability: An Ill-defined Concept and Its Assessment Using Fuzzy Logic. Ecol. Econ. 37(3), 435–456 (2001)
3. Andriantiatsaholiniaina, L.A., Kouikoglou, V.S., Phillis, Y.A.: Evaluating Strategies for Sustainable Development: Fuzzy Logic Reasoning and Sensitivity Analysis. Ecol. Econ. 48(2), 149–172 (2004)
4. Kouloumpis, V., Kouikoglou, V.S., Phillis, Y.A.: Sustainability Assessment of Nations and Related Decision Making Using Fuzzy Logic. IEEE Syst. J. 2(2), 224–236 (2008)
5. Phillis, Y.A., Kouikoglou, V.S.: Fuzzy Measurement of Sustainability. Nova Science, New York (2009)
6. Phillis, Y.A., Grigoroudis, E., Kouikoglou, V.S.: Sustainability Ranking and Improvement of Countries. Ecol. Econ. 70(3), 542–553 (2011)
7. Sage, A.P., Biemer, S.M.: Processes for System Family Architecting, Design, and Integration. IEEE Syst. J. 1(1), 5–16 (2007)
8. DeLaurentis, D., Callaway, R.K.: A System-of-Systems Perspective for Public Policy Decisions. Rev. Policy Res. 21(6), 829–837 (2004)
9. Agusdinata, D.B., Dittmar, L.: Adaptive Policy Design to Reduce Carbon Emissions: A System-of-Systems Perspective. IEEE Syst. J. 3(4), 509–519 (2009)
10. Arrhenius, O.: Species and Area. J. Ecol. 9(1), 95–99 (1921)
11. Millenium Ecosystem Assessment: Ecosystem and Human WellBeing: Synthesis. Island Press, Washington, D.C. (2005)
12. Beattie, A., Ehrlich, P.: The Missing Link in Biodiversity Conservation. Science 328(5976), 307–308 (2010)
13. Brooks, T.M., Pimm, S.L., Collar, N.J.: Deforestation Predicts the Number of Threatened Birds in Insular Southern Asia. Conserv. Biol. 11(2), 382–394 (1997)
14. Millenium Ecosystem Assessment: Ecosystems and Human WellBeing: Biodiversity Synthesis. World Resources Institute (2005)
15. Wilson, K.A., McBride, M.F., Bode, M., Possingham, H.P.: Prioritizing Global Conservation Efforts. Nature 440, 337–340 (2006)
16. Bode, M.: Decision Theory in Conservation Biology—Case Studies in Mathematical Conservation. Ph.D. Thesis, University of Queensland, Australia (2007)
17. Hartl, R., Sethi, S., Sethi, S.P.: A Survey of the Maximum Principles for Optimal Control Problems with State Constraints. SIAM Rev. 37(2), 181–218 (1995)

PART I

Databases and Information Systems Integration

Clustering Documents with Maximal Substrings

Tomonari Masada[1], Atsuhiro Takasu[2], Yuichiro Shibata[1], and Kiyoshi Oguri[1]

[1] Nagasaki University, 1-14 Bunkyo-machi, Nagasaki-shi, Nagasaki, Japan
[2] National Institute of Informatics, 2-1-2 Hitotsubashi, Chiyoda-ku, Tokyo, Japan
{masada,shibata,oguri}@nagasaki-u.ac.jp,
takasu@nii.ac.jp

Abstract. This paper provides experimental results showing that we can use maximal substrings as elementary building blocks of documents in place of the words extracted by a current state-of-the-art supervised word extraction. Maximal substrings are defined as the substrings each giving a smaller number of occurrences even by appending only one character to its head or tail. The main feature of maximal substrings is that they can be extracted quite efficiently in an unsupervised manner. We extract maximal substrings from a document set and represent each document as a bag of maximal substrings. We also obtain a bag of words representation by using a state-of-the-art supervised word extraction over the same document set. We then apply the same document clustering method to both representations and obtain two clustering results for a comparison of their quality. We adopt a Bayesian document clustering based on Dirichlet compound multinomials for avoiding overfitting. Our experiment shows that the clustering quality achieved with maximal substrings is acceptable enough to use them in place of the words extracted by a supervised word extraction.

Keywords: Maximal substring, Unsupervised method, Document clustering, Suffix array, Bayesian modeling.

1 Introduction

Recently, researchers propose a wide variety of large scale data mining methods, where documents originating from SNS environments or DNA/RNA sequences provided by next generation sequencing are a typical target of their proposals. Many of those methods adopt an *unsupervised* learning, because it is often difficult to prepare a sufficient amount of training data for a *supervised* learning. This paper focuses on text mining, where we have various useful unsupervised methods, e.g. document clustering [15], topic extraction [2], topical trend analysis [23], etc. However, most of such unsupervised methods assume that each document is already represented as a *bag of words*, i.e., as a set of the numbers of occurrences of words. Therefore, we should first extract elementary building blocks that can be called words from documents.

With respect to English, French, German, etc, we can easily obtain such building blocks, because each character sequence separated by white spaces can be regarded as a word. While we may further conduct a stemming to obtain a canonical form of the words, this causes no serious burden.

R. Zhang et al. (Eds.): ICEIS 2011, LNBIP 102, pp. 19–34, 2012.

However, with respect to Japanese, Chinese, Korean, etc, it is far from a trivial task to extract such elementary building blocks from documents. Japanese and Chinese sentences contain no white spaces and thus give no word boundaries. While Korean sentences contain many white spaces, most of the character sequences separated by white spaces consist of two or more words [4].

Therefore, various word extraction methods have been proposed. However, many of such methods are a *supervised* one. They require a hand-maintained dictionary that should be constantly updated or are based on a mathematical model of character sequences that should be trained with a sufficient amount of training data, where supervised signals (e.g. 0/1 labels giving word boundaries, categorical labels giving grammatical roles, etc) are assigned by human annotators. Therefore, any mining method sitting on a supervised word extraction will show difficulty in scaling up to larger data sets even when the mining method itself is an unsupervised one.

This paper provides experimental results showing that we can use *maximal substrings* [17] as elementary building blocks of documents in place of the words extracted by a current state-of-the-art supervised word extraction. The most important feature of maximal substrings is that they can be extracted in an *unsupervised* manner. Therefore, we need no training data aside target data. Further, maximal substrings can be extracted quite efficiently.

From here, when we use the words extracted by a supervised method to represent each document as a bag of words, we simply call this *bag of words representation* and distinguish it from *bag of maximal substrings representation*.

For evaluating the effectiveness of maximal substrings, we compare bag of maximal substrings representation with bag of words representation in *document clustering*, where the latter representation is obtained by using a state-of-the-art supervised word extraction. We compare these two types of representation based on the quality of document clustering. We run the same Bayesian clustering algorithm on the same document set and obtain two different clustering results depending on whether we use bag of maximal substrings representation or bag of words representation. We then compare the clustering quality in F-scores and clarify the effectiveness of maximal substrings.

As far as we know, this paper firstly gives a quantitative comparison between bag of maximal substrings representation and bag of words representation in document clustering. While Chumwatana et al. [5,6] conduct a similar experiment with respect to Thai documents, the authors fail to make evaluation reliable, because the data set only contains tens of documents. Further, they do not compare bag of maximal substrings representation with bag of words representation.

Our comparison was conducted on a set of tens of thousands of Korean and Chinese newswire articles. To compare with maximal substrings, we extracted words by applying a dictionary-based morphological analyzer [8] to Korean documents and by applying a word segmenter, implemented by us based on linear conditional random fields (CRF) [19], to Chinese documents. Both are a supervised word extraction. The former requires a hand-maintained dictionary, and the latter requires a sufficient amount of human annotated training data.

Our experiment will provide the following observations:

- Both for Korean and Chinese documents, maximal substrings are as effective as the words extracted by a current state-of-the-art supervised method as long as we remove high and low frequency maximal substrings with a little care.
- Document clustering requires longer time and larger memory when we use maximal substrings, because the number of maximal substrings is larger than that of the words extracted by a supervised method. This is the cost we should pay in performing various text mining tasks with maximal substrings.

The rest of the paper is organized as follows. Section 2 reviews the works related to the extraction of elementary building blocks of documents. Section 3 describes the details of maximal substrings and of document clustering used in our evaluation experiment. Section 4 includes the procedure and the results of our experiment. Section 5 concludes the paper with discussions and future work.

This paper improves our preceding paper [11] with respect to the following three aspects. First, we added two data sets to make our experiment more reliable. Second, we provided an additional method for reducing the variety of maximal substrings extracted from Chinese documents. While we did not obtain any good results in [11] for Chinese documents, this new reduction method made maximal substrings as effective as the words extracted by a CRF-based supervised method. Third, we conducted an MCMC sampling aside the EM algorithm in [11] for document clustering and made our experiment more comprehensive.

2 Previous Works

Most text mining methods require *word extraction*, i.e., extraction of elementary building blocks that can be called words, as a preprocessing of documents. For English, French, German, etc, we have words as the character sequences separated by white spaces. Therefore, we at most need to apply stemming for obtaining a canonical form of the words. In contrast, for Japanese, Chinese, Korean, etc, word extraction is never a trivial task.

Word extraction can be conducted, for example, by analyzing language-specific word sequence structures with a hand-maintained dictionary [8], or by labeling character sequences with an elaborated probabilistic model whose parameters are in advance optimized with respect to a human annotated training data set [21]. However, recent research trends point to increasing need for large scale text mining. Therefore, an intensive use of such *supervised* methods becomes less realistic, because it becomes more difficult to prepare a hand-maintained data set of size and quality sufficient to serve as a dictionary or as a training data set for exploring very large scale *unknown* data.

Actually, we already have important results for *unsupervised* word extraction.

Poon et al. [18] propose an unsupervised word segmentation by using log-linear models, which are often adopted for supervised word segmentation, in an unsupervised learning framework. However, when computing the expected count, which is required in learning process, the authors exhaustively enumerate all segmentation patterns. Consequently, this approach is only applicable to the languages whose sentences are given as a set of short character sequences separated by white spaces (e.g. Arabic and Hebrew), because the total number of segmentation patterns is not so large for each of such short character sequences. In other words, this approach may be extremely inefficient for the languages whose sentences contain no white spaces (e.g. Chinese and Japanese).

Mochihashi et al. [13] provide a sophisticated Bayesian probabilistic model for segmenting given sentences into words in a totally unsupervised manner. The authors improve the generative model of Teh [20] and utilize it for modeling both character n-grams and word n-grams. The proposed model can cope with the data containing so-called out-of-vocabulary words, because the generative model of character n-grams serves as a new word generator for that of word n-grams. However, highly complicated sampling procedure, including MCMC for the nested n-gram models and segmentation sampling by an extended forward-backward algorithm, may encounter an efficiency problem when we try to implement this method by ourselves, though the proposed model is well designed enough to prevent any exhaustive enumeration of segmentation candidates.

Okanohara et al. [17] propose an unsupervised method from a completely different angle. The authors extract *maximal substrings*, i.e., the substrings each giving a smaller number of occurrences even by appending only one character to its head or tail, as elementary building blocks of documents. The extraction can be efficiently implemented and conducted as is shown in the works related to suffix array or Burrows-Wheeler transform [7,1,14,16]. While Zhang et al. [25] also provide a method for extracting a special set of substrings, this is not the set of maximal substrings. Further, their method has many control parameters and thus is guided not by a principled methodology, but by a heuristic intuition.

In this paper, we adopt maximal substrings as elementary building blocks of documents by following the line of [17] and evaluate the effectiveness of maximal substrings in *document clustering*, because previous works [17,25] have proved the effectiveness only in document classification.

While we can find several works employing maximal substrings in document clustering, this paper firstly gives a quantitative comparison between bag of maximal substrings representation and bag of words representation as far as we know. Zhang et al. [24] present a Chinese document clustering method using maximal substrings. However, the authors give no quantitative evaluation. Especially, maximal substrings are not compared with the words extracted by some elaborated supervised method. While Li et al. [9] also propose a document clustering based on the maximality of subsequences, the authors focus not on character sequences, but on word sequences. Further, the proposed method utilizes WordNet, i.e., an external knowledge base, for reducing the variety of maximal subsequences. Therefore, their method is not an unsupervised one.

This paper will show what kind of effectiveness maximal substrings can provide in document clustering. In the evaluation experiment, we prepared a set of tens of thousands of documents as an input for clustering and made our evaluation reliable. We only appealed to a simple frequency-based reduction of the variety of maximal substrings and used no external knowledge base. Further, we compared the clustering quality achieved with maximal substrings to that achieved with the words extracted by an elaborated supervised method.

3 Clustering Documents with Maximal Substrings

3.1 Maximal Substrings

Maximal substrings are defined as a substring whose number of occurrences is reduced even by appending only one character to its head or tail. We can discuss more formally as follows. Let S denote a string of length $l(S)$ over a lexicographically ordered character set Σ. At the tail of S, a special character \$, called sentinel, is attached, i.e., $S[l(S)] = \$$. The sentinel \$ does not appear in the given original string and is smaller than all other characters in lexicographical order. For a pair of strings S and T over Σ, we define the set of all occurrence positions of T in S as follows:

$$Pos(S,T) \equiv \{i : S[i+j-1] = T[j] \text{ for } j = 1,\dots,l(T)\} . \quad (1)$$

We denote the nth smallest element in $Pos(S,T)$ by $pos_n(S,T)$. Further, we define $RPos(S,T)$ as follows:

$$RPos(S,T) \equiv \{(n, pos_n(S,T) - pos_1(S,T)) : n = 1,\dots,|Pos(S,T)|\} . \quad (2)$$

That is, $RPos(S,T)$ is the set of all occurrence positions of T in S *relative to* the first smallest occurrence position. Then, T is a *maximal substring* of S when

- $|RPos(S,T)| > 1$,
- $RPos(S,T) \neq RPos(S,T')$ for any T' such that $l(T') = l(T) + 1$ and $T[j] = T'[j], j = 1,\dots,l(T)$, and
- $RPos(S,T) \neq RPos(S,T')$ for any T' such that $l(T') = l(T) + 1$ and $T[j] = T'[j+1], j = 1,\dots,l(T)$.

The last condition corresponds to "left expansion" discussed in [17].

When we extract maximal substrings from a document set, we first concatenate all documents by inserting a special character, which does not appear in the given document set, between the documents. The concatenation order is irrelevant to our discussion. We put a sentinel at the tail of the resulting string and obtain a string S from which we extract maximal substrings. We can efficiently extract all maximal substrings from S in time proportional to $l(S)$ [17].

After the extraction, the maximal substrings containing special characters put between the documents are removed. However, the number of the resulting maximal substrings is in general far larger than the number of the words extracted by a state-of-the-art supervised method from the same document set. Therefore, we further reduce the variety of maximal substrings by removing the maximal substrings containing white spaces, delimiters (e.g. comma, period, question mark, etc), and other functional characters (e.g. parentheses, hyphen, center dot, etc).

Even after the above reduction, we still have a large number of maximal substrings. Therefore, we propose a simple frequency-based strategy for reducing the variety by using three integer parameters n_L, r_H, and r_h as follows:

1. Remove the maximal substrings whose frequencies are smaller than n_L;
2. Remove the top r_H highest frequency maximal substrings; and

3. Remove the maximal substrings *of length one* among the top r_h highest frequency maximal substrings, where r_h should be larger than r_H.

The third reduction using r_h was not proposed in [11]. However, this additional reduction made maximal substrings as effective as the words extracted by the supervised word segmenter for Chinese documents. Consequently, we could obtain more interesting results than in [11] with respect to Chinese documents.

While we tried various settings for n_L, r_H, and r_h, this paper provides a limited number of settings, because other settings gave no remarkable improvement. Our reduction strategy was also applied to the words extracted by a supervised method, because we could obtain better evaluation results with this reduction.

3.2 Bayesian Document Clustering

Dirichlet Compound Multinomial (DCM). When we represent documents as a bag of maximal substrings or of words, multinomial distribution [15] is a natural choice for document modeling, because we can identify each document with a frequency histogram of maximal substrings or of words. However, it is often discussed that multinomial distributions are likely to overfit to *sparse* data. Here the term "sparse" means that the number of different maximal substrings or of different words appearing in each document is far less than the total number observable in the entire document set.

Therefore, we use a Bayesian document model called *Dirichlet compound multinomial* (DCM) [10] and avoid overfitting. Let K denote the number of clusters. We prepare K multinomial distributions each modeling a frequency distribution for a different document cluster. Further, a Dirichlet prior distribution is applied to each multinomial distribution. By marginalizing out the multinomial parameters, we obtain a DCM for each document cluster. The parameters of these K DCMs and their mixing proportions are estimated by the EM algorithm described below.

EM Algorithm. We prepare notations for discussions. We assume that the given document set contains J documents and that W different words (or maximal substrings) can be observed in the document set. Let c_{jw} be the number of occurrences of the wth word (or maximal substring) in the jth document. The sparseness in our case means that $c_{jw} = 0$ holds for most w. Let $\alpha_k = (\alpha_{k1}, \ldots, \alpha_{kW})$ be the hyperparameters of the Dirichlet prior prepared for the kth document cluster. The probability that the jth document belongs to the kth cluster is denoted by p_{jk}. Note that $\sum_k p_{jk} = 1$. We define $\alpha_k \equiv \sum_w \alpha_{kw}$ and $c_j \equiv \sum_w c_{jw}$. We update the cluster assignment probabilities and the hyperparameters with the EM algorithm described below.

E step: For each j, update p_{jk}, $k = 1, \ldots, K$ by

$$p_{jk} \leftarrow \frac{\sum_j p_{jk}}{\sum_j \sum_k p_{jk}} \cdot \frac{\Gamma(\alpha_k)}{\Gamma(c_j + \alpha_k)} \prod_w \frac{\Gamma(c_{jw} + \alpha_{kw})}{\Gamma(\alpha_{kw})}$$

and then normalize p_{jk} by $p_{jk} \leftarrow p_{jk} / \sum_k p_{jk}$.

M step: For each k, update α_{kw}, $w = 1, \ldots, W$ by

$$\alpha_{kw} \leftarrow \alpha_{kw} \cdot \frac{\sum_j p_{jk}\{\Psi(c_{jw} + \alpha_{kw}) - \Psi(\alpha_{kw})\}}{\sum_j p_{jk}\{\Psi(c_j + \alpha_k) - \Psi(\alpha_k)\}}$$

where $\Gamma(\cdot)$ is gamma function and $\Psi(\cdot)$ is digamma function. The M step is based on Minka's discussion [12]. We ran 200 iterations of the E and M steps.

Before entering into the loop of E and M steps, we initialize all α_{jk} to 1, because this makes every Dirichlet distribution a uniform distribution. Further, we initialize p_{jk} not randomly but by the EM algorithm for multinomial mixtures [15]. In the EM for multinomial mixtures, we use a random initialization for p_{jk}. The execution of the EM for multinomial mixtures is repeated 30 times. Each of the 30 executions of the EM for multinomial mixtures gives a different estimation of p_{jk}. Therefore, we choose the estimation giving the largest likelihood as the initial setting of p_{jk} in the EM algorithm for DCM. We conduct this entire procedure three times. Among the three results, we select the one giving the largest likelihood as the final output of our EM algorithm. We then assign each document to the cluster giving the largest value among $p_{j1}, \ldots, p_{jK}$ in this final output. The time complexity of this EM is $O(IKM)$, where I is the number of iterations and M is the number of unique pairs of document and word (or the number of unique pairs of document and maximal substring). Note that M is far smaller than $J \times W$ due to the sparseness discussed above.

MCMC Sampling. We also employed *Gibbs sampling*, a widely used class of MCMC samplings, for inference. Our Gibbs sampling updates cluster assignments by picking up the documents in a random order. The assignment of the jth document is a random multinomial draw determined by the following probabilties for $k = 1, \ldots, K$:

$$p_{jk} \propto m_k^{\neg j} \cdot \frac{\Gamma(c_k^{\neg j} + \alpha_k)}{\Gamma(c_k^{\neg j} + c_j + \alpha_k)} \prod_w \frac{\Gamma(c_{kw}^{\neg j} + c_{jw} + \alpha_{kw})}{\Gamma(c_{kw}^{\neg j} + \alpha_{kw})}, \quad (3)$$

where m_k is the number of documents assigned to the kth cluster, c_{kw} is the number of occurrences of the wth word (or maximal substring) in the documents assigned to the kth cluster, and c_k is defined as $\sum_w c_{kw}$. The notation "$\neg j$" in Eq. (3) means that we use the corresponding statistics after removing the jth document. The probabilities $p_{j1}, \ldots, p_{jK}$ for each j should be normalized so that $\sum_k p_{jk} = 1$ is satisfied. Based on these K probabilities, we draw a new cluster assignment of the jth document.

We repeat a series of 50 iterations of this MCMC sampling ten times from different initializations. We then choose the run giving the largest likelihood among the ten runs and continue the chosen run until we reach 300 iterations. We regard the cluster assignments at the 300th iteration of the chosen run as the final output of our MCMC sampling. The time complexity of the MCMC sampling is $O(IKM)$, where I is the number of iterations.

4 Evaluation Experiment

4.1 Document Sets

We used four document sets in our experiment: two sets of Korean newswire articles and two sets of Chinese newswire articles. Each set consists of already categorized articles downloaded from the Web. Our task for evaluation is to guess the categories by clustering documents. No documents belong to more than one categories. Below we describe how we collected each set.

1. The first set is a set of Korean newswire articles downloaded from the Web site of *Seoul Newspaper*[1]. We denote this set as SEOUL1. This set consists of 35,783 articles from the six categories: Economy, Sports, International, Entertainment, Politics, and Culture. We collected this data set so that the numbers of the documents contained in each category is almost the same. Consequently, the ranges of document dates are different for each category. For example, while the dates observed in Entertainment category range from July 2007 to May 2011, those in Politics category range from July 2010 to May 2011. This is because the per day number of articles in Politics category is larger than that in Entertainment category. Table 1 gives the numbers of documents in each category. This table also includes the numbers for the other three document sets.
2. The second one is also a set of Korean newswire articles downloaded from the Web site of Seoul Newspaper. However, we collected the articles from the same range of the dates for all categories. We denote this set as SEOUL2. SEOUL2 consists of 52,730 articles whose dates range from January 2008 to September 2009. Each article belongs to one among the following four categories: Economy, Local Issues, Sports, and Politics.
3. The third one is a set of Chinese newswire articles downloaded from the Web site of *China News*[2]. This set, denoted as CNEWS, consists of 47,171 articles whose dates range from June to December in 2010. Each article belongs to one among the following six categories: Economy, International, Entertainment, Information & Technology, Domestic Issues, and Social Issues.
4. The fourth one is a set of Chinese newswire articles downloaded from *Xinhua Net*[3]. We denote this data set as XINHUA. This set consists of 20,127 articles whose dates range from May to December in 2009. Each article belongs to one among the following three categories: Economy, International, and Politics. For this set, it was relatively difficult to discriminate between Economy category and International category. Therefore, the evaluation results were not so good even though the number of categories is only three.

For each data set, we set the number of clusters K to the number of categories and ran the EM algorithm and the MCMC sampling described in Section 3.2. We regarded article categories as the ground truth for evaluation.

[1] `http://www.seoul.co.kr/`
[2] `http://www.chinanews.com/`
[3] `http://www.xinhuanet.com/`

Table 1. Number of documents belonging to each category in the four document sets prepared for our experiment, i.e., SEOUL1, SEOUL2, CNEWS, and XINHUA

SEOUL1 Korean document set						
Economy	Sports	International	Entertainment	Politics	Culture	total
5,870	5,129	6,309	6,206	6,242	6,027	35,783

SEOUL2 Korean document set				
Economy	Local	Sports	Politics	total
13,058	22,993	6,621	10,058	52,730

CNEWS Chinese document set						
Economy	International	Entertainment	Info&Tech	Domestic	Social	total
11,285	5,515	9,448	10,589	6,955	3,379	47,171

XINHUA Chinese document set			
Economy	International	Politics	total
3,290	10,230	6,607	20,127

4.2 Extraction and Reduction

For every document in each document set, we obtained two representations, i.e., a bag of maximal substrings representation and a bag of words representation. We obtained the former representation by extracting all maximal substrings from the document set and then counting their numbers of occurrences in each document. The latter was obtained by applying a supervised word extraction sentence by sentence and then count their numbers of occurrences in each document.

We applied KLT morphological analyzer [8] to SEOUL1 and SEOUL2. To CNEWS and XINHUA, we applied a word segmenter implemented based on an L1-regularized linear conditional random fields (CRF) [19]. The parameter optimization in training this Chinese word segmenter is based on a stochastic gradient descent algorithm with exponential decay scheduling [22]. This segmenter achieved the following F-scores for the four data sets of SIGHAN Bakeoff 2005 [21]: 0.943 (AS), 0.941 (HK), 0.929 (PK) and 0.960 (MSR). In our experiment, we used the segmenter trained with MSR data set, because this gave the highest F-score. For Korean language, we could not find any training data comparable with SIGHAN training data in its size and quality. Therefore, we used a dictionary-based morphological analyzer for Korean documents.

The wall clock time required for extracting all maximal substrings was only a few minutes for all data sets on a PC equipped with Intel Core i7 920 CPU. This wall clock time is not widely different from the time required for word extraction by our CRF-based Chinese word segmenter, though the time required for training the segmenter is not included. However, the wall clock time required for extracting all maximal substrings is much less than the time required by the Korean morphological analyzer, because this morphological analyzer achieves its excellence by dictionary lookups. While this morphological analyzer can provide part-of-speech tags, they are not used in the experiment.

Both for maximal substrings and the words extracted by the supervised method, we reduce the varieties based on their frequencies as Table 2 presents. Both in SEOUL1 and SEOUL2, we only removed low frequency maximal substrings by setting n_L to 50 or 100. For example, when $n_L = 50$, we remove all maximal substrings whose frequencies

表	关	其	实	同	们	品	还	面	与	事	内	据	已	天	示	都	最	商	目
区	民	理	主	外	度	但	务	此	子	定	小	合	：	之	加	当	重	报	力
得	司	体	政	法	员	展	名	手	入	《	》	金	%	信	从	水	次	并	增
被	道	期	因	相	万	间	比	（	企	提	所	如	）	情	利	没	应	制	很
数	位	明	点	好	平	调	联	安	心	正	今	费	i	格	计	然	及	e	受
三	量	收	n	化	海	两	保	建	学	消	起	看	至	o	济	影	着	更	些
台	东	持	投	总	果	户	问	意	北	基	门	性	近	管	达	第	视	认	南
里	向	接	件	去	该	交	强	由	，	称	口	无	解	演	系	广	种	式	车
西	a	布	购	规	设	题	P	息	城	特	告	只	；	局	代	亿	文	流	社
回	游	导	任	各	指	统	她	张	营	运	查	站	服	少	处	物	京	销	常
打	女	立	求	程	省	身	样	组	己	做	推	使	路	原	未	山	显	直	团
股	周	续	需	预	专	造	线	标	活	每	集	支	院	江	给	结	华	售	灾
权	二	话	客	？	完	传	让	份	先	么	气	士	际	低	知	府	非	王	众
技	别	首	整	片	超	想	老	警	证	州	放	战	级	c	几	单	斯	速	项
再	界	带	转	创	络	取	议	供	世	空	约	势	友	领	较	节	步	术	降
头	共	易	改	涨	快	变	案	或	委	风	难	S	s	办	采	引	始	准	观
r	施	防	那	军	责	决	备	一	质	李	确	升	房	包	感	率	十	D	选
响	源	则	黄	模	票	救	亚	况	款	德	争	反	光	昨	值	科	货	店	乐
随	型	何	获	t	某	农	注	博	球	米	环	研	尔	深	l	半	d	G	把
h	才	买	A	论	马	划	言	书	银	形	具	队	构	雨	媒	走	号	监	存

Fig. 1. A part of the maximal substrings of length one removed from CNEWS data set by our new reduction method proposed for Chinese documents

are less than 50. We did not remove any high frequency maximal substrings, because this gave no remarkable improvement. With respect to both SEOUL1 and SEOUL2, we applied the same reduction procedure to the words extracted by the morphological analyzer.

In CNEWS and XINHUA, we removed low frequency maximal substrings by setting n_L to 50 or 100. Further, we removed high frequency ones by setting r_H to 100, which means that we removed the top 100 highest frequency maximal substrings. The same reduction is also employed for reducing the variety of the words extracted by our CRF-based word segmenter. However, only for maximal substrings, we additionally reduced their variety by setting r_h to 1,000. That is, we removed the maximal substrings *of length one* from the top 1,000 highest frequency maximal substrings. We did not use this reduction in [11] and could not obtain any good results for maximal substrings. Figure 1 presents a part of the maximal substrings of length one removed from CNEWS data set by this new reduction method. As Figure 1 shows, many of the maximal substrings of length one have no power to discriminate topics. They may relate to a specific topic as a part of the words of length two or more. While this reduction using r_h led to a drastic improvement for maximal substrings, we could not obtain any remarkable improvements for the words extracted by our segmenter. This may be because the supervised segmenter did not give so many words of length one. Therefore, we employed the reduction using r_h only for maximal substrings.

Table 2 provides the number of different words (or different maximal substrings) W and the number of unique document word pairs (or unique document maximal substring pairs) M for all document sets. The number M is important, because the running time of our clustering algorithm is proportional to this number. Table 2 shows that M is increased roughly by factor of five when we use maximal substrings in place of the words extracted by the supervised method, i.e., KLT morphological analyzer or our

Table 2. Specifications of the four data sets used in our experiment

data set name	J	K	extraction method	n_L	r_H	r_h	W	M
SEOUL1	35,783	6	MaxSubstr	50	-	-	72,544	36,462,658
			MaxSubstr	100	-	-	44,048	34,813,328
			Morph	50	-	-	16,908	6,548,876
			Morph	100	-	-	10,165	6,196,036
SEOUL2	52,730	4	MaxSubstr	50	-	-	72,104	34,562,947
			MaxSubstr	100	-	-	45,360	33,037,750
			Morph	50	-	-	20,068	7,312,519
			Morph	100	-	-	12,411	6,913,269
CNEWS	47,171	6	MaxSubstr	50	100	1,000	220,107	42,187,771
			MaxSubstr	100	100	1,000	103,815	35,406,367
			WordSeg	50	100	-	19,998	7,155,607
			WordSeg	100	100	-	12,990	6,796,572
XINHUA	20,127	3	MaxSubstr	50	100	1,000	52,530	8,324,321
			MaxSubstr	100	100	1,000	24,635	6,775,577
			WordSeg	50	100	-	8,518	2,018,329
			WordSeg	100	100	-	5,444	1,862,819

CRF-based segmenter. Consequently, the running time of the document clustering is also increased roughly by factor of five. This is the price we should pay when we adopt bag of maximal substrings representation in place of bag of words representation.

4.3 Evaluation Measure

We evaluated the quality of document clustering as follows:

1. We calculate precision and recall for each cluster. Precision is defined as

$$\frac{\#(\text{true positive})}{\#(\text{true positive}) + \#(\text{false positive})},$$

   and recall is defined as

$$\frac{\#(\text{true positive})}{\#(\text{true positive}) + \#(\text{false negative})};$$

2. We calculate *F-score* as the harmonic mean of precision and recall; and
3. The F-score is micro-averaged over all clusters.

The above micro-averaged F-score is our evaluation measure. From here, we denote this micro-averaged F-score simply as F-score.

We ran document clustering 50 times and obtained 50 F-scores for each setting. Table 2 gives four rows for each document set. That is, we tried four settings for each set. Further, we conducted two types of inference, i.e., the EM algorithm and the MCMC sampling. Consequently, we tried eight settings for each data set and had a set of 50 F-scores for each of these eight settings. The evaluation result was represented by the mean and standard deviation of 50 F-scores for each of the eight settings with respect to each data set.

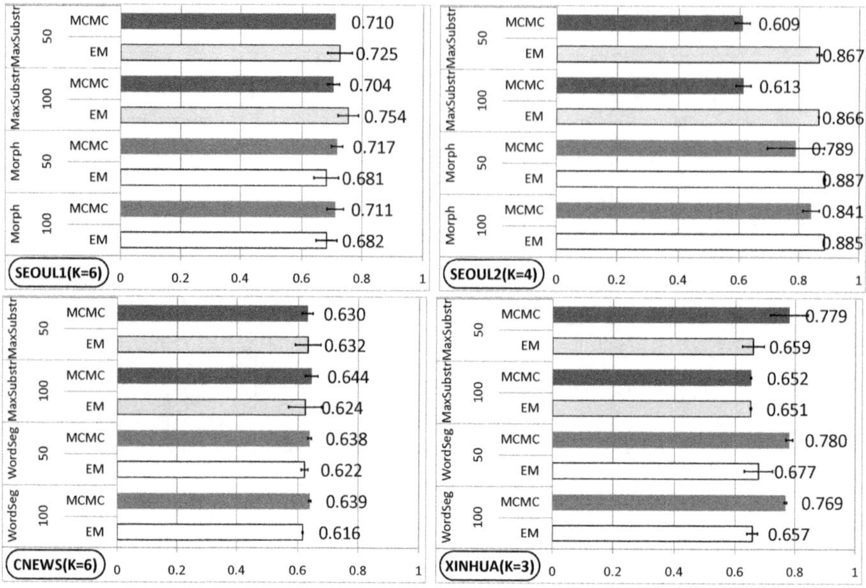

Fig. 2. Comparing between the F-scores achieved with bag of maximal substrings representation and those achieved with bag of words representation

4.4 Analysis

Figure 2 presents all results with four charts corresponding to four data sets.

The top left chart gives the results for SEOUL1 data set. Each bar accompanied with an error bar shows the mean and standard deviation of 50 F-scores obtained by running the clustering algorithm 50 times for each setting. The four bars in the upper half gives the results obtained when we use maximal substrings as elementary building block of documents, and the four bars in the lower half gives the results obtained when we use the words extracted by the morphological analyzer. For both cases, we tested the two settings, $n_L = 50$ and $n_L = 100$, for n_L and ran the two types of inference, the EM algorithm and the MCMC sampling. Therefore, we have eight settings in total. Also for the other data sets, we have eight settings. With respect to SEOUL1, we achieved the best mean F-score 0.754 when we used maximal substrings, reduced their variety by setting $n_L = 100$, and ran the EM algorithm. The difference from the mean F-scores obtained with the words extracted by the morphological analyzer is statistically significant based on a two-tailed Student's t-test with p value less than 0.01.

The top right chart presents the results for SEOUL2. For this data set, the EM algorithm led to a better result than the MCMC sampling for every setting. We could obtain the best mean F-score 0.887 when we used the words extracted by the morphological analyzer, reduced their variety by setting $n_L = 50$, and ran the EM algorithm for clustering. The difference from the best result obtained with maximal substrings is statistically significant based on a two-tailed Student's t-test with p value less than 0.01. However, the difference is at most 0.020 ($= 0.887 - 0.867$). On the other hand, for SEOUL1, the difference of the best mean F-score obtained with maximal substrings from that obtained with the words given by the morphological analyzer amounts to 0.037 (= 0.754 − 0.717).

The bottom left chart shows the results for CNEWS. Recall that we employed an additional reduction of the variety of maximal substrings for CNEWS and XINHUA. To be specific, we remove the maximal substrings of length one from the 1,000 highest frequency maximal substrings. For CNEWS, the chart shows that all mean F-scores are almost the same. In fact, the best mean F-score obtained with maximal substrings and that obtained with the words extracted by our CRF-based word segmenter gave no significant difference based on a one-tailed Student's t-test with p value less than 0.05.

The bottom right chart provides the results for XINHUA. For this data set, the MCMC sampling is likely to give better results than the EM. The best mean F-score obtained with maximal substrings and that obtained with the words extracted by our CRF-based word segmenter gave no significant difference based on a one-tailed Student's t-test with p value less than 0.05. With respect to bag of maximal substrings representation, the mean F-score dropped when we set n_L to 100, though, for CNEWS data set, the two settings of n_L gave no significant differences. Therefore, we need a little care in reducing the variety of maximal substrings for Chinese documents lest we remove too many low frequency ones.

Based on Figure 2, we can draw the following considerations. First, we should try both the EM algorithm and the MCMC sampling in document clustering, because which one performs better depends on the data. For example, we can conduct a rough comparison on a hold out document set. This argument applies both to maximal substrings and the words extracted by a supervised method.

Second, with respect to the comparison between the clustering quality given by bag of maximal substrings representation and that given by bag of words representation, which one performs better again depends on the data. However, the difference is not so large. Therefore, we can use one among the two representations consistently. When we have a hand-maintained dictionary or a human annotated training data set of large enough size for the tasks we envision, we can consistently use a supervised word extraction, because M in Table 2 is far smaller for bag of words representation than for bag of maximal substrings representation and thus can conduct text mining tasks efficiently.

However, out of vocabulary words, i.e., the words not contained in training data sets, may have a serious effect on text mining sitting on a supervised word extraction. This is the very reason why an elaborated word n-gram model was proposed in [13]. Further, text data available from SNS environments are a typical example where we can observe a wide variety of out of vocabulary words, because SNS users are likely to coin new terms, e.g. hard-to-understand abbreviations and homophones derived from widely used words, without hesitation. In such a case, unsupervised word extraction will show an advantage.

5 Conclusions

As text data originating from SNS environments come to show a wider diversity in writing style or vocabularies, unsupervised extraction of elementary building blocks from documents becomes more important as a preprocessing for various text mining techniques than before. This paper provided the results where we compare bag of maximal substrings representation with bag of words representation in a typical text mining task, i.e., in document clustering, because maximal substrings can be efficiently extracted in an unsupervised manner.

Our results showed that bag of maximal substrings representation was as effective as bag of words representation. While the two representations may show a statistically significant difference in their effectiveness, the winner changes from data to data. Further, the difference is not so large to prevent us from adopting one representation consistently. With respect to the running time and memory space of document clustering, bag of maximal substrings representation showed no advantage, because the number of maximal substrings is far larger than that of the words extracted by a supervised method from the same document set. However, when we use a supervised word extraction, we should update a training data set constantly, because it is a fact that many new words are coined day by day especially in SNS environments.

Therefore, it must be an important future work to acquire a more realistic insight with respect to the trade-off between the following two types of cost:

- the execution time and memory space required for a text mining task conducted on a set of documents represented as bags of maximal substrings; and
- the hours and money required for preparing and constantly updating training data sets used in a supervised word extraction.

In addition, a method for further reducing the variety of maximal substrings is required to reduce the running time of mining tasks using maximal substrings.

We also have a plan to conduct experiments where we use maximal substrings as elementary building blocks of DNA/RNA sequences. We would like to propose a multi-topic analysis, e.g. by using latent Dirichlet allocation [2], with maximal substrings and to revise the results reported in [3], where the authors simply use k-mers of fixed length as elementary building blocks of DNA/RNA sequences.

Acknowledgements. This work was done as a joint research with National Institute of Informatics (NII) and was also supported in part by Nagasaki University Strategy for Fostering Young Scientists with funding provided by Special Coordination Funds for Promoting Science and Technology of the Ministry of Education, Culture, Sports, Science and Technology (MEXT).

References

1. Abouelhoda, M., Ohlebusch, E., Kurtz, S.: Optimal Exact String Matching Based on Suffix Arrays. In: Laender, A.H.F., Oliveira, A.L. (eds.) SPIRE 2002. LNCS, vol. 2476, pp. 31–43. Springer, Heidelberg (2002)
2. Blei, D., Ng, A., Jordan, M.: Latent Dirichlet Allocation. Journal of Machine Learning Research 3, 993–1022 (2003)
3. Chen, X., Hu, X., Shen, X., Rosen, G.: Probabilistic Topic Modeling for Genomic Data Interpretation. In: Park, T., Tsui, S.K.-W., Chen, L., Ng, M.K., Wong, L., Hu, X. (eds.) IEEE International Conference on Bioinformatics and Biomedicine, pp. 18–21. IEEE (2010)

4. Choi, K.-S., Isahara, H., Kanzaki, K., Kim, H., Pak, S.M., Sun, M.: Word Segmentation Standard in Chinese, Japanese and Korean. In: 7th Workshop on Asian Language Resources, pp. 179–186. Association for Computational Linguistics (2009)
5. Chumwatana, T., Wong, K., Xie, H.: An Automatic Indexing Technique for Thai Texts Using Frequent Max Substring. In: Imsombut, A. (ed.) Eighth International Symposium on Natural Language Processing, pp. 67–72. IEEE (2009)
6. Chumwatana, T., Wong, K., Xie, H.: A SOM-Based Document Clustering Using Frequent Max Substrings for Non-Segmented Texts. Journal of Intelligent Learning Systems & Applications 2, 117–125 (2010)
7. Kasai, T., Lee, G., Arimura, H., Arikawa, S., Park, K.: Linear-Time Longest-Common-Prefix Computation in Suffix Arrays and Its Applications. In: Amir, A., Landau, G.M. (eds.) CPM 2001. LNCS, vol. 2089, pp. 181–192. Springer, Heidelberg (2001)
8. Gang, S.: Korean Morphological Analyzer KLT Version 2.10b (2009), `http://nlp.kookmin.ac.kr/HAM/kor/`
9. Li, Y., Chung, S.M., Holt, J.D.: Text Document Clustering Based on Frequent Word Meaning Sequences. Data & Knowledge Engineering 64, 381–404 (2008)
10. Madsen, R., Kauchak, D., Elkan, C.: Modeling Word Burstiness Using the Dirichlet Distribution. In: Raedt, L.D., Wrobel, S. (eds.) 22nd International Conference on Machine Learning, pp. 545–552. ACM (2005)
11. Masada, T., Shibata, Y., Oguri, K.: Documents as a Bag of Maximal Substrings: An Unsupervised Feature Extraction for Document Clustering. In: 13th International Conference on Enterprise Information Systems, pp.5–13. INSTICC (2011)
12. Minka, T.: Estimating a Dirichlet Distribution (2000), `http://research.microsoft.com/en-us/um/people/minka/papers/dirichlet/`
13. Mochihashi, D., Yamada, T., Ueda, N.: Bayesian Unsupervised Word Segmentation with Nested Pitman-Yor Language Modeling. In: Joint Conference of the 47th Annual Meeting of the Association for Computational Linguistics and the Fourth International Joint Conference on Natural Language Processing of the Asian Federation of Natural Language Processing, pp. 100–108. Association for Computational Linguistics (2009)
14. Navarro, G., Mäkinen, V.: Compressed Full-Text Indexes. ACM Comput. Surv. 39(1) (2007)
15. Nigam, K., McCallum, A., Thrun, S., Mitchell, T.: Text Classification from Labeled and Unlabeled Documents Using EM. Machine Learning 39(2/3), 103–134 (2000)
16. Nong, G., Zhang, S., Chan, W.H.: Two Efficient Algorithms for Linear Time Suffix Array Construction. IEEE Transactions on Computers 99(PrePrints) (2008)
17. Okanohara, D., Tsujii, J.: Text Categorization with All Substring Features. In: Ninth SIAM International Conference on Data Mining, pp. 838–846. Society for Industrial and Applied Mathematics (2009)
18. Poon, H., Cherry, C., Toutanova, K.: Unsupervised Morphological Segmentation with Log-Linear Models. In: Human Language Technologies: The 2009 Annual Conference of the North American Chapter of the Association for Computational Linguistics, pp. 209–217. Association for Computational Linguistics (2009)
19. Sutton, C., McCallum, A.: An Introduction to Conditional Random Fields for Relational Learning. In: Getoor, L., Taskar, B. (eds.) Introduction to Statistical Relational Learning, pp. 93–128. The MIT Press (2007)
20. Teh, Y.W.: A Hierarchical Bayesian Language Model Based on Pitman-Yor Processes. In: The 21st International Conference on Computational Linguistics and 44th Annual Meeting of the Association for Computational Linguistics, pp. 985–992. Association for Computational Linguistics (2006)

21. Tseng, H., Chang, P., Andrew, G., Jurafsky, D., Manning, C.: A Conditional Random Field Word Segmenter for SIGHAN Bakeoff 2005. In: Fourth SIGHAN Workshop on Chinese Language Processing, pp. 168–171. Association for Computational Linguistics (2005)
22. Tsuruoka, Y., Tsujii, J., Ananiadou, S.: Stochastic Gradient Descent Training for L1-Regularized Log-Linear Models with Cumulative Penalty. In: Joint Conference of the 47th Annual Meeting of the Association for Computational Linguistics and the fourth International Joint Conference on Natural Language Processing of the Asian Federation of Natural Language Processing, pp. 477–485. Association for Computational Linguistics (2009)
23. Wang, X., McCallum, A.: Topics over Time: a Non-Markov Continuous-Time Model of Topical Trends. In: 12th ACM SIGKDD International Conference on Knowledge Discovery and Data Mining, pp. 424–433. ACM (2006)
24. Zhang, D., Dong, Y.: Semantic, Hierarchical, Online Clustering of Web Search Results. In: Yu, J.X., Lin, X., Lu, H., Zhang, Y. (eds.) APWeb 2004. LNCS, vol. 3007, pp. 69–78. Springer, Heidelberg (2004)
25. Zhang, D., Lee, W.: Extracting Key-Substring-Group Features for Text Classification. In: 12th ACM SIGKDD International Conference on Knowledge Discovery and Data Mining, pp. 474–483. ACM (2006)

Imbalanced Classification Problems: Systematic Study, Issues and Best Practices

Camelia Lemnaru and Rodica Potolea

Technical University of Cluj-Napoca, Computer Science Department
26 Baritiu St., Room C9, 400027, Cluj-Napoca, Romania
{Camelia.Lemnaru,Rodica.Potolea}@cs.utcluj.ro

Abstract. This paper provides a systematic study of the issues and possible solutions to the class imbalance problem. A set of standard classification algorithms is considered and their performance on benchmark data is analyzed. Our experiments show that, in an imbalanced problem, the imbalance ratio (IR) can be used in conjunction with the instances per attribute ratio (IAR), to evaluate the appropriate classifier that best fits the situation. Also, MLP and C4.5 are less affected by the imbalance, while SVM generally performs poorly in imbalanced problems. The possible solutions for overcoming these classifier issues are also presented. The overall vision is that when dealing with imbalanced problems, one should consider a wider context, taking into account several factors simultaneously: the imbalance, together with other data-related particularities and the classification algorithms with their associated parameters.

Keywords: Class imbalance, Metrics, Classifiers, Comprehensive study.

1 Introduction

One of the current important issues in data mining research, triggered by the rapid shift in status from academic to applied science, is that of class imbalance. It appears in areas where the classifier has to identify a rare but important case [1], such as detecting fraudulent phone calls, intrusions, failures in the manufacturing process, or in diagnosing rare medical diseases. In such domains, the imbalance hinders the capability of traditional classification algorithms to identify cases of interest most of the time.

A problem is imbalanced if, in the available data, a specific class is represented by a very small number of instances compared to other classes [2]. It is common practice to consider only binary problems when dealing with imbalance (any multi-class problem can be converted to one/more binary problems). The majority class is usually referred to as the negative class and the minority class as the positive class, since it is the one of interest, possessing the same or (often) greater importance than the negative class.

The first step in providing viable solutions for imbalanced domains is to understand the problem: what is the real issue with the imbalance? Recent studies suggest that the nature of the imbalance problems is actually manifold. In [3], two issues are considered as being crucial: (1) insufficient data to build a model, in case

R. Zhang et al. (Eds.): ICEIS 2011, LNBIP 102, pp. 35–50, 2012.

the minority class has only a few examples (similar to dealing with small samples/small data sets), (2) too many "special cases" in the minority class, so that in the class itself, some kind of sub-clustering occurs, which might lead again to insufficient examples for correctly identifying such a sub-cluster.

An important theoretical result related to the nature of class imbalance is presented in [2], where it is concluded that the imbalance problem is a relative problem, which depends on: (1) the imbalance ratio, i.e. the ratio of the majority to the minority instances, (2) the complexity of the concept represented by the data, (3) the overall size of the training set and (4) the classifier involved. The experiments there were conducted on artificially generated data, in the attempt to simulate different imbalance ratios, complexities and data set sizes. The results have indicated that C5.0 is the most sensitive learner to the imbalance problem, while the Multilayer Perceptron showed a less categorical sensitivity pattern and the Support Vector Machine seemed to be insensitive to the problem.

In this paper we perform a set of experiments on real world benchmark data sets, to study the effect of the class imbalance problem on several classes of algorithms: Decision Trees, instance based learning, Bayesian methods, ensemble methods, Artificial Neural Networks and Support Vector Machines. Our initial analysis focuses on the factors described in [2] – data set size, imbalance ratio, complexity and learning algorithm, in an attempt to address some of the open questions presented there, related to the applicability of the conclusions drawn on artificial data in real-world settings. We conducted our experiments by evaluating various performance metrics. The results of this first investigation suggest that a more meaningful analysis can be performed by considering another data set meta-feature, which combines size and complexity information. The new meta-feature allows for a faster and easier initial assessment of a particular data set. Also, we review the main options for improving the behavior of classifiers in imbalanced problems available in literature.

2 Metrics

Almost all metrics are represented in terms of the elements of the confusion matrix generated by the model on a test sample (Table 1). A column represents an actual class, while a row represents the predicted class. The total number of instances in the test set is represented on the top of the table (P=total number of positive instances, and N=total number of negative instances), while the number of instances predicted to belong to each class are represented to the left of the table (p= total number of instances classified as positive; n=total number of instances classified as negative). TP (*true positives*) is the number of correctly classified positive examples. In a similar fashion, FN (*false negatives*), is the number of positive examples classified as negative, TN (*true negatives*) – the number of correctly classified negative examples, and finally, FP (*false positives*) – the negative examples for which the positive class was predicted.

Perhaps the most popular performance metric for classification problems is the accuracy of the induced model on a test sample. It provides a good general estimation of the prediction capabilities of a model, but it has been recently declared inadequate by the scientific community for imbalanced or cost-sensitive problems [4]. A classical example of why the accuracy is not an appropriate metric in imbalanced problem is the classification of pixels in mammogram images [5].

Table 1. The confusion matrix

<table>
<tr><td colspan="3" rowspan="3">Total number of instances</td><td>P</td><td>N</td></tr>
<tr><td colspan="2">Actual Class</td></tr>
<tr><td>positive</td><td>negative</td></tr>
<tr><td>p</td><td rowspan="2">Predicted Class</td><td>positive</td><td>TP</td><td>FP</td></tr>
<tr><td>n</td><td>negative</td><td>FN</td><td>TN</td></tr>
</table>

Recent studies suggest using new approaches for evaluating the performance in such problems. In [6, 7, 8], the *area under the ROC curve* (AUC) is employed to assess the performance of several sampling techniques. The ROC curve measures the performance of a learner under all possible trade-offs between the true positive rate ($TP_{rate} = TP/P$) and the false positive rate ($FP_{rate} = FP/N$). It is considered to be a consistent measure, even under highly skewed class distributions. The AUC provides a scalar summary performance assessment for learning algorithms, based on the ROC curve. However, it evaluates all possible decision thresholds, while in imbalanced domains the focus should be on the performance at a high decision threshold.

In [1], the *geometric mean* (GM) is proposed as a metric for evaluating classifiers in imbalanced domains. It is computed as the geometric mean of TP_{rate} and TN_{rate} ($TN_{rate} = TN/N$) and it provides a more objective estimation of the prediction capabilities of a model than the accuracy. It has been employed in several studies on imbalanced problems [6, 9].

The average accuracy obtained on either/each class also known as *balanced accuracy*, is another symmetric measure which is more suited for imbalanced problems [14]. If a classifier performs equally well on both classes, the balanced accuracy reduces to its conventional correspondent. If, on the other hand, the classifier favors one class – the majority class – in an imbalanced problem, and performs weakly on the other, then the balanced accuracy will drop accordingly, while the conventional accuracy will still be high.

Another metric is the *f-measure*, or *f-score* [4, 9], i.e. the harmonic mean between the *precision* ($Prec = TP/p$) and *recall* ($Rec = TP/P = TP_{rate}$). It provides a trade-off between the correct identification of the positive class and the cost (in number of FP errors) of false alarms. A generalization of the metric – the f_β*-measure* – can be tuned to put more emphasis on either the recall or precision: $f_\beta\text{-}measure = (1+\beta^2) * precision * recall / (\beta^2 * recall + precision)$; $\beta>1$ when we need to accentuate recall more. For a specific problem, the goal is to identify the appropriate β such that the right amount of penalization for the false negatives is provided.

For an imbalanced problem, the TP_{rate} is usually the most important. In [4], the strategy to follow in imbalanced problems is to maximize recall (i.e. TP_{rate}) while keeping precision under control. Grzymala [11] suggests that in imbalanced problems more attention should be given to sensitivity (TP_{rate}) than to specificity (TN_{rate}). This is rather natural, since usually the TN_{rate} is high while the TP_{rate} is low in such problems. Therefore the goal is to increase the sensitivity, without degrading of specificity.

Careful and correct selection of the metric in imbalanced problems is essential for the success of a data mining effort in such domains. The metric should also reflect the goal of the classification process, not just the data imbalance. Thus, if we are also dealing with imbalance at the level of the error costs, then a cost-sensitive metric should be more appropriate (e.g. associate a cost parameter to the balanced accuracy or geometric mean). If, on the other hand, we have the interest in identifying both classes correctly, then an equidistant metric, such as the geometric mean, or balanced accuracy, provides a fair estimation.

3 The Effect of Class Imbalance on Different Classifiers: Empirical Study

As concluded in [2], the nature of the imbalance problem resides in more than just the imbalance ratio (IR). Our set of experiments tries to validate the statement on benchmark problems.

In order to study the nature of the imbalance problem, we have considered 34 data sets from the UCI machine learning data repository [12] (Table 2). A number of problems were modified to obtain binary classification problems from multi-class data. Also, three of the relatively large data sets were under-sampled to generate higher IR values (contain *_IR* in their name).

Table 2. Benchmark data sets employed in the experiments

Data set	No. Att.	No. Inst.	IR	IAR	C	Data set	No. Att.	No. Inst.	IR	IAR	C
Bupa	6	345	1	58	3	Ecoli_im_rm	8	336	3	42	2
Haberman_1	4	367	1	92	3	Glass_NW	11	214	3	19	4
Cleve	14	303	1	22	5	Vehicle_van	19	846	3	45	4
Monk3	7	554	1	79	4	Chess_IR5	37	2002	5	54	5
Monk1	7	556	1	79	5	Segment_1	20	1500	6	75	3
Australian	15	690	1	46	5	Ecoli_imu	8	336	9	42	4
Crx	16	690	1	43	5	Segment_1 _IR10	20	1424	10	71	3
Chess	37	3196	1	86	5	Tic-tac-toe_IR10	10	689	10	69	6
Mushrooms	23	8124	1	353	4	German_IR10	21	769	10	37	7
Breast-cancer	10	286	2	29	2	Sick-euthyroid	26	3163	10	122	5
Glass_BWNFP	11	214	2	19	3	Glass_VWFP	11	214	12	19	3
Glass_BWFP	11	214	2	19	4	Sick	30	3772	15	126	5
Vote	17	435	2	26	3	Ecoli_bin	8	336	16	42	3
Wisconsin	10	699	2	70	4	Caravan	86	5822	16	68	11
Pima	7	768	2	110	4	Ecoli_im_rm	8	336	3	42	2
Tic-tac-toe	10	958	2	96	7	Glass_NW	11	214	3	19	4
German	21	1000	2	48	7	Vehicle_van	19	846	3	45	4

The complexity of each data set was approximated, as suggested in [2], to $C = \log_2 L$, where L is the number of leaves generated by the C4.5 decision tree learner. Also, the values for IR, IAR and C have been rounded.

In this study, learning algorithms belonging to 6 different classes were considered: instance based learning – kNN (k Nearest Neighbor), Decision Trees – C4.5, Support Vector Machines – SVM, Artificial Neural Networks – MLP (Multilayer Perceptron), Bayesian learning – NB (Naïve Bayes) and ensemble learning – AB (AdaBoost.M1). We have employed the implementation in the Weka framework [13] for the six methods selected, and their default parameter values. The evaluations have been performed using a 10-fold cross validation loop, and the average values obtained are reported. The following metrics were recorded: the accuracy (Acc), TP_{rate}, and TN_{rate}. Also, the geometric mean (GM), the balanced accuracy (BAcc) and the Fmeasure (Fmeas) have been computed. The minority class in all problems is the positive class.

An initial analysis was carried out on the data grouped by size, IR and complexity (C), into the categories presented in Table 3. Not all combinations of the three categories can be found in the data sets we have evaluated: for example, a very large complexity is only represented in the large data sets category. Table 4 presents a summary of the results obtained by the learning algorithms on the different categories of problems. Shaded rows represent data categories sensitive to imbalance, while non-shaded rows represent groups of problems on which classifiers have a robust behavior, under TP_{rate}. We have selected this metric to assess robustness since, as suggested in [2], performance degradation is related to a large drop in the TP_{rate}. Also, for each data set category we have marked the best performance (bolded) and the worst performance (underlined).

Table 3. Data set grouping on size, IR, C

Dimension Category	*Very small*	*Small*	*Medium*	*Large*	*Very large*
Size (no. of instances)	<400	400-1500	2000-5000	>5000	-
Rounded IR	-	<9	-	>=9	-
Rounded C	-	<=2	[3,4]	[5,9]	>=10

Table 4. TPrates obtained by classifiers on the different categories of problems

Set Size	IR	Complexity	kNN	C4.5	SVM	MLP	NB	AB
very small		*Small*	.53	.5	.5	.61	**65**	.57
	<9	*Medium*	**.72**	**.71**	.3	.61	.65	.65
		Large	.73	.72	.79	.76	**.8**	**.81**
	>=9	*Medium*	.52	.6	.15	.59	**.83**	.4
small	<9	*Medium*	.88	**.89**	**.89**	**.9**	**.89**	.83
		Large	.81	.77	**.85**	.81	.62	.67
	>=9	*Medium*	**.98**	.94	**.98**	**.99**	.98	**.99**
		Large	.24	.09	.47	**.65**	.09	.0
medium	<9	*Large*	.74	**.97**	.92	**.98**	.69	.85
	>=9	*Medium*	.6	**.91**	.5	.86	.78	.89
		Large	.57	**.88**	.04	.73	.84	.82
large	<9	*Large*	**1**	**1**	**1**	**1**	.92	.98
	>=9	*Very Large*	.06	.0	.01	.0	**.39**	.0

The results agree with the conclusions presented in [2], that the value of the IR plays an important role in the performance of the classifiers. However, an increase in the complexity does not necessarily lead to classifier performance degradation: for very small data sets, one would expect that a large complexity significantly affects the capacity of classifiers to achieve acceptable performance scores, even for small IRs. As it can be observed from Fig. 1 - 4, the behavior of classifiers on large complexity data sets is better than on categories of problems of smaller complexity (in Fig. 3 almost all classifiers seem to be robust to the imbalance problem). Still, for the other set size categories (small, medium and large), a large imbalance (IR>=9) associated with increased complexity (large, large and very large, respectively) always affects the learning process (Table 3).

The results suggest that neither data set size, nor the complexity alone represent good (i.e. monotonic) indicators of the IR's influence in the classification process. We consider that poor concept identification is related to the lack of information caused by insufficient examples to learn from. However, a relation between problem size, complexity and classifier performance is revealed, i.e. the larger the data set size, the higher the complexity for which the performance degradation becomes clear. This suggests the existence of another meta-feature which better discriminates the classifier robustness when faced with imbalanced problems. Such a meta-feature, the instance per attribute ratio (IAR), will be introduced shortly.

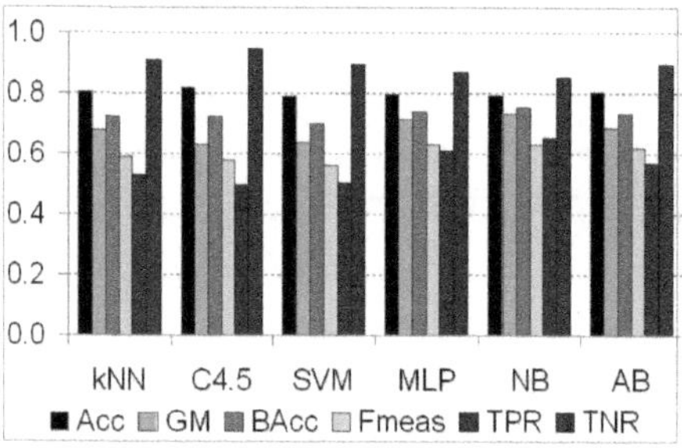

Fig. 1. Size very small, IR<9, C small

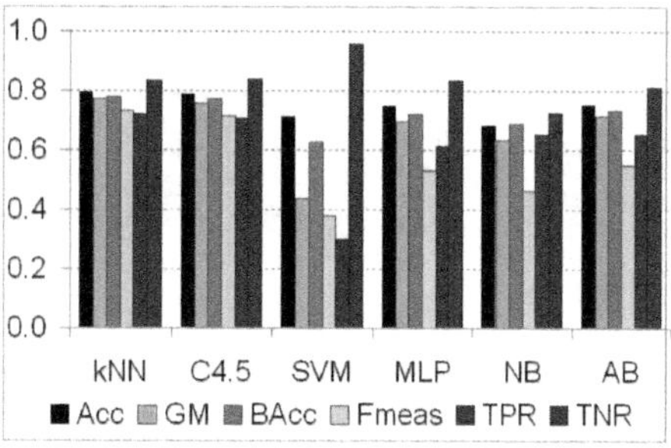

Fig. 2. Size very small, IR<9, C medium

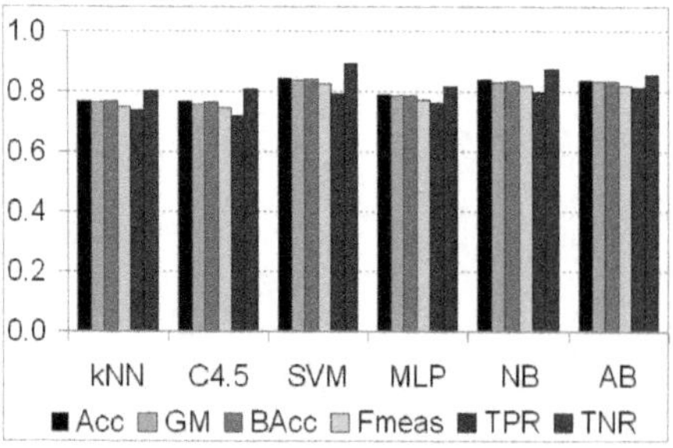

Fig. 3. Size very small, IR<9, C large

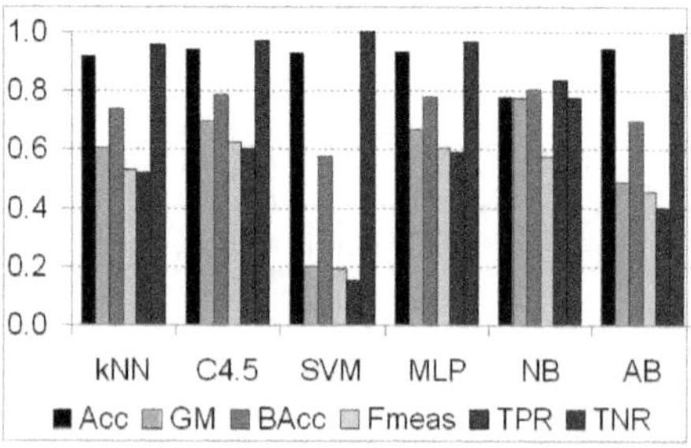

Fig. 4. Size very small, IR>=9, C medium

The diagrams in Fig. 5 - 7 present the performance of the different classifiers, under different metrics, on the problem categories which affect their learning capacity. The accuracy alone is not a good measure of performance. The analysis should focus on the following criteria: high values for TP_{rate}, GM, BAcc and Fmeasure indicate a good classification, while high TN_{rate} values reveal a classification which is biased towards the majority class. Moreover, the larger the difference between the TN_{rate} and the TP_{rate}, the more biased the classification process is.

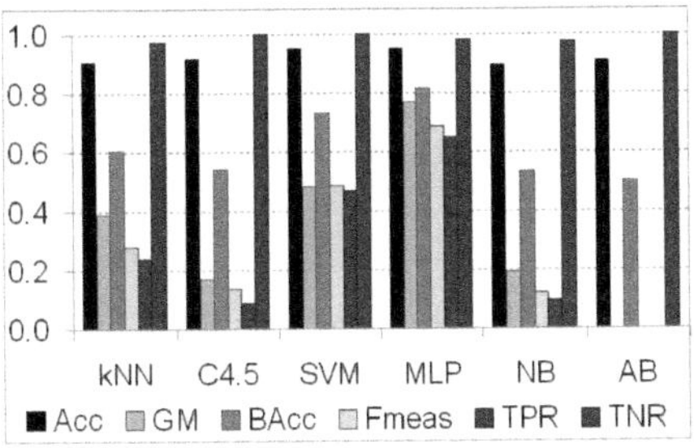

Fig. 5. Size small, C large

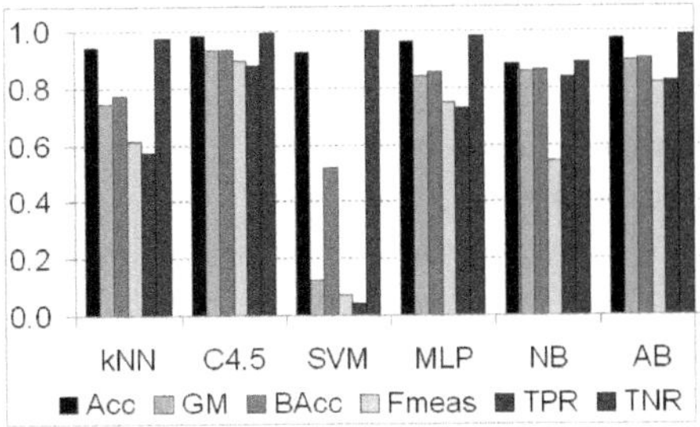

Fig. 6. Size medium, C large

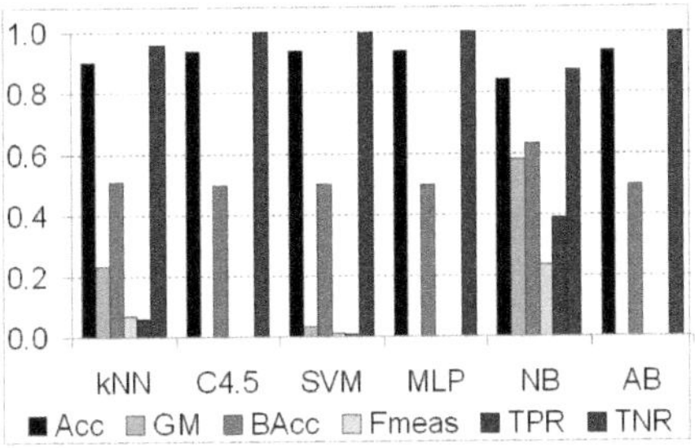

Fig. 7. Size large, C v. large

The results prove that the learning capabilities of the classifiers considered are affected to some extent by an increased imbalance in conjunction with the other data-related particularities. It can be observed that, like in [2], MLPs are generally more robust than C4.5 to the imbalance problem. Moreover, they are the least affected by the imbalance-related factors, in most cases. As an exception, C4.5 performs noticeably better than MLP (and all the others, actually) on medium sized data sets, with large IR and C (Fig. 6).

The analysis also reveals that the NB classifiers have a good general behavior when dealing with a very large imbalance. In some cases they even yield the best performance (Fig. 1, 4, 7 – all with IR>=9). However, they are not as robust as MLPs, since, in some cases, they achieve a very poor performance (Fig. 5). Although not always the best classifier, MLPs yield at least the second best performance in all cases, which makes them the most robust out of all the classifiers evaluated. None of the kNN and AB show remarkable results in any of the cases studied, which makes them suitable only for baseline problem assessment.

The above observations provide an affirmative answer to one of the open questions in [2], whether the conclusions presented there can be applied to real-world domains. However, our results also indicate that SVM are the most sensitive to imbalance. This means that, for the particular case of SVMs, the conclusion drawn from experiments on artificial data cannot be extended to real data sets. A justification for this could be the following: in the case of artificial data sets, even for large IRs, the examples which represent reliable support vectors are present in the data, due to the systematic data generation process, while in the case of real problems, these vital learning elements might be missing. This makes SVMs the weakest classifiers in mostreal-world imbalanced problems.

We have performed a second analysis for studying the effect of imbalanced problems on the performance of the classifiers, using another data set grouping: by IR and by the ratio between the number of instances and the number of attributes (IAR). We consider this new meta-feature successfully combines size and complexity information: a small IAR should yield a higher classifier sensibility to the imbalance problem, while a very large IAR should provide more robustness to the imbalance. The categories for this second analysis are summarized in Table 5.

By re-grouping the evaluations according to this new criterion, we noticed a more clear separation between the different categories and that classifiers better learn with larger IARs. Indeed, as we can observe from Table 6, the larger the IAR, the larger the IR for which the TP_{rate} value of the classifiers decreases. Also, for the same IR, as IAR increases, classifiers are more robust to the imbalance. The different levels of shading used for the rows indicate the performance level (more shading, better average performance). Again, we have marked the highest and lowest TP_{rate} values for each problem category (bolded and underlined, respectively).

Fig. 8 – 11 present the performance of the classifiers under this second categorization, for all metrics considered, on the relevant groups (problems which are affected the most by the imbalance related issues). The diagrams indicate again that SVM are unstable classifiers for imbalanced problems (strongly biased towards the majority class). Out of all classifiers, MLP are the most robust, yielding either the best or second best performance. The NB classifier generally achieves the best recognition of the minority class (maximum TP_{rate}).

Table 5. Data set grouping on IR, IAR

Category	*Rounded IR*			*Rounded IAR*			
Type	Balanced	Small IR	Large IR	Small	Medium	Large	Very large
Value	1	[2,3]	>=4	<=60	(60,110]	(110,200]	>200

Table 6. TPrateson IR and IAR grouping

IR	IAR	kNN	C4.5	SVM	MLP	NB	AB
Balanced	*Small*	.68	.71	.72	.7	<u>.58</u>	**.75**
	Medium	**.94**	**.95**	.8	.86	<u>.78</u>	.85
	Very large	**1**	**1**	**1**	**1**	<u>.92</u>	.98
Small	*Small*	.71	.69	<u>.53</u>	.72	**.78**	.65
	Medium	.81	.77	**.82**	**.83**	.67	<u>.63</u>
Large	*Small*	.5	.55	<u>.27</u>	.62	**.64**	.4
	Medium	.53	.52	**.72**	**.73**	.59	<u>.49</u>
	Large	.58	**.89**	<u>.19</u>	.74	.82	.84

However, it is not the best classifier due to poor recognition of the majority class (lowest TN_{rate} in all cases). This makes the NB classifier the most appropriate for imbalanced problems in which the minority class possesses a significantly larger importance than the majority class. Similar to the previous analysis, kNN and AB have a variable behavior, which hinders the identification of a situation in which they could guarantee quality results. If we have found that a large IAR improves the behavior of classifiers for the same IR, it appears that C4.5 is the most responsive to a large IAR, as it can be observed from Fig. 11. All the above measurements refer to pruned versions of C4.5.

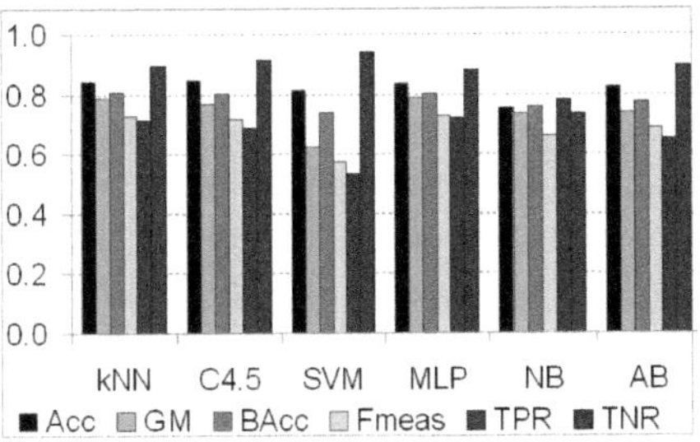

Fig. 8. IR small imbalance, IAR small

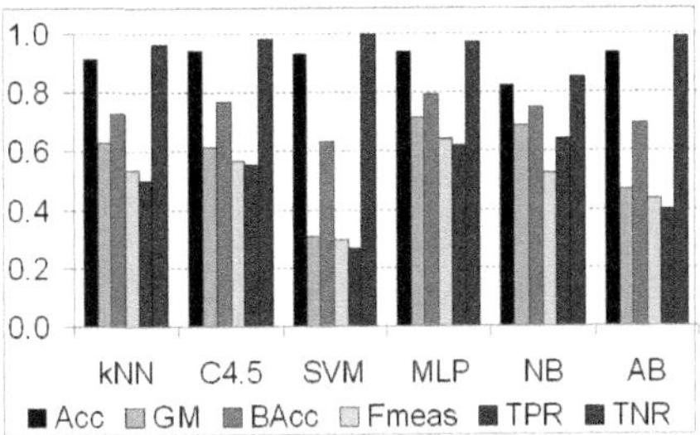

Fig. 9. IR large, IAR small

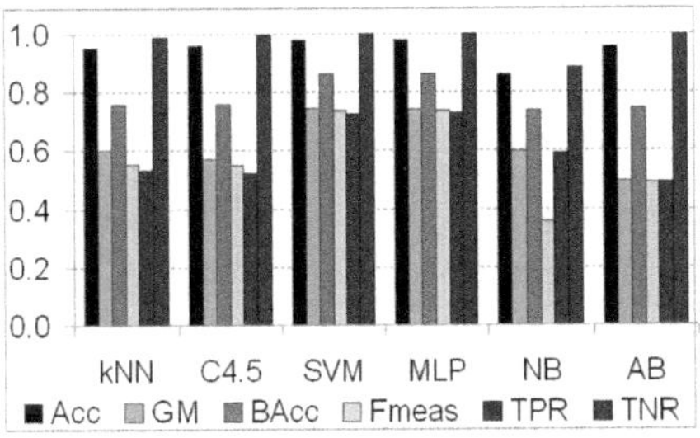

Fig. 10. IR large, IAR medium

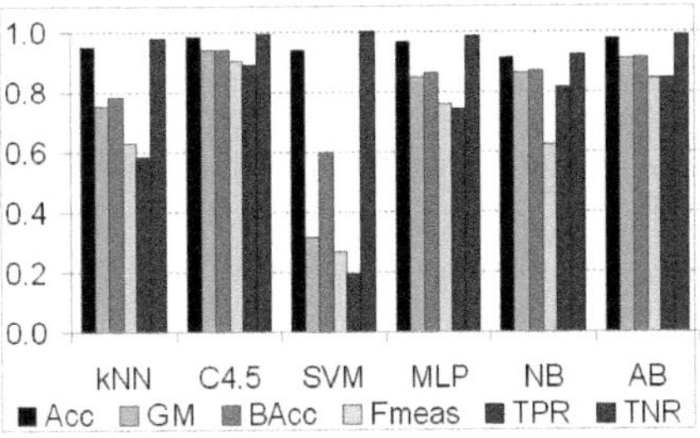

Fig. 11. IR large, IAR large

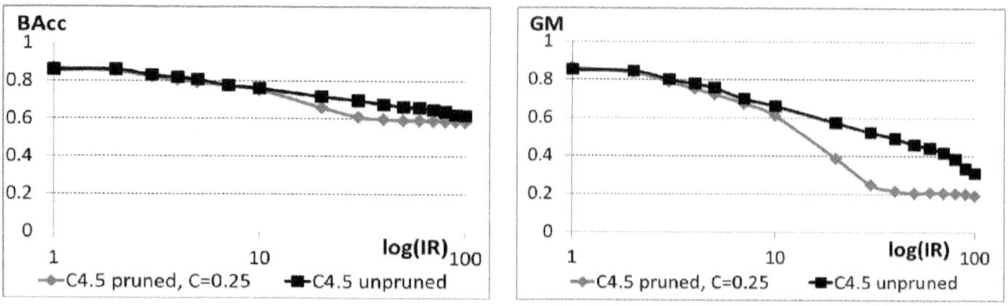

Fig. 12. Performance degradation for C4.5 on mushrooms data set, under the balanced accuracy (BAcc) and the geometric mean (GM)

In [2], it is argued that, for large IRs, unpruned C4.5 models are better than the pruned versions. We have performed an evaluation to validate this statement, using the mushrooms problem – large size, balanced data set – by varying the IR up to 100. The evaluation was performed in a 10-fold cross validation loop. The results are presented in the diagrams from Fig. 12. We have employed the logarithmic scale for the x axis (IR), to better differentiate between the two curves at smaller IRs. By comparing the two diagrams we notice that GM is more fitted for this situation, as it is more realistic in estimating the performance (BAcc being overoptimistic), and it better differentiates between the pruned/unpruned versions. This is due to the fact that a larger difference between two variables is more visible in the product than the sum of their values. This makes GM a better metric than BAcc in imbalanced problems.

Also, as IR increases, pruning deteriorates the performance of the decision tree model. This result supports the statement in [3], that pruning might eliminate rare and important cases, thus affecting the correct identification of the minority class. However, no pruning at all results in an increase of complexity for the majority class as well, which might lead to overfitting in that area. A more sophisticated approach is therefore required for imbalanced domains, an intelligent pruning mechanism, which adjusts the level of pruning for branches according to the number of minority cases they contain.

4 Approaches for Dealing with Class Imbalance

This section provides an overview of the most prominent approaches for dealing with imbalanced problems. The first part of the discussion focuses on the limitations of traditional learning methods. It is followed by data-oriented strategies and algorithm-related approaches.

4.1 Limitations of Traditional Learning Techniques

As shown by the experiments performed, most traditional machine learning methods are affected by class imbalance. This is mostly because the assumptions on which they are designed do not hold in this domain. Firstly, they are built to maximize accuracy, which is not the most appropriate measure for imbalanced problems. Secondly, they presume that the distributions of the train and test sets are the same. This entails two pitfalls: the built model is customized for a given distribution which may fail to identify the true patterns in data; moreover, the actual distribution of the data could be unknown at the time the model is generated. Therefore, we might need to find an optimal distribution which leads to the best model from the available data. A very good reason for doing so is that data is usually costly, and rare cases are even more costly; therefore, the correct strategy is to make the most of the available data.

Out of the existing methods, some are affected more seriously by the imbalance problem. Decision trees perform the worst when the data is imbalanced. This major drawback is thought of being rooted in the pruning stage. As opposed to the conclusions found in [2, 14], we found that support vector machines (SVMs) are strongly affected by the imbalance problem, while the artificial neural networks (ANN) are not. Out of the methods we have evaluated, ANNs have proved to be the most robust to the imbalance problem. Our experimental results are in agreement with the observations found in [2], that the multilayer perceptron is not sensitive to the class imbalance problem, while decision trees are strongly affected by the imbalance. However, they are in disagreement with respect to the behavior of SVMs in imbalanced problems.

These observations entail an evident requirement of either redesigning the algorithms, to adapt them to the specific situations, or design new, dedicate algorithms to face the new assumptions. The alternative solution is to alter the data distribution such as to provide a more appropriate distribution in the training set (via resizing).

4.2 Data-Oriented Techniques

One natural solution for dealing with an imbalanced problem is to rebalance the training data. There are several known sampling techniques, all with advantages and limitations, and with specific applicability scope. Extensive and thorough efforts have focused on proposing and evaluating sampling techniques comparatively. However, it is important to mention that many of them are suited for specific situations (i.e. type of rarity), and for a subset of classifiers. Here we enumerate the most prominent sampling strategies, indicating valuable sources of exhaustive and systematic evaluation of particular methods.

Sampling techniques follow two major strategies: oversampling and undersampling. Oversampling reduces the imbalance rate by adding examples. Important drawbacks of oversampling refer to the fact that it may lead to overfitting, increase the time required to build the classifier, or it may even harm the learning process [15]. Algorithms less affected by the oversampling techniques are Naive Bayes and ANN. Undersampling performs rebalancing by removing examples from the majority class. While this helps narrowing the search space, by reducing the data size, it may cause loss of information. A guided undersampling could limit this drawback. There are different opinions regarding which technique is better, some researchers being in favor of oversampling [2] while others advocate for undersampling [6].

However, sampling should be considered in the wider context consisting of the problem itself and the adequate classifier for the problem. Different classifiers perform better in conjunction with specific sampling techniques, guided by the intrinsic mechanism they employ (i.e. rely on the number of instances that cover some rule – decision trees, or on a better representation of the boundary – SVM). Another important aspect which influences sampling is the noise associated with the data, which has been shown to affect the rare classes more [3].

A comprehensive study of sampling techniques can be found in [7]. Several efficiently guided oversampling and undersampling techniques are compared. Complex methods, resulting from the combination of different basic techniques are briefly described, and thoroughly evaluated on thirteen benchmark data sets. Although most of them have yielded an increase in performance, as expected, there is no technique which dominates all the other on all data sets. Moreover, based on the results of the evaluations, it has been concluded that "random over-sampling provided competitive results with the more complex methods". Another important study suggests that the improvements produced by under/over sampling are more significant for larger imbalance rates [2]. In [6], an evolutionary undersampling technique is proposed and comparative evaluations with other existing techniques are presented. The performance is validated using an instance based learner as classification method and AUC and GM as metrics.

A very important issue regarding sampling techniques refers to the appropriate volume of over/under sampling required [16], and whether this amount is problem, domain, and/or data-dependent. Most learning algorithms employ the distribution of the available data, assuming it is the naturally occurring distribution of the problem. This strategy could be faulty for two reasons: firstly, the real distribution could be unknown (or time-variable) and secondly it may not be the most appropriate distribution for learning [17]. In [16] it is suggested that using wrappers to perform a guided search for the correct percentage of undersampling the majority class or synthetic oversampling the minority class may improve the performance. Other evaluations [17] prove that if there is a best distribution for the training set, it needs more positive examples as the dimension of the training set decreases. Moreover, the same performance could be acquired with a smaller training set, if the distribution is balanced in favor of the minority class, up to 90%. Another important technique is suggested in [18]. A sampling technique which uses only actual data would suffer neither from information loss, nor from information distortion, due to the addition of new (duplicate or synthetic) instances. Moreover, it does not enlarge the data set.

Another data-related mechanism in handling imbalance is data segmentation, in which the original problem is separated into sub-problems. This way, we may isolate the rare cases in a single partition, which is assigned special treatment, while for the other(s) regular reasoning methods are employed [3].

Among the various pre-processing tasks, feature selection is one of the most effective in enhancing the data mining process. It not only reduces the data dimensionality, by discarding attributes, thus reducing the search space, but it also improves the knowledge extraction task most of the time [19]. Moreover, it proves to be valuable when dealing with imbalanced problems as well, since a large number of features is most usually accompanied by skew in the class distribution. Feature selection could be beneficial in such cases, by selecting the features which "can capture the high skew in the class distribution" [14, 15]. Also, the experiments we have performed have shown that data sets with a large number of instances per number of attributes ratio (IAR) behave better when faced with the imbalanced problem. Feature selection reduces the number of features, thus leading to an increased IAR value.

4.3 Adapting Learning Techniques

It is widely accepted that the accuracy is a weak estimator for an imbalanced problem [3, 6, 14]. As stated in [14], it is commonly agreed that current learning methods "are heavily biased in recognizing mostly the majority class since they are built to achieve overall accuracy to which the minority class contributes very little."

Therefore, a first important step in adapting the existing algorithms to the new conditions is to choose the most appropriate metric for attaining the novel objective. This could be done by analyzing the particularities of the data and the specific problem requirements. Some problems could require a large TP, with equal weights on the generated errors, while others, most often require a higher penalization for the errors which fail to identify a positive example – i.e. require a low false negative rate (e.g. medical diagnosis). There are situations in which a low false positive rate is also important (e.g. in contextual advertising).

In addition to changing the performance estimator of the method, altering the optimization criterion (such as the info gain in decision trees) to one which better allows the promotion of rare patterns is another viable option. Also, modifying the decision threshold in the algorithm (e.g. from the default 50% at leaves in decision trees) might prove beneficial. The new threshold should be customized to the particular problem under observation (data set), so that it better detects rare cases (decrease the threshold in favor of the positives). Moreover, making the algorithms interactive for specific tasks (such as setting the threshold) could prove beneficial. In many cases, human interaction may give insights that help boosting the process of mining data. Several studies indicate this approach can be more efficient than data-related strategies, such as sampling [20].

Another observation which refers to decision trees can be made about the pruning process. It has been observed that pruning is not a good option for imbalanced problems [17]. Our experiments show that simply disabling the pruning option on evaluations with C4.5 lead to a constant improvement. It is worth mentioning that branches which cover small disjuncts would benefit from this change mostly. Therefore, we expect that a weighted pruning, focused on keeping those branches which are sensitive to the number of cases they cover, should be more adequate.

In [3], the idea of changing the algorithm so that examples at the boundary of the domain are classified as belonging to the positive class is presented. This change of strategy fosters the identification of the positive class, with a possible penalty in increasing the number of false positives; however, as mentioned before, in most of the cases, an increase in FP is preferable to an increase in FN.

Important improvements have been reported when using boosting for increasing the performance of the algorithms [21]. This statement is sustained by mathematical arguments as well.

Cost-sensitive learning has been shown to outperform any kind of sampling in imbalanced problems [3]. However, if the costs are not known, or the costs often change values, it is not applicable. Current commercial data mining systems handle cost-sensitive with complex misclassification functions, and dynamic adjusting of thresholds for induced classifiers. The importance of cost sensitive learning is related also to the costs of acquiring data. A more refined approach [22] should be considered: minimize the costs associated with both acquiring and learning from data and/or maximize performance with respect to some reduced training set. The training set could either be provided, in which case the best sampling technique should be employed, or its optimal dimension should be identified based on some specific optimality objective, and only the minimum amount of data should be requested.

One-class learning is beneficial for imbalanced data sets as it avoids overfitting on the majority class [19]. A good method could be to generate a model for each single class, rather than generating a complete model with a unique strategy. Taking this proposal further, different inducers could be employed for learning different classes. For example, employ SVMs or decision trees for the majority class and ANN for the minority class. The advantages here are two-fold: improve the performance by employing a method which is more robust to the class imbalance for the minority class, and the speed, by employing fast methods on the majority class.

5 Conclusions

Starting from the observation that when dealing with imbalanced classification problems there is no winner strategy for all data sets (neither in terms of sampling, nor algorithm), special attention should be paid to the particularities of the data in hand. In doing so, one should focus on a wider context, taking into account several factors simultaneously: the imbalance rate, together with other data-related meta-features, the algorithms and their associated parameters.

Our experiments show that, in an imbalanced problem, the IR can be used in conjunction with the IAR factor to evaluate the appropriate classifier that best fits the situation. Moreover, a good metric to assess the performance of the model built is important; again, it should be chosen based on the particularities of the problem and of the goal established for it.

All classification algorithms are affected to some extent by the class imbalance problem. The results indicate that the MLP is the most robust to the imbalance on real world benchmark data. This comes as a confirmation to the conclusions presented in [2]. On the other hand, the SVM is largely affected by the imbalance in our experiments. This contradiction with previous studies may be explained through the nature of the experimental data: on artificial data, the SVMs performed well because the systematic process of generating the data allows the existence of good support vectors (even at high imbalance ratios), whereas the existence of such vectors in real world imbalanced data sets is less probable.

In terms of solutions, since the performance is not expected to improve significantly with a more sophisticated sampling strategy, more focus should be allocated to algorithm related improvements, rather than to data improvements. The choice of the evaluation metric should be based on the data particularities (i.e. imbalance), but also on the goal of the classification process (are we dealing with a cost-sensitive classification or are all errors equally serious?).

Acknowledgements. The work for this paper has been partially supported by research grant no. 12080/2008 – SEArCH, founded by the Ministry of Education, Research and Innovation.

References

1. Barandela, R., Sanchez, J.S., Garcia, V., Rangel, E.: Strategies for Learning in Class Imbalance Problems. Pattern Recognition 36(3), 849–851 (2003)
2. Japkowicz, N., Stephen, S.: The Class Imbalance Problem: A Systematic Study. Intelligent Data Analysis Journal 6, 429–449 (2002)
3. Weiss, G.: Mining with Rarity: A Unifying Framework. SIGKDD Explorations 6(1), 7–19 (2004)
4. Chawla, N.V.: Data Mining from Imbalanced Data Sets. In: Data Mining and Knowledge Discovery Handbook, ch. 40, pp. 853–867. Springer US (2006)
5. Woods, K., Doss, C., Bowyer, K., Solka, J., Priebe, C., Kegelmeyer, P.: Comparative Evaluation of Pattern Recognition Techniques for Detection of Microcalcifications in Mammography. Int. Journal of Pattern Rec. and AI 7(6), 1417–1436 (1993)
6. Garcia, S., Herrera, F.: Evolutionary Undersampling for Classification with Imbalanced Datasets: Proposals and Taxonomy. Evolutionary Computation 17(3), 275–306 (2009)
7. Batista, G.E.A.P.A., Prati, R.C. Monard, M.C.: A Study of the Behavior of Several Methods for Balancing Machine Learning Training Data, 20–29 (2004)
8. Chawla, N.V., Bowyer, K.W., Hall, L.O., Kegelmeyer, W.P.: SMOTE: Synthetic Minority Over-Sampling Technique. Journal of Artificial Intelligence Research 16, 321–357 (2002)
9. Guo, H., Viktor, H.L.: Learning from Imbalanced Data Sets with Boosting and Data Generation: The DataBoost-IM Approach. Sigkdd Explorations 6, 30–39 (2004)
10. Brodersen, K.H., Ong, C.S., Stephen, K.E., Buhmann, J.M.: The balanced accuracy and its posterior distribution. In: Proceedings of the 20th Int. Conf. on Pattern Recognition, pp. 3121–3124 (2010)
11. Grzymala-Busse, J.W., Stefanowski, J., Wilk, S.: A Comparison of Two Approaches to Data Mining from Imbalanced Data. Journal of Intelligent Manufacturing 16, 65–573 (2005)
12. UCI Machine Learning Data Repository, `http://archive.ics.uci.edu/ml/`
13. Witten, I., Frank, E.: Data Mining: Practical machine learning tools and techniques, 2nd edn. Morgan Kaufmann (2005)
14. Visa, S., Ralescu, A.: Issues in mining imbalanced data sets -a review paper. In: Proceedings of the Sixteen Midwest Artificial Intelligence and Cognitive Science Conference, pp. 67–73 (2005)
15. Chawla, N.V., Japkowicz, N., Kolcz, A.: Editorial: special issue on learning from I imbalanced data sets. SIGKDD Explorations Special Issue on Learning from Imbalanced Datasets 6(1), 1–6 (2004)

16. Hall, L.O., Joshi, A.: Building Accurate Classifiers from Imbalanced Data Sets. In: IMACS 2005, Paris (2005)
17. Weiss, G., Provost, F.: Learning when Training Data are Costly: The Effect of Class Distribution on Tree Induction. Journal of Artificial Intelligence Research 19, 315–354 (2003)
18. Chan, P., Stolfo, S.: Toward scalable learning with non-uniform class and cost distributions: a case study in credit card fraud detection. In: Proceedings of the Fourth International Conference on Knowledge Discovery and Data Mining, pp. 164–168. AAAI Press, Menlo Park (1998)
19. Vidrighin Bratu, C., Muresan, T., Potolea, R.: Improving Classification Accuracy through Feature Selection. In: Proceedings of the 4th IEEE International Conference on Intelligent Computer Communication and Processing, ICCP 2008, pp. 25–32 (2008)
20. Provost, F.: Learning with Imbalanced Data Sets. Invited paper for AAAI 2000 Workshop on Imbalanced Data Sets (2000)
21. Joshi, M.V., Agarwal, R.C., Kumar, V.: Predicting rare classes: can boosting make any weak learner strong? In: Proceedings of the Eighth International Conference on Knowledge Discovery and Data Mining, pp. 297–306 (2002)
22. Weiss, G.M., Hirsh, H.: A quantitative study of small disjuncts. In: Proceedings of the Seventeenth National Conference on Artificial Intelligence, pp. 665–670. AAAI Press (2000)

Adaptive Information Integration: Bridging the Semantic Gap between Numerical Simulations

Tobias Meisen[1], Philipp Meisen[2], Daniel Schilberg[1], and Sabina Jeschke[1]

[1] Institute of Information Management in Mechanical Engineering
RWTH Aachen University, Dennewartstraße 27, 52068, Aachen, Germany
{tobias.meisen,daniel.schilberg,
sabina.jeschke}@ima-zlw-ifu.rwth-aachen.de
[2] Inform GmbH, Pascalstraße 23, 52076, Aachen, Germany
philipp.meisen@inform-ac.com

Abstract. The increasing complexity and costs of modern production processes makes it necessary to plan processes virtually before they are tested and realized in real environments. Therefore, several tools facilitating the simulation of different production techniques and design domains have been developed. On the one hand there are specialized tools simulating specific production techniques with exactness close to the real object of the simulation. On the other hand there are simulations which simulate whole production processes, but in general do not achieve prediction accuracy comparable to such specialized tools. Hence, the interconnection of tools is the only way, because otherwise the achievable prediction accuracy would be insufficient. In this chapter, a framework is presented that helps to interconnect heterogeneous simulation tools, considering their incompatible file formats, different semantics of data and missing data consistency.

Keywords: Application integration, Data integration, Simulation tools, Ontology, Framework.

1 Introduction

Within the enterprising environment, the necessity to couple deviating applications being used in a company was recognized early. As a consequence, various concepts were developed that were subsumed under the collective term "Data Integration Techniques" [28]. One of those techniques, "Enterprise Application Integration" (EAI), focuses on integrating business processes based on IT along the value chain of an enterprise without taking into account the platform, the architecture as well as the generation of the applications being used in these processes [4]. Especially in the widely spread field of enterprise resource planning [8] EAI technologies are well established. These technologies are the foundation for such systems concerning data and application integration. In other fields, e.g. Business Intelligence (BI) or Enterprise Performance Management (EPM), other data integration techniques (i.e. ETL, EII) are mainly used to gain information about cross-applicational business processes [19].

R. Zhang et al. (Eds.): ICEIS 2011, LNBIP 102, pp. 51–65, 2012.

The combination of those integration techniques to analyze more complex business processes, like simulation processes, is seldom taken into account [23]. Simulation itself is a well-established field in research and development and different simulations for specific tasks as e.g. casting, welding or cooling and also for whole processes (e.g. transformation or heat-treatment processes) are available. Nevertheless, those simulations have to be seen as isolated applications. They are often specialized for a single purpose (e.g. a specific task) and have neither standardized interfaces nor standardized data formats. Therefore, different results that were received within a simulation can only be integrated into a simulation process if they are checked manually and are adapted to the needs of the subsequent simulations. Current data integration techniques cannot easily be applied to the simulation context because a combination of different techniques and solutions is required. Huge data volumes which are characteristic for simulation processes tend to use ETL techniques, whereby those do not support the important concept of message-oriented transactions. These message-oriented transactions are realized in the field of EAI (e.g. ESB). Although within the field of EAI, huge data volumes cannot be handled satisfactorily. Another problem is the adaption of the data integration process concerning changes within the simulation process (e.g. the integration of a new application, the modification of a simulated object) and the semantics of data that have to be considered by the integration.

In this chapter, a framework will be described which provides the possibility of simulating a production process by making use of existing isolated applications. The integration is based on ontologies, which describe the domain specific knowledge (e.g. material processing simulations) and planning algorithms used to identify how the data can be transferred between different heterogeneous simulation tools. Thereby, the chapter focuses on the integration of data that was generated during applications' usage, whereas the applications' linkup technique, which can be handled with the help of modern middleware [18], will not be stressed.

The framework has been validated on the foundation of the simulation of three production processes, namely a line-pipe, a gear wheel and a top-box. The framework was developed within the project "Integrated Platform for Distributed Numerical Simulation", which is part of the Cluster of Excellence "Integrative Production Technology for High-Wage Countries".

The chapter is structured as follows: In section 2, the current state of technology will be outlined in order to provide a foundation for section 3, in which one of the simulated production processes is exemplarily presented. Section 4 consists of a description of the architecture of the framework that is completed in section 5 by a specification of the used information integration method. Section 6 points out how the framework needs to be extended with regard to the presented use case. In section 7, a conclusion and outlook will be drawn from the insights generated in this chapter.

2 State of the Art

Since the nineties, data integration belongs to the most frequented topics with reference to finding answers to questions which are raised across application boundaries [9]. Today, a multitude of data integration products can be found which are used in different fields of application, whereby each technology can be assigned to one of three techniques [28] (cf. Fig. 1): data propagation, data federation or data consolidation.

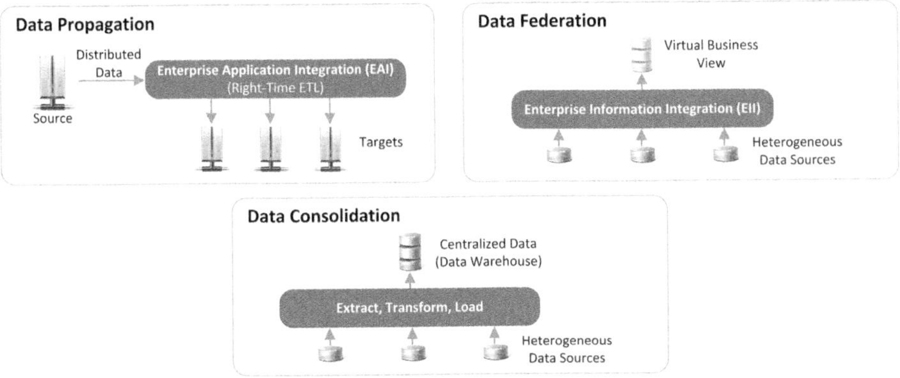

Fig. 1. Main areas of data integration [28]

With regard to the operational section, data propagation is applied in order to make use of data on a cross-application basis, which is often realized via EAI. As already presented in [28], EAI mainly focuses on small data volumes like messages and business transactions that are exchanged between different applications. In order to realize EAI, a contemporary architecture concept exists, which was developed in connection with service-based approaches [3] and which will be emphasized within this contribution – the so-called Enterprise Service Bus (ESB). The basic idea of ESB, which can be compared to the usage of integration brokers, comprises the provision of services within a system [25]. Within an ESB different services provide a technical or technological functionality with the help of which business processes are supported. A service can be a transformation or a routing service, whereby all services are connected with each other via an integration bus. Transformation services provide general functions in order to transfer data from one format and/or model into another. In contrast, routing services are used to submit data to other services. Both transformation and routing services are used by adapters in order to transfer data provided by the integration bus into the format and the model of an application. Consequently, transformation services support the reuse of implemented data transformations. The advantage of solutions based on ESB is to be seen in the loose coupling of several services, whereas the missing physical data coupling can be regarded as a disadvantage [20]: If recorded data has to be evaluated subsequently, it has to be read out and to be transformed once again. According to this fact, a historic or at least long-term oriented evaluation of data is unconvertible, even though such an evaluation is often required.

In order to realize such a unified examination on a cross-data basis, other techniques belonging to the field of data integration need to be taken into consideration (cf. Fig. 1). Data federation, which is studied within the field of Enterprise Information Integration (EII), might serve as one possible solution to enable a unified examination. With the help of EII, data from different data sources can be unified in one single view [1]. This single view is used to query for data based on a virtual, unified data schema. The query itself is processed by mediators and divided in several queries fired against the underlying data sources. Because of the fact that most EII do not support advanced data consolidation techniques, the implementation will only be successful if the data of the different data sources can be unified, the data quality is sufficient and if access to the data is granted (e.g. via standard query interfaces).

If a virtual view is not applicable, techniques belonging to the field of data consolidation need to be utilized. Data consolidation comprises the integration of differing data into a common, unified data structure. Extract Transform Load (ETL) can be seen as one example for data consolidation, which is often used in the field of data warehousing [27]. ETL starts with the extraction of data from one or several – mostly operational – data sources. The extracted data is than transformed (e.g. joined, modified, aggregated) and the data model is adapted to a final schema (often a so called star schema). During the last phase the data is loaded into a target database (in general a data warehouse).

The presented techniques of data integration have in common that - independent of the technique - the heterogeneity of data has to be overcome. In literature, different kinds of heterogeneity are distinguished [7, 14, 16]. In this chapter, the well-established kinds of heterogeneity, technical, syntactic, data model, structural and semantic heterogeneity, listed in [16] are considered.

3 Use Case

Within this chapter, the manufacture of a line-pipe will be stressed as example use case. During the manufacture several simulation tools that are specialized for these techniques are used. The goal is the simulation of the whole production process, whereby the results of each specialized tool will be considered across the whole simulation process. The production process which will be used to exemplify the example use case is illustrated in Fig. 2.

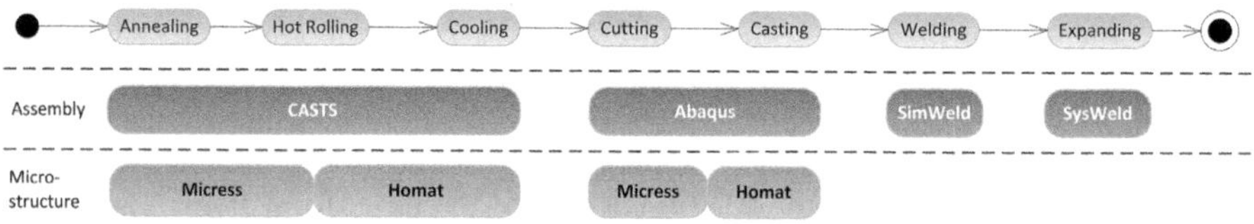

Fig. 2. Production process of a line-pipe (top) and the used simulation tools (middle & bottom)

The use case starts with a simulation of the annealing, the hot rolling as well as the controlled cooling of the components via the simulation tool CASTS (Access). The next step consists in representing the cutting and the casting with the help of Abaqus (Dassault Systems), whereas the welding and the expanding of the line-pipe will be simulated via SimWeld (ISF - RWTH Aachen University), and via SysWeld (ESI-Group). Furthermore, the simulation of modifications in the microstructure of the assembly will be realized by making use of Micress and Homat (Access). All in all, the use case contains six different kinds of tools, each based on different formats and simulation models. Thereby, the required integration solution has to take different requirements into account [22]. Two requirements, which turned out to be central with reference to the framework presented in this chapter, are on the one hand, the possibility of data propagation, focusing the semantic data exchange between the applications, and, on the other hand, the necessity of a process-oriented data consolidation. Both are used to facilitate a subsequent visualization and analysis of data collected within the process.

4 Architecture of the Framework

4.1 System Architecture

The framework's architecture is based on the requirements described in section 3. The architecture is depicted in Fig. 3. As illustrated, the framework follows the architecture concept of ESB, whereby the possibility of data consolidation was realized by implementing a central data storage (CDS) [21].

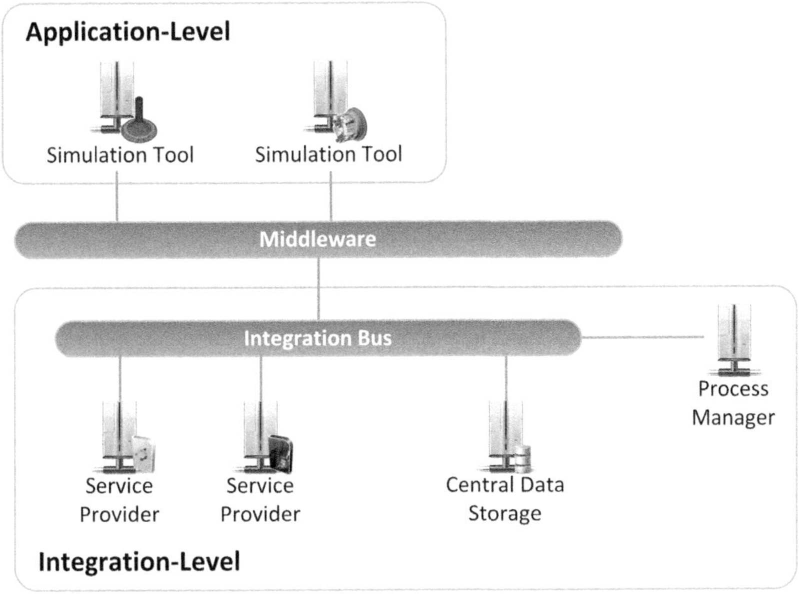

Fig. 3. System-architecture of the framework

In order to realize a communication (e.g. concerning the exchange of files and overcome the technical heterogeneity) between the integration bus and the different simulation tools, a middleware is used that encapsulates the functionality of routing services which are typical of those used in ESB concepts[1]. Hence, routing services are not considered in this framework, as the integration of a standard middleware is straight forward. The framework is employed with the intention of realizing an integration level, at which service providers, which are directly linked to the integration

[1] Within the use case mentioned in section 3 the application-oriented middleware Condor [2] is used.

bus, offer different services. With the help of these services, data can be integrated, extracted and transformed. As the connection is realized via a platform independent messaging protocol, it is not bound to the operating system in use. The employment of a process manager as well as of a CDS marks an important difference between the architecture described in this section and the architectural pattern of an ESB. The process manager receives all data transferred by the middleware, analyses it and, subsequently, makes it available for each of the service providers via the integration bus. In turn, the service providers tap the required data in order to process it. After a step of processing is finished, the consistency of the data is checked and the next processing step is determined by the process manager.

Consequently, with regards to the processes of data integration and data extraction, the process manager has the task of a central supervisory authority. The service providers as well as the process manager have access to the central data storage, whereby data consolidation and, as a result, analyses of data collected during the process become possible.

4.2 Software Architecture

The framework comprises three main components: the middleware communication, the process manager and the service provider. In order to guarantee a connection between those components, a codebase component is needed, in which a cross-component functionality is encapsulated. In the following, these components will be described in detail.

Middleware Communication. The Middleware Communication component supports the realization of communication processes between the middleware and the integration bus. It contains adapters, which facilitate the transmission of demands to the integration bus by making use of different communication protocols, such as JMS, RMI or SOAP [13]. As far as a concrete use case is concerned, which is not covered by technologies that were already integrated, the component is modular expandable, which enables the implementation of additional separate adapters (cf. section 5).

Process Manager. The Process Manager comprises the implementation of a management component, which functions as a service provider and a central control unit for integration, extraction and conversion processes. The services provided by this component involve the integration, the extraction and the transformation of data. For each of these services, a service process is stored, which is started and processed as soon as a query is sent to the process manager. A service process describes which services need to be handled with the purpose of providing the requested functionality. The service processes realized within the framework are illustrated in Fig. 4.

The conversion process is defined by an integration process and an extraction process which are both based upon extended ETL process. Within the integration process, a post-processing of integrated data is succeeded, whereas the extraction process makes use of a data enrichment that is carried out prior to the actual ETL process. Thereby, the process manager is used as a mediator with the help of which data is exchanged to those service providers that feature the postulated functionality and capacity. As a consequence, the algorithms, which are important for the process of information integration and which are depending on the use case in question, are encapsulated within the specified service providers. Additionally, the process manager realizes a process-related integration of data. Thereby, the process manager controls the assignment of data to the process step and transmits the context of the process in question to the service providers.

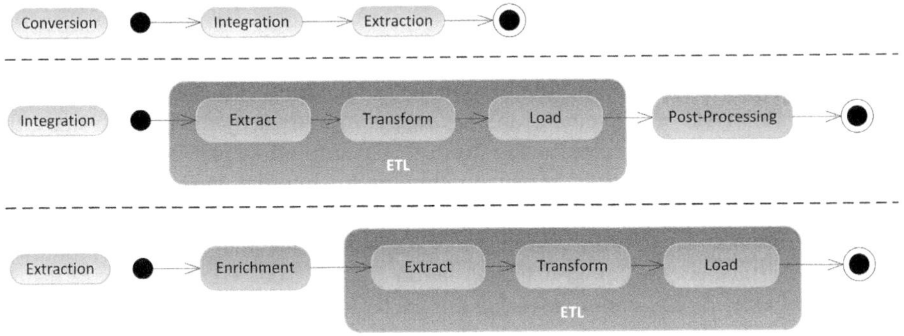

Fig. 4. Service Processes of the framework

Service Provider. The functionality provided by a service provider always depends on the provided services and therefore on the concrete use case. For instance, the integration of FE data on the one hand and the integration of data of molecular structures on the other hand are based upon different data schemas, even though these processes of integration consist in the same physical object and deal with comparable physical entities.

The framework offers interfaces to common ETL tools as, for example, the Pentaho Data Integrator (PDI) [15]. Thus, the integration and extraction of data, and therefore the overcoming of the syntactical and data model heterogeneity, can be created on the basis of these tools. Furthermore, additional tools can be implemented in order to realize the processes of integration and extraction in the case that this way of proceeding is convenient and necessary within a concrete use case.

Apart from services which provide an ETL process, the framework supports additional services in order to post-process and enrich data. For instance, the post-processing service allows the implementation of plausibility criteria, which need to be fulfilled by the integrated data without reference to their original source. During the process of enrichment, data transformations are carried out with the purpose of editing data stored within the central data store in such a way that the data is able to meet the requirements demanded with regard to the extraction process. Therefore an adaptive information integration process [17] is used, which is described in the next section.

5 Adaptive Information Integration

5.1 Concept

The main goal of the adaptive information integration is to overcome the problems of structural and semantic heterogeneity considering domain specific knowledge.

The adaptive information integration is part of the enrichment process step in the extended ETL process being used during the extraction of data. The goal of the process is to extract data in a defined data format, regarding the data model and structure, as well as the semantics, of this format and the domain. Therefore, the implemented enrichment enables the discovery and exploitation of domain specific knowledge. The concept is based upon ontologies and planning algorithms used in the field of artificial intelligence.

First, the existing data is analyzed. The goal of the analysis is the determination of so called features that are fulfilled by the data. A feature is domain specific and expresses structural or semantic properties that are satisfied by the data. Besides, the analysis step determines features that have to be fulfilled by the data to satisfy the requirements of the specific output format. Following the analysis the planning algorithms are used to find a data translation that transforms and enriches the data, so that the enriched data fulfills the features needed by the output format. After the planning is finished, the found data translation is processed. The data transformation algorithms used for the data transformation are realized as a service. The information about the existing transformations and features is expressed in an ontology. The basic structure of this ontology is described in the following section.

5.2 Ontology

The information used by the enrichment process is subdivided among a *framework ontology* and a *domain ontology*. The *domain ontology* holds information about the concrete transformations, features and applications used in the context of a specific domain. Besides, information about the domain specific data schema is stored. An extract of the domain ontology used to implement the use case is described in section 6, using the Web Ontology Language (OWL).

The *domain ontology* specialize the concepts of the framework ontology in order to specify the conceptualization of the domain. Hence, the framework ontology is a specification of the concepts used in the framework to enable the enrichment process. These main concepts are *data*, *feature*, *application* and *transformation*, which are introduced shortly.

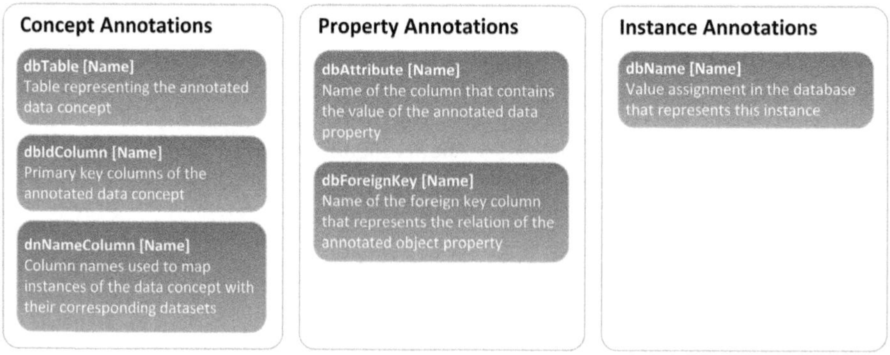

Fig. 5. Ontology annotations

The concept *data* is the generalization of all data concepts used in the domain. More precisely each concept in the domain ontology used to describe the data schema of the domain has to be a specialization of the concept *data*. The mapping between data concepts and the data schema of the domain is realized by using a predefined set of annotations. Because of the single mapping between a well-known ontology and a well-known database schema, automatic schema matching algorithms are not used. Instead this approach follows the concept of annotation-based programming. Fig. 5 gives an overview of the main annotations.

Defining domain specific features is done by creating a specialization of the concept *feature*. Such a specialization is a listing of the requirements that have to be satisfied by a set of data, so that the represented feature is fulfilled.

For each definition of applications and their requirements, instances of the concept *application* have to be expressed in the domain ontology. An instance of the concept *application* can have additional object properties to express domain specific information of an application. Similar to an application, a transformation has requirements that have to be satisfied. Otherwise, the transformation cannot be used. Therefore, each instance of the concept *transformation* has to outline the requirements by defining instances of *feature* concepts. In addition, a transformation changes the features of data. This is realized by expressing the effects of the transformation in the ontology. The concept *transformation* and its main relations are depicted in Fig. 6.

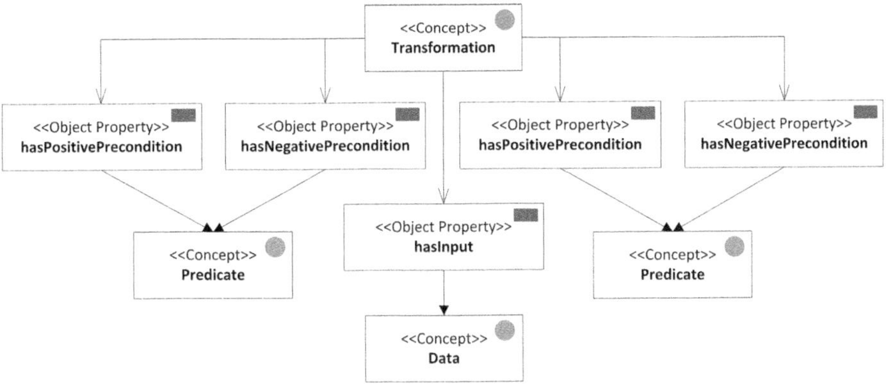

Fig. 6. Fragment of framework ontology - transformation concept

The input is set by an instance of the concept *data*, whereby the requirements are expressed by instances of either *hasPositivePrecondition* or *hasNegativePrecondition*. These object properties realize relations between the concrete transformation and feature instances. The framework ontology provides a set of logical connectives and quantifiers to express complex requirements like *feature1* **or** *feature2*. Similarly, the effects of the transformation are expressed.

5.3 Components

The concept of the adaptive information integration is realized by three services: the data analyzer, the plan generator and the plan processor. Each service implements one of the previously described steps of the enrichment process.

The data analyzer loads the ontology and establishes a connection to the CDS. By using the domain ontology, the features are determined by querying all defined specializations of the concept *feature*. The implementation of this service makes use of the OWL API [12] and the reasoner Pellet [26]. The fulfillment of a feature is checked by querying once again the CDS. The queries are generated by using the annotation based mapping. The result of the query is analyzed according to the feature definition.

The fulfilled features define the initial state of the data. In addition, the goal state is determined by the data analyzer by reasoning. This means that the current context (required output format and domain specific parameters) is used to query the required features by using the information stored in the domain ontology.

Hence, the result of the data analyzer consists of the initial and the goal state. This information is passed to the plan generator to determine the needed data translation. Therefore, the plan generator queries the existing data transformations from the domain ontology and generates a problem description using the Planning Domain Definition Language (PDDL) [5]. The defined planning problem is than solved by a planner component, which generates a solution plan. More detailed, the planner is used to determine a sequence of, so called actions that lead from the initial state to a goal state. The framework supports different planning algorithms like forward, backward and heuristic search, STRIPS algorithm or Planning Graphs [6, 10]. If the planner succeeds a plan is generated that contains the transformations and their parameterization as well as their ordering to transform the data, so that the required *features* are fulfilled by the data after having processed the plan. Finally, the processing of the plan is realized by the plan processor.

6 Application of the Framework

Within the domain of the use case described in section 3 and the requirements resulting from the examination of four additional use cases in the domain of FE-simulations, an integration platform has been implemented in parallel to the implementation of the framework. The integrated applications are simulations based upon the finite-element-method. In order to implement the integration platform a domain specific data schema, adapters for integration and extraction, the transformation library and the domain ontology have been provided. In the following, some selected examples will be presented.

Data Schema. The domain specific data schema has been determined by analyzing the different input and output formats of the simulations used in the use case. Within this data schema, a grid structure, representing the abstraction of the assembly that is simulated, is the central entity. It consists of nodes, cells and attributes. The latter ones exhibit attribute values, which are assigned to individual cells or nodes depending on the class of attributes available in the whole mesh. The integration services, which were specified within the use case, read in the mesh data provided by the simulation, transform it into the central data model and store it into the CDS. In contrast, the extraction services proceed as follows: The mesh data is read out from the CDS and transformed into the required format. Finally, the data is saved into the destination file or into the target database. Because of the prior enrichment, all of the structural and semantic data transformations have been performed. Hence, most of the data transformations formerly performed by the adapter services are omitted.

Adapter Service. Most of the adapter services have been implemented using the Pentaho Data Integrator (PDI). If more complex data have been given, or binary formats that can only be read by programming interfaces of the manufacturer, either the PDI functionality have been extended using the provided plug-in architecture or the needed functionality has been implemented using Java or C++. For example, the simulation results generated within the simulation tool CASTS are stored in the Visualization Toolkits (VTK) format [24]. Hence, an integration service was implemented, which is based on the programming interface provided by the developers of VTK using the provided functionality of the framework. Furthermore, an extraction service was developed with regard to the Abaqus input format, whereby, in this case, the aforementioned ETL tool PDI was used.

Transformation Library. In order to realize the information integration, different sorts of data transformations for FE data were implemented into the application, for example the conversion of attribute units, the deduction of attributes from those ones that are already available, the relocating of the mesh within space, the modification of cell types (e.g. from a hexahedron to a tetrahedron) or the re-indexing of nodes and cells.

Domain Ontology. The domain specific information has been expressed in the domain ontology. As described previously in section 5, the domain ontology uses the concept of the framework ontology to express the data schema, the transformations, the applications and the features of the domain. Fig. 7 sketches a fragment of the concept *Mesh*.

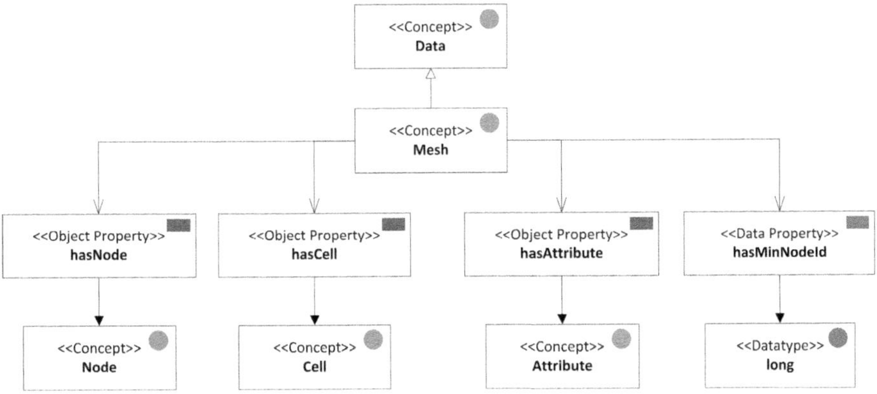

Fig. 7. Fragment of the concept *Mesh* and related concepts

Because of the number of data and object properties, only a few are depicted. Most interesting is the data property *hasMinNodeId*, which is a sub-property of the *hasMinimumValueProperty*. This kind of data property can be used to prompt the data analyzer to use the SQL *MIN* function, whenever a classification requires such information. Analogous data properties for average and maximum exist within the framework ontology. The depicted object properties *hasNode*, *hasCell* and *hasAttribute* represent the relation between the concept *Mesh* and the concept referred to by the object property. Using the previously described annotations the metadata of the relationship like primary and foreign keys are expressed.

The defined data schema is used to point out different data features of the domain. As described, a feature is a kind of classification of existing data. More precisely, if all conditions of a feature are fulfilled, the data belongs to the concept represented by the feature. One feature is the already mentioned *PlainMeshFeature*. It expresses that a mesh belongs to the class of plain meshes if all nodes of the mesh have a z-coordinate of zero. The feature is illustrated in Fig. 8 as well as expressed by the OWL Manchester Syntax [11].

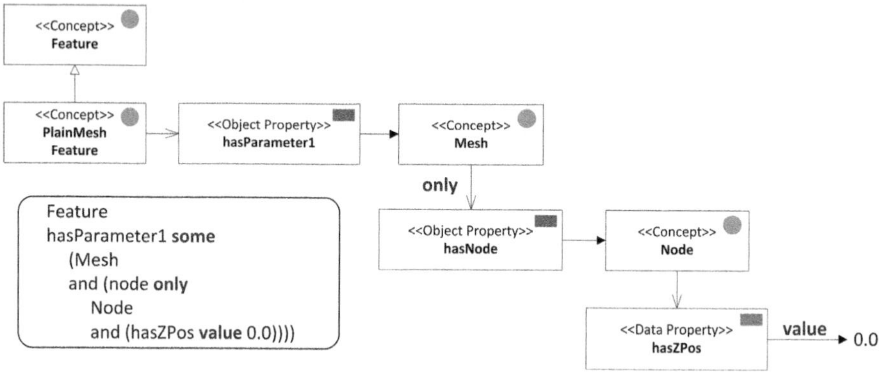

Fig. 8. Expression of the *PlainMeshFeature*

Besides the data schema and the features the ontology also contains information about the available transformations and the used applications. One example of a transformation is *HexaToTetra* that transforms a mesh that is based on hexahedrons into a mesh of tetrahedrons. The transformation searches all occurrences of hexahedrons within the mesh and splits them into tetrahedrons without creating new nodes. Hence, the precondition of the transformation is that at least one hexahedron exists in the mesh. The effect is that all hexahedrons are replaced by tetrahedrons. Preconditions and effects are expressed by using features. The expression of the transformation *HexaToTetra* in the domain ontology is illustrated in Fig. 9.

As described previously a concrete transformation is expressed by an instance of the concept *transformation*, whereby the input, preconditions and effects are expressed by instances of the corresponding concepts. The instance *HTTMesh* of the concept *Mesh* describes that the input of the transformation is some mesh. The precondition is an instance of the concept *CellTypeFeature* expressing that the transformation is only valid if the *HTTMesh* has cells of the cell type hexahedron, which is a concrete instance of the concept *CellType*. Also, the effects are expressed using *CellTypeFeature*. The positive effect is that the resulting mesh contains cells of the type tetrahedron, whereas the negative effect is, that the concrete *CellTypeFeature* representing the hexahedron is forfeited.

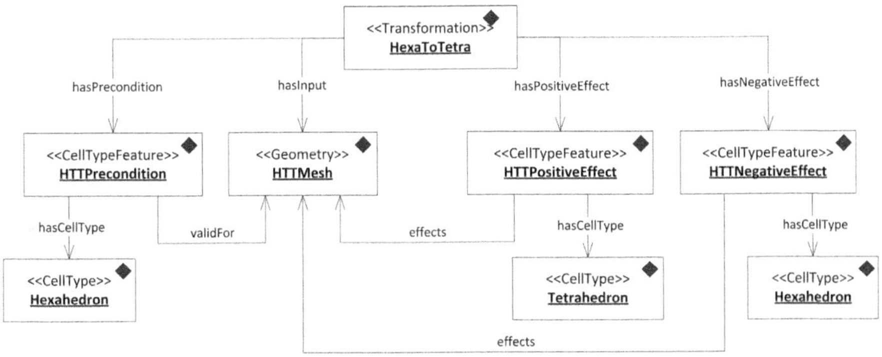

Fig. 9. Expression of the transformation *HexaToTetra*

Example. Concluding this section, a small example of the data provision of results generated by the simulation CASTS to the simulation Abaqus is presented. The example focuses on the structural changes of the data that are needed, in order to enable the usage of the data in Abaqus. Using the VTK data format, the indexing of nodes and cells begins with zero. Instead, Abaqus requires a sorted indexing starting with one. Additionally, in CASTS, vectors are decomposed into single components and stored as attribute values assigned to nodes, whereas in Abaqus, vectors need to be quoted entirely. Due to the data enrichment, the needed data transformations have been determined autonomously (cf. Fig. 10).

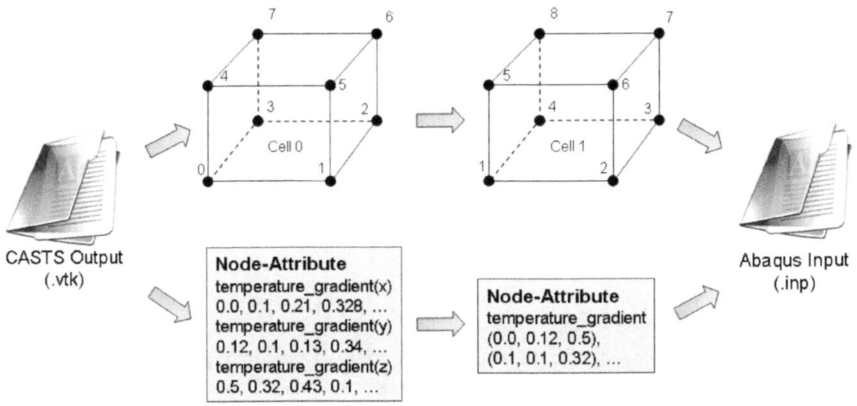

Fig. 10. Simplified illustration of the resulting data translation from CASTS to Abaqus

7 Conclusions

The development of the framework presented in this chapter can be regarded as an important step in the establishment of integrated simulation processes using heterogeneous simulations. Both, data losses as well as manual, time-consuming data transformations from one data format to another are excluded from this approach. The suggested framework facilitates the interconnection of simulation tools, which were - until now - developed independently and which are specialized for certain production processes or methods. Furthermore, the integration of data generated in the course of the simulation is realized in a unified and process-oriented way. Apart from the integration of further simulation tools into an application, which was already established, it is essential to extend the domain of simulations reflected upon with additional simulations covering the fields of machines and production. In this way, a holistic simulation of production processes is provided. Thereby, a major challenge consists in generating a central data model, which provides the possibility of illustrating data uniformly and in consideration of its significance in the overall context, which comprises the levels of process, machines as well as materials. Due to the methodology presented in this chapter, it is not necessary to adapt applications to the data model aforementioned. On the contrary, this step is realized via the integration application, which is to be developed on the basis of the framework. Because of the unified data view and the particular logging of data at the process level, the framework facilitates a comparison between the results of different simulation processes and those of simulation tools. Furthermore, conclusions can be drawn much easier from potential sources of error - a procedure which used to be characterized by an immense expenditure of time and costs. The realization of this procedure requires the identification of Performance Indicators, which are provided subsequently within the application. In this context, the development of essential data exploration techniques on the one hand and of visualization techniques on the other hand turns out to be a further challenge. Concepts and methods focusing this challenge will be developed and summarized under the term *Virtual Production Intelligence*. This term is motivated by the notion of *Business Intelligence*, which refers to computer-based techniques used to handle business data in the aforementioned manner.

Acknowledgements. The approaches presented in this chapter are supported by the German Research Association (DFG) within the Cluster of Excellence "Integrative Production Technology for High-Wage Countries".

References

1. Bernstein, P.A., Haas, L.M.: Information integration in the enterprise. Communications of the ACM - Enterprise Information Integration and Other Tools for Merging Data 51(9), 72–79 (2008)
2. Cerfontaine, P., Beer, T., Kuhlen, T., Bischof, C.H.: Towards a Flexible and Distributed Simulation Platform. In: Gervasi, O., Murgante, B., Laganà, A., Taniar, D., Mun, Y., Gavrilova, M.L. (eds.) ICCSA 2008, Part I. LNCS, vol. 5072, pp. 867–882. Springer, Heidelberg (2008)
3. Chappell, D.: Enterprise Service Bus. Theory in Practice. O'Reilly, Beijing (2004)
4. Conrad, S.: Enterprise Application Integration: Grundlagen, Konzepte, Entwurfsmuster, Praxisbeispiele. Elsevier, Spektrum, Akad. Verl., Heidelberg (2005)
5. Fox, M., Long, D.: PDDL2.1: An Extension to PDDL for Expressing Temporal Planning Domains. Journal of Artificial Intelligence Research 20(1), 61–124 (2003)

6. Ghallab, M., Nau, D.S., Traverso, P.: Automated planning. Theory and Practice. Elsevier/Morgan Kaufmann, Amsterdam (2004)
7. Goh, C.H.: Representing and reasoning about semantic conflicts in heterogeneous information systems. PhD thesis, Massachusetts Institute of Technology (1997)
8. Gronau, N.: Enterprise Resource Planning: Architektur, Funktionen und Management von ERP-Systemen, Oldenbourg, München (2010)
9. Halevy, A., Rajaraman, A., Ordille, J.: Data integration: the teenage years. In: Proceedings of the 32nd International Conference on Very Large Data Bases (VLDB), pp. 9–16. VLDB Endowment (2006)
10. Hoffmann, J., Nebel, B.: The planning system: Fast plan generation through heuristic search. Journal of Artificial Intelligence Research 14(1), 253–302 (2001)
11. Horridge, M., Patel-Schneider, P.F.: OWL 2 Web Ontology Language Manchester Syntax, W3C Working Group Note, W3C, October 27 (2009), `http://www.w3.org/TR/owl2-manchester-syntax/`
12. Horridge, M., Bechhofer, S.: The OWL API: A Java API for Working with OWL 2 Ontologies. In: Proceedings of the 5th International Workshop on OWL: Experiences and Directions (OWLED). CEUR Workshop Proceedings, vol. 529 (2009)
13. Kashyap, V., Bussler, C., Moran, M.: The Semantic Web, Semantics for Data and Services on the Web. Springer, Heidelberg (2008)
14. Kim, W., Seo, J.: Classifying schematic and data heterogeneity in multidatabase systems. Computer 24(12), 12–18 (1991)
15. Lavigne, C.: Advanced ETL with Pentaho Data Integration. Whitepaper, Breadboard BI (2006)
16. Leser, U.: Informationsintegration: Architekturen und Methoden zur Integration verteilter und heterogener Datenquellen. Dpunkt-Verl., Heidelberg (2007)
17. Meisen, T., Schilberg, D., Henning, K.: Planner Based Data Integration for Simulation Chains in Virtual Production. In: Proceedings of the International Conference on Science, Technology and Innovation for Sustainable Well-Being (STISWB), pp. 100–108. Klung NaNa Vithya Press Limited Partnership (2009)
18. Myerson, J.M.: The Complete Book of Middleware. Auerbach Publications, Boston (2002)
19. Panian, Z.: Supply chain intelligence in ebusiness environment. In: Proceedings of the 9th WSEAS International Conference on Computers (ICCOMP), pp. 1–6. World Scientic and Engineering Academy and Society (2005)
20. Rademakers, T., Dirksen, J.: Open-Source ESBs in Action. Manning Publications Co., Greenwich (2008)
21. Schilberg, D., Gramatke, A., Henning, K.: Semantic Interconnection of Distributed Numerical Simulations via SOA. In: Proceedings of the World Congress on Engineering and Computer Science (WCECS), pp. 894–897 (2008)
22. Schilberg, D.: Architektur eines Datenintegrators zur durchgängigen Kopplung von verteilten numerischen Simulationen. PhD thesis, RWTH Aachen University (2010)
23. Schmitz, G., Prahl, U.: Toward a virtual platform for materials processing. JOM Journal of the Minerals, Metals and Materials Society 61, 19–23 (2009)
24. Schroeder, W., Martin, K., Lorensen, B.: The Visualization Toolkit, Kitware Inc. (2004)
25. Schulte, R.W.: Predicts 2003: Enterprise service buses emerge. Technical report, Gartner (2003)
26. Sirin, E.: Pellet: A practical owl-dl reasoner. Web Semantics: Science, Services and Agents on the World Wide Web 5(2), 51–53 (2007)
27. Vassiliadis, P., Simitsis, A., Skiadopoulos, S.: Conceptual modeling for ETL processes. In: Proceedings of the 5th ACM International Workshop on Data Warehousing and OLAP (DOLAP), pp. 14–21. ACM, New York (2002)
28. White, C.: Data Integration: Using ETL, EAI and EII Tools to Create an Integrated Enterprise. Technical report, The Data Warehousing Institute (2005)

PAR-COM: A New Methodology for Post-processing Association Rules

Veronica Oliveira de Carvalho[1], Fabiano Fernandes dos Santos[2], Solange Oliveira Rezende[2], and Renan de Padua[1]

[1] Univ. Estadual Paulista (Unesp), Rio Claro SP, Brasil
[2] Universidade de São Paulo (USP), São Carlos SP, Brasil
{veronica,padua}@rc.unesp.br,
{fabianof,solange}@icmc.usp.br

Abstract. The post-processing of association rules is a difficult task, since a huge number of rules that are generated are of no interest to the user. To overcome this problem many approaches have been developed, such as objective measures and clustering. However, objective measures don't reduce nor organize the collection of rules, therefore making the understanding of the domain difficult. On the other hand, clustering doesn't reduce the exploration space nor direct the user to find interesting knowledge, therefore making the search for relevant knowledge not so easy. In this context this paper presents the PAR-COM methodology that, by combining clustering and objective measures, reduces the association rule exploration space directing the user to what is potentially interesting. An experimental study demonstrates the potential of PAR-COM to minimize the user's effort during the post-processing process.

Keywords: Association rules, Post-processing, Clustering, Objective measures.

1 Introduction

Association rules are widely used due to its ability to discover the frequent relationships that occur among sets of items stored in databases. Although this characteristic along with its inherent comprehensibility motivates its use, the main weakness of association technique occurs when it is necessary to analyze the mining result. The huge number of rules that are generated makes the user's exploration a difficult task. Many approaches have been developed to overcome this problem, as *Querying* (Q), *Evaluation Measures* (EM), *Pruning* (P), *Summarizing* (S) and *Grouping* (G) [1,5,7,12]. These post-processing approaches aid the exploration process by reducing the exploration space (**RES**), as Q, P and S, by directing the user to what is potentially interesting (**DUPI**), as EM, or by structuring the domain (**SD**), as G.

One of the more popular approaches to estimate the interestingness of a rule is the application of evaluation measures [7,12], which are usually classified as objective or subjective. Objective measures are more general and independent on the domain in which the data mining process is carried out and, thus, are more used. In this approach, the rules are ranked according to a selected measure and an ordered list of potentially interesting knowledge is shown to the user. Although this **DUPI** approach highlights

R. Zhang et al. (Eds.): ICEIS 2011, LNBIP 102, pp. 66–80, 2012.

the potentially interesting knowledge, it doesn't reduce nor organize the collection of rules, therefore making the understanding of the domain difficult.

Grouping is a relevant approach related to **SD**, since it organizes the rules in groups that contain, somehow, similar knowledge. These groups improve the presentation of the mined patterns, providing the user a view of the domain to be explored [8,9]. However, this approach doesn't reduce the exploration space nor direct the user to find interesting knowledge, making the search for relevant knowledge not so easy. Grouping can be done: (i) based on a user criteria; (ii) by using a clustering technique. While in case (i) the user describes how the groups will be formed, in case (ii) the user "let the rules speak for themselves" [7].

Clustering is the process of finding groups in data [6]. A cluster is a collection of objects that are similar to each other within the group and dissimilar towards the objects of the other groups[1]. Some steps have to be carried out in a clustering process as: (i) the selection of a similarity/dissimilarity measure, used to calculate the proximity among the objects; (ii) the selection/execution of a clustering algorithm, which is basically divided in two families: partitional and hierarchical.

Considering the exposed arguments, this work presents the PAR-COM (Post-processing Association Rules with Clustering and Objective Measures) methodology that, by combining clustering (**SD**) and objective measures (**DUPI**), reduces the association rule exploration space by directing the user to what is potentially interesting. Thus, PAR-COM, which was initially presented in [2], improves the post-processing process since it adheres **RES** and **DUPI**. Besides, different from the approaches related to **RES**, PAR-COM doesn't only show the user a reduced space through a small subset of groups but also highlights the potentially interesting knowledge.

The paper is structured as follows: Section 2 presents some concepts and related works; Section 3 the PAR-COM methodology; Section 4 the configurations used in experiments to apply PAR-COM; Section 5 the results and discussion; Section 6 a case study using PAR-COM; Section 7 the conclusions and future works.

2 Related Works

Since PAR-COM combines clustering and objetive measures, this section presents some works related to the clustering approach. The works regarding objective measures are all associated with the ranking of rules and due to its simplicity are not described here (for details see [10]).

In order to structure the extracted knowledge, different clustering strategies have been used for post-processing association rules. In [8] clustering is demonstrated through partitional (K-means, PAM, CLARANS) and hierarchical (AGNES) algorithms using Jaccard as the similarity measure. In this case, the Jaccard between two rules r and s, presented in Equation 1, is calculated considering the common transactions (t) the rules match (in our work we refer to this similarity measure as Jaccard with Rules by Transactions (J-RT)). A rule matches a transaction t if all the rule's items are contained in t. Jorge [5] demonstrates the use of clustering through hierarchical algorithms (Single Linkage, Complete Linkage, Average Linkage) also using Jaccard as the similarity

[1] The words cluster and group will be used as synonyms in this work.

measure. However, in this case, the Jaccard between two rules r and s, presented in Equation 2, is calculated considering the items the rules share (in our work we refer to this measure as Jaccard with Rules by Items (J-RI)). Toivonen et al. [11] propose a similarity measure based on transactions and use a density algorithm to carry out the clustering of the rules. Sahar [9] also proposes a similarity measure based on transactions considering the Toivonen et al. [11] work, although it uses a hierarchical algorithm to do the clustering.

$$\text{J-RT(r,s)}=\frac{\{t\ matched\ by\ r\} \cap \{t\ matched\ by\ s\}}{\{t\ matched\ by\ r\} \cup \{t\ matched\ by\ s\}} \tag{1}$$

$$\text{J-RI(r,s)}=\frac{\{items\ in\ r\} \cap \{items\ in\ s\}}{\{items\ in\ r\} \cup \{items\ in\ s\}} \tag{2}$$

However, all the described works, related to **SD**, are only concerned with the domain organization. Thus, a methodology as PAR-COM that take it as an advantage to reduce the exploration space, by directing the user to relevant knowledge, is useful.

3 PAR-COM Methodology

The PAR-COM (Post-processing Association Rules with Clustering and Objective Measures) methodology aims at combining clustering and objetive measures to reduce the association rule exploration space by directing the user to what is potentially interesting. For this purpose, PAR-COM considers that there is a subset of groups that contains all the h-top interesting rules, so that a small number of groups have to be explored. The h-top interesting rules are the h rules that have the highest values regarding an objective measure, where h is a number to be chosen. Besides, it is also considered that if some rules within a group express interesting knowledge, than the other rules within the same group also tend to express interesting knowledge. This assumption is taken considering the concept of cluster: a collection of objects that are similar to one another. So, if the rules are similar regarding a similarity measure, an interesting rule within a group indicates that its similar rules are also potentially interesting. Based on the exposed arguments, PAR-COM can reduce the exploration space by directing the user to the groups that are ideally interesting. As as consequence, PAR-COM can allow the discovery of additional interesting knowledge within these groups.

The PAR-COM methodology, presented in Figure 1, is described as follows:

Step A: the value of an objective measure is computed for all rules in the association set.

Step B: the h-top rules are selected considering the computed values.

Step C: after selecting a clustering algorithm and a similarity measure the rule set is clustered.

Step D: a search is done to find out the clusters that contain one or more h-top rules selected in Step B. These clusters are the ones that contain the potentially interesting knowledge (PIK) of the domain. The more h-top rules a cluster has, the more interesting it is.

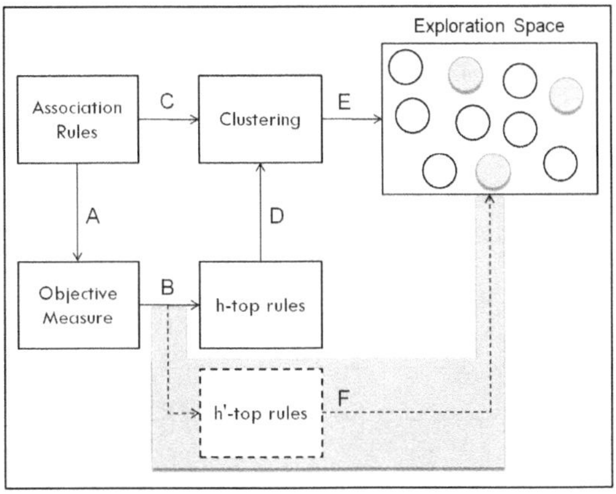

Fig. 1. The PAR-COM methodology

Step E: only the m first interesting clusters are shown to the user, who is directed to a reduced exploration space that contains the PIK of the domain, where m is a number to be chosen.

Step F, described in the next section, is a validation step used to evaluate the experiment's results. As will be noted in Sections 5 and 6, the combination of clustering with objective measures used in PAR-COM aids the post-processing process, therefore minimizing the user's effort.

4 Experiments

Some experiments were carried out to evaluate the performance of PAR-COM. However, in order to validate the results presented in Section 5 an additional step was added to the methodology. Step F, highlighted in gray in Figure 1, considers all the h'-top interesting rules to be also selected in Step B. The h'-top rules are the first h rules that immediately follow the previously selected h-top rules. Thus, the aim of Step F is to demonstrate that the m clusters presented to the user really contain PIK. For this purpose, a search is done to find out if these m clusters contain one or more h'-top rules. It is expected that these m clusters cover all the h'-top rules, since by definition a cluster is a collection of objects that are similar to one another. So, as mentioned before, if the rules are similar regarding a similarity measure, an interesting rule within a group indicates that its similar rules are also potentially interesting. It is important to note that PAR-COM doesn't aid the exploration as an ordered list of PIK, which is the case when objective measures are used (see Section 6). For that reason, PAR-COM can allow the discovery of additional interesting knowledge within the m groups.

The four data sets used in experiments are presented in Table 1. The first three data sets are available in *R Project for Statistical Computing*[2] through "arules" package[3].

[2] `http://www.r-project.org/`
[3] `http://cran.r-project.org/web/packages/arules/index.html`

Table 1. Details of the data sets used in experiments

Data set	# of transactions	# of distinct items	Brief description
Adult	48842	115	This set is a R pre-processed version for association mining of the "Adult" database available in [3]. It was originally used to predict whether income exceeds USD 50K/yr based on census data.
Income	6876	50	This set is also a R pre-processed version for association mining of the "Marketing" database available in [4]. It was originally used to predict the anual income of household from demographics attributes.
Groceries	9835	169	This set is also available in R and contains 1 month (30 days) of real-world point-of-sale transaction data from a typical local grocery outlet.
Sup	1716	1939	This set contains 1 day of real-world transaction data from a supermarket located in São Carlos city in Brazil.

The last one was donated by a supermarket located in São Carlos city, Brazil. All the transactions of the Adult and Income contain the same number of items (referred here as standardized-transactions data sets), different from Groceries and Sup (referred here as non-standardized-transactions data sets). Thus, PAR-COM was evaluated on different types of data. The rules were mined using an *Apriori* implementation developed by Christian Borgelt[4] with a maximum number of 5 items per rule and excluding the rules of type $TRUE \Rightarrow X$, where X is an item contained in data. With the Adult set 6508 rules were generated using a minimum support (min-sup) of 10% and a minimum confidence (min-conf) of 50%; with Income 3714 rules considering a min-sup of 17% and a min-conf of 50%; with Groceries 2050 rules considering a min-sup of 0.5% and a min-conf of 0.5%; with Sup 7588 rules considering a min-sup of 0.7% and a min-conf of 0.5%. These parameter values were chosen experimentally.

Since the works described in Section 2 only use one family of clustering algorithms and one similarity measure to cluster the association rules, it was decided to apply PAR-COM with one algorithm of each family and with the two most used similarity measures (J-RI and J-RT (Equations 1 and 2)). The Partitioning Around Medoids (PAM) was chosen within the partitional family and the Average Linkage within the hierarchical family. In the partitional case, a medoid algorithm was chosen because the aim is to cluster the most similar rules in one group; thus, the ideal is that the centroid group be a rule and not, for example, the mean, as in the K-means algorithm (same argument of [8]). In the hierarchical case, the traditional algorithms were applied (Single, Complete and Average) and the one that had the best performance is here presented. PAM was executed with k ranging between 5 to 100 considering a step of 5. The dendrograms generated by Average Linkage were cut in the same ranges (5 to 100 considering a step of 5). The range was chosen based on some results presented in [2], that by considering a short range (6 to 15, step of 1) didn't lead to a final conclusion about the combinations "algorithm + similarity measure".

To apply PAR-COM it was also necessary to choose the values of h (Step B), m (Step E) and an objective measure (Step A). h was set to 0.5% of the total of the rules in order to make the comparisons more fair; therefore, each data set has its own value that it is proportional in all of them. m was set to 3 based on the amount of information a human

[4] `http://www.borgelt.net/apriori.html`

Table 2. Configurations used to evaluate PAR-COM

Data sets	Adult; Income; Groceries; Sup
Algorithms	PAM; Average Linkage
Similarity measures	J-RI; J-RT
k	5 to 100, step of 5
h	0.5% of the rules
m	3
Objective measures	Average rating obtained through the measures Added Value, Certainty Factor, Collective Strength, Confidence, Conviction, IS, ϕ-coefficient, Gini Index, J-Measure, Kappa, Klosgen, λ, Laplace, Lift, Mutual Information (asymmetric), Novelty, Support, Odds Ratio

can assimilate simultaneously in a short period (cognitive science). Since it is expected that any measure produces good results, instead of choosing a specific measure, the average rating obtained through 18 objective measures (see Table 2) was considered as follows: (i) the value of the 18 measures is computed for each rule; (ii) each rule receives 18 ID's, each one corresponding to position in one of the ranks related to a measure; (iii) the average is then calculated based on the rank position (ID's). Details about the measures can be found on [10]. Table 2 summarizes the configurations applied to evaluate PAR-COM.

5 Results and Discussion

Considering the configurations presented in Table 2, PAR-COM was applied and the results are presented in Figures 2 to 9. The results were grouped by algorithm for each data set. Figures 2 and 6 present the results for the Adult data set, Figures 3 and 7 for Income, Figures 4 and 8 for Groceries, Figures 5 and 9 for Sup, all using, respectively, PAM and Average. Each figure contains 2 sub-figures: one related to the J-RI similarity measure and one to J-RT. The x axis of each graphic represents the range considered for k. The y axis represents the percentage of h-top and h'-top rules contained in the m first interesting clusters (lines h-top and h'-top) and also the percentage of reduction in the exploration space (line R). Each graphic title indicates the used configuration.

In order to facilitate the interpretation of the graphics consider Figure 2(b). It can be observed that for a $k = 10$: (i) the first 3 interesting clusters (m=3) contain 100% of the 33-top rules (h=33 (0.5%*6508)) using J-RT; (ii) the first 3 interesting clusters contain 91% of the 33'-top rules; thus, by the validation step (Step F), these 3 clusters are ideal the 3 most interesting subsets; (iii) the first 3 interesting clusters cover 37% (100%-63%) of the rules, leading to a reduction of 63% in the exploration space; in order words, if the user explores these 3 clusters, he will explore 37% of the rule space.

Evaluating the results, in relation to PAM algorithm, it can be noticed that:

- in Figures 2 and 3 the J-RT similarity measure presented better results compared with J-RI in relation to the h-top and h'-top rules. However, J-RI and J-RT had a similar behavior regarding the exploration space reduction.

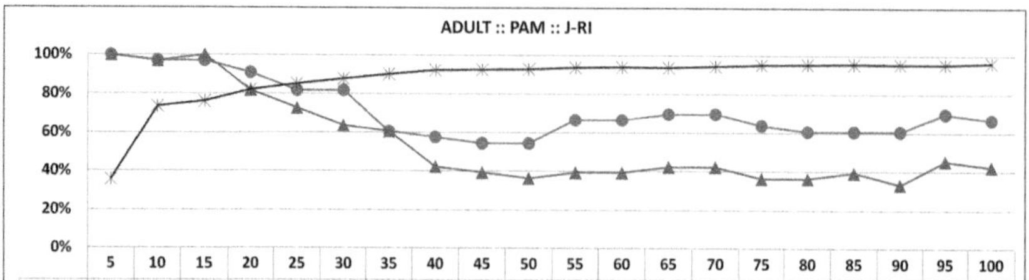

	5	10	15	20	25	30	35	40	45	50	55	60	65	70	75	80	85	90	95	100
h-top	100%	97%	97%	91%	82%	82%	61%	58%	55%	55%	67%	67%	70%	70%	64%	61%	61%	61%	70%	67%
h'-top	100%	97%	100%	82%	73%	64%	61%	42%	39%	36%	39%	39%	42%	42%	36%	36%	39%	33%	45%	42%
R	36%	73%	76%	82%	85%	88%	90%	92%	92%	93%	94%	94%	94%	94%	95%	95%	95%	95%	95%	96%

(a)

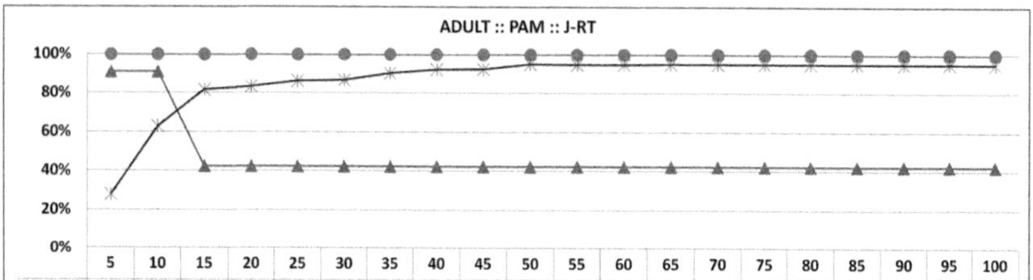

	5	10	15	20	25	30	35	40	45	50	55	60	65	70	75	80	85	90	95	100
h-top	100%	100%	100%	100%	100%	100%	100%	100%	100%	100%	100%	100%	100%	100%	100%	100%	100%	100%	100%	100%
h'-top	91%	91%	42%	42%	42%	42%	42%	42%	42%	42%	42%	42%	42%	42%	42%	42%	42%	42%	42%	42%
R	28%	63%	82%	83%	86%	86%	90%	92%	92%	95%	95%	95%	95%	95%	95%	95%	95%	95%	95%	95%

(b)

Fig. 2. PAM's results in the ADULT data set

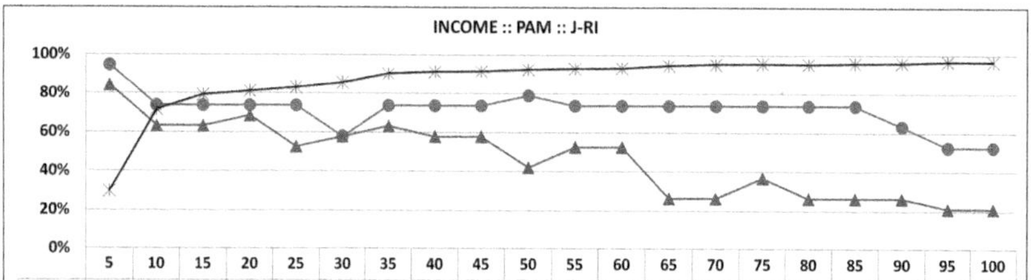

	5	10	15	20	25	30	35	40	45	50	55	60	65	70	75	80	85	90	95	100
h-top	95%	74%	74%	74%	74%	58%	74%	74%	74%	79%	74%	74%	74%	74%	74%	74%	74%	63%	53%	53%
h'-top	84%	63%	63%	68%	53%	58%	63%	58%	58%	42%	53%	53%	26%	26%	37%	26%	26%	26%	21%	21%
R	30%	72%	79%	81%	83%	85%	90%	91%	91%	92%	93%	93%	94%	95%	95%	95%	96%	96%	97%	97%

(a)

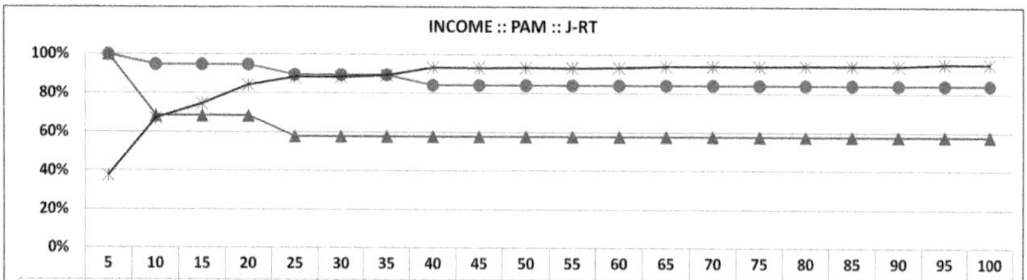

	5	10	15	20	25	30	35	40	45	50	55	60	65	70	75	80	85	90	95	100
h-top	100%	95%	95%	95%	89%	89%	89%	84%	84%	84%	84%	84%	84%	84%	84%	84%	84%	84%	84%	84%
h'-top	100%	68%	68%	68%	58%	58%	58%	58%	58%	58%	58%	58%	58%	58%	58%	58%	58%	58%	58%	58%
R	37%	67%	74%	84%	88%	88%	89%	93%	93%	93%	93%	93%	94%	94%	94%	94%	94%	94%	95%	95%

(b)

Fig. 3. PAM's results in the INCOME data set

- in Figure 4 the J-RI similarity measure presented better results compared with J-RT in relation to the h-top and h'-top rules. Although J-RI and J-RT had, in general, a similar behavior regarding the exploration space reduction, J-RT had a slightly better performance.
- in Figure 5 the J-RI similarity measure presented better results compared with J-RT in relation to the h-top and h'-top rules. However, J-RI and J-RT had a similar behavior regarding the exploration space reduction.

Summarizing the results in Figures 2, 3, 4 and 5, it can be seen that with PAM, considering non-standardized-transactions data sets, the similarity measure that had the best performance was J-RI regarding h and h'; on the contrary, for standardized-transactions data sets, J-RT was the best regarding h and h'. However, considering the exploration space reduction, both similarity measures presented similar behavior. On the other hand, in relation to the Average algorithm, it can be noticed that:

- in Figure 6 the J-RT similarity measure presented better results compared with J-RI in relation to the h-top and h'-top rules. However, J-RI and J-RT had a similar behavior regarding the exploration space reduction.
- in Figure 7 the J-RT similarity measure presented better results compared with J-RI in relation to the h-top and h'-top rules. Although J-RI and J-RT had, in general, a similar behavior regarding the exploration space reduction, J-RT had a slightly better performance.
- in Figures 8 and 9 the J-RT similarity measure presented better results compared with J-RI in relation to the h-top and h'-top rules. However, J-RI had a better performance regarding the exploration space reduction.

Summarizing the results in Figures 6, 7, 8 and 9, it can be seen that with Average the similarity measure that had the best performance was J-RT regarding h and h', regardless of the data set type (standardized-transactions or non-standardized-transactions). However, considering the exploration space reduction, J-RI presented better results in Groceries and Sup and the measures presented similar behavior in Adult and Income. Thus, since PAM had a better performance with J-RT in Adult and Income and with J-RI in Groceries and Sup two comparisons were done: one for the Adult and Income data sets considering PAM+J-RT with Average+J-RT and one for the Groceries and Sup data sets considering PAM+J-RI with Average+J-RT. It can be noticed that:

- in the Adult data set, while the Average algorithm had a better performance regarding h and h', PAM presented better results considering the reduction exploration space (compare Figures 2(b) and 6(b)). However, Average can also obtain good results for $k \geq 25$ regarding R (above 70%), being indicated in these cases. Finally, in cases where $k < 25$, it is better to use PAM, since it presents a good tradeoff among h, h' and R.
- in the Income data set, while the Average algorithm had a better performance regarding h and h', PAM presented better results considering the reduction exploration space (compare Figures 3(b) and 7(b)). However, Average can also obtain good results for $k \geq 30$ regarding R (above 70%), being indicated in these cases. Finally, in cases where $k < 30$, it is better to use PAM, since it presents a good tradeoff among h, h' and R.

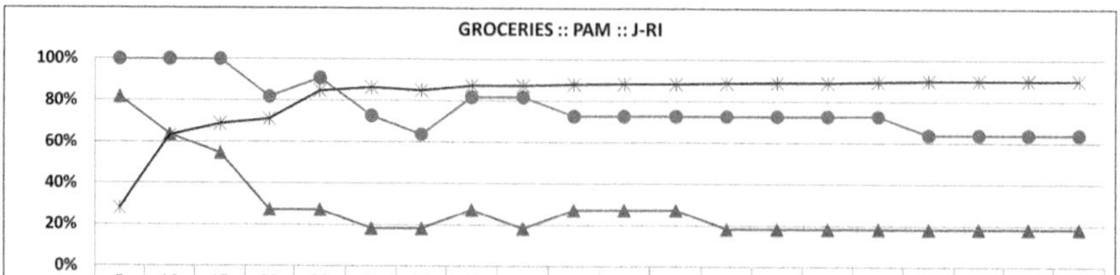

	5	10	15	20	25	30	35	40	45	50	55	60	65	70	75	80	85	90	95	100
h-top	100%	100%	100%	82%	91%	73%	64%	82%	82%	73%	73%	73%	73%	73%	73%	73%	64%	64%	64%	64%
h'-top	82%	64%	55%	27%	27%	18%	18%	27%	18%	27%	27%	27%	18%	18%	18%	18%	18%	18%	18%	18%
R	28%	63%	69%	71%	85%	86%	85%	87%	87%	88%	88%	88%	89%	89%	89%	90%	90%	90%	90%	90%

(a)

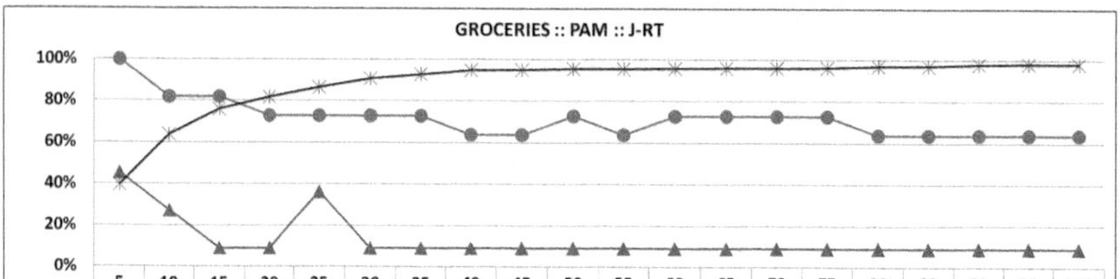

	5	10	15	20	25	30	35	40	45	50	55	60	65	70	75	80	85	90	95	100
h-top	100%	82%	82%	73%	73%	73%	73%	64%	64%	73%	64%	73%	73%	73%	73%	64%	64%	64%	64%	64%
h'-top	45%	27%	9%	9%	36%	9%	9%	9%	9%	9%	9%	9%	9%	9%	9%	9%	9%	9%	9%	9%
R	40%	64%	76%	82%	86%	91%	93%	95%	95%	95%	95%	96%	96%	96%	96%	97%	97%	98%	98%	98%

(b)

Fig. 4. PAM's results in the GROCERIES data set

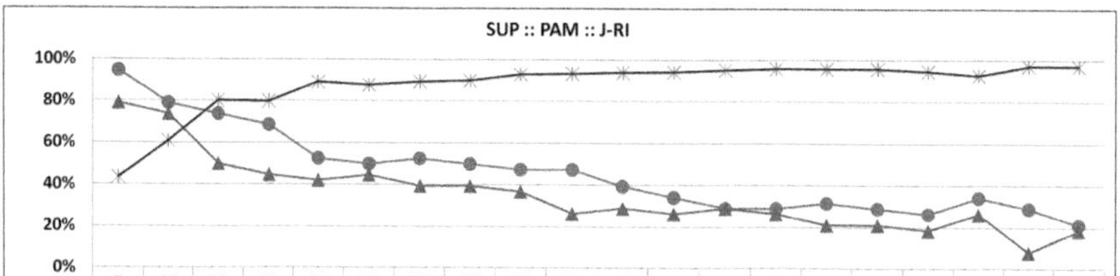

	5	10	15	20	25	30	35	40	45	50	55	60	65	70	75	80	85	90	95	100
h-top	95%	79%	74%	68%	53%	50%	53%	50%	47%	47%	39%	34%	29%	29%	32%	29%	26%	34%	29%	21%
h'-top	79%	74%	50%	45%	42%	45%	39%	39%	37%	26%	29%	26%	29%	26%	21%	21%	18%	26%	8%	18%
R	43%	61%	80%	80%	89%	88%	89%	90%	93%	93%	94%	94%	95%	96%	96%	96%	94%	93%	97%	97%

(a)

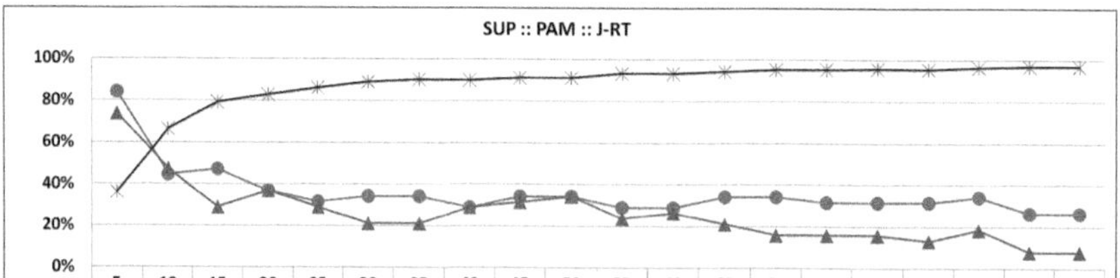

	5	10	15	20	25	30	35	40	45	50	55	60	65	70	75	80	85	90	95	100
h-top	84%	45%	47%	37%	32%	34%	34%	29%	34%	34%	29%	29%	34%	34%	32%	32%	32%	34%	26%	26%
h'-top	74%	47%	29%	37%	29%	21%	21%	29%	32%	34%	24%	26%	21%	16%	16%	16%	13%	18%	8%	8%
R	36%	66%	79%	83%	86%	89%	90%	90%	91%	91%	93%	93%	94%	95%	95%	96%	95%	96%	97%	97%

(b)

Fig. 5. PAM's results in the SUP data set

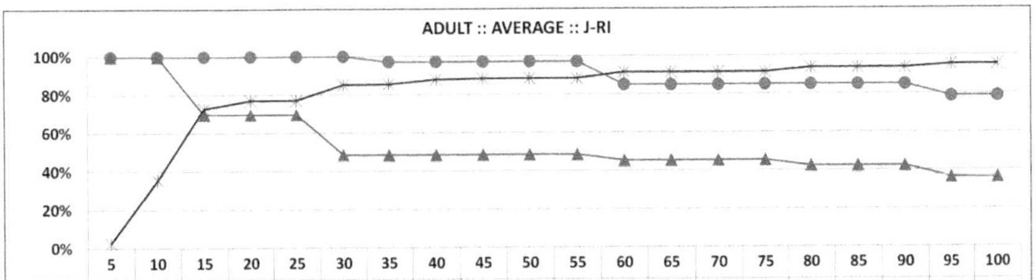

	5	10	15	20	25	30	35	40	45	50	55	60	65	70	75	80	85	90	95	100
h-top	100%	100%	100%	100%	100%	100%	97%	97%	97%	97%	97%	85%	85%	85%	85%	85%	85%	85%	79%	79%
h'-top	100%	100%	70%	70%	70%	48%	48%	48%	48%	48%	48%	45%	45%	45%	45%	42%	42%	42%	36%	36%
R	3%	36%	73%	77%	77%	85%	85%	88%	88%	88%	88%	91%	91%	91%	91%	93%	93%	93%	95%	95%

(a)

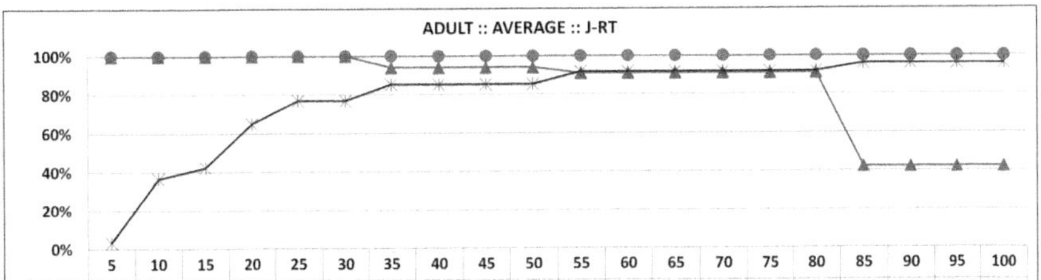

	5	10	15	20	25	30	35	40	45	50	55	60	65	70	75	80	85	90	95	100
h-top	100%	100%	100%	100%	100%	100%	100%	100%	100%	100%	100%	100%	100%	100%	100%	100%	100%	100%	100%	100%
h'-top	100%	100%	100%	100%	100%	100%	94%	94%	94%	94%	91%	91%	91%	91%	91%	91%	42%	42%	42%	42%
R	3%	36%	42%	65%	77%	77%	85%	85%	85%	85%	92%	92%	92%	92%	92%	92%	96%	96%	96%	96%

(b)

Fig. 6. AVERAGE's results in the ADULT data set

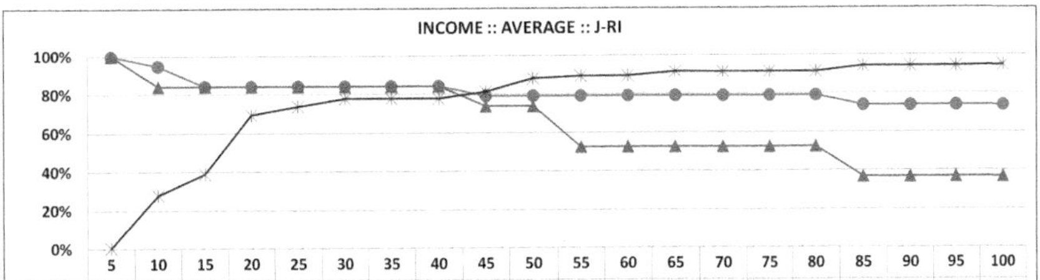

	5	10	15	20	25	30	35	40	45	50	55	60	65	70	75	80	85	90	95	100
h-top	100%	95%	84%	84%	84%	84%	84%	84%	79%	79%	79%	79%	79%	79%	79%	79%	74%	74%	74%	74%
h'-top	100%	84%	84%	84%	84%	84%	84%	84%	74%	74%	53%	53%	53%	53%	53%	53%	37%	37%	37%	37%
R	0%	28%	39%	69%	74%	78%	78%	78%	81%	88%	89%	89%	91%	91%	91%	91%	94%	94%	94%	95%

(a)

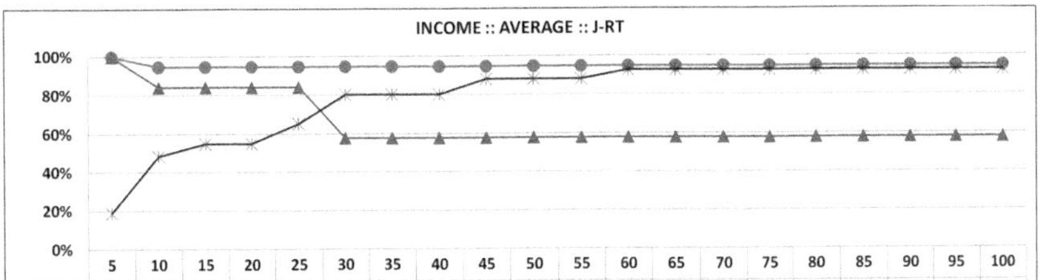

	5	10	15	20	25	30	35	40	45	50	55	60	65	70	75	80	85	90	95	100
h-top	100%	95%	95%	95%	95%	95%	95%	95%	95%	95%	95%	95%	95%	95%	95%	95%	95%	95%	95%	95%
h'-top	100%	84%	84%	84%	84%	58%	58%	58%	58%	58%	58%	58%	58%	58%	58%	58%	58%	58%	58%	58%
R	19%	49%	55%	55%	65%	80%	80%	80%	88%	88%	88%	93%	93%	93%	93%	93%	93%	93%	93%	93%

(b)

Fig. 7. AVERAGE's results in the INCOME data set

- in the Groceries data set, while the Average algorithm had a better performance regarding h and h', PAM presented better results considering the reduction exploration space (compare Figures 4(a) and 8(b)). Moreover, Average needs greater values of k to obtain good results regarding R: it is necessary a $k \geq 50$ to get a reduction above 70%. Therefore, if the user wants to obtain higher reductions with fewer groups (for example, compare $k = 20$) it is better to use PAM even if some interesting information (h+h') is lost; on the other hand, if the combination number-of-groups+R is not a problem, Average is preferable.
- in the Sup data set, while the Average algorithm had a better performance regarding h and h', PAM presented better results considering the reduction exploration space (compare Figures 5(a) and 9(b)). Moreover, Average needs greater values of k to obtain good results regarding R: it is necessary a $k \geq 90$ to get a reduction above 50%. Therefore, if the user wants to obtain higher reductions with fewer groups (for example, compare $k = 20$) it is better to use PAM even if some interesting information (h+h') is lost; on the other hand, if the combination number-of-groups+R is not a problem, Average is preferable.

Based on the exposed discussion, it can be observed that: (i) for standardized-transactions data sets, the user can apply PAR-COM considering the combination PAM:J-RT for small values of k ($k < 30$) or Average:J-RT for greater values of k ($k \geq 30$); (ii) for non-standardized-transactions data sets, the user can apply PAR-COM considering the combination PAM:J-RI if it is needed to lose some h+h' information to increase R; otherwise, Average:J-RT.

6 Case Study

This section presents a case study that was done to illustrate the proposed methodology and to compare the obtained results with a **DUPI** approach, since PAR-COM combines **SD+DUPI** to obtain a potentially interesting reduced space (**RES**).

The study was done with the Sup data set. All the obtained rules (7588) were evaluated by two specialists. Since a high number of rules were available and that, in most of the cases, each pair of rules contained a variation of the same items, the rules were alternately presented: while one specialist evaluated the patterns of type $A \Rightarrow B$ the other evaluated the types $B \Rightarrow A$. Each rule received a value according to the specialist's knowledge: **-1** if the rule was common or not interesting; **0** if the rule was a little interesting; **1** if the rule was very interesting. In the end, the 38 rules that received the values **0** and **1** were selected as baseline.

PAR-COM was applied considering the same configurations presented in Figure 5(a): PAM; J-RI; k ranging from 5 to 100, step of 5; h of 0.5% (also leading to 38 rules (0.5%*7588)); the same 18 objective measures (see Table 2). The combination PAM+J-RI was selected considering the conclusions presented in Section 5 and the specialists's needs. However, in this case, the value of m was not considered. That is because a web environment, named RulEE-AREC, was implemented to support PAR-COM. In this environment all the groups are presented to the user considering its interesting order: the more h-top rules a cluster has, the more interesting it is (see Steps D and E in

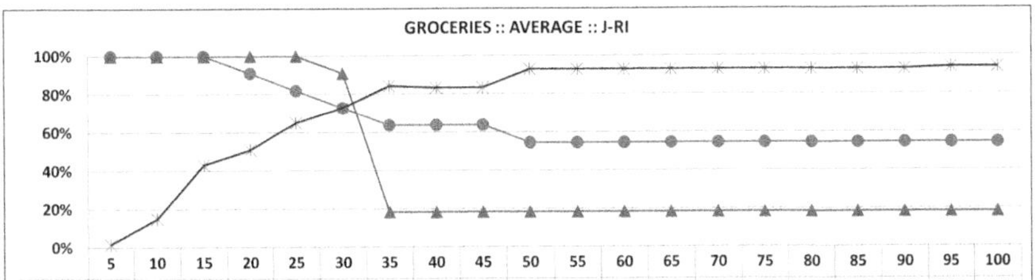

	5	10	15	20	25	30	35	40	45	50	55	60	65	70	75	80	85	90	95	100
h-top	100%	100%	100%	91%	82%	73%	64%	64%	64%	55%	55%	55%	55%	55%	55%	55%	55%	55%	55%	55%
h'-top	100%	100%	100%	100%	100%	91%	18%	18%	18%	18%	18%	18%	18%	18%	18%	18%	18%	18%	18%	18%
R	2%	15%	43%	51%	65%	73%	84%	83%	83%	93%	93%	93%	93%	93%	93%	93%	93%	93%	94%	94%

(a)

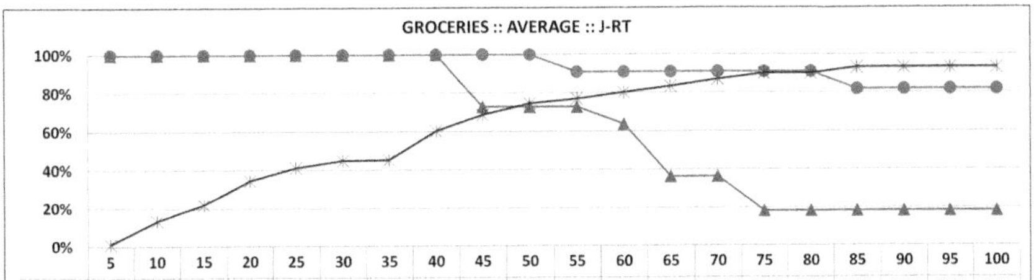

	5	10	15	20	25	30	35	40	45	50	55	60	65	70	75	80	85	90	95	100
h-top	100%	100%	100%	100%	100%	100%	100%	100%	100%	100%	91%	91%	91%	91%	91%	91%	82%	82%	82%	82%
h'-top	100%	100%	100%	100%	100%	100%	100%	100%	73%	73%	73%	64%	36%	36%	18%	18%	18%	18%	18%	18%
R	1%	13%	22%	34%	41%	45%	45%	60%	68%	74%	77%	80%	83%	87%	90%	90%	93%	93%	93%	93%

(b)

Fig. 8. AVERAGE's results in the GROCERIES data set

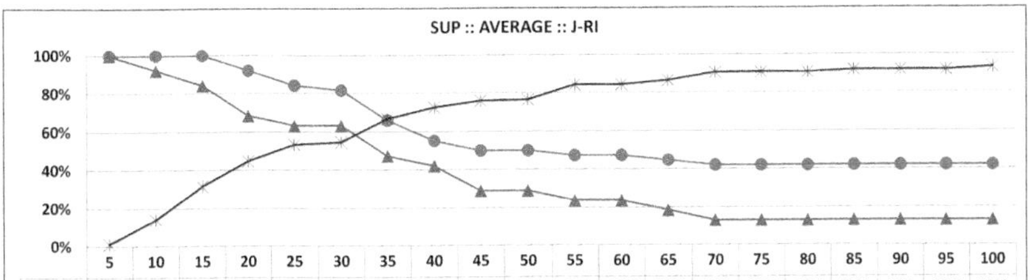

	5	10	15	20	25	30	35	40	45	50	55	60	65	70	75	80	85	90	95	100
h-top	100%	100%	100%	92%	84%	82%	66%	55%	50%	50%	47%	47%	45%	42%	42%	42%	42%	42%	42%	42%
h'-top	100%	92%	84%	68%	63%	63%	47%	42%	29%	29%	24%	24%	18%	13%	13%	13%	13%	13%	13%	13%
R	1%	14%	32%	45%	53%	55%	67%	72%	76%	76%	84%	84%	86%	90%	91%	91%	92%	92%	92%	93%

(a)

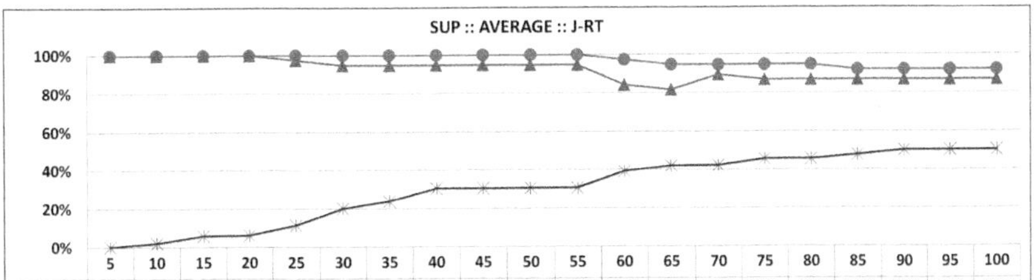

	5	10	15	20	25	30	35	40	45	50	55	60	65	70	75	80	85	90	95	100
h-top	100%	100%	100%	100%	100%	100%	100%	100%	100%	100%	100%	97%	95%	95%	95%	95%	92%	92%	92%	92%
h'-top	100%	100%	100%	100%	97%	95%	95%	95%	95%	95%	95%	84%	82%	89%	87%	87%	87%	87%	87%	87%
R	0%	2%	6%	6%	11%	20%	24%	31%	31%	31%	31%	39%	42%	42%	46%	46%	48%	50%	50%	50%

(b)

Fig. 9. AVERAGE's results in the SUP data set

AREC Exploration

Group number	Label	Exploration space	Exploration space (accumulated)	h-top rules	h-top rules (accumulated)	Most similar group
8	CREME_DE_LEITE_NESTLE,LEITE_MOCA LEITE_MOCA,CREME_DE_LEITE_NESTL	5.09 %	5.09 %	21.05 %	21.05 %	25
7	CREME_DE_LEITE_NESTLE,FARTRIGO_RENATA FARTRIGO_RENATA,CREME_DE_LEITE_NESTL	3.82 %	8.91 %	18.42 %	39.47 %	25
17	LEITE_MOCA,BOMBRI	2.20 %	11.11 %	13.16 %	52.63 %	24
10	ACHOCNESCAU,LEITE_MOCA LEITE_MOCA,ACHOCNESCA	4.22 %	15.33 %	10.53 %	63.16 %	23
25	COCA_COLA,LEITE_MOCA LEITE_MOCA,COCA_COL	3.66 %	18.99 %	10.53 %	73.69 %	24
23	BISCNESTLE,LEITE_MOCA LEITE_MOCA,BISCNESTL	2.45 %	21.44 %	7.89 %	81.58 %	25
3	FERMROYAL,MAIONESE_HELLMANN_S MAIONESE_HELLMANN_S,FERMROYA	9.77 %	31.21 %	5.26 %	86.84 %	19
2	DETERGLIMPOL,LEITE_MOCA LEITE_MOCA,DETERGLIMPO	3.53 %	34.74 %	2.63 %	89.47 %	20
5	LEITE_MOCA,SAL_CISNE SAL_CISNE,LEITE_MOC	8.12 %	42.86 %	2.63 %	92.10 %	24
9	BISCNESTLE,PAPEL_HIGPERSONAL PAPEL_HIGPERSONAL,BISCNESTL	4.09 %	46.95 %	2.63 %	94.73 %	18
18	LEITE_MOCA,PAPEL_HIGPERSONAL PAPEL_HIGPERSONAL,LEITE_MOC	2.83 %	49.78 %	2.63 %	97.36 %	24
24	COCA_COLA,LEITE_MOCA LEITE_MOCA,COCA_COL	3.08 %	52.86 %	2.63 %	99.99 %	25
1	ACUCAR_UNIAO,COCA_COLA COCA_COLA,ACUCAR_UNIA	7.24 %	60.10 %	0.00 %	---	24

Fig. 10. Part of PAR-COM results presented in RulEE-AREC considering the combination PAM+J-RI+k=25

Section 3). Thus, the first listed clusters are potentially the more interesting. Figure 10 presents part of the PAR-COM results, in RulEE-AREC, considering the combination PAM+J-RI+k=25. Each line corresponds to a group. The columns present the following information: (i) "Group number" the number of the group that, in this case, ranges from 1 to 25; (ii) "Label" a summary of the concepts covered by the rules in the group – the idea is to facilitate the user's navigation, since a view of the groups is obtained before the rules are explored; (iii) "Exploration Space" the percentage of rules contained in the group – this means that if only the first group is explored the exploration space will be reduced in 94.91% (100%-5.09%); (iv) "Exploration space (accumulated)" the cumulative total of rules – this means, for example, if the user explores only the first three clusters, that contains, respectively, 5.09%, 3.82%, 2.20% of the rules, the exploration space will be reduced in 88.89% (100%-11.11%), where 11.11% represents the sum of the three mentioned values (check with the result presented in Figure 5(a)); (v) "h-top rules" the percentage of h-top rules contained in the group; (vi) "h-top rules (accumulated)" the cumulative total of h-top rules, as in (iv) – the first group contains, for example, 21.05% of the h-top rules and along with the second group a total of 39.47% (21.05%+18.42%); (vii) "Most similar group" the number of the group that is more similar to the one presented – the idea is that if a group contains interesting knowledge its similar group (neighbor group) also contains interesting knowledge. This similarity is obtained in the same way of Average Linkage. To view the rules of a group the user simply selects the group label. It is important to note that the labels presented in column (ii) are automatically generated by a labeling method, for example, the simplest one that selects the medoid of the group. Moreover, any method can be applied. The labeling methods will not be covered since it isn't the scope of the paper.

After applying PAR-COM, a search was done to find out the clusters where the 38 rules selected by the specialists were. It was expected that these rules were in some of the most interesting clusters; in case of Figure 10, somewhere until "group number" 24.

In the presented configuration, 87% of the 38 rules were in "group number" 3 and 16% in "group number" 5, reducing the exploration space in 57.14% (100%-42.86%) (see Figure 10).

To compare the PAR-COM results with a **DUPI** approach, objective measures were used. Therefore, the following methodology was applied: (i) all the 7588 rules were ranked in the same way described in Section 4, i.e., according to their average rating obtained through the 18 objective measures considered in Table 2; (ii) considering the same number n of rules contained in the first cluster, a search was done in the ranked list to find out the percentage of the 38 selected rules that were in the n first positions of the list; (iii) considering the next m rules contained in the second cluster, a search was done in the ranked list, starting from the last visited position, to find out the percentage of the 38 selected rules that were in the m next positions of the list; (iv) the same process was done until the last cluster; (v) finally, the percentage of retrieved interesting rules obtained by the **DUPI** approach was observed when PAR-COM achieved its 100% of recovery. It was expected that PAR-COM achieved 100% before **DUPI**, since its idea is to obtain a potentially interesting reduced space.

To understand the methodology, consider the results presented in Figure 10. The first cluster contains 386 rules of 7588 (5.09%*7588). Thus, the ranked list was searched until position 386 to find out the percentage of the 38 selected rules contained until this position. After that, starting from position 387, the next 290 positions, corresponding to the total of rules in the second cluster (3.82%*7588), were searched to find out the next percentage of the 38 selected rules contained until this position (from 1 to 676 (386+290); the percentage is accumulative); the process was done until the last cluster. In the end, it was observed that when PAR-COM achieved 100% of recovery, in this case, in "group number" 5 as mentioned above, the **DUPI** approach obtained 21%. In other words, while PAR-COM explored only 42.86% of the rules, it would be necessary to explore 97.65% of the space to find out all the 38 selected interesting rules in the **DUPI** approach.

Finally, it could be observed that although the 38 interesting rules had not been presented in the first three clusters, PAR-COM presented a good result since: (i) **DUPI** doesn't reduce nor organize the collection of rules (PAR-COM does); (ii) in **RES** some patterns can be removed (P), the user has to provide an extra knowledge (S) or state its needs (Q) (PAR-COM doesn't); (iii) **SD** doesn't reduce the exploration space nor direct the user to find interesting knowledge (PAR-COM does).

7 Conclusions

This work presented the PAR-COM methodology that by combining clustering (**SD**) and objective measures (**DUPI**) provides a powerful tool to aid the post-processing. PAR-COM can present the user only a small subset of the rules, providing a view to what is really interesting. Thereby, PAR-COM adheres **RES** and **DUPI**. PAR-COM has a good performance, as observed in Sections 5 and 6, in: (i) highlighting the potentially interesting knowledge (PIK); (ii) reducing the exploration space. Moreover, considering the results presented in Section 5, PAR-COM with PAM:J-RT for small values of k ($k < 30$) or Average:J-RT for greater values of k ($k \geq 30$) is indicated to standardized-transactions data sets. For non-standardized-transactions data sets, PAR-COM with PAM:J-RI is indicated if it is needed to lose some information in order to increase exploration space reduction; otherwise, Average:J-RT.

Regarding the case study, PAR-COM demonstrates the potential to minimize the user's effort during the post-processing process when compared with a DUPI approach. In future works, we intend to expand the evaluation to other PAR-COM configurations. Also, as a future work, some labeling methodologies will be studied and implemented that, along with PAR-COM, will direct the user to the potentially interesting "topics" (PIT) in the domain.

Acknowledgements. We wish to thank Fundação de Amparo à Pesquisa do Estado de São Paulo (FAPESP) for the financial support (process number 2010/07879-0).

References

1. Baesens, B., Viaene, S., Vanthienen, J.: Post-processing of association rules. In: Proceedings of the Special Workshop on Post-processing, The 6th ACM SIGKDD International Conference on Knowledge Discovery and Data Mining, pp. 2–8 (2000)
2. Carvalho, V.O., Santos, F.F., Rezende, S.O.: Post-processing association rules with clustering and objective measures. In: Proceedings of 13th International Conference on Enterprise Information Systems, vol. 1, pp. 54–63 (2011)
3. Frank, A., Asuncion, A.: UCI machine learning repository. University of California, Irvine, School of Information and Computer Sciences (2010), `http://archive.ics.uci.edu/ml`
4. Hastie, T., Tibshirani, R., Friedman, J.: The Elements of Statistical Learning: Data Mining, Inference, and Prediction, 2nd edn. Springer Series in Statistics. Springer (2009), `http://www-stat.stanford.edu/~tibs/ElemStatLearn/`
5. Jorge, A.: Hierarchical clustering for thematic browsing and summarization of large sets of association rules. In: Berry, M.W., Dayal, U., Kamath, C., Skillicorn, D. (eds.) Proceedings of the 4th SIAM International Conference on Data Mining, 10p. (2004)
6. Kaufman, L., Rousseeuw, P.J.: Finding Groups in Data: An Introduction to Cluster Analysis. Wiley Interscience (1990)
7. Natarajan, R., Shekar, B.: Interestingness of association rules in data mining: Issues relevant to e-commerce. SĀDHANĀ – Academy Proceedings in Engineering Sciences (The Indian Academy of Sciences) 30(parts 2&3), 291–310 (2005)
8. Reynolds, A.P., Richards, G., de la Iglesia, B., Rayward-Smith, V.J.: Clustering rules: A comparison of partitioning and hierarchical clustering algorithms. Journal of Mathematical Modelling and Algorithms 5(4), 475–504 (2006)
9. Sahar, S.: Exploring interestingness through clustering: A framework. In: Proceedings of the IEEE International Conference on Data Mining, pp. 677–680 (2002)
10. Tan, P.-N., Kumar, V., Srivastava, J.: Selecting the right objective measure for association analysis. Information Systems 29(4), 293–313 (2004)
11. Toivonen, H., Klemettinen, M., Ronkainen, P., Hätönen, K., Mannila, H.: Pruning and grouping discovered association rules. In: Workshop Notes of the Workshop on Statistics, Machine Learning, and Knowledge Discovery in Databases, pp. 47–52. MLnet (1995)
12. Zhao, Y., Zhang, C., Cao, L.: Post-Mining of Association Rules: Techniques for Effective Knowledge Extraction. Information Science Reference, 372p. (2009)

Ubiquitous Resource-Aware Clustering of Data Streams

Ching-Ming Chao[1] and Guan-Lin Chao[2]

[1] Department of Computer Science & Information Management,
Soochow University
56 Kueiyang St., Sec. 1, Taipei, 100, Taiwan
chao@csim.scu.edu.tw
[2] Department of Electrical Engineering,
National Taiwan University
No. 1, Sec. 4, Roosevelt Road, Taipei, 106, Taiwan
guanlinchao@gmail.com

Abstract. With the advance of wireless networks and mobile devices, the concept of ubiquitous data mining was proposed. Because mobile devices are resource-constrained, mining data streams with mobile devices poses a great challenge. Therefore, ubiquitous data stream mining has become one of the newest research topics in data mining. Previous research on ubiquitous data stream clustering mainly adopts the AOG approach. Although the AOG approach can continue with mining under a resource-constrained environment, it sacrifices the accuracy of mining results. In this paper, we propose the RA-HCluster algorithm that can be used in mobile devices for clustering stream data. It adapts algorithm settings and compresses stream data based on currently available resources, so that mobile devices can continue with clustering at acceptable accuracy even under low memory resources. Experimental results show that not only is RA-HCluster more accurate than RA-VFKM, it is able to maintain a low and stable memory usage.

Keywords: Ubiquitous data mining, Data stream mining, Ubiquitous data stream clustering, Resource-aware.

1 Introduction

Due to rapid progress of information technology, the amount of data is growing very fast. How to identify useful information from these data is very important. Data mining is to discover useful knowledge from large amounts of data. Data generated by many applications are scattered and time-sensitive. If not analyzed immediately, these data will soon lose their value; e.g., stock analysis [1] and vehicle collision prevention [2]. How to discover interesting patterns via mobile devices anytime and anywhere and respond to the user in real time faces major challenges, resulting in the concept of ubiquitous data mining (UDM).

With the advance of sensor devices, many data are transmitted in the form of streams. Data streams are large in amount and potentially infinite, real time, rapidly

R. Zhang et al. (Eds.): ICEIS 2011, LNBIP 102, pp. 81–97, 2012.

changing, and unpredictable [3] and [4]. Compared with traditional data mining, ubiquitous data mining is more resource-constrained, such as constrained computing power and memory size. Therefore, it may result in mining failures when data streams arrive rapidly. Ubiquitous data stream mining thus has become one of the newest research topics in data mining.

Previous research on ubiquitous data stream clustering mainly adopts the AOG (Algorithm Output Granularity) approach [5], which reduces output granularity by merging clusters, so that the algorithm can adapt to available resources. Although the AOG approach can continue with mining under a resource-constrained environment, it sacrifices the accuracy of mining results. In this paper, we propose the RA-HCluster (Resource-Aware High Quality Clustering) algorithm that can be used in mobile devices for clustering stream data. It adapts algorithm settings and compresses stream data based on currently available resources, so that mobile devices can continue with clustering at acceptable accuracy even under low memory resources.

The rest of this paper is organized as follows. Section 2 reviews related work. Section 3 presents the RA-HCluster algorithm. Section 4 shows our experimental results. Section 5 concludes this paper.

2 Related Work

Aggarwal et al. [6] proposed the CluStream clustering framework that consists of two components. The online component stores summary statistics of the data stream. The offline component uses summary statistics and user requirements as input, and utilizes an approach that combines micro-clustering with pyramidal time frame to clustering.

The issue of ubiquitous data stream mining was first proposed by [7]. They analyzed problems and potential applications arising from mining stream data in mobile devices and proposed the LWC algorithm, which is an AOG-based clustering algorithm. LWC performs adaptation process at the output end and adapts the minimum distance threshold between a data point and a cluster center based on currently available resources. When memory is full, it outputs the merged clusters.

Shah et al. [8] proposed the RA-VFKM algorithm, which borrows the effective stream clustering technique from the VFKM algorithm and utilizes the AOG resource-aware technique to solve the problem of mining failure with constrained resources in VFKM. When the available memory reaches a critical stage, it increases the value of allowable error (ε^*) and the value of probability for the allowable error (δ^*) to decrease the number of runs and the number of samples. Its strategy of increasing the value of error and probability compromises on the accuracy of the final results, but enables convergence and avoids execution failure in critical situations.

The RA-Cluster algorithm proposed by [9] extends the idea of CluStream and adapts algorithm settings based on currently available resources. It is the first threshold-based micro-clustering algorithm and it adapts to available resources by adapting its output granularity.

3 RA-HCluster

As shown in Figure 1, RA-HCluster consists of two components: online maintenance and offline clustering. In the online maintenance component, summary statistics of stream data are computed and stored, and then are used for mining by the offline clustering component, thereby reducing the computational complexity. First, the sliding window model is used to sample stream data. Next, summary statistics of the data in the sliding window are computed to generate micro-clusters, and summary statistics are updated incrementally. In addition, the calculation of correlation coefficients is included in the process of merging micro-clusters to improve the problem of declining accuracy caused by merging micro-clusters. Finally, a hierarchical summary frame is used to store cluster feature vectors of micro-clusters. The level of the hierarchical summary frame can be adjusted based on the resources available. If resources are insufficient, the amount of data to be processed can be reduced by adjusting the hierarchical summary frame to a higher level, so as to reduce resource consumption.

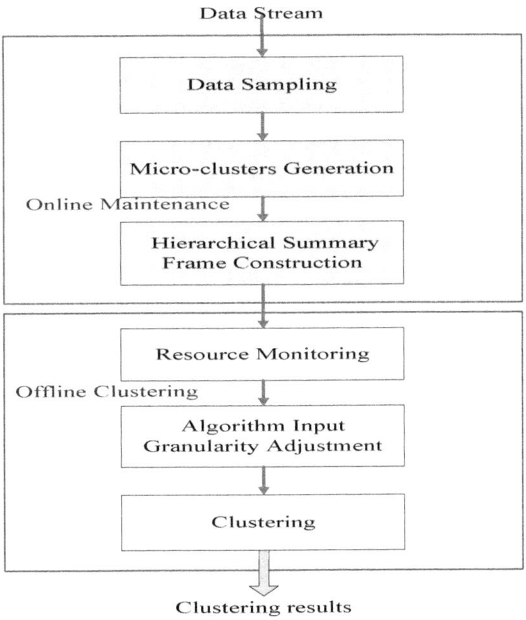

Fig. 1. RA-HCluster

In the offline clustering component, algorithm settings are adapted based on currently available memory, and summary statistics stored in the hierarchical summary frame are used for clustering. First, the resource monitoring module computes the usage and remaining rate of memory and decides whether memory is sufficient. When memory is low, the size of the sliding window and the level of the hierarchical summary frame are adjusted using the AIG (Algorithm Input Granularity) approach. Finally, clustering is conducted. When memory is low, the distance threshold is decreased to reduce the amount of data to be processed. Conversely, when memory is sufficient, the distance threshold is increased to improve the accuracy of clustering results.

3.1 Online Maintenance

3.1.1 Data Sampling

The sliding window model is used for data stream sampling. Figure 2 shows an example of sliding window sampling, in which Stream represents a data stream and t_0, t_1, …, t_9 each represents a time point. Suppose the window size is set to 3, which means three data points from the stream are extracted each time. Thus, the sliding window first extracts three data points A, B, and C at time points t_1, t_2, and t_3, respectively. After the data points within the window are processed, the window moves to the right to extract the next three data points. In this example, the window moved a total of three times and extracted a total of nine data points at time points from t_1 to t_9. Table 1 shows the sampled stream data.

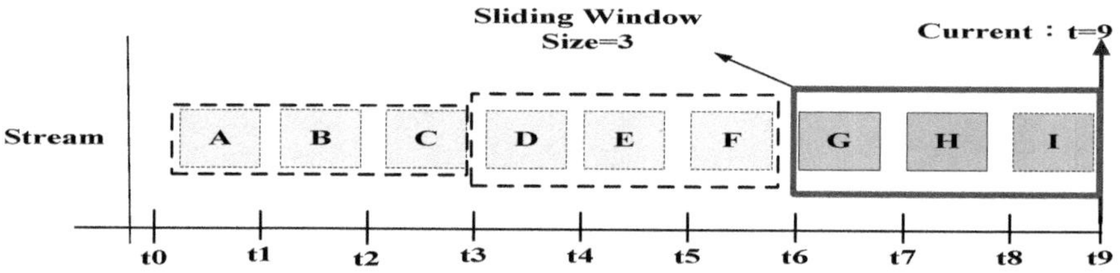

Fig. 2. Example of sliding window sampling

Table 1. Sampled stream data

Data point	Age	Salary (in thousands)	Arrival timestamp
A	36	34	t1
B	30	21	t2
C	44	38	t3
D	24	26	t4
E	35	27	t5
F	35	31	t6
G	48	40	t7
H	21	30	t8
I	50	44	t9

3.1.2 Micro-cluster Generation

For sampled data points, we use the K-Means algorithm to generate micro-clusters. Each micro-cluster is made up of *n* *d*-dimensional data points $x_1 \ldots x_n$ and their arrival timestamp $t_1 ... t_n$. Next, we compute summary statistics of data points of each micro-cluster to obtain its cluster feature vector, which consists of $(2 \times d + 3)$ data entries and is represented as ($\overline{CF2^x}$, $\overline{CF1^x}$, $CF2^t$, $CF1^t$, n). Data entries are defined as follows:

- $\overline{CF2^x}$ is the squared sum of dimensions, and the squared sum of the eth dimension can be expressed as $\sum_{j=1}^{n} (x_j^e)^2$
- $\overline{CF1^x}$ is the sum of dimensions, and the sum of the eth dimension can be expressed as $\sum_{j=1}^{n} x_j^e$.
- $CF2^t$ is the squared sum of timestamp $t_1 ... t_n$, and can be expressed as $\sum_{j=1}^{n} t_j^2$.
- $CF1^t$ is the sum of timestamp $t_1 ... t_n$, and can be expressed as $\sum_{j=1}^{n} t_j$.
- n is the number of data points

The following are the steps for generating micro-clusters:

Step 1: Compute the mean of sampled data.

Step 2: Compute the square distance between the mean and each data point, and find the data point nearest to the mean as a center point. Then move the window once to extract data.

Step 3: If the current number of center points is equal to the user-defined number of micro-clusters q, execute Step 4; otherwise, return to Step 1.

Step 4: Use the K-Means algorithm to generate q micro-clusters with q center points as cluster centroids, and compute the summary statistics of data points of each micro-cluster.

Assume that the user-defined number of micro-clusters is three. Table 2 shows the micro-clusters generated from the data points of Table 1, in which the micro-cluster Q_1 contains three data points B (30, 21), D (24, 26), and H (21, 30) and the cluster feature vector is computed as {($30^2 + 24^2 + 21^2$, $21^2 + 26^2 + 30^2$), (30+24+21, 21+26+30), $2^2 + 4^2 + 8^2$, 2+4+8, 3} = {(1917,2017), (75,77), 84, 14, 3}.

Table 2. Micro-clusters generated

Micro-cluster	Data points	Cluster feature vector
Q_1	B, D, H	((1917,2017), (75,77), 84, 14, 3)
Q_2	A, E, F	((3746,2846), (106,92), 62, 12, 3)
Q_3	C, G, I	((6740,4980), (142,122), 139, 19, 3)

Next, we set a maximum radius boundary λ. When a new data point p arrives at the data stream, if the square distance $d^2(p, m_i)$ between p and its nearest micro-cluster center m_i is less than λ, p is merged into micro-cluster M_i; otherwise, a new micro-cluster is generated for p. When the current number of micro-clusters is greater than the user-defined number, two of the micro-clusters must be merged. In the merge process, we not only compute the distance similarity between micro-clusters, but also use Pearson correlation coefficient γ to identify the two most similar micro-clusters to merge in order to improve the problem of reduced accuracy caused by merge. Equation (1) is the calculation formula for Pearson correlation coefficient and is used for computing the direction and level of change of data points for each micro-cluster. The value of γ is between -1 and 1. A greater γ means a greater level of change; that is, the degree of correlation between two micro-clusters is greater.

$$\frac{\sum\frac{(X-\overline{X})(Y-\overline{Y})}{n-1}}{\sqrt{\sum\left(\frac{(X-\overline{X})^2}{n-1}\right)}\times\sqrt{\sum\left(\frac{(Y-\overline{Y})^2}{n-1}\right)}}=\frac{\sum XY-n\overline{XY}}{\sqrt{\sum X^2-n\overline{X}^2}\times\sqrt{\sum Y^2-n\overline{Y}^2}} \tag{1}$$

3.1.3 Hierarchical Summary Frame Construction

After micro-clusters are generated, we propose the use of a hierarchical summary frame to store cluster feature vectors of micro-clusters and construct level 0 (L = 0), which is the current level, of the hierarchical summary frame. In the offline clustering component, the cluster feature vectors stored at the current level of the hierarchical summary frame will be used as virtual points for clustering. In addition, the hierarchical summary frame is equipped with two functions: data aggregation and data resolution. When memory is low, it performs data aggregation to aggregate detailed data of lower level into summarized data of upper level to reduce the consumption of memory space and computation time for clustering. But if there is sufficient memory, it will perform data resolution to resolve summarized data of upper level back to detailed data of lower level.

The representation of the hierarchical summary frame is shown in Figure 3.

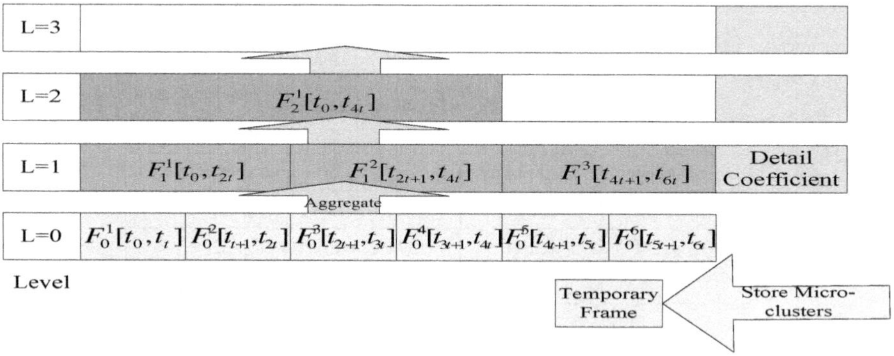

Fig. 3. Hierarchical summary frame

- L is used to indicate a level of the hierarchical summary frame. Each level is composed of multiple frames and each frame stores the cluster feature vector of one micro-cluster.
- Each frame can be expressed as $F_i^j[t_s, t_e]$, in which t_s is the starting timestamp, t_e is the ending timestamp, and i and j are the level number and frame number, respectively.
- A detail coefficient field is added to each level above level 0 of the hierarchical summary frame, which stores the difference of data and is used for subsequent data resolution.

The process of data aggregation and data resolution utilizes the Haar wavelet transform, which is a data compression method characterized by fast calculation and easy understanding and is widely used in the field of data mining [10]. This transform can be regarded a series of mean and difference calculations. The calculation formula is as follows:

- The use of wavelet transform to aggregate frames in the interval can be expressed as $W(\beta) = \frac{\sum_{i=1}^{\beta} F_i}{|\beta|}$, in which F represents the frame.
- k wavelet transforms can be expressed as

$$W^k = \frac{\left(\sum_{i=1}^{k} W(\beta_i) \times |\beta_i|\right)}{\left(\sum_{i=1}^{k} |\beta_i|\right)} \quad (2)$$

Figure 4 shows an example of hierarchical summary frame, in which the aggregation interval β is set to 2, indicating that two frames are aggregated in each data aggregation process. Suppose the current level $L = 0$ stores four micro-clusters, and the sums of dimension are 68, 12, 4, and 24, respectively, represented as $L_0 = \{68,12,4,24\}$. When memory is low, data aggregation is performed. Because the aggregation interval is 2, it first computes the average and difference of the first frame F_0^1 and the second frame F_0^2 of level 0, resulting in the value (12+68)/2=40 and detail coefficient (12-68)/2=-28 of the first frame F_1^1 of level 1, and then derives the timestamp $[0,3]$ of F_1^1 by storing the starting timestamp of F_0^1 and the ending timestamp of F_0^2. It then moves on to the third frame F_0^3 and the fourth frame F_0^4 of level 0, resulting in the value (24+4)/2=14, detail coefficient (24-4)/2=10, and timestamp $[4,7]$ of the second frame F_1^2 of level 1. After all frames of level 0 are aggregated, the data aggregation process ends and level 1 of the hierarchical summary frame is constructed, which is represented as $L_1 = \{40, 14\}$. Other levels of the hierarchical summary frame are constructed in the same way. In addition, we can obtain the Haar transform function $H(f(x)) = (27, -13, -28, 10)$ by storing the value and detail coefficient of the highest level of the hierarchical summary frame, which can be used to convert the aggregated data back to the data before aggregation.

When there is sufficient memory, data resolution is performed to convert the aggregated data back to the detailed data of lower level, using the Haar transform function obtained during data aggregation. To illustrate, assume that the current level of the hierarchical summary frame is L=2. $L_1 = \{40,14\}$ is obtained by performing subtraction and addition on the value and detail coefficient of level 2, {40, 14}={[27-(-13), 27+(-13)]}. L_0= {68, 12, 4, 24} is obtained in the same way, except that there are two values and detail coefficients at level 1. Therefore, to obtain {68, 12, 4, 24} = {[40-(-28), 40+(-28), 14-10, 14+10]}, we first perform subtraction and addition on the first value and detail coefficient, then perform the same calculation on the second value and detail coefficient.

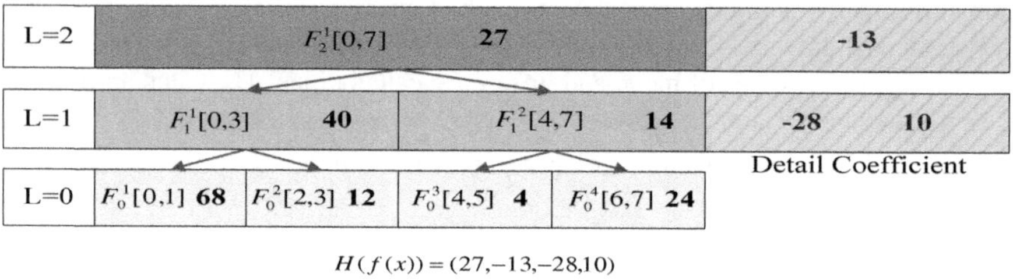

Fig. 4. Example of hierarchical summary frame

3.2 Offline Clustering

3.2.1 Resource Monitoring and Algorithm Input Granularity Adjustment

In the offline clustering component, we use the resource monitoring module to monitor memory. This module has three parameters N_m, U_m, and LB_m, which represent the total memory size, current memory usage, and lowest boundary of memory usage, respectively. In addition, we compute the remaining rate of memory $R_m = (N_m - U_m)/N_m$. When $R_m < LB_m$, meaning that memory is low, we will adjust the algorithm input granularity. Algorithm input granularity adjustment refers to reducing the detail level of input data of the algorithm in order to reduce the resources consumed during algorithm execution. Therefore, when memory is low, we will adjust the size of the sliding window and the level of the hierarchical summary frame in order to reduce memory consumption.

First, we adjust the size of the sliding window. A larger window size means a greater amount of stream data to be processed, which will consume more memory. Thus, we multiply the window size w by the remaining rate of memory R_m to obtain the adjusted window size. As R_m gets smaller, so is the window size. Figure 5 shows an example of window size adjustment, with the initial window size w set to 5. In scenario 1, the memory usage U_m is 20 and the computed R_m is 0.8. Then, through $R_m \times w = 0.8 \times 5$ we obtain the new window size of 4, so we reduce the window size

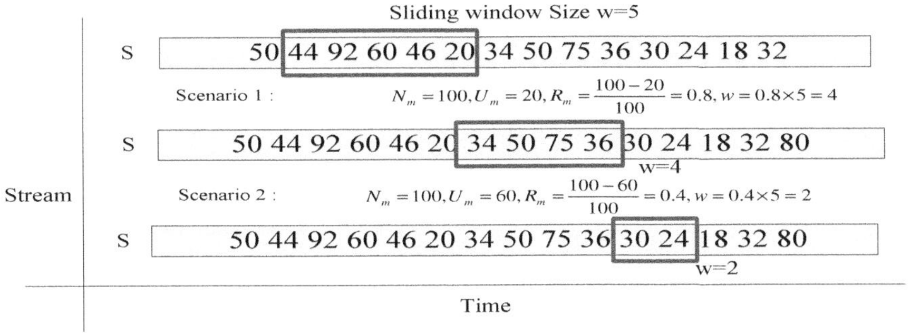

Fig. 5. Example of window size adjustment

from 5 to 4. In scenario 2, the memory usage U_m is 60 and the computed R_m is 0.4. Then, through $R_m \times w = 0.4 \times 5$ we obtain the new window size of 2, so we reduce the window size from 5 to 2.

Next, we perform data aggregation to adjust the level of the hierarchical summary frame. This process will be done only when R_m < 20% because it will reduce the accuracy of clustering results. On the other hand, we will perform data resolution when $(1-R_m)$ < 20%, which indicates there is sufficient memory. The process of data aggregation and data resolution has been described in details in Section 3.1.3.

3.2.2 Clustering

Figure 6 shows the proposed clustering algorithm. The algorithm inputs the number of clusters k, the distance threshold $\bar{d}$, the lowest boundary of memory usage LB_m, and the cluster feature vectors stored in the current level of the hierarchical summary frame as virtual points x. The algorithm outputs the finally generated k clusters C. The steps of the algorithm are divided into three parts. The first part is for cluster generation (line 4-10). Every virtual point is attributed to the nearest cluster center to generate k clusters. The second part is for the adjustment of distance threshold $\bar{d}$ (line 11-14). The adjustment of $\bar{d}$ is based on the current remaining rate of memory. A smaller $\bar{d}$ implies that virtual points are more likely to be regarded as outliers and discarded in order to reduce memory usage. The third part is for determination of the stability of clusters (line 15-31). Recalculate cluster centers of the clusters generated in the first part and use the sample variance and total deviation to determine the stability of clusters. Output the clusters if they are stable; otherwise repeat the process by returning to the first part.

The parameters of the clustering algorithm are defined as follows:

- k is the user-defined number of clusters.
- $\bar{d}$ is the user-defined distance threshold.
- LB_m is the user-defined lowest boundary of memory usage.
- $x = \{x_i | 1 \le i \le n\}$ is the set of virtual points stored in the current level of the hierarchical summary frame.

- $C = \{C_j | 1 \le j \le k\}$ is the set of k clusters generated by the algorithm.
- N_m is the total memory size
- $c = \{c_j | 1 \le j \le k\}$ is the set of k cluster centers.
- $d^2(x_i, c_j)$ is the Euclidean distance between virtual point x_i and cluster center c_j.
- $D_i = \{d^2(x_i, c_j) | 1 \le i \le n, 1 \le j \le k\}$ is the set of Euclidean distances between virtual point x_i and each cluster center, with the initial value of ∅.
- $Min\ [D_i]$ is the Euclidean distance between virtual point x_i and its nearest cluster center.
- U_m is the memory usage.
- R_m is the remaining rate of memory.
- E is the total deviation.
- S^2 is the sample variance.
- $count(C_j)$ is the number of virtual points in the cluster C_j.
- E' is the total deviation calculated from the new cluster center.
- $\hat{S}^2$ is the sample variance calculated from the new cluster center.

The following is a detailed description of the steps of the clustering algorithm.

Step 1 (line 1): Use a system built-in function to compute the total memory size.

Step 2 (line 2): Use a random function to randomly select k virtual points as initial cluster centers.

Step 3 (line 4-10): For each virtual point, compute the Euclidean distance between it and each cluster center. If the Euclidean distance between a virtual point and its nearest cluster center is less than the distance threshold, the virtual point is attributed to the cluster to which the nearest cluster center belongs; otherwise, the virtual point is deleted.

Step 4 (line 11-14): Compute the memory usage U_m and the remaining rate of memory R_m. If $R_m < LB_m$, meaning that memory is low, then decrease $\bar{d}$ by subtracting the value of multiplying $\bar{d}$ by the memory usage rate $(1 - R_m)$. When the memory usage rate is higher, $\bar{d}$ is decreased more. On the other hand, if $(1 - R_m)$ <20%, meaning that memory is sufficient, then increase $\bar{d}$ by adding the value of multiplying $\bar{d}$ by the remaining rate of memory R_m. When the remaining rate of memory is higher, $\bar{d}$ is increased more.

Step 5 (line 15-31): Steps 5.1 and 5.2 are executed for each cluster.

Step 5.1 (line 16-18): Compute the sample variance S^2 and the total deviation E of virtual points contained in the cluster. Next, compute the mean of virtual points contained in the cluster as the new cluster center c'_j.

Input: k, $\bar{d}$, LB_m, x
Output: C
compute N_m;
$c \leftarrow Random(x)$;
Repeat
  For each $x_i \in x$ **do**
    For each $c_j \in c$ **do**
      $D_i \leftarrow D_i \cup \{d^2(x_i, c_j)\}$;
    If $Min[D_i] < \bar{d}$ **then**
      $C_j \leftarrow C_j \cup \{x_i\}$ s.t. $d^2(x_i, c_j) = Min[D_i]$;
    Else
      delete x_i;
  compute U_m;
  $R_m \leftarrow (N_m - U_m) / N_m$;
  If $R_m < LB_m$ **then** $\bar{d} \leftarrow \bar{d} - \bar{d} \times (1 - R_m)$;
  If $(1 - R_m) < 20\%$ **then** $\bar{d} \leftarrow \bar{d} + \bar{d} \times R_m$;
  For each C_j **do**
    $E \leftarrow \sum_{x_i \in C_j} \sqrt{(x_i - c_j)^2}$;
    $S^2 \leftarrow \left(\sum_{x_i \in C_j} (x_i - c_j)^2 \right) / (count(C_j) - 1)$;
    $c'_j \leftarrow (\sum_{x_i \in C_j} x_i) / count(C_j)$;
    If $c'_j \neq c_j$ **then**
      $E' \leftarrow \sum_{x_i \in C_j} \sqrt{(x_i - c'_j)^2}$;
      $\hat{S}^2 \leftarrow \left(\sum_{x_i \in C_j} (x_i - c'_j)^2 \right) / (count(C_j) - 1)$;
      If ($\hat{S}^2 < S^2$) and ($E' < E$) **then**
        $c_j \leftarrow c'_j$;
      Else
        output C_j;
        $\forall x_i \in C_j \quad x \leftarrow x - \{x_i\}$;
        $c \leftarrow c - \{c_j\}$;
    Else
      output C_j;
      $\forall x_i \in C_j \quad x \leftarrow x - \{x_i\}$;
      $c \leftarrow c - \{c_j\}$;
Until $\forall C_j \; (c'_j = c_j)$ or $(\hat{S}^2 \geq S^2)$ or $(E' \geq E)$
return;

Fig. 6. Clustering algorithm

Step 5.2 (line 19-31): If the new cluster center c'_j is the same as the old cluster center c_j, then output the cluster C_j, meaning that C_j will not change any more, and delete the virtual points and cluster center of C_j; otherwise, use c'_j to recalculate the sample variance $\hat{S}^2$ and the total deviation E', and determine whether both $\hat{S}^2$ and E' are decreased. If yes, replace the old cluster center with the new one; otherwise, output the cluster C_j and delete the virtual points and cluster center of C_j.

Repeat the execution of Step 3 to Step 5 until for every cluster the cluster center is not changed or the sample variance or total deviation is not decreased.

Assume k = 2, $\bar{d}$ = 10, LB_m = 30%, and the virtual points stored in the current level of the hierarchical summary frame are A (2,4), B (3,2), C (4,3), D (5,6), E (8,7), F (6,5), G (6,4), H (7,3), I (7,2), the algorithm output two clusters C_1 = [A, B, C] and C_2 = [D, F, G, H, I].

4 Performance Evaluation

4.1 Experimental Environment and Data

To simulate the environment of mobile devices, we use Sun Java J2ME Wireless Toolkit 2.5 as the development tool to write programs and conduct performance evaluation on the J2ME platform. Table 3 shows the experimental environment.

Table 3. Experimental environment

Component	Specification
Processor	Pentium D 2.8 GHz
Memory	1 GB
Hard disk	80 GB
Operating system	Windows XP

Table 4. Generating parameters of synthetic data

Parameter	Description
B	Number of data points
C	Number of clusters
D	Number of dimensions

We use the ACM KDD-CUP 2007 consumer recommendations data set as the real data set. This data set contains 480,000 customer data, 17,000 movie data, and 1 million recommendations data recorded between October 1998 and December 2005. We use 200,000 recommendations data for the experiments. Furthermore, in order to use a variety of number of data points and dimensions to carry out the experiments, we use Microsoft SQL Server 2005 with Microsoft Visual Studio Team Edition for Database Professional to generate synthetic data sets, which are in uniform distribution. Table 4 shows the description of generating parameters of synthetic data. All data points are sampled evenly from C clusters. All sampled data points show a normal distribution. For example, B100kC10D5 represents that this data set contains 100k data points belonging to 10 different clusters and each data point has 5 dimensions.

4.2 Comparison and Analysis

As RA-VFKM is also a ubiquitous data stream clustering algorithm that can continue with mining under constrained resources, we compare the performance between RA-HCluster and RA-VFKM in terms of stream processing efficiency, accuracy, and memory usage.

4.2.1 Stream Processing Efficiency

We use the number of data points processed per second to measure the stream processing efficiency with the consumer recommendations data set as experimental data. Figure 7 and Figure 8 show the comparison of stream processing efficiency between RA-HCluster and RA-VFKM, where the horizontal axis is the elapsed data processing time in seconds and the vertical axis is the number of data points processed per second.

As shown in Figure 7, because RA-HCluster needs to generate micro-clusters and compute cluster feature vectors as soon as stream data arrive, the initial stream processing is more inefficient. After 20 seconds while micro-clusters have been generated, the stream processing efficiency of RA-HCluster increases and stabilizes. In contrast, because RA-VFKM uses Hoeffding Bound to limit the sample size, the initial stream processing efficiency is better. But over time, the stream processing efficiency of RA-VFKM is worse than that of RA-HCluster.

As shown in Figure 8, for a longer elapsed time, the stream processing efficiency of RA-HCluster is poor only initially. By the 60th second, its stream processing efficiency is about the same as RA-VFKM, and it gradually overtakes RA-VFKM in terms of stream processing efficiency after 80 seconds.

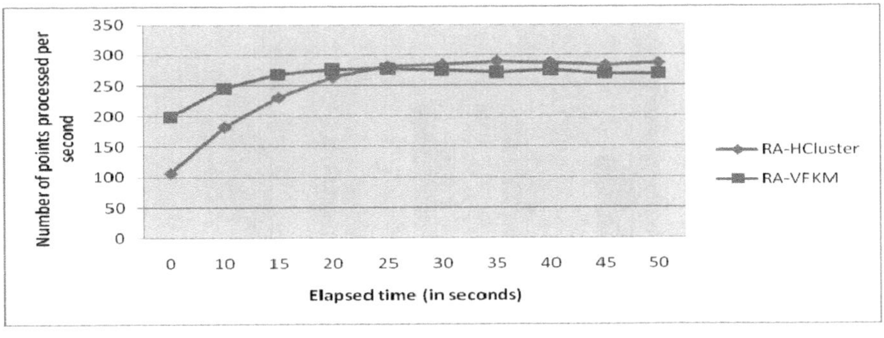

Fig. 7. Comparison of stream processing efficiency

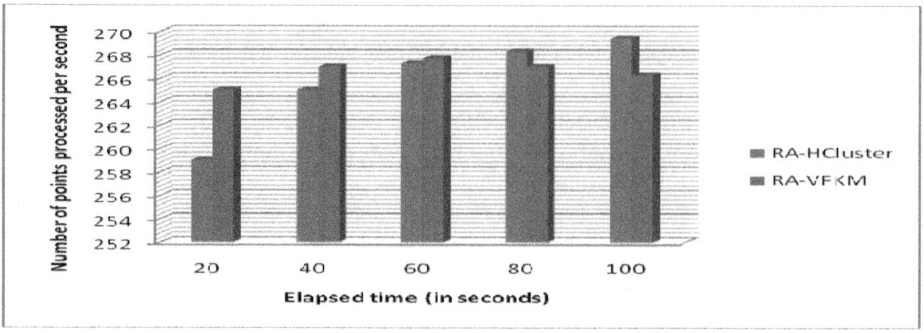

Fig. 8. Comparison of stream processing efficiency for a longer elapsed time

4.2.2 Accuracy

We use the average of the sum of square distance (Average SSQ) to measure the accuracy of clustering results. Suppose there are n_h data points in the period h before the current time T_c. Find the nearest cluster center c_{ni} for each data point n_h in the period h and compute the square distance $d^2(n_i, c_{ni})$ between n_i and c_{ni}. The $Average\ SSQ(T_c, h)$ for the period h before the current time T_c equals to the sum of all square distances between every data point in h and its cluster center divided by the number of clusters. A smaller value of Average SSQ indicates a higher accuracy.

Figure 9 and Figure 10 show the comparison of accuracy between RA-HCluster and RA-VFKM with the consumer recommendations data set and synthetic data set, respectively. The horizontal axis is the data rate (e.g., data rate 100 means that stream data arrive at the rate of 100 data points per second) and the vertical axis is the Average SSQ. As shown in Figure 9 and Figure 10, the accuracy of RA-HCluster is about the same as that of RA-VFKM only when the data rate is from 50 to 100. When the data rate is over 200, the accuracy of RA-HCluster is higher than that of RA-VFKM.

In Figure 10, the differences in Average SSQ are not obvious because synthetic data of the same distribution are used, but we can still see that the Average SSQ of RA-HCluster is smaller. The reason is that RA-HCluster uses the distance similarity between micro-clusters as the basis for merge, and employs the sample variance to

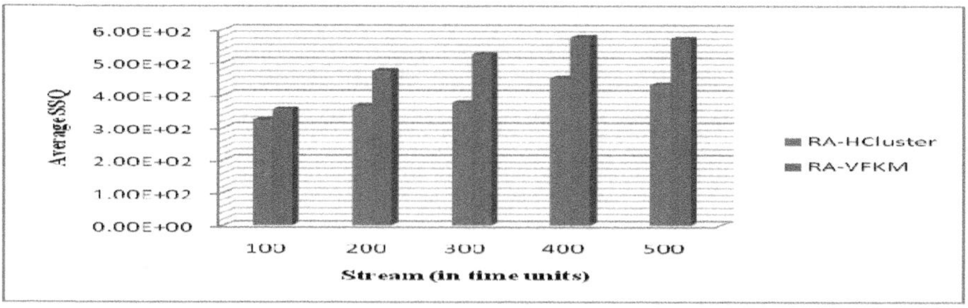

Fig. 9. Comparison of accuracy with consumer recommendations data set

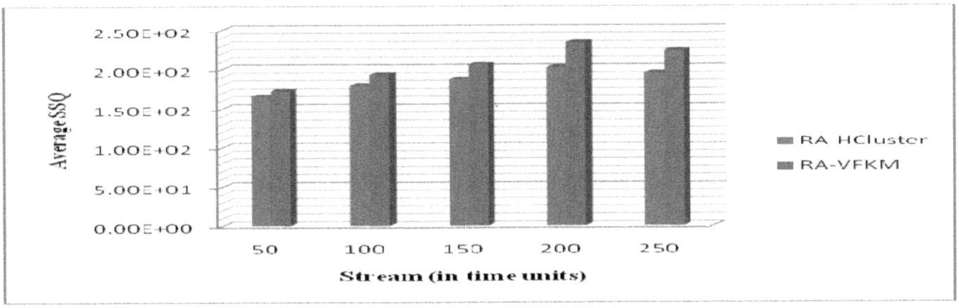

Fig. 10. Comparison of accuracy with synthetic data set

identify more dense clusters in the offline clustering component, so as to increase the clustering accuracy. In contrast, RA-VFKM increases the error value ε to reduce the sample size and merges clusters to achieve the goal of continuous mining, so as to reduce the clustering accuracy.

4.2.3 Memory Usage

Because the greatest challenge in mining data streams using mobile devices lies in the constrained memory of mobile devices and insufficient memory may lead to mining interruption or failure, we compare the capability of continuous mining of algorithms by analyzing their memory usage. Figure 11 shows the comparison of memory usage among RA-HCluster, RA-VFKM, and traditional K-Means, where the horizontal axis is the elapsed data processing time in seconds and the vertical axis is the remaining memory in megabytes (MB). The experimental data is the consumer recommendations data set, with a parameter setting of C = 10, data rate = 100, and N_m = 100 MB. As shown in Figure 11, traditional K-Means is not able to continue with mining and mining interruption occurs after 450 seconds. Although RA-VFKM is able to continue with mining, it is incapable of adapting to the evolution of data stream effectively because the fluctuation in memory usage is very large. In contrast, even though RA-HCluster uses more memory in the beginning, it is able to maintain low and stable

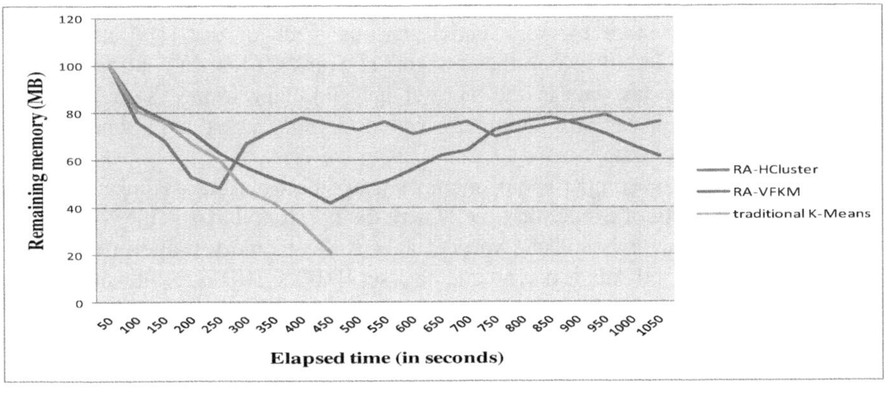

Fig. 11. Comparison of memory usage

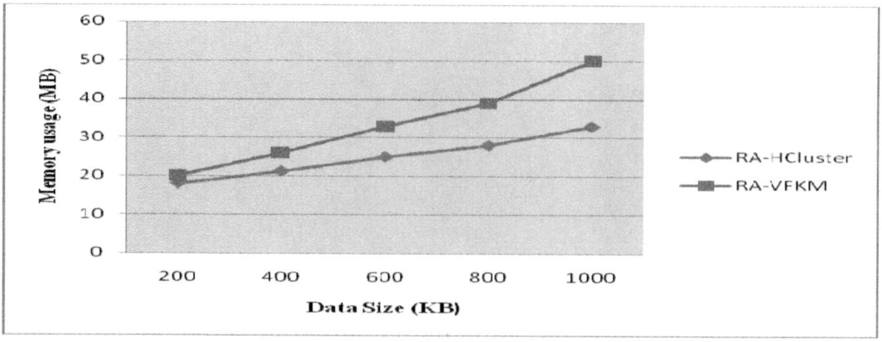

Fig. 12. Comparison of memory usage by data size

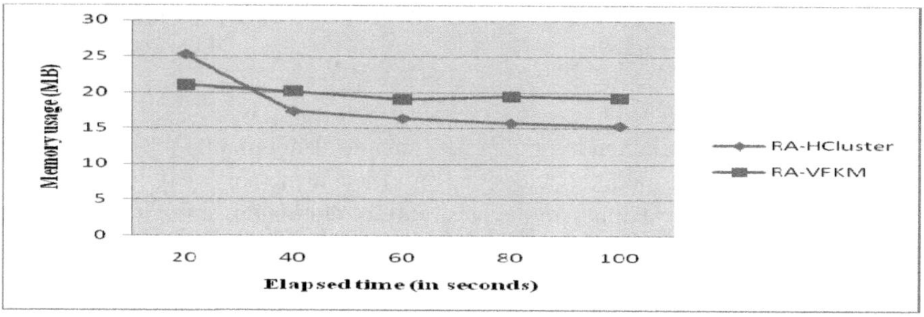

Fig. 13. Comparison of memory usage by execution time

memory usage thereafter. The reason is that RA-VFKM releases resources by merging clusters at the end of the clustering process, but RA-HCluster adapts algorithm settings during the clustering process so that mining can be stable and sustainable.

Figure 12 shows the comparison of memory usage between RA-HCluster and RA-VFKM under a variety of data size, where the horizontal axis is the data size in kilobytes (KB) and the vertical axis is the memory usage in megabytes (MB). The experimental data is the consumer recommendations data set. As shown in Figure 12, RA-VFKM requires more memory under various sizes of data and its memory usage increases significantly when the data size is over 600 KB. In contrast, because RA-HCluster compresses data in the hierarchical summary frame through the data aggregation process, it can still maintain a stable memory usage even when dealing with larger amounts of data.

Figure 13 shows the comparison of memory usage between RA-HCluster and RA-VFKM under a variety of execution time, where the horizontal axis is the elapsed data processing time in seconds and the vertical axis is the memory usage in megabytes (MB). The experimental data is a synthetic data set B100kC10D5. As shown in Figure 13, even though RA-HCluster uses more memory in the beginning, it then decreases the memory usage by reducing the input granularity. After 40 seconds, therefore, the memory usage is decreased and stabilized. In contrast, RA-VFKM uses less memory than RA-HCluster only in the beginning, and it uses more memory after 37 seconds.

5 Conclusions

In this paper, we have proposed the RA-HCluster algorithm for ubiquitous data stream clustering. This algorithm adopts the resources-aware technique to adapt algorithm settings and the level of the hierarchical summary frame, which enables mobile devices to continue with mining and overcomes the problem of lower accuracy or mining interruption caused by insufficient memory in traditional data stream clustering algorithms. Furthermore, we include the technique of computing the correlation coefficients between micro-clusters to ensure that more related data points are attributed to the same cluster during the clustering process, thereby improving the accuracy of clustering results. Experimental results show that not only is the accuracy of RA-HCluster higher than that of RA-VFKM, it can also maintain a low and stable memory usage.

References

1. Kargupta, H., Park, B.H., Pittie, S., Liu, L., Kushraj, D., Sarkar, K.: MobiMine: Monitoring the Stock Market from a PDA. ACM SIGKDD Explorations Newsletter 3(2), 37–46 (2002)
2. Kargupta, H., Bhargava, R., Liu, K., Powers, M., Blair, P., Bushra, S., Dull, J., Sarkar, K., Klein, M., Vasa, M., Handy, D.: VEDAS: a Mobile and Distributed Data Stream Mining System for Real-Time Vehicle Monitoring. In: Proceedings of the 4th SIAM International Conference on Data Mining, Florida, USA, pp. 300–311 (2004)
3. Babcock, B., Babu, S., Motwani, R., Widom, J.: Models and Issues in Data Stream Systems. In: Proceedings of the 21st ACM SIGMOD Symposium on Principles of Database Systems, Madison, Wisconsin, USA, pp. 1–16 (2002)
4. Golab, L., Ozsu, T.M.: Issues in Data Stream Management. ACM SIGMOD Record 32(2), 5–14 (2006)
5. Gaber, M.M., Zaslavsky, A., Krishnaswamy, S.: Towards an Adaptive Approach for Mining Data Streams in Resource Constrained Environments. In: Kambayashi, Y., Mohania, M., Wöß, W. (eds.) DaWaK 2004. LNCS, vol. 3181, pp. 189–198. Springer, Heidelberg (2004)
6. Aggarwal, C.C., Han, J., Wang, J., Yu, P.S.: A Framework for Clustering Evolving Data Streams. In: Proceedings of the 29th International Conference on Very Large Data Bases, Berlin, Germany, pp. 81–92 (2003)
7. Gaber, M.M., Krishnaswamy, S., Zaslavsky, A.: Ubiquitous Data Stream Mining. In: Proceedings of the 8th Pacific-Asia Conference on Knowledge Discovery and Data Mining, Sydney, Australia (2004)
8. Shah, R., Krishnaswamy, S., Gaber, M.M.: Re-source-Aware Very Fast K-Means for Ubiquitous Data Stream Mining. In: Proceedings of 2nd International Workshop on Knowledge Discovery in Data Streams, Porto, Portugal, pp. 40–50 (2005)
9. Gaber, M.M., Yu, P.S.: A Framework for Resource-aware Knowledge Discovery in Data Streams: A Holistic Approach with Its Application to Clustering. In: Proceedings of the 2006 ACM Symposium on Applied Computing, Dijon, France, pp. 649–656 (2006)
10. Dai, B.R., Huang, J.W., Yeh, M.Y., Chen, M.S.: Adaptive Clustering for Multiple Evolving Streams. IEEE Transactions on Knowledge and Data Engineering 18(9), 1166–1180 (2006)

UF-Evolve: Uncertain Frequent Pattern Mining

Shu Wang and Vincent Ng

Department of Computing, The Hong Kong Polytechnic University
Hung Hom, Kowloon, Hong Kong
{csswang,cstyng}@comp.polyu.edu.hk

Abstract. Many frequent-pattern mining algorithms were designed to handle precise data, such as the FP-tree structure and the FP-growth algorithm. In data mining research, attention has been turned to mining frequent patterns in uncertain data recently. We want frequent-pattern mining algorithms for handling uncertain data. A common way to represent the uncertainty of a data item in record databases is to associate it with an existential probability. In this paper, we propose a novel uncertain-frequent-pattern discover structure, the mUF-tree, for storing summarized and uncertain information about frequent patterns. With the mUF-tree, the UF-Evolve algorithm can utilize the shuffling and merging techniques to generate iterative versions of it. Our main purpose is to discover new uncertain frequent patterns from iterative versions of the mUF-tree. Our preliminary performance study shows that the UF-Evolve algorithm is efficient and scalable for mining additional uncertain frequent patterns with different sizes of uncertain databases.

Keywords: Uncertain frequent pattern mining, Tree, Shuffling and Merging.

1 Introduction

Data uncertainty is often found in real-world applications because of measurement inaccuracy, sampling discrepancy, outdated data sources, or other errors. One type of data uncertainty is existential uncertainty. In existential uncertainty, there are applications in which it is uncertain about the presence or absence of some items or events. For example, we may highly suspect, while cannot guarantee, that a patient suffers from an illness based on a few symptoms. The uncertainty of such suspicion can be expressed in terms of existential probability. If R_i represents a patient record, then each item within R_i represents an illness and is associated with an existential probability expressing the likelihood of the patient suffering from that illness in R_i. As an example, in R_i, the patient can have an 80% likelihood of suffering from fever, and a 60% likelihood of suffering from H1N1.

Han et al. [8] proposed the FP-tree structure, which is an extended prefix-tree structure for storing compressed, crucial information about frequent patterns, and developed an efficient FP-growth algorithm. In our work, we extend the FP-tree for mining uncertain data. The key contributions are (i) the development of the mUF-tree structure to summarize the content of records consisting of uncertain data, and (ii) the

R. Zhang et al. (Eds.): ICEIS 2011, LNBIP 102, pp. 98–116, 2012.

idea of shuffling and merging nodes of mUF-tree, whose difference is small, to derive more uncertain frequent patterns by the UF-Evolve algorithm.

The remainder of the paper is organized as follows. Section 2 gives a literature review and Section 3 gives the problem statement. Section 4 introduces the mUF-tree and its construction algorithm. Next, Section 5 discusses an mUF-tree-based uncertain-frequent-pattern mining algorithm, the UF-Evolve algorithm, and Section 6 presents our performance study. Finally, Section 7 concludes our work.

2 Literature Review

For uncertain data representation, Antova et al. [2] proposed U-relations, a succinct and purely relational representation system for uncertain databases. U-relations support attribute-level uncertainty using vertical partitioning. When considering positive relational algebra extended by an operation for computing possible answers, a query on the logical level can be translated into, and evaluated as, a single relational algebra query on the U-relation representation. The approach takes full advantage of query evaluation and optimization techniques on vertical partitions. Chui et al. [6] proposed an algorithm called U-Apriori. They also introduced a trimming strategy to reduce the number of candidates that need to be counted based on the Apriori approach. The Apriori heuristic achieves good performance gained by (possibly significantly) reducing the size of candidate sets. However, in situations with a large number of frequent patterns, long patterns, or low minimum support thresholds, an Apriori-like algorithm may suffer from the following two nontrivial issues: it is costly to handle a huge number of candidate sets; and it is tedious to repeatedly scan the database and check a large set of candidates by pattern matching, which is especially true for mining long patterns.

Han et al. [8] proposed the FP-tree structure and the FP-growth algorithm for efficiently mining frequent patterns without generation of candidate itemsets for precise data. It consists of two phases. The first phase focuses on constructing the FP-tree from the database, and the second phase focuses on applying FP-growth to derive frequent patterns from the FP-tree. Each node in the FP-tree consists of three attributes, item-name, count and node-link. In the FP-tree, each entry in the header table consists of two fields: (1) item-name, and (2) head of node-links (a pointer pointing to the first node in the FP-tree carrying the item-name). Below, an example is used to illustrate the uses of the FP-tree. Suppose there is a precise transaction database as shown in Table 1, and the minimum support threshold is 3. The FP-tree together with the associated node-links are shown in Fig. 1.

Table 1. A precise transaction database

TID	Items
1	f, a, c, d, g, i, m, p
2	a, b, c, f, l, m, o
3	b, f, h, j, o
4	b, c, k, s, p
5	a, f, c, e, l, p, m, n

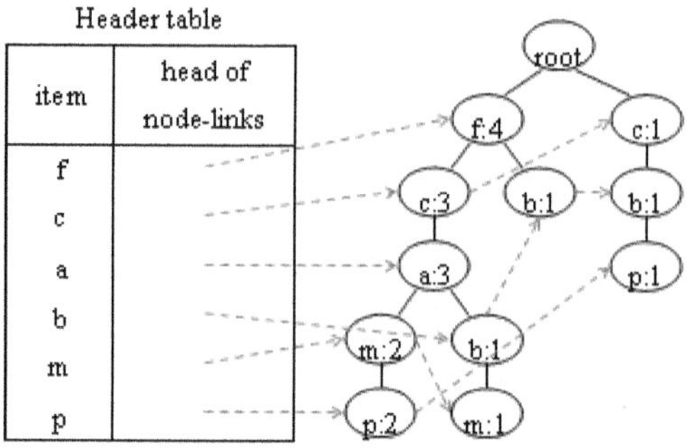

Fig. 1. The FP-tree for data in Table 1

Leung et al. [10, 11] proposed the UF-tree structure, a different tree structure than the FP-tree for capturing the content of transactions consisting of uncertain data, and the UF-growth algorithm, a mining algorithm for finding frequent patterns from the UF-tree. Each node in the UF-tree stores item, expected support and occurrence (i.e. the number of transactions containing such an item). UF-growth computes expected supports of itemsets and finds frequent patterns from the UF-tree. The expected support of an itemset in a transaction is the expected probability (over all "possible worlds") of coexistence of all the items in the itemset. The expected support of an itemset in a database is the sum of the expected probabilities of the itemset over all transactions. This calculation incurs much information loss.

3 Problem Statement

Here, in this section, we give some definitions of uncertain data before introducing our target problem. First, we define what an uncertain record and an uncertain database are.

Definition 1. Uncertain Record (R). Let I = $\{a_1, a_2, \ldots, a_k\}$ be a set of items. An uncertain record R = $\{(a_1{:}p_1), (a_2{:}p_2), \ldots, (a_m{:}p_m)\}$, where $(a_i \in I) \wedge$ (a_i appears once with p_i as the probability indicating its existence).

Definition 2. Uncertain Database (UDB). An uncertain database UDB consists of multiple uncertain records, i.e. UDB = $<R_1, R_2, \ldots, R_n>$.

An example uncertain database is shown in Table 2.

In an uncertain database, it is often that an item with a probability appears in a record while the same item with another probability appears in another record. For example, in Table 2, (d:0.4) appears in the 10th record while (d:0.5) appears in the 11th record. Given a predefined minimum support threshold, an item with a specific probability may not have sufficient support (i.e. the number of records containing it in UDB) to be a frequent pattern.

In order to improve the chance of having more and longer frequent patterns, one can consider to merge the same items with only small differences in their various probabilities for satisfying the support. For example, we can merge (d:0.4) and (d:0.5) as d with a probability range [0.4-0.5]. Hence, for a group of item:probability pairs in which all items are the same, we can use [lowerbound-upperbound] to represent the spread of probabilities for the item. Once the item:probability pairs are grouped, more general frequent patterns can be found.

With the above arrangement, we define what a maximum merging threshold and an uncertain frequent pattern are.

Table 2. An uncertain database

Record ID	Item:probability pairs
1	(a:0.2), (f:0.8), (g:0.1), (d:0.3), (c:0.2)
2	(a:0.2), (d:0.3), (c:0.2), (f:0.8)
3	(b:0.3), (f:0.8), (a:0.2)
4	(a:0.4), (c:0.7), (d:0.6), (f:0.8)
5	(f:0.8)
6	(a:0.7), (c:0.4), (b:0.5)
7	(a:0.7)
8	(f:0.8), (a:0.4), (c:0.7), (d:0.6)
9	(b:0.5), (a:0.7), (c:0.4)
10	(d:0.4), (e:0.5), (f:1.0), (a:0.1)
11	(e:0.6), (c:0.3), (d:0.5), (a:0.1), (f:1.0)
12	(a:0.1), (f:1.0), (c:0.3), (d:0.5)
13	(a:0.1), (f:1.0)
14	(f:1.0)
15	(d:0.4), (c:0.4), (b:0.2)
16	(b:0.2)
17	(b:0.2), (f:0.6)
18	(b:0.2)

Definition 3. Maximum Merging Threshold (γ). A maximum merging threshold γ is used to determine whether two item:probability pairs can be merged. Assume that an item with a probability ($a:p_1$) appears in a record while the same item with another probability ($a:p_2$) appears in another record. If abs($p_1 - p_2$) $\leq \gamma$, then ($a:p_1$) and ($a:p_2$) can be merged as (a:[l-u]), where ($l = \min(p_1, p_2)$) $\wedge$ ($u = \max(p_1, p_2)$). Here, (a:[l-u]) denotes the item with its [lowerbound-upperbound].

Definition 4. Uncertain Frequent Pattern (UFP). Let an item with its [lowerbound-upperbound] be denoted as (a:[l-u]). An uncertain frequent pattern UFP is represented as $(a_1{:}[l_1\text{-}u_1])(a_2{:}[l_2\text{-}u_2])\ldots(a_k{:}[l_k\text{-}u_k]){:}s$, where (s is the support for UFP) $\wedge$ (s $\geq$ a predefined minimum support threshold). A record R contains a UFP if for each $(a_i{:}[l_i\text{-}u_i]) \in$ UFP, $\exists$ $(a_j{:}p_j) \in$ R, such that $(a_i = a_j) \wedge (l_i \leq p_j \leq u_i)$.

Given an uncertain database, a minimum support threshold and a maximum merging threshold, we are interested in mining a possible set of uncertain frequent patterns. Our approach is to solve the problem in two phases.

- In the first phase, an mUF-tree is constructed for storing summarized and uncertain information about frequent patterns.
- In the second phase, the UF-Evolve algorithm, which utilizes the shuffling and merging techniques to generate iterative versions of the mUF-tree, is applied for discovering new uncertain frequent patterns.

4 mUF-Tree: Design and Construction

Given an uncertain database, we propose to use an mUF-tree to store summarized and uncertain information about frequent patterns. An mUF-tree with its header table is shown in Fig. 2.

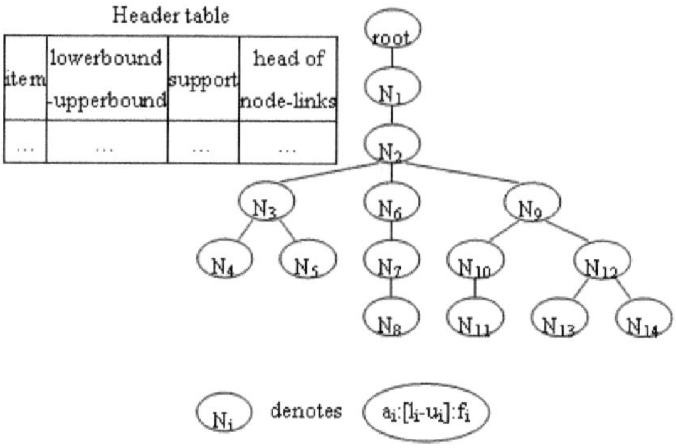

Fig. 2. mUF-tree

Definition 5. Uncertain Frequent Pattern Tree (mUF-tree). An mUF-tree has the following characteristics.

1. An mUF-tree has a virtual root. Each node in the mUF-tree consists of five attributes, item, lowerbound, upperbound, frequency and node-link. Lowerbound and upperbound register the spread of probabilities of the corresponding item. To facilitate tree traversal, nodes with the same item:[lowerbound-upperbound] are linked in sequence via node-links. In Fig. 2, a_i:[l_i-u_i]:f_i in each node N_i represents item:[lowerbound-upperbound]:frequency.
2. In the mUF-tree, each entry in the header table consists of four fields: (1) item, (2) lowerbound-upperbound, (3) support (the cumulative frequency of the item: [lowerbound-upperbound] in the mUF-tree), and (4) head of node-links (a pointer pointing to the first node in the mUF-tree carrying the item:[lowerbound-upperbound]).
3. In the header table, item:[lowerbound-upperbound] pairs are in the descending order of supports.

The UF-Construct algorithm is used to construct an mUF-tree from an uncertain database, and its output is the initial mUF-tree. Unlike the FP-tree construction algorithm, UF-Construct scans the database without specifying a minimum support threshold. With this change, the mUF-tree constructed contains all information. Compared with FP-tree, the mUF-tree stores uncertain information about items, and maintains the structure to be further modified for discovering more uncertain frequent patterns. Fig. 3 shows the steps of the UF-Construct algorithm.

With the records in Table 2, the mUF-tree together with the associated node-links are shown in Fig. 4. Since the constructed mUF-tree is large, we split it into two parts. Fig. 4(a) shows the header table with the left half of the mUF-tree, and Fig. 4(b) shows the right half of the mUF-tree. For the ease of understanding, we only show several node-links.

```
UF-Construct algorithm.
Input: A UDB.
Output: An mUF-tree T.

Procedure UF-Construct(UDB)
(1)   scan UDB once and collect a_set = the set of item:probability pairs with their
         respective supports in descending order;
(2)   create T with a root;
(3)   for each record R in UDB do {
(4)      R' = item:probability pairs in R putting in the same order as in a_set;
(5)      r = root(T);
(6)      for i = 1 to length(R') do {
(7)         (a_i:p_i) = the i^th item:probability pair of R';
(8)         find N_c = child(r), where (N_c.a_c = a_i) ∧ (N_c.l_c = p_i);
(9)         if ∃ N_c then N_c.f_c ++;
(10)        else {
(11)           create node N_c with (N_c.a_c = a_i) ∧ (N_c.l_c = N_c.u_c = p_i) ∧ (N_c.f_c = 1);
(12)           insert N_c as the rightmost child of r;
            }
(13)        update header table and node-links within T;
(14)        r = N_c;
         }
      }
(15)  return T;
```

Fig. 3. UF-Construct

Header table

item	lowerbound-upperbound	support	head of node-links
f	0.8-0.8	6	
f	1.0-1.0	5	
a	0.1-0.1	4	
b	0.2-0.2	4	
a	0.2-0.2	3	
a	0.7-0.7	3	
c	0.4-0.4	3	
d	0.3-0.3	2	
c	0.2-0.2	2	
a	0.4-0.4	2	
c	0.7-0.7	2	
d	0.6-0.6	2	
b	0.5-0.5	2	
d	0.4-0.4	2	
c	0.3-0.3	2	
d	0.5-0.5	2	
g	0.1-0.1	1	
b	0.3-0.3	1	
e	0.5-0.5	1	
e	0.6-0.6	1	
f	0.6-0.6	1	

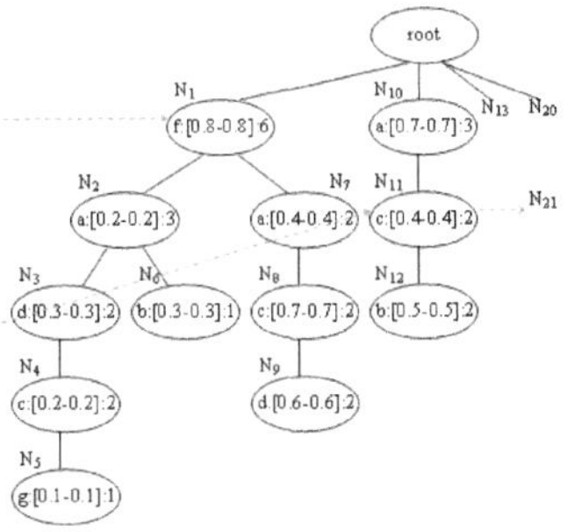

(a) mUF-tree(left).

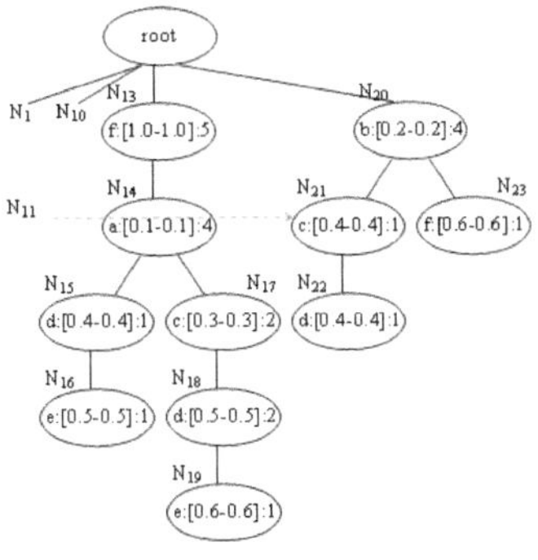

(b) mUF-tree(right).

Fig. 4. The mUF-tree for data in Table 2

5 Discovering New Uncertain Frequent Patterns

If we want to use the FP-growth algorithm to mine frequent patterns with mUF-tree(right) in Fig. 4(b), we can consider a_i:[l_i-u_i] as an item. Then FP-growth will discover a set of frequent patterns {(b:[0.2-0.2]):4, (a:[0.1-0.1]):4, (f:[1.0-1.0])(a:[0.1-0.1]):4, (f:[1.0-1.0]):5} with the minimum support threshold be 3.

In an mUF-tree, it is often that an item with a [lowerbound-upperbound] appears in a node while the same item with another [lowerbound-upperbound] appears in another node. For example, in Fig. 4(b), d:[0.4-0.4] appears in N_{15} while d:[0.5-0.5] appears in N_{18}. One can consider to merge the same items with only small differences in their various [lowerbound-upperbound] for satisfying the support. For example, we can merge d:[0.4-0.4] and d:[0.5-0.5] as d:[0.4-0.5]. Hence, for a group of item:[lowerbound-upperbound] pairs of the same item, we can use a combined [lowerbound-upperbound] to represent it. Once the item:[lowerbound-upperbound] pairs are grouped, more general frequent patterns can be found.

Hence, we are proposing to further discover new uncertain frequent patterns by utilizing shuffling and merging of the mUF-tree. Nodes can be merged to evolve into another mUF-tree for further pattern mining. The steps can be repeated until merging is not possible.

5.1 Preliminary Definitions

For the ease of future discussion, we have further definitions before presenting the algorithms.

Definition 6. Within Range. Given a maximum merging threshold γ, we define two nodes N_b and N_c are **within range** if $(N_b.a_b = N_c.a_c) \wedge (abs(N_b.u_b - N_c.l_c) \leq \gamma) \wedge (abs(N_c.u_c - N_b.l_b) \leq \gamma)$.

In Fig. 4(b), given a maximum merging threshold 0.3, then N_{15} and N_{18} are within range, as well as N_{16} and N_{19} are within range.

Definition 7. Common Items (CI). Given a pair of paths PB = $\langle N_{b1}N_{b2}\ldots N_{bk}\rangle$ and PC = $\langle N_{c1}N_{c2}\ldots N_{cm}\rangle$, we define CI(PB, PC) = {a_1, a_2, ..., a_n} as a sequence of ordered items, where $(n \leq k) \wedge (n \leq m) \wedge (\forall\, i \in \{1, 2, \ldots, n\}$, there is a node in PB and a node in PC, such that these two nodes contain a_i and are within range).

In Fig. 4(b), given a pair of paths PB = $\langle N_{15}N_{16}\rangle$ and PC = $\langle N_{17}N_{18}N_{19}\rangle$, then CI(PB, PC) = {d, e}.

We want to merge the nodes corresponding to common items in the two paths. However, it is difficult to merge N_{15} with N_{18} and N_{16} with N_{19} directly. We need to shuffle these nodes to be in the same order. Here, we define the Maximum Attainable Peak (MAP) of a node in a path first.

Definition 8. Maximum Attainable Peak (MAP). Given a_set = {a_{11}, a_{12}, ..., a_{1k}} as a sequence of ordered items, and a path PB = $\langle N_{21}N_{22}\ldots N_{2m}\rangle$, where the items in a_set is a subset of the items in PB. We take out each item a_{1i} in a_set sequentially and trace along PB. If the position of a_{1i} in PB is not as in a_set, the node N_{2j} containing a_{1i} will be shuffled upward until the position of a_{1i} in PB is as in a_set. The final position is called the MAP of N_{2j} in PB.

Now, we are ready to describe two cases for shuffling the node N_{2j} with its parent node N_q.

- Case 1: $N_{2j}.f_{2j} = N_q.f_q$. Swap N_{2j} and N_q.
- Case 2: $N_{2j}.f_{2j} < N_q.f_q$. Create a new node, N_r, with the same property of N_q except $N_r.f_r = N_q.f_q - N_{2j}.f_{2j}$. Make N_r as another child of the parent of N_q. Set $N_q.f_q = N_{2j}.f_{2j}$. Update the header table and node-links within the mUF-tree, and then follow the handling of Case 1 for N_{2j} and N_q.

The node N_{2j} will be shuffled until it reaches its MAP in PB.

In Fig. 4(b), given a_set = {d, e}, then the MAP of N_{18} in the path <$N_{17}N_{18}N_{19}$> is the 1st position. We shuffle N_{18} with N_{17}, which follows Case 1. mUF-tree(right) evolves into mUF-tree(right)$_2$, as shown in Fig. 5.

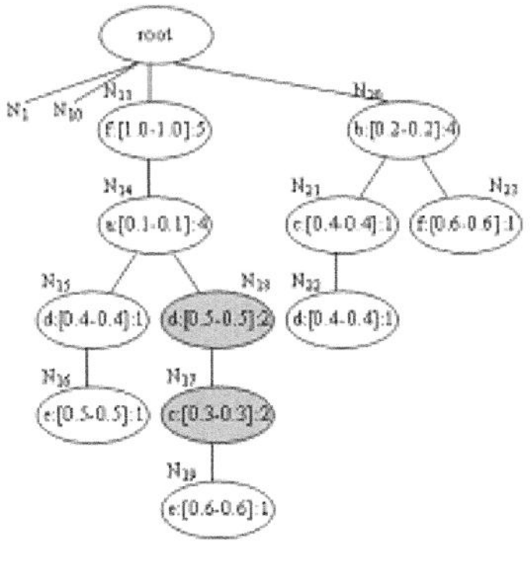

Fig. 5. mUF-tree(right)$_2$

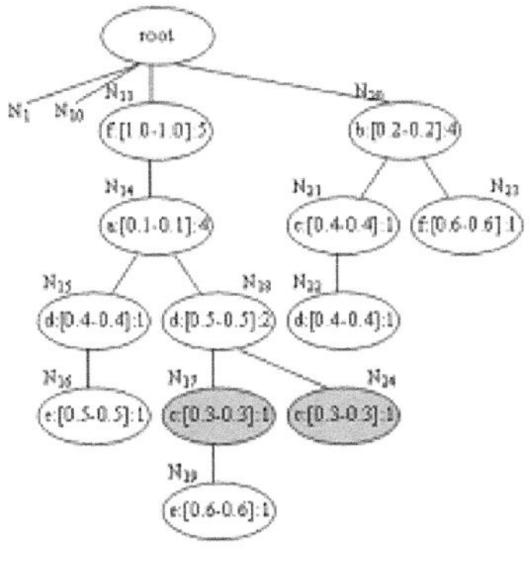

Fig. 6. mUF-tree(right)$_3$

After shuffling N_{18} to its MAP, the MAP of N_{19} in the updated path <$N_{18}N_{17}N_{19}$> is the 2nd position. We shuffle N_{19} with N_{17}, which follows Case 2. We create a new node N_{24} and modify N_{17}, which evolves into mUF-tree(right)$_3$, as shown in Fig. 6. Then we shuffle N_{19} with N_{17}, which evolves into mUF-tree(right)$_4$, as shown in Fig. 7.

After shuffling, the nodes corresponding to common items are above the other nodes in the two paths. It is much easier to merge N_{15} with N_{18} and N_{16} with N_{19}.

Next, we define the merging criteria, which determine how two candidate nodes can be merged to a new node.

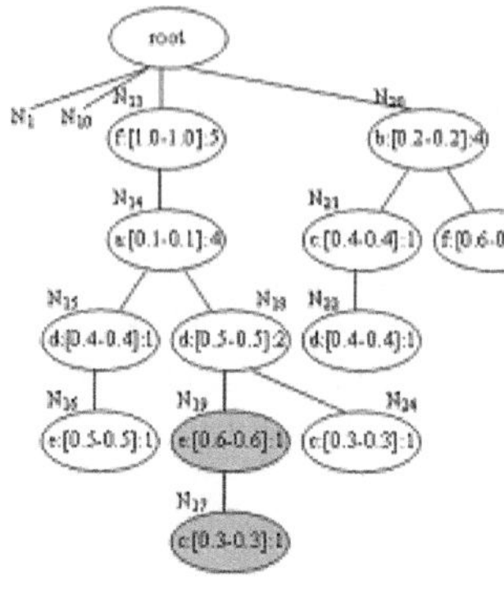

Fig. 7. mUF-tree(right)$_4$

Definition 9. Merging Criteria. If two nodes N_b and N_c are within range, they can be merged as a new node N_q, where $(N_q.a_q = N_b.a_b) \wedge (N_q.l_q = \min(N_b.l_b, N_c.l_c)) \wedge (N_q.u_q = \max(N_b.u_b, N_c.u_c)) \wedge (N_q.f_q = N_b.f_b + N_c.f_c)$.

We merge N_{15} with N_{18} as a new node N_{25}, which evolves into mUF-tree(right)$_5$, as shown in Fig. 8. And then we merge N_{16} with N_{19} as a new node N_{26}, which evolves into mUF-tree(right)$_6$, as shown in Fig. 9.

Definition 10. Overlap. Given a path PB, overlap(PB) is true if PB shares common nodes with any other path in the mUF-tree.

In Fig. 4(b), given PB = $<N_{13}N_{14}N_{15}N_{16}>$, PC = $<N_{13}N_{14}N_{17}N_{18}N_{19}>$ and PD = $<N_{17}N_{18}N_{19}>$, then overlap(PB) since PB shares N_{13} and N_{14} with PC, and !overlap(PD) since PD does not share common nodes with any other path.

Definition 11. Above. Given a_set = $\{a_{11}, a_{12}, \ldots, a_{1k}\}$ and a path PB = $<N_{21}N_{22}\ldots N_{2m}>$, above(a_set , PB) is true if $(k \leq m) \wedge (\forall\ i \in \{1, 2, \ldots, k\}, a_{1i} = N_{2i}.a_{2i})$.

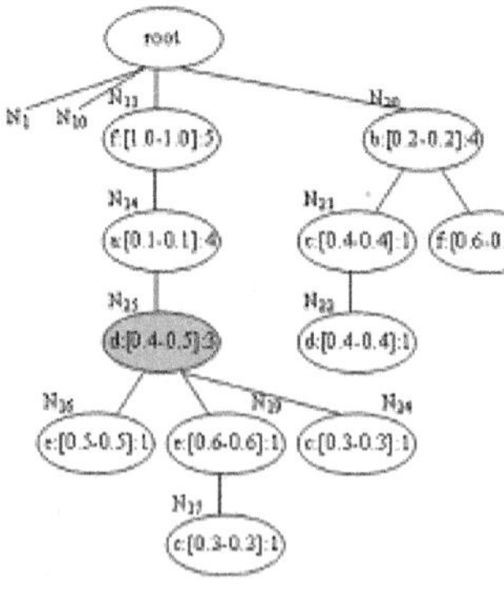

Fig. 8. mUF-tree(right)$_5$

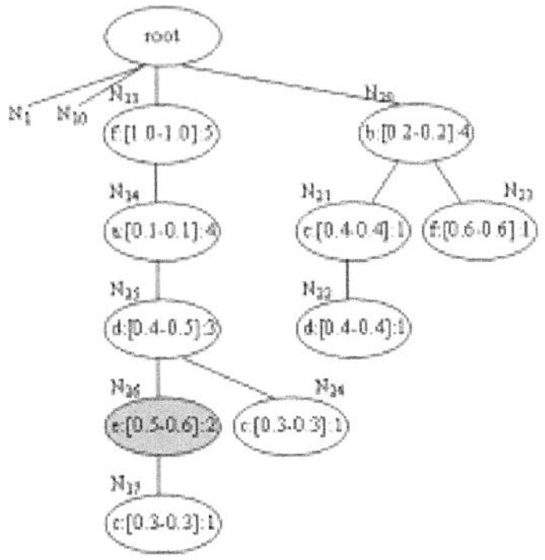

Fig. 9. mUF-tree(right)$_6$

In Fig. 4(b), given a_set = {d, e}, PB = <$N_{15}N_{16}$> and PC = <$N_{17}N_{18}N_{19}$>, then above(a_set, PB) since d and e are above other items in PB, and !above(a_set, PC) since d and e are not above other items in PC.

There can be five cases for shuffling a pair of paths PB and PC. In Case 1, both PB and PC do not share common nodes with any other path in the mUF-tree. Therefore, PB and PC can be shuffled without influencing others. In Case 2, PB does not share common nodes with any other path, but PC does. However, in PC, the nodes with common items are above other nodes. Therefore, we do not need to shuffle PC. Case 3 is similar to Case 2 with the information in PB and PC inter-changed. In Case 4, both PB and PC share common nodes with other paths, but with nodes having common items above other nodes. Therefore, neither PB nor PC needs to be shuffled. For all the four cases, PB and PC can be merged after shuffling if necessary.

All other conditions besides the above are considered as Case 0. In Case 0, shuffling is not allowed. Since shuffling in the two paths may induce much effort in re-structuring of the whole mUF-tree.

Definition 12. Shuffle Case (SC). Given a pair of paths PB and PC, and a_set = CI(PB, PC), there are five shuffle cases.

- SC(PB, PC) = 1 if !overlap(PB) $\wedge$!overlap(PC).
- SC(PB, PC) = 2 if !overlap(PB) $\wedge$ overlap(PC) $\wedge$ above(a_set, PC).
- SC(PB, PC) = 3 if overlap(PB) $\wedge$ above(a_set, PB) $\wedge$!overlap(PC).
- SC(PB, PC) = 4 if overlap(PB) $\wedge$ above(a_set, PB) $\wedge$ overlap(PC) $\wedge$ above(a_set, PC).
- SC(PB, PC) = 0 for other conditions.

For the ease of understanding, the shuffle cases are shown in Table 3.

Table 3. Shuffle cases

SC(PB, PC)	!overlap(PC)	overlap(PC) $\wedge$ above(a_set, PC)
!overlap(PB)	1	2
overlap(PB) $\wedge$ above(a_set, PB)	3	4

Take the mUF-tree in Fig. 4 as an example. Given a maximum merging threshold 0.3, then the shuffle cases with the corresponding path pairs are shown in Table 4.

Table 4. Shuffle cases with corresponding path pairs

PB	PC	CI(PB, PC)	SC(PB, PC)
$<N_{15}N_{16}>$	$<N_{17}N_{18}N_{19}>$	{d, e}	1
$<N_{10}N_{11}N_{12}>$	$<N_{20}N_{21}N_{22}>$	{b, c}	2
$<N_2N_3N_4N_5>$	$<N_7N_8N_9>$	{a, d}	3
$<N_1N_2N_3N_4N_5>$	$<N_{13}N_{14}N_{15}N_{16}>$	{f, a, d}	4
$<N_{10}N_{11}N_{12}>$	$<N_{13}N_{14}N_{17}N_{18}N_{19}>$	{c}	0
$<N_1N_7N_8N_9>$	$<N_{20}N_{23}>$	{f}	0
$<N_1N_2N_6>$	$<N_{10}N_{11}N_{12}>$	{b}	0
$<N_1N_2N_6>$	$<N_{20}N_{23}>$	{b, f}	0
$<N_1N_7N_8N_9>$	$<N_{20}N_{21}N_{22}>$	{c, d}	0

Definition 13. Common Ancestor Path (CAP). Given a pair of paths PB = $<N_{b1}N_{b2}...N_{bk}>$ and PC = $<N_{c1}N_{c2}...N_{cm}>$, we define CAP(PB, PC) = $<N_{b1}N_{b2}...N_{bn}>$, where $(n \leq k) \wedge (n \leq m) \wedge (\forall\ i \in \{1, 2, ..., n\}$, N_{bi} and N_{ci} are the same node).

In Fig. 4(b), given a pair of paths PB = $<N_{13}N_{14}N_{15}N_{16}>$ and PC = $<N_{13}N_{14}N_{17}N_{18}N_{19}>$, then CAP(PB, PC) = $<N_{13}N_{14}>$.

Definition 14. Single Prefix-Path Part and Multipath Part. The single prefix-path part of an mUF-tree consists of a single path from the root to N_k, the first node containing more than one child. The multipath part of an mUF-tree consists of the descendants of N_k, with a virtual root connecting to the children of N_k as the parent.

For the mUF-tree shown in Fig. 2, the single prefix-path part and the multipath part are shown in Fig. 10.

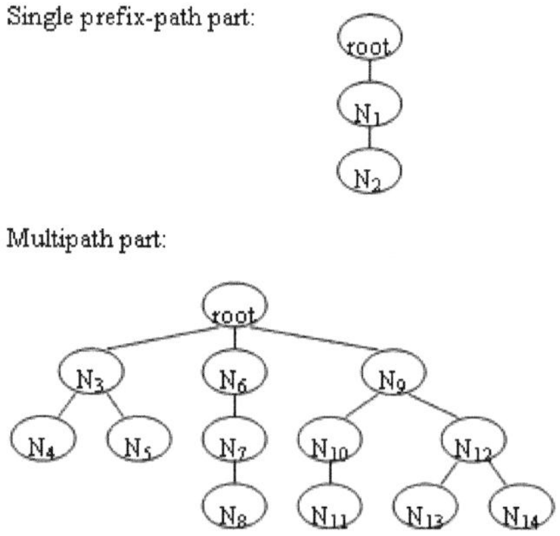

Fig. 10. Single prefix-path part and multipath part of mUF-tree

5.2 The UF-Evolve Algorithm

With the aforementioned definitions, we present the UF-Evolve algorithm for mining frequent patterns in an uncertain database by using an mUF-tree. The algorithm integrates the UF-Mine algorithm for finding out the possible frequent patterns and the UF-Shuffle algorithm for moving and merging the nodes in the mUF-tree iteratively. Fig. 11 shows the steps of the UF-Evolve algorithm.

```
UF-Evolve algorithm.
Input: An mUF-tree T, a minimum support threshold σ, and a maximum merging
  threshold γ.
Output: A set of uncertain frequent patterns.

Procedure UF-Evolve(T, σ, γ)
(1)   FPS = ϕ;  // Frequent pattern set
(2)   do {
(3)     FPS = FPS ∪ UF-Mine(T, null, σ);
(4)     T = UF-Shuffle(T, γ);
(5)   } while T has been modified;
(6)   return FPS;
```

Fig. 11. UF-Evolve

The UF-Mine algorithm is a variant of the FP-growth algorithm [8]. It has two phases. It first tries to find frequent patterns in the single prefix-path part of the given mUF-tree, and then continues to work out the multipath part. The details are shown in Fig. 12.

In line (16) of Fig. 12, (FPS(P) × FPS(Q)) means concatenating each frequent pattern FP_i in FPS(P) with each frequent pattern FP_j in FPS(Q), with support equal to FP_j.support.

In order to illustrate how the different algorithms work, we will use a running example with mUF-tree(right) in Fig. 4(b). Suppose the minimum support threshold is 3,

```
UF-Mine algorithm.
Input: An mUF-tree T, an uncertain frequent pattern α = (a1:[l1-u1])(a2:[l2-u2])...(ak:[lk-
  uk]):s, and a minimum support threshold σ.
Output: A set of uncertain frequent patterns.

Procedure UF-Mine(T, α, σ)
(1)   P = the single prefix-path part of T;
(2)   Q = the multipath part of T;
(3)   FPS(P) = ϕ;  // Frequent pattern set in P
(4)   FPS(Q) = ϕ;  // Frequent pattern set in Q
(5)   for each pattern β formed from P where all nodes in β have sufficient supports
        do {
(6)     β.support = minimum support of nodes in β;
(7)     append α to the end of β;
(8)     FPS(P) = FPS(P) ∪ β;
      }
(9)   for each (ai:[li-ui]) in Q with sufficient support do {
(10)    β = (ai:[li-ui]);
(11)    β.support = (ai:[li-ui]).support;
(12)    append α to the end of β;
(13)    FPS(Q) = FPS(Q) ∪ β;
(14)    find cond_tree from Q constructed with the conditional pattern-base of β;
          // Conditional mUF-tree of β
(15)    if ∃ cond_tree then FPS(Q) = FPS(Q) ∪ UF-Mine(cond_tree, β, σ);
      }
(16)  return FPS(P) ∪ FPS(Q) ∪ (FPS(P) × FPS(Q));
```

Fig. 12. UF-mine

and the maximum merging threshold is 0.3. UF-Evolve calls UF-Mine, and UF-Mine returns a set of uncertain frequent patterns, which is {(b:[0.2-0.2]):4, (a:[0.1-0.1]):4, (f:[1.0-1.0])(a:[0.1-0.1]):4, (f:[1.0-1.0]):5}.

The core algorithm is the UF-Shuffle algorithm, which is shown in Fig. 13. Each time it is called by UF-Evolve, it collects the set of paths under the root and finds the most suitable pair of paths to shuffle and merge.

There can be different versions of the UF-Shuffle algorithm. Fig. 14 shows UF-Shuffle_2, which is a variant of UF-Shuffle. Each time it is called by UF-Evolve, it collects the set of paths under the root and tries to shuffle and merge each pair of paths. If a pair of paths are shuffled and merged, they will be removed from the set of paths since they have been modified and no longer exist.

```
UF-Shuffle algorithm.
Input: An mUF-tree T, and a maximum merging threshold γ.
Output: A shuffled mUF-tree T.

Procedure UF-Shuffle(T, γ)
(1)   scan T once and collect P_set = the set of paths under root(T);
(2)   for each pair of paths PB and PC in P_set do {
(3)       P = CAP(PB, PC);
(4)       PB = PB excludes P;
(5)       PC = PC excludes P;
(6)       get CI(PB, PC) and SC(PB, PC);
      }
(7)   suppose (PB', PC') is a pair of paths that (has maximum length(CI(PB, PC))) ∧
          (length(CI(PB', PC')) > 0) ∧ (SC(PB', PC') > 0);
(8)   if ∃ (PB', PC') then {
(9)       switch SC(PB', PC') {
(10)          case 1: shuffle the nodes corresponding to CI(PB', PC') to their MAP in PB'
                  and PC';
(11)          case 2: shuffle the nodes corresponding to CI(PB', PC') to their MAP in PB';
(12)          case 3: shuffle the nodes corresponding to CI(PB', PC') to their MAP in PC';
(13)          case 4: do nothing;
          }
(14)      T = UF-Merge(T, PB', PC', length(CI(PB', PC')));
      }
(15)  return T;
```

Fig. 13. UF-Shuffle

```
Procedure UF-Shuffle_2(T, γ)
(1)   scan T once and collect P_set = the set of paths under root(T);
(2)   for each pair of paths PB and PC in P_set do {
(3)       P = CAP(PB, PC);
(4)       PB = PB excludes P;
(5)       PC = PC excludes P;
(6)       if (length(CI(PB, PC)) > 0) ∧ (SC(PB, PC) > 0) then {
(7)           switch SC(PB, PC) {
(8)               case 1: shuffle the nodes corresponding to CI(PB, PC) to their MAP in PB
                      and PC;
(9)               case 2: shuffle the nodes corresponding to CI(PB, PC) to their MAP in
                      PB;
(10)              case 3: shuffle the nodes corresponding to CI(PB, PC) to their MAP in
                      PC;
(11)              case 4: do nothing;
              }
(12)          T = UF-Merge(T, PB, PC, length(CI(PB, PC)));
(13)          remove PB and PC from P_set;   // Updates will be used in loop at line (2)
          }
      }
(14)  return T;
```

Fig. 14. UF-Shuffle_2

After shuffling, candidate nodes can then be merged with some updating. The algorithm of UF-Merge is shown in Fig. 15.

In continuing the example, UF-Evolve calls UF-Shuffle to shuffle mUF-tree(right) in Fig. 4(b), and UF-Shuffle generates mUF-tree(right)$_4$, as shown in Fig. 7.

```
UF-Merge algorithm.
Input: An mUF-tree T, a pair of paths PB = <N_b1 N_b2...N_bl> and PC = <N_c1 N_c2...N_cm>, and
  n, the number of nodes to be merged in each path.
Output: A merged mUF-tree T.

Procedure UF-Merge(T, PB, PC, n)
(1)    for i = 1 to n do {
(2)       N_q = the new node formed by merging N_bi and N_ci and updating its item,
             lowerbound, upperbound, frequency, node-link, parent and children;
(3)       remove N_bi and N_ci from T;
(4)       update header table and node-links within T;
       }
(5)    return T;
```

Fig. 15. UF-Merge

UF-Shuffle calls UF-Merge and recommends the pair of paths to be merged (i.e. $<N_{15}N_{16}>$ and $<N_{18}N_{19}N_{17}>$). UF-Merge merges the pair of paths, and returns the generated mUF-tree(right)$_6$, as shown in Fig. 9.

UF-Evolve calls UF-Mine, and UF-Mine returns a new set of uncertain frequent patterns, which is {(d:[0.4-0.5]):3, (a:[0.1-0.1])(d:[0.4-0.5]):3, (f:[1.0-1.0])(d:[0.4-0.5]):3, (f:[1.0-1.0])(a:[0.1-0.1])(d:[0.4-0.5]):3, (b:[0.2-0.2]):4, (a:[0.1-0.1]):4, (f:[1.0-1.0])(a:[0.1-0.1]):4, (f:[1.0-1.0]):5}.

UF-Evolve combines the original set of uncertain frequent patterns with the new set. Now, the set of uncertain frequent patterns becomes {(b:[0.2-0.2]):4, (a:[0.1-0.1]):4, (f:[1.0-1.0])(a:[0.1-0.1]):4, (f:[1.0-1.0]):5, (d:[0.4-0.5]):3, (a:[0.1-0.1])(d:[0.4-0.5]):3, (f:[1.0-1.0])(d:[0.4-0.5]):3, (f:[1.0-1.0])(a:[0.1-0.1])(d:[0.4-0.5]):3}.

The algorithms continue to attempt building new mUF-trees until not successful. At the end, the patterns are stabilized.

6 Performance Study

6.1 Experimental Environment and Data Preparation

In this section, we present some performance comparison of UF-Evolve with FP-growth. All the experiments are performed on a 2.83 GHz Xeon server with 3.00 GB of RAM, running Microsoft Windows Server 2003. The programs are written in Java. Runtime here means the total execution time, i.e. the period between input and output, instead of CPU time. Also, all the runtime measurements of UF-Evolve/FP-growth included the time of constructing mUF-trees/FP-trees from the original databases.

The experiments are done on a synthetic database (T10.I4.D3K), which is generated by using the methods in [13]. In this database, the average record length is 10, the average length of pattern is 4, and the number of records is 3K. Besides, we set the number of items as 1000. All the probabilities for the items are randomly generated.

For UF-Evolve, each record in the database consists of multiple item:probability pairs. However, for FP-growth, each record in the database consists of multiple items. These two representations have different semantic meanings. In order to carry out a consistent comparison of UF-Evolve with FP-growth, we make the following arrangements.

- First we generate UDB for UF-Evolve. Each record in UDB consists of multiple $(a_i:p_i)$.
- Based on UDB, we generate a special database UDB' for FP-growth. Each record in UDB' consists of multiple $(a_j:[l_j-u_j])$, where $a_j = a_i$, and $l_j = u_j = p_i$. FP-growth treats each $(a_j:[l_j-u_j])$ as an item.
- While constructing an mUF-tree from UDB, we keep the Record IDs in the corresponding nodes. When UF-Evolve generates iterative versions of the mUF-tree, we record the changes of [lowerbound-upperbound] in the nodes together with their Record IDs.
- We use the Record IDs to trace back to the records in UDB' and change the corresponding l_j and u_j. Then there will be iterative versions of UDB' for discovering new frequent patterns by FP-growth.

With these arrangements, we will have a consistent comparison for the runtime and number of mined frequent patterns from the two algorithms.

6.2 Experiments

In the first experiment, we measured the runtime, number of shuffles and number of mined frequent patterns with different numbers of records for UF-Evolve and FP-growth. The number of records varies from 0.1K to 3K, the minimum support threshold is 3%, and the maximum merging threshold is 0.3. The runtime of UF-Evolve and FP-growth are shown in Fig. 16. UF-Evolve is faster and more scalable than FP-growth. The number of shuffles of UF-Evolve is shown in Fig. 17. Since when the number of records increases, UF-Evolve shuffles a bigger mUF-tree. The numbers of mined frequent patterns of UF-Evolve and FP-growth are shown in Fig. 18. The two algorithms mined the same numbers and the same sets of frequent patterns.

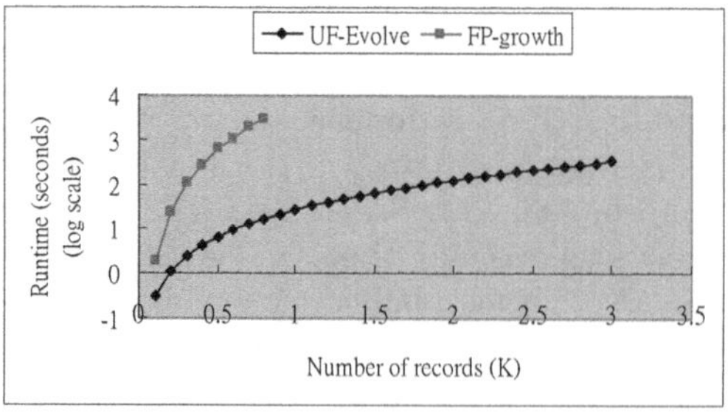

Fig. 16. Runtime with number of records for UF-Evolve and FP-growth

In the second experiment, we measured the runtime, number of shuffles and number of mined frequent patterns with different minimum support thresholds for UF-Evolve and FP-growth. The minimum support threshold varies from 0.1% to 8%, the number of records is 3K, and the maximum merging threshold is 0.3. The runtime of UF-Evolve and FP-growth are shown in Fig. 19. UF-Evolve is faster and more scalable than FP-growth. When the minimum support threshold increases, the runtime of both UF-Evolve and FP-growth decreases. Since when the minimum support threshold is high, UF-Evolve processes fewer and smaller conditional mUF-trees. The number of shuffles of UF-Evolve is shown in Fig. 20. When the minimum support threshold increases, the number of shuffles of UF-Evolve remains the same. This is because UF-Evolve always shuffles the same mUF-tree. The numbers of mined frequent patterns of UF-Evolve and FP-growth are shown in Fig. 21. The two algorithms mined the same numbers and the same sets of frequent patterns. When the minimum support threshold increases, the numbers of mined frequent patterns of both UF-Evolve and FP-growth decrease. This is because when the minimum support threshold is high, the frequent patterns are short and the set of such patterns is not large.

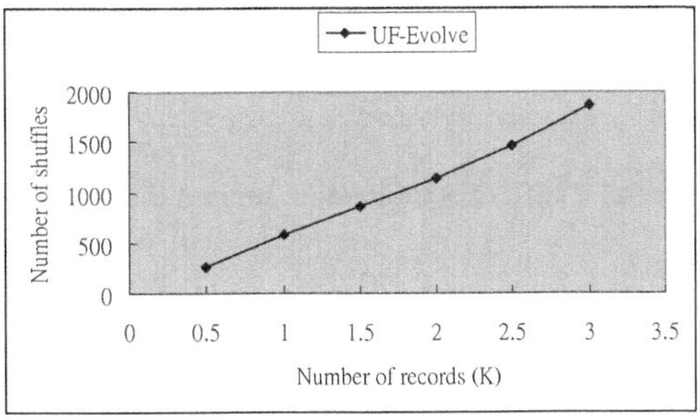

Fig. 17. Number of shuffles with number of records for UF-Evolve

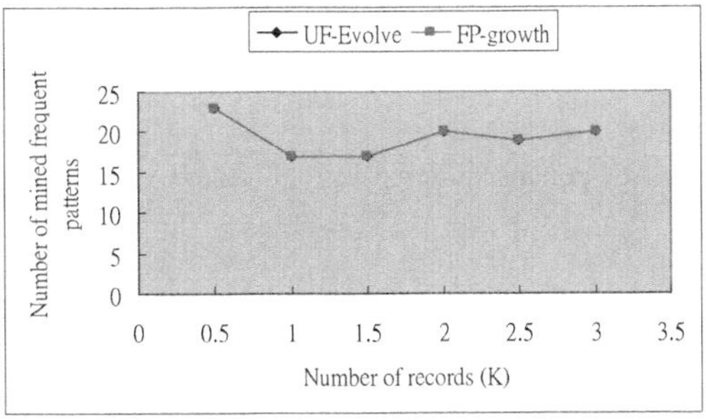

Fig. 18. Number of mined frequent patterns with number of records for UF-Evolve and FP-growth

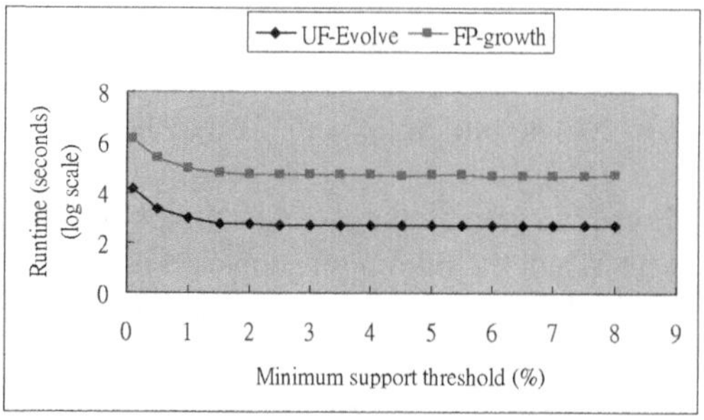

Fig. 19. Runtime with minimum support threshold for UF-Evolve and FP-growth

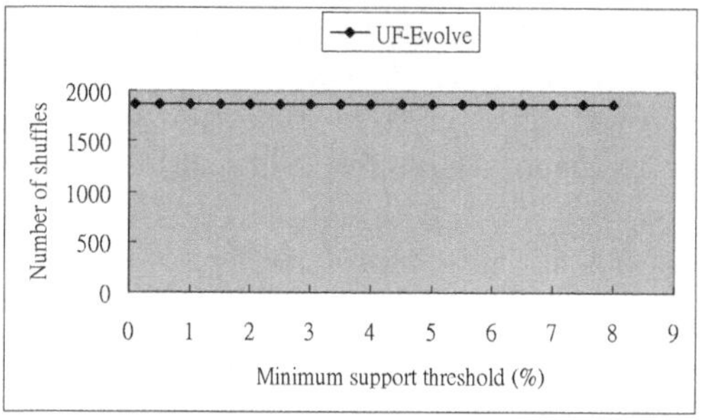

Fig. 20. Number of shuffles with minimum support threshold for UF-Evolve

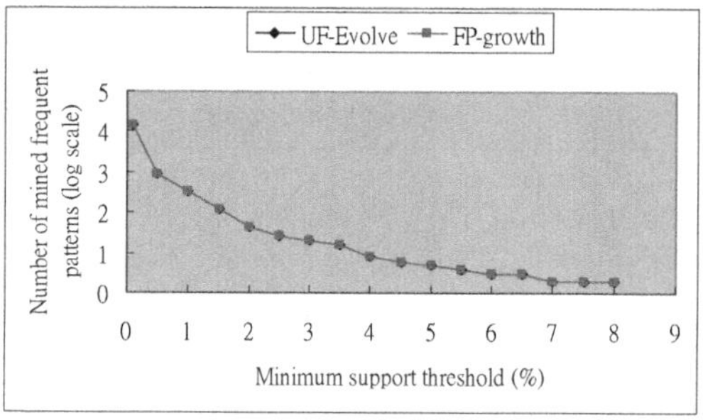

Fig. 21. Number of mined frequent patterns with minimum support threshold for UF-Evolve and FP-growth

In the third experiment, we measured the number of mined frequent patterns in each iteration for UF-Evolve. The number of records is 3K, the minimum support threshold is 0.1%, and the maximum merging threshold is 0.3. As shown in Fig. 22, UF-Evolve discovers new frequent patterns from iterative versions of the mUF-tree, and the number of mined frequent patterns keeps increasing until stabilized.

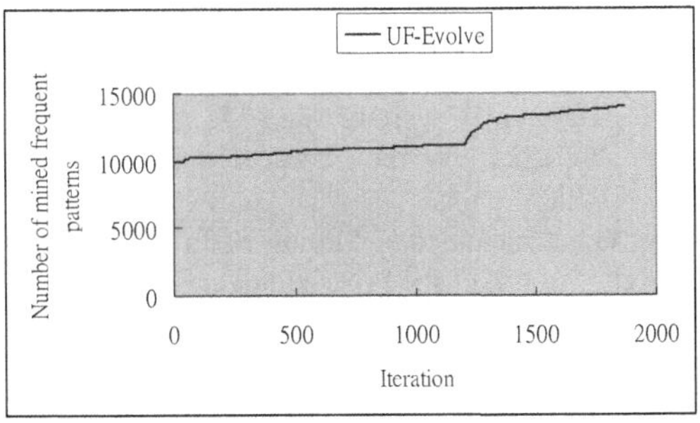

Fig. 22. Number of mined frequent patterns in each iteration for UF-Evolve

For the above experiments, UF-Evolve and FP-growth mined the same numbers and the same sets of frequent patterns. Some of the discovered frequent patterns are shown in Table 5. Here, the supports for frequent patterns are shown as (support count)/(number of records in UDB) in percentage.

Table 5. Discovered frequent patterns

Frequent patterns mined in 1st iteration	New frequent patterns mined in 2nd iteration	New frequent patterns mined in 3rd iteration
(59757:[0.3-0.3]):4%	(29340:[0.1-0.3]):3%	(45973:[0.2-0.3]):4%
(45370:[0.7-0.7]):5%	(59757:[0.3-0.4])	(38212:[0.8-0.8])
…	(22360:[0.3-0.3])	(8885:[0.2-0.5])
	(18474:[0.5-0.7])	(45973:[0.2-0.3]):4%
	(29340:[0.1-0.3]):3%	…
	…	

7 Conclusions

We have proposed the mUF-tree structure, which is a novel uncertain-frequent-pattern discover structure, and the UF-Evolve algorithm, which utilizes the shuffling and merging techniques on the mUF-tree for iteratively discovering new uncertain frequent patterns. Also, we proposed a variant of the UF-Shuffle algorithms. Our preliminary performance study shows that the UF-Evolve algorithm is efficient and scalable for mining additional uncertain frequent patterns with different sizes of uncertain databases.

References

1. Adnan, M., Alhajj, R., Barker, K.: Constructing Complete FP-Tree for Incremental Mining of Frequent Patterns in Dynamic Databases. In: Ali, M., Dapoigny, R. (eds.) IEA/AIE 2006. LNCS (LNAI), vol. 4031, pp. 363–372. Springer, Heidelberg (2006)
2. Antova, L., Jansen, T., Koch, C., Olteanu, D.: Fast and Simple Relational Processing of Uncertain Data. In: ICDE 2008, pp. 983–992 (2008)

3. Borgelt, C.: An Implementation of the FP-growth Algorithm. In: OSDM 2005, Chicago, Illinois, USA, August 21, pp. 1–5 (2005)
4. Chau, M., Cheng, R., Kao, B.: Uncertain Data Mining: A New Research Direction. In Proceedings of the Workshop on the Sciences of the Artificial, Hualien, Taiwan, December 7-8, pp. 1–8 (2005)
5. Cheung, W., Zaiane, O.R.: Incremental Mining of Frequent Patterns Without Candidate Generation or Support Constraint. In: Proceedings of the Seventh International Database Engineering and Applications Symposium (IDEAS 2003), pp. 111–116 (2003)
6. Chui, C.K., Kao, B., Hung, E.: Mining Frequent Itemsets from Uncertain Data. In: Zhou, Z.-H., Li, H., Yang, Q. (eds.) PAKDD 2007. LNCS (LNAI), vol. 4426, pp. 47–58. Springer, Heidelberg (2007)
7. Ezeife, C.I., Su, Y.: Mining Incremental Association Rules with Generalized FP-Tree. In: Cohen, R., Spencer, B. (eds.) Canadian AI 2002. LNCS (LNAI), vol. 2338, pp. 147–160. Springer, Heidelberg (2002)
8. Han, J., Pei, J., Yin, Y., Mao, R.: Mining Frequent Patterns without Candidate Generation: A Frequent-Pattern Tree Approach. Data Mining and Knowledge Discovery 8, 53–87 (2004)
9. Hong, T.P., Lin, C.W., Wu, Y.L.: Incrementally fast updated frequent pattern trees. Expert Systems with Applications 34, 2424–2435 (2008)
10. Leung, C.K.S., Carmichael, C., Hao, B.: Efficient Mining of Frequent Patterns from Uncertain Data. In: ICDM-DUNE 2007, pp. 1–19 (2007)
11. Leung, C.K.-S., Mateo, M.A.F., Brajczuk, D.A.: A Tree-Based Approach for Frequent Pattern Mining from Uncertain Data. In: Washio, T., Suzuki, E., Ting, K.M., Inokuchi, A. (eds.) PAKDD 2008. LNCS (LNAI), vol. 5012, pp. 653–661. Springer, Heidelberg (2008)
12. Li, H.F., Lee, S.Y., Shan, M.K.: An Efficient Algorithm for Mining Frequent Itemsets over the Entire History of Data Streams, `http://citeseerx.ist.psu.edu/viewdoc/summary?doi=10.1.1.81.9955`
13. IBM Quest Market-Basket Synthetic Data Generator, `http://www.cs.loyola.edu/~cgiannel/assoc_gen.html`

Formal Fact-Oriented Model Transformations for Cooperative Information Systems Semantic Conceptualisation

Mario Lezoche, Alexis Aubry, and Hervé Panetto

Research Centre for Automatic Control (CRAN), Nancy-University, CNRS
Campus Scientifique, Faculté des Sciences et Technologies, BP 70239
54506, Vandoeuvre-lès-Nancy Cedex, France
{mario.lezoche,alexis.aubry,herve.panetto}@cran.uhp-nancy.fr

Abstract. Information in enterprise is, now more than ever, a fundamental resource. In order to increase enterprise performance, economics paradigms focus on how to better manage it. Information Systems (IS) are systems whose activities are devoted to capture and to store data, to process them and produce knowledge, used by any stakeholders within an enterprise or among different networked enterprises. The modern architecture of information systems is based on distributed networks. An important challenge, to reach higher performance, is to represent and share knowledge managed by those ISs. One of the main issues in making such heterogeneous Cooperative Information Systems (CIS) working together is to remove semantics interoperability barriers. This paper firstly analyses interoperability issues between CISs and then proposes a systematic approach for data models conceptualisation for knowledge explicitation, based on initial conceptual model cleaning rules, expert knowledge injection rules and finally fact-oriented transformation rules. A case study is proposed, related to a work order process in an Enterprise Resource Planning application, Sage X3.

Keywords: Conceptual modelling, Cooperative information systems, Formal verification, Data model conceptualisation.

1 Introduction

The actual archetype for the Information Systems (ISs) involves large number of ISs distributed over large, complex computer/ communication networks. Such cooperative information systems (CIS) have access to large amount of information and have to interoperate to achieve their purpose. The cooperative information systems architects and developers have to face a hard problem: interoperability.

Interoperability can be defined as the ability for two or more systems to share, to understand and to consume information [20]. Some work [8] in the INTEROP NoE project has identified three different levels of barriers for interoperability: technical, conceptual and organisational. Organisational barriers are still an important issue but

R. Zhang et al. (Eds.): ICEIS 2011, LNBIP 102, pp. 117–131, 2012.

out of scope of this paper. The technological barriers are strongly studied by researchers in computer science and the solution is generally based on models transformation [14].

Our research [24] focuses on the conceptual level of interoperability that is the ability to understand the exchanged information. A concept is a cognition unit of meaning [39], an abstract idea, a mental symbol. It is created through the action of conceptualisation, that is, a general and abstract mental representation of an object. During the history of human effort to model knowledge, different conceptualisation approaches regarding different application domains were developed [1].

This paper is dealing with a first step from a more general work focusing on the study of the semantic loss during the exchange of information representing business concepts. Quantifying the semantic gap between interoperating ISs implies enacting their semantics through their normalized conceptual models. Indeed, in this context, the starting point for semantics interoperability is related to models conceptualisation.

We will present a conceptualisation approach to make explicit the finest-grained semantics embedded into conceptual models for finally enabling two different information systems seamlessly interoperating.

Next section presents the general context of our work. Then, the following section details the fundamental pillars of our conceptualisation process. Then, we will propose a knowledge explicitation process starting from an implemented relational model to a fact-oriented conceptual one. This process allows us emphasizing the finest-grained semantics that must be enacted to study semantics interoperability between collaborating ISs.

Finally, to validate our proposal, a practical case study is presented based on an Enterprise Resource Planning application involved in a B2M (Business to Manufacturing) interoperation process.

2 Cooperative Information Systems

Information Systems are systems whose activities are devoted to capture and to store data, to process them and produce knowledge, used by any stakeholders within an enterprise or among different networked enterprises. It is commonly agreed that Cooperative Information Systems provide a backbone for the Integrated Information Infrastructure [35]. Fully understanding and exploiting the advances in computing is the only way to encompass the complexity of constructing and maintaining such systems.

Although the progress made in information technology considerably improved the efficiency of applications development, its drawbacks and limitations are obvious and serious. In fact, the application models involved in a single application are numerous and different, each coping only with particular and partial aspects of the overall task. Moreover, the components technologies are heterogeneous, platform- and machine-dependant. The above-mentioned limitations and barriers measurably hinder the development and the maintenance process.

There is a growing demand to integrate such systems tightly with organizational work so that these information systems can be directly and immediately used by the business activity.

Here, the need of interoperation clearly appears. In fact, to achieve the purpose of the cooperation between the different Information Systems, information must be physically exchanged (technical interoperability), must be understood (conceptual interoperability) and must be used for the purpose that they have been produced (conceptual and organisational interoperability). When trying to assess the understanding of an expression coming from a system to another system, there are several possible levels of interoperability [12]:

- *encoding:* being able to segment the representation in characters;
- *lexical:* being able to segment the representation in words (or symbols);
- *syntactic:* being able to structure the representation in structured sentences (or formulas or assertions);
- *semantic:* being able to construct the propositional meaning of the representation;
- *semiotic:* being able to construct the pragmatic meaning of the representation (or its meaning in context).

This tiered structure is arguable in general; it is not as strict as it seems. It makes sense because each level cannot be achieved if the previous levels have not been completed [12].

The encoding, lexical and syntactic levels are the most effective solutions for removing technical barriers for interoperability, but not sufficient, to achieve a practical interoperability between computerised systems. Dealing with trying to enable a seamless data and model exchange at the semantic level is still a big issue that needs conceptual representation of the intended exchanged information and the definition of the pragmatic meaning of that exchanged information in the context of the source and destination applications.

Different cooperation types have been investigated in ISO 14528 [21]. In fact, this standard considers that models could be related in three ways:

(1) integration when there exists a standard or pivotal format to represent these models;

(2) unification when there exists a common meta-level structure establishing semantic equivalence between these models; and

(3) federation when each model exists per se, but mapping between concepts could be done at an ontology level to formalise the interoperability semantics.

Integration is generally considered to go beyond mere interoperability to involve some degree of functional dependence. Classifying interoperability problems [38] may help in understanding the degree of development needed to solve, at least partially, these problems but conceptualisation and semantics extraction is still an important issue because of the various contextual understanding of tacit knowledge embedded into those applications. The main prerequisite for achievement of interoperability of information systems is to maximise the amount of semantics which can be used and make it increasingly explicit [29], and consequently, to make the systems semantically interoperable. To highlight this issue, the paper is based on a referenced scenario involving enterprise systems applications.

Most of reverse engineering approaches [13] [9] return the information structure but present a model with tacit semantics. The ADM (Architecture-Driven Modernization) initiative [30] from OMG [5] is tackling this problem by promoting a common Knowledge Discovery Meta-model to facilitate discovering tacit knowledge embedded inside existing software. In our scenario, those applications are still implemented and running using databases. We can extract, from them, by using reverse engineering approaches, some knowledge in a form of a conceptual model. We have then to enrich that model with enterprise applications best practices (knowledge coming from users). Finally, we make explicit all disclosed knowledge hidden in the resulting model.

3 Our Approach for Semantics Enactment in Conceptual Models

In order to cooperate, two (or more) Information Systems have to interoperate. As previously discussed, we focus our interest on the conceptual level of interoperability letting different information systems to share and use knowledge models that they represent. Our principal issues are, therefore, first to understand the conceptual relationships between those models in the context of their use and secondly how, through conceptualisation, to unhide the tacit knowledge buried inside them. A usual approach for making explicit the tacit knowledge, concealed in attributes and classes, is the relationships-oriented perspective composed of a set of transformation rules. In that transformation method, an attribute a_1 of type T_1 pertaining to a class C_1 is modelled as a relationship between the class C_1 and a standard type T_1. This approach does not resolve entirely the semantics elicitation problem because it focuses its point of view on the values instead of on the concepts. The attribute semantics is somewhat yet hidden in the relationship just created.

In literature, [27] presented the definition of two different objects types, *a lexical object (LOT),* a term, *is an object in a certain reality that can be written down. LOTs always consist of letters, numbers, symbols or other characters. They can be used as names for or references to other objects. A non-lexical object (NOLOT),* a concept, *is an object in a certain reality that cannot be written down. Non-lexical objects must be named by lexical objects or referred to by means of lexical objects.*

Applying these definitions, we can flatten the nested knowledge embedded in a model to simplify semantic enactment resulting from a set of modelling transformations. Our contribution is to have at our disposal an approach letting us to fragment knowledge through the transformation of attributes into entities and relationships, and thus to emphasize some fine-grained knowledge atoms. In the proposed approach, that is the first part (Figure 1) of our general methodology, the starting point can be various: an application, a data model, a logical view, a model. We have already mentioned that there are several reverse engineering methods, such as in [13] and in [9], through which a model from the application or schema level can be derived (Step 1). Then, the resulted initial model is enriched and corrected through an Expert Knowledge Injection step (Step 2). In fact, the model is examined with the help of a domain expert or an end-user, who are the most qualified persons to describe the context of the peculiar domain and to put in evidence the contextual knowledge. According to the enterprise best practices and its data, they would clean and better organise the knowledge represented in the derived model. However, the obtained

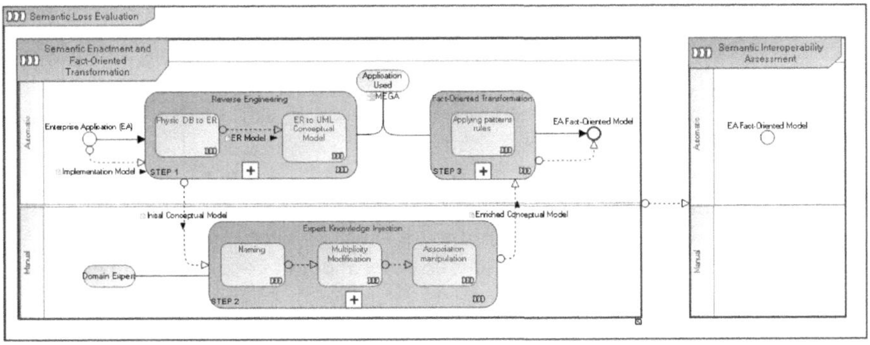

Fig. 1. Conceptualisation approach

initial conceptual model, in the form of a UML class diagram, has yet a major limit. In fact, its semantics is in a tacit form because all the attributes are buried inside single classes and it is then difficult to make their semantics explicit.

Thus, the next step of our approach (Step 3) is a Fact-Oriented Transformation [16] through the application of a set of rules for transforming the enriched conceptual model to a fact-oriented model (FOM) with its semantics completely displayed. The consequence is that all the classes and their attributes are transformed into respectively LOTs and NOLOTs objects. The resulting fact-oriented model, displaying the finest-grained semantic atoms, is then used as an input for the second part of our methodology for semantic loss evaluation (not presented in this paper).

In the following sub-sections, we will discuss, in detail, the proposed 3 steps.

3.1 Step 1: Reverse Engineering

Conceptualisation is a decision process [15], a view, in which studied part of reality knowledge, usually in an implicit and complex form, is reorganised in different aggregates usually simpler to be represented.

According to [11], developing conceptual models means specifying the essential objects or components of the system to be studied, the relationships of the objects that are recognised and what kinds of changes in the objects or their relationships affect the functioning of the system and in which ways.

Conceptual models range in type from the more precise, such as the mental image of a familiar physical object, to the abstractness of mathematical models that do not appear to the mind as an image. Conceptual models also range in terms of the scope of the subject matter that they are taken to represent. The variety and scope of conceptual models is due to the variety of purposes that people had while using them.

Conceptualisation approaches are numerous and have been developed in different knowledge domains [23].

Our scenario assumes that we start from enterprise application database. So, the first studied approach is the Reverse engineering. It is, in database (DB) community, an approach to extract the domain semantics from the existing database structures. Typically, it concerns making the reverse transformation from logical to conceptual schema. In [13], the authors propose a general algorithm based on several old attempts to make explicit the logical structure buried into DB schemas, application programs and in the minds of designers and developers. [9] presents a methodology for extracting an extended Entity-Relationship model from a relational database, through a combination of data schema and data instance analysis. In our study we will consider at profit the reverse engineering experiences developed in the past. These methods are, by now, acquired by the software industry that produces countless tools. We choose MEGA Suite (http://www.mega.com), a modelling management environment to transform relational models into conceptual ones. MEGA Suite implements a parameterised reverse engineering method coping with major existing approaches from direct database metadata analysis to a semi-automatic conceptual models building from existing database schemas.

3.2 Step 2: Expert Knowledge Injection

After the reverse engineering process has created a conceptual model, the current step concerns enriching it by injecting the enterprise knowledge, expressed by users' best practices or experts. These stakeholders know the domain peculiarities and they are capable to embed specific constraints into the new conceptual model. The first stage is the renaming process. Usually the database tables, and the derived concepts, have not standard names. The renaming process is essential to bring coherence and semantics in concepts that otherwise would be of very difficult comprehension. The following stage is the redefinition of the attributes and of the associations' roles multiplicities according to the enterprise users' best practices. This step is fundamental to define the real constraints that are not always made explicit into the implementation model. As an example, considering a particular attribute a_1, two cases can be considered:

1) a_1 is a non-mandatory attribute in the conceptual model but, as users are requested to always fill it with a specific value, the enriched model must formalise that this attribute a_1 is to be treated as mandatory;

2) a_1 is defined as mandatory in the conceptual model but, by practice, the users never care about its value and fill it with some dummy one. In such case, the enriched model may formalise that this attribute is not mandatory.

Note that the same cases may happen also to the roles of associations.

The last stage concerns of making explicit some implicit associations. Those implicit associations relate some concepts but they are defined only by enterprise practices even if they are not expressed in the model itself.

At this time, the enriched conceptual model formalises the whole application semantics (both the explicit one and the users' implicit one).

3.3 Step 3: Fact-Oriented Transformation

The quality of a conceptual model is often influenced by the conceptual language used for its specification. Most conceptual languages for data modelling are based on a version of Entity-Relationship modelling (E-R) [3] [10] [19]. However, these modelling languages are making a distinction between entities, attributes and relationships. On the contrary, in order to normalise the way that knowledge is represented, NIAM (Natural-language Information Analysis Method) [28] proposed to model the world in term of facts (either presenting terms (real things), or representing characteristics (attributes) of these real things), and relationships between facts. NIAM is attribute-free, it does not use explicitly the notion of attribute, treating all elementary facts as relationships. Some authors have extended the concepts and notations developed by NIAM with object orientation. It is the case of ORM (Object Role Modelling) [17]. Our purpose is to adapt this fact-oriented modelling approach to enriched conceptual models represented using the UML [31] class notation. Thus, we developed a set of transformation modelling rules, to be applied to selected UML patterns (Table 1).

Let us refer to the definitions of LOT and NOLOT facts given in the beginning of section 3. Transforming a particular conceptual model in a fact-oriented model must follow these rules:

1. all classes are transformed into LOT facts. Using UML Class notation, a LOT fact is represented by a UML Class.
2. all attributes are transformed into NOLOT facts. Using the UML Class notation, a NOLOT fact is represented as a UML Class.
3. for each attribute *a* belonging to a UML Class *C*, an association is created between the corresponding LOT *a* and the corresponding NOLOT *C*, created by the two previous rules.
4. the multiplicity associated to each attribute *a* is copied as the multiplicity of the role of the previous (rule 3) association attached to the NOLOT *a*. The opposite role of the same association must have a constraint multiplicity equal to one.
5. all "simple" associations between classes are transformed into "simple" associations between NOLOTs.
6. all generalisation relationships between classes are transformed into "simple" associations with a constraint multiplicity equal to one on the role attached to generalised NOLOT and a non constraint multiplicity equal to * on the opposite role. In order to trace the fact that this association was coming from a generalisation, we annotate semantically the new corresponding association with a logical rule using OCL (Object Constraint Language) notation. Moreover, the inheritance feature of the generalisation association is mapped as new associations between LOTs representing the attributes of the generalised NOLOT, and all the specialised NOLOTs (sub-classes).
7. composition and aggregation relationships are transformed into simple association (rule 3) that keep unchanged the existing roles' multiplicities but trace their specific semantics through an attached semantic annotation formalised with an OCL logical rule.
8. association classes are transformed into a LOT fact with two associations linked to the corresponding initial LOT facts. The multiplicities of the roles of these two associations are determined inverting the ones initially formalised on the roles of the previous association.
9. any other specific constraints (generally modelled using OCL logical rules) are kept during the transformation process.
10. we did not take into account special cases of constraints in generalisations because they are not usually used in data conceptual modelling.

One of the conceptual modelling requirements is that a conceptual model must have formal foundations, which allow comparing that model with other conceptual models in a formal and exact way.

3.4 Patterns Represented in FOL

[4] and [38] formalise UML class constructs semantics in First Order Language (FOL) axioms. We propose to adapt these works to formalise the fact-oriented model patterns (presented previously) in FOL axioms.

We will present only one pattern rule formalisation in FOL: the "Class and Attributes" rule as presented in Table 1.

A class in UML designates a set of object with common features. Formally a *class C* corresponds to a FOL *unary predicate C.*

An *attribute a* of type *T* for a *class C* associates to each instance of *C* a set of instance of *T*, its multiplicity *[i..j]* specifies that *a* associates to each instance of *C* at least *i* and at most *j* instances of *T*. Formally, an attribute *a* of type *T* for *class C* corresponds to a binary predicate.

An association in UML is a relation between the instances of two or more classes. The multiplicity *[m..n]* attached to the role of a binary association specifies that each instance of the class *C* can participate at least *m* times and at most *n* times to the related association.

Table 1. Fact-Oriented modelling patterns using UML notation

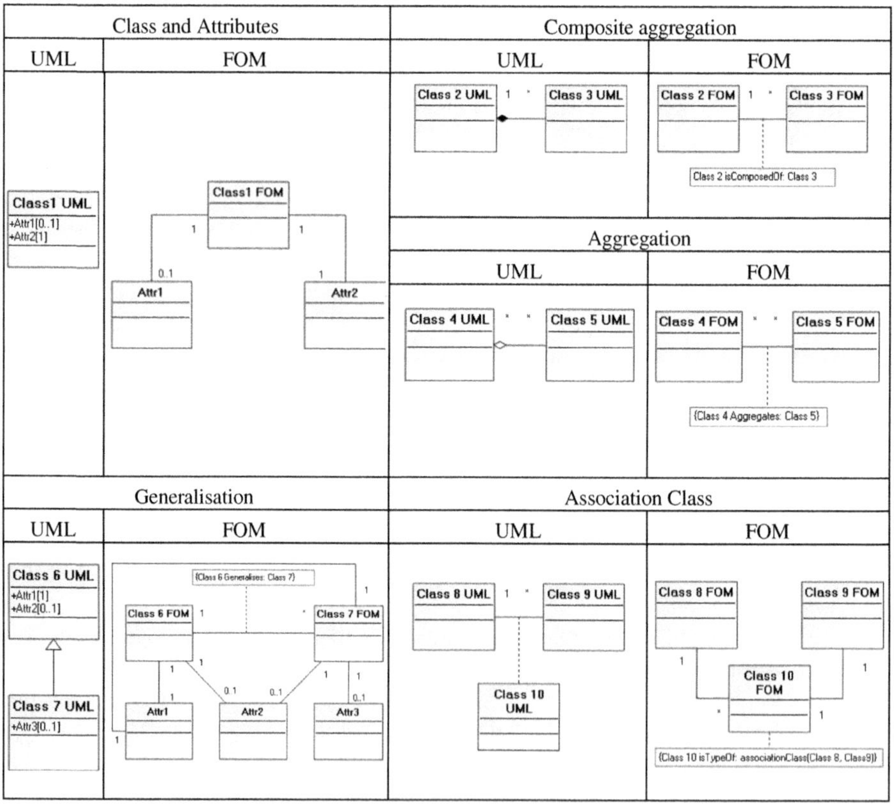

An association A between two classes can be formalised as a binary predicate. In the studied pattern, we formalise a class C_1 containing two attributes A_1 and A_2 with respectively a multiplicity of 1 and [0..1], and with associated types respectively, A_1Type and A_2Type.

Its formalisation in FOL assertions is the following:

$$\forall x, y, (C_1(x) \wedge A_1(x, y)) \supset A_1Type(y)$$
$$\forall x, z, (C_1(x) \wedge A_2(x, z)) \supset A_2Type(z)$$
$$\forall x, C_1(x) \supset (1 \{y | A_1(x, z)\})$$
$$\forall x, C_1(x) \supset (0 \leq 1 \{y | A_1(x, y)\})$$

Applying the transformation rule, presented in section 3.3, to the class C_1, and to the two attributes A_1 and A_2, we will obtain the Fact-Oriented Model (FOM) in UML notation as shown in Table 1 "Class and Attributes".

Its formalisation in FOL assertions is the following:

$$\forall x_1, x_2, Assoc_1(x_1, x_2) \supset C_1(x_1) \wedge A_1(x_2)$$
$$\forall x_1, C_1(x_1) \supset (1 \{y | Assoc_1(x_1, y)\})$$
$$\forall x_2, A_1(x_2) \supset (1 \{y | Assoc_1(x_2, y)\})$$
$$\forall x_1, x_2, Assoc_2(x_1, x_2) \supset C_1(x_1) \wedge A_2(x_2)$$
$$\forall x_1, C_1(x_1) \supset (0 \leq 1 \{y | Assoc_2(x_1, y)\})$$
$$\forall x_2, A_2(x_2) \supset (1 \{y | Assoc_2(x_2, y)\})$$

We used as demonstration tools Prover9, an automated theorem prover for first-order and equational logic, and Mace4 searcher for finite models and counterexamples. We implemented our models in prover9 syntax to verify them in FOL formalised transformation models rules.

These artefacts are the constituent basis to represent the transformation rules in First Order Logic. After the translation, we own two sets of FOL expression facts. We named them A and B. They represent the formalised semantics of UML and FOM models. They can be used to verify the models semantic equality. We will use a standard verification algorithm based on set theory. The verification algorithm takes as input assumptions the two expression sets, A and B.

The goal of the verification task is to demonstrate $\forall x\, A(x) \wedge \neg B(x) \rightarrow \emptyset$.

With this evaluation method we are able to demonstrate that the semantics formalised in the initial conceptual model is equivalent or included into the one transformed in FOM and so it is sufficient for our verification purpose.

4 Case Study

Interoperability between organisational and manufacturing activities is crucial in manufacturing enterprises. Production services have to produce, quickly and efficiently, the good product at the right moment. For this reason, they need at time information coming from others services, which need in return precise and update data on production.

We propose here to study and present the first part of such a B2M interoperability issue by considering a particular IS implemented in a real manufacturing environment: Sage X3 as an Enterprise Resource Planning (ERP) application.

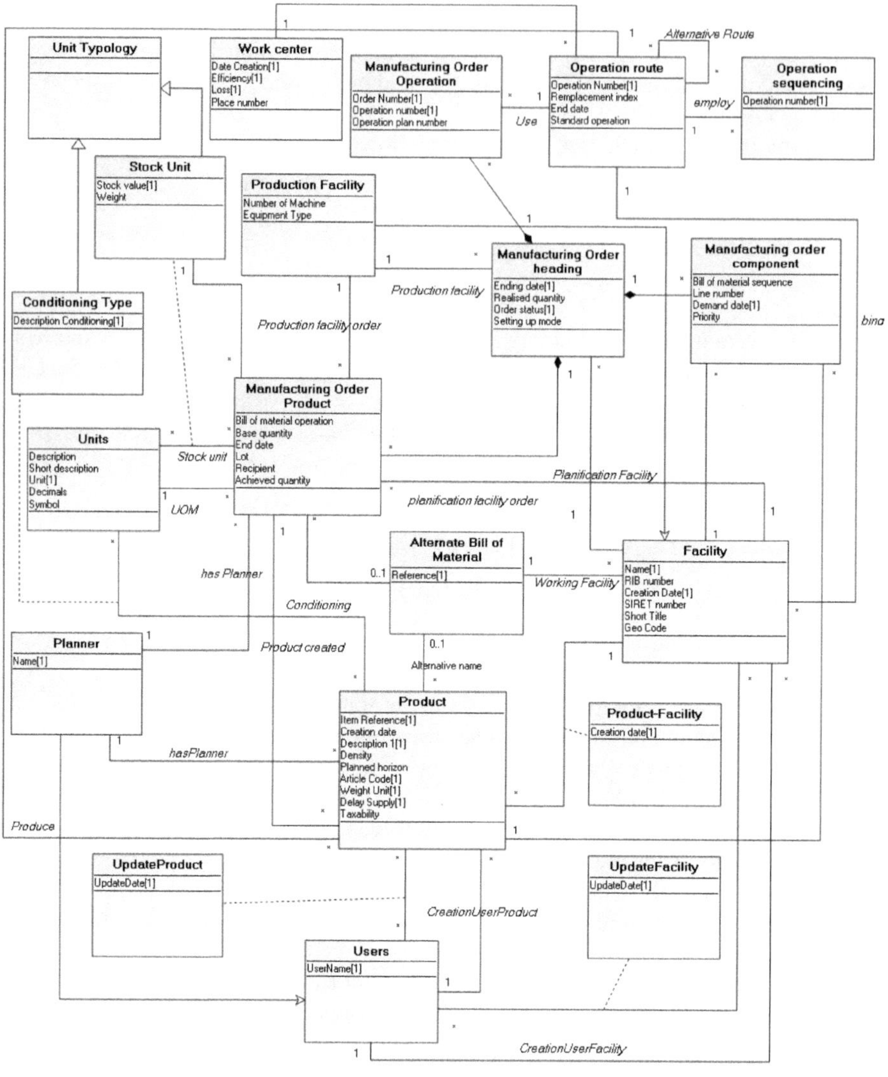

Fig. 2. Sage X3 work order enriched process model

4.1 Specific Analysed Enterprise Information System: Sage X3 ERP

An Enterprise Resource Planning (ERP) is an integrated computer-based system used to manage internal and external resources including tangible assets, financial resources, materials, and human resources [6]. Its purpose is to facilitate the flow of information between all business functions inside the boundaries of the organization and manage the connections to outside stakeholders. Built on a centralized database, ERP systems centralise all business operations into a uniform system environment. Sage X3 presents different enterprise management functions: finance, commercial, industrial and services.

The focus for this case study is (i) to analyse how the work order process inside the Sage X3 application is modelled, (ii) to use the proposed modelling process to externalise the implicit knowledge in the model structure.

The model depicted in figure 2 is already the result from the two first steps of our approach. This means that we have already passed the "Reverse Engineering" and the "Expert knowledge injection" stages. The "Manufacturing Order Heading" concept is the management function of production orders and planned activities. It allows the generation of a production order by variation of one or more classifications and a single production line. For each production order, the achievement of the material benefits and sequencing operations is possible. This block captures general information about the work order, such as, planning facility and facility of production, status of the order (manufacturing order product). It allows entering general information about the production order. The availability of components is checked through the information given by the bill of material related with the launched products.

Once that initial information is determined, the system updates the list of materials and operations of the created or modified orders.

Step 1: Reverse Engineering. All these information are coded in the Sage application database. The first step of our method is the reverse engineering to extract the initial conceptual model.

Step 2: Expert Knowledge Injection. Currently the model depicted in Figure 2 is the result of the reverse engineering step enriched by a domain expert because the architecture of the Sage X3 ERP is built with all the database relationships implemented directly into the application layer and not in the database. The reverse engineering result, as shown in the lower part of the Figure 3, creates a model containing unlinked classes with coded names.

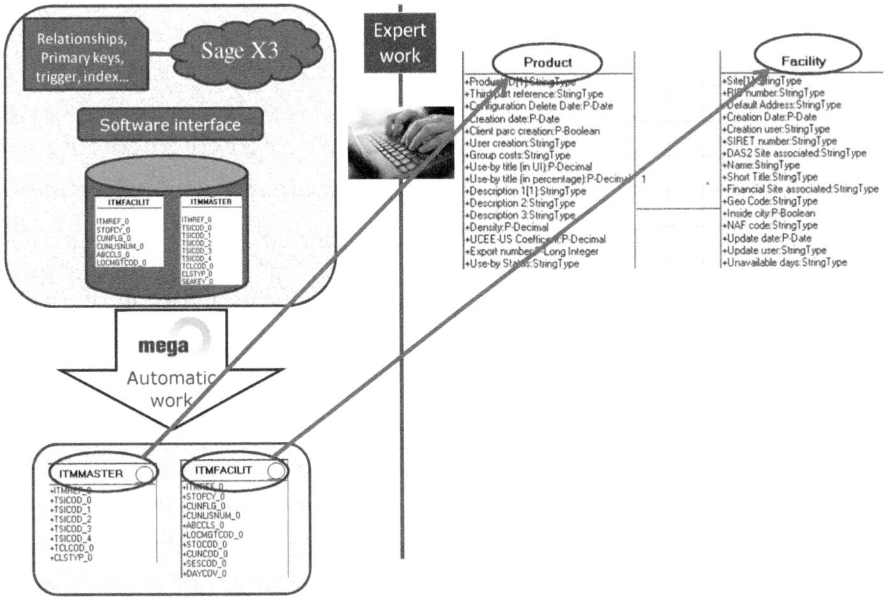

Fig. 3. Sage X3 architecture and expert knowledge injection

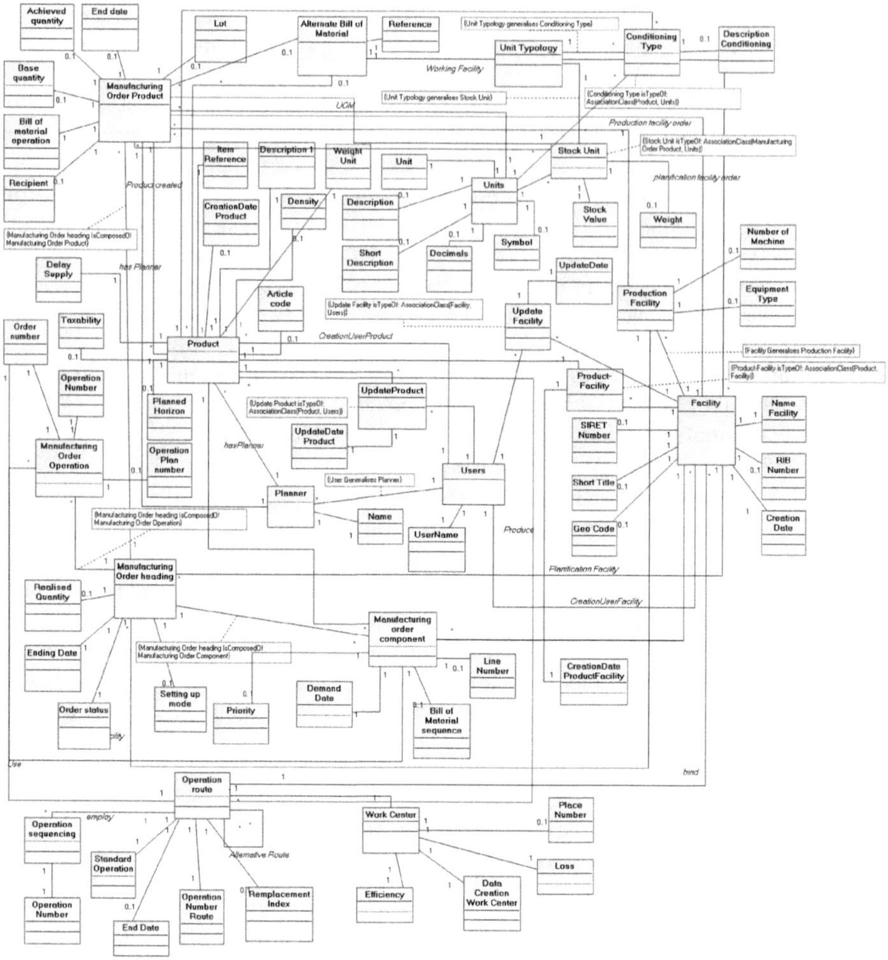

Fig. 4. Sage X3 work order process model part transformed with fact-oriented approach

The expert work was about cleaning this conceptual model according to the best practices in the enterprise, modifying the attributes multiplicity, adding explicit names to the concepts, the attributes and the associations and others operations to fit the conceptual model to the "real" use of the Enterprise Information System. A usual case that requests the domain expert attention is about the mandatory properties in forms' attributes.

Step 3: Fact-Oriented Transformation. Applying the pattern transformation rules, presented in the previous section, class attributes are transformed into NOLOTs to increase the atomic representation of the knowledge embedded into the model. These rules have been coded using a programming language and then automatically executed inside MEGA Suite.

Figure 4 shows an extract of the resulting FOM after applying our approach to the Sage X3 work order process. The resulting full FOM is composed of 23 NOLOTs, 56

LOTs and 46 associations. It seems then that the resulting model is much more complex than the initial one, which it is true in a visual point of view but it is false in term of expressiveness of its semantics. Indeed, the fine-grained atoms of semantics are now made explicit, which helps any automatic computing. An important result is that such semantically detailed model will help automating the next part of our methodology for semantic gap evaluation, as presented in [41].

5 Conclusions

In this article, a conceptualisation approach for enacting implicit semantics from Enterprise Information Systems is proposed. Our approach if divided into 3 steps from the traditional reverse engineering process, through a knowledge elicitation and model enrichment by domain experts, till making use of fact-oriented modelling patterns to externalise tacit knowledge. These patterns have been formalised in FOL axioms to verify their semantic coherence. Our contribution can be assimilated to a reverse engineering methodology. However, the main objective is to formalize the whole semantics of such models in order to help automatic knowledge computing. An industrial case study, related to an enterprise information system implemented into an ERP system demonstrates the applicability of our approach.

Our current work concerns applying this approach for evaluating the (non)-interoperation through the measurement of the semantic gap occurring between CISs interoperability [40] and [41].

References

1. Aspray, W.F.: The Scientific Conceptualization of Information: A Survey. Annals of the History of Computing 7, 117–140 (1985)
2. Badia, A.: Conceptual Modeling for Semistructured Data. In: Proceedings of the 3rd International Conference on Web Information Systems Engineering Workshops (WISE 2002 Workshops), Singapore, pp. 170–177 (2002)
3. Barker, R.: CASE* Method: Entity Relationship Modelling. Addison-Wesley, Wokingham (1990)
4. Berardi, D., Calvanese, D., De Giacomo, G.: Reasoning on UML class diagrams. Artificial Intelligence 168(1-2), 70–118 (2005)
5. Bézivin, J., Kurtev, I.: Model-based Technology Integration with the Technical Space Concept. In: Proceedings of the Metainformatics Symposium, Esbjerg, Denmark, November 8-11. Springer (2005)
6. Bidgol, H.: The Internet Encyclopedia, vol. 1, p. 707. John Wiley & Sons, Inc. (2004)
7. Carney, D., Fisher, D., Morris, E., Place P.: Some current Approaches to Interoperability. Technical note CMU/SEI-2005-TN-033 (2005)
8. Chen, D., Dassisti, M., Elvesaeter, B., Panetto, H., et al.: DI.2: Enterprise Interoperability Framework and knowledge corpus, Interoperability Research for Networked Enterprises Applications and Software Network of Excellence, IST 508-011 (2006)
9. Chiang Roger, H.L., Barron, T.M., Storey Veda, C.: Reverse engineering of relational databases: Extraction of an EER model from a relational database. Data & Knowledge Engineering 12(2), 107–142 (1994)

10. Czejdo, B., Elmasri, R., Rusinkiewicz, M., Embley, D.W.: A graphical data manipulation language for an extended entity-relationship model. IEEE Computer, 26–37 (March 1990)
11. Engelbart, D.C.: Augmenting human intellect: a conceptual framework. Stanford Research Institute, Menlo Park (1962)
12. Euzenat, J.: Towards a principled approach to semantic interoperability. In: CEUR Proceedings of the IJCAI 2001 Workshop on Ontologies and Information Sharing, Seattle, USA, August 4-5, vol. 47, pp. 19–25 (2001) ISSN 1613-0073
13. Fonkam, M.M., Gray, W.A.: An Approach to Eliciting the Semantics of Relational Databases. In: Loucopoulos, P. (ed.) CAiSE 1992. LNCS, vol. 593, pp. 463–480. Springer, Heidelberg (1992) ISBN 3-540-55481-5
14. Frankel, D.S.: Model Driven Architecture: Applying MDA to Enterprise Computing. John Wiley & Sons (2003)
15. Guarino, N.: Formal Ontology in Information Systems (Ed.). IOS Press (1998)
16. Halpin, T.A.: A Fact-Oriented Approach to Schema Transformation. In: Thalheim, B., Gerhardt, H.-D., Demetrovics, J. (eds.) MFDBS 1991. LNCS, vol. 495. Springer, Heidelberg (1991)
17. Halpin, T.: In: Bernus, P., Mertins, K., Schmidt, G. (eds.) Handbook on Architectures of Information Systems, ch. 4. Springer, Berlin (1998)
18. Henrard, L., Hainaut, J.-L.: Data Dependency Elicitation in Database Reverse Engineering Software Maintenance and Reengineering. In: Fifth European Conference on Software Maintenance and Reengineering, p. 11 (2001)
19. Hohenstein, U., Engels, G.: Formal semantics of an entity-relationship-based query language. In: Kangassalo, H. (ed.) Proc. 9th ER Conf. on Entity-Relationship Approach: The Core of Conceptual Modelling. Elsevier Science Pub., Amsterdam (1991)
20. IEEE: Standard Computer Dictionary. A Compilation of IEEE Standard Computer Glossaries, NY. 610-1990 (1990). ISBN: 1559370793
21. International Organization for Standardization. ISO 14528: Industrial Automation Systems – Concepts and rules for Enterprise Models, TC 184/SC5/WG1, Geneva, Switzerland (1999)
22. International Organization for Standardization. ISO 16100: Manufacturing Software Capability Profiling for interoperability. In Part 1: Framework, TC 184/SC5/WG4, Geneva, Switzerland (2002)
23. LaOngsri, S.: Semantic Extensions and a Novel Approach to Conceptual Modelling, Ph.D. Thesis, School of Computer Science, Engineering and Mathematics, The Flinders University of South Australia (2009)
24. Lezoche, M., Panetto, H., Aubry, A.: Conceptualisation approach for Cooperative Information Systems interoperability. In: 13th International Conference on Enterprise Information Systems ICEIS, Beijing, P.R. China, pp. 101-110 (2011), doi:10.5220/0003508401010110
25. Mani, M.: ERеX: A Conceptual Model for XML. In: Bellahsène, Z., Milo, T., Rys, M., Suciu, D., Unland, R. (eds.) XSym 2004. LNCS, vol. 3186, pp. 128–142. Springer, Heidelberg (2004)
26. Manola, F., Miller, E.: RDF Primer. World Wide Web Consortium, Recommendation REC-rdf-primer-20040210 (2004)
27. De Bo, J., Spyns, P., Meersman, R.: Creating a "DOGMAtic" Multilingual Ontology Infrastructure to Support a Semantic Portal. In: Meersman, R. (ed.) OTM-WS 2003. LNCS, vol. 2889, pp. 253–266. Springer, Heidelberg (2003)
28. Nijssen, G.M., Halpin, T.A.: Conceptual Schema and Relational Database Design. Prentice Hall, Sydney (1989)

29. Obrst, L.: Ontologies for semantically interoperable systems. In: Proceedings of the 12th International Conference on Information and Knowledge Management, New Orleans, USA (2003)
30. OMG. Object Management Group. Architecture-Driven Modernization specification (2003), http://adm.omg.org
31. OMG. Object Management Group. UML 2.0 Superstructure Specification (2004), http://uml.omg.org
32. Rumbaugh, J., Blaha, M., Premerlani, W., Eddy, F., Lorensen, W.: Object Oriented Modeling and Design. Prentice Hall, New York (1991)
33. Russel, S., Norvig, P.: Artificial Intelligence. A Modern Approach. Prentice-Hall, Inc. (1995)
34. Seeley, R.S.: Manufacturing execution systems in Med. Device Diagn. Ind. 19(11), 64–68 (1997)
35. Sheth, A.: Changing Focus on Interoperability in Information Systems: From System, Syntax, Structure to Semantics. In: Goodchild, M., Egenhofer, M., Fegeas, R., Kottman, C. (eds.) Interoperating Geographic Information Systems, pp. 5–30. Kluwer (1998)
36. Smith, M.K., Welty, C., McGuinness, D.L.: OWL Web Ontology Language Guide. World Wide Web Consortium, Recommendation REC-owl-guide-20040210 (2004)
37. Tolk, A., Diallo, S.Y., Turnitsa, C.D.: Applying the Levels of Conceptual Interoperability Modelling Support of Integrability, Interoperability, and Composability for System-of-Systems Engineering. Journal of Systemics, Cybernetics and Informatics 5(5), 65–74 (2007)
38. Tursi, A., Panetto, H., Morel, G., Dassisti, M.: Ontological approach for Products-Centric Information System Interoperability in Networked Manufacturing Enterprises. IFAC Annual Reviews in Control 33(2), 238–245 (2009) ISSN: 1367-5788
39. Vyvyan, E.: Lexical Concepts, Cognitive Models and Meaning-Construction. Cognitive Linguistics 17(4), 491–534 (2006)
40. Yahia, E., Lezoche, M., Aubry, A., Panetto, H.: Semantics enactment in Enterprise Information Systems. In: 18th IFAC World Congress, Milan, Italy. IFAC PapersOnline (2011)
41. Yahia E.: Contribution à l'Evaluation de l'Interopérabilité Sémantique entre Systèmes d'Information d'Entreprises: Application aux Systèmes d'Information de Pilotage de la Production. PhD Thesis, Université Henri Poincaré, Nancy I (2011) (in French)

Incorporating Data Concerns into Query Languages for Data Services*

Muhammad Intizar Ali[1], Reinhard Pichler[1],
Hong-Linh Truong[2], and Schahram Dustdar[2]

[1] Database and Artificial Intelligence Group, Vienna University of Technology, Vienna, Austria
[2] Distributed Systems Group, Vienna University of Technology, Vienna, Austria
{intizar,pichler}@dbai.tuwien.ac.at,
{truong,dustdar}@infosys.tuwien.ac.at

Abstract. More and more organizations provide their data on the web via data services – also referred to as Data as a Service (DaaS). Data services combine the strength of database systems and query languages on the one hand with the benefits of service-oriented architecture on the other hand. Data services are increasingly used for data integration. The data provided via data services is often associated with data concerns like privacy, licensing, pricing, quality of data, etc. Hence, data integration tools not only have to mitigate the heterogeneity in data formats and query languages. In addition, also the various data concerns should be preserved when data is published and utilized. Moreover, data service selection and data selection should be based on these data concerns. Current Data Integration systems using data services lack the ability to preserve data concerns while querying multiple services in an integrated environment. In this paper, we design a new querying system which takes data concerns into account. To this end we discuss several models of data concern aware querying and select the best suited one for our system. We describe a querying system where data concern awareness is integrated directly into the XQuery language. We also report on an implementation and experimental evaluation of this system.

1 Introduction

More and more data providers are reaping the benefits of Web 2.0 technology and provide their data on the web either through web services, APIs (REST/SOAP), or data services – also referred to as *Data as a Service* (DaaS) [1,2]. Data services combine the strength of database systems and query languages on the one hand with the benefits of service-oriented architecture on the other hand. Many big companies have started to publish their data via query interfaces (rather than simple forms in html) so that the data can be easily reused, composed and integrated with other data sources. Amazon Public Data Sets on AWS [1], Google Squared [2] and UN data API's [3] are some prominent examples of publicly available data services.

* This work was supported by the Vienna Science and Technology Fund (WWTF), project ICT08-032.

[1] http://aws.amazon.com/publicdatasets/

[2] http://www.google.com/squared

[3] http://www.undata-api.org/

R. Zhang et al. (Eds.): ICEIS 2011, LNBIP 102, pp. 132–145, 2012.

Data services are increasingly used for data integration. Many tools and techniques are available to dynamically compose, integrate and execute different data services or sources[3,4]. These tools help to create situational applications by composing existing data services. The data thus published and processed is often associated with data concerns like privacy, licensing, pricing, quality of data, etc. Hence, data integration tools not only have to mitigate the heterogeneity in data formats and query languages. In addition, also the various data concerns should be preserved when data is published and utilized. Moreover, data service selection and data selection should be based on these data concerns. Consider for example, a meta-search query (a query that is posed against many data sources and selects the best possible integrated results among them). A user query will be executed on multiple data services registered at the integrated application. After integrating the results of all the data services, usually top-k results (where k is a constant value defined by the application) are returned. Now consider that different users have different priorities for the data selection, e.g., one user may be more interested in quality of data while another user is more concerned about the pricing. There is a clear need for an explicit system that (semi)automatically selects the most appropriate data service as well as data items for each user according to various data concerns.

Some data concerns like data quality, privacy, and quality of service (QoS) have long been studied in their respective domains of databases, data mining and web services. However, data services are different. Recently, the importance of distinguishing data services from web services has been recognized [5]. For instance, while licensing and quality of data are usually *static* for web services, they are dynamic for data services. Indeed, as the data gets "older", the licensing and the data quality (of which the up-to-dateness may be an important aspect) will most probably change. Moreover data concerns can be dynamically updated. Hence static information about usage permission or privacy cannot deal with the requirements of the dynamic integration application created by composing data services on the fly. Hence, new techniques are required to integrate data concerns into data services.

Among the various data concerns, *privacy* has received most attention. It has been studied in many different areas like data integration [6,7], data mining [8], and web services [9,10]. In [11] and similarly in [12], privacy has been studied in the context of data services. However a systematic integration of data concern awareness into data services is still missing to date. Moreover, previous approaches of dealing with data concerns like privacy do not directly integrate the data concern awareness into the query language, even though this would be very important for enabling the querying system to select the best suited data source for various parts of a given query. The goal of this work is to design a querying system (i) which can take arbitrary data concerns into account, (ii) which integrates the data concern awareness into the query language, and (iii) which automatically selects the appropriate data sources depending on current context, user requirements and data concerns.

Structure and Summary of Results. The main results of this paper are as follows.

- ***Roles and Concerns.*** In Section 2, we lay the foundations of our study by identifying the actors involved in data services and their specific concerns. In contrast to common web services, there are normally *three* actors involved, namely consumer, service provider, and also a data provider.

- ***Models.*** In Section 3, we present four possible models of data concern aware querying. We discuss the characteristics and virtues of each model and select the best suited one for our system.

- ***System.*** In Section 4, we come up with our data concern aware querying system. We describe how meta-data is organized and stored by this system and how data concern awareness is integrated directly into the XQuery language.

- ***Implementation and Evaluation.*** We report on an implementation of our data concern aware querying system and an evaluation on benchmark tests in Section 5.

- ***Conclusion.*** Finally, in Section 6, we give a conclusion and point out directions for future work.

Related Work. In [5], the authors give an overview of data concerns and discuss the different parties and their roles in data service creation and utilization. As mentioned above, there have been attempts to incorporate privacy concerns into data services [11,12]. Data source selection has been long discussed in the database and information retrieval community and different algorithms have been developed for optimal selection of the database [13]. Different frameworks and techniques are available for the best service selection in a web service environment [14]. In [15], the authors consider user preferences for data source selection while [16] used QoS attribute for the service selection. Selection of data services based on data concerns has not been considered so far. A query language extension method has been used to provide additional functionality for the integrated applications. A framework for data quality aware queries is presented by extending SQL query language [17] while privacy aware querying language has been designed for preserving privacy in distributed query evaluation [18]. To the best of our knowledge, there is no querying system available for data concern aware querying to integrate data services.

2 Data Services: Roles and Data Concerns

The concept of data services is based upon the service-oriented architecture (SOA), which includes standardized processes for accessing data "where it resides" irrespective of the platform. Data services take advantage of service-oriented architecture to offer users a mediator for integrating information from database systems and other structured or non-structured data sources. Data services thus realize a layer of software between the physical, distributed data sources and the applications or services which want to access the data. The data is exposed to the customer via a virtual data model. It is the responsibility of the data service to connect to the back-end data sources via the available interfaces and to map the physical data schema to the virtual data model. The applications and services using the data service leverage this virtual data model to access the required information and the data service software handles the collection and distribution of the data as needed from the physical instances of the data. Figure 1 gives an overview of the conceptual architecture of the data services.

The traditional approach to the design of data services is that the service provider and consumer agree on how the service shall be used. The terms of this agreement

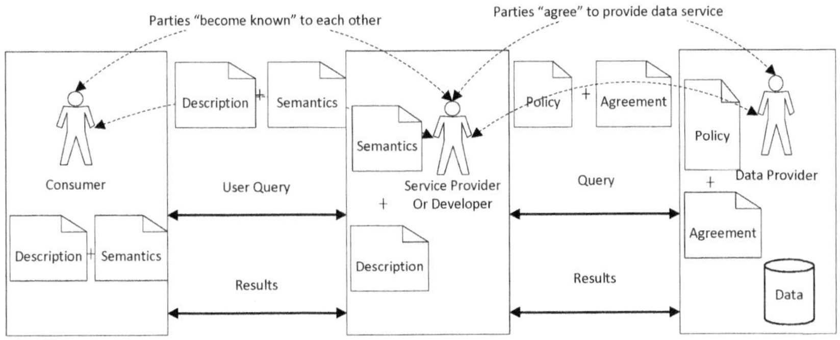

Fig. 1. Conceptual architecture of the data services

are usually static and are not altered over time. Typically, data services in the form of integration server products have connectors or adaptors built to connect applications together. A number of them have added or will add new connectors for data service applications such as salesforce (see `http://salesforce.com`). However, the static nature of agreements on data concerns is a severe drawback of the existing technology – in particular in dynamic data integration scenarios using mashups or cloud strategy. Moreover, several important aspects of data integration applications are not addressed in these solutions, such as (1) automatic updates, (2) changes of regulations, and (3) changes of the location of the data.

2.1 Roles of the Data Service

As can be seen in Figure 1, there are three actors involved in a data service architecture, namely Data Provider (DP), Service Provider (SP), and Consumer. Below we discuss each of them briefly.

Data Provider. The Data Provider is responsible to provide the actual data for the service. The DP is not necessarily the owner of the data, since data can also be outsourced. But it is the responsibility of the DP to ensure the availability of the data for the usage by the data service. All the concerns related to the data must also be communicated to the service provider. Some data concerns for the data provider like the privacy and permission concerns can vary from data item level to the whole data source level.

Service Provider. The Service Provider entity is the person or organization that provides an appropriate agent to implement a particular service. Service Provider is owner of the data service. After making the arrangement with the DP, the SP defines the functionality of the service. It is responsibility of the SP to make sure that all the concerns defined by the various data providers are preserved while the service is used.

Consumer. The consumer is a person or organization that wishes to make use of the data service. It will use a requester agent to exchange messages with the provider agent.

Table 1. Some data concerns associated with data services

Category	Scope	Data Concern	Description
Data Quality	Data Level	Timeliness	Defines the life time and freshness of the data
		Accuracy	Data correctness and consistency
		Completeness	Missing information in terms of null values etc.
		Availability	Defines possible access limitations
Quality of Service	Service Level	Performance	Defines performance of the data service, e.g. execution time, response time
		Reliability/availability	What is the failure probability and what is the recovery time in case of failure
		Dependability/Trust	Reputation, how trustful is the data service
		Service Location	Location of the service execution
License	Data Level	Usage Permission/Rights	How a data service can be used
		Data Location	Defines where the data resides
		Usage Fee	Defines the fee associated with the usage of the data or data service
		Law Enforcement	Defines laws which are used to deal with the use of the service

In most cases, the requester agent interacts with the provider agent to exchange messages. The requester entity and provider entity agree on the service description (e.g. a WSDL document) and the semantics that will govern the interaction between the requester agent and the provider agent.

2.2 Data Concerns for Data Services

Data services have different requirements and concerns compared with traditional web services. Data provided through data services is usually associated with many data concerns [5,19]. These concerns must be precisely described, organized and stored in such a way that the SP is capable of preserving these concerns while querying a data source.

For the sake of simplicity we have chosen a few of the most important concerns as shown in Table 1. Each concern can be categorized into a particular category depending on the type of the concern. We categorized the chosen data concerns into three categories namely (1) Data Quality, (2) Quality of Service, and (3) Licensing. Every category of the data concerns has its scope which will be either service level or data level (for further details, see Section 4.1). For example in Table 1, data concerns belonging to the category of quality of service have service level scope while data concerns belonging to the categories of data quality and licensing have data level scope.

2.3 DaaS Architecture with Data Concerns

Figure 2 describes the activities in a data service system with data concerns. As an initial step, both DP and SP mutually agree to provide the facility of the data service. The data provider is required to provide accessibility to its data for the service operations. The DP should provide a mechanism to access its data and additionally provide data

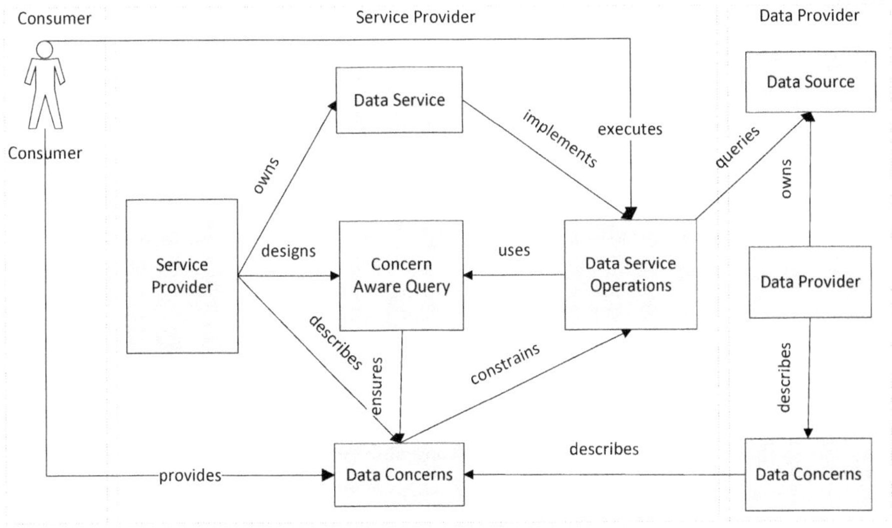

Fig. 2. Activities in data concern aware data service systems

concerns associated with the data. The user can also contribute to the data concerns meta-data by providing her preferences. Such information can be easily managed using profiling techniques. The service provider describes the service operations to access the data sources. This access can be realized via a query language, REST/SOAP or a parameterized query for structured data. The SP has to make sure that all the concerns defined by the DP are preserved.

3 Models of Data Concern Aware Querying

Figure 3 depicts four possible models for querying data services with concerns. As already discussed in Section 2 there are three actors/roles involved. For the sake of simplicity we assume that Data Provider and Service Provider have already agreed on the storage format of the data concerns: we assume that this information is stored in the form of an XML document whose schema will be described in Section 4.1.

The main difference between the models presented in Figure 3 is due to the way how the data concerns are associated with the queries that are posed against the data sources: The models in Figure 3(a) and (b) use the *"Querying With Concerns"* paradigm. In this case, the system sends a pair $\langle Q, C\rangle$ to the data source, where Q is the query for the data service and C is the collection of data concerns associated with the query. Each data service must be capable of preserving these concerns by using its own individual querying system. The models in Figure 3(c) and (d) are based on *"Concern Aware Querying"*. The service provider has the concerns either stored locally or fetched dynamically and is capable of writing queries in such a way that they preserves all the data concerns associated with the particular query and its relevant data source.

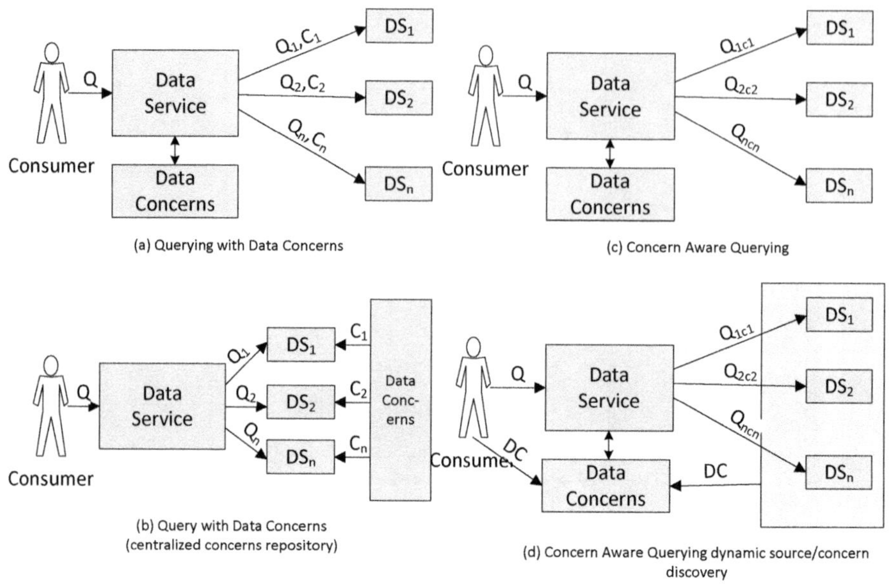

Fig. 3. Data concerns aware querying models

Below we briefly discuss each of the models shown in Figure 3

Model (a): Querying with Data Concerns. Figure 3(a) shows the basic model of querying with data concerns. DP and SP have mutually agreed and have accumulated their data concerns. These data concerns are stored by the SP. A user query Q is subdivided into multiple sub-queries for multiple data sources. The SP must be capable of retrieving the data concerns meta-data of a particular data source and attaching it to the query. The data provider must be capable of taking care of the supplied concerns while executing the query and returning the results.

Model (b): Query with Data Concerns with Centralized Repository. This model deals with the generic data concerns stored in a centralized repository. Such a model is best suited for an inter-organization data integration system, where data concerns are homogeneous for all of the data sources of the organization. As shown in Figure 3(b) this model is very similar to the existing data integration systems. The SP sends user queries to multiple data sources and assumes that the data sources are capable of preserving the data concerns by accessing a centralized repository of data concerns.

Model (c): Concern Aware Querying. The concern aware querying model of Figure 3(c) is a data service capable of re-writing user queries in such a way that all the concerns associated with a particular data service are incorporated into the query itself. All the data sources and their concerns are already registered at the SP and the required meta-data information is locally stored by the SP. The SP divides a user query into multiple sub-queries in such a way that all the applicable data concerns (which are stored within meta-data file locally stored at the SP) are incorporated into these sub-queries.

Model (d): Concern aware Querying Model with Dynamic Discovery. Contrary to the legacy data integration systems for databases, data services usually have no prior knowledge of the schema or the data source. Mostly data sources are discovered dynamically and the most suitable data source has to be selected. Of course, storing meta-data information of all data sources at internet scale is out of the question. Figure 3(d) shows the model for concern aware querying with dynamic discovery of data sources and their associated data concerns. The SP stores data concerns meta-data as in the concern aware querying model, but at the same time it is capable of discovering data services dynamically and creating meta-data of data concerns by fetching them dynamically. These concerns are then applied to queries for a particular data source. This model also allows the consumer to provide her concerns and preferences within the query.

4 Concern Aware Querying

For our system, we have chosen the concern aware querying model as shown in Figure 3(d) since it is the most flexible and most powerful of the models discussed in the previous section. Our system stores the meta-data information of the concerns of all three stake holders of the data service and is capable of querying data concerns dynamically. All the three actors of a data service have the possibility to contribute their concerns to the meta-data. Each data provider provides its data concerns associated with its data along with its data. Similarly each consumer has the option to add her preferences/concerns with her query. The service provider can add its concerns to form an aggregated data concerns meta-data which will be utilized by the query language to write concern aware queries. A data concern tree (dct) is generated from the available meta-data and is associated with each of the data sources.

We have extended the XQuery language to make it concern aware, with the introduction of special keywords for mentioning data concerns within the query. The query parser looks into the data concern trees attached to the available data sources and executes the query by selecting the most suitable data sources and data items for the particular user query. Below we discuss the concern aware querying system in detail.

4.1 Data Concerns Collection

For storing the meta-data information of data concerns of a particular data source, we have decided to use XML because of its standardization and platform independence. Figure 4 shows the schema definition for the meta-data for the concern aware querying. A data concern tree will be generated by using the meta-data information available in the attached XML file. The schema shown in Figure 4 describes the data concerns as shown in Table 1. The data concern collection file can be expanded to any number of concerns depending on the type and requirement of the SP or DP. The data concern tree can be subdivided into two categories based on the scope of the data concerns.

Service Level Concerns. Data concerns whose scope is the entire data service are called service level concerns. The data concerns tree of a data service contains exactly one value for any of the service level concerns. For instance, consider the performance concern of QoS category of a service. Clearly, a data service can have only one calculated value for its performance data concern.

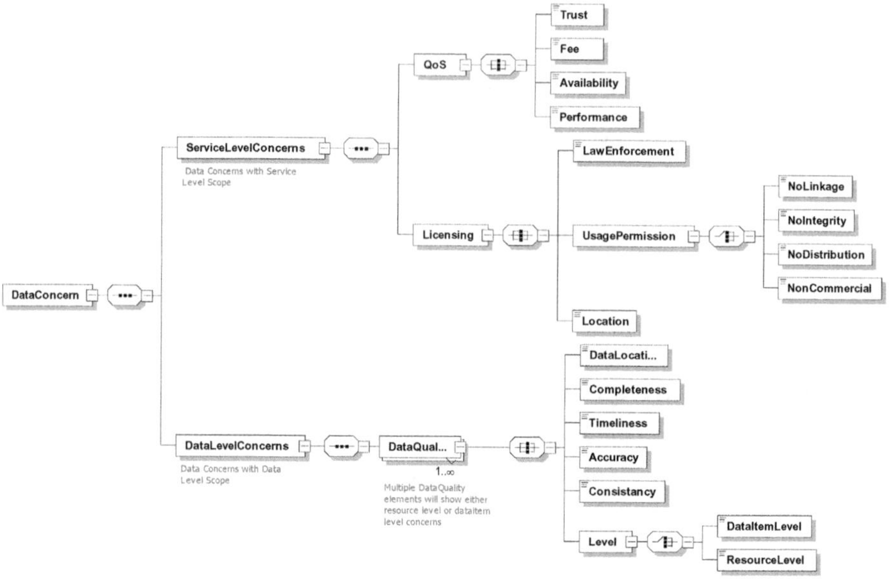

Fig. 4. Data Concerns Tree

Data Level Concerns. Data concerns whose scope is a single data item or a collection of data items are called data level concerns. Data level concerns can have multiple values in the data concern tree attached to some data source. If a data source returns a node or a list of nodes of an XML document as a result of a user query (written in XQuery), then a data level concern can be described for each of the nodes in this result and for each element in the subtrees rooted at these nodes.

The data concern tree is populated by the values of data concerns depending on the type of each data concern. There are two possible types of data concerns based on their value, namely (i) *boolean data concerns*, which can have either the value true or false, e.g. usage permission for commercial purposes can either be allowed or restricted by the data provider, and (ii) *value based data concerns*, which can have any value within a specific range e.g. the performance concern of QoS of a data service or the completeness concern of a data item can have a specific value inside a pre-described range. Different algorithms are available for the calculation of QoS values of a data service or data quality measurements for a data item, which is outside the scope of this paper. We assume that after applying any of the available algorithms and techniques a fixed value (positive integer) is provided for the value based data concerns within a range between 1 and 10, where 10 is the highest level.

4.2 Query Processing

If concern aware querying is used and a query contains data concerns, then the SP iterates through the data concern trees of all available data sources. Using data concern information provided in the query and the meta-data tree of data concerns, the data concern aware querying system is able to select the most suitable data service for a

```
input : Concern Aware Query Q, DS = {ds1, ds2,...,dsn}
output: DS′ ⊆ DS

DS′ = {ϕ};
for each dsi ∈ DS do
    flag = true;
    for each Q.SLCb do
        if Q.SLCb ≠ ds.SLCb then flag = false
        end
    end
    if flag == true then
        for each Q.SLCb do
            if Q.SLCv ≥ ds.SLCv then flag = false
            end
        end
    end
    if flag == true then DS′ ← dsi
    end
end
Return DS′;
```

Algorithm 1. Data Source Selection based on SLC

particular query. Algorithm 1 shows the data source selection by assuring both types (i.e., boolean and value based) of service level concerns. A concern aware query and a set of available data sources is provided as input. After evaluating the Algorithm 1, the most suitable data source or set of data sources (in case multiple data sources assure the desired concerns) is returned for data querying. Once the input is provided, the algorithm starts iterating through the available data sources. For each of the service level concerns mentioned inside a concern aware query the system verifies whether that particular service level concern is also supported by the data source. If a particular service level concern is supported by a certain data source, as a next step the system compares the required value of service level concern mentioned inside the query with the value of service level concern of the data source in its data concern tree. If both conditions are met, a data source is included in the list of suitable data sources for that particular query. Similarly, DLCs are also evaluated using the same technique mentioned in Algorithm 1 for data selection to assure data level concerns.

4.3 Concern Aware XQuery

We have chosen XQuery because it is the de facto standard language for XML data and because of its capability to execute distributed queries over heterogeneous data sources [20]. Now consider a dynamic data sources integration system as described in Figure 3(d), where a user query can be executed on multiple data sources which perform the same task and one data concern tree is attached to each data source. Current query languages for semi-structured data like XQuery or SPARQL need to provide the URI or location of the data source manually. In order to select the most appropriate data source from the available data sources which perform the same task, we have extended the XQuery syntax by providing additional keywords to make it concern aware.

For service level concerns we introduce a new keyword "SLC". A comma separated list of service level concerns inside square brackets will immediately follow the "doc" function of the XQuery language or wherever the URI for the location of data sources is provided. The syntax can be illustrated as

doc("xmldoc.xml")
SLC [ServiceLevelConcern1 op value, ... , ServiceLevelConcernN op value]

where N is a finite number of service level concerns in a concern aware query (formulated in XQuery) and op can be any of the basic comparison operators.

For data level concerns we used the simple notation of attaching each data level concern with the variables defined within concern aware XQuery. Variables having data level concerns will be written inside square brackets with one data level concern attached with the variable. The syntax can be illustrated as

[$varA.DataLevelConcern op value]

where $varA can be any variable defined within XQuery and op can be any of the basic comparison operators.

5 Implementation and Evaluation

5.1 Implementation

We have implemented a data concern aware XQuery tool to support the idea of concern aware querying. To store XML data sources, we use the open source native XML database system eXist-db[4] (release 1.4.0). Our concern aware querying tool prototype is implemented in Java (JDK 6) on top of the XQuery processing facility provided by eXist-db. When a concern aware query is submitted to the tool it implements the methods described above and selects the most suitable data sources for a particular query. Once the most suitable data sources have been selected, our tool excludes concern aware querying clauses and sends standard XQuery to the selected data sources.

Figure 5 shows a sample query over the XMARK benchmark data of a web application for auctions, which return a list of person names and items bought by them within Europe. A comma separated list of all the service level concerns is described within square brackets using additional keywords defined for the service level concerns immediately after the URL/location of the data source mentioned in XQuery. In the above example two service level concerns are evaluated. The statement "performance > 7" will select only those data services which have a performance attribute value greater than 7 in their data concern tree, while statement "CommercialUsagePermission=true" will make sure that data returned as a result from the query will have no restriction on the commercial usage of the data. For the purpose of simple illustration we allow using data level concerns related to particular data elements within an XQuery [QName.DLC]

[4] `http://exist.sourceforge.net/`

```
let $auction :=
doc("auction.xml") SLC[performance > 7,
CommercialUsagePermission = true]
 return let [$ca.timeliness] :=
$auction/site/closed_auctions/closed_auction return
let
    [$ei.completeness > 4] := $auction/site/regions/europe/item
for $p in $auction/site/people/person
let $a :=
  for $t in $ca
  where $p/@id = $t/buyer/@person
  return
    let $n := for $t2 in $ei
    where $t/itemref/@item = $t2/@id return $t2
    return <item>{$n/name/text()}</item>
return <person name="{$p/name/text()}">{$a}</person>
```

Fig. 5. Sample Concern Aware XQuery

as part of concern aware querying. For example the statement, "$ei.completeness > 4" in the above example of Figure 5 will make sure that only those values of the variable "ei" are selected which have completeness data concern value greater than 4. Boolean data concerns can have either a true or false value. Basic comparison operators can be applied for the calculation of value based data concerns.

5.2 Experimental Application: Distributed Extended XQuery for Data Integration (DeXIN)

Our data concern aware XQuery tool is built upon the DeXIN system [20,21], which is a web based system to integrate data over heterogeneous data sources. DeXIN extends the XQuery language to support SPARQL queries inside XQuery, thus facilitating the integration of data modeled in XML, RDF, and OWL. DeXIN supports the data integration of XML and RDF data without the need of transforming large data sources into common format. It is a powerful tool for knowledgeable users or web applications to facilitate querying XML data and reasoning over Semantic Web data simultaneously.

To build our data concern aware XQuery system, we have incorporated the data concern awareness into DeXIN. Now DeXIN can integrate heterogeneous distributed data sources while preserving their individual data concerns. It is worth mentioning that by incorporating data concerns into the DeXIN system not only XQuery capabilities are enhanced for data concern assurance but SPARQL is also enhanced with data concern awareness using the DeXIN tool.

5.3 Evaluation

In order to evaluate the performance and concreteness of our concern aware querying tool, we have conducted tests with realistically large data sets. As a proof of concept we

Table 2. Data sources with varying size and data concerns

Data Source Name	File Size	No. of Copies	No. of SLC	No. of DLC
Auction1.xml	30 MB	20	3	5
Auction2.xml	70 MB	30	3	8
Auction3.xml	100 MB	10	3	4

have evaluated our system on XML benchmark data. We used the XMARK [5] benchmark data set for experimental analysis. XMARK is a popular XML benchmark and models an internet auction application. We made three subsets of varying size of auction data provided by XMARK. Table 2 shows the details of the data services used for experimental analysis. We made further copies of the subset of the XMARK auction data and defined each as a data service. Each data service assures a varying number of service level concerns and data level concerns. The resulting data services were constructed with the same functionality but with different concerns.

Due to the unavailability of data services which support data concerns, we randomly generated data concern tree meta-data for each data service and assigned different values to both service and data level concerns. To assure the distribution of the data services we set up a testbed which includes 3 computers (Intel(R) Core(TM)2 CPU, 1.86 Ghz, 2GB RAM), one running SUSE Linux with kernel version 2.6 while the other two running Windows XP. The machines were connected over a standard 100Mbit/S network connection. An open sources native XML database eXist is installed on each system to store XML data. We utilize the eXist XQuery processor to execute XQuery queries.

We used 20 different sample queries [6] provided with the benchmark and executed each of them with different data concern values. There was no reported failure in the concern aware query execution and all the provided data concerns were assured, which proves the suitability of our tool and the potential for its incorporation into any data service integration application.

6 Conclusions and Future Work

In this work, we have designed a querying system which is capable of taking several kinds of data concerns into account. We have provided a basic model in which we concentrate on three concerns, namely data quality, quality of service, and licensing. However, our approach is generic in the sense that one can incorporate arbitrary data concerns. Indeed, one item on our agenda for future work will be to integrate further data concerns like pricing, data security, auditing model, etc. Another important goal for future work is the integration of our querying system into a powerful mash-up tool. So far, our querying system is designed to access data sources via XQuery. In the future, we want our system to access also data sources which expose their data via web services.

[5] `http://www.xml-benchmark.org/`

[6] `http://www.ins.cwi.nl/projects/xmark/Assets/xmlquery.txt`

References

1. Dan, A., Johnson, R., Arsanjani, A.: Information as a service: Modeling and realization. In: Proc. SDSOA 2007. IEEE Computer Society (2007)
2. Hacigümüs, H., Mehrotra, S., Iyer, B.R.: Providing database as a service. In: Proc. ICDE 2002. IEEE Computer Society (2002)
3. Mykletun, E., Tsudik, G.: Aggregation Queries in the Database-As-a-Service Model. In: Damiani, E., Liu, P. (eds.) DBSec 2006. LNCS, vol. 4127, pp. 89–103. Springer, Heidelberg (2006)
4. Virtuoso universal server, http://virtuoso.openlinksw.com/
5. Truong, H.L., Dustdar, S.: On analyzing and specifying concerns for data as a service. In: Proc. APSCC 2009, pp. 87–94. IEEE (2009)
6. Bhowmick, S.S., Gruenwald, L., Iwaihara, M., Chatvichienchai, S.: Private-iye: A framework for privacy preserving data integration. In: Proc. ICDE Workshops 2006, p. 91. IEEE Computer Society (2006)
7. Clifton, C., Kantarcioglu, M., Doan, A., Schadow, G., Vaidya, J., Elmagarmid, A.K., Suciu, D.: Privacy-preserving data integration and sharing. In: Proc. DMKD 2004, pp. 19–26. ACM (2004)
8. Zhang, N., Zhao, W.: Privacy-preserving data mining systems. IEEE Computer 40, 52–58 (2007)
9. Kobsa, A.: Tailoring Privacy to Users' Needs. In: Bauer, M., Gmytrasiewicz, P.J., Vassileva, J. (eds.) UM 2001. LNCS (LNAI), vol. 2109, pp. 303–313. Springer, Heidelberg (2001)
10. Creese, S., Hopkins, P., Pearson, S., Shen, Y.: Data Protection-Aware Design for Cloud Services. In: Jaatun, M.G., Zhao, G., Rong, C. (eds.) CloudCom 2009. LNCS, vol. 5931, pp. 119–130. Springer, Heidelberg (2009)
11. Mrissa, M., Tbahriti, S.E., Truong, H.L.: Privacy model and annotation for daas. In: Proc. ECOWS 2010, pp. 3–10. IEEE Computer Society (2010)
12. McSherry, F.: Privacy integrated queries: an extensible platform for privacy-preserving data analysis. In: Proc. SIGMOD 2009, pp. 19–30. ACM (2009)
13. French, J.C., Powell, A.L., Callan, J.P., Viles, C.L., Emmitt, T., Prey, K.J., Mou, Y.: Comparing the performance of database selection algorithms. In: Proc. SIGIR 1999, pp. 238–245. ACM (1999)
14. Maximilien, E.M., Singh, M.P.: A framework and ontology for dynamic web services selection. IEEE Internet Computing 8, 84–93 (2004)
15. Boulakia, S.C., Lair, S., Stransky, N., Graziani, S., Radvanyi, F., Barillot, E., Froidevaux, C.: Selecting biomedical data sources according to user preferences. In: ISMB/ECCB 2004, pp. 86–93 (2004)
16. Liu, Y., Ngu, A.H., Zeng, L.Z.: Qos computation and policing in dynamic web service selection. In: Proc. WWW Alt. 2004, pp. 66–73. ACM (2004)
17. Yeganeh, N.K., Sadiq, S.W., Deng, K., Zhou, X.: Data Quality Aware Queries in Collaborative Information Systems. In: Li, Q., Feng, L., Pei, J., Wang, S.X., Zhou, X., Zhu, Q.-M. (eds.) APWeb/WAIM 2009. LNCS, vol. 5446, pp. 39–50. Springer, Heidelberg (2009)
18. Farnan, N.L., Lee, A.J., Yu, T.: Investigating privacy-aware distributed query evaluation. In: Proc. WPES 2010, pp. 43–52. ACM (2010)
19. Truong, H.L., Dustdar, S.: On evaluating and publishing data concerns for data as a service. In: Proc. APSCC 2010, pp. 363–370. IEEE Computer Society (2010)
20. Ali, M.I., Pichler, R., Truong, H.L., Dustdar, S.: DeXIN: An Extensible Framework for Distributed XQuery over Heterogeneous Data Sources. In: Filipe, J., Cordeiro, J. (eds.) ICEIS 2009. LNBIP, vol. 24, pp. 172–183. Springer, Heidelberg (2009)
21. Ali, M.I., Pichler, R., Truong, H.L., Dustdar, S.: On Using Distributed Extended XQuery for Web Data Sources as Services. In: Gaedke, M., Grossniklaus, M., Díaz, O. (eds.) ICWE 2009. LNCS, vol. 5648, pp. 497–500. Springer, Heidelberg (2009)

PART II

Artificial Intelligence and Decision Support Systems

A Study on Noisy Typing Stream Analysis Using Machine Learning Approach

Jun Li

Department of Land Economy, University of Cambridge
19 Silver Street, Cambridge, CB1 2AB, U.K.
Jl601@cam.ac.uk

Abstract. People's behaviors on using computer keyboard are different. This is particularly the case within disabled community. The differences are reflected by individual's distinct typing characters such as speed and error patterns, and the environment around. This paper studies features such as keyboard layout, key distance and time gap and provides evidence that these features significantly affect people's typing performance. A specific user typing behavior, i.e. 'Hitting Adjacent Key Errors', is selected from categorized typing behaviors and simulated based on a probabilistic neural network algorithm to correct typing mistakes. Results demonstrate a high performance of the designed model, about 70% of all tests score above Basic Correction Rate, and simulation also shows a very unstable trend of user's 'Hitting Adjacent Key Errors' behavior with specific datasets used by the research. Further work is suggested in the conclusion.

Keywords: QWERTY keyboard, Probabilistic neural network, Backpropagation, Key distance, Time gap, Error margin distance.

1 Introduction

People's behaviors on using computer keyboard are different. This is particularly the case within disabled community. For example, Computer users with disabilities or some elderly people may have difficulties in accurately manipulating the QWERTY keyboard [11]. Motor disability can cause significant typing mistakes. These issues haven't been well addressed by current technologies. Although alternative input devices or software such as keyguard [6] [15] and Dasher [3] [17] are available for use, none of them prove more efficient or comfortable than the conventional QWERTY keyboard. Some efforts associated with standard keyboard has been made such as Windows' Accessibility Options [16], ProtoType [10], however the solution to remedy typing difficulties encountered by disabled people hasn't been achieved as yet.

Ouazzane and Li [5] provided a comprehensive report and classified user performance as four categories, i.e. Motor disability, Dyslexia, Unfamiliar with Computer and Others performance. For instance, the 'Miss-stroke' or 'Press Additional Keys' error is classified as sub-category three within category one. However, in the paper only a brief model framework is given based on multi-technologies to tackle the typing errors as a whole, while there is no specific solution

R. Zhang et al. (Eds.): ICEIS 2011, LNBIP 102, pp. 149–161, 2012.

and convincing results for solving specific errors such as 'Miss-stroke' errors. This paper is written to tackle these issues by carrying out a pilot research in the filed.

In computer science, a neural network [1] [14] is a mathematical model or computational model that is inspired by the structure and/or functional aspects of biological neural networks. Modern neural networks are non-linear statistical data modeling tools. They are usually used to model complex relationships between inputs and outputs or to find patterns in data. There are three major learning paradigms, i.e. supervised learning, unsupervised learning and reinforcement learning, while BackPropagation [2] is a supervised learning method and most popular used in practice. It is an implementation of the Delta rule, whose architecture belongs to feedforward network. Probabilistic Neural Networks (PNN) [8] [20] is a type of radial basis network suitable for classification problems. It is a feedforward network built with three layers, and offers a series of advantages, including rapid training speed, incremental training, and robustness to noisy examples.

In the following sections, a Time Gap model and a Prediction using Time Gap model based on BackPropagation are developed respectively to verify the influence of parameters such as keyboard layout, key distance and time gap on human typing behavior. Then, an innovative model named Distance, Angle and Time Gap model based on Probabilistic Neural Network is developed to simulate and predict a specific user typing behavior – 'Hitting Adjacent Key Errors'.

2 Time Gap Modeling

From Fitts'law [9], users input performance ***IP*** in bits per second is proportional to the variable movement time ***ID***, which has a direct relation with the moving distance from one point to another. Let's consider a standard keyboard layout, the time gap between two consecutive strokes directly depends upon the distance between those two keys. As observed, the last key's position represented by the distance and angle with the target typing key could affect some of the disabled users' judgment on their typing accuracy and speed, which would be reflected by the time gap recorded on the computer log. Given the user's typing history, a *1*-gram neural network model named as Time Gap Neural Network (TGNN) is designed here to simulate and predict the two consecutive typing letters' time gap. A typical structure of generated log is shown below.

```
01929 KeyPress    20080605-132149-593 "T" Status=(down) Key(84) Extra(0x14) KeyDistance(3.500000) TimeGap(307)
01930 KeyPress    20080605-132149-655 "T" Status=(up) Key(84) Extra(0xc014) KeyDistance(0.000000) TimeGap(62)
01931 KeyPress    20080605-132149-658 "H" Status=(down) Key(72) Extra(0x23) KeyDistance(2.500000) TimeGap(3)
01932 KeyPress    20080605-132149-694 "H" Status=(up) Key(72) Extra(0xc023) KeyDistance(0.000000) TimeGap(36)
01933 KeyPress    20080605-132149-804 "A" Status=(down) Key(65) Extra(0x1e) KeyDistance(5.000000) TimeGap(110)
01934 KeyPress    20080605-132149-992 "A" Status=(up) Key(65) Extra(0xc01e) KeyDistance(0.000000) TimeGap(188)
```

Fig. 1. Example structure of a generated log. Each line contains nine columns, i.e., 1: sequence number; 2: key press – used to distinguish from mouse action; 3: action date and time (ms); 4: key pressed; 5: key status (up or down); 6: the value of Virtual Key Code [19]; 7: key press information from lParam; 8: distance between two keys of a standard keyboard; 9: time gap between two consecutive key presses.

It is extracted from a charity helpline keystroke log. The associated computer is routinely used as a question recording, database query and email writing tool by a disabled volunteer. According to Windows system, each key stroke evokes two messages, namely, key-pressed (either WM_KEYDOWN or WM_SYSKEYDOWN) and key-released (either WM_KEYUP or WM_SYSKEYUP), which are associated with two 32 byte parameters, *wParam* and *lParam*. In Figure 1, every couple of lines marked with status equal to 'up' or 'down' represents a complete key press. The time gap is the margin value of each two rows in Column 3. The key distance is the sum of horizontal and vertical distance from one key to another. A half key (*0.5*) distance is counted if two keys' distance is not an integer multiple of one-key distance.

From the reflected keystroke log, the typing mistakes are predominantly about adjacent key press errors. The keystroke recording tool used in this research is KeyCapture software [12] [13], which has been modified and adjusted for the purpose of this research. It runs in background under Windows environment to collect keystrokes without interfering with user's work. System environment including computational capability and memory capacity may have a great influence on the intelligent models' testing process. In this research, all experiments are carried out based on Lenovo T60 (IBM) platform, Windows XP operating system, and MATLAB (Version 7.4.0, R2007a) and its Neural Network Toolbox.

A function - *OnBnClickedsuggesttimegap* is programmed to pre-process the dataset. A fifty-four virtual key codes set is considered, which includes fifty-three visible symbols such as alphabet, numbers and space. The other symbols are classified as an assumed symbol - 'Other'.

OnBnClickedsuggesttimegap function only extracts the keystrokes whose time gaps is in a range of [*0, 3000*] ms. The rest keystrokes which have been considered as either out of range or computer system related problems are ignored. *2*-gram dataset is created with their corresponding time gaps. This requires *108* (i.e. NumberOfSymbols * Gram) neurons in the input layer. All the time gap values are normalized into a range of [*-1, 1*] according to Min-Max Normalization before they are used by the Time Gap Neural Network model (TGNN). The normalization equation is shown below,

$$v' = (v - V_{min})*(V'_{max} - V'_{min})/(V_{max} - V_{min}) + V'_{min} \quad (1)$$

Where $V'_{max} = 1, V'_{min} = -1$ and variable v is the time gap value extracted from the dataset. The results of TGNN model will be reversed to their natural values based on the same equation.

Then, a traditional BackPropagation neural network is designed with a *108-7-1* three layer structure. The input includes two consecutive symbols represented by unary codes [18], and the output is the expected time gap between these two consecutive symbols. MATLAB neural network toolbox is used for programming. The '*tansig*' and '*purelin*' functions are considered as the hidden and output layer's activation function.

A reconstructed dataset extracted from the log file is used as neural network's training dataset; another two datasets, i.e. English alphabets in an alphabetical order and QWERTY keyboard layout order respectively, 'abcdefghijklmnopqrstuvwxyz' and 'qwertyuiopasdfghjklzxcvbnm', are used as two testing cases. The experimental results generated by TGNN model then demonstrated on these two datasets are shown in Figure 2 and 3.

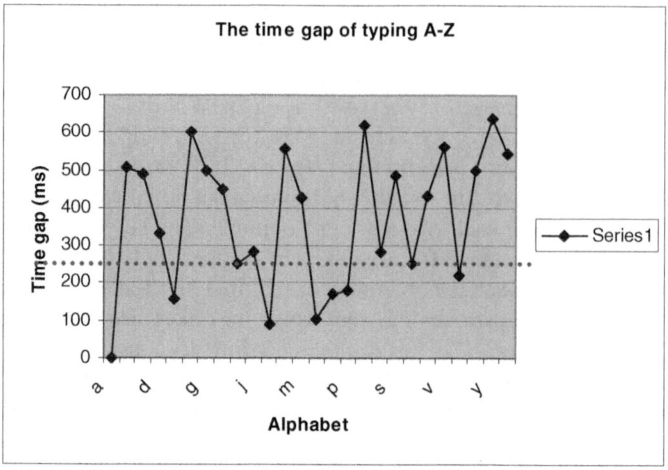

Fig. 2. Modeling time gap using A➔Z sequence. This shows a simulation of the user's typing behaviour by typing an Alphabet sequence. The cost of typing an alphabet order sequence is *384.44ms* as shown in dashed line.

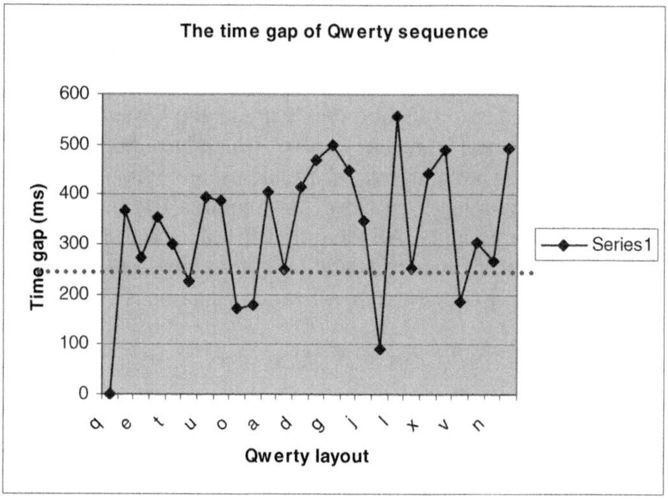

Fig. 3. Modeling time gap using QWERTY sequence. This shows a simulation of the user's typing behavior by typing a QWERTY sequence. The cost of typing an alphabet order sequence is *342.50ms* as shown in dashed line.

Firstly, the TGNN (Time Gap Neural Network) model is trained based on the log file. Then the Alphabet and QWERTY sequences are applied to the TGNN model. Figure 2 shows a simulation of the user's typing behavior (e.g. speed and time gap) by typing an Alphabet sequence; Figure 3 shows a simulation of the user's typing behaviors (e.g. speed and time gap) by typing a QWERTY sequence. Due to no predecessors, both corresponding time gaps of the first keystrokes in sequence (in Figure 2 is 'a'; and in Figure 3 is 'q') are counted as zero.

In Figure 2 and 3, x-axis represents user's typing sequence; y-axis represents the time gap in milliseconds. Between each two consecutive alphabets, a blue line (or a line connecting two points, in the case of black and white printing) is drawn to illustrate the elapsed time. The maximum time gap (*637.4ms*) occurs in Figure 2 when the finger moves from key '*x*' to '*y*'; while the minimum time gap (*89.9ms*) appears in both figures, when the finger moves from '*j*' to '*k*'.

These two figures show that the current keystroke's predecessor affects the user's typing behavior (e.g. time gap) if one ignores the user's keystroke action itself and behavior randomicity that human may have. Due to the distance difference between each two keys in computer QWERTY keyboard, the time gap of each two consecutive keys during user strokes varies.

The red lines (or dashed lines, in the case of black and white printing) in Figure 2 and 3 represent the average time cost of all twenty-five movements, which show that the cost of typing an alphabet order sequence is *384.44ms* (see Figure 2), whereas the cost of typing a QWERTY order sequence is *342.50ms* (see Figure 3). The test shows typing an Alphabet sequence is more time consuming based on a standard keyboard. This can be explained by movement cost, meaning that an alphabet order sequence would require more time for a user to locate the keys from one to another.

This research gives a glance at the idea that the Time Gap between two consecutive keystrokes is influenced by current symbol's predecessor. A further research tracing back more than one gram history accompanied with a larger dataset is necessary.

3 Prediction Using Time Gap

As mentioned in the introduction, people with motor disability or Parkinson disease using keyboard may press adjacent keys or stick keys. These can be shown from the time gap between each two consecutive key strokes. For example, a time gap between the windows keyboard messages caused by sticking keys can be much smaller than the user's normal typing speed; the opposite case may also happen when more time can be spent by disabled people aiming at the target before making up their mind. From observation, interestingly it is rare for those people to completely miss typing a symbol. According to these distinct behaviors, a neural network model using BackPropagation (*newff*) is designed by adding an extra Time Gap variable in the input layer, called Prediction using Time Gap (PTG). Here, a small sample typed by a Parkinson person is used to demonstrate the idea. The target typing sample is,

the quick brown fog jumped over the lazy dog

The user's true typing sample is,

hthe quick brrooownn fgow jummppefd iobverethe lwqazy dooggfg

The typed sample is reconstructed for preprocessing,

@the quick br@o@@wn@ @@f@ox@ jum@p@e@d @@o@ver the l@@azy do@g@@@

Where the symbol '@' represents an error or a NULL, compared to the right sample which should be recognized by PTG model. During preprocessing, the time gap value which is one of the input parameters is categorized into three levels and converted into three bits unary codes. In this case,

'<= 10 milliseconds'	*over-fast => 001*
'10< && <=1000 milliseconds'	*user-Speed => 010*
'>1000 milliseconds'	*over-slow => 100*

The user's typing has been recorded both by Notepad and KeyCapture software.

Prediction using Time Gap model is designed with three layers *30-7-28* structure, where the input requirement of PTG model is twenty seven length unary coding symbol *{'a'...'z', space}* and three length unary coding time gap, and the output requirement is twenty eight length unary coding limited in symbol set *{'a'...'z', space, '@'}*, where the symbol '@' is added to represent an additional or missed symbol.

The correction rate distribution within one hundred times training is shown in Figure 4, which has a mean value of *0.8480* and a deviation of *0.0501*. The x-axis represents the correction rate based on the comparison between the target dataset and PTG generating dataset; the y-axis represents the absolute frequency of the one hundred times training results, which illustrates the number of times a particular outcome occurs.

Figure 4 demonstrates the range that PTG model's correction rate lies on. It shows that the results lie predominantly between *65%* and *90%*. Under this test sample there is about twenty-seven times where the correction rate has reached near *90%* and only once the correction rate happens to be less than *65%*.

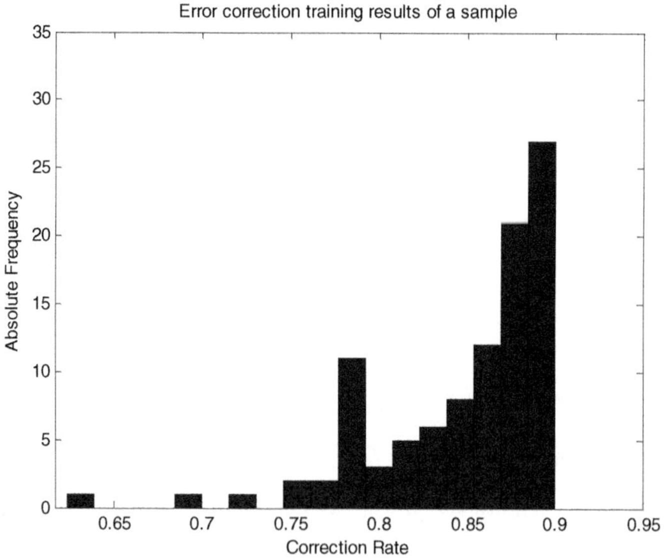

Fig. 4. Absolute Frequency of PTG model Correction Rate. The x-axis represents the correction rate based on the comparison between the target dataset and PTG generating dataset; the y-axis represents the absolute frequency of the one hundred times training results.

This test indicates that the time gap can be considered as an input element used by neural network model to correct wrong typed symbols. Due to no gram consideration and the size limitation of training dataset, the relationship built between input and output is a pure right-wrong relationship. This could lead to a further research on the *n*-gram language modeling with larger training and testing dataset.

4 Probabilistic Neural Network Modeling

♦ **Assumption:** The research carried out in this section is based on one finger typing user case. User's each key press and move rely entirely on a single finger. Skilful users' typing behavior in controlling fingers may vary, and the distance of fingers move between two consecutive keystrokes could be more complex.

♦ **Key Distance Definition:** According to the layout of a computer QWERTY keyboard, there exists a physical distance between each two keys. Let $d_{i,j}$ be the distance between *key i* and *key j*, and define the measure unit as key-distance. Then, $d_{a,s} = 1$ shows that the distance between key '*A*' and key '*S*' is one key-distance; $d_{a,f} = 3$ means there are three key-distances between key '*A*' and key '*F*'. Users move their fingers toward the next key as soon as they finish current key press. The distance between two keys affects a user's typing performance.

♦ **Error Margin Distance (EMD) Definition:** Based on Key Distance, a variable $\Delta d_{s,f}$ is further defined as a distance between a user's typed key - key_s and target key - key_f and called Error Margin Distance. The Error Margin Distance is mainly caused by the user's 'Hitting Adjacent Key Error'.

♦ **Key Distance Class Definition:** Let's define a class, $C_{key_i,j} = \{\overline{key_{ij}} \mid key_i\}$, by giving $key_i, \overline{key_{ij}} \in \{key_1, ..., key_n\}$, where $i, j \le n$, *n* is the number of keys related to a computer QWERTY keyboard, $\overline{key_{ij}}$ represents a key set around key_i within *j* key-distances. For instance, a one key-distance set corresponding to key '*s*' is, $C_{s,1} = \{\overline{s_1} \mid s\} \approx \{'D', 'E', 'W', 'A', 'Z', 'X'\}$.

Noisy data prediction models such as Neural Network models not only can be generally used to analyze a language text, but also can be explored to analyze some specific problems. For example, again let's take the helpline data as a real scenario. As shown in the data, a typist is frequently making 'Hitting Adjacent Key Errors' mistakes. Therefore, all the typing mistakes are extracted from the log file and used to identify the possible rules. A sample of it is shown below,

```
"Q" Status=(*) Key(*) Extra(*) KeyDistance(*) TimeGap(*)
"S" Status=(*) Key(*) Extra(*) KeyDistance(*) TimeGap(*)
"BACK" Status=(*) Key(*) Extra(*) KeyDistance(*) TimeGap(*)
"D" Status=(*) Key(*) Extra(*) KeyDistance(*) TimeGap(*)
```

Fig. 5. A sample of 'Hitting Adjacent Key Errors'. "Q","S", "BACK", and "D" are the typed keys in order. Other values such as key distances and time gaps are not shown here for simplification reason.

This is a typical 'Hitting Adjacent Key Errors' typing mistake that occurred within a user's typing stream. The user's intention is to type a letter 'd' following letter 'q', but the letter 's' is mistakenly pressed. So the user has to go back and make a correction by pressing 'backspace' key shortly after the mistake is made (in virtual key code, the 'backspace' is represented by 'BACK'). Both Key Distance and Time Gap are calculated and recorded in the log.

The user investigation shows users' Hitting Adjacent Key behaviour is related to the positions of both the last key and the current key if one ignores the stroke randomicity that users' symptoms may cause. It also shows that a user's typing speed moving from one key to another also plays an important role in making such errors. For example, although a faster typing speed than a user's normal speed increases the occurrence of 'Hitting Adjacent Key Errors', the users' hesitation which leads to much slower typing speed does not always help to an increase of right typing rate, as shown in the log file.

Here, the idea is to use these essential parameters, namely, Key Distance, Time Gap and Error Margin Distance to discover the fundamental rules behind uses' typing mistakes. Let's start with the introduction of QWERTY keyboard layout, and consider Figure 6 and 7,

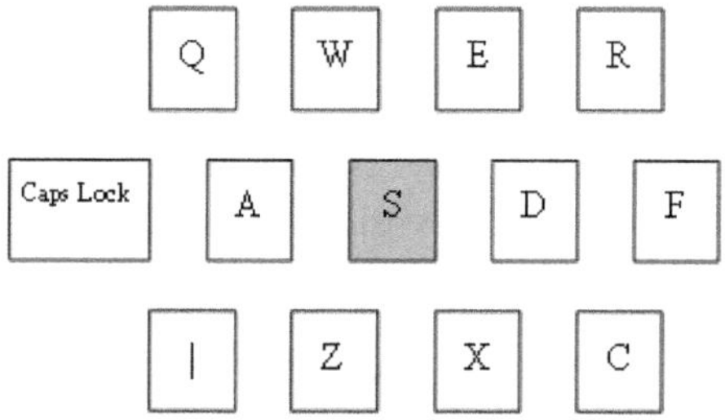

Fig. 6. A QWERTY keyboard layout sample. Key *'S'* is surrounded by one key-distance dataset *{'W', 'E', 'A', 'D', 'Z', 'X'}* and two key-distance dataset *{'Q', 'R', 'caps lock', 'F', '|', 'C'}*.

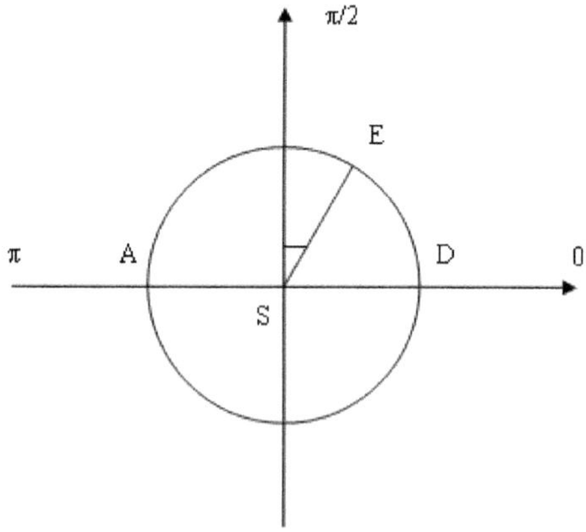

Fig. 7. Relationship – angle between keys and its surrounding keys D, E, A. The key *'D'* is expressed as *{key='S', distance=1, angle=0}* and the key 'A' is expressed as {*key='s', distance=1, angle=π*}.

In Figure 6, key *'S'* is surrounded by one key-distance dataset *{'W', 'E', 'A', 'D', 'Z', 'X'}* and two key-distance dataset *{'Q', 'R', 'caps lock', 'F', '|', 'C'}*. Given certain inputs, if one requires the neural network model to be able to produce the right symbol that a user intends to type, the designed model not only need to deduce the dataset which the right symbol belongs to, but also the right angle the user intends to move towards. This is illustrated in Figure 7. All keys surrounding *'S'* are positioned with different angles. Let's assume the circle starts from right-hand side of *'S'* and turns in an anticlockwise direction. Then the key *'D'* can be expressed by a three dimensions vector, key_d = *{key='S', distance=1, angle=0}*, where *key='S'* illustrates the dataset surrounding key *'S'*, *distance=1 & angle =0* represent the key which is one key-distance away from key *'S'* with an angle of zero degree. The key *'A'* can be expressed as key_a = *{key='s', distance=1, angle=π}*, *distance=1, angle=π* means the key is one key-distance away from key *'S'* with an angle of π degree.

The key distance and time gap between last two grams could determine the error margin between the wrong key and the right key. In order to prove this hypothesis, a Neural Network Topology with Distance, Angle and Time Gap vectors in the input layer, and the Error Margin Distance vector between the typed key and target key in the output layer is designed. These require a precise measurement on both input and output parameters. However, given the difficulty of QWERTY keyboard and its associated operating system to respond to an accurate simulation of users' movement and the difficulty of a neural network to provide a precise output, this solution, as it stands, is not practical. For example, the difference in angle between key *'S'* → key *'E'* and key *'S'* → key *'R'* is not significant. This high precision requirement raises the design difficulty of a neural network model.

In order to overcome these obstacles, a more robust neural network model with re-designed vectors on both input and output layers is developed in this research. The input of neural network model uses (x, y) coordinate expression instead of distance and angle, where x represents x-axis key-distance (i.e. horizontal distance), and y represents y-axis key-distance (i.e. vertical distance). X-axis key-distance refers to a user's horizontal move toward the typed key; y-axis key-distance refers to a user's vertical move toward the typed key. The time gap parameter is kept unchanged, which represents the time difference (*ms*) between two consecutive key strokes. When the error margin is calculated, the coordinate centre lies at the current typed key. When the distance of last typed key and current typed key is calculated, the coordinate centre lies at the last typed key. The sign of key distance will be determined as soon as the coordinate centre is fixed.

In QWERTY keyboard there are maximum of six one key-distance keys around each key. The user investigation records suggest that most of 'Hitting Adjacent Key Errors' occur in an area where the keys are equal or less than one key-distance away from the target keys. Therefore, instead of computing a precise error margin $\Delta d_{t,f}$, the output of neural network model can be designed as a six-classes classifier. If one counts the class in a wise-clock direction according to traditional coordinate, then, from Figure 7, *'d'* belongs to class one, *'e'* belongs to class two and so on. Thus the question can be interpreted as finding an appropriate neural network model to solve a classification issue associated with input vectors: Distance, Angle and Time Gap.

It is well known that radial basis networks can require more neurons than standard feedforward BackPropagation networks, but quite often they can be designed in a fraction of the time it takes to train standard feedforward networks. One of Radial basis networks is Probabilistic Neural Networks (PNN) which can be used for classification problems. As PNN is a time-efficient and classification-solving solution, in this research a *3-N-1* structure model, i.e. Distance, Angle and Time Gap PNN model (DATP model) is designed based on PNN to predict where the target key could possibly lie against the wrong key press.

The DATP model consists of three layers, input layer, hidden layer and output layer. The hidden layer – radbas layer compute the distance between the input vector and the hidden weights vector, and then produces a distance vector which indicates how close the input is against the correct letter. The third layer would classify the results of radbas layer and produces the right class.

In this experiment, thirty three 'Hitting Adjacent Key Errors' are identified from log file, and are converted into the format training dataset manually. At the same time another ten samples are used as test samples. Here an example is given to show the pre-processing procedure,

```
"C" Status=(*) Key(*) Extra(*) KeyDistance(*) TimeGap(78)
"J" Status=(*) Key(*) Extra(*) KeyDistance(*) TimeGap(108)
"BACK" Status=(*) Key(*) Extra(*) KeyDistance(*) TimeGap(78)
"H" Status=(*) Key(*) Extra(*) KeyDistance(*) TimeGap(923)

➔     3.5      1      108      4
```

Fig. 8. An example of pre-processing procedure

The first four lines are extracted from log file. The line following an arrow is the data transformed manually from the lines above, which has four parameters, namely, horizontal distance, vertical distance, time gap between two consecutive keystroke, and class.

The first line shows that the horizontal distance from '*C*' to '*J*' is *3.5* key-distances, however, if the move are from '*J*' to '*C*', the key-distance would be *-3.5*; the vertical distance is one key-distance; the time gap from '*C*' to '*J*' is *108ms* (shown in red) and the class is '*4*' as the key '*H*' is at the left hand side of key '*J*'. In the case of overlapping keys, a half key-distance can be counted. For example,

```
"D" Status=(*) Key(68) Extra(*) KeyDistance(*) TimeGap(93)
"G" Status=(*) Key(71) Extra(*) KeyDistance(*) TimeGap(218)
"H" Status=(*) Key(72) Extra(*) KeyDistance(*) TimeGap(3)

➔      2.5      0      218      4
```

Fig. 9. An example of overlapping keys pre-processing

This is a typical key press with overlapped key '*G*' and key '*H*'. The time gap between '*G*' press and '*H*' press is *3ms*, which is much less than the user's usual typing speed. This has been proved by the user's correction which happened afterwards, as shown in the log file. The horizontal key-distance between key '*D*' and key '*G*' is two key-distances, however, another *0.5* key-distance is added in pre-processing by taking into consideration the overlapping. The vertical distance between these two keys is zero, while the time gap is *218ms* and the output class is *4*.

The experimental results show a correction rate of *50%* which is five out of the ten testing samples. However, due to the highness of user's typing disorder and the small size of training dataset, a random training and testing dataset selection strategy is further adopted. The thirty three training samples and ten testing samples are mixed up and the random function *iRand* is applied to randomly pick up the training dataset and testing dataset in a proportion of *2/3* and *1/3* respectively. Two groups of trials are carried out, and each group of them includes ten training and testing samples. The corresponding plots are shown in Figure 10.

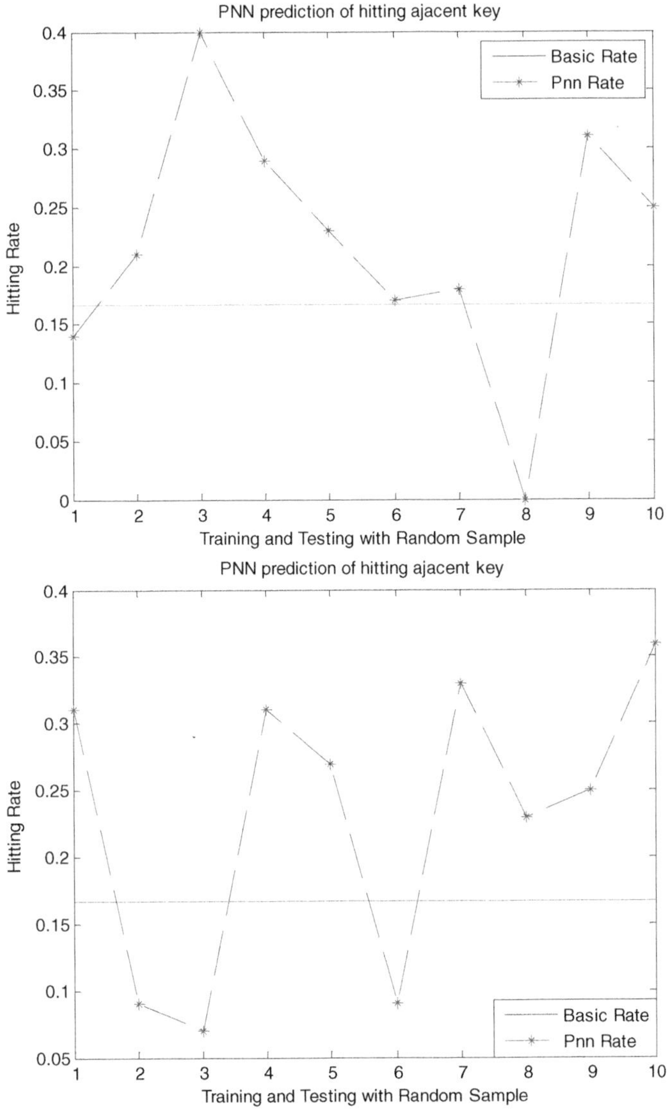

Fig. 10. Hitting Adjacent Key prediction rates based on PPN network. The top and the beneath plots are generated from group one and two trials respectively.

The x-axis refers to training and testing samples that are picked up randomly; the y-axis refers to the prediction rate of the DATP model. The dashed lines in red show the prediction rate of each testing dataset according to its training dataset; the lines in blue (or the horizontal lines in the middle of the figures, in the case of black and white printing) is the random prediction rate which has been named as Basic Rate.

The first plot of Figure 10 demonstrates that there are six rounds out of eight whose prediction rates are above Basic Rate, while the rest are below Basic Rate. The highest score (*40%*) occurs at the third round, while the lowest score occurs at eighth round (*0%*). The second plot indicates that there are seven rounds whose prediction rates are above Basis Rate, while the three remaining rounds are below Basic Rate. The highest score (*36%*) occurs at the tenth round while the lowest score (*7%*) occurs at the third round.

Both plots show that there are *70%* of all tests scoring above Basic Rate. They also demonstrate a very unstable trend of user's 'Hitting Adjacent Key Errors' behaviour. It recommends that the training dataset with a small size of data may not be able to give a high prediction rate as the dataset has a bad convergence. In that case, several rounds of training with a random dataset selection strategy is required.

5 Conclusions

In this paper the influence of time gap on user's typing performance is studied, and a unique Time Gap model is developed. Experimental results show that the current keystroke's predecessor affected the user's typing behaviour, and the Time Gap between two consecutive keystrokes is influenced by current symbol's predecessor. Inspired by this conclusion, a fundamental PTG model is developed. Its experimental results indicate that the correction rates predominantly lie in between *65%* and *90%* with the current testing sample.

Furthermore, an innovative Distance, Angle and Time Gap PNN model based on Probabilistic Neural Network is developed to simulate a specific user typing behaviour – 'Hitting Adjacent Key Errors' based on unique factors such as key distances. Results demonstrate that about *70%* of all tests score above Basic Correction Rate. Results also show a very unstable trend of user's 'Hitting Adjacent Key Errors' behaviour, which suggest that several training trials with a random dataset selection strategy could be applied.

Further work to be carried out should focus on two areas: the DATP model development with larger scaled data to obtain a more accurate prediction rate, and a touch keyboard combining the sensitivity of touch screen and functionality of QWERTY layout to detect the users' finger movement more precisely to calculate the accurate $\Delta d_{s,f}$.

Acknowledgements. The research is funded by Disability Essex [4] and Technology Strategy Board [7]. Thanks to Richard Boyd, Pete Collings and Ray Mckee for helpful advice and discussions.

References

1. Artificial neural network, December 31 (2010), http://en.wikipedia.org/wiki/Artificial_neural_network (January 12, 2010)
2. BackPropagation, January 10 (2008), Wikipedia, http://en.wikipedia.org/wiki/Back_propagation (accessed January 20, 2008)
3. Ward, D.J., Blackwell, A.F., et al.: Dasher-a Data Entry Interface Using Continuous Gestures and Language Models. In: Proceedings of the 13th Annual ACM Symposium on User Interface Software and Technology, UIST 2000 (2000)
4. Disability Essex, http://www.disabilityessex.org (accessed January 18, 2009)
5. Ouazzane, K., Li, J., Brouwer, M.: A hybrid framework towards the solution for people with disability effectively using computer keyboard. In: IADIS International Conference Intelligent Systems and Agents 2008, pp. 209–212 (2008)
6. Keyguards and Keyboards, Maxess Products, http://www.maxesssite.co.uk/html/mpkeykey.html (accessed July 20, 2011)
7. Knowledge Transfer Partnership, http://www.ktponline.org.uk/ (accessed January 18, 2009)
8. Nikolaev, N.Y.: Probabilistic Neural Networks, Goldsmiths, University of London, October 1 (2008), http://homepages.gold.ac.uk/nikolaev/311pnn.htm (accessed January 23, 2009)
9. Fitts, P.M.: The information capacity of the human motor system in controlling the amplitude of movement. Journal of Experimental Psychology 47(6), 381–391 (1954)
10. Prototype, http://www.sensorysoftware.com/prototype.html (accessed March 03, 2008)
11. QWERTY, November 13 (2009), http://en.wikipedia.org/wiki/QWERTY (accessed November 13, 2009)
12. Soukoreff, R.W., MacKenzie, I.S.: KeyCapture, http://dynamicnetservices.com/~will/academic/textinput/keycapture/ (accessed January 18, 2009)
13. Soukoreff, R.W., MacKenzie, I.S.: Input-based language modelling in the design of high performance text input techniques. In: Proceedings of Graphics Interface 2003, pp. 89–96 (2003)
14. Haykin, S.: Neural Networks – A comprehensive Foundation, 2nd edn. Tom Robbins (1999)
15. Trewin, S.: An invisible keyguard. In: ACM SIGACCESS Conference on Assistive Technologies, pp.143–149 (2002)
16. Trewin, S., Pain, H.: A Model of Keyboard Configuration Requirements. In: Proceedings of International ACM Conference on Assistive Technologies, pp. 173–181 (1998)
17. The Dasher Project, Inference Group of Cambridge, November 14 (2007), http://www.inference.phy.cam.ac.uk/dasher/ (accessed March 03, 2008)
18. Unary coding, December 23 (2009), http://en.wikipedia.org/wiki/Unary_coding (January 12, 2010)
19. Virtual key codes, http://api.farmanager.com/en/winapi/virtualkeycodes.html (accessed February 5, 2009)
20. Bengio, Y., Ducharme, R., Vincent, P., Janvi, C.: A neural probabilistic language model. The Journal of Machine Learning Research 3, 1137–1155 (2003)

Intelligent Information Acquisition and Utilization in Safety Evaluation Decision Making Process of Power Generation Enterprises

Dongxiao Gu[1], Changyong Liang[1,4], Jinhong Zhong[1], Jun Wang[2], Wenxing Lu[1], Junyuan Song[3], Wenwen Lv[5], and Yifeng Wu[6]

[1] School of Management at Hefei University of Technology
193 Tunxi Road, Hefei, Anhui, 230009, China
[2] Department of Computer Science at University of Wisconsin at Milwaukee
2200 E. Kenwood Blvd, Milwaukee, WI 53201, U.S.A.
[3] Department of Economy and Trade at Chuzhou Vacational and Technical College
64 N. Fengle Road, Chuzhou, Anhui, 239000, China
[4] Key Laboratory of Process Optimization and Intelligent Decision-making of Ministry of Education of China, 193 Tunxi Road, Hefei, Anhui, 230009, China
[5] Department of Economy and Management at Chuzhou University
2 Langya Road, Chuzhou, Anhui, 239000, China
[6] Department of Business Administration of Anhui Sanlian University
Hefei, Anhui, 230601, China
mikehfut@gmail.com, cyliang@163.com

Abstract. Modern information technologies are playing an increasing importantly role in safety production assessment of thermal power plants (TPPs). This paper investigates historical knowledge acquisition and utilization issue in safety evaluation of power generation enterprise and provides a case-based approach for the safety assessment decision making of TPPs (MSSATPP). A case matching method named CBR-Grey which ingrates Delphi approach and Grey System theory is proposed. Based on this method, we implement a prototype of information acquisition and utilization system (CBRSYS-TPP) for MSSATPP. We use this system to complete two distinct comparative experiments and validate the effectiveness and excellent comprehensive performance of CBR-Grey. CBRSYS-TPP is hopeful to be a powerful decision tool for panel of experts during their evaluation.

Keywords: Information acquisition, Intelligent decision making, Power generation system, Safety evaluation, Information management, Data mining.

1 Introduction

Thermal Power Plants (TPPs) equip numerous industrial departments and their productive process is very complicated [1]. As one of the strongest nations in electric power generation, due to various limitations and causes, China produces its electric power mainly from coal [2]. In Turkey as well, 80% of the total electricity is generated from thermal power plants [3]. For the purpose of reducing major and extraordinarily large accidents in TPPs and ensuring the security of electric power production, an

R. Zhang et al. (Eds.): ICEIS 2011, LNBIP 102, pp. 162–177, 2012.

increasing number of power generation enterprises in China pay more attention to the safety assessment issue. Safety assessment of power generation enterprises mainly concerns three different aspects: Production Equipment Systems (PES), Working Circumstance Systems (WCS), and Management Systems in production. The latter is also referred to as the Management System (MS) in current research.

Along with the increasing perfection of safety assessment rules and the development of information technologies, new techniques are being applied to almost all aspects of power systems to improve efficiency [4]. First, common evaluation issues concerning the power industry have been reported in the literature. In view of the special importance of production security for TPPs, it is important to study scientific approaches that fit the characteristic features of the production and management of power generation enterprises for safety assessment. However, few research studies focus on the safety assessment of TPPs in production - the inside security itself. Most of the literature focuses on the operational performance [5], energetic and exergetic performance analyses [6], the selection of an optimum power plant [7], air quality impact[8][9], and ecological efficiency [10]. Second, as far as content assessment is concerned, few studies concern safety evaluation of management work. In terms of evaluation approaches, few approaches are actually able to solve the problems of providing powerful and helpful information support for experts' decision making and the reuse of domain knowledge. Until now, rare contributions have been made to the assessment approaches for management security of thermal power plants. As an important technology in artificial intelligence, CBR can provide an information support for the whole decision making process of management safety assessment of TPPs (MSSATPP). Part of its advantage lies in that it can capture expert knowledge, provide methods for knowledge management, and give suggestions for fast problem-solving. Different from ANNs and decision trees, CBR can address the problem of over fitting.

In the area of evaluation research, there are also many articles concerning CBR, such as the applications of CBR to software cost estimation [11], software effort estimation[12], risk assessment in audit judgment[13], risk analysis for electronic commerce[14], web break sensitivity evaluation in a paper machine [15], safety risk analysis in information security systems [16], safety evaluation of process configuration[17], and so forth. In this article, we apply CBR to MSSATPP, and propose a whole evaluation approach integrating weight derivation approaches and case retrieval algorithms for MSSATPP. The research novelty of our work lies in that by taking the management system of whole power systems as an example, we integrate Grey System Theory and Delphi method into case-based reasoning, and then apply the optimized CBR to historical knowledge acquisition and utilization intelligent decision support system for MSSATPP (IDSS-MSSATPP).

The rest of our article is organized as follows. Section2 presents a framework of case knowledge acquisition and utilization system. This section describes several performance evaluation statistics and the case-based evaluation process and evaluation index, and presents IDSS-MSSATPP functional structure. Section3 is methodology. In this section, we firstly investigate the decision information acquisition method and Delphi weight derivation method. And then we introduce the data set for subsequent experiments. Section4 introduce related experiments and provides main results. We also perform some discussions based on the experimental results. In the last section, we conclude our current study.

2 The Framework

After defining the concepts used in the framework presentation, this section firstly describe several related concepts and statistics, and then presents the main steps of the case-based evaluation process, evaluation indexes, and IDSS-MSSATPP functional structure.

2.1 Related Concepts and Statistics

In this section, several related concepts shall be defined. Definition1 to Definition 4 are the statistics for performance evaluation of the new case retrieval method. Suppose NR1 denotes the number of true positives according to the retrieval requirements, and NUR2 denotes the number of true negatives. Meanwhile, suppose NR2 and NUR1 represent the number of false positives and the number of false negatives respectively. Then we introduce Definition3, Definition4, and Definition5.

Definition 1. Accuracy [18] is the proportion of true results (both true positives and true negatives) in the population. As a parameter of the test, it is often used as a statistical measure of how well a binary classification test correctly identifies or excludes a condition (see formula (1)).

$$Accuracy = \frac{NR_1 + NUR_2}{NR_1 + NR_2 + NUR_1 + NUR_2} \tag{1}$$

Definition 2. Precision is the proportion of positives in a binary classification test which are correctly identified, which can be calculated by formula (2).

$$\text{Precision} = NR1 / (NR1 + NR2) \tag{2}$$

Definition 3. Recall is the fraction of the cases that are relevant to the query that are successfully retrieved in a binary classification test, which can be computed by formula (3).

$$\text{Recall} = NR1 / (NR1 + NUR1) \tag{3}$$

Precision and recall can be microscopic or macroscopic. Formula (2) and Formula (3) are microscopic statistics used to evaluate the effect of one retrieval episode. Accordingly, there are also macroscopic precision and recall, as shown in Formula (4) and Formula (5), which can be used to evaluate the effect of multiple retrieval episodes.

$$\text{Precisionmacro} = \Sigma\, NR1 / (NR1 + NR2) \tag{4}$$

$$\text{Recall macro} = \Sigma\, N\, R1 / (NR1 + NUR1) \tag{5}$$

Definition 4. Fmacro-value is a statistic that is used for a comprehensive assessment of retrieval algorithms. It can simultaneously reflect the effects of both sensitivity and specificity. It can be computed via Formula (6).

$$F_{macro}\text{-value} = \frac{2 * Precision_{macro} * Recall_{macro}}{Precision_{macro} + Recall_{macro}} \quad (6)$$

Additional information for Precision, Recall and Fmacro-value can be acquired from the research work by García-Nieto, Alba, Jourdan and Talbi [19]. In this study, two statistics are simultaneously used to evaluate the performances of different case matching methods. One is the accuracy, the most commonly popular index for the evaluation of performance. The other is the Fmacro-value. In the area of statistics and information retrieval, the sensitivity and specificity are generally used for evaluating an algorithm [20]. The combined effect can be evaluated by the Fmacro-value.

2.2 The Case-Based Evaluation Process

Most of the electric power incorporations currently complete their internal thermal power plants safety evaluation work through external experts' evaluation. The complete evaluation steps are approximately as follows:

Step1: organize an experts' group to conduct the assessment. The experts can come from a technical layer, a management layer of the electric power companies, the institutes of the electric power, or universities or government departments related to electric power. Step2: determine the weights associated with the evaluation index or the total score of each index by DELPHI method [21]; Step3: organize the experts' visit to the thermal power plants and their scoring through the fact-finding inspection; Step4: gather the score, conduct group discussions, and finally make decisions. Usually, the evaluation can end in one of two ways: qualified with minor correction and remedy or unqualified with major correction and remedy[1]. It is vital for a group of experts to have intelligent information and knowledge support during decision making. Following, one important purpose of our current research is to present a more effective case matching method different from those commonly used in case-based reasoning for the safety assessment issue of thermal power plants. Another aim of our current study is to develop a case-based intelligent system based on historical knowledge to assist the panel of experts in reaching a right decision making for MSSATPP. The knowledge acquisition process of historical cases is shown in Fig.1.

2.3 Evaluation Indexes

On the basis of actual investigations of coal-fired thermal power enterprises, currently, the safety evaluation of thermal power plants mainly concerns the following six aspects, which are generally regarded as evaluation indexes.

The first is the safety goal: the implementation of security principles or policies in production and the security goal management. Concretely, the implementation of

[1] This kind of division is not very strict. There is also an exception. A minority of the electric power enterprises only score and do not draw the specific conclusions: qualified or unqualified. However generally, there are only two outcomes: major correction and remedy or not.

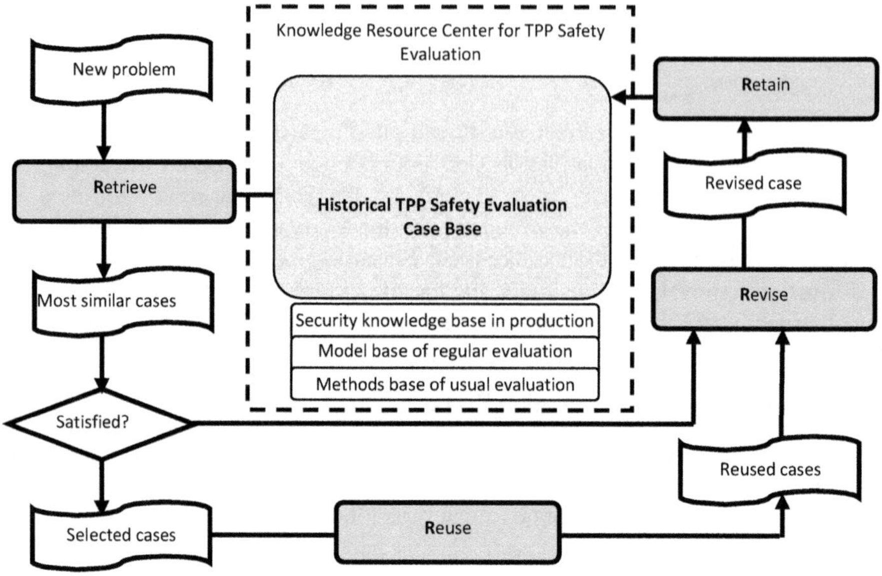

Fig. 1. Case-based reasoning process of TPP safety evaluation

security policies encompass dimensions such as "Safety first", "Precaution is crucial", and "Comprehensive harnessing", the hierarchical decomposition and pertinence of safety goal management, the familiarity of workers with all potentially unsafe factors in operations locations, and the clarity of supervision and certification systems for safety in production. The second is the responsible system (ResponsSys): the implementation of the responsibility system for safety in production. It includes the implementation of the responsibility of "The-First-Responsible-Person-In- Production", the security responsibility of functional departments and workshop directors, the responsibility system of the security in production for group leaders, and the responsibility system of safety in production of production directions and technical support. The third is the supervision system for safety in TPPs production (Supervision). It principally contains the implementation of regular security meetings planning, the implementation of the security supervision activities, the implementation of the activities related to security bulletin reports, and the implementation of other security related supervision systems. The fourth is the basic activities for production security (BasicWork). The specific fundamental activities include the use and management of work order and operation order, the management of major hazard installations, the classified performance assessment and management, the production safety management of outsourced projects and contracted projects, and the contingency management of production security.The fifth is the training and education about production safety (SafeEdu). It includes the management of training and education production safety, the "Factory-Workshop-Group" three different levels of enrollment safety education, the training for recruits and workers replacing the guards and special operational personnel.The last item is the integrated management (IntergratedM) in which are included mainly the reward and punishment system for production security and the security culture creation in enterprises.

In IDSS-MSSATPP, the cases represent actual historical evaluation reports which have been structured. Not only the attributes (i.e. Goal, ResponsSys, Supervision, BasicWork, SafeEdu, and IntergratedM) are included as evaluation indexes, but also other important attributes, such as the Number of Items with Deducted Marks, the Number of Major Problems, the Assessment Result, the Suggested Amendment Opinions, are represented. In Fig.2, the six indexes on the left are input variables, and four extra attributes on the right are the output variables. The values of input variables are acquired by expert group scoring.

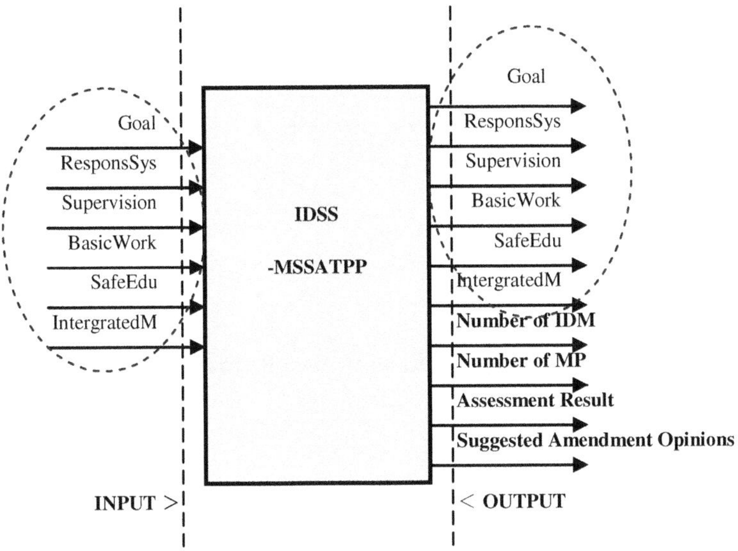

Fig. 2. Evaluation indexes and four extra output attributes in IDSS-MSSATPP

Then, the similar cases including ten rather than six attributes are able to be acquired by case matching. The four extra attributes on the right in Fig.2 are extremely important and valuable. The former three items, i.e. Number of Items with Deducted Marks (IDM), Number of Major Problems (MP), and Assessment Result, are influential for the decision results of the current evaluation problem. The last one, i.e. Suggested Amendment Opinions, is extremely helpful as reference for the expert group to derive their suggested corrective and remedial measures based on the specific conditions of the thermal power plant.

The four extra attributes on the right in Fig.2 are extremely important and valuable. The former three items, i.e. Number of Items with Deducted Marks (IDM), Number of Major Problems (MP), and Assessment Result, are influential for the decision results of the current evaluation problem. The last one, i.e. Suggested Amendment Opinions, is extremely helpful as reference for the expert group to derive their suggested corrective and remedial measures based on the specific conditions of the thermal power plant. Accordingly, IDSS-MSSATPP is able to be used by all the expert group members to effectively acquire their knowledge and decision support. The entire safety evaluation procedure of thermal power plants will be eventually completed with the powerful aid and support of IDSS-MSSATPP.

2.4 IDSS-MSSATPP Functional Structure

The system developed is an intelligent decision support system for safety assessment of TPPs (IDSS-MSSATPP). A case base is the core of the whole system [20].

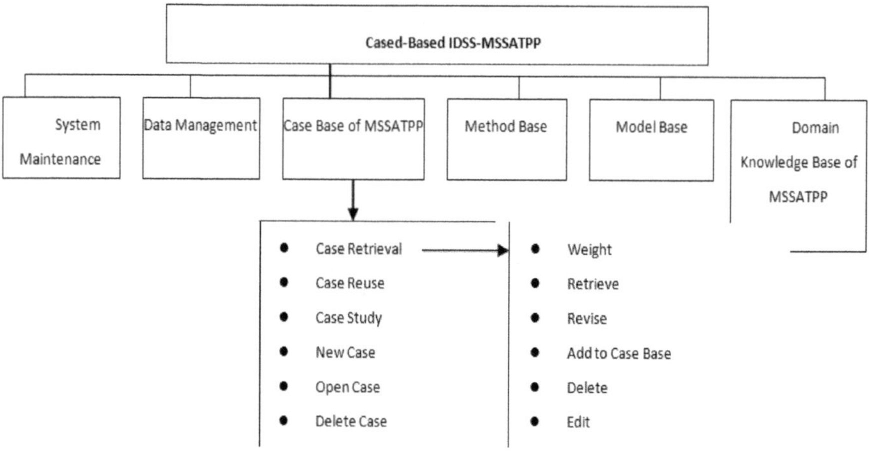

Fig. 3. Main functional structure of Cased-Based IDSS-MSSATPP

3 Methodology

Research methodology is presented in four parts. Part one proposes the retrieval method based on grey system theory and our improvement on it. Part two introduce how to use Delphi method to derive weight. Part three defines several statistics for performance evaluation and the last part describes our used data set.

3.1 Decision Information Acquiring Method

In our study, we use grey system theory combining Delphi approach to complete the acquisition of decision information. In CBR systems, the information acquisition is also called case matching or case retrieval. The most famous case matching method is the traditional CBR retrieval algorithm which is based on Euclidean distance. Besides, other methods such as neural networks, genetic algorithms and fuzzy logic are also studied in previous literatures [22] [23] [24].

However, there still exists a gap between the abilities of these techniques and the real requirement to improve their accuracy and to provide more detailed decision information. In this article, grey system theory and Delphi method are integrated into case-based reasoning technology and CBR-KNN is introduced as a novel case matching method.

Grey System Theory was first built by Ju-Long Deng in 1982 [25]. All systems with incomplete information can be regarded as grey systems [26]. The case retrieval algorithm for knowledge acquisition of MSSATPP has been based on grey relationship analysis. As one of the system analysis techniques, grey relationship analysis is an approach for analyzing the degree of association among different factors. Here, we integrated it into CBR for MSSATPP and proposed CBR-Grey. The fundamental steps using grey relationship analysis for case retrieval in MSSATPP are as follows [27].

Step 1. Determine the evaluation index system according to the evaluation purpose, and then collect evaluation data.

Suppose there are m data series which form the following matrix:

$$\left(X_1, X_2, \wedge, X_{\mathrm{m}}\right) = \begin{pmatrix} x_{11} & \cdots & x_{1n} \\ \vdots & \ddots & \vdots \\ x_{m1} & \cdots & x_{mn} \end{pmatrix}$$

where n denotes the number of evaluation indexes, and m is the number of historical MSSATPP cases in the case base.

Step 2. Use Delphi method and obtain all weight values of the indexes. The Delphi method is a systematic, interactive forecasting method which relies on a panel of experts. This technique is based on the principle that forecasts from a structured group of experts are more accurate than those from unstructured groups or individuals [28].

Step 3. Determine the reference data series. The reference data series should be an ideal contrast standard. They can be composed of the optimal value or worst-case value of the indexes as well as other reference values that are selected according to the evaluation purpose. In our current research, the reference data series is the target case to be solved and the attribute values are those of the objective case to be solved. Let X0 denote the reference data series.

Step 4. Normalize the data.

Step 5. Compute the absolute differences between the corresponding elements of reference data series and comparisons from the case base, namely |x0k- xik| , i=1, 2, …, m ; k=1, 2, …, n., where k denotes the number of attributes, and i denotes the number of evaluation objects.

Step 6. Derive the values of and.

Step 7. Compute the correlation coefficient. By Formula (1), respectively compute the correlation coefficients between each comparative series and reference series. In Formula (1), denotes the resolution ratio, and its values range from zero to one. The smaller is, the bigger the differences among correlation coefficients are, and the stronger the separating capacity is. Generally, the value of is 0.5. i denotes the case number in the case base. represents the correlation between the target case and case i in the case base for index k.

$$\zeta_i(k) = \frac{\min\limits_i \min\limits_k |x_{0\mathrm{k}} - x_i| + \rho \cdot \max\limits_i \max\limits_k |x_{0\mathrm{k}} - x_{i\mathrm{k}}|}{|x_{0\mathrm{k}} - x_{i\mathrm{k}}| + \rho \cdot \max\limits_i \max\limits_k |x_{0\mathrm{k}} - x_{i\mathrm{k}}|} \tag{7}$$

Step8. Compute correlative series. Respectively compute the average value of the correlation coefficients between the corresponding elements of the reference series and every evaluation object (comparative series). This average value, named correlation series, can reflect the correlation relationship between the reference series and the comparative series denoted by i. We mark it as follows.

$$r_{0i} = \frac{1}{\text{n}} \sum_{k} \zeta_i(k) \quad \text{(k=1, 2... n)} \tag{8}$$

Step9. When the indexes have different roles and importance in comprehensive assessment, we can compute weighted means which can be shown as follows.

$$S_{global}(\text{i}) = \frac{1}{\text{n}} \sum_{k} \text{w}_k \cdot \zeta_i(k) \quad \text{(k=1, 2 ... n)} \tag{9}$$

where w_k denotes the weight of index k.

Step10. Derive the comprehensive assessment result on the basis of the correlation series of all the objects of observation: $S_{global}(1)$, $S_{global}(2)$, ... $S_{global}(\text{m})$.

In the above descriptions, the local similarity is represented by the grey association degree of the characteristic attributes. The global similarity is derived by the weighted addition of all the local similarities. For the different importance of the evaluation indexes of thermal power plants, the weight can be integrated into the computing process of a comparative environment when the local similarities are being computed. Therefore an improved local grey association algorithm is derived and further expressed as follows in equation (4).

$$\zeta_{\text{i}}'(k) = \frac{\min\limits_{i} \min\limits_{k} \text{X(i, k)} + \rho \cdot \max\limits_{i} \max\limits_{k} w_k * \text{X(i, k)}}{(w_k * \text{X(i, k)}) + \rho \cdot \max\limits_{i} \max\limits_{k} w_k * \text{X(i, k)}} \tag{10}$$

Where $\text{X(i, k)} = w_k \left| x_0(k) - x_i(k) \right|$. The local grey similarity of the index k between the objective case and historical evaluation case can be defined as follows.

$$\zeta_i^{dist}(k) = \frac{1}{\zeta_{\text{i}}'(k)} - 1 \tag{11}$$

According to the definition of the Euclidean distance, the global similarity between two cases can be defined as follows.

$$\zeta_{\text{i}}^{\text{global}} = \sum_{k=1}^{m} (\zeta_i^{\text{dist}}(k))^2 \tag{12}$$

Thereby, the global similarity of two cases can be derived by the following formula. The case chosen for reuse is the one maximizing the global similarity.

$$S_{\text{i}}^{\text{global}} = \frac{1}{\zeta_i^{\text{global}} + 1} \tag{13}$$

3.2 Weight Derivation of MSSATPP Cases

In general, to obtain a composite indicator a decision needs to be made upon the weight to assign to each indicator. In the index literature, numerous weighting determination methods can be found. In general, indicator weights can be determined based on correlations (factor analysis), experts' opinions (such as Delphi method), optimization models (data envelopment analysis) or equally distributed (equal weighting) [29]. Herman [30] focused on weights which can represent the idea of experts concerning the importance of the indicators. In the analytic hierarchy process (AHP) [31] experts are asked to judge the relative contribution of one indicator compared to another one. These pairwise comparisons are somewhat time consuming and may involve some level of inconsistency.

Therefore, we opt for the more simple design of Delphi method. The Delphi process today exists in two distinct forms: conventional Delphi and real-lucre Delphi. The former is the paper-and-pencil version which is commonly referred to as a "Delphi Exercise." This form is the most commonly used in practice. Real-lucre Delphi, a newer form, sometimes called a "Delphi Conference," replaces the monitor team to a large degree by a computer which has been programmed to carry out the compilation of the group results. This latter approach may eliminate the delay caused in summarizing each round of Delphi, thereby turning the process into a real-time communications system. However it requires that the characteristics of the communication be well defined before Delphi is undertaken, whereas in a paper-and-pencil Delphi exercise the monitor team can adjust these characteristics as a function of the group responses. Hence, in our research, we use the conventional Delphi. To a degree, this form of Delphi is a combination of a polling procedure and a conference procedure which attempts to shift a significant portion of the effort needed for individuals to communicate from the larger respondent group to the smaller monitor team. A selected panel of experts is asked to mark a weight value for each characteristic index respectively. After a series of procedural steps, the final weight values will be acquired. The higher feature weight value implies the more importance of this index. In our study, the evaluation panel members consist of six experts selected from both inside and outside of the power enterprise. The selected company for the current research is GreatT Power Generation Group of China (GreatT), one of the largest power generation corporations in Asia. Amongst the experts, four are from corporate headquarter, another one ever worked at a thermal power plant and currently retired, and the last one from a university of electric power. The detailed steps for the weight values of MSSATPP by the conventional Delphi method In our study, the respondent group is given three opportunities to re-evaluate its original answers based upon examination of the group response. We performed nonparametric tests (K related samples) by SPSS 16.0.

3.3 Data Set

The data set for our experiments are mainly collected from a mega electric power enterprise group, GreatT Power Generation Group of China (GreatT). As one of the largest power generation corporations in Asia, she owns over one hundred power plants, most of which are coal-fired thermal power plants. The data set are mainly the historical security assessment data of TPP of GreatT over the years. Most of the data are the newest assessment reports of SATPP occurring between 2007 and 2009. Since these TPPs vary in their degree of informatization and electronic data were not even available in parts of them, the task of collecting the data was hard. The current project team collected a total of 120 MSSATPP records, and 106 complete and valid cases were acquired after displaying and analyzing. Among them, the number of positive cases is 56, and the number of negative cases is 50. The assessment reports from the same thermal plants but occurring in different years will be regarded as two different records. In this research, we conducted the experiments by 10-fold-cross-validation. The test data are extracted randomly. For each test, 96 cases will be used as historical data in the case base, and the remaining 10 cases represent the testing data (five positive cases and five negative cases respectively). For each experiment, the tests will be repeated ten times. Although the data set is not very large, since there are only six attributes in the cases, according to the usual requirement: number of attributes / number of data should equal 1:10~1:20, it can satisfy the experimental requirements (6 / 106 = 0.057).

4 Experiments

We implemented a prototype of CBRSYS-TPP and used it to complete the following experiment regarding the performance of information acquisition. In this section, we completed two different experiments. The first one is to test the accuracy, sensitivity and specificity as well as calculate the F_{macro}-Value of our proposed case matching methods which combines Delphi method and grey system theory. And the second one is to test several common classification methods using the same data set. 10-fold-cross-validation tests were conducted. The performance of the methods is evaluated by accuracy, F_{macro}-value, sensibility and specificity. In each 10-fold-cross-validation, the data set was divided into ten mutually exclusive subsets with the same distribution using Matlab R2008a. Each fold should be used only once to test the performance of the retrieval algorithms. The most similar cases were generated from the remaining nine folds.

Firstly, we used Delphi method to derive weight values. We acquired the original weight values from experts and then tested the consistency by nonparametric tests. The test results are shown in Table1, in which Asymp. Sig. is zero smaller than 0.5 and Kendall's W[a] is 0.97 bigger than 0.71. Thereby the group of data from the six experts have favourable highly consistency. By calculating the means of six groups of data by column and then divided the sum of the means, we obtained the weight values for the six feature attributes as shown in Table 2.

Table 1. Kendall's W test result

Test Statistics	
N	6
Kendall's W[a]	.910
Chi-Square	27.304
df	5
Asymp. Sig.	.000

a.Kendall's Coefficient of Concordance

Table 2. The cases attribute weights of MSSATPP (DELPHI)

Attribute	Goal	ResponsSys	Supervision	BasicWork	SafeEdu	IntergratedM
Weight	0.12	0.4467	0.0633	0.2317	0.0267	0.1116

4.1 Comparison Tests with KNN

In the first experiment, tests compare different case matching methods: the traditional case retrieval method and our proposed approach. By the tests, the accuracy of CBR-Grey is 94%. The average sensitivity, average specificity, recall and Fmacro-value are 96%, 92%, 92.3%, 96%, and 94.11% respectively. Meanwhile, the traditional KNN based on Euclidean distance algorithms is used as the second retrieval method to acquire similar cases. In this experiment, the value of K selected is seven. The accuracy of CBR-KNN is 90%. The average sensitivity, average specificity, precision, recall and Fmacro-value are 91%, 90%, 91%, 91.07%, and 90.03% respectively. The results are still acceptable. But by comparison, CBR-Grey has significantly higher accuracy and better comprehensive performance.

4.2 Comparison with Other Methods

Neural networks (especially RBF Network), decision trees and logistic regression are also common methods for different assessment issues, especially binary classification evaluations [32] [33] [34].

In the current study, comparative experiments were conducted between CBR-Grey and the other two methods: RBF Network and logistic regression. The first tool for this experiment is Weka 3.6.2 in which RBF Network is integrated. The second tool is SPSS15 which is the platform for logistic regression analysis. The data set used here are still the GreatT TPP data set. 10-fold-cross-validation tests were conducted. The experimental results are shown in Table3. Among them, CBR-Grey has the best accuracy (94%) and F-value (94.11%). Logistic regression has 91.50 % of accuracy and 91.89% of F-value. Nevertheless, RBF Network only has 84.90% of accuracy and 84.39% of F-value. Accordingly, RBF Network is not recommended for real applications in MSSATPP.

In our proposed approach, Delphi method is also regarded as part of the case retrieval method. Our experimental results highlight that, as far as practical aspects of decision support for expert panel members are concerned, in comparison with KNN based on Euclidean distance algorithm, the most popular retrieval algorithm, our proposed approach seems to present the advantage of combining the strength of Delphi method and grey system theory to complement the weaknesses of traditional case matching approaches. Meanwhile, we completed the comparative experiments among our proposed approach and three other common methods for binary classification evaluation issues. The conclusion is that CBR-Grey is the best both in accuracy and Fmacro-value. This further illustrates the validity and high performance of CBR applied to MSSATPP. At the methodological level, the potential advantage of CBR-Grey is in its ability to acquire and reuse the historical knowledge whenever the available information is complete or incomplete.

Table 3. the comparative experimental results of four different approaches (based on Great TPP dataset)

Method	Accuracy	Precision	Recall	F-value	Exp. Tool
CBR-Grey	94.00%	92.30%	96.00%	94.11%	CBRsys-TPP, Matlab R2008a
Logistic Regression#	91.50%	91.07%	92.73%	91.89%	SPSS15
RBF Network*	84.90	80.00%	89.30%	84.39%	Weka3.6.2

#: The cut value is .500 which is the standard and default cutoff value. We can rerun the analysis with a series of cutoff values such as 0.4, 0.45, 0.55 and 0.65 to see if the cutoff value could be adjusted for a better fit. For this particular model, these alternate cutoff values do not lead to better predictions. In this case, the default 0.5 cutoff value is deemed sufficient.

*: Logistic regression applied to K-means clusters as basic functions here.

5 Conclusions

Our proposed method integrating grey system theory and Delphi method into CBR methodologies and intelligent knowledge reuse system may provide intelligent decision support for MSSATPP, and the evaluation cycles of experts may be reduced with an improved efficiency. This paper provides a novel and effective way for the security assessment of thermal power plants as well as a new perspective on the use of prototypes through case aggregation which is one of the popular trends of CBR systems in recent years [35]. From a practical perspective, this approach can not only provide the suggested conclusion but also a whole set of evaluation and improvement alternatives for both expert panel members and TPPs.

By further trials in Luodian, one of high-power stations in China, the practical results have verified its availability and high performance again. The computerized system works well in providing the knowledge and decision making support for experts during the process of MSSATPP. According to an anonymous survey of 32 assessment experts, 29 of them (90.6%) replied that they were mainly satisfied with the effects of the CBRSYS-TPP system. All the experts expressed that they got valuable information support during the decision making and the conclusions are more scientific and acceptable than those without the support of CBRSYS-TPP. This further inflects the application values of CBR in the safety assessment of TPPs.

Compared to the direct expert evaluation approach, the most commonly used approach in which experts first evaluate each item of safety management work using an evaluation index system then reach a conclusion through face-to-face discussion, our approach has a number of advantages. Firstly, it is more objective than the expert evaluation approach. Furthermore, compared to expert evaluation approach and other common classification methods, our method has the following features and advantages: i) more helpful to the utilization of historical knowledge; ii) higher comprehensive performance; iii) based on real cases and easy to be understood and operated.

For future research directions, we have several thoughts. First, a new, more objective, approach should be explored for weight determination of case retrieval. Second, it is also necessary to integrate the weight determination and case retrieval methods into one system and implement a more powerful CBR system. It is also important to note that the issue of implementation and usability of the CBR systems for MSSATPP are also an interesting and promising direction for future research in this area. In addition, further communications with the electric power enterprises should be strongly encouraged. It is hoped to be able to acquire larger datasets for further experiments, especially to evaluate the performance of retrieval algorithms under the condition of large-scale data. The above problems provide broad horizon for further study. Researchers of this topic could be the professors who are interested in the safety assessment of power systems, the scholars who would like to further improve the performance of case retrieval algorithms, or PHD students who are doing the projects or research on semantic data mining or the case matching under incomplete information.

Acknowledgements. This research is partially supported by the National Natural Science Foundation of China under Grant No. 70771037, No. 90924021 and No. 70871032, China National "863" Plan Program (2006AA04A126), Anhui Provincial Natural Science Foundation under Grant No. 090416249, the MOE Project of Key Research Institute of Humanities and Social Science in University of Anhui Province and Science Research &Development Foundation of Hefei University of Technology of China (2009HGXJ0039). We thank Dr Shen Pan (Department of Computer Science at Hokkaido University, Japan) and Lucy Zhang (Senior Engineer in Canada China Computer Company) for their assistance in developing the experimental tools. And we also would like to express our thanks to Mu Xia (Assistant professor in School of Business at Santa Clara University) for his help on an improved version of our paper. Specially, we are grateful to the editors for their excellent work for the publication of this paper.

References

1. Yang, Y.P., Guo, X.Y., Wang, N.L.: Power generation from pulverized coal in China. Energy 35(11), 4336–4348 (2010)
2. Williams, R.H.: Toward zero emissions from coal in China. Energy for Sustainable Development 5(4), 39–65 (2001)
3. Oktay, Z.: Investigation of coal-fired power plants in Turkey and a case study: Can plant. Applied Thermal Engineering 29(2-3), 550–557 (2009)
4. Zhao, Y., Wang, S.X., Nielsen, C.P., Li, X.H., Hao, J.M.: Establishment of a database of emission factors for atmospheric pollutants from Chinese coal-fired power plants. Atmospheric Environment 44(12), 1515–1523 (2010)
5. Liu, C.H., Lin, S.J., Lewis, C.: Evaluation of thermal power plant operational performance in Taiwan by data envelopment analysis. Energy Policy 38(2), 1049–1058 (2010)
6. Erdem, H.H., Akkaya, A.V., Cetin, B., et al.: Comparative energetic and exergetic performance analyses for coal-fired thermal power plants in Turkey. International Journal of Thermal Sciences 48(11), 2179–2186 (2009)
7. Garg, R.K., Agrawal, V.P., Gupta, V.K.: Coding, evaluation and selection of thermal power plants – A MADM approach. International Journal of Electrical Power & Energy Systems 29(9), 657–668 (2007)

8. Kumar, R., Mahur, A.K., Sengupta, D., Prasad, R.: Radon activity and exhalation rates measurements in fly ash from a thermal power plant. Radiation Measurements 40(2-6), 638–641 (2005)
9. Petkovšek, S.A.S., Batič, F., Lasnik, C.R.: Norway spruce needles as bioindicator of air pollution in the area of influence of the Šoštanj Thermal Power Plant, Slovenia. Environmental Pollution 151(2), 287–291 (2008)
10. Lora, E.E.S., Salomon, K.R.: Estimate of ecological efficiency for thermal power plants in Brazil. Energy Conversion and Management 46(7-8), 1293–1303 (2005)
11. Zhuang, Z.Y., Churilov, L., Burstein, F., Sikaris, K.: Combining data mining and case-based reasoning for intelligent decision support for pathology ordering by general practitioners. European Journal of Operational Research 195(3), 662–675 (2009)
12. Mukhopadhyay, T., Vicinanaza, S.S., Prieutula, M.J.: Examining the feasibility of a case-based reasoning model for software effort estimation. MIS Quarterly 16(2), 155–172 (1992)
13. Chang, P.-C., Lai, C.-Y., Lai, K.R.: A hybrid system by evolving case-based reasoning with genetic algorithm in wholesaler's returning book forecasting. Decision Support Systems 42(3), 1715–1729 (2006)
14. Jung, C., Han, I., Shu, B.: Risk Analysis for Electronic Commerce Using Case-Based Reasoning. International Journal of Intelligent Systems in Accounting, Finance & Management 8(1), 61–73 (1999)
15. Ahola, T., Leiviskä, K.: Case-based reasoning in web breaks sensitivity evaluation in a paper machine. Journal of Advanced Computational Intelligence and Intelligence Informatics 9, 555–561 (2005)
16. Bang, Y.-H., Kim, J.-G., Hwang, I.-S.: CBR (Case-Based Reasoning) Evaluation Modelling for Security Risk Analysis in Information Security System. In: 2008 International Conference on Security Technology, pp. 66–70 (2008)
17. Gu, D.X., Liang, C.Y., Li, X.G., et al.: Intelligent Technique for Knowledge Reuse of Dental Medical Records Based on Case-Based Reasoning. Journal of Medical Systems 34(2), 213–222 (2010)
18. Ivanov, K.: A subsystem in the design of informatics: Recalling an archetypal engineer. In: Dahlbom, B. (ed.) The Infological Equation: Essays in Honor of Börje Langefors, pp. 1101–7422. Gothenburg University, Dept. of Informatics, Gothenburg (1995) ISSN 1101-7422
19. García-Nieto, J., Alba, E., Jourdan, L., Talbi, E.: Sensitivity and specificity based multiobjective approach for feature selection: Application to cancer diagnosis. Information Processing Letters 109(6), 887–896 (2009)
20. Rowe, G., Wright, G.: Expert Opinions in Forecasting. Role of the Delphi Technique. In: Armstrong (ed.) Principles of Forecasting: A Handbook of Researchers and Practitioners. Kluwer Academic Publishers, Boston (2001)
21. Kayacan, E., Ulutas, B., Kaynak, O.: Grey system theory-based models in time series prediction. Expert Systems with Applications 37(2), 1784–1789 (2010)
22. Aamodt, A., Plaza, E.: Case-Based Reasoning: Foundational Issues, Methodological Variations, and System Approaches. Artificial Intelligence Communications 7(1), 39–59 (1994)
23. de Mántaras, R.L., McSherry, D., et al.: Retrieval, reuse, revision, and retention in case-based reasoning. Knowledge Engineering Review 20(3), 215–240 (2005)
24. Bichindaritz, I., Marling, C.: Case-based Reasoning in the Health Sciences: What's Next? Artificial Intelligence in Medicine, Special Issue on Case-based Reasoning in the Health Sciences 36(2), 127–135 (2006), Bichindaritz, I. (ed.)

25. Deng, J.L.: Control problems of grey systems. Systems & Control Letters 1(5), 288–294 (1982)
26. Liu, P.D., Wang, T.J.: Research on Risk Evaluation in Supply Chain Based on Grey Relational Method. Journal of Computers 3(10), 28–35 (2008)
27. Lu, Y., He, X., Du, J.J.: Malfunction case retrieval algorithm based on Grey System Theory. Chinese Computer Engineering of China 34(9), 28–32 (2008)
28. Harman, D.: Evaluation issues in Information Retrieval. Information Processing & Management 28(4), 439–528 (1992)
29. Kumar, R., Mahur, A.K., Sengupta, D., Prasad, R.: Radon activity and exhalation rates measurements in fly ash from a thermal power plant. Radiation Measurements 40(2-6), 638–641 (2005)
30. Hermans, E., Ruan, D., Brijs, T., Wets, G., Vanhoof, K.: Road safety risk evaluation by means of ordered weighted averaging operators and expert knowledge. Knowledge-Based Systems 23(1), 48–52 (2010)
31. Petkovšek, S.A.S., Batič, F., Lasnik, C.R.: Norway spruce needles as bioindicator of air pollution in the area of influence of the Šoštanj Thermal Power Plant, Slovenia. Environmental Pollution 151(2), 287–291 (2008)
32. Boyen, X., Wehenkel, L.: Automatic induction of fuzzy decision trees and its application to power system security assessment. Fuzzy Sets and Systems 102(1), 3–19 (1999)
33. Kim, H., Singh, C.: Power system probabilistic security assessment using Bayes classifier. Electric Power Systems Research 74(1), 157–165 (2005)
34. Amjady, N.: Dynamic voltage security assessment by a neural network based method. Electric Power Systems Research 66(3), 215–226 (2003)
35. Nilsson, M., Sollenborn, M.: Advancements and trends in medical case-based reasoning: an overview of systems and system development. In: Barr, V., Markov, Z. (eds.) Proceedings of the 17th International Florida Artificial Intelligence Research Society Conference—Special Track on Case-based Reasoning, pp. 178–183. AAAI Press, Menlo Park (2004)

Outperforming Mutation Operator with Random Building Block Operator in Genetic Algorithms

Ghodrat Moghadampour

VAMK, University of Applied Sciences, Wolffintie 30, 65200, Vaasa, Finland
ghodrat.moghadampour@puv.fi

Abstract. The refinement process in genetic algorithms is carried out mainly by crossover and mutation operators. In their classical forms these operators need to be tuned through parameters and they are not efficient enough. Moreover, lack of sufficient variation in the population causes genetic algorithms to stagnate at local optima. In this work a new dynamic mutation operator called random building block operator with variable mutation rate proportionate to the number of variables in the problem is proposed. This operator does not require any pre-fixed parameter. At runtime it dynamically takes into account the length of the binary presentation of the individual and the number of variables in the problem and replaces a randomly selected section of the individual by a randomly generated bit string of the same size. Experimentation with 33 test functions, 231 test cases and 11550 test runs proved the superiority of the proposed dynamic mutation operator over single-point mutation operator with 1%, 5% and 8% mutation rates and the multipoint mutation operator with 5%, 8% and 15% mutation rates. Based on the experimentation results the random building block operator can be proposed as a better substitution of single-point and multipoint mutation operators.

Keywords: Evolutionary algorithm, Genetic algorithm, Function optimization, Random building block operator, Mutation operator, Multipoint mutation operator, Random building block operator, Fitness evaluation and analysis.

1 Introduction

Evolutionary algorithms are heuristic algorithms, which imitate the natural evolutionary process and try to build better solutions by gradually improving present solution candidates. It is generally accepted that any evolutionary algorithm must have five basic components: 1) a genetic representation of a number of solutions to the problem, 2) a way to create an initial population of solutions, 3) an evaluation function for rating solutions in terms of their "fitness", 4) "genetic" operators that alter the genetic composition of offspring during reproduction, 5) values for the parameters, e.g. population size, probabilities of applying genetic operators [8].

A genetic algorithm is an evolutionary algorithm, which starts the solution process by randomly generating the initial population and then refining the present solutions through natural like operators, like crossover and mutation. The behaviour of the

R. Zhang et al. (Eds.): ICEIS 2011, LNBIP 102, pp. 178–192, 2012.

genetic algorithm can be adjusted by parameters, like the size of the initial population, the number of times genetic operators are applied and how these genetic operators are implemented. Deciding on the best possible parameter values over the genetic run is a challenging task, which has made researchers busy with developing even better and efficient techniques than the existing ones.

2 Genetic Algorithms

Most often genetic algorithms (GAs) have at least the following elements in common: populations of chromosomes, selection according to fitness, crossover to produce new offspring, and random mutation of new offspring.

A simple GA works as follows: 1) A population of n l-bit strings (chromosomes) is randomly generated, 2) the fitness $f(x)$ of each chromosome x in the population is calculated, 3) chromosomes are selected to go through crossover and mutation operators with p_c and p_m probabilities respectively, 4) the old population is replace by the new one, 5) the process is continued until the termination conditions are met.

However, more sophisticated genetic algorithms typically include other intelligent operators, which apply to the specific problem. In addition, the whole algorithm is normally implemented in a novel way with user-defined features while for instance measuring and controlling parameters, which affect the behaviour of the algorithm.

2.1 Genetic Operators

For any evolutionary computation technique, the representation of an individual in the population and the set of operators used to alter its genetic code constitute probably the two most important components of the system. Therefore, an appropriate representation (encoding) of problem variables must be chosen along with the appropriate evolutionary computation operators. The reverse is also true; operators must match the representation. Data might be represented in different formats: binary strings, real-valued vectors, permutations, finite-state machines, parse trees and so on. Decision on what genetic operators to use greatly depends on the encoding strategy of the GA. For each representation, several operators might be employed [9]. The most commonly used genetic operators are crossover and mutation. These operators are implemented in different ways for binary and real-valued representations. In the following, these operators are described in more details.

2.1.1 Crossover

Crossover is the main distinguishing feature of a GA. The simplest form of crossover is single-point: a single crossover position is chosen randomly and the parts of the two parents after the crossover position are exchanged to form two new individuals (offspring). The idea is to recombine building blocks (schemas) on different strings. However, single-point crossover has some shortcomings. For instance, segments exchanged in the single-point crossover always contain the endpoints of the strings; it treats endpoints preferentially, and cannot combine all possible schemas. For example, it cannot combine instances of 11*****1 and ****11** to form an instance of 11***11*[10]. Moreover, the single-point crossover suffers from "positional bias" [10]: the location of the bits in the chromosome determines the schemas that can be created or destroyed by crossover.

Consequently, schemas with long defining lengths are likely to be destroyed under single-point crossover. The assumption in single-point crossover is that short, low-order schemas are the functional building blocks of strings, but the problem is that the optimal ordering of bits is not known in advance [10]. Moreover, there may not be any way to put all functionally related bits close together on a string, since some particular bits might be crucial in more than one schema. This might happen if for instance in one schema the bit value of a locus is 0 and in the other schema the bit value of the same locus is 1. Furthermore, the tendency of single-point crossover to keep short schemas intact can lead to the preservation of so-called hitchhiker bits. These are bits that are not part of a desired schema, but by being close on the string, hitchhike along with the reproduced beneficial schema [10].

In two-point crossover, two positions are chosen at random and the segments between them are exchanged. Two-point crossover reduces positional bias and endpoint effect, it is less likely to disrupt schemas with large defining lengths, and it can combine more schemas than single-point crossover [10]. Two-point crossover has also its own shortcomings; it cannot combine all schemas.

Multipoint-crossover has also been implemented, e.g. in one method, the number of crossover points for each parent is chosen from a Poisson distribution whose mean is a function of the length of the chromosome. Another method of implementing multipoint-crossover is the "parameterized uniform crossover" in which each bit is exchanged with probability, typically [10]. In parameterized uniform crossover, any schemas contained at different positions in the parents can potentially be recombined in the offspring; there is no positional bias. This implies that uniform crossover can be highly disruptive of any schema and may prevent co-adapted alleles from ever forming in the population [10].

There has been some successful experimentation with a crossover method, which adapts the distribution of its crossover points by the same process of survival of the fittest and recombination [8]. This was done by inserting into the string representation special marks, which keep track of the sites in the string where crossover occurred. The hope was that if a particular site produces poor offspring, the site dies off and vice versa.

The one-point and uniform crossover methods have been combined by some researchers through extending a chromosomal representation by additional bit. There has also been some experimentation with other crossovers: segmented crossover and shuffle crossover [4], [8]. Segmented crossover, a variant of the multipoint, allows the number of crossover points to vary. The fixed number of crossover points and segments (obtained after dividing a chromosome into pieces on crossover points) are replaced by a segment switch rate, which specifies the probability that a segment will end at any point in the string. The shuffle crossover is an auxiliary mechanism, which is independent of the number of the crossover points. It 1) randomly shuffles the bit positions of the two strings in tandem, 2) exchanges segments between crossover points, and 3) unshuffles the string [8]. In gene pool recombination, genes are randomly picked from the gene pool defined by the selected parents.

There is no definite guidance on when to use which variant of crossover. The success or failure of a particular crossover operator depends on the particular fitness function, encoding, and other details of GA. Actually, it is a very important open problem to fully understand interactions between particular fitness function, encoding, crossover and other details of a GA. Commonly, either two-point crossover or parameterized uniform crossover has been used with the probability of occurrence [10].

Generally, it is assumed that crossover is able to recombine highly fit schemas. However, there is even some doubt on the usefulness of crossover, e.g. in schema analysis of GA, crossover might be considered as a "macro-mutation" operator that simply allows for large jumps in the search space [10].

2.1.2 Mutation

The common mutation operator used in canonical genetic algorithms to manipulate binary strings $a=(a_1,...a_\ell)\in I=\{0,1\}^\ell$ of fixed length ℓ was originally introduced by Holland [6] for general finite individual spaces $I=A_1\times...A_\ell$, where $A_i=\{\alpha_{i_1},...,\alpha_{i_{k_l}}\}$.

By this definition, the mutation operator proceeds by:

1. determining the position $i_1,...,i_h (i_j\in\{1,...,l\})$ to undergo mutation by a uniform random choice, where each position has the same small probability p_m of undergoing mutation, independently of what happens at other position.
2. forming the new vector $a_i'=(a_1,...,a_{i_1-1},a_{i_1}',a_{i_1+1},...,a_{i_h-1},a_{i_h}',a_{i_h+1},...a_\ell)$, where $a_i'\in A_i$ is drawn uniformly at random from the set of admissible values at position i.

The original value a_i at a position undergoing mutation is not excluded from the random choice of $a_i'\in A_i$. This implies that although the position is chosen for mutation, the corresponding value might not change at all [1].

Mutation rate is usually very small, like 0.001 [10]. A good starting point for the bit-flip mutation operation in binary encoding is $P_m={}^1\!/_L$, where L is the length of the chromosome [13]. Since ${}^1\!/_L$ corresponds to flipping one bit per genome on average, it is used as a lower bound for mutation rate. A mutation rate of range $P_m\in[0.005,0.01]$ is recommended for binary encoding [17]. For real-value encoding the mutation rate is usually $P_m\in[0.6,0.9]$ and the crossover rate is $P_m\in[0.7,1.0]$ [17].

Crossover is commonly viewed as the major instrument of variation and innovation in GAs, with mutation, playing a background role, insuring the population against permanent fixation at any particular locus [10], [1]. Mutation and crossover have the same ability for "disruption" of existing schemas, but crossover is a more robust constructor of new schemas [16], [10]. The power of mutation is claimed to be underestimated in traditional GA, since experimentation has shown that in many cases a hill-climbing strategy works better than a GA with crossover [13], [10].

While recombination involves more than one parent, mutation generally refers to the creation of a new solution form one and only one parent. Given a real-valued representation where each element in a population is an n-dimensional vector $x\in\Re^n$, there are many methods for creating new offspring using mutation. The general form of mutation can be written as:

$$x' = m(x) \tag{1}$$

where x is the parent vector, m is the mutation function and x' is the resulting offspring vector. The more common form of mutation generated offspring vector:

$$x' = x + M \tag{2}$$

where the mutation M is a random variable. M has often zero mean such that

$$E(x') = x \tag{3}$$

The expected difference between the real values of a parent and its offspring is zero [1]. Some forms of evolutionary algorithms apply mutation operators to a population of strings without using recombination, while other algorithms may combine the use of mutation with recombination. Any form of mutation applied to a permutation must yield a string, which also presents a permutation. Most mutation operators for permutations are related to operators, which have also been used in neighbourhood local search strategies [18]. Some other variations of the mutation operator for more specific problems have been introduced in Chapter 32 in [1]. Some new methods and techniques for applying crossover and mutation operators have also been presented in [11].

It is not a choice between crossover and mutation but rather the balance among crossover, mutation, selection, details of fitness function and the encoding. Moreover, the relative usefulness of crossover and mutation change over the course of a run. However, all these remain to be elucidated precisely [10].

Crossover is commonly viewed as the major instrument of variation and innovation in GAs, with mutation, playing a background role, insuring the population against permanent fixation at any particular locus [10], [1]. Mutation and crossover have the same ability for "disruption" of existing schemas, but crossover is a more robust constructor of new schemas [16], [10]. The power of mutation is claimed to be underestimated in traditional GA, since experimentation has shown that in many cases a hill-climbing strategy works better than a GA with crossover [13], [10].

2.1.3 Other Operators and Mating Strategies

In addition to common crossover and mutation there are some other operators used in GAs including inversion, gene doubling and several operators for preserving diversity in the population. For instance, a "crowding" operator has been used in [2], [10] to prevent too many similar individuals ("crowds") from being in the population at the same time. This operator replaces an existing individual by a newly formed and most similar offspring. In [7] a probabilistic crowding niching algorithm, in which subpopulations are maintained reliably, is presented. It is argued that like the closely related deterministic crowding approach, probabilistic crowding is fast, simple, and requires no parameters beyond those of classical genetic algorithms.

The same result can be accomplished by using an explicit "fitness sharing" function [10], whose idea is to decrease each individual's fitness by an explicit increasing function of the presence of other similar population members. In some cases, this operator induces appropriate "speciation", allowing the population members to converge on several peaks in the fitness landscape [10]. However, the same effect could be obtained without the presence of an explicit sharing function [15], [10].

Diversity in the population can also be promoted by putting restrictions on mating. For instance, distinct "species" tend to be formed if only sufficiently similar individuals are allowed to mate [10]. Another attempt to keep the entire population as diverse as possible is disallowing mating between too similar individuals, "incest" [4], [10]. Another solution is to use a "sexual selection" procedure; allowing mating only between individuals having the same "mating tags" (parts of the chromosome that identify prospective mates to one another). These tags, in principle, would also evolve to implement appropriate restrictions on new prospective mates [6].

Another solution is to restrict mating spatially. The population evolves on a spatial lattice, and individuals are likely to mate only with individuals in their spatial neighbourhoods. Such a scheme would help preserve diversity by maintaining spatially isolated species, with innovations largely occurring at the boundaries between species [10].

The efficiency of genetic algorithms has also been tried by imposing adaptively, where the algorithm operators are controlled dynamically during runtime [5]. These methods can be categorized as deterministic, adaptive, and self-adaptive methods [3], [5]. Adaptive methods adjust the parameters' values during runtime based on feedbacks from the algorithm [5], which are mostly based on the quality of the solutions or speed of the algorithm [14].

3 The Random Building Block Operator

The *random building block* (RBB) operator was originally presented in [11] and [12], where promising results were also reported. In this paper we modify the original idea of the operator by taking into account the number of variables in the function. By building block we refer to any arbitrary section in the binary representation of the individual. During the classical crossover operation, building blocks of two or more individuals of the population are exchanged in the hope that a better building block from one individual will replace a worse building block in the other individual and improve the individual's fitness value. However, the random building block operator involves only one individual. The random building block operator resembles more the multipoint mutation operator, but it lacks the frustrating complexity of such an operator. The reason for this is that the random building block operator does not require any pre-defined parameter value and it automatically takes into account the number of variables in the problem and the length of the binary representation of the individual at hand. In practice, the random building block operator selects a section of random length from the individual at hand and replaces it with a randomly produced building block of the same length. However, the length of the random building block is inversely proportionate to the dimension (the number of variables) of the problem. It should be noted that regardless of the number of variables in the problem, each candidate solution (individual in the population) will be represented as one binary string. For instance, if there are 5 variables in the problem, the random building block will be generated from 1/5 of the length of the binary representation of the individual, which naturally includes all variables. If the number of variables in the problem is denoted as v and the length of the individual as l, the length of the building block is randomly determined according to the following formula:

$$RBB_{length} = rand(\frac{1}{v} \times l) \tag{4}$$

The random building block operator can help breaking the possible deadlock when the classic crossover operator fails to improve individuals. It can also refresh the population by injecting better building blocks into individuals, which are not currently found from the population. Figure 1 describes the random building block operator.

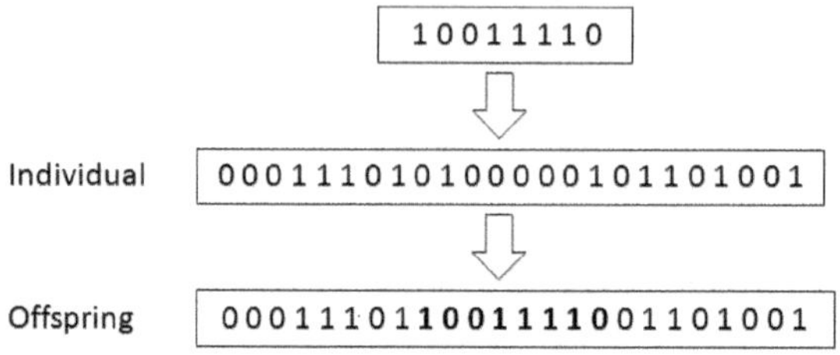

Fig. 1. The random building block operator. A random building block is generated and copied to an individual to produce a new offspring.

4 Experimentation

The random building block operator, three versions of single-point mutation operator (with 1%, 5% and 8% mutation rates) and three versions of multipoint mutation operator (with 5%, 8% and 15% mutation rates) were implemented as prat of a genetic algorithm to solve the following demanding minimization problems: Ackley's ($\forall x_i : -32.768 \le x_i \le 32.768$), Colville's ($\forall x_i : -10 \le x_i \le 10$), Griewank's F1 ($\forall x_i : -600 \le x_i \le 600$), Rastrigin's ($\forall x_i : -5.12 \le x_i \le 5.12$), Rosenbrock's ($\forall x_i : -100 \le x_i \le 100$) and Schaffer's F6 ($\forall x_i : -100 \le x_i \le 100$). Some of these functions have a fixed number of variables and some others are multidimensional in which the number of variables could be determined by the user. For multidimensional problems with an optional number of dimensions (n), the algorithm was tested for $n = 1, 2, 3, 5, 10, 30, 50, 100$. The exception to this was the Rosenbrock's function for which the minimum number of variables is 2. The efficiency of each of the operators in generating better fitness values was studied.

During experimentation only one operator was tested at each time. To simplify the situation and clarify interpretation of experimentation results the operators were not combined with other operators, like crossover.

Single-point mutation operator was implemented so that the total number of mutation points ($total\_mutation\_points$) was calculated by multiplying the mutation rate (m_rate) by the binary length of the individual (ind_bin_length) and the population size (pop_size):

$$total\_mutation\_points = m\_rate \times ind\_bin\_length \times pop\_size \tag{5}$$

Then during each generation for the total number of mutation points one gene was randomly selected from an individual in the population and mutated. Multipoint mutation operator was implemented so that during each generation for the total number of mutation points ($total\_mutation\_points$) a random number of mutation points ($sub\_mutation\_points$) from a random number of individuals in the population was selected and mutated. This process was continued until the total number of mutation points was consumed:

$$total\_mutation\_points = \sum_{i=1}^{n} sub\_mutation\_points_i \tag{6}$$

For each test case the steady-state algorithm was run for 50 times. The population size was set to 9 and the maximum number of function evaluations for each run was set to 10000. The exception to this was the Rosenbrock's function for which the number of function evaluations was set to 100000 in order to get some reasonable results.

The mapping between binary strings into floating-point numbers and vice versa was implemented according to the following well-known steps:

1. The distance between the upper and the lower bounds of variables is divided according to the required precisions, $precision$ (e.g. the precision for 6 digits after the decimal point is $1000000_{(10)}$) in the following way:

$$(upperbound - lowerbound) \times precision \tag{7}$$

2. Then an integer number l is found so that:

$$(upperbound - lowerbound) \times precision \leq 2^l \tag{8}$$

Thus, l determines the length of binary representation, which implies that each chromosome in the population is l bits long.

Therefore, if we have a binary string x' of length l, in order to convert it to a real value x, we first convert the binary string to its corresponding integer value in base 10, $x'_{(10)}$ and then calculate the corresponding floating-point value x according to the following formula:

$$x = lowerbound + x'_{(10)} \times \frac{upperbound - lowerbound}{2^l - 1} \tag{9}$$

The variable and solution precisions set for different problems were slightly different, but the same variable and solution precisions were set the same for all operators. During each run the best fitness value achieved during each generation was recorded. This made it possible to figure out when the best fitness value of the run was actually found. Later at the end of 50 runs for each test case the average of the best fitness values and the required function evaluations were calculated for comparison. In the following, test results for comparing the efficiency of random building block operator with different versions of mutation operator are reported.

Table 1 summarizes test results achieved with single-point mutation operator and the random building block operator on Ackley's, Griewank's and Colville's functions. In the table the average of the best fitness values and required function evaluations by single-point mutation operator (with 1%, 5% and 8% mutation rates) and the building block operator are reported.

Table 1. Comparison of the average of the best fitness values achieved for Ackley's (A1-A100), Griewank's (G1-G100) and Colville's (C4) functions by single-point mutation (SPM) operator with 1%, 5% and 8% mutation rates and the random building block (RBB) operator. In the table *Fn.* stands for function, *F.* for fitness and *FE.* for function evaluations.

Fn.	Operator							
	SPM (1%)		SPM (5%)		SPM (8%)		RBB	
	F.	FE.	F.	FE.	F.	FE.	F.	FE.
A1	0.0	472	0.0	625	0.0	517	0.0	925
A2	0.38	3172	0.23	2330	0.44	3559	0.0	3233
A3	1.4	6735	0.62	4513	1.02	5510	0.0	6194
A5	2.0	8645	1.96	7878	1.69	7641	0.0	9310
A10	2.4	9810	2.51	9804	2.47	9784	0.0	10000
A30	2.65	10000	2.71	10000	2.71	10000	0.32	10000
A50	2.73	10000	2.70	10000	2.76	10000	2.0	10000
A100	6.83	10000	6.8	10000	6.57	10000	5.2	10000
G1	0.02	5091	0.0	5815	0.0	6544	0.0	1078
G2	0.47	10000	0.8	10000	0.7	10000	0.0	6990
G3	0.16	10000	2.1	10000	2.0	10000	0.0	9287
G5	5.7	10000	5.6	10000	5.8	10000	0.02	9974
G10	11.1	10000	11.1	10000	10.7	10000	0.06	10000
G30	33	10000	32.6	10000	33.2	10000	0.9	10000
G50	56	10000	56.3	10000	53.4	10000	1.6	10000
G100	125	10000	120	10000	118	10000	10.4	10000
C4	51.0	10000	88.0	10000	52.5	10000	1.4	9963

Comparing results in Table 1 indicates that the random building block operator has produced better results than different versions of the single-point mutation operator in almost all test cases. The difference seems not to be significant for A1, but in all other cases the random building block apparently beats different versions of single point mutation operator. The difference in performance seems to be particularly significant for Colville's function and Griewank's function when the number of variables increases. The following Table contains the summary of statistical comparison of test results.

Table 2. The summary of statistical comparison of test results achieved by single-point mutation (SPM) operator with 1%, 5% and 8% mutation rates and the random building block (RBB) operator for Ackley's, Griewank's and Colville's functions

Test	Operators		
	RBB & SPM (1%)	RBB & SPM (5%)	RBB & SPM (8%)
T-Test	0.029	0.024	0.026
F-Test	0.000	0.000	0.000

As it can be seen from Table 2 very low p-values for T-test and F-test indicate that the performance values achieved by Random Building Block operator are significantly smaller than the ones achieved by other operators.

The performance of the random building block operator against the single-point mutation operator was also tested on Rastrigin's, Rosenbrock's and Schaffer's F6 functions. Table 3 summarizes the test results.

Table 3. Comparison of the average of the best fitness values achieved for Rastrigin's (Ra1-Ra100), Rosenbrock's (Ro2-Ro100) and Schaffer's F6 (S2) functions by single-point mutation (SPM) operator with 1%, 5% and 8% mutation rates and the random building block (RBB) operator. In the table *Fn.* stands for function, *F.* for fitness and *FE.* for function evaluations.

Fn.	Operator							
	SPM (1%)		SPM (5%)		SPM (8%)		RBB	
	F.	FE.	F.	FE.	F.	FE.	F.	FE.
Ra1	0.0	1375	0.0	1609	0.0	1436	0.0	402
Ra2	0.85	7992	1.2	8589	1.1	7988	0.0	1697
Ra3	3.1	9656	4.2	9931	3.7	9912	0.0	3665
Ra5	11.2	10000	10.2	10000	11.8	10000	0.0	8275
Ra10	24.8	10000	23.7	10000	24.8	10000	0.0	10000
Ra30	74.4	10000	72.2	10000	75.9	10000	2.1	10000
Ra50	131	10000	129	10000	129	10000	16.1	10000
Ra100	300.1	10000	292	10000	304	10000	91.4	10000
Ro2	10.9	100000	10.9	100000	18.2	100000	0.02	87254
Ro3	644	100000	1093	100000	194	100000	16.1	100000
Ro5	218	100000	1044	100000	438	100000	23.8	100000
Ro10	80	100000	353	100000	129	100000	79	100000
Ro30	649	100000	260	100000	291	100000	230	100000
Ro50	365 (712)	100000	1132 (832)	100000	351 (455)	100000	416 (185)	100000
Ro100	542 (1189)	100000	521 (946)	100000	342 (1264)	100000	929 (359)	100000
S2	0.02	6770	0.01	9810	0.01	6365	0.008	8313

Studying data presented in Table 3 proves that the random building block operator has been able to produce significantly better results in more than 78% of test cases. According to the results it seems that for Ro50 and Ro100 the random building block has on average produced worse results than the single mutation point operator. However, studying the results shows that there are huge differences between the median values (in parentheses) of test results for the benefit of the random building block. For R050 in 70% of test cases the fitness value achieved by random building block operator was less than 351, which is the average of fitness values achieved by single mutation operator with 8% mutation rate. This means that in 70% of test cases random building block has had a better performance in finding the best fitness value for Rosenbrock's function with 50 variables.

For R0100 in 70% of test cases the fitness value achieved by random building block operator was less than 521, which is the average of fitness values achieved by single mutation operator with 5% mutation rate. This means that in 70% of test cases random building block had a better performance over mutation operator with 1% and 5% mutation rates in finding the best fitness value for Rosenbrock's function with 100 variables.

Again for R0100 in 46% of test cases the fitness value achieved by random building block operator was less than 342, which is the average of fitness values achieved by single mutation operator with 8% mutation rate. This means that in 46% of test cases random building block had a better performance over mutation operator with 1% and 5% and 8% mutation rates in finding the best fitness value for Rosenbrock's function with 100 variables. The following table contains the summary of statistical comparison of test results without Ro50 and Ro100.

Table 4. Summary of statistical comparison of test results achieved by single-point mutation (SPM) operator with 1%, 5% and 8% mutation rates and the random building block (RBB) operator for Rastrigin's, Rosenbrock's (Ro2-Ro30) and Schaffer's F6 functions

Test	Operators		
	RBB & SPM (1%)	RBB & SPM (5%)	RBB & SPM (8%)
T-Test	0.076	0.065	0.060
F-Test	0.000	0.000	0.008

As it can be seen from Table 4 very low p-values for T-test and F-test indicate that the performance values achieved by random building block operator are significantly smaller than the ones achieved by other operators. The following table contains the summary of statistical comparison of test results with Ro50 and Ro100.

Table 5. Summary of statistical comparison of test results achieved by single-point mutation (SPM) operator with 1%, 5% and 8% mutation rates and the random building block (RBB) operator for Rastrigin's, Rosenbrock's (Ro2-Ro100) and Schaffer's F6 functions

Test	Operators		
	RBB & SPM (1%)	RBB & SPM (5%)	RBB & SPM (8%)
T-Test	0.367	0.117	0.663
F-Test	0.906	0.048	0.079

According to Table 5 the average of test results for Rosenbrock's function with 50 and 100 variables have a significant effect on the results of statistical analyses. But, if we take the median of test results for Rosenbrock's function with 50 and 100 variables and carry out the statistical analyses again, the differences become statistically significant for the benefit of random building block operator as in the following table.

Table 6. Summary of statistical comparison of test results achieved by single-point mutation (SPM) operator with 1%, 5% and 8% mutation rates and the random building block (RBB) operator for Rastrigin's, Rosenbrock's (Ro2-Ro100) and Schaffer's F6 functions. Notice that for Ro50 and Ro100 the median of test results have been used.

Test	Operators		
	RBB & SPM (1%)	RBB & SPM (5%)	RBB & SPM (8%)
T-Test	0.055	0.029	0.102
F-Test	0.000	0.000	0.000

The performance of the random building block operator was also compared against the multipoint mutation operator in which several points of the individual were mutated during each mutation operator. As it was earlier mentioned the number of points to be mutated during each mutation operation was randomly determined. Mutation cycles were repeated until total mutation points were utilized. Clearly, the total number of mutation points was determined by the mutation rate, which was 5%, 8% and 15% for different experimentations.

Table 7. Comparison of the average of the best fitness values achieved for Ackley's (A1-A100), Griewank's (G1-G100) and Colville's (C4) functions by multipoint mutation (MPM) operator with 5%, 8% and 15% mutation rates and the random building block (RBB) operator. In the table *Fn.* stands for function, *F.* for fitness and *FE.* for function evaluations.

Fn.	Operator							
	MPM (5%)		MPM (8%)		MPM (15%)		RBB	
	F.	FE.	F.	FE.	F.	FE.	F.	FE.
A1	0.0	1063	0.0	1173	0.0	1428	0.0	925
A2	0.0	6613	0.0	7343	0.0	8855	0.0	3233
A3	0.01	7695	0.0	9986	0.01	10000	0.0	6194
A5	0.51	7770	0.46	10000	0.5	10000	0.0	9310
A10	4.28	7806	3.5	10000	4.2	10000	0.0	10000
A30	15.18	7840	14.7	10000	15.1	10000	0.32	10000
A50	17.93	7849	17.6	10000	17.9	10000	2.0	10000
A100	19.62	7847	19.39	10000	19.6	10000	5.2	10000
G1	0.0	3256	0.0	3295	0.0	2956	0.0	1078
G2	0.02	9850	0.01	9493	0.02	9934	0.0	6990
G3	0.07	10000	0.08	9996	0.08	10000	0.0	9287
G5	0.6	10000	0.44	9999	0.4	10000	0.02	9974
G10	6.9	10000	6.6	10000	7.3	10000	0.06	10000
G30	80.6	10000	80.9	10000	89.0	10000	0.9	10000
G50	269	10000	266	10000	300	10000	1.6	10000
G100	978	10000	1005	10000	1076	10000	10.4	10000
C4	5.11	7483	4.99	9859	6.15	10000	1.4	9963

Comparing results reported in Table 7 proves that the fitness values achieved by the building block operator have been better than the ones achieved by different versions of multipoint mutation operator in all cases. Differences between the average fitness values achieved for Ackley's and Griewank's functions with 30, 50 and 100 variables by the random building block and different versions of multipoint mutation operator are even more substantial. The following table contains the summary of statistical comparison of test results.

Table 8. Summary of statistical comparison of test results achieved by multipoint mutation (MPM) operator with 5%, 8% and 15% mutation rates and the random building block (RBB) operator for Ackley's, Griewank's and Colville F6 functions

Test	Operators		
	RBB & MPM (5%)	RBB & MPM (8%)	RBB & MPM (15%)
T-Test	0.183	0.187	0.184
F-Test	0.000	0.000	0.000

As it can be seen from Table 8 low p-values for T-test and very low p-values for F-test indicate that the performance values achieved by random building block operator are significantly smaller than the ones achieved by other operators.

The performance of the random building block operator against the multipoint mutation operator was also tested on Rastrigin's, Rosenbrock's and Schaffer's F6 functions. Table 9 summarizes the test results.

Table 9. Comparison of the average of best fitness values achieved for Rastrigin's (Ra1-Ra100), Rosenbrocks's (Ro2-Ro100) and Schaffer's F6 (S2) functions by multipoint mutation (MPM) operator with 5%, 8% and 15% mutation rates and the random building block (RBB) operator. In the table *Fn.* stands for function, *F.* for fitness and *FE.* for function evaluations.

Fn.	Operator							
	MPM (5%)		MPM (8%)		MPM (15%)		RBB	
	F.	FE.	F.	FE.	F.	FE.	F.	FE.
Ra1	0.0	775	0.0	793	0.0	954	0.0	402
Ra2	0.0	4873	0.0	5114	0.0	6690	0.0	1697
Ra3	0.28	9963	0.23	9989	0.32	10000	0.0	3665
Ra5	3.0	10000	2.7	10000	3.4	10000	0.0	8275
Ra10	18.3	10000	17.7	10000	21.8	10000	0.0	10000
Ra30	159.9	10000	163.1	10000	179.2	10000	2.1	10000
Ra50	392.4	10000	388.3	10000	407.5	10000	16.1	10000
Ra100	1049	7842	1041	10000	1085	10000	91.4	10000
Ro2	0.3	98173	0.33	93046	0.37	96276	0.02	87254
Ro3	4.9	100000	9.5	100000	10.6	100000	16.1	100000
Ro5	98	100000	69.2	100000	68	100000	23.8	100000
Ro10	795	100000	693	100000	1222	100000	79	100000
Ro30	1.58E+05	100000	1.89E+05	100000	5.76E+05	100000	230	100000
Ro50	4.12E+07	100000	3.90E+07	100000	9.16E+07	100000	416	100000
Ro100	3.35E+09	100000	3.32E+09	100000	4.42E+09	100000	929	100000
S2	0.008	6079	0.006	7229	0.007	9551	0.008	8313

Studying results presented in Table 9 proves that compared to different versions of the multipoint mutation operator, the random building block operator has achieved better fitness values in 90% of test cases. Again the differences in the average of the best fitness values achieved are apparently very significant for Rastrigin's and Rosenbrock's functions with 10, 30, 50 and 100 variables. The following table contains the summary of statistical comparison of test results.

Table 10. Summary of statistical comparison of test results achieved by multipoint mutation (MPM) operator with 5%, 8% and 15% mutation rates and the random building block (RBB) operator for Rastrigin's, Rosenbrock's and Schaffer's F6 functions

Test	Operators		
	RBB & MPM (5%)	RBB & MPM (8%)	RBB & MPM (15%)
T-Test	0.327	0.327	0.323
F-Test	0.000	0.000	0.000

As it can be seen from Table 10 a small p-value for T-test and very low p-value for F-test indicate that the performance values achieved by random building block operator are significantly smaller than the ones achieved by other operators.

5 Conclusions

In this paper a dynamic mutation operator, namely random building block operator for genetic algorithms was proposed. The operator was described and utilized in solving six well-known test problems. The operator was test on 33 instances of six test functions for 1650 test runs. For each test case, the performance of the random building block operator was tested against single-point mutation operator with 1%, 5% and 8% mutation rates and multipoint mutation operator with 5%, 8% and 15% mutation rates. The maximum limit of the function evaluations was set to a pre-defined value to compare the ability of the operators to make the population converge. Runs for each test case were repeated 50 times and the average of the best fitness values and the average numbers of function evaluations required for achieving the best fitness values were calculated. Comparing test results revealed that the random building block operator was capable of achieving better fitness values compared to different versions of single-point and multipoint mutation operators. The fascinating feature of random building block is that it is dynamic and therefore does not require any pre-defined fixed parameter by the user. However, for mutation operators the mutation rate and the number of mutation points should be set in advance. The random building block can be used straight off the shelf without needing to know its best recommended rate. Hence, it lacks frustrating complexity, which is typical for different versions of the mutation operator. Therefore, it can be claimed that the random building block is superior to the mutation operator and capable of improving individuals in the population more efficiently.

5.1 Future Research

The proposed operator can be developed more and combined with other operators and applied to new problems and its efficiency in helping the search process can be evaluated more with new functions. Moreover, the random building block operator can be adopted as part of the genetic algorithm to compete with other state-of-the-art algorithms on solving more problems.

As part of the future plan the random building block operator will be improved to be even more efficient by including more useful actions in its process. In combination with other heuristic operators the random building block operator can boost the efficiency of GA.

References

1. Bäck, T., Fogel, D.B., Whitely, D., Angeline, P.J.: Mutation operators. In: Bäck, T., Fogel, D.B., Michalewicz, Z. (eds.) Evolutionary Computation 1, Basic Algorithms and Operators. Institute of Physics Publishing Ltd., United Kingdom (2000)
2. De Jong, K.A.: An Analysis of the Behavior of a Class of Genetic Adaptive Systems. Ph.D. thesis, University of Michigan. Ann Arbor, Michigan (1975)
3. Eiben, Smith, J.: Introduction to Evolutionary Computing, 2nd edn. Natural Computing Series. Springer (2007)

4. Eshelman, L.J., Schaffer, J.D.: Preventing premature convergence in genetic algorithms by preventing incest. In: Belew, R.K., Booker, L.B. (eds.) Proceedings of the Fourth International Conference on Genetic Algorithms. Morgan Kaufmann Publishers, San Mateo (1991)
5. Eiben, G., Schut, M.C.: New Ways To Calibrate Evolutionary Algorithms. In: Advances in Metaheuristics for Hard Optimization, pp. 153–177 (2008)
6. Holland, J.H.: Adaptation in Natural and Artificial Systems. University of Michigan Press, Ann Arbor (1975)
7. Mengshoel, O.J., Goldberg, D.E.: The crowding approach to niching in genetic algorithms. Evolutionary Computation 16(3) (Fall 2008) ISSN:1063-6560
8. Michalewicz, Z.: Genetic Algorithms + Data Structures = Evolution Programs. Third, Revised and Extended Edition. Springer, USA (1996) ISBN 3-540-60676-9
9. Michalewicz, Z.: Introduction to search operators. In: Bäck, T., Fogel, D.B., Michalewicz, Z. (eds.) Evolutionary Computation 1, Basic Algorithms and Operators. Institute of Physics Publishing Ltd., United Kingdom (2000) ISBN 0750306645
10. Mitchell, M.: An Introducton to Genetic Algorithms. A Bradford Book. First MIT Press Paperback Edition, United States of America (1998)
11. Moghadampour, G.: Genetic Algorithms, Parameter Control and Function Optimization: A New Approach. PhD dissertation. Acta Wasaensia 160, Vaasa, Finland (2006) ISBN 952-476-140-8
12. Moghadampour, G.: Random Building Block Operator For Genetic Algorithms. In: 13th International Conference on Enterprise Information Systems (ICEIS 2011), Beijing, China, June 08-11 (2011)
13. Mühlenbein, H.: How genetic algorithms really work: 1. mutation and hill-climbing. In: Männer, R., Manderick, B. (eds.) Parallel Problem Solving from Nature 2, North-Holland (1992)
14. Smit, S.K., Eiben, A.E.: Comparing Parameter Tuning Methods for Evolutionary Algorithms. In: IEEE Congress on Evolutionary Computation (CEC), pp. 399–406 (May 2009)
15. Smith, R.E., Forrest, S., Perelson, A.S.: Population diversity in an immune system model: implications for genetic search. In: Whitely, L.D. (ed.) Foundations of Genetic Algorithms 2. Morgan Kaufmann (1993)
16. Spears, W.M.: Crossover or mutation? In: Whitely, L.D. (ed.) Foundations of Genetic Algorithms 2. Morgan Kaufmann (1993)
17. Ursem, R.K.: Models for Evolutionary Algorithms and Their Applications in System Identification and Control Optimization (PhD Dissertation). A Dissertation Presented to the Faculty of Science of the University of Aarhus in Partial Fulfillment of the Requirements for the PhD Degree. Department of Computer Science, University of Aarhus, Denmark (2003)
18. Whitley, D.: Permutations. In: Bäck, T., Fogel, D.B., Michalewicz, Z. (eds.) Evolutionary Computation 1, Basic Algorithms and Operators. Institute of Physics Publishing Ltd., United Kingdom (2000) ISBN 0750306645

Automating Texas Hold'em Poker with *PLICAS*

Michael Schwind[1] and Christian Friedrich[2]

[1] IT-based Logistics, Institute for Information Systems, Goethe University Frankfurt
Grüneburgplatz 1, 60323 Frankfurt Main, Germany
[2] Business Information Systems and Operations Research, Technical University Kaiserslautern
Erwin-Schrödinger-Str., D-67663 Kaiserslautern, Germany

Abstract. Influenced by the possibilities of the Internet poker has become a popular online game. Spurred by this development, automated poker got into the focus of research in *game theory* (GT), *artificial intelligence* (AI) and *multi-agent systems* (MAS). This paper describes the development and evaluation of *PLICAS*, a poker bot designed for the 'Texas Hold'em Fixed Limit Heads-up' variant. The poker bot integrates approaches, such as opponent modeling, abstraction techniques, and case-based reasoning. *PLICAS* also introduces simulation-based methods for the exploitation of the opponent's play. Participation in the 2010 *AAAI Computer Poker Competition (ACPC)* shows that *PLICAS* has a lot of potential but suffers from a vulnerable opponent modeling strategy.

Keywords: Multi-agent systems, Artificial intelligence, Game theory.

1 Introduction

In contrast to games with perfect information such as chess or checkers, poker is a game with imperfect information [7,16]. While for perfect information games there are solution approaches that can compete with the world's best human players, games with imperfect information did not enter the research focus until the end of the nineties [9]. However, in the recent years a lot of poker bots have been developed including the 'Texas Hold'em Fixed Limit' variant.[1] This has resulted in a significant improvement in the quality of playing poker bots driven by the *AAAI Computer Poker Competition (ACPC)*[2]. Recent bots use abstraction methods to handle the complexity of poker [5] or employ classical AI approaches for opponent modeling and decision making [1]. While these approaches mostly specialize on a single particular aspect or phase of the poker game and the implementation of suitable solution methods derived from GT, AI, and MAS, such as learning and reasoning techniques, we follow a holistic hybrid approach. For that reason, this paper presents the concept, architecture, and evaluation of the poker bot *PLICAS*[3], which uses a combination of case and rule-based reasoning together with simulation, abstraction, learning, and opponent modeling techniques to create a decision making process for the relevant phases of the poker game. Additionally, *PLICAS* uses preflop ranges for determining the optimal bluffing frequency, which is a new approach. After an overview of the literature on automated poker play, we present the

[1] Poker rules & variants: `www.pagat.com/poker/rules/`
[2] `www.computerpokercompetition.org`
[3] 'Fold' (lat. plicare) describes the action of laying down cards and quitting the game.

R. Zhang et al. (Eds.): ICEIS 2011, LNBIP 102, pp. 193–207, 2012.

architecture, methods, and algorithms of *PLICAS* followed by the presentation of some experiments in order to initially evaluate the bot and the results of 2010 ACPC which *PLICAS* participated in.

2 A Short Overview of Automated Poker Play

The seminal scientific work on poker is mainly based on GT. The pioneers of GT, such as Neumann [13], Kuhn [10] and Nash [12] present some game theoretic analysis for simplified versions of poker in their early work. Due to the complexity of poker it was merely impossible to think about using their work for building automated poker players until the last decade. Koller and Pfeffer [9] are the first to analyze poker and imperfect information games from a game theoretical point of view with respect to automated play. They present the design for the theory-based GALA system which is able to deal with the imperfect information problem in poker. However, this system remains purely theoretical.

Billings et al. [2] published the first article about a poker bot implementation called LOKI. This bot introduces *opponent modeling* which allows an adaptive playing style trying to exploit the weaknesses of the opponent. The decision making process of LOKI is rule-based. A revised version of LOKI is the poker bot POKI which uses neural net-based opponent modeling [4], efficient hand strength simulation and probability triples for probabilistic decision making [3,5].

Opponent modeling is often coupled with bluffing which is essential in real-world poker. Southey et al. [19] present a opponent modeling poker bot which uses bluffing strategies. Von Neumann and Morgenstern [13, p. 189] characterize bluffing as follows: ‘Of the two motives for bluffing, the first is the desire to give a (false) impression of strength in (real) weakness; the second is the desire to give a (false) impression of weakness in (real) strength.’

Another technique used to enhance poker play in connection with opponent modeling is abstraction. The poker bot PsOpti uses an abstraction technique named *bucketing* where hands are classified into ‘buckets’ in accordance with their strength. Additionally a betting round reduction is realized by merging pre- and postflop behavior. These techniques are combined with a pseudo-optimal playing strategy which tries to approximate a *Nash equilibrium* for poker [1].

Approximating the Nash equilibrium (ϵ-equilibrium) strategy is a very common technique in automated poker play. A Nash equilibrium strategy is designed to avoid losing for the poker bot in contrast to the opponent modeling strategy which aims at winning a game by exploiting weaknesses. This is because no matter what playing strategy the opponent adopts, the *ϵ-equilibrium strategy* ensures that the opponent can not win more than the equilibrium solution allows for. The approximation is needed because of the large size of the game tree [1].

After having substantial success with PsOpti while playing against human poker players of even world-class level, Billings et al. [1] present a further bot called BR-Player. This bot employs heuristic search and uses the ‘expectimax’ algorithm to exploit the opponents’ strategies [17]. The ‘expectimax’ strategy is a subtype of the *min-max strategy*. In a min-max strategy each player tries to minimize the maximum payoff possible for the opponent. If the game is a zero-sum game, this strategy also maximizes minimum payoff of the player. Expectimax is a min-max strategy that works with expected values due to the stochasticity of poker. Another type of min-max strategy is the *min-regret approach* that minimizes the worst-case regret. Regret is defined as the difference between the actual payoff and the payoff that could have been obtained if the player would have chosen another action. Min-max strategies are usually employed to find the ϵ-equilibrium strategy in a Nash game.

Latest poker bots with successful playing strategies use case-based reasoning to make playing decisions. In 2008 Watson and Rubin [20], published CASPER, a bot which introduces case-based reasoning in multi-player poker. A heads-up version of CASPER (SARTRE) was fairly successful in the 2010 ACPC [14,15].

3 Essential Techniques for Automated Poker Play

Summarizing the models for playing automated poker that have been presented in the previous section, we give a short overview of standard techniques, that are currently used to design poker bots:

- **Case-based reasoning** is used to find suitable action in the playing process. Without bucketing large databases are needed to cover all situations.
- **ϵ-equilibrium** is an approximation to the Nash equilibrium strategy. The strategy is designed to avoid losing the game. ϵ-equilibrium strategy is often used together with min-max optimization.
- **Min-max strategy** minimize the maximum payoff possible for the opponent. The *min-regret* and the *expectimax* strategy are variants of this approach.
- **Opponent modeling** is an adaptive playing style that tries to exploit the weaknesses of the opponent. In contrast to the ϵ-equilibrium strategy, opponent modeling is designed to win the game while increasing the risk of losing.
- **Learning** refers to all memory-based techniques which are designed to exploit former experience for finding better future playing strategies.
- **Bluffing** has the goal to cause at least one opponent who holds a better hand to quit the game.
- **Simulation** produces pre-play results which are stored in a memory and can be exploited for better strategy selection in the course of a poker game.
- **Bucketing** is an abstraction technique that reduces the complexity of the game. Several decision situations in the game are treated in the same way.

Because *bucketing* is an essential technique for *PLICAS*, we will give an example how it works together with the ranking of *starting hands*. Tab. 1 shows an example using eight equivalence classes. The term 'suited' and 'off suit' means that a hand has the same color (e.g. $8\diamondsuit, 9\diamondsuit$) respectively different colors (e.g. $8\heartsuit, 9\spadesuit$). Class one includes the strongest starting hands: $A\diamondsuit A\spadesuit$, $K\diamondsuit K\spadesuit$, $Q\diamondsuit Q\spadesuit$, $J\diamondsuit J\spadesuit$ and $A\diamondsuit K\diamondsuit$. These hands can bet handled with the same strategies in the first round. The higher the number in Tab. 1 is, the weaker is the starting hand class. A hand such as $J\heartsuit, 8\spadesuit$ is considered as just playable. Hands marked in gray are falling into class eight and are considered as not playable.

Table 1. Ranking of starting hands into buckets (numbers denote classes)

		suited												
		A	K	Q	J	T	9	8	7	6	5	4	3	2
off suite	A	1	1	2	2	3	4	4	5	5	5	5	5	5
	K	2	1	2	3	3	5	6	6	6	6	6	6	6
	Q	3	4	1	3	4	5	6						
	J	4	5	5	1	4	5	6	7					
	T	4	5	5	5	2	5	6						
	9	7	7		6	6	3	6	6	7				
	8	7			7	7	6	4	6	7	7			
	7							7	5	7	6	7		
	6								7	6	7	6		
	5									7	6	7	7	
	4										7	6	6	7
	3												6	7
	2													6

4 System Architecture and Playing Algorithms

The *general system architecture* of *PLICAS* is depicted in Fig. 1. Several *decision units* influence the decision process that can end in a 'fold', 'call', or 'raise' action.

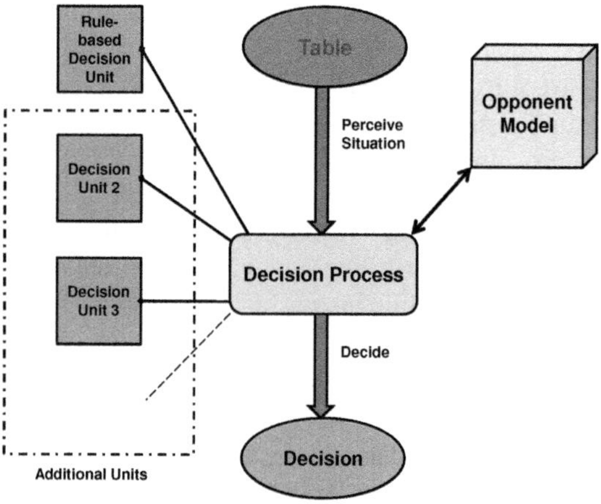

Fig. 1. System architecture of the *PLICAS* poker bot

A *rule-based based unit* contains the logic for these decisions. *PLICAS* uses basically rules that are generically derived from classical expert rules for poker play [18]. These decisions also depend on the data collected by the *opponent model* unit in the course of the game. Poker play in general has four phases: the *flop*, the *turn*, the *river* and the *showdown*. These can be grouped into two main phases: the *preflop* phase before the flop cards are dealt and the *postflop* phase afterwards (including turn, river, and showdown). For this reason the *PLICAS* bot uses two decision units, one for the *preflop* phase and another for the *postflop* phase (including turn, river, and showdown).

The dichotomy of the decision units produces interdependencies: observations made in the preflop phase (opponent's played hand ranges[4]) influence decisions in the postflop phase and vice versa (opponents postflop aggression influences preflop play).

4.1 The Preflop Model

PLICAS' decision model for the preflop phase is depicted in Fig. 2.

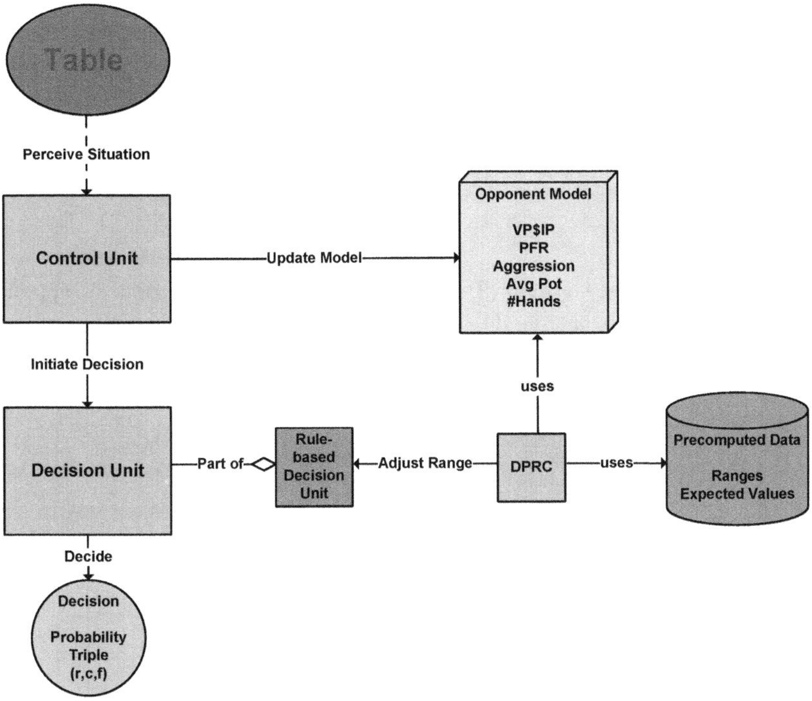

Fig. 2. System architecture of the *PLICAS* preflop decision model

Information gathered in the preflop phase is very important for getting an idea of how the opponent plays. For this purpose, *PLICAS* has been given an opponent model, which registers how often the opponent *raises* and *calls* before the flop. The opponent's aggression, the proportion of raises and calls during the game, is also measured. The information about the percentage of hands (*range*) the opponent does not fold before the flop is the most essential for adapting play. The output of the preflop phase decision process is a probability triple $pt(r, c, f)$. This triple helps *PLICAS* to decide when to fold, call, or raise during the game. *PLICAS*' preflop system is endowed with the simulation-based *dynamic preflop range control (DPRC)* and a rule-based decision unit.

[4] A hand range is a subset of all possible starting hands.

Rule-Based Decision Unit (Preflop). This unit provides the basic rules for decision making process of *PLICAS*. The preflop decisions are rational decisions based on the opponent's actions and an hand ranking according to expected values (EV). The EV is the probability that a starting hand will win the game (*pot*) against another starting hand at the showdown, without knowing any postflop cards. Decisions whether to call, fold or raise are made on base of expert-knowledge for Texas Hold'em Poker, which is represented as a rules set.

PLICAS classifies 169 starting hands according to their approximated EV against a large number of other starting hands. The calculation of the EV is done by using the 'Pokerstove'[5] tool and the result is comparable to the starting hand ranking presented in Tab. 1. There are other popular hand ranking approaches like the Sklansky [18] ranking for multi-player matches which does not use the EV as a main attribute. We decided to use an EV-based hand ranking mechanism because the EV is important in heads-up matches. Because there are only two players involved in heads-up matches, the EV can be used to assess whether run a bet, call, or raise has a positive or negative return in the long run.

Dynamic Preflop Range Control. The DPRC unit automatically adapts the opponent's preflop hand ranges by balancing the cost of preflop folding and the increase in the EV at the flop deriving from a *tighter* preflop range.[6] The following function is used for the calculation of the adapted preflop range:

$$\begin{aligned} f(r_p, r_o, p_{avg}) = \quad & EV(r_p, r_o)(p_{avg}/2) \\ & +(1 - EV(r_p, r_o))(-p_{avg}/2) \\ & +(r_o - r_p)(-1) \end{aligned}$$

r_p : one's own preflop range
r_o : the opponents' preflop range
p_{avg} : the average pot size

In this formula $EV(r_p, r_o)$ gives the percentage of how often range r_p defeats range r_o at the showdown without knowing any postflop cards. For example a range of 0.1 (10%) has an EV of 55% against a range of 0.15 (15%). A range of 0.1 represents the set of hands: $\{88_+, A9s_+, KTs_+, QTs_+, AJo_+, KQo\}$, whereas the range 0.15 represents the set of hands: $\{77_+, A7s_+, K9s_+, QTs_+, JTs, ATo_+, KTo_+, QJo\}$[7] The rest of the formula can be explained as follows: The first addend $EV(r_p, r_o)(p_{avg}/2)$ represents the chance of winning the pot postflop multiplied by the possible winnings, which is half the pot size. By contrast, the second addend $(1 - EV(r_p, r_o))$ $(-p_{avg}/2)$ is the chance of loosing the pot postflop multiplied by the possible loss, which is also

[5] www.pokerstove.com

[6] Range is called tight if the number of starting hands is small and loose if it is high.

[7] The nomenclature is as follows: 's' means that the cards' suits are the same, 'o' means that the suits are different. '+' means that hands that dominate the stated hand are also included in the range. A pocket pair is dominated by other pocket pairs with a higher rank. A non-pair hand is dominated by a hand with the same high-card and a higher kicker.

half the pot size. The third addend $(r_o - r_p)(-1)$ is the amount *PLICAS* looses by folding more often than the opponent in the preflop betting round. For example, *PLICAS*' range r_p is 0.5 and the opponents range r_o is broader with 0.6. So *PLICAS* folds in 10% ($r_o - r_p = 0.1$) of the cases when the opponent would not. In these cases he looses 1 SB[8], which is an average loss of $-0.1 \cdot SB$ per hand. The function represents a trade-off between gaining - by having an EV-advantage postflop based on a tighter preflop range - and loosing - by having a higher folding rate in the preflop phase. For performance reasons, the simulation for determining the EV is not performed at runtime. A *lookup table* holds the precalculated *simulation* results for 169 preflop ranges playing against each other in a 169×169 matrix. The starting hands categories are abstracted to 169 following the *position equivalency isomorphism* and the *suit equivalency isomorphism* described by Billings et al. [1]. *Algorithm* 1 describes the DPRC process. A relation is defined on the set of ranges. It specifies the dominance relationship of two ranges r_p and r_o based on the function $f(r_p, r_o, p_{avg})$ introduced above. If a specified number of hands $n \in \mathbb{N}$ was processed by the opponent model, the DPRC maximizes $f(r_p, r_o, p_{avg})$ using fixed values for r_o and p_{avg}. The adapted level of one's own hand range r_p is the local maximum of $f(r_p, r_o, p_{avg})$.

Algorithm 1. Dynamic Preflop Range Control

$\forall r_o \in [0,1] : \exists r_p \in [0,1] : r_p \geq r_o$
$r_p \geq r_o \Leftrightarrow r_p \ dominates \ r_o \Leftrightarrow f(r_p, r_o, p_{avg}) \geq 0$
if $OpponentModel.numHands > n$ **then**
  $r_o = OpponentModel.range$
  $p_{avg} = OpponentModel.avgPot$
  $r_p \in [0,1] \ with \ r_p \geq r_o$
  $f(r_p, r_o, p_{avg}) \rightarrow max!$
end if

4.2 The Postflop Model

The function the postflop decision model is shown in Fig. 3. After the three flop cards are dealt the size of the decision tree of the game increases significantly and decision making becomes more difficult. *PLICAS* uses the abstraction technique *bucketing* to keep the complexity at a level which can still be handled. The postflop decision process also involves a rule-based decision unit. Additionally, a case-based decision unit, a simulation-based unit for bluffing, and a unit for adapting the opponents aggression affect the postflop decision process. These units enable *PLICAS* to pursue a flexible return maximizing strategy [1] by exploiting the opponents style of play. As for preflop, the postflop decision model generates a value triple $pt(r, c, f)$ that contains the probabilities for *PLICAS*'s actions fold, call, or raise.

Rule-Based Decision Unit (Postflop). The rule-base contains rules that form a basic playing strategy. On the one hand, these rules enable the bot to avoid unprofitable play

[8] A 'small blind' (SB) is the smallest money unit that can be bet with, a 'big blind' (BB) has the double value of a SB.

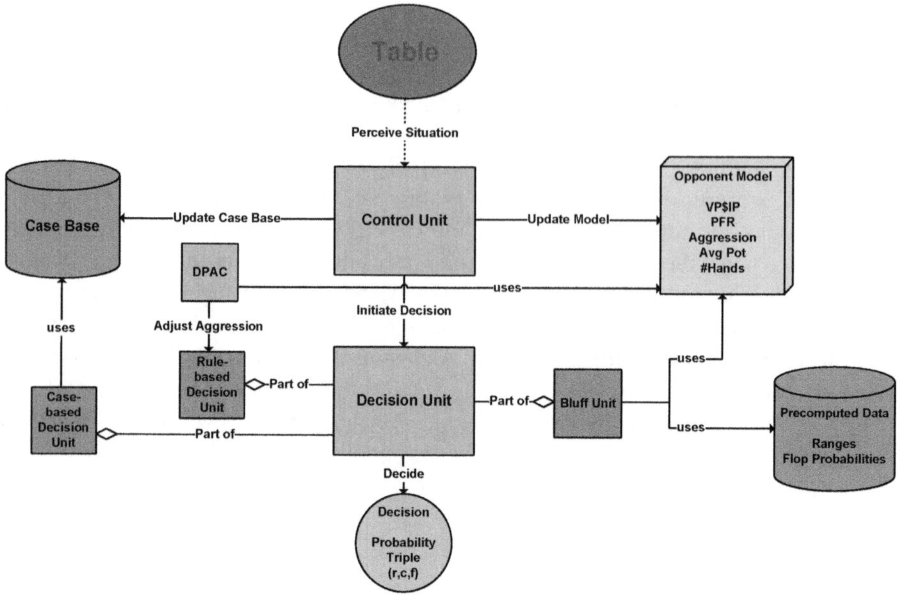

Fig. 3. Postflop decision model of the *PLICAS* poker bot

Algorithm 2. Postflop Decision Process

$Perceive\ situation\ s$
if $isFirstAction \wedge isNotPlayableHand$ **then**
  $bluff(opponentModel.range)$
else $pt(r, c, f) = ruleBase.getTriple(s)$
end if
if $|CaseBase| > n$ **then**
  $pt = merge(pt(r,c,f), CaseBase.getTriple(s))$
  $decide(pt(r, c, f))$
end if

in order to minimize losses, on the other hand, the rules produce static playing behavior which is not capable of exploiting the opponents weaknesses to maximize *PLICAS*'s profit. To do this, *Algorithm* 2 periodically perceives the situation s during the game and checks, whether the situation is suitable for bluffing. This is the case, if the opponent did not yet actively invest in the 'pot' (*isFirstAction*) and the own hand is classified as '*isNotPlayableHand*'. If the situation allows bluffing, *PLICAS* performs a bluff with a probability that depends on the opponent's preflop range (see Sec. 4.2). In the 'not bluffing' case, the rule base computes the appropriate probability triple $pt(r, c, f)$ for the situation s according to a set of rules based on [18]. Additionally, if the case-based decision unit (see Sec. 4.2) contains more than n previously recorded playing cases (threshold of operation) a second probability triple is generated. Both probability triples are then merged and used for decision making.

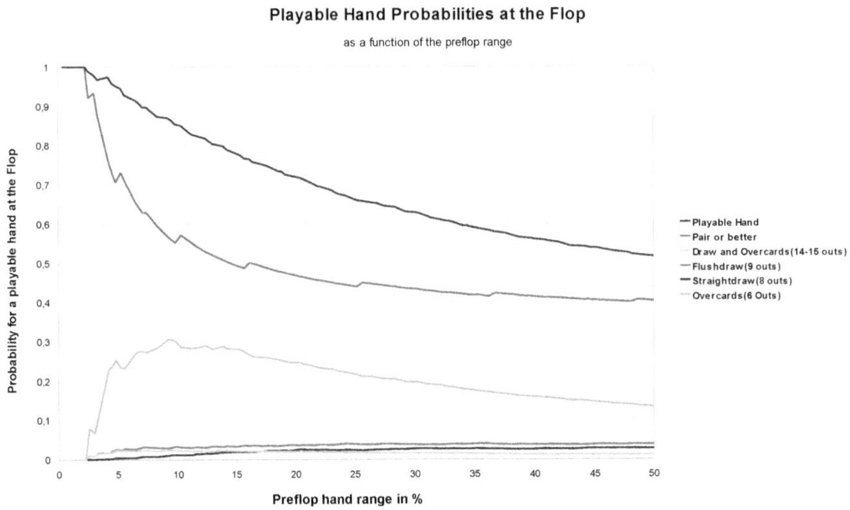

Fig. 4. Range model of the *PLICAS* poker bot

Algorithm 3. Case-based Decision with Bucketing

Perceive situation s
$c_s = createCase(s)$
if $\exists C \subset CB$ *with* $|C| > n : \forall c \in C : c \approx c_s$ **then**
  $\forall c \in C :$ *checkOpponentBucket*(c)
  return $pt(r, c, f)(ownBucket, opponentBuckets)$
else *return null*
end if

Case-Based Decision Unit. Hands going to the showdown are evaluated and stored in the case base. A case contains one's own and one's opponent's betting pattern for a hand and the opponent's hand strength shown at the showdown. This hand strength is represented by a corresponding bucket. In addition to the heuristic decision making process for playing a hand, the case base can be checked for similar cases corresponding to the hand that is currently being played. Based on the opponent's hand strength at the showdown in similar cases, the case-based decision unit influences the probability distribution of the resulting probability triple. This helps to exploit and to adapt similar patterns of the opponent's play. A more complex case-based reasoning is used by the bot CASPER [20] and SARTRE [14].

Algorithm 3 shows the procedure of the case-based decision process with bucketing. First, a case c is created for a playing situation s that is perceived by *PLICAS*. If there are more than $n \in \mathbb{N}$ cases stored in the case base that are similar to c, the algorithm checks each of these cases with respect to the behavior that is stored in the opponent modeling buckets. In order to do this, a similarity relation $c_i \approx c_j$ is defined for the cases $c_i, c_j \in C$. A similarity for a case (situation) is given if the opponent takes the same action pattern like for another situation. For all current states of the game the opponent's buckets in the corresponding situation are checked. A better average bucket of the opponent leads to a higher probability of folding for *PLICAS*. A new case is put into the case-base if it was played and recorded until showdown. A probability triple is generated based on the opponent's hand strength observed for playing situations with similar hands (which have been recorded in previous games) and the own hand strength in the current situation.

Bluff Unit. Although *bluffing* is not a part of a loss minimizing pseudo-optimal strategy it can be integrated into the player's strategy to maximize the profit. An opponent with a pseudo-optimal strategy plays an *ϵ-Nash equilibrium* strategy where ϵ is an approximation factor to the theoretical Nash equilibrium. As this opponent can never reach a real Nash equilibrium *PLICAS* can adapt to this strategy and take advantage of the instability factor ϵ.

The bluff unit provides the ability to determine whether and how probable *PLICAS* should play a bluff[9]. A situation where this can be used profitably is the first action on the flop. In correspondence with the opponent model, *PLICAS* knows the preflop range of the opponent and is able to derive the probability that the opponent is holding a hand he is willing to continue playing with. As the counter-probability expresses how probable it is that the opponent will fold to a bet, *PLICAS* can use this probability to determine its own optimal bluffing frequency. These probabilities are calculated by simulating all possible preflop hand ranges at a big number of random flops. This simulation approximates the probability that a starting hand and the flop form a playable hand. Fig. 4 shows these probabilities as a function of the preflop hand range. The blue curve represents the probability of a playable hand. The probability is the disjunction of the probabilities for holding a pair or better[10] (red curve), two overcards (light blue curve), a *flush draw* (green curve) or a *straight draw* (purple curve).[11] The number of *outs*[12] determines how probable it is that these hands will improve at the turncard. As the definition of a playable hand can vary amongst different players the probabilities are not always precise. *PLICAS* accesses these previously simulated probabilities in the form of a lookup table.

Dynamic Postflop Aggression Control. As aggression describes the proportion of raises and calls of a player, one's own aggression should vary between different opponent types. Against very aggressive opponents (*maniacs*) a more passive play is useful whereas being aggressive should be preferred against very passive players (*calling stations*). In addition to the opponent's aggression, the *dynamic postflop aggression control (DPAC)* also considers the preflop range of the opponent. A tight range yields a higher probability of the opponent holding a playable hand after the flop and thus a higher aggression. The DPAC adjusts *PLICAS*' aggression in order to maximize profit against the opponent's strategy. *PLICAS*' strategy is modified by an intentional variation of the

---

[9] Our case: getting the opponent to fold the better hand.

[10] Including *three of a kind, flush, straight* or a better hand.

[11] A draw is a situation where a card is missing for flush / straight. 2 overcards have a higher rank than all board cards.

[12] A card which is still in the deck and can improve the player's hand is called an 'out'.

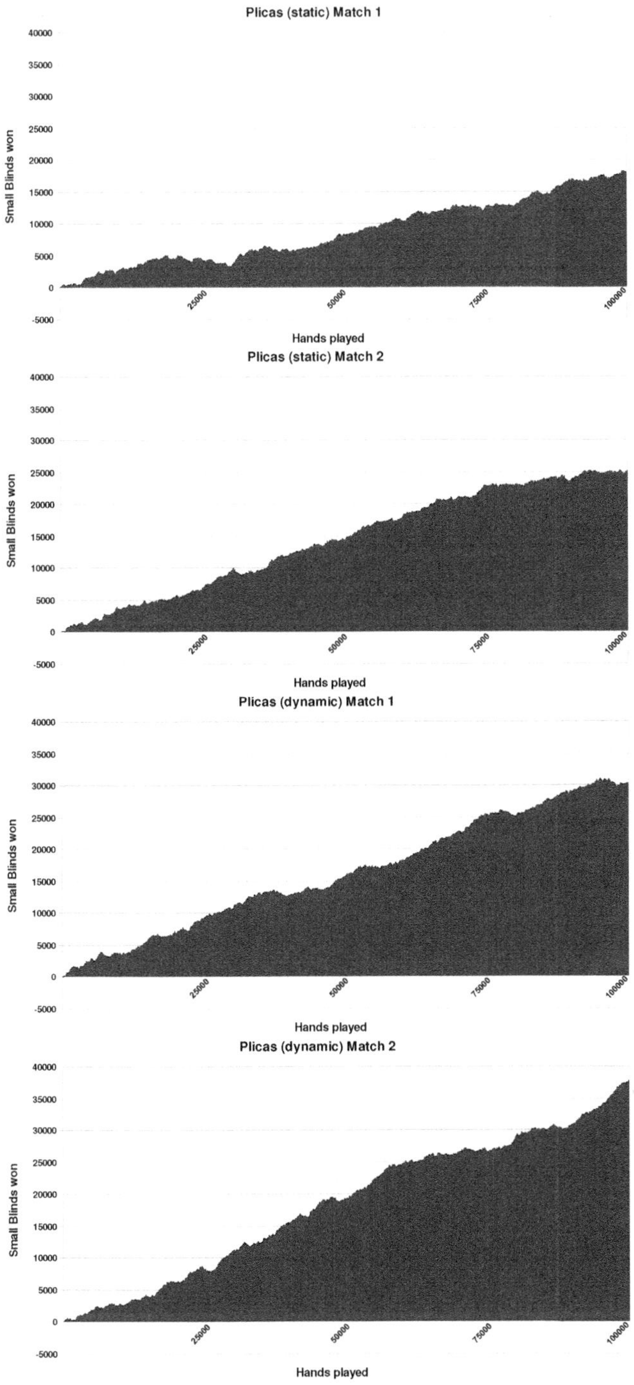

Fig. 5. Simulation results of *PLICAS* (static (up) and dynamic (down)) vs. *dpp*

original strategy based on observations of the opponent's aggression and preflop ranges. This is realized by a modification of the bucket mapping. If *PLICAS*'s aggression is increased, hands can be put into buckets representing a higher strength. If *PLICAS* is supposed to play less aggressive, hands can be put into a bucket representing a lower strength. Bucket mapping is probabilistic to avoid exploitation.

5 Experiments

The evaluation of *PLICAS* took place in two phases: In a *first step* we used a bot called '*dpp*', developed by the University of Darmstadt, Germany[13] to perform pretests and in a *second step* *PLICAS* participated in the 2010 ACPC.

5.1 Pretests with the *'dpp'* Poker Bot

Unfortunately the availability of poker bots outside the ACPC is very limited. Due to this fact, we used the freely available poker bot *dpp* for a first evaluation of *PLICAS*. *Dpp* is a 'mathematically fair' poker bot without opponent modeling which is specialized on 3-Player Texas Hold'em Limit (it made the third place in the 2009 ACPC). Despite the fact that *dpp* is playing an ϵ-equilibrium strategy and has no opponent modeling module, it can be considered as a good initial benchmark to investigate the impact of *PLICAS*' dynamic units on its performance.

The framework used for the simulations is the poker server of the ACPC. A poker match comprises $100,000$ hands including a rematch of the same size. In a rematch exactly the same hands are played but with switched positions.

Fig. 5 shows *PLICAS*' performance against *dpp* in the original match (left) and the rematch (right). *PLICAS* has a winning rate of 0.302 SB per hand in the first match and 0.377 SB per hand in the rematch. The average winning rate in both matches is 0.340 SB per hand. Another run is performed while DPRC and DPAC units of *PLICAS* are switched off. This leads to a static playing style without adaptation to the opponent's strategy. In this case the winning rate dropped to 0.179 SB per hand (Fig. 5, top) and to 0.250 SB per hand (Fig. 5, bottom) resulting in an average winning rate of 0.215 SB per hand. Comparing the dynamic and the static version of *PLICAS* the average winning rate drops by 37% from 0.34 to 0.215 SB per hand. The results show that *PLICAS*' dynamic adaptive systems have a positive influence on the winning rate. Even in a static standard playing mode *PLICAS* is able to frequently win against an average playing bot. After this initial evaluation of PLICAS, we decided to participate in the 'Heads-up Limit Texas Hold'em' category of the 2010 ACPC.

5.2 2010 Computer Poker Competition

The results of *PLICAS* in the 2010 ACPC are depicted in Tab. 2 and Tab. 3. Tab. 2 shows the total bankroll results in *big blinds (BB)* per hand including their variance.[14]

[13] `http://www.ke.tu-darmstadt.de/resources/poker`
[14] The rules and the results of the 2010 ACPC can also be seen on: `www.computer-pokercompetition.org`

Table 2. Total bankroll results in BB per hand

Rank	*Poker Bot*	*Bankroll*
1	PULPO	0.225 ± 0.003
1	Hyperborean.tbr	0.207 ± 0.002
2	Sartre	0.203 ± 0.002
3	Rockhopper	0.200 ± 0.002
4	Slumbot	0.199 ± 0.002
5	GGValuta	0.193 ± 0.003
6	Jester	0.164 ± 0.003
7	Arnold2	0.160 ± 0.003
8	GS6.tbr	0.139 ± 0.004
9	LittleRock	0.118 ± 0.003
10	**PLICAS**	-0.046 ± 0.005
11	ASVP	-0.320 ± 0.006
12	longhorn	-1.441 ± 0.005

Table 3. Ranking limit heads up runoff

Poker Bot	*Literature*
Rockhopper	not available
GGValuta	not available
Hyperborean	[8,21]
Slumbot	not available
PULPO	not available
Sartre	[15,14]
GS6.tbr	[6]
Arnold2	not available
Jester	not available
LittleRock	not available
PLICAS	this paper
ASVP	not available
longhorn	[11]

All results are significant within a 95% confidence interval. Tab. 3 shows the ranking of the poker bots after the runoff phase. Additionally, literature related to the poker bots is given in Tab. 3, if available. While making the tenth place out of twelve, *PLICAS* was not as successful as we initially expected. However, one should consider that the most poker bots in the 2010 competition have participated in previous ACPC tournaments and therefore presumably have an advantage in development.

In order to analyze the performance of *PLICAS* we categorized the bots participating in the 2010 ACPC 'Heads-up Fixed Limit' competition according to the decision methods used in the playing process. The classification of the poker bots is given in Tab. 4. The decision methods are discussed in Sec. 3. It is interesting to see that with the exception of *SARTRE*, the top ranking poker bots employ ϵ-equilibrium strategies

Table 4. Decision methods of the poker bots

Poker Bot	*Decision Method*
PULPO	learning, ϵ-equilibrium
Hyperborean	min-regret, ϵ-equilibrium
Sartre	case-based reason., opponent model
Rockhopper	not available
Slumbot	fictitious play, ϵ-equilibrium
GGValuta	not available
Jester	min-max , bucketing, ϵ-equilibrium
Arnold2	min-regret, simulation, ϵ-equilibrium
GS6.tbr	bucketing ϵ-equilibrium
LittleRock	regret-min., bucketing, ϵ-equilibrium
PLICAS	case-based reason., bucketing, learning, simulation, opponent model
ASVP	learning, simulation, opponent model
longhorn	learning, opponent model

(bots with unknown decision methods are not considered here). Poker bots using the ϵ-equilibrium strategy seem to have an advantage over opponent modeling bots unless the opponent modeling bot is able to significantly exploit the ϵ-deviations from the perfect equilibrium. From this perspective *PLICAS* is the second best performing opponent modeling poker bot in the 2010 ACPC 'Heads-up Fixed Limit' competition. We believe that the success of opponent modeling poker bots is directly related to the adaptivity of their playing strategies and the quality of the case base. The *SARTRE* bot used in the 2010 ACPC is a opponent modeling poker bot in the third generation of development that might be reason for a high adaptivity to the ACPC competitors and can be seen as a source for its success.

6 Conclusions

The 'Heads-up Texas Hold'em Fixed Limit Bot' *PLICAS* presented here is based on the computer poker competition framework of the poker research group at University of Alberta. *PLICAS* integrates approaches such as case-based reasoning, simulation-based bluffing, dynamic range control, and automated aggression adaption. The participation in the 2010 *AAAI Computer Poker Competition (ACPC)* showed that the overall performance *PLICAS* has a lot of room for improvement. However, in a differentiated analysis of the 2010 ACPC results, we find that the performance of poker bots that operate by using a ϵ-equilibrium strategy is mostly superior to poker bots that use opponent modeling strategies. From this point of view, *PLICAS*, is the second best performing participant in the group of opponent modeling poker bots. One way to improve *PLICAS*' performance is to evaluate and optimize the direct impact of the functional components (bluff unit, preflop range control, etc.) on the overall playing strength of the poker bot, by switching them on and off, while avoiding functional interferences of the modules. With a lot of training and improvement of the components *PLICAS* should be a real successful poker bot in future ACPC competitions.

References

1. Billings, D., Burch, N., Davidson, A., Holte, R., Schauenberg, T., Schaeffer, J., Szafron, D.: Approximating game-theoretic optimal strategies for full-scale poker. In: Proc. of the Int. Joint Conf. on Artificial Intelligence (ICAI 2003), Las Vegas, NV, pp. 661–668 (2003)
2. Billings, D., Papp, D., Schaeffer, J., Szafron, D.: Opponent modeling in poker. In: Proc. of the Fifteenth Nat. Conf. on Artificial Intelligence (AAAI 1998), Madison, WI, pp. 493–499. AAAI Press (1998)
3. Billings, D., Pena, L., Schaeffer, J., Szafron, D.: Using probabilistic knowledge and simulation to play poker. In: Proc. of the Sixteenth Nat. Conf. on Artificial Intelligence (AAAI 1999), Orlando, FL, pp. 697–703 (1999)
4. Davidson, A.: Using artificial neural networks to model opponents in texas hold'em. Res. Proj. Review CMPUT 499, Poker Res. Group, Univ. of Alberta, CA (1999)
5. Davidson, A., Billings, D., Schaeffer, J., Szafron, D.: Improved opponent modeling in poker. In: Proceedings of the Int. Conf. on Artificial Intelligence (ICAI 2000), Las Vegas, Nevada, pp. 493–499 (2000)
6. Gilpin, A., Sorensen, T.B., Sandholm, T.: Potential-aware automated abstraction of sequential games, and holistic equilibrium analysis of texas hold'em poker. In: Proc. of the Nat. Conf. on Artificial Intelligence (AAAI 2007), Vancouver, CA (2007)
7. Hamilton, S., Garber, L.: Deep blue's hardware-software synergy. Computer 30, 29–35 (1997)
8. Johanson, M.: Robust strategies and counter-strategies: Building a champion level computer poker player. Master's thesis, University of Alberta (2007)
9. Koller, D., Pfeffer, A.: Representations and solutions for game-theoretic problems. Artificial Intelligence 94, 167–215 (1997)
10. Kuhn, H.W.: Simplified two-person poker. In: Kuhn, H.W., Tucker, A.W. (eds.) Contributions to the Theory of Games, vol. 1, pp. 97–103. Princeton University Press (1950)
11. Lockett, A., Miikkulainen, R.: Evolving opponent models for texas hold'em. In: Proc. of the 2008 IEEE Conf. on Computational Intelligence in Games, Perth. IEEE (2008)
12. Nash, J.F., Shapley, L.S.: A simple 3-person poker game. In: Kuhn, H.W., Tucker, A.W. (eds.) Contributions to the Theory of Games, vol. 1, pp. 105–116. Princeton University Press (1950)
13. Neumann, J.V., Morgenstern, O.: Theory of Games and Economic Behavior. John Wiley (1944)
14. Rubin, J., Watson, I.: A Memory-Based Approach to Two-Player Texas Hold'em. In: Nicholson, A., Li, X. (eds.) AI 2009. LNCS, vol. 5866, pp. 465–474. Springer, Heidelberg (2009)
15. Rubin, J., Watson, I.: Similarity-Based Retrieval and Solution Re-use Policies in the Game of Texas Hold'em. In: Bichindaritz, I., Montani, S. (eds.) ICCBR 2010. LNCS, vol. 6176, pp. 465–479. Springer, Heidelberg (2010)
16. Schaeffer, J.: One jump ahead: challenging human supremacy in checkers. Springer, NY (1997)
17. Schauenberg, T.: Opponent modeling and search in poker. Master's thesis, University of Alberta, Department of Computing Science, Edmonton, Alberta (2006)
18. Sklansky, D.: Hold'em Poker: A Complete Guide to Playing the Game. Two Plus Two Publishing, Henderson, NV, USA (1997)
19. Southey, F., Bowling, M., Larson, B., Piccione, C., Burch, N., Billings, D., Rayner, C.: Bayes' bluff: Opponent modeling in poker. In: Proc. of the Twenty-First Conf. on Uncertainty in Artificial Intelligence (UAI), pp. 550–558 (2005)
20. Watson, I., Rubin, J.: CASPER: A Case-Based Poker-Bot. In: Wobcke, W., Zhang, M. (eds.) AI 2008. LNCS (LNAI), vol. 5360, pp. 594–600. Springer, Heidelberg (2008)
21. Zinkevich, M., Johanson, M., Bowling, M., Piccione, C.: Regret minimization in games with incomplete information. In: Advances in Neural Information Processing Systems 20 (NIPS), pp. 1729–1736 (2008)

An Event-Based Service Framework for Learning, Querying and Monitoring Multivariate Time Series

Chun-Kit Ngan, Alexander Brodsky, and Jessica Lin

Department of Computer Science, George Mason University
4400 University Drive MSN 4A5, Fairfax, 22030-4422, Virginia, U.S.A.
{cngan,brodsky,jessica}@gmu.edu

Abstract. We propose an event-based service framework for Multivariate Time Series Analytics (MTSA) that supports model definition, querying, parameter learning, model evaluation, monitoring, and decision recommendation on events. Our approach combines the strengths of both domain-knowledge-based and formal-learning-based approaches for maximizing utility on events over multivariate time series. More specifically, we identify multivariate time series parametric estimation problems, in which the objective function is dependent on the time points from which the parameters are learned. We propose an algorithm that guarantees to find the optimal time point(s), and we show that our approach produces results that are superior to those of the domain-knowledge-based approach and the logit regression model. We also develop MTSA data model and query language for the services of parameter learning, querying, and monitoring.

Keywords: Event-based service framework, Multivariate time series, Parameter learning, Decision support.

1 Introduction

Making decisions over multivariate time series is an important topic which has gained significant interest in the past decade, as two or more time series are often observed simultaneously in many fields. In business and economics, financial analysts and researchers monitor daily stock prices, weekly interest rates, and monthly price indices to analyze different states of stock markets. In medical studies, physicians and scientists measure patients' diastolic and systolic blood pressure over time and electrocardiogram tracings to evaluate the patients' health of respiratory systems. In social sciences, sociologists and demographers study annual birth rates, mortality rates, accident rates, and various crime rates to dig out hidden social problems within a community. The purpose of these measures over multivariate time series is to assist the specialists in understanding the same problem in different perspectives within particular domains. For those significant events to be identified and detected over multivariate time series, the events can lead the professionals to make better decisions and take more reasonable actions promptly. Those events may include index bottoms and tops in financial markets, irregular readings on blood pressure and pulse

R. Zhang et al. (Eds.): ICEIS 2011, LNBIP 102, pp. 208–223, 2012.

anomalies on electrocardiogram, as well as low birth but high death rates in a population region. To support such event-based decision-making and determination over multivariate time series, we propose a service framework, Multivariate Time Series Analytics (MTSA), which consists of services for model definition, querying, parameter learning, model evaluation, monitoring, and decision recommendation on events. Our technical focus of this work is on the problem of event detection; namely, the parameter learning, data monitoring, and decision recommendation services.

Currently, existing approaches to identifying and detecting those interesting events can be roughly divided into two categories: domain-knowledge-based and formal-learning-based. The former relies solely on domain expert knowledge. Based on their knowledge and experiences, domain experts determine the conditions that trigger the events of interest. Consider one particular example of the timely event detection of certain conditions in the stock market, e.g., the bear market bottom, that can provide investors a valuable insight into the best investment opportunity. Such identification and detection can aid in the task of decision-making and the determination of action plans. To assist users in making better decisions and determinations, domain experts have identified a set of financial indices that can be used to determine the event, i.e., the bear market bottom or the "best buy" opportunity. The indices include the S&P 500 percentage decline (SPD), Coppock Guide (CG), Consumer Confidence point drop (CCD), ISM Manufacturing Survey (ISM), and Negative Leadership Composite "Distribution" (NLCD) [1]. If these indices satisfy the pre-defined, parameterized conditions, e.g., SPD < -20%, CG < 0, etc., [1], it signals that the best period for the investors to buy the stocks is approaching. Often these parameters may reflect some realities since they are set by the domain experts based on their past experiences, observations, intuitions, and domain knowledge. However, they are not always accurate. In addition, the parameters are static, but the problem that we deal with is often dynamic in nature. The market is constantly impacted by many unknown and uncontrollable factors from the business surroundings. Thus, this approach lacks a formal mathematical computation that dynamically learns the parameters to meet the needs of the changing environment.

An alternative approach is to utilize formal learning methods such as non-linear logit regression models [2, 3, 4]. The logit regression models are used to predict the occurrence of an event (0 or 1) by learning parametric coefficients of the logistic distribution function of the explanatory variables. This is done based on the historical data by applying nonlinear regression models and Maximum Likelihood Estimation (MLE). The main challenge concerning using formal learning methods to support decision-making is that they do not always produce satisfactory results, as they do not consider incorporating domain knowledge into their formal learning approaches. Without domain experts' knowledge, formal learning methods become computationally intensive and time consuming. The whole model building is an iterative and interactive process, including model formulation, parameter estimation, and model evaluation. Despite enormous improvements in computer software in recent years, fitting such nonlinear quantitative decision model is not a trivial task, especially if the parameter learning process involves multiple explanatory variables, i.e., high dimensionality. Working with high-dimensional data creates difficult challenges, a phenomenon known as the "curse of dimensionality". Specifically, the amount of observations required in order to obtain good estimates increases exponentially with the increase of dimensionality. In addition, many learning algorithms do not scale well on high dimensional data due to the high computational cost. The parameter computations by formal-learning-based approaches, e.g., logit regression model, are complicated and costly, and they lack the consideration of integrating experts' domain knowledge into the learning process – a step that could potentially reduce the dimensionality. Clearly, both approaches, domain-knowledge-based and formal-learning-based, do not take advantage of each other to learn the optimal decision parameters, which are then used to monitor the events and make better recommendations.

To mitigate the shortcomings of the existing approaches, the proposed MTSA service framework combines the strengths of both the domain-knowledge-based and the formal-learning-based approaches. The service framework supports quick implementation of services towards decision recommendation on events over multivariate time series. More specifically, the *MTSA Model Definition Service* takes the template of conditions, which determines the occurrence of an event, identified by domain experts - such template consists of inequalities of values in the time sequences - and the *Learning Service* "parameterizes" it, e.g., SPD $< p_1$. The goal of the learning service is to efficiently learn parameters that maximize the objective function, e.g., earnings in our financial example. The *Monitoring and Recommendation Service* continuously monitors the data stream for data that satisfy the parameterized conditions, in which the parameters have been instantiated by the learning service. We also propose an extension of the relational database model and SQL with high-level MTSA constructs to support querying, monitoring, and parameter learning.

To this end, we identify multivariate time series parametric estimation problems, in which the objective function is dependent on the time points from which the parameters are learned. With the potentially large data size and multiple variables, classic branch-and-bound approaches have exponential complexity in the worst-case scenario. We develop a new algorithm that guarantees a true optimal time point, with complexity of *O(kNlogN)*, where N is the size of the learning data set, and k is the number of parametric time series. To demonstrate the effectiveness and the efficiency of our algorithm, we compare our method with the domain-knowledge-based approach and the logit regression model. As a proof of concept, we conduct an experiment in the financial domain, but note that our framework is applicable to solve problems in different domains. We show that our algorithm is more effective and produces results that are superior to those of the two approaches mentioned above. More specifically, in our experiments we show that our algorithm outperforms the financial experts' recommendation and the logit regression model, resulting in higher earnings for our imaginary investor.

The rest of the paper is organized as follows. In Section 2, we provide an overview on the MTSA service framework. We discuss the learning and monitoring services by defining the Expert Query Parametric Estimation (EQPE) model in Section 3. Section 4 explains the domain-knowledge-inspired learning algorithm and shows the experimental evaluation on stock market data. In Section 5, we describe the MTSA data model and query language. Section 6 contains the conclusions and future work.

2 An Event-Based Service Framework for Multivariate Time Series Analytics (MTSA)

Fig. 1 shows a range of common services that is desirable to be offered over the internet. The *MTSA Model Definition Service* provides a parametric model template, which determines the occurrence of an event, identified by the domain experts. In the financial example that predicts the event, i.e., market bottom, the model template may consist of indices such as S&P 500 percentage decline (SPD), Coppock Guide (CG), etc. These indices are associated with their respective inequality constraints, for example, SPD < p_1 and CG < p_2. Given such a parametric model template in a given domain, the *Monitoring and Recommendation Service* continuously screens the incoming data stream for indices that satisfy *all* the constraints which specify when the event of interest, e.g., the market bottom, has occurred, and recommends an action, e.g., buying stock. Note that in the traditional approach, the decision parameters p_1 and p_2 are specified by the domain experts, e.g., SPD < -20% and CG < 0. However, using such hard-set parameters cannot capture the dynamics of the rapidly changing market. The *Parameter Learning Service* parameterizes the template, e.g., SPD < p_1 and CG < p_2, and supports learning of the parameters from the historic time series. The accuracy of the decision parameters are ensured through the *Model Accuracy and Quality Evaluation Service*, which validates the prediction, i.e., market bottom, with the observed real data, and updates the model if necessary. The *Querying Service* allows the service developers and database programmers to express the complex information services over multivariate time series mentioned above in a high-level abstraction.

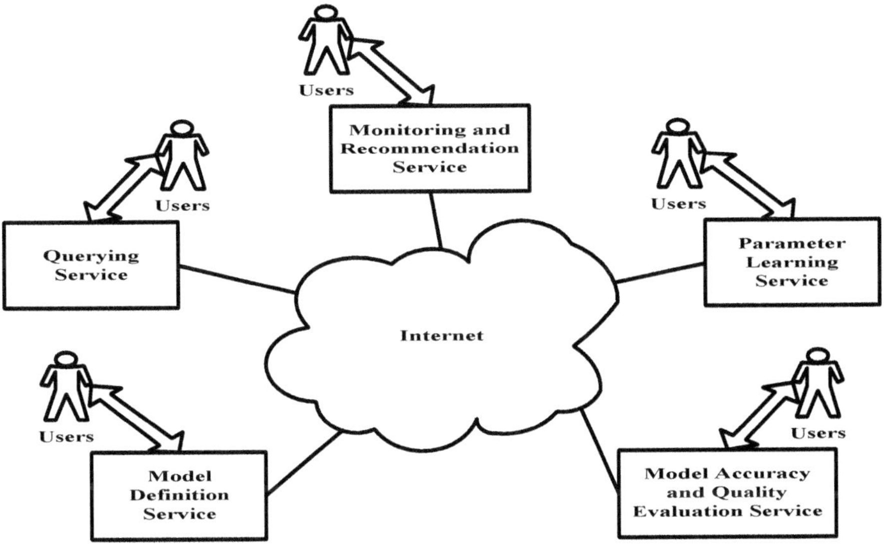

Fig. 1. Services for Multivariate Time Series Over Internet

The event-based service framework for multivariate time series analytics (MTSA) provides a medium that supports quick implementation of the services described above. The MTSA service framework is illustrated in Fig. 2. It consists of three layers: data integration, information processing, and query language. The top layer is the MTSA Model Definition and Query Language, which extends the relational database model with time series and events, and SQL with MTSA constructs. The middle layer supports the MTSA constructs including MTSA model template definition, querying, parameter learning, model evaluation, data monitoring, and decision recommendation. The bottom, Data Integration Layer, allows service providers to interact with external data services and collect time series data from heterogeneous sources, as well as from local repositories. This integration layer provides a concentric view of the collected data. The integration of the model template and the learned parameters, which may be available both locally and through external services, is also supported by the Data Integration Layer.

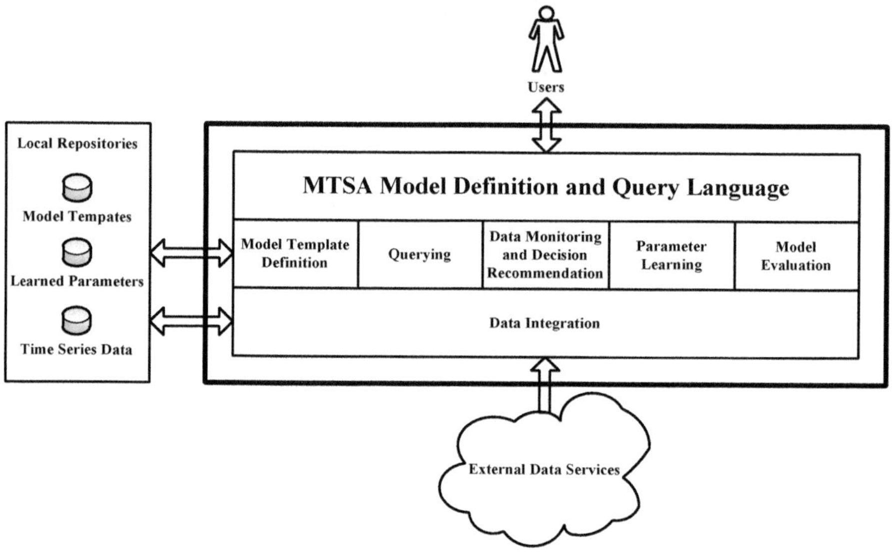

Fig. 2. An Event-Based Service Framework for Multivariate Time Series Analytics

3 Expert Query Parametric Estimation (EQPE) Model

In this section, we discuss in detail the methodologies used in the *Parameter Learning Service* and the *Monitoring and Recommendation Service* in the MTSA framework. More specifically, we review the mathematical formulations of the Expert Query Parametric Estimation (EQPE) problem and solution. We also use the examples to explain them in detail.

The goal of an EQPE problem is to find optimal values of decision parameters that maximize an objective function over historical, multivariate time series. For an EQPE problem being constructed, we need to define a set of mathematical notations and a model for it. We assume that the time domain **T** is represented by a set of natural numbers: **T** = **N**, and that we are also given a vector of n real-valued parameter variables $(p_1, p_2,\ldots, p_n)$.

Definition 1. *Time Series*: A time series S is a function S: T → R, where T is the time domain, and R is the set of real numbers.

Definition 2. *Parametric Monitoring Constraint*: A parametric monitoring constraint $C(S_1(t), S_2(t),\ldots, S_k(t), p_1, p_2,\ldots, p_n)$ is a symbolic expression in terms of $S_1(t), S_2(t),\ldots, S_k(t), p_1, p_2,\ldots, p_n$, where $S_1(t), S_2(t),\ldots, S_k(t)$ are time series, $t \in T$ is a time point, and $(p_1, p_2,\ldots, p_n)$ is a vector of parameters.

We assume a constraint C written in a language that has the truth-value interpretation I: $R^k \times R^n \rightarrow$ {True, False}, i.e., $I(C(S_1(t), S_2(t),\ldots, S_k(t), p_1, p_2,\ldots, p_n))$ = True if and only if the constraint C is satisfied at the time point $t \in T$ and with the parameters $(p_1, p_2,\ldots, p_n) \in R^n$. In this paper, we focus on conjunctions of inequality constraints: $C(S_1(t), S_2(t),\ldots, S_k(t), p_1, p_2,\ldots, p_n) = \wedge_i (S_i(t)\ op\ p_j)$, where op $\in \{<, \leq, =, \geq, >\}$.

Definition 3. *Time Utility Function*: A time utility function U is a function U: T → R.

Definition 4. *Objective Function*: Given a time utility function U: T → R and a parametric constraint C, an objective function O is a function O: $R^n \rightarrow R$, which maps a vector of n parameters on R^n to a real value R, defined as follows. For $(p_1, p_2,\ldots, p_n) \in R^n$, $O(p_1, p_2,\ldots, p_n) \stackrel{\text{def}}{=} U(t)$, where U is the utility function, and $t \in T$ is the earliest time point that satisfies C, i.e.,

(1) $S_1(t)\ op_1\ p_1 \wedge S_2(t)\ op_2\ p_2 \wedge \ldots \wedge S_n(t)\ op_n\ p_n$ is satisfied, and

(2) There does not exist $0 \leq t' < t$, such that $S_1(t')\ op_1\ p_1 \wedge S_2(t')\ op_2\ p_2 \wedge \ldots \wedge S_n(t')\ op_n\ p_n$ is satisfied.

Definition 5. *Expert Query Parametric Estimation (EQPE) Problem*: An EQPE problem is a tuple <***S, P, C, U***>, where $\boldsymbol{S} = \{S_1, S_2\ldots, S_k\}$ is a set of k time series, $\boldsymbol{P} = \{p_1, p_2,\ldots, p_n\}$ is a set of n real-value parameter variables, ***C*** is a parametric constraint in ***S*** and ***P***, and ***U*** is a time utility function.

Intuitively, a solution to an EQPE problem is an instantiation of values into the vector ***P*** of n real-value parameters that maximizes the objective ***O***.

Definition 6. *Expert Query Parametric Estimation (EQPE) Solution*: A solution to the EQPE problem <***S, P, C, U***> is *argmax* $\boldsymbol{O}(p_1, p_2,\ldots, p_n)$, i.e., the (estimated) values of parameters, $p_1, p_2,\ldots, p_n$, that maximize ***O***, where ***O*** is the objective function corresponding to ***U***.

The base time series in our financial example are shown in Table 1. We suppose that the first starting date in any time-series data set is **t** = 0. Note that some base time series are the direct inputs, whereas some are used to derive another set of time series. For instance, the derived time series in our case study are shown in Table 2. The decision parameters used in the case study are defined in Table 3. Let us consider the following constraint C as an illustration:

$$C(SPD(t), CG(t), CCD(t), ISM(t), NLCD(t), p_1, p_2, p_3, p_4, p_5) =$$
$$SPD(t) < p_1 \wedge CG(t) < p_2 \wedge CCD(t) < p_3 \wedge ISM(t) < p_4 \wedge NLCD(t) > p_5$$

It means that the parametric monitoring constraint ***C*** is satisfied, i.e., its interpretation is True, if the above inequalities with the decision parameters are satisfied at the time point t. The interpretation also indicates that the monitoring event occurs. We assume that the investor buys the S&P 500 index fund at the decision variable time t and sell it at the given t_S, which is the last day of the given training data set. The earning function $SP(t_S)/SP(t) - 1 \in R$ is the utility, which is maximized by choosing the optimal value $t \in T$, where $SP(t_S)$ and SP(t) are the sell and buy value of the S&P 500 index fund at the time t_S and t respectively. The EQPE problem and solution for our example can be constructed by putting the considered time series, parameters, constraints, and functions to the definitions shown in Table 4.

Table 1. Base Time-Series Data

Base Time Series S	Abbreviation
S&P 500	SP(t)
Coppock Guide	CG(t)
Consumer Confidence	CC(t)
ISM Manufacturing Survey	ISM(t)
Negative Leadership Composite	NLC(t)

Table 2. Derived Time-Series Data

Derived Time Series S	Abbreviation
Percentage decline in SP(t) at the time point t	SPD(t)
Points drop in CC(t) at the time point t	CCD(t)
Number of consecutive days in Bear Market "DISTRIBUTIOIN" of NLC(t) at and before the time point t	NLCD(t)
Time Utility Earning at the time point t, i.e., the index fund is bought at t and sold at t_s, where t_s is the last day of the learning data set	Earning(t)

Table 3. Decision Parameters

Parameter	Interpretation
p_1	Test if SPD(t) is less than p_1 at t.
p_2	Test if CG(t) is less than p_2 at t.
p_3	Test if CCD(t) is less than p_3 at t.
p_4	Test if ISM(t) is less than p_4 at t.
p_5	Test if NLCD(t) is greater than p_5 at t.

Table 4. EQPE Problem and Solution Formulation for S&P 500 Index Fund

Problem and Solution
Problem: $\langle \boldsymbol{S}, \boldsymbol{P}, \boldsymbol{C}, \boldsymbol{U} \rangle$, where $\boldsymbol{S} = \{\text{SPD, CG, CCD, ISM, NLCD}\}$ $\boldsymbol{P} = \{p_1, p_2, p_3, p_4, p_5\}$ $\boldsymbol{C} = \text{SPD}(t) < p_1 \wedge \text{CG}(t) < p_2 \wedge \text{CCD}(t) < p_3 \wedge \text{ISM}(t) < p_4 \wedge \text{NLCD}(t) > p_5$ $\boldsymbol{U} = \text{SP(ts)/SP}(t) - 1$ Solution: $\text{argmax}\ \boldsymbol{O}(p_1, p_2, p_3, p_4, p_5) \stackrel{\text{def}}{=} \boldsymbol{U}(t)$

The values of the optimal decision parameters can be determined by using the learning algorithm, Checkpoint. Before explaining the Checkpoint algorithm in detail, we first review the concept of *Dominance*.

Definition 7. *Dominance* $\succ$: Given an EQPE problem <***S, P, C, U***> and any two time points t, $t' \in$ T, we say that t' dominates t, denoted by $t' \succ t$, if the following conditions are satisfied:

(1) $0 \leq t' < t$, and

(2) $\forall(p_1, p_2,\ldots, p_n) \in R^n$, $C(S_1(t), S_2(t), \ldots, S_k(t), p_1, p_2,\ldots, p_n) \rightarrow C(S_1(t'), S_2(t'),\ldots, S_k(t'), p_1, p_2, \ldots, p_n)$.

Intuitively, t' dominates t if for any selection of parametric values, the query constraint satisfaction at t implies the satisfaction at t'. Clearly, the dominated time points should be discarded when the optimal time point is being determined. We formally claim that: **Claim 1** - Given the conjunctions of inequality constraints, $S_1(t)\ op_1\ p_1 \wedge S_2(t)\ op_2\ p_2 \wedge \ldots \wedge S_k(t)\ op_k\ p_k$ and the two time points t', t such that $0 \leq t' < t$, $t' \succ t$ if and only if $S_1(t')\ op_1\ S_1(t) \wedge S_2(t')\ op_2\ S_2(t) \wedge \ldots \wedge S_k(t')\ op_k\ S_k(t)$. The proof is shown in **Appendix**.

For example, suppose there are three time series S_1, S_2, S_3 and three decision parameters p_1, p_2, p_3. And the constraints are $C(S_1(t), S_2(t), S_3(t), p_1, p_2, p_3) = S_1(t) \geq p_1 \wedge S_2(t) \geq p_2 \wedge S_3(t) \leq p_3$. Also assume the values for S_1, S_2, and S_3 at the time point t_1, t_2, and t_3 respectively in Table 5 shown in the next page.

In this case, the time point t_3 is dominated because there is a time point t_1 that make the inequality, $S_1(t_1) \geq S_1(t_3) \wedge S_2(t_1) \geq S_2(t_3) \wedge S_3(t_1) \leq S_3(t_3)$, equal to true.

On the contrary, for all $t' < t$, if $S_1(t')\ \neg op_1\ S_1(t) \vee S_2(t')\ \neg op_2\ S_2(t) \vee \ldots \vee S_n(t')\ \neg op_n\ S_n(t)$ is satisfied, t is not dominated by t' denoted by $t' \nsucc t$. Let us consider the same example above. Because $S_1(t_1) < S_1(t_2) \vee S_3(t_1) > S_3(t_2)$, t_2 is not dominated.

4 Checkpoint Algorithm and Experimental Evaluation

Conceptually, we can search a particular set of parameters $\{p_1, p_2, \ldots, p_n\}$ which is at the earliest time point t that is not dominated by *any* t' such that the value of the objective function ***O*** is maximal among all the instantiations of values into parameters. However, the problem of this approach is that for every single parameter set at t in a learning data set, the parameter set at t has to be examined with all the previous sets of parameters at t' for checking the non-dominance before the optimal solution can be found. In fact, due to the quadratic nature, the conceptual approach is time consuming and expensive particularly if the size of the learning data set is significantly large. Instead, the Checkpoint algorithm uses the KD-tree data structure and searching algorithm [5, 6, 7] to evaluate whether a time point t is dominated based on the Claim 1 for checking the non-dominance. The pseudo code of the algorithm is:

```
Input:          <S, P, C, U>
Output: p[1…k] is an array of the optimal parameters that
        maximizes the objective.
Data Structure:
                1.  N is the size of the learning data set.
                2.  T_kd is a KD tree that stores the parameter vectors
                    that are not dominated so far.
                3.  MaxT is the time point that gives the maximal U so
                    far, denoted by MaxU.
Processing:
STEP 1: T_kd := <S_1(0), S_2(0),…, S_k(0)>;
                MaxT := 0;
                MaxU := U(0);
STEP 2: FOR t := 1 TO N - 1 DO {
                    Non-Dominance Test: Query the T_kd to find if there
                    exists a point (p_1, p_2,…, p_k) in the T_kd, which is in
                    the range [S_1(t),∞) x [S_2(t),∞) x … x [S_k(t),∞).

                    IF (NOT AND t is not dominated AND U(t) > MaxU) THEN
                    Add <S_1(t), S_2(t),…, S_k(t)> to T_kd;

                    MaxT := t;
                    MaxU := U(t);}
STEP 3: FOR i := 1 TO k DO {
                    p[i] := S_i(MaxT);}
STEP 4: RETURN p[1…k];
```

Clearly, the first time point is not dominated because there is no time point preceding it. Therefore, $<S_1(0), S_2(0), \ldots, S_k(0)>$ can be added to T_{kd}. 0 and U(0) can be assigned to MaxT and MaxU respectively.

Using the Checkpoint algorithm step by step for the problem shown in Table 5, we can search through a particular set of parameters $\{p_1, p_2, p_3\}$ which is at the earliest time point t that is not dominated by any t' such that the value of the utility function $\boldsymbol{U}$ is maximal. In **STEP 1**, the $<S_1(t_1), S_2(t_1), S_3(t_1)>$ is added to the T_{kd} since it is the first time point. Then t_1 and U(t_1) are assigned to MaxT and MaxU respectively. In **STEP 2**, t_2 is *not dominated* because $S_1(t_1) < S_1(t_2) \wedge S_2(t_1) > S_2(t_2) \wedge S_3(t_1) > S_3(t_2)$ does not satisfy the Claim 1. However, t_3 is *dominated* because $S_1(t_1) > S_1(t_3) \wedge S_2(t_1) > S_2(t_3) \wedge S_3(t_1) < S_3(t_3)$ does satisfy the Claim 1. $<S_1(t_2), S_2(t_2), S_3(t_2)>$ is added to the T_{kd} because t_2 is *not dominated* and U(t_2) > U(t_1). Thus t_2 and U(t_2) are assigned to MaxT and MaxU respectively. In **STEP 3**, p[1] := $S_1(MaxT)$, p[2] := $S_2(MaxT)$, and p[3] := $S_3(MaxT)$ in the for-loop statement. In **STEP 4**, the algorithm returns 25, 15, and 2 respectively.

The time complexity for the range search and insertion of a parameter vector in the T_{kd} tree is $O(klogN)$ respectively.

Theorem 1: For N parameter vectors in the data set, the Checkpoint algorithm correctly computes an EQPE solution, i.e., *argmax* $\boldsymbol{O}(p_1, p_2, p_3, p_4, p_5)$, where $\boldsymbol{O}$ is the objective function of the EQPE problem, with the complexity $O(kNlogN)$. The proof of the theorem is shown in **Appendix**.

Using the Checkpoint algorithm, we can obtain the optimal decision parameters and the maximal earning from the training data set for the financial problem shown in Table 6. The time complexity of the MLE for the logit regression model is $O(k^2N)$, where k is the number of decision parameters, and N is the size of the learning data set. For the Checkpoint algorithm, the complexity is *O(kNlogN)*. Using the decision parameters from the financial expert (i.e., -20%, 0, -30, 45, 180 days), the logit regression model, and the Checkpoint algorithm, the "Best Buy" opportunities in stock and their earnings are shown in Table 7. Note that the Checkpoint algorithm considerably outperforms both the financial expert's criteria and the logit regression model.

Table 5. Values of S_1, S_2, S_3, and U at the time point t_1, t_2, and t_3

Time	S_1	S_2	S_3	U
t_1	13	27	3	10
t_2	25	15	2	200
t_3	10	20	5	150

Table 6. Optimal Decision Parameters and Maximum Earning (%) from the Learning Data Set[1]

p_1	p_2	p_3	p_4	p_5	$O(p_1,p_2,p_3,p_4,p_5)$
-29.02	-20.01	-26.61	49	70	53.37

Table 7. Investors' Earning of the S&P 500 Index Fund from the Test Data Set[2]

Decision Approach	Best Buy	S&P 500 Index	Earning %
Financial Expert's Criteria	10/09/08	909.92	1.03
Logit Regression Model	11/26/08	887.68	3.56
Checkpoint Algorithm with Financial Expert's Template	03/10/09	719.6	27.8

5 MTSA Data Model and Query Language

5.1 Data Model

The time-series (TS) data model is an extension of the relational database model with specialized schemas. A time-series schema is of the form TSname(T:Time, Vname:Vtype), where Time and Vtype are data types, Vtype is either Real or Integer, and TSname and Vname are names chosen by users.

A time-event (TE) schema is of the form TEname(T:Time, Ename:Binary), where Binary is the binary type corresponding to the domain {0,1}, and TEname and Ename are names chosen by users.

A TS database schema is a set of relational schemas which may include (specific) TS and/or TE schemas.

A TS tuple over a schema TSname(T:Time, Vname:Vtype) is a relational tuple over that schema, i.e., a mapping m: {T, Vname} → Dom(Time) x Dom(Vtype), such that m(T) ∈ Dom(Time) and m(Vname) ∈ Dom(Vtype).

[1] The learning data set is from 06/01/1997 to 06/30/2005.

[2] The test data set is from 07/01/2005 to 06/30/2009 that is the sell date of the fund with the value of 919.32.

A TE tuple over a similar schema TEname(T:Time, Ename:Binary) is a mapping m: {T, Ename} → Dom(Time) x Dom(Binary), such that m(T) ∈ Dom(Time) and m(Ename) ∈ Dom(Binary).

Let us consider our financial example. In the market-bottom scenario, the service provider can use the querying service to create the base, derived, and related time-series tables as inputs and store them in the database. The base time-series tables are SP(T, Index), CG(T, Index), CC(T, Index), ISM(T, Index), and NLC(T, Index).

5.2 Querying Service

Using the base time series tables, we can generate derived time series tables (if any) by the traditional SQLs. In our case study, some derived time series tables, e.g., SPD(t), CCD(t), etc., are:

```
CREATE VIEW SPD AS (
       SELECT After.T, After.Average /
              Before.Average - 1 AS Value
       FROM   (SELECT SP1.T, AVG(SP2.Index) AS Average
              FROM SP SP1, SP SP2
              WHERE  SP2.T <= SP1.T AND SP2.T >= SP1.T - 6
                     AND SP1.T - 6 >= 0
              GROUP BY SP1.T) After,

              (SELECT SP1.T, AVG(SP2.Index) AS Average
              FROM SP SP1, SP SP2
              WHERE  SP2.T <= SP1.T - 150 AND SP2.T >=
              SP1.T - 156 AND SP1.T - 156 >= 0
              GROUP BY SP1.T) Before
       WHERE After.T = Before.T);


CREATE VIEW CCD AS (
       SELECT After.T, (After.Average -
              Before.Average) AS Value
       FROM   (SELECT CC1.T, AVG(CC2.Index) AS Average
              FROM CC CC1, CC CC2
              WHERE  CC2.T <= CC1.T AND CC2.T >= CC1.T - 6
                     AND CC1.T - 6 >= 0
              GROUP BY CC1.T) After,

              (SELECT CC1.T, AVG(CC2.Index) AS Average
              FROM CC CC1, CC CC2
              WHERE  CC2.T <= CC1.T - 150 AND CC2.T >=
              CC1.T - 156 AND CC1.T - 156 >= 0
              GROUP BY CC1.T) Before
       WHERE After.T = Before.T);
```

5.3 Monitoring and Recommendation Service

Using the monitoring and recommendation service over the new incoming data, the financial analyst can recommend the investors whether or not they should buy the stock. In our example, the input parametric time series tables for monitoring are

SPD(T, Value), CG(T, Index), CCD(T, Value), ISM(T, Index), and NLCD(T, Value). The monitoring and recommendation service can be expressed by a monitoring view and executed by the **MONITOR** command.

```
CREATE VIEW MarketBottomTable AS (
       SELECT SPD.T,  (CASE   WHEN    SPD.Value < PR.p1 AND
                              CG.Index < PR.p2 AND
                       CCD.Value < PR.p3 AND
               ISM.Index < PR.p4 AND
       NLCD.Value >   PR.p5
                              THEN    '1' ELSE '0' END) AS MB
       FROM    SPD, CG, CCD, ISM, NLCD, Para PR
       WHERE   SPD.T = CG.T AND CG.T = CCD.T AND CCD.T =
       ISM.T AND ISM.T = NLCD.T);

CREATE VIEW MB_Monitoring_Recommendation AS (
       SELECT MBT.T,  (CASE   WHEN MBT.MB = '1'
                              THEN 'Market Bottom Is
                                     Detected. Buy Stock Is
                                     Recommended.'
                              END) AS Action
       FROM MarketBottomTable MBT);

MONITOR MB_Monitoring_Recommendation;
```

where Para is a table to store the decision parameters, e.g., $p_1 = -20$, $p_2 = 0$, $p_3 = -30$, $p_4 = 45$, and $p_5 = 180$. If the parametric monitoring constraint in the "CASE WHEN" clause is satisfied at the current time point t, the value of the attribute "MB" indicates "1". The service then recommends the financial analysts to buy the index fund for the investors since the market bottom is predicted.

5.4 Parameter Learning Service

As we discussed, the expert's suggested parameters (-20. 0, -30, 45, 180) are not accurate enough to monitor the dynamic financial market at all time; thus, the parameter learning service should be adopted by expressing as follows:

```
STEP 1: Store base TS tables, e.g., SP, CG, CC, ISM,
        and NLC, in the database.

STEP 2: Define SQL views for derived TS tables, e.g, SPD, CCD,
etc., shown in Section 5.2.

STEP 3: Create a parameter table which stores the optimal
        decision parameters.

               CREATE VIEW Para (
                      p1 REAL, p2 REAL, p3 REAL, p4 REAL, p5 REAL);

STEP 4: Create a TS view for the time utility.

               CREATE VIEW Earning AS (
                      SELECT SP1.T, ((Last.Index/SP1.Index - 1) *
                                          100) AS Percent
```

```
                  FROM SP SP1, (SELECT SP2.Index
                                FROM SP SP2 WHERE SP2.T >= ALL
                                     (SELECT SP3.T
                                     FROM SP SP3)) Last);

STEP 5: Create a learning event and then execute the event
        construct to learn the parameters.

             CREATE EVENT LearnMarketBottomParameter (
                    LEARN Para PR
                    FOR MAXIMIZE E.Percent
                    WITH   SPD.Value < PR.p1 AND CG.Index < PR.p2
                           AND CCD.Value < PR.p3 AND ISM.Index <
                           PR.p4 AND NLCD.Value > PR.p5
                    FROM SPD, CG, CCD, ISM, NLCD, Earning E
                    WHERE  SPD.T = CG.T AND CG.T = CCD.T AND
                    CCD.T = ISM.T AND ISM.T = NLCD.T AND
                    NLCD.T = E.T;)

             EXECUTE LearnMarketBottomParameter;
```

when the event "LearnMarketBottomParameter" is executed, the command "LEARN" will call for the Checkpoint algorithm to solve the corresponding EQPE problem and will put its solution in the Para table, where all parameters, e.g., p_1, p_2, p_3, p_4, and p_5 are instantiated with optimal values.

6 Conclusions and Future Work

To the best of our knowledge, this is the first paper to propose an event-based service framework for multivariate time series analytics that provides model definition, querying, parameter learning, model evaluation, monitoring, and decision recommendation on events over multivariate time series. The parameter learning services combine the strengths of both domain-knowledge-based and formal-learning-based approaches for maximizing utility on events over the time series. It includes a mathematical model and a learning algorithm for solving Expert Query Parametric Estimation problems. Using the framework, we conduct a preliminary experiment in the financial domain to demonstrate that our model and algorithm are more effective and produce results that are superior to the two approaches mentioned above. We also develop MTSA data model and query language for the services of querying, monitoring, and parameter learning. There are still many open research questions, e.g., which model can capture and integrate multiple, inter-related events, what algorithm can simultaneously learn decision parameters optimally for those events, and how those events will impact the services that the framework provides.

References

1. Stack, J.B.: Technical and Monetary Investment Analysis. InvesTech Research 9(3 & 5) (2009)
2. Dougherty, C.: Introduction to Econometrics, 3rd edn. Oxford University Press (2007)

3. Hansen, B.E.: Econometrics. University of Wisconsin (2010), http://www.ssc.wisc.edu/~bhansen/econometrics/Econometrics.pdf
4. Heij, D., De Boer, P., Franses, P.H., Kloek, T., Van Dijk, H.K.: Econometric Methods with Applications in Business and Economics. Oxford University Press (2004)
5. Bentley, J.L.: Multidimensional Binary Search Trees Used for Associative Searching. Communications of the ACM 18(09), 509–517 (1975)
6. Bentley, J.L.: Multidimensional Binary Search Trees in Database Applications. IEEE Transactions on Software Engineering 5(04), 333–340 (1979)
7. Samet, H.: Foundations of Multidimensional and Metric Data Structures. Morgan Kaufmann (2006)
8. Bellman, R.: Adaptive Control Processes: A Guided Tour. University Press, Princeton (1961)
9. Brodsky, A., Bhot, M.M., Chandrashekar, M., Egge, N.E., Wang, X.S.: A Decisions Query Language (DQL): High-Level Abstraction for Mathematical Programming over Databases. In: Proceedings of the 35th SIGMOD International Conference on Management of Data (2009)
10. Brodsky, A., Henshaw, S.M., Whittle, J.: CARD: A Decision-Guidance Framework and Application for Recommending Composite Alternatives. In: 2nd ACM International Conference on Recommender Systems (2008)
11. Brodsky, A., Wang, X.S.: Decision-Guidance Management Systems (DGMS): Seamless Integration of Data Acquisition, Learning, Prediction, and Optimization. In: Proceedings of the 41st Hawaii International Conference on System Sciences (2008)
12. Dumas, M., O'Sullivan, J., Heravizadeh, M., Edmond, D., Hofstede, A.: Towards a Semantic Framework for Service Description. In: Proceedings of the IFIP TC2/WG2.6 Ninth Working Conference on Database Semantics: Semantic Issues in E-Commerce Systems (2001)
13. Erl, T.: Service-Oriented Architecture (SOA): Concepts, Technology, and Design. Prentice Hall (2005)
14. Erradi, A., Anand, S., Kulkarni, N.: SOAF: An Architectural Framework for Service Definition and Realization. In: IEEE International Conference on Services Computing, SCC 2006 (2006)
15. Harrington, J.: Relational Database Design and Implementation, 3rd edn. Morgan Kaufmann (2009)
16. Holyfield, S.: Non-technical Guide to Technical Frameworks. JISC CETIS (2005), http://www.elearning.ac.uk/features/nontechguide1
17. Josuttis, N.: SOA in Practice: The Art of Distributed System Design. O'Reilly Media (2007)
18. Ngan, C.K., Brodsky, A., Lin, J.: Decisions on Multivariate Time Series: Combining Domain Knowledge with Utility Maximization. In: The 15th IFIP WG8.3 International Conference on Decision Support Systems (2010)
19. Nicholls, P.: Enterprise Architectures and the International e-Framework. e-framework Organization (2009), http://www.e-framework.org/Portals/9/docs/EAPaper_2009-07.pdf
20. Olivier, B., Roberts, T., Blinco, K.: The e-Framework for Education and Research: An Overview. e-framework Organization (2005), http://www.e-framework.org/Portals/9/Resources/eframeworkrV1.pdf
21. Ort, E.: Service-Oriented Architecture and Web Services: Concepts, Technologies, and Tools. Sun Developer Network Technical Articles and Tips, http://java.sun.com/developer/technicalArticles/WebServices/soa2/

22. Papazoglou, M., Heuvel, W.: Service Oriented Architectures: Approaches, Technologies, and Research Issues. The VLDB Journal (June 2005)
23. Quartel, D., Steen, M., Pokraev, S., Sinderen, M.: COSMO: A Conceptual Framework for Service Modelling and Refinement. Journal of Information Systems Frontiers 9(2-3), 225–244 (2007)
24. Sprague Jr., R.H.: A Framework for the Development of Decision Support Systems. MIS Quarterly 4(4), 1–26 (1980)
25. Stephen, B., et al.: Database Design: Know It All. Morgan Kaufmann (2008)
26. Wilson, S., Blinco, K., Rehak, D.: Service-Oriented Frameworks: Modelling the Infrastructure for the Next Generation of e-Learning Systems. JISC CETIS (2004), `http://www.jisc.ac.uk/uploaded_documents/AltilabServiceOrientedFrameworks.pdf`
27. Zhang, T., Ying, S., Cao, S., Jia, S.: A Modeling Framework for Service-Oriented Architecture. In: Proceedings of the Sixth International Conference on Quality Software, QSIC 2006 (2006)

Appendix

Claim 1 - Given the conjunctions of inequality constraints, $S_1(t)\ op_1\ p_1 \wedge S_2(t)\ op_2\ p_2 \wedge \ldots \wedge S_k(t)\ op_k\ p_k$ and the two time points t', t such that $0 \le t' < t$, $t' \succ t$ if and only if $S_1(t')\ op_1\ S_1(t) \wedge S_2(t')\ op_2\ S_2(t) \wedge \ldots \wedge S_k(t')\ op_k\ S_k(t)$.

Proof

Without loss of generality, we assume that op_i = "$\le$", for all $1 \le i \le k$. It is because "$\ge$" can be replaced with $\le$ by changing a corresponding time series $S_i(t)$ to - $S_i(t)$. For op_i = "=", we can use the conjunction with both $\ge$ and $\le$.

If Direction

Assume that $S_1(t') \le S_1(t) \wedge S_2(t') \le S_2(t) \wedge \ldots \wedge S_k(t') \le S_k(t)$. For any $(p_1, p_2, \ldots, p_k) \in R^k$ and every i = 1, 2, …, k, if $S_1(t) \le p_1$, then $S_1(t') \le p_1$ because $S_1(t') \le S_1(t)$. Therefore, $S_1(t) \le p_1 \wedge S_2(t) \le p_2 \wedge \ldots \wedge S_k(t) \le p_k \rightarrow S_1(t') \le p_1 \wedge S_2(t') \le p_2 \wedge \ldots \wedge S_k(t') \le p_k$ and then $t' \succ t$.

Only If Direction

Assume that $t' \succ t$. Then $S_1(t) \le p_1 \wedge S_2(t) \le p_2 \wedge \ldots \wedge S_k(t) \le p_k \rightarrow S_1(t') \le p_1 \wedge S_2(t') \le p_2 \wedge \ldots \wedge S_k(t') \le p_k$. Therefore, for any $(p_1, p_2, \ldots, p_k) \in R^k$ and every i = 1, 2, …, k, we have $S_i(t) \le p_i \rightarrow S_i(t') \le p_i$.

Proof of Theorem 1: The Checkpoint algorithm correctly solves the EQPE problem, i.e., if $argmax\ \boldsymbol{O}(p_1, p_2, p_3, p_4, p_5)$, where $\boldsymbol{O}$ is the objective function of the EQPE problem.

The time complexity is $O(kNlogN)$, where k is the number of time series and N is the size of the learning data set.

Proof: To prove the correctness of the algorithm if it is sufficient to show **Claim 2**: The Non-Dominance test in STEP 2 of the Checkpoint Algorithm is satisfied at the time point t if and only if there does not exist t' that dominates t, where $0 \le t' < t$.

We prove it by induction on t, where $1 \leq t \leq N$. For $t = 1$, $T_{kd} = \emptyset$, and $t = 1$ is not dominated; therefore, the "if and only if" condition holds. Assuming the correctness for 1, 2,..., t - 1; it follows the STEP 2 of the algorithm that T_{kd} at the point t contains all the non-dominated time points t', where $t' \leq t - 1$.

If Direction

The IF part of the Claim 2 is straightforward since if t is not dominated by an earlier time point t', such point cannot appear on the T_{kd} tree; therefore, the Non-Dominance Test must be satisfied by the Claim 1.

Only If Direction

For the ONLY IF part of the Claim 2, assume that the Non-Dominance test in STEP 2 of the algorithm is satisfied. Then there does not exist the time point t' on T_{kd} for which $(S_1(t'), S_2(t'),..., S_k(t')) \in [S_1(t), \infty) \times [S_2(t), \infty) \times ... \times [S_k(t), \infty)$, where $0 \leq t' < t$. Assume that T_{kd} at the time t contains the time points $t_{1_i} < t_{2_i} < \cdots < t_{m_i}$ and assume, by contradiction, that there exists t' that dominates t, $t' \succ t$, where $0 \leq t' < t$. Clearly, t' is not one of $t_{1_i} < t_{2_i} < \cdots < t_{m_i}$ because they do not dominate t by the induction hypothesis. Because t' was not added to the T_{kd} tree and the induction hypothesis, $t_{j_i} \succ t'$ for some j = 1, 2, ..., m. From the contradiction assumption $t' \succ t$ and the transitivity of $\succ$, it follows that $t_{j_i} \succ t$. Thus, by the Claim 1, $S_1(t_{j_i}) \leq S_1(t) \wedge S_2(t_{j_i}) \leq S_2(t) \wedge \cdots \wedge S_k(t_{j_i}) \leq S_k(t)$ which contradicts the fact that the Non-dominance test in STEP 2 was satisfied for t. This completes the proof of the Claim 2 and of the correctness of the algorithm.

Time Complexity: The algorithm performs N iterations in STEP 2, spending time $O(k \log N)$ using the T_{kd} algorithm for the T_{kd} range query in Non-Dominance Test. Thus the overall complexity is $O(kN \log N)$.

From Natural Language Software Specifications to UML Class Models

Imran Sarwar Bajwa[1] and M. Abbas Choudhary[2]

[1] School of Computer Science, University of Birmingham
B15 2TT, Birmingham, U.K.
[2] University of Engineering and Technology
47050, Taxila, Pakistan
i.s.bajwa@cs.bham.ac.uk, vc@uettaxila.edu.pk

Abstract. Software specifications are typically captured in natural languages and then software analysts manually analyzed and produce the software models such class models. Various approaches, frameworks and tool have been presented for automatic translation of software models such as CM-Builder, Re-Builder, NL-OOML, GOOAL, etc. However, the experiments with these tools show that they do not provide with high accuracy in translation. Major reason of less accuracy reported in the literature is the ambiguous and informal nature of the natural languages. In this article, we aim to address this issue and present a better approach for processing natural languages and produce more accurate UML software models. The presented approach is based on Semantic Business Vocabulary and Rules (SBVR) recently adopted standard by OMG. Our approach works as the natural language software specifications are first mapped to SBVR rules representation. SBVR rules are easy to translate other formal representations such as OCL and UML as SBVR is based on higher order logic. A case study solved with our tool NL2UMLviaSBVR is also presented and the a comparative analysis of our tools research with other available tools show that use of SBVR in NL to UML translation helps to improve the accuracy.

Keywords: Automated software modelling, UML class models, Natural language software specifications, SBVR.

1 Introduction

Since the early days of computer history, automated processing of the natural languages (NL) is a dream for computer scientists. Where, the scientists are introducing new frameworks and approaches for better understanding of NL text at the same time NL interfaces are also being introduced to simplify the software engineering process. Major efforts in last a few decades are NL-OOPS [3], D-H [4], NL2SBVR [5], RCR [6], LIDA [7], GOOAL [8], CM-Builder [9], Re-Builder [10], NL-OOML [11], UML-Generator [12], etc. The focus of all such efforts has been automatic analysis of the NL specification of software requirements and generation of the UML software models. However, a challenge of NL community is the accurate object oriented (OO) analysis [19], [20], [22], [23]. The presented research in this domain attributes that the inherent ambiguity of NL such as English makes processing

R. Zhang et al. (Eds.): ICEIS 2011, LNBIP 102, pp. 224–237, 2012.

difficult. English is ambiguous because English sentence structure is informal [12]. Similarly, English is inconsistent as majority of English words have multiple senses and a single sense can be reflected by multiple words.

In this paper, the major contribution is three folds. Firstly, a Semantic Business vocabulary and Rule (SBVR) [13] based approach is presented to generate a controlled (unambiguous and consistent) representation of natural language software specification. Secondly, we report the structure of the implemented tool NL2UML*via*SBVR that is able to automatically perform object-oriented analysis of SBVR software specifications. Thirdly, a case study is solved that was originally solved with CM-Builder [9] and the results of the case study are compared with available tools (used for automated OOA) to evaluate the tool.

Our approach works as the user inputs a piece of English specification of software and the NL to SBVR approach generates SBVR (an adopted standard of the OMG) based controlled representation of English software specification. To generate a SBVR representation such as SBVR rule, first the input English text is lexically, syntactically and semantically parsed and SBVR vocabulary is extracted. Then, the SBVR vocabulary is further processed to construct a SBVR rule by applying SBVR's *Conceptual Formalization* [13] and *Semantic Formulation* [13]. The last phase is extraction of the OO information (such as classes, methods, attributes, associations, generalizations, etc) from the SBVR's rule based representation.

The remaining paper is structured into the following sections: Section 2 explains that how SBVR provides a controlled representation to English. Section 3 illustrates the architecture of NL2UML*via*SBVR. Section 4 presents a case study. The evaluation of our approach is presented in section 5. Finally, the paper is concluded to discuss the future work.

2 SBVR Based Controlled Natural Language

SBVR was originally presented for business people to provide a clear and unambiguous way of defining business policies and rules in their native language [13]. The SBVR based controlled representation is useful in multiple ways such as due to its natural language syntax, it is easy to understand for developers and users. Similarly, SBVR is easy to machine process as SBVR is based on higher order logic (first order logic). We have identified a set of characteristics of SBVR those can be used to generate a controlled natural language representation of English:

2.1 Conceptual Formalization

SBVR provides rule-based conceptual formalization that can be used to generate a syntactically formal representation of English. Our approach can formalize two types of requirements: The structural requirements can be represented using SBVR structural business rules, based on two alethic modal operators [13]: "*it is* necessary *that...*" and "*it is* possible *that...*" for example, **It is possible** that a <u>customer</u> *is a* <u>member</u>. Similarly, the behavioural requirements can be represented using SBVR operative business rule, based on two deontic modal operators [13]: "*it is* obligatory *that* ..." and "*it is* permitted *that* ..." for example, **It is obligatory** that a <u>customer</u> *can borrow* **at most** two <u>books</u>.

2.2 Semantic Formulation

SBVR is typically proposed for business modeling in NL. However, we are using the formal logic based nature of SBVR to semantically formulate the English software statements. A set of logic structures called semantic formulations are provided in SBVR to make English statements controlled such as atomic formulation, instantiate formulation, logical formulation, quantification, and modal formulation. For more details, we recommend user SBVR 1.0 document [13].

3 Generating Class Models from NL Specification via SBVR

This section explains how English text is mapped to SBVR representation, object oriented analysis and finally generation of a class model. The used approach works in five phases (see fig. 1):

a. Processing natural language specification
b. Extracting Business Vocabulary from NL text
c. Generating Business Rules from business vocabulary
d. Performing object oriented analysis
e. Generating UML Class models.

3.1 Parsing NL Software

The first phase of NL2UML*via*SBVR is NL parsing that involves a number of sub-processing units (organized in a pipelined architecture) to process complex English statements. The NL parsing phase tokenizes English text and lexically, syntactically and semantically processes the English text [24].

Morphological Processing. The NL parsing starts with the lexical processing of a plain text file containing English software specification. The lexical processing phase comprises following four sub-phases [16]:

1. The input is processed to identify the margins of a sentence and each sentence is stored in an arraylist.
2. After sentence splitting, each sentence goes through the tokenization. Tokenization works as a sentence "A member can borrow at most two books." is tokenized as [A] [member] [can] [borrow] [at] [most] [two] [books] [.]
3. The tokenized text is POS (Parts-of-Speech) tagged using Stanford POS tagger [14] v3.0 to identify the basic POS tags e.g. A/DT member/NN can/MD borrow/VB at/IN most/JJS two/CD books/NNS ./. The Stanford POS tagger v3.0 can identify 44 POS tags.
4. In morphological analysis, the suffixes attached to the nouns and verbs are segregated e.g. a verb "applies" is analyzed as "apply+s" and similarly a noun "students" is analyzed as "student+s".

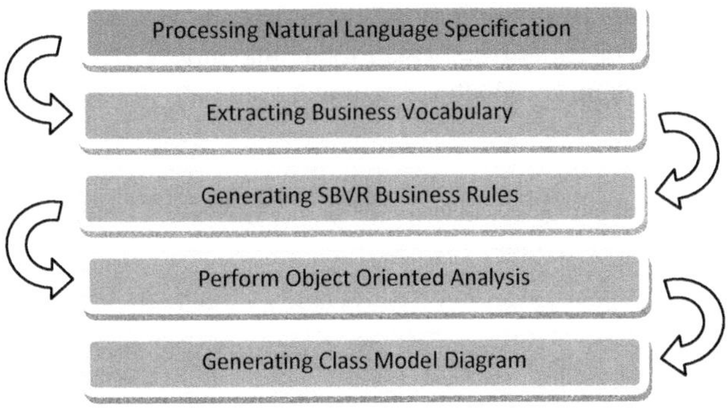

Fig. 1. The NL to UML via SBVR Framework

Syntactic Processing. We have used an enhanced version of a rule-based bottom-up parser for the syntactic analyze of the input text used in [21]. English grammar rules are base of used parser. The text is syntactically analyzed and a parse tree is generated for further semantic processing, shown in Figure 2.

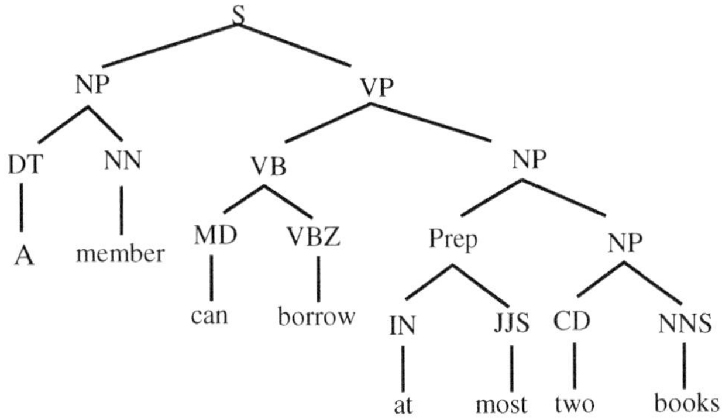

Fig. 2. Parsing English text and generating a parse tree

Semantic Interpretation. In this semantic interpretation phase, role labelling [21] is performed. The desired role labels are actors (nouns used in subject part), co-actor (additional actors conjuncted with '*and*'), action (action verb), thematic object (nouns used in object part), and a beneficiary (nouns used in adverb part) if exists, (see figure 3). These roles assist in identifying SBVR vocabulary and exported as an xml file. We have used following thematic roles in semantic interpretation:

Agent: The 'actor' or initiator of the action.
Co-agent: The additional actor with the agent.
Patient: The 'recipient' of the action.
Theme: The entity that is moved by the action.
Goal: The location or entity in the direction of which something moves.

Beneficiary: The entity that benefits from the action.
Source: The location or entity from which something moves
Instrument: The medium by which the action carried out.

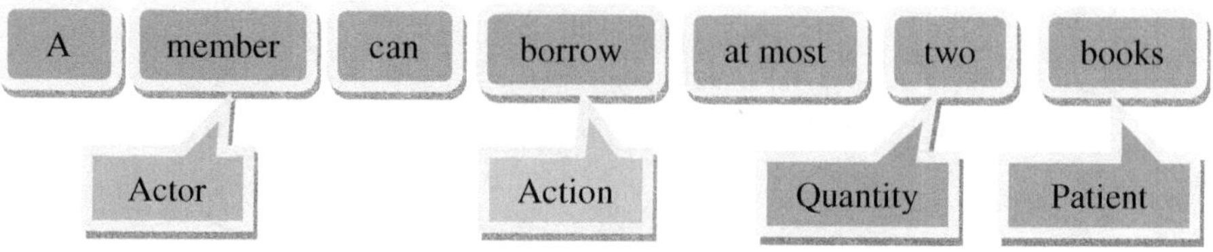

Fig. 3. Semantic interpretation of English text

3.2 SBVR Vocabulary Extraction

The similar rules to extract SBVR vocabulary from English text, we used in [5]. We have extended the rules to use in NL to UML translation via SBVR. In NL to SBVR translation phase, the basic SBVR vocabulary e.g. noun concept, individual concept, object type, verb concepts, fact type, etc are identified from the English input that is preprocess in the previous phase. The extraction of various SBVR elements is described below:

Extracting Object Types. All common nouns (actors, co-actors, thematic objects, or beneficiaries) are represented as the object types or general concept (see figure 4) e.g. belt, user, cup, etc. In conceptual modelling, the object types are mapped to classes.

Extracting Individual Concept. All proper nouns (actors, co-actors, thematic objects, or beneficiaries) are represented as the individual concepts.

Extracting Fact Types. The auxiliary and action verbs are represented as verb concepts. To constructing a fact types, the combination of an object type/individual

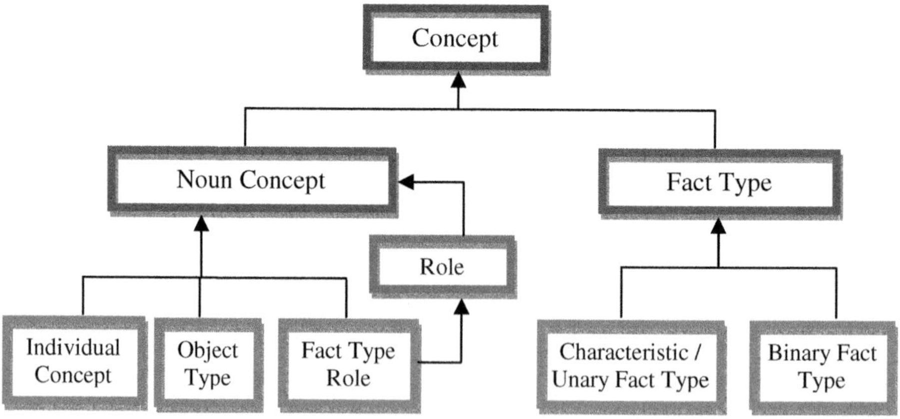

Fig. 4. An extract of the SBVR metamodel: concepts

concept + verb forms a unary fact type e.g. "vision system senses". Similarly, the combination of an object type/individual concept + verb + object type forms a binary fact type e.g. belt conveys part is a binary fact type.

Extracting Characteristics. In English, the characteristic or attributes are typically represented using is-property-of fact type e.g. "name is-property-of customer". Moreover, the use of possessed nouns (i.e. pre-fixed by's or post-fixed by of) e.g. student's age or age of student is also characteristic.

Extracting Quantifications. All indefinite articles (a and an), plural nouns (prefixed with s) and cardinal numbers (2 or two) represent quantifications.

Extracting Associative Fact Types. The associative fact types (OMG, 2008) (section 11.1.5.1) (see figure 4) are identified by associative or pragmatic relations in English text. In English, the binary fact types are typical examples of associative fact types e.g. "The belt conveys the parts". In this example, there is a binary association in belt and parts concepts. This association is one-to-many as 'parts' concept is plural. In conceptual modeling of SBVR, associative fact types are mapped to associations.

Extracting Partitive Fact Type. The partitive fact types (OMG, 2008) (section 11.1.5.1) (see figure 4) are identified by extracting structures such as "is-part-of", "included-in" or "belong-to" e.g. "The user puts two-kinds-of parts, dish and cup". Here 'parts' is generalized form of 'dish' and 'cup'. In conceptual modeling of SBVR, partitive fact types are mapped to aggregations.

Extracting Categorization Fact Types. The categorization fact types (OMG, 2008) (section 11.1.5.2) (see figure 4) are identified by extracting structures such as "is-category-of" or "is-type-of", "is-kind-of" e.g. "The user puts two-kinds-of parts, dish and cup". Here 'parts' is generalized form of 'dish' and 'cup'. In conceptual modeling of SBVR, categorization fact types are mapped to generalizations. All the extracted information shown in figure 5 is stored in an arraylist for further analysis.

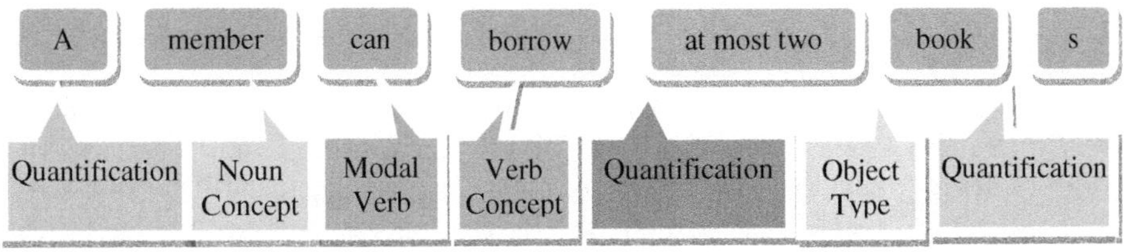

Fig. 5. Semantic interpretation of English text

3.3 SBVR Rules Generation

In this phase, a SBVR representation such as SBVR rule is generated from the SBVR vocabulary in previous phase. SBVR rule is generated in two phases as following:

Applying Semantic Formulation. A set of semantic formulations are applied to each fact type to construct a SBVR rule. There are five basic semantic formulations proposed in SBVR version 1.0 (OMG, 2008) but we are using following three with respect to the context of the scope of proposed research:

1. *Logical Formulation*: A SBVR rule can be composed of multiple fact types using logical operators e.g. AND, OR, NOT, implies, etc. For logical formulation (OMG, 2008), the tokens '*not*' or '*no*' are mapped to negation ($\neg$ a). Similarly, the tokens '*that*' & '*and*' are mapped to conjunction (a $\wedge$ b). The token '*or*' is mapped to disjunction (a $\vee$ b) and the tokens '*imply*', '*suggest*', '*indicate*', '*infer*' are mapped to implication (a $\Rightarrow$ b).

2. *Quantification*: Quantification (OMG, 2008) is used to specify the scope of a concept. Quantifications are applied by mapping tokes like "*more than*" or "*greater than*" to at least n quantification; token "less than" is mapped to at most n quantification and token "*equal to*" or a positive statement is mapped to exactly n quantification.

3. *Modal Formulation*: In SBVR, the modal formulation (OMG, 2008) specifies seriousness of a constraint. Modal verbs such as '*can*' , '' or '*may*' are mapped to possibility formulation to represent a structural requirement and the modal verbs '*should*', '*must*' or verb concept "*have to*" are mapped to obligation formulation to represent a behavioural requirement.

Applying Structured English Notation. The last step in generation of a SBVR is application of the Structured English notation in SBVR 1.0 document, Annex C (OMG, 2008). Following formatting rules were used: The noun concepts are underlined e.g. student; the verb concepts are italicized e.g. *should be*; the SBVR keywords are bolded e.g. at most; the individual concepts are double underlined e.g. Ahmad, England. Attributes are also italicized but with different colour: e.g. *name*. RuleSpeak (OMG, 2008) is the other available notation in SBVR. The NL2UML*via*SBVR tool supports both notations.

3.4 Object-Oriented Analysis

In this phase, finally the SBVR rule is further processed to extract the OO information. The extraction of each OO element from SBVR representation is described below:

1. *Extracting Classes:* All SBVR object types are mapped to classes e.g. library, book, etc.
2. *Extracting* Instances: The SBVR individual concepts are mapped to instances.
1. *Extracting Class Attributes*: All the SBVR characteristics or unary fact types (without action verbs) associated to an object type are mapped to attributes of a class.
2. *Extracting Class Methods*: All the SBVR verb concepts (action verbs) associated to a noun concept are mapped to methods for a particular class e.g. issue() is method of library class.
3. *Extracting Associations*: A unary fact type with action verb is mapped to a unary relationship and all associative fact types are mapped to binary relationships. The use of quantifications with the respective noun concept is employed to identify *multiplicity* e.g. library and book(s) will have one to many association. The associated verb concept is used as caption of association as shown in fig. 6.

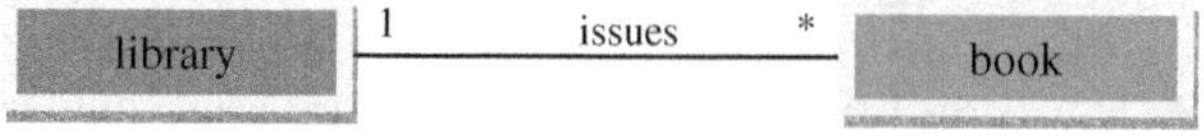

Fig. 6. Extracting class associations

4. *Extracting Generalization*: The partitive fact types are specified as generalizations. The subject-part of the fact type is considered the main class in generalization and object-part of the fact types is considered as the sub class.

5. *Extracting Aggregations*: The categorization fact types are mapped to aggregations. The subject-part of the fact type is considered the main class in aggregation and object-part of the fact types is considered as the sub class.

3.5 Drawing UML Class Model

This phase draws a UML class model by combining class diagram symbols with respect to the information extracted of the previous phase. In this phase, the java graphics functions (drawline(), drawrect(), etc) are used to draw the class diagram symbols.

4 A Case Study

A case study is discussed from the domain of library information systems that was originally presented by [17] (1994) and later on solved by [9]. The problem statement for the case study is as follows:

> *A library issues loan items to customers. Each customer is known as a member and is issued a membership card that shows a unique member number. Along with the membership number other details on a customer must be kept such as a name, address, and date of birth. The library is made up of a number of subject sections. Each section is denoted by a classification mark. A loan item is uniquely identified by a bar code. There are two types of loan items, language tapes, and books. A language tape has a title language (e.g. French), and level (e.g. beginner). A book has a title, and author(s). A customer may borrow up to a maximum of 8 items. An item can be borrowed, reserved or renewed to extend a current loan. When an item is issued the customer's membership number is scanned via a bar code reader or entered manually. If the membership is still valid and the number of items on loan less than 8, the book bar code is read, either via the bar code reader or entered manually. If the item can be issued (e.g. not reserved) the item is stamped and then issued. The library must support the facility for an item to be searched and for a daily update of records.*

The problem statement of the case study was given as input to the NL2UML*via*SBVR tool that is an Eclipse plugin implemented in java as a proof of concept. The generated SBVR representation is:

> A library *issues* loan items to each customer. Each customer *is known* as a member and *is issued* a membership card that *shows* a unique member number. It is necessary that the membership number and other details on a customer *must be kept* such as a *name*, *address*, and *date-of-birth*. The library *is made up* of a number of subject sections. Each section *is denoted* by a *classification-mark*. A loan item *is identified* by a *bar-code*. There *are* exactly two types of loan items, language tapes, and books. A language tape *has* a *title-language*, and *level*. A book *has* a *title*, and *author*(s). It is possibility that each customer *may borrow* up to at most 8 items. It is possibility that each item *can be borrowed*, *reserved* or *renewed* to *extend* a current loan. When an item *is issued* the customer's *membership-number is scanned* via a bar code reader or *entered* manually. If the membership *is valid* and the number of items on loan at most 8, the book's *bar-code is read*, either via the bar code reader or *entered* manually. It is possibility that if the item *can be issued* the item *is stamped* and then *issued*. It is necessary that the library *must support* the facility for an item to *be searched* and for a daily *update* of records.

After generating the SBVR representation, OOA was performed to extract following information:

Table 1. Object Oriented Analysis results

Type	Count	Details
Classes	10	Library, Loan_Items, Member_Number, Customer, Book, Language_Tape Member, Bar_Code_Reader, Subject_Section, Membership_Card
Attributes	10	name, address, date-of-birth, bar_code, classification_mark, title, author, Level, membership-number, valid
Methods	11	issue(), show(), denote(), identify(), extend(), scan(), enter(), read_barcode(), stamp(), search(). update()
Associations	07	Library issues Loan_Items; Member_Card issued to Member; Library made up of Subject_sections; Customer borrow Loan_items; customer renew Loan_item; customer reserve_Loan_item; Library support facility
Generalizations	02	Loan Items is type-of Language_tapes, Loan Items is type-of Books
Aggregations	00	-
Instances	00	-

There were some synonyms for the used classes such as Item and Loan_Item, Section and Subject_Section. Our system keeps only one of the similar classes. Here, customer and member are also synonyms, but our system is not able to handle such similarities. There is only one wrong class that is Member_Number as it is an attribute. There are two incorrect associations: "Library support facility" is not an association and "Library made up of Subject_sections" is an aggregation but classified as an association.

A screen shot of a class model generated for the case study shown in fig. 7.

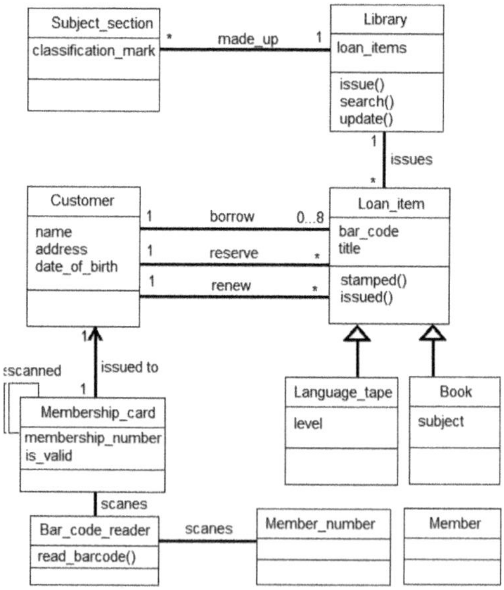

Fig. 7. A class model of case study generated by NL2UML*via*SBVR

5 Evaluation

We have done performance evaluation to evaluate the accuracy of NL2UML*via*SBVR tool. An evaluation methodology, for the performance evaluation of NLP tools, proposed by Hirschman and Thompson [18] is based on three aspects:

- Criterion specifies the interest of evaluation e.g. precision, error rate, etc.
- Measure specifies the particular property of system performance someone intends to get at the selected criterion e.g. percent correct or incorrect.
- Evaluation method determines the appropriate value for a given measure and a given system.

As we want to compare the results of performance evaluation with other tools such as CM-Builder [9], we have a used a similar evaluation methodology used for CM-Builder. Following is the evaluation methodology used to evaluate the performance of NL2UML*via*SBVR.

5.1 Evaluation Methodology

Our evaluation methodology is based on three items, described in [9]:

Criterion. For evaluation of the designed system, a criterion was defined that how close are the NL2UML*via*SBVR output to the opinion of the human expert (named sample results). Different human experts produce different representations and can be good or bad analysis. However, we gained a human expert's opinion for the target input and used it as a sample result.

Measure. We have used two evaluation metrics: recall and precision. These metrics are extensively employed to evaluate NL based knowledge extraction systems. We can define these metrics as following:

Recall: The completeness of the results produced by system is called recall. Recall can be calculated by comparing the correct results produced by the system's with the human expert's opinion (sample results), such as:

$$R = \frac{N_{correct}}{N_{sample}}$$

Where $N_{correct}$ is the number of correct results generated by the tool and N_{sample} is the number of sample results (opinion of human expert).

Precision: The second metrics precision expresses accuracy of the designed system where system accuracy means the correct number of results produced by the system. Precision is measured by comparing designed system's number of correct results by all (incorrect and correct) results produced by the system. Precision is calculated as:

$$P = \frac{N_{correct}}{N_{incorrect} + N_{correct}}$$

Where $N_{incorrect}$ is the number of incorrect results and $N_{correct}$ is the number of correct results.

F-measure: The F-measure is defined as a mean of *Precision* and *Recall.* F-measure is the *harmonic mean* or the "standard" average of total, correct, and incorrect results.

$$F = \frac{2(P)(R)}{P + R}$$

Where *P* is the precision value and the *R* is the recall value.

Method. To evaluate the results of NL2UMLviaSBVR, each outcome (class names, attributes names, method names, associations, multiplicity generalizations, aggregations, and instance names) of the NL2UML*via*SBVR's output was matched with the expert's opinion (N_{sample}) (sample solution). The outcome that accurately classified into respective category was declared correct ($N_{correct}$) otherwise incorrect ($N_{incorrect}$). Additionally, the information that was not extracted (or missed) by the NL2SBVR tool but it was given in the human expert's opinion (N_{sample}) was categorized as the missing information ($N_{missing}$).

5.2 Evaluation Results

We solved five different case studies of various lengths. The length of largest case study was 157 words and the smallest case study had 63 words. The results of all the case studies were used to calculate recall, precision and the F-value shown in table 2.

Table 2. Evaluation results of NL 2 UML Translation via SBVR

Example	N_{sample}	$N_{correct}$	$N_{incorrect}$	$N_{missing}$	***Rec%***	***Prec%***	***F-Value***
Case Study 1	67	52	11	4	77.61	82.53	80.06
Case Study 2	40	35	3	2	87.50	92.10	89.73
Case Study 3	37	28	6	3	75.67	82.35	78.86
Case Study 4	53	42	8	3	79.24	84.00	81.55
Case Study 5	49	41	7	2	83.67	85.41	84.53
				Average	80.73	85.27	82.95

Average recall for English requirement specification is calculated 80.73% while average precision is calculated 85.27%. These results are very encouraging for the future enhancements.

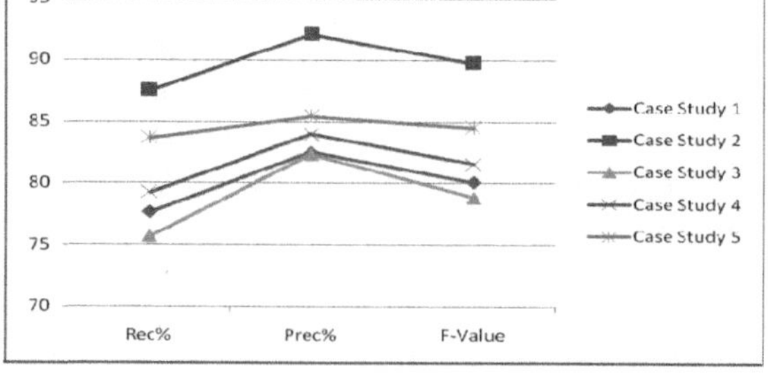

Fig. 8. Results of solved case studies using NL2UML via SBVR

We have also compared the results of NL2UML*via*SBVR with other available tools that can perform automated analysis of the NL requirement specifications. Recall value was not available for some of the tools. We have used the available recall and precision values of the tools for comparison as shown in table 3:

Table 3. A comparison of performance evaluation - NL2UML*via*SBVR vs other tools

NL Tools for Class Modelling	Recall	Precision
CM-Builder (Harmain, 2003)	73.00%	66.00%
GOOAL (Perez-Gonzalez, 2002)	-	78.00%
UML-Generator (Bajwa, 2009)	78.29%	81.17%
NL-OOML (Anandha, 2006)	-	82.00%
LIDA (Overmyer, 2001)	71.32%	63.17%
NL2UML*via*SBVR	80.73%	85.27%

Here, we can note that the accuracy of other NL tools used for information extraction and object oriented analysis is well below than NL2UML*via*SBVR. Moreover, the various tools' functionalities (if available, is automated or user involved) are also compared with NL2UML*via*SBVR as shown in Table 4:

Table 4. Comparison of NL2UML*via*SBVR with other tools

Support	CM Builder	LIDA	GOOAL	NL OOML	NL2UML*via*SBVR
Classes	Yes	User	Yes	Yes	Yes
Attributes	Yes	User	Yes	Yes	Yes
Methods	No	User	Yes	Yes	Yes
Associations	Yes	User	Semi-NL	No	Yes
Multiplicity	Yes	User	No	No	Yes
Aggregation	No	No	No	No	Yes
Generalization	No	No	No	No	Yes
Instances	No	No	No	No	Yes

Table 4 shows that besides NL2UML*via*SBVR, there are very few tools those can extract information such as multiplicity, aggregations, generalizations, and instances from NL requirement. Thus, the results of this initial performance evaluation are very encouraging and support both the approach adopted in this paper and the potential of this technology in general.

6 Conclusions

The primary objective of the paper was to address the challenge of addressing ambiguous nature of natural languages (such as English) and generate a controlled representation of English so that the accuracy of machine processing can be improved. To address this challenge we have presented a NL based automated approach to parse English software specifications and generated a controlled representation using SBVR. Automated object oriented analysis of SBVR specifications of software using the NL2UML*via*SBVR provides a higher accuracy as compared to other available NL-based tools. Besides better accuracy, SBVR has also enabled to extract OO information such as association multiplicity, aggregations, generalizations, and instances as other NL-based tools can't process and extract this information.

Some non-functional in the case study such as "*If the membership is still valid and the number of items on loan less than 8, the book bar code is read*" and "*If the item can be issued (e.g. not reserved) the item is stamped and then issued.*" are not part of the output class model. These are basically constraints and it is our future work to also generate Object Constraint language (OCL) for these natural language constraints.

References

1. Bryant, B.R., Lee, B.S., et al.: From Natural Language to Executable Models of Software Components. In: Workshop on S. E. for Embedded Systems, pp. 51–58 (2008)
2. OMG. Unified Modelling Language (UML) Standard version 2.1.2. Object Management Group (2007), `http://www.omg.org/mda/`
3. Mich, L.: NL-OOPS: from natural language to object oriented using the natural language processing system LOLITA. Natural Language Engineering 2(2), 167–181 (1996)
4. Delisle, S., Barker, K., Biskri, I.: Object-Oriented Analysis: Getting Help from Robust Computational Linguistic Tools. In: 4th International Conference on Applications of Natural Language to Information Systems, Klagenfurt, Austria, pp. 167–172 (1998)
5. Bajwa, I.S., Lee, M.G., Bordbar, B.: SBVR Business Rules Generation from Natural Language Specification. In: AAAI Spring Symposium 2011, San Francisco, USA, pp. 2–8 (2011)
6. Börstler, J.: User - Centered Engineering in RECORD - An Overview. In: Nordic Workshop on Programming Environment Research NWPER 1996, Aalborg, Denmark, pp. 149–156 (1999)
7. Overmyer, S.V., Rambow, O.: Conceptual Modeling through Linguistics Analysis Using LIDA. In: 23rd International Conference on Software Engineering (July 2001)
8. Perez-Gonzalez, H.G., Kalita, J.K.: GOOAL: A Graphic Object Oriented Analysis Laboratory. In: 17th Annual ACM SIGPLAN Conference on Object-oriented Programming, Systems, Languages, and Applications (OOPSLA 2002), NY, USA, pp. 38–39 (2002)
9. Harmain, H.M., Gaizauskas, R.: CM-Builder: A Natural Language-Based CASE Tool for Object- Oriented Analysis. Automated Software Engineering 10(2), 157–181 (2003)
10. Oliveira, A., Seco, N., Gomes, P.: A CBR Approach to Text to Class Diagram Translation. In: TCBR Workshop at the 8th European Conference on Case-Based Reasoning, Turkey (September 2006)
11. Anandha Mala, G.S., Uma, G.V.: Automatic Construction of Object Oriented Design Models [UML Diagrams] from Natural Language Requirements Specification. In: Yang, Q., Webb, G. (eds.) PRICAI 2006. LNCS (LNAI), vol. 4099, pp. 1155–1159. Springer, Heidelberg (2006)
12. Bajwa, I.S., Samad, A., Mumtaz, S.: Object Oriented Software modeling Using NLP based Knowledge Extraction. European Journal of Scientific Research 35(01), 22–33 (2009)

13. OMG. Semantics of Business vocabulary and Rules (SBVR) Standard v.1.0. Object Management Group (2008), http://www.omg.org/spec/SBVR/1.0/
14. Toutanova, K., Manning, C.D.: Enriching the Knowledge Sources Used in a Maximum Entropy Part-of-Speech Tagger. In: Joint SIGDAT Conference on Empirical Methods in Natural Language Processing and Very Large Corpora, pp. 63–70 (2000)
15. Li, K., Dewar, R.G., Pooley, R.J.: Object-Oriented Analysis Using Natural Language Processing. Linguistic Analysis (2005)
16. Bajwa, I.S., Hyder, I.S.: UCD-generator - A LESSA application for use case design. In: International Conference on Information and Emerging Technologies, ICIET 2007 (2007)
17. Callan, R.E.: Building Object-Oriented Systems: An introduction from concepts to implementation in C++. Computational Mechanics Publications (1994)
18. Hirschman, L., Thompson, H.S.: Chapter 13 evaluation: Overview of evaluation in speech and natural language processing. In: Survey of the State of the Art in Human Language Technology (1995)
19. Berry, D.M.: Ambiguity in Natural Language Requirements Documents. In: Martell, C. (ed.) Monterey Workshop 2007. LNCS, vol. 5320, pp. 1–7. Springer, Heidelberg (2008)
20. Ormandjieva, O., Hussain, I., Kosseim, L.: Toward A Text Classification System for the Quality Assessment of Software written in Natural Language. In: 4th International Workshop on Software Quality Assurance (SOQUA 2007), pp. 39–45 (2007)
21. Bajwa, I.S., Choudhary, M.A.: A Rule Based System for Speech Language Context Understanding. Journal of Donghua University (English Edition) 23(6), 39–42 (2006)
22. Denger, C., Berry, D.M., Kamsties, E.: Higher Quality Specifications through Natural Language Patterns. In: Proceedings of IEEE International Conference on Software-Science, Technology & Engineering (SWSTE 2003), pp. 80–85 (2003)
23. Ilieva, M.G., Ormandjieva, O.: Automatic Transition of Natural Language Software Requirements Specification into Formal Presentation. In: Montoyo, A., Muńoz, R., Métais, E. (eds.) NLDB 2005. LNCS, vol. 3513, pp. 392–397. Springer, Heidelberg (2005)
24. Bajwa, I.S.: A Framework for Urdu Language Translation using LESSA. In: WASET Spring International Conference, WASET 2011, vol. 75, pp. 309–312 (2011)

PART III

Information Systems Analysis and Specification

On the Use of Software Visualization to Analyze Software Evolution: An Interactive Differential Approach

Renato Lima Novais[1,2], Glauco de F. Carneiro[1], Paulo R.M. Simões Júnior[1], and Manoel Gomes Mendonça[1]

[1] Computer Science Department, Federal University of Bahia, Bahia, Brazil
[2] Information Technology Department, Federal Institute of Bahia
Campus Santo Amaro, Bahia, Brazil
{renatoln,glauco.carneiro,pauloroberto,mgmendonca}@dcc.ufba.br

Abstract. Software evolution is one of the most important topics in modern software engineering research. This activity requires the analysis of large amounts of data describing the current software system structure as well as its previous history. Software visualization can be helpful in this scenario, as it can summarize this complex data into easy to interpret visual scenarios. This paper presents an interactive differential approach for visualizing software evolution. The approach builds multi-view structural descriptions of a software system directly from its source code, and uses colors to differentiate it from any other previous version. This differential approach is highly interactive allowing the user to quickly brush over many pairs of versions of the system. As a proof of concept, we used the approach to analyze eight versions of an open source system and found out it was useful to quickly identify hot spot and code smell candidates in them.

Keywords: Software visualization, Software evolution.

1 Introduction

Most of the software engineering costs are associated with software evolution and maintenance [11]. Software evolution has been studied for different purposes – reengineering, refactoring, and maintenance – from different point of views – process, architecture, and reuse – and it is one of the most important topics in modern software engineering research.

Maintenance tasks are heavily dependent on comprehension activities. Before the programmer can execute any maintenance, he/she has to understand how the software works and how it is internally structured. Researchers have pointed out that 50% of the time spent in the maintenance phase is devoted to software comprehension activities [13].

Software visualization is a field of software engineering that aims to help people to understand software through the use of visual resources [9]. Most of the current software visualization tools use the source code as its main information source. Source code is the most formal and unambiguous artifact developed and handled by humans during the software development process.

R. Zhang et al. (Eds.): ICEIS 2011, LNBIP 102, pp. 241–255, 2012.

One should expect that software visualization can also be effectively used to analyze and understand how software evolves. In fact, there are many applications for software evolution visualization. Some we have found in the literature are the identification of: (1) hot-spots of design erosion and code decay [25]; (2) elements that are inducing code decay [10]; and, (3) code smells [22] in the software. Independent of the portrayed information, high or low level, the common goal of these applications is to provide the user with a natural, instinctive and easy way to understand problems that permeate the software evolution process.

As mentioned before, source code is a key information source for data gathering. Current software configuration management (SCM) systems keep track of code releases and versions as they evolve. For this reason, this information is readily accessible from those systems. Notwithstanding its appeal, visualizing software evolution through its source code is not a trivial task. One important problem is the large amount of data with which one has to cope [28].

In spite of the difficulties, many researches are trying to identify how software visualization can help with software evolution [2][29][20][8]. The majority of them only analyze the high level information provided by SCM systems such as CVS, SVN and GIT. Information such as the number of changes in a file, co-changed (or logical) coupling, the growth in a file size, or how many authors has worked on it. To obtain this information, one does not have to analyze the source code itself, as it can be directly extracted from the SCM metadata.

A few other works analyze the source code itself [20] [6]. This approach is also very promising. Through it, one can extract precious software evolution information – such as code size and module dependency – that is not readily available as SCM metadata. Unfortunately, this approach is also more complex. In order to understand how the code evolves, one has to extract information over many versions of the source code and organize it for automated or human-based data analysis. Our work tackles this problem.

During the past three years, we have been developing a multi-perspective software visualization environment named SourceMiner [4][5][3]. This is a general purpose software visualization environment that is integrated into an industrial strength IDE (Eclipse). It provides several different integrated views to visualize Java software projects.

The work presented in this paper augments SourceMiner with a differential approach for visualizing software evolution. Although, it is tailored to SourceMiner, this approach is, in theory, applicable to other source code visualization tools. It consists of loading several code versions into the environment and allowing the user to compare any two versions through the visualization environment. Upon the selection of two versions, the views of the environment show the most recent one and use its colors to highlight the changes on this version with respect to the other one.

Although the approach is differential, comparing only two versions at a given moment, it is highly interactive. A range bar widget can be used to dynamically select any two of the available versions. Views are then instantaneously updated for user analysis. This allows the user to quickly browse over any pair of versions, from several different visualization perspectives.

The current work uses three visualization metaphors to present evolution from three different perspectives: structure, inheritance and dependency. A software layer was developed to access information directly from the SubVersion (SVN) configuration management system.

This paper presents the approach, describes the resources provided by SourceMiner for its support, and discusses ways of using them for software evolution analysis. The remainder of the paper is organized as follows. Section 2 introduces some background concepts. Section 3 discusses our approach. Section 4 shows the approach in action. Section 5 discusses related works. And, Section 6 concludes the paper with an outlook at future work.

2 Background

This section presents some basic concepts related to this work. Section 2.1 focuses on software evolution and Section 2.2 focuses on software visualization.

2.1 Software Evolution

The IEEE Standard 1219 [15] definition for software maintenance is "the modification of a software product after delivery to correct faults, to improve performance or other attributes, or to adapt the product to a modified environment". The term software evolution has been used as a preferable substitute for software maintenance [1]. In general, software evolution is related to why or how software changes over the time.

According to the continuous change law stated by Lehman in the seventies, software change is inevitable; otherwise the software would die [23]. Software needs to change for many reasons. New requirements emerge when the software is being used. Bugs are detected and must be fixed. Functional and non-functional improvements are needed to fulfill new requirements in the business environment. The software system must work on new hardware and software platforms.

On top of this all, the size and complexity of modern software systems are continuously increasing to keep up with the pace of hardware evolution and new functionalities requested by users. This has demanded a greater concern about the management of software evolution. Thousands of lines of code and documentation must be kept up to date as systems evolve, and tool support is fundamental in this context.

Considering the importance of software evolution and the need for software change, new methodologies, processes and tools to efficiently manage software evolution are urgent necessities in modern software engineering organizations.

2.2 Software Visualization

Software visualization (SoftVis) can be defined as the mapping from any kind of software artifact to graphical representations [18][27]. SoftVis is very helpful because it transforms intangible software entities and their relationships into visual metaphors that are easily interpretable by human beings. Consider coupling among software modules as an example. Using a graph as a visual metaphor, these modules can be represented as nodes and the coupling information can be represented as directed edges to build an intuitive visual metaphor for their dependency. Without a visual representation, the only way to analyze this information would be to look inside the source code or at a table of software metrics, in a potentially labor and cognitive intensive effort.

There are several classification taxonomies for SoftVis. Some divide SoftVis according to type of visualized object. Diehl [9], for example, divides software visualization into visualizing the structure, behavior and evolution of the software. Structure refers to visualizing static parts of the software. Behavior refers to visualizing the execution of the software. Evolution refers to visualizing how software evolves [9].

Software can also be visually analyzed from different perspectives [4]. In this case, visualization can be classified according to the point of views it provides to engineers to explore a software system.

SoftVis can also be classified according to the metaphors it uses to represent software. Among others, visualizations can use iconographic, pixel-based, matrix-based, graph-based and hierarchical metaphors [17][12].

This paper focuses on the static visualization of source code of object-oriented systems using multiple perspectives and different types of metaphors. Multiple perspectives are needed for analyzing the different static characteristics of the source code. On the same token, certain types of metaphors are best suited to certain perspectives, and it would be confusing if the same metaphor is used to represent two different perspectives [5].

For example, one can be interested in investigating software according to its structure. This structural perspective reveals how the software is organized into packages, classes and methods. The IDEs usually provide a hierarchical view for this purpose. Eclipse's package explorer is a very well known example of such a view. It uses an iconographic tree to represent the system's package and file structure.

SourceMiner uses treemaps as its own visual metaphor to represent the software from a structural perspective, see Figure 1. A Treemap is a hierarchical 2D visualization that maps a tree structure into a set of nested rectangles [16]. In SoftVis, the nested rectangles can represent software entities, like packages, classes and methods. Rectangles representing methods of the same class are drawn together inside the rectangle of the class. Likewise, the rectangles of the classes that belong to the same package are drawn together inside the rectangle of the package.

Treemaps are constructed recursively and fits well in a reduced space. A computer screen can fit thousands of small rectangles. This is a clear advantage over the package explorer tree structure. Another bonus of this approach is that the size and the color of the rectangles can be easily associated to metrics such as module size and complexity.

Another perspective of interest in OO systems is the inheritance tree. It is important to visually show which classes extends others or implement certain interfaces. In this case, it is also desirable to use a hierarchical metaphor, but SourceMiner does not use treemaps in order to avoid confusion. Instead, it uses a metaphor called polymetric views for this purpose, see Figure 1. A polymetric view uses a forest of rectangles to represent the inheritance trees formed by classes and interfaces in a software system [21]. Rectangles are linked by edges representing the inheritance relation between them. The length and width of the rectangles can be used to represent software attributes such as the size and number of methods of a class.

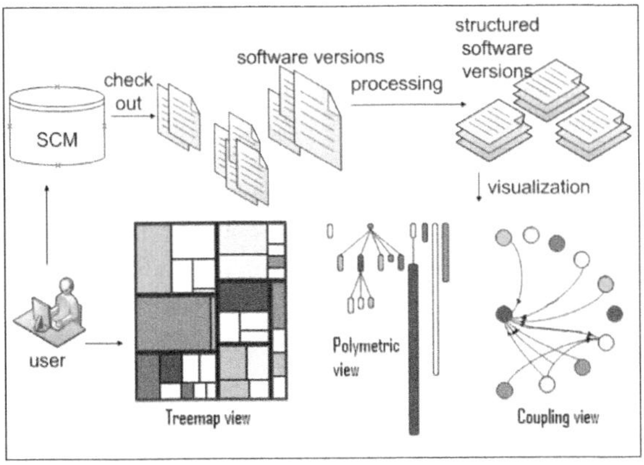

Fig. 1. Views, Perspectives and Overview of the Approach

The third perspective discussed here is the dependency perspective. It represents the coupling between software entities, in this case, software modules that depends on other modules. One of the most useful views to describe this kind of information is interactive directed graphs (IDG), see Figure 1. IDG's coupling views use nodes to represent software modules and directed edges to represent the dependency between them. Like in the other views, the visual attributes can be used to express the attributes of the represented software entities. The size of a graph node can be associated to the size of a module, for example.

Observe that each perspective represents the software from a different point of view. This way, views from different perspectives can be used to complement each other. Also, different views – views that use different metaphors – may be used to represent the software from the same perspective. SourceMiner uses, for example, relationship matrixes and egocentric graphs as complementary views to the dependency perspective. This paper, however, will focus only on the use of the three views previously discussed – polymetric, treemaps and IDGs – to represent the inheritance, structural and dependency perspectives. Its goal is to use them to analyze software evolution under distinct points of view.

3 A Differential Approach to Understand Software Evolution

This section presents the differential approach to visualize software evolution attributes. The goal is to use a multiple view software visualization approach to identify hot-spots of design erosion and structural decay in the code [25].

3.1 Using Colors to Represent Evolution Attributes

Several attributes can be used to characterize software evolution. Size, coupling and inheritance hierarchy are examples of these attributes and the important issue here is how they evolve over time. Visual elements in SourceMiner's views are decorated with colors to denote this scenario and therefore support its analysis. Users can dynamically select any two versions of a software system. Elements that appeared from one version to the other are painted in blue. Elements that disappeared are painted in gray. Elements that decreased or increase are painted in a color scale that ranges from bright green (decreased a lot) to bright red (increased a lot), using white to denote elements that have not changed. Figure 2 portrays the element differential decoration colors. As colors perception may depend on cultural, linguistic, and physiological factors [24], the choice of colors is a configurable item in the visualization tool.

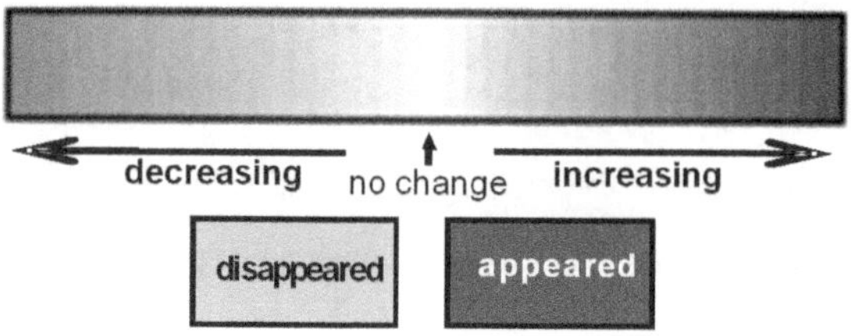

Fig. 2. Colors used to decorate changing software elements

Color interpolation is used to show the size variation as follows. The greater the growth/decrease the brighter the color used. To smoothly interpolate a color from an initial color IC (e.g. green representing decrease) to a final color FC (e.g. red representing growth) going through a neutral color ZC (e.g. white representing no variation), based on the value of a certain metric value, SourceMiner uses the expressions represented in (1). Where NC = new color, FC = final color, IC = initial color, and $_{R,G,B}$ is the RGB value of that color (e.g. FC_G is the green RG_B value of the final color FC).

$$
\begin{aligned}
NC_R &= (FC_R * ratio) + IC_R * (1 - ratio) \\
NC_G &= (FC_G * ratio) + IC_G * (1 - ratio) \\
NC_B &= (FC_B * ratio) + IC_B * (1 - ratio) \\
ratio &= (itemValue - minValue)/(maxValue - minValue).
\end{aligned} \tag{1}
$$

minValue is the minimal value associated to IC. *maxValue* the maximal value associated to FC. *itemValue* is the value for which the color is being calculated and *zeroValue* is the value associated to ZC (the neutral color).

$$minValue <= itemValue <= maxValue.$$

If $itemValue < zeroValue$ one should use the *maxValue* as *zeroValue*, FC as ZC, in (1). The rest of the equation remains the same. If $itemValue \geq zeroValue$, one should use *minValue* as *zeroValue*, IC as ZC, and the rest of the equation remains the same. At the end, the interpolated color for the item with an *itemValue* value is the RGB color represented by $\{NC_R, NC_G, NC_B\}$.

All these values are positive integers, because they are represented as RGB values. In the context of software evolution, metrics can be either positive or negative. So, sometimes the system will need to shift values to a positive scale. The procedure presented in (2) is used for that. *zeroValue* is set as the module of the *minValue*.

maxValue is added with module of *minValue*, and *minValue* receives the value 0. For consistency, the *itemValue*, for which one wants to calculate the interpolated color, should also be shifted by the module of *minValue*.

$$\begin{aligned} zeroValue &= |\, minValue \,| \\ maxValue &= maxValue + zeroValue \\ minValue &= 0. \end{aligned} \tag{2}$$

3.2 A Differential Approach to Visualize Software Evolution

Our approach, summarized on Figure 1, starts when the user checks out the versions of the software he/she wants to analyze from the SCM system. SourceMiner then analyses all versions. The analyzer reads the Eclipse's Abstract Syntax Tree for each system and stores the gathered information in internal data structures for fast access and search. This process is depicted on the top of Figure 1.

The user can now select a metric of interest and operate a range bar widget to interactively select any two of the analyzed versions. The system calculates the amount of change on the selected metric (e.g. size), between the two chosen versions, for each one of the software elements that exist in the system.

In this differential approach, the views always show the most recent of the selected versions of the analyzed software. The views are decorated with the changing colors as discussed in the previous section. Although our approach treats elements that have appeared and disappeared, the current implementation does not yet display elements that disappeared (grey elements).

The source code of the most recent of the selected versions is readily accessible from the views graphical elements. Clicking on any visual element will bring forth the source code of this element on the Eclipse Editor, so the user can obtain details on demand directly from the source code.

One important question that emerges here, which can be seen as a limitation of the approach, is that it just takes into account two of the processed versions to decorate the views. The visualization shows the *diff* between these two versions, but it misses intermediate values. Consider three versions – *1*, *j* and *n* – as an example. Consider that $1 < j < n$ and some values $M1 = 5$, $Mj = 3$ and $Mn = 9$ for a certain metric of a given software entity. In the example, the system only considers the versions *1* and *n*, and portrays the difference $Mn - M1 = 4$. The views do not explicitly show what happened between *1* and *j* or between *j* and *n*.

This is in fact a limitation, but it is not a major problem. The user can easily and quickly select any other two versions among the analyzed ones. The elapsed time between version selection and the construction of new views are instantaneous for all practical purposes. This allows for fast interactive exploration of different versions and the differences among them. Moreover, this can be done using all three different perspectives of SourceMiner and the metrics that are currently implemented in it (size, cyclomatic complexity, number of methods, and afferent and efferent coupling). In any case, all three views are consistently colored with respect to the metrics selected.

3.3 Using Multiple Perspectives

Figure 3 depicts the SourceMiner plug-in in action. There are three views presented in this picture: Package Explorer, an original Eclipse view, on the top left. It is showing eight versions of a Software Product Line (SPL). These versions were sequentially analyzed by the SourceMiner, and data were extracted from each project. At the left bottom, there's the *EvolutionFilters* view. Through this view, the user can select the two versions to be differentially analyzed, using a range bar. This widget is highlighted on the picture. This view also allows the user to select the metric he wants to analyze and the colors that will be used in the views.

The right side of Figure 3 is filled by the generated Treemap view. This view is showing the evolution in lines of code from version 7 to version 8 of the system. The user can use it to visually identify elements (methods, in this view) that had its size changed, and how they are spread in the project. It also highlights the elements with the highest decrease – brightest green – and highest increase – brightest red.

Mind that other metrics can be used as well. If the selected metric is complexity, dark red show elements that had a steep increase in complexity with respect to the other version, and so on so forth.

Observe that the other (polymetric and dependency) views are also present in Figure 3. They are hidden under the treemap view to facilitate its readability. The Eclipse environment allows for many layouts for the views. SourceMiner views can be configured and mingled with Eclipse views and resources. These layouts can then be saved for specific tasks.

As a generic data exploration strategy, we recommend the use of the treemap view to understand the big picture of system evolution. Several situations can be represented in this *structural* view: 1) the software is growing if the majority of the colors are red; 2) a module is a hotspot for decaying analysis if it is bright red for complexity metrics when other are behaving differently; 3) a sub-system was under refactoring or redesign if the majority of its elements are green or white; 4) an element is possibly losing functionality, or reducing its role in a system, if they are bright green.

The Polymetric view can also help with the big picture, showing how the inheritance structure of a system is changing over the time. In order to illustrate some situations that can be detected through the *inheritance* view, suppose that a class A is inherited by classes B, C and D. If A grows too much (bright red), it may be adding extraneous functionality and have a negative impact in its descendants. If B, C and D grows as A remains the same this might represent a pull-up refactoring opportunity. The opposite scenario may indicate a push-down refactoring opportunity. If A grows as B, C, and D decreases this might indicate the occurrence of pull-up refactoring operation. The opposite scenario may indicate a push-down refactoring operation, and so on so forth.

The *Coupling* view shows the afferent and efferent coupling between classes. With this metaphor, one can analyze the impact of an element in their dependents, or in the elements it depends on. Consider that a class A is coupled with other modules of the system. If there is an increasing afferent coupling to A (more and more modules uses resources of A), the maintenance costs of this part of the system is increasing. If there is an increasing efferent coupling from A (A uses more and more resources from other modules), A is a candidate for God Class [22] and there might be a class extraction refactoring opportunity.

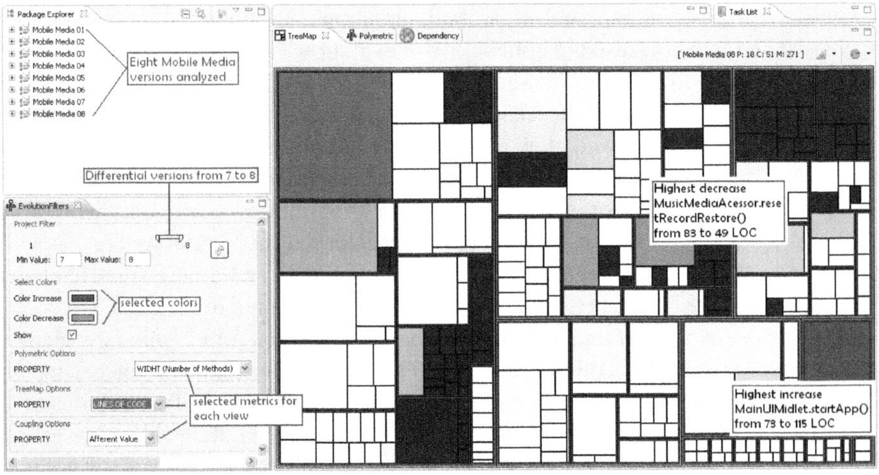

Fig. 3. SourceMiner plug-in in action

4 SourceMiner in Action

To test SourceMiner, we analyzed the evolution of eight versions of a SPL called MobileMedia (MM). This SPL manipulates photo, music, and video on mobile devices. MM is an open source system and has been used in many software engineering studies [3][7]. Our analysis considered the changes of MM version to version (from version 1 to 2, 2 to 3, 3 to 4, and so on so forth). Three views and five metrics were used in the analysis process as described on Table 1.

Table 1. Metrics used in each view

View	Metrics	Versions
TreeMap	Complexity	1-2, 2-3, 3-4, 4-5, 5-6, 6-7, 7-8
	Lines of code (LOC)	
Polymetric	Number of Methods (NOM)	
	Lines of code (LOC)	
Dependency	*Afferent Coupling (AC)*	
	Efferent Coupling (EC)	

The combination of versions, view and metrics generated forty two snapshots of the MM evolution – comprising seven version differentials, three views per differential, and two metrics per view. All these pictures and their comments are available at the study website (http://softvis.dcc.ufba.br/MobileMediaEvolutionStudy January2011). Due to the space constraints of this paper, we discuss only six analyses here.

The *TreeMap-Complexity analysis* showed that the cyclomatic complexity of the software modules evolved little from version to version. Only a few elements showed variation in the analysis. There was no variation in evolutions 2–3 and 3–4. Just new elements have appeared during them. Only one element increased in complexity in evolutions 1–2, 4–5, 5–6 and 6–7. And, as shown in Figure 4.a, two elements increased and two decreased in complexity in evolution 7–8.

The *TreeMap-LOC analysis* showed that the evolution of this metric is easily perceived. The majority of the elements changed along the evolution, increasing in size. Evolution 1–2 showed that the methods `BaseController.showImage` and `ImageUtil.getImageInfoFromBytes` have increased in size but decreased in complexity. The element `BaseController.handleCommand( Command c, Displayable d)` had the highest increase (brighter red) in evolutions 1–2 , 2–3, 3–4 (see Figure 4.b). This element disappeared in version 5, and a new smaller element `BaseController.handleCommand(Command c)` appeared in its place.

The *Polymetric–NOM analysis* showed that from version 1 to 2 only new elements have appeared (the Exception package). There are elements with increasing and decreasing behavior in almost every analysis. It's possible to identify variations on the inheritance tree from version 4 on. For example, on evolution 4–5, the element `BaseController` has decreased in number of methods (from 22 to 4). This is the only green rectangle in Figure 4.c. This class inherits from `AbstractController`, an abstract class created in version 5. So, one can easily infer that some functionalities of `BaseController` was pulled-up to `AbstractController`.

The *Polymetric–LOC analysis* confirmed that the majority of the classes increase at each new version. In evolution 4–5, `BaseController` has decreased from 629 to 93 lines of code. Almost all elements of the `Controller` inheritance tree showed variation in evolution 7–8. This is shown on the third tree from the left to the right of Figure 4.d. Three elements in this tree showed significant a growth: `SelectMediaController` (from 32 to 110), `PhotoViewController` (from 119 to 153) and `MediaController` (from 391 to 470). Following our strategy, the software engineer should investigate if there is any pull-up refactoring opportunity in these classes.

The *Dependency–AC analysis* showed that the afferent coupling metric has changed only in few elements along the versions. There were no variation in evolutions 1–2 and 3–4. Although there were not many changes, the afferent coupling generally increased when this change happened. Only two elements have decreased their AC values: `BaseController`, in evolution 4–5 and `AlbumListScreen`, in evolution 6–7. The highest growths were observed in evolution 4–5 (see Figure 4.e): `MainUIMidlet` (from 1 to 6), `AlbumData` (from 4 to 9) and `AlbumListScreen` (from 1 to 6). This evolution had a major impact on this subsystem, as maintenance activities in these elements can now impact a much larger number of elements than before.

The *Coupling* view shows the afferent and efferent coupling between classes. With The *Dependency–EC analysis* showed that, like the AC metric, the efferent coupling metric has also changed only in few elements along the versions. There were no variations in evolutions 1–2, 3–4 and 5–6. The highest growth was again observed in evolution 4–5: `PhotoController` (from 3 to 6). The decrease behavior happened only in evolution 6–7 where the class `AbstractController` has decreased its afferent coupling value from 4 to 3 (see Figure 4.f).

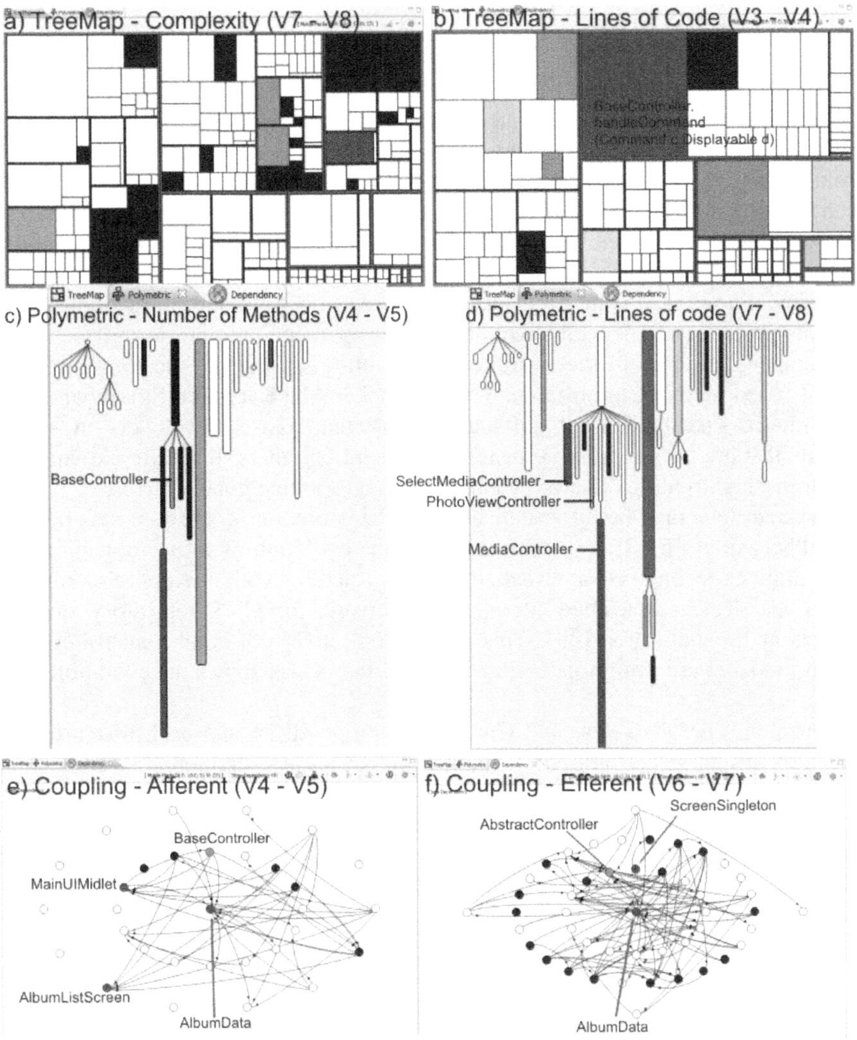

Fig. 4. Six snapshots of Mobile Media evolution analysis

The following interesting points were observed in the study:

- The system elements increased significantly all over the board in number of lines, but their complexity increased only in some instances;
- When compared to size, afferent and efferent coupling changes sporadically, however it almost always increases when it does so. This means that the system is getting more and more tangled along its evolution;
- Some elements appeared recurrently in the study, pointing out the hot spots of the system with respect to evolution.
- All this information was gathered rather quickly and in most part did not require any source code inspection at all.

5 Related Works

The recognition that the use of software visualization can help software evolution is not new. During the recent years, a growing body of relevant work is being developed in this area. Lanza [20] proposed an Evolution Matrix to visualize the software evolution. He used an astronomy metaphor to analyze some aspects of the evolution of the classes. D'Ambros et al. [8] proposed Evolution Radar, a visualization-based approach that integrates both file-level and module-level logical coupling information.

Ripley, Sarma and van der Hoek [26] proposed a visualization approach for software project awareness and evolution. Their approach presents an overview of the development activities of the entire team, providing insight into the evolution of the project based on SCM information. On same token, the Evolution Storyboards [2] is an animated visualization of software history that assists developers in spotting artifacts that are becoming more or less dependent on others. It tries to explain decay symptoms, highlighting refactoring candidates and spotting good structure.

A system for graph-based visualization of the evolution of software was proposed by Collberg et al. [6]. This system visualizes the evolution of software using a novel graph drawing technique for visualizing large structures with a temporal component. Vonea and Telea developed an open framework for CVS repository querying, analysis and visualization [29]. This multi-perspective tool is an n-snapshot matrix that shows software evolution. Each column of the matrix shows the evolution of one metric.

Gonzalez, Theron, Telea, and Garcia [14] proposed an approach that presents a four-view design visualization combined with metrics-and-structure data for software evolution analysis. The four views focus on different tasks and use-cases, showing: an overview of the project commits structure and related metrics (timeline view); a comparison of package or class hierarchy structures evolving over time (structure evolution view); a trend analysis of metrics (metric view); and a detailed code inspection (visualization of the indirect class coupling integrating source code viewing).

Wu, Holt and Hassan [30] used spectrographs to explore software evolution. The evolution spectrograph combines time, spectrum and property measurement coded in colors to characterize software evolution. The coloring technique used is aimed to easily distinguish patterns in the evolutionary data.

Considering that the evolution data is multi-dimensional, some authors propose the use of animated visualization. The work of Langelier, Sahraoui and Poulin [19] is an example of this. They proposed an approach that uses animated visualization to explore the evolution of software quality.

Most of the approaches discussed in this section analyze high level information based on commits on the SCM. Our approach differs from the others because it represent the evolution of metrics directly extracted from the source code, using different perspectives, like structure, inheritance and dependency, to present the software through cross referenced views focused on its basic elements (methods, classes and packages). With them, one can analyze information like the basic elements' complexity, size and coupling evolution using an interactive differential approach.

6 Final Remarks

This paper presented a highly interactive differential approach for visualizing software evolution using SourceMiner, a multi-perspective software visualization environment. Three of the SourceMiner views, one for each perspective, were augmented to deal with software evolution.

The paper discussed how to enhance a multiple view environment with an interactive differential approach to understand software evolution. It showed how five different colors and a color interpolation were used to portray the evolution of software elements across their different versions and from different perspectives. It also presented some strategies to detect code evolution problems and related issues using this differential approach.

The proposed approach has some limitations. It currently does not control the elements that have disappeared from one version to the other. This requires quite a bit of extra work, as they have to be discovered and maintained across different versions. We plan to do that in our next version of the tool. We believe that this will provide the user with more accurate information about what happened during the evolution of a system.

We are extending the system with temporal views. Contrary to the differential views, they will show the timeline of a set of metrics of a chosen software element across all its versions. A parallel coordinate visual metaphor will be used for that and the new view will be completely integrated with the others.

We are also planning to extend the approach with new information. Firstly, we want to augment the views with high level information and metadata from the SCM. Secondly, we want to augment them with history sensitive metrics [7]. We want to investigate how useful those metrics are to further characterize software evolution.

Lastly, we are planning a series of experimental studies to further investigate the usefulness of the approach to identify code smells, refactoring opportunities, system hot-spots and code decay.

Acknowledgements. This work was partially supported by the National Institute of Science and Technology for Software Engineering (INES - http://www.ines.org.br/), funded by CNPq and FACEPE, grants 573964/2008-4 and APQ-1037-1.03/08.

References

1. Bennett, K.H., Rajlich, V.T.: Software maintenance and evolution: a roadmap. In: Proc. of the Conference on The Future of Software Engineering (ICSE 2000), pp. 73–87. ACM, New York (2000)
2. Beyer, D., Hassan, A.E.: Animated Visualization of Software History using Evolution Storyboards. In: Proc. of the 13th Working Conference on Reverse Engineering, WCRE, pp. 199–210. IEEE Computer Society, Washington, DC (2006)
3. de F. Carneiro, G., Sant'Anna, C.N., Garcia, A.F., von F.G. Chavez, C., Mendonça, M.G.: On the Use of Software Visualization to Support Concern Modularization Analysis. In: Proc. of the 3rd Workshop on Assessment of Contemporary Modularization Techniques, Co-located with OOPSLA, Florida, USA (2009)

4. de F. Carneiro, G., Silva, M., Mara, L., Figueiredo, E., Sant'Anna, C., Garcia, A., Mendonça, M.: Identifying Code Smells with Multiple Concern Views. In: Soft. Eng. Brazilian Symposium, pp. 128–137 (2010a)
5. de F. Carneiro, G., Sant'Anna, C., Mendonça, M.: On the Design of a Multi-Perspective Visualization Environment to Enhance Software Comprehension Activities. In: Proc. of the VII Workshop on Modern Software Maintenance, Co-located with SBQS (2010b)
6. Collberg, C., Kobourov, S., Nagra, J., Pitts, J., Wampler, K.: A system for graph-based visualization of the evolution of software. In: Proc. of the 2003 ACM Symposium on Software Visualization, SoftVis 2003, pp. 77–86. ACM, New York (2003)
7. Silva, L.M., Dantas, F., Honorato, G., Garcia, A., Lucena, C.: Detecting Modularity Flaws of Evolving Code: What the History Can Reveal? In: Proc. of the 4th Brazilian Symposium Software Components, Architectures and Reuse, SBCARS (2010)
8. D'Ambros, M., Lanza, M., Lungu, M.: Visualizing Co-Change Information with the Evolution Radar. IEEE Trans. Softw. Eng. 35(5), 720–735 (2009)
9. Diehl, S.: Software Visualization - Visualizing the Structure, Behavior and Evolution of Software. Springer (2007)
10. Eick, S.G., Graves, T.L., Karr, A.F., Marron, J.S., Mockus, A.: Does Code Decay? Assessing the Evidence from Change Management Data. IEEE Trans. Softw. Eng. 27(1), 1–12 (2001)
11. Erlikh, L.: Leveraging legacy system dollars for e-business. IEEE IT Pro., 17–23 (2000)
12. Ferreira de Oliveira, M.C., Levkowitz, H.: From visual data exploration to visual data mining: a survey. IEEE Transactions on Visualization and Computer Graphics 9(3), 378–394 (2003)
13. Fjeldstad, R., Hamlen, W.: Application program maintenance: Report to our respondents. In: Parikh, G., Zvegintzov, N. (eds.) Tutorial on Software Maintenance, pp. 13–27. IEEE Computer Soc. Press (1983)
14. Gonzalez, A., Theron, R., Telea, A., Garcia, F.J.: Combined visualization of structural and metric information for software evolution analysis. In: Proc. of the Joint international and Annual ERCIM Workshops on Principles of Software Evolution (Iwpse) and Software Evolution (Evol) Workshops, IWPSE-Evol 2009, pp. 25–30. ACM, New York (2009)
15. IEEE Std. 1219: Standard for Software Maintenance. IEEE Computer Society Press, Los Alamitos CA (1993)
16. Johnson, B., Shneiderman, B.: Tree-Maps: a space-filling approach to the visualization of hierarchical information structures. In: Nielson, G.M., Rosenblum, L. (eds.) Proc. of the 2nd Conference on Visualization 1991, pp. 284–291 (1991)
17. Keim, D.A.: Information visualization and visual data mining. IEEE Transactions on Visualization and Computer Graphics 7(1), 100–107 (2002)
18. Koschke, R.: Software visualization in software maintenance, reverse engineering, and reengineering: a research survey. Journal of Software Maintenance 15(2), 87–109 (2003)
19. Langelier, G., Sahraoui, H., Poulin, P.: Exploring the evolution of software quality with animated visualization. In: Proc. of the 2008 IEEE Symposium on Visual Languages and Human-Centric Computing, VLHCC, Washington, DC, pp. 13–20 (2008)
20. Lanza, M.: The evolution matrix: recovering software evolution using software visualization techniques. In: Proc. of the 4th International Workshop on Principles of Software Evolution, IWPSE 2001, pp. 37–42. ACM, New York (2001)
21. Lanza, M., Ducasse, S.: Polymetric Views - A Lightweight Visual Approach to Reverse Engineering. IEEE Trans. Softw. Eng. 29(9), 782–795 (2003)
22. Lanza, M., Marinescu, R., Ducasse, S.: Object-Oriented Metrics in Practice. Springer-Verlag New York, Inc. (2005)

23. Lehman, M.M.: On Understanding Laws, Evolution, and Conservation in the Large-Program Life Cycle. Journal of Systems and Software 1, 213–221 (1980)
24. Mazza, R.: Introduction to Information Visualization. Springer, London (2009)
25. Ratzinger, J., Fischer, M., Gall, H.: EvoLens: Lens-view visualizations of evolution data. In: Proc. of the Int. Workshop on Principles of Software Evolution, pp. 103–112. IEEE Comp. Soc. (2005)
26. Ripley, R.M., Sarma, A., van der Hoek, A.: A Visualization for Software Project Awareness and Evolution. In: 4th IEEE International Workshop on Visualizing Software for Understanding and Analysis, VISSOFT 2007, June 24-25, pp. 137–144 (2007)
27. Roman, G.-C., Cox, K.C.: Program visualization: the art of mapping programs to pictures. In: Proc. of the 14th ICSE. ACM, New York (1992)
28. Voinea, L., Telea, A.: An open framework for CVS repository querying, analysis and visualization. In: Proc. of the MSR 2006, pp. 33–39. ACM, New York (2006a)
29. Voinea, L., Telea, A.: Multiscale and multivariate visualizations of software evolution. In: Proc. of the 2006 ACM Symposium on Software Visualization, Brighton, United Kingdom (2006b)
30. Wu, J., Holt, R.C., Hassan, A.E.: Exploring Software Evolution Using Spectrographs. In: Proc. of the 11th Working Conference on Reverse Engineering, WCRE, pp. 80–89. IEEE Computer Society, Washington, DC (2004)

Temporal Management of WS-BPEL Processes

Amirreza Tahamtan[1], Christian Österle[1],
A. Min Tjoa[1], and Abdelkader Hameurlain[2]

[1] Institute of Software Technology & Interactive Systems,
Information & Software Engineering Group,
Vienna University of Technology,
Favoritenstrasse 9-11/188, A-1040 Vienna, Austria
[2] Université Paul Sabatier, 118, Route de Narbonne,
31062 Toulouse Cedex, France
tahamtan@ifs.tuwien.ac.at
http://www.ifs.tuwien.ac.at/~tahamtan

Abstract. WS-BPEL is de-facto industry standard for business processes. One of its major shortcomings is lack of temporal management capabilities. WS-BPEL offers no possibility for definition, calculation and monitoring of temporal values such as activity duration and deadlines as well as checking the temporal conformance of processes. This paper tackles temporal management of WS-BPEL based on two different techniques: interval-based and probabilistic. This paper describes temporal management of cooperating WS-BPEL abstract and executable processes. We have implemented a temporal management prototype as a WS-BPEL extension.

Keywords: WS-BPEL, Time, Temporal management, Extension, Conformance.

1 Introduction

Temporal conformance and compliance are important quality criteria for business processes and interorganizational workflows. Processes may have deadlines. The assigned deadlines may be part of the service level agreement between partners or enforced by law or organizational policies. It must be ensured that the right information is delivered to the right activity at the right time and the process executes in a timely manner in order to be able to hold the deadlines. Temporal conformance on the one hand increases the QoS and on the other hand reduces the cost of process execution as costly exception handling mechanisms can be avoided. Temporal management can be used for three different purposes [1]:

- Predictive time management: to predict the possible temporal behavior of the system and pre-calculate future possible violations of temporal constraints.
- Pro-active time management: to detect potential future violations and raise alarm in these cases such that counter-measure mechanisms can be triggered early enough.
- Reactive time management: to react and trigger exception handling mechanisms if a temporal failure has already occurred.

R. Zhang et al. (Eds.): ICEIS 2011, LNBIP 102, pp. 256–269, 2012.

Web Services and SOA offer several advantages for implementation of business processes such as interoperability, loosely coupling and composition. WS-BPEL has become the accepted standard for description end execution of business processes based on Web Services. In the realm of web services we mainly talk about two concepts: choreographies and orchestrations or in the WS-BPEL notation, abstract and executable processes.

A WS-BPEL executable process or orchestration is controlled and run by one partner. A partner's internal logic and business know-how are contained in his executable process. Other tasks such as data transformations, data handling, arithmetic operations and the actual performed work are as well contained in this process. An executable process is solely visible to its owner and other external partners have no view on and knowledge about it. An executable process is a process viewed only from the perspective of its owner.

On the other hand, a choreography, which is called abstract process in WS-BPEL, describes business protocols. An abstract process may be used to describe observable message exchange behavior of each of the parties involved, without revealing their internal implementation [2]. An abstract process can use all the construct of an executable process and have the same expressive power but it is not intended to be executed. It has merely a descriptive role. An abstract process defines a collaboration among involved partners to reach an overall business goal. It contains only visible exchanged messages between partners in course of a business process.

In order to ensure that cooperating business processes are temporally compliant, it must be guaranteed that both the tasks performed in executable processes and the protocols described in abstract processes have a compliant temporal behavior. In our previous work [3] we have implemented a time management extension for WS-BPEL, called BPEL-TIME. In this work we describe how BPEL-TIME handles temporal management of a set of cooperating WS-BPEL abstract and executable processes. BPEL-TIME consists of two components, a design time component and a run time component. The design time component allows the definition of temporal constraints. At design time it is checked if the model is temporally feasible, i.e. if there is a solution that satisfies all the temporal constraints. If the system is temporally not feasible, it can be detected at design time and necessary modifications performed. We calculate a valid temporal window for each activity in this phase. If an activity executes within its valid temporal window it is guaranteed that the whole process terminates successfully. The run time component monitors the execution of the process and informs the process manager if any deviation from valid temporal windows is detected. Based on the calculations at design time, the run time component predicts the future temporal behavior of the flow and informs the process manager about its status. Our approach is based on prevention of errors rather than repairing them after their occurrence. By predicting the behavior of a flow appropriate measures can be triggered in order to guarantee its successful execution. BPEL-TIME offers two different possibilities: an interval-based and a probabilistic approach, The interval-based approach allows the definition of fixed and/or variable temporal constraints such as deadlines and durations. The probabilistic approach enables a probabilistic representation of temporal constraints and takes also branching probabilities into account.

2 Model Description

For modeling and calculation of temporal plans of WS-BPEL executable and abstract processes three types of constraints have to be considered:

- **Implicit constraints** are derived implicitly from the structure of a process, e.g. an activity can start execution if and only if all of its predecessors have finished execution.
- **Explicit constraints**, e.g. assigned deadlines, can be set explicitly by the process designer or enforced by law, regulations or business rules.
- **Dependencies with other processes** may impose a temporal restriction on a process. It is not enough to perform a temporal analysis in isolation.

The first two constraints are needed to calculate the temporal plan of one single process. Note that abstract and executable processes are both handled uniformly. From the point of view of temporal management it makes no difference if the WS-BPEL process is abstract or executable. The third constraint must be considered in order to check the temporal conformance and calculate the temporal plans of a set cooperating processes. We model the first two constraints using two different modeling approaches: the interval-based and the probabilistic approach.

2.1 Interval-Based Approach

As the basic modeling language, we adapt the model presented in [1]. It is a timed graph augmented with start and end events for activities. Timed graphs are familiar workflow graphs where nodes correspond to activities and edges to the dependencies between activities, enriched with temporal information. Fig. 1 shows an example of the model. All activities have a unique name, duration and two corresponding events: start and end event. $a.d$ denotes the duration of an activity a and a_s and a_e its start event and end event respectively. Because BPEL-processes are full-blocked [4], in this work we restrict the graphs to full-blocked ones, i.e. each split node has a counterpart join node and vice versa.

The interval-based approach allows modeling of fixed and variable durations of activities. The duration of an activity can take any value within an interval bounded by minimum and maximum durations, e.g. $a.d = [a.d_{min}, a.d_{max}]$, where $a.d$ refers to duration of an activity a. We use upper-bound and lower-bound constraints [5] to model this interval. Let a be the source event and b the destination event.

Lower-bound constraint identifies the minimum temporal distance between two events. $lbc(a, b, \delta)$ denotes that between a and b at least δ time points must pass.
Upper-bound constraint identifies the maximum temporal distance between two events. $ubc(a, b, \delta)$ denotes that between a and b at most δ time points can pass.

$a.d_{min}$ and $a.d_{max}$ can be modeled by defining the minimum and maximum allowed time points between start event and end event of an activity respectively. This scenario as depicted in fig. 2, where $a.d = [2, 7]$. Obviously an activity can also be assigned a fixed value, if $a.d_{min} = a.d_{max}$. Note that in the rest of this paper, for the sake of

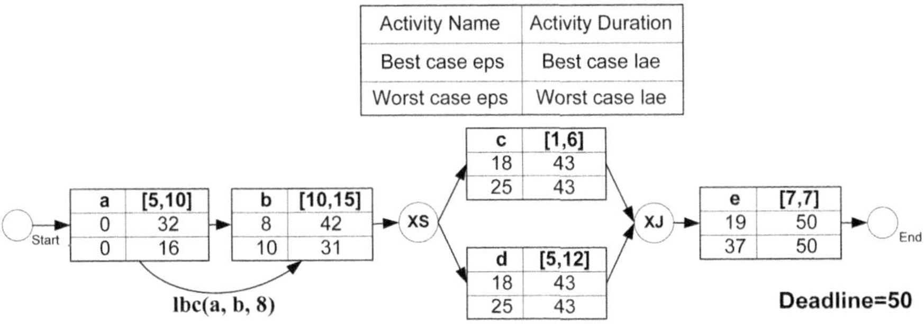

Fig. 1. An example of a timed graph with deadline= 50

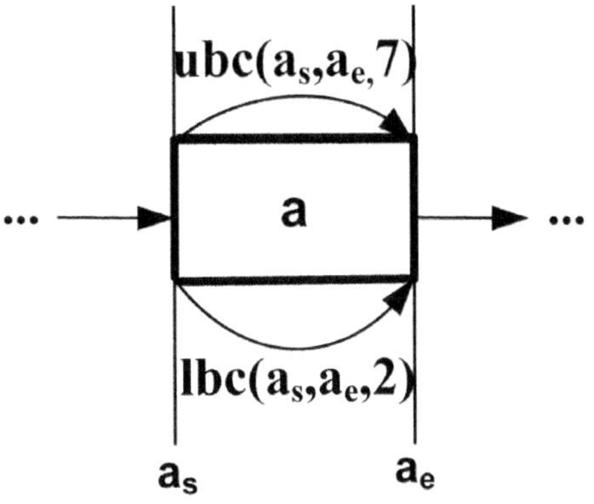

Fig. 2. Modeling d_{min} and d_{max} by lbc and ubc

brevity, we do not illustrate *lbc* and *ubc* as well as start and end events in the graphs, unless it contributes to a better understanding. lbc and ubc are not only used for modeling d_{min} and d_{max} of activities. They can also be used for modeling temporal constraints between different activities. For example to model requirements such as approval or rejection of an application may take at most one week after its receipt and sending a notification to the applicant takes at least three days.

For calculation of temporal values, we extend the algorithms developed in our previous works [6, 7]. An interval in which an activity may execute is calculated. This interval is delimited by *earliest possible start* (eps-value) and *latest allowed end* (lae-value). $a.eps$ denotes the eps-value of an activity a and is the earliest point in time in which the activity a can start execution. eps-values reflect the implicit constraints of a flow. $a.lae$ represents the latest point in time in which an activity a can finish execution in order to hold the assigned deadline. lae-values reflect the explicit constraints of a flow. Both eps and lae values are calculated for *best case* and *worst case*. Best case and worst case identifies the execution of the shortest and longest path of a flow respectively. $a.bc.eps$ refers to best case eps and $a.wc.eps$ refers to worst case eps of an activity a. The same applies to lae-values. Temporal values of a simple graph are depicted in fig. 1. The algorithms and techniques for calculation of the interval-based temporal values are described in our previous works [1, 3, 6] and omitted here.

Given known activity durations, in addition we can calculate *earliest possible end* (epe-values) and *latest allowed start* (las-values) for an activity, using the following formulas: $a.epe = a.eps + a.d$ and $a.las = a.lae - a.d$. We refer to eps-values and epe-values as e-values and to lae-values and las-values as l-values. In this approach we handle loops as complex activities. For calculation of the temporal plan at design time we consider only one iteration. Because the actual iterations of a loop is not known at design time, its execution is monitored at run time and process manager receives notifications about the temporal status of the process.

2.2 Probabilistic Approach

In some use cases one may need to consider branching probabilities. The probabilistic approach described in this subsection caters for probabilistic representation of temporal constraints.

In order to express variable duration of activities, the notion of time histograms [8, 9] is used. A duration histogram is a data structure for representation of the (probabilistic and variable) duration of basic activities, complex activities, subworkflows and workflow itself. A duration histogram is a tuple (p, d), where p is a probability and d a duration. For example the probabilistic duration of an activity can be represented as $\{(0.1, 10), (0.25, 12), (0.32, 15), (0.33, 20)\}$. This duration can be interpreted as follows: the duration of this activity is with the probability 10%, 10 time points, with the probability 25%, 12 time points, with the probability 32%, 15 time points and with the probability 33%, 20 time points. If a duration histogram contains any tuples whose time values are the same, these tuples must be merged by adding the probabilities of tuples with the same duration. A workflow graph augmented with probabilistic temporal information for activities and nodes is referred to as probabilistic timed graph (PTG). Fig. 3 illustrates an example of such a probabilistic timed graph. The duration of activities are given in the table above the graph.

The deadline of the workflow is also given in form of a (probability, duration) tuple. Analogous to duration histograms (d-histograms), [8] defines e-histograms for presentation of e-values and l-histograms for presentation of l-values. Note that for probabilistic calculations we do not consider best and worst case or *lbc* and *ubc*. The calculation of the probabilistic temporal values has been described in [3] and hence omitted here.

3 Temporal Management of WS-BPEL Executable and Abstract Processes

The interval-based and the probabilistic approach can be used to calculate the temporal plan of one single process in isolation. However, in order to calculate the temporal plans of a set of cooperating processes and check their temporal conformance, it is necessary to consider the dependencies between them. Processes may be linked in several ways. As a generic architecture we use the model described in [10–12]. This architecture (see fig. 4) is generic enough for modeling different relationships between executable and abstract processes. It covers scenarios as e.g. described in [13, 14], one shared abstract

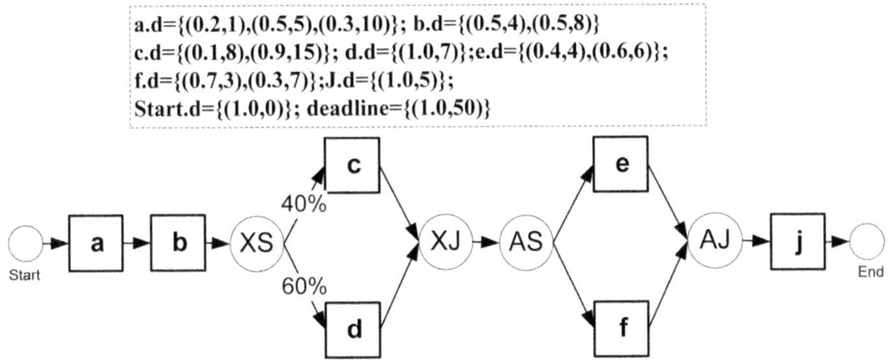

Fig. 3. A sample probabilistic timed graph (PTG)

process among a set of executable processes. This scenario is depicted in fig. 5. The generic architecture in fig. 4 covers also other scenarios as depicted in fig. 6.

The architecture in fig. 4 is a two layered model. The first layer consists of abstract processes. An abstract process may support another abstract process. This means the former contributes to the latter and partially elaborates it. The first abstract process may describe the business process in details needed for a specific group of partners and the second abstract process describes the same process in more details for another group of partners involved in the process. In this way different groups of partners can have different views on the same process. The second layer consists of executable processes that realize the abstract processes. The presented approach is fully distributed and there is no need for central coordination.

The most important issue to consider regarding the dependency between two nodes (abstract and/or executable processes) is the greatest common divisor (GCD) of their activities. GCD identifies the set of common activities in two nodes. A dependency between two nodes implies that GCD of activities of two nodes is not empty, i.e. these two nodes have at least one activity in common. Dependencies between activities are depicted using links between them as in fig. 4 and fig. 6. Fig. 8 depicts the abstract process *C* and the executable process *O1* in fig. 5. The GCD of two graphs include the activities *Receive request* and *Reply request*. For the sake of brevity the the executable process O2 is omitted. Note that even if *O*1 and *O*2 has no direct link with each other, through their common activities with *C* they may affect each other indirectly. This is due to the fact that *O*1 may affect *C* and change its temporal value and this change may in turn affect *O*2 or vice versa.

If two nodes have no common activities, these two nodes are temporally independent and their temporal plans can be calculated in isolation. If GCD of two nodes is not empty these two nodes affect each other through the common activities. In this case a cycle of calculation-assignment-recalculation must be repeated. In the assignment phase, temporal values of the activities of GCD are assigned from the source node to the target node. The assignment is only performed if e-values of the source node are greater than e-values of the target node. l-values are assigned if l-values of the source node are smaller than those of the target node. In other words an assignment is only

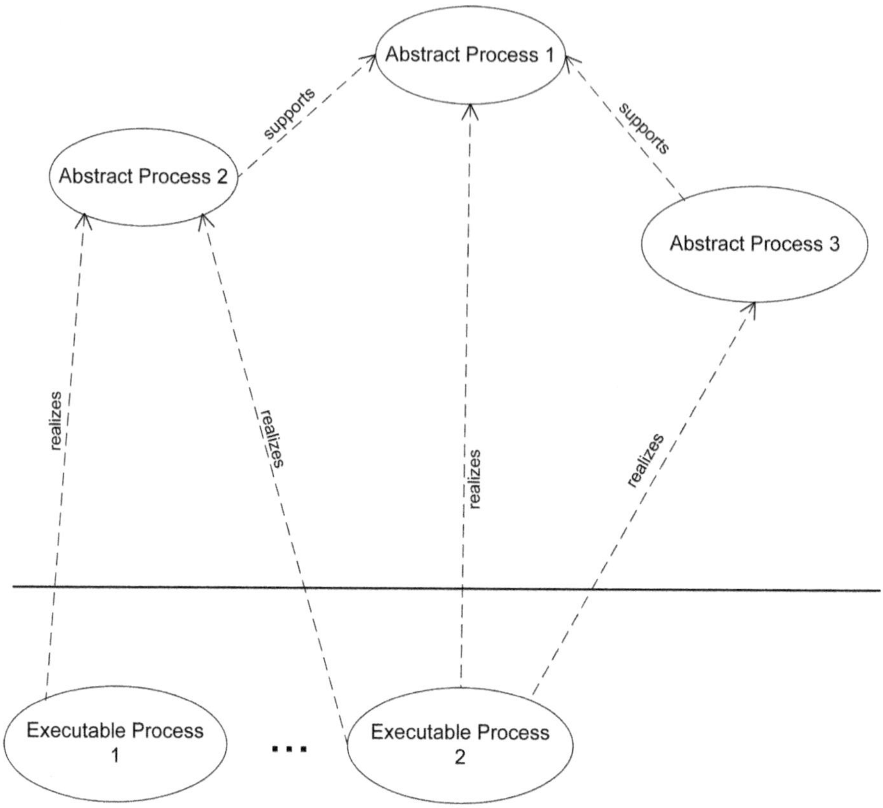

Fig. 4. A Generic architecture for abstract and executable processes

allowed if the current valid execution interval of an activity in the target node becomes tighter. The idea of assignment is depicted in fig. 7. The assignment uses the concept of event correspondence. Event correspondence describes if different events in different graphs are actually the same. $e_1 \equiv e_2$ denotes that event e_1 corresponds to event e_2. Note that e_1 and e_2 may belong to different abstract and/or executable processes. In the top part of the fig. 7 (case *a*), event correspondence is used for propagation of the temporal values of a complex activity *a*. Start of the complex activity *a* corresponds to the start of the first activity *i* and its end to the activity *j*. Case *b* shows how event correspondence is used for propagation of the temporal values of the same activity in different abstract and executable processes.

If any temporal value changes after the assignment, the temporal plan of the graph must be recalculated. Again here, current values can be overwritten if newly calculated e-values are greater than current values and newly calculated l-values are smaller than current l-values. How the cycle of calculation-assignment-recalculation works can be seen in fig. 8. The dependency between these processes is illustrated in fig. 5. The top part of the fig. 8 illustrates the graphs after calculation of *C* and *O1* and assignment of values from *C* to *O1*. The bottom part of the figure illustrates the values after

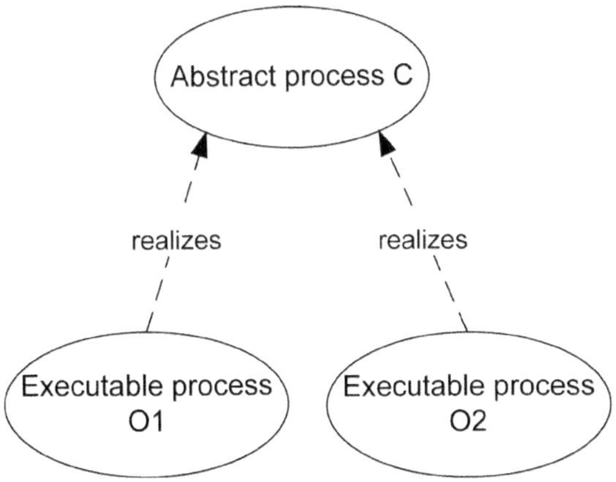

Fig. 5. A typical scenario of Web Service composition

recalculation at *O1*, assignment of the values from *O1* to *C*. A recalculation at *C* does not change the values at *C* and hence these values are final values. As you can see the same activities in different graphs have the same final temporal values. The arrows only shows the assigned values. For example in the top part of the figure the e-values of the activity *Receive request* in the abstract process *C* are equal to those in the executable process O1 and hence not assigned.

Calculation of a set of cooperating abstract and executable processes consists of two phases: the initialization and precalculation phase and the recalculation and conformance checking phase. In the following we refer to the abstract process with no outgoing links, the *global abstract process* (e.g. abstract process 1 in fig. 4).

In the initialization and precalculation phase after initialization of the global abstract process, its graph is calculated without considering other nodes. That means only implicit and explicit constraints are considered. If there is more than one global abstract process present in the model, any of them can be chosen randomly for beginning the calculations. The temporal graphs are initialized by setting e-values to 0 and l-values to ∞. Maximum duration $d.max$ is considered for calculating the deadline of other nodes than the global abstract process. Analogous to the maximum duration of activities, maximum duration of the whole process identifies the maximum duration during which a process can execute whereas a deadline denotes a point in time. Like deadlines, $d.max$ is given a priori. It suffices in this phase to assign the values to each node only once. These values just serve as initial values for further calculations. A variable *change* indicates the change of a graph, i.e. if any temporal value in a graph is changed due to assignment and/or recalculation. If *change* becomes true all incoming and outgoing links of the corresponding node are marked. Start and target node of each marked link must be revisited and recalculated if any value is changed. Multiple marks on an edge has no additional effect.

The recalculation and conformance checking phase consists of recalculation of the precalculated graphs in the previous phase. For all marked edges, the cycle of assignment-recalculation is repeated until a stable state is reached or the conformance condition is violated. A stable state is reached if all marked edges are unmarked.

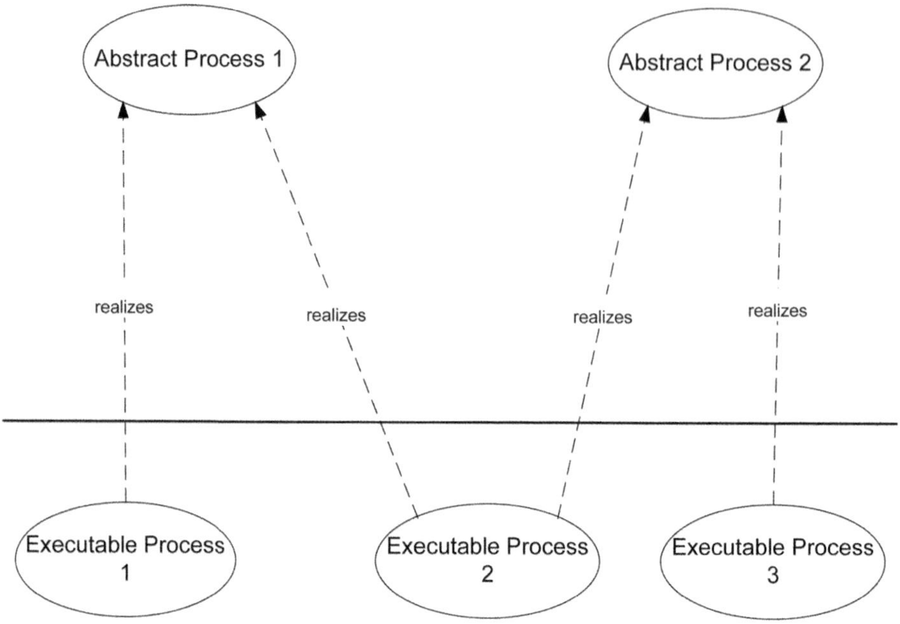

Fig. 6. A special case of the generic architecture in fig. 4

The conformance condition is violated if e-value of an activity (no matter in which process) becomes greater that its corresponding l-value.

The probabilistic approach, as well, uses the same concept for assignment and calculation of temporal plans. Due to the presence of probabilities in this approach an additional parameter *certainty* must be considered for comparison of nodes and propagation of values. A detailed discussion can be found in [3]. Note that in addition to temporal conformance, other conformance issues of processes may also be verified. Structural conformance has been studies in [15].

4 Prototypical Implementation

Our prototype has been implemented based on the open source softwares Eclipse BPEL designer and Apache ODE (Orchestration Director Engine). The prototype consists of two components: A design time component that allows the definition of cooperating processes, their dependencies and temporal constraints (deadline, activity durations, lower and upper bound constraints between activities). The design time component also checks the temporal satisfiability of the model. It checks if there exists a solution that satisfies temporal constraints of all processes. If such a solution does not exist the user will be informed which part of the process has temporal conflicts. In this case process structure or temporal constraints should be redefined such that the temporal constraints can be satisfied. Design time component calculates a valid temporal window for each activity. If activities execute within their valid temporal window it can be guaranteed

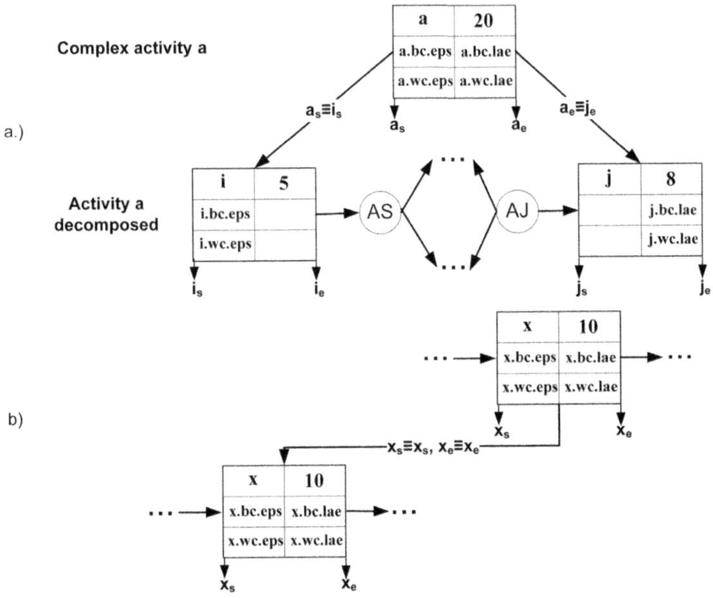

Fig. 7. Assignment of values using event correspondence

that all cooperating processes execute and terminate in a temporally compliant way. The run time component monitors the execution of each activity and checks if it executes within its valid temporal window. If any deviation is found the user receives an alarm about the process status. We use the traffic light model presented in [5]. If all activities executes within their valid temporal window the traffic light is green and everything is ok. If some activities deviate from their precalculated valid temporal window but it is still possible to hold the deadline and satisfy the temporal constraints (e.g. by executing the shortest path of a conditional structure) the traffic light turns to yellow. If some activities took longer than expected and in any case, even in best case scenario, temporal constraints will be violated, the traffic light turns to red. In this case the process manager can decide to cancel the execution prematurely or skip some activities. The prototype, an installation and troubleshooting guide and an introduction how to perform basic tasks such as defining BPEL-process, preparing wsdl-files and setting up variables can be found on our homepage [16].

4.1 Design Time Component

The design time component is prototyped under Eclipse Helios. The required functionalities are implemented under *properties* as depicted in fig. 9. After definition of the structure of the processes, the dependencies between processes can be defined using the property *choreography*. A supported process can be chosen using *Select Process*. A supported process identifies processes that have a link to this process, i.e. their GCD is

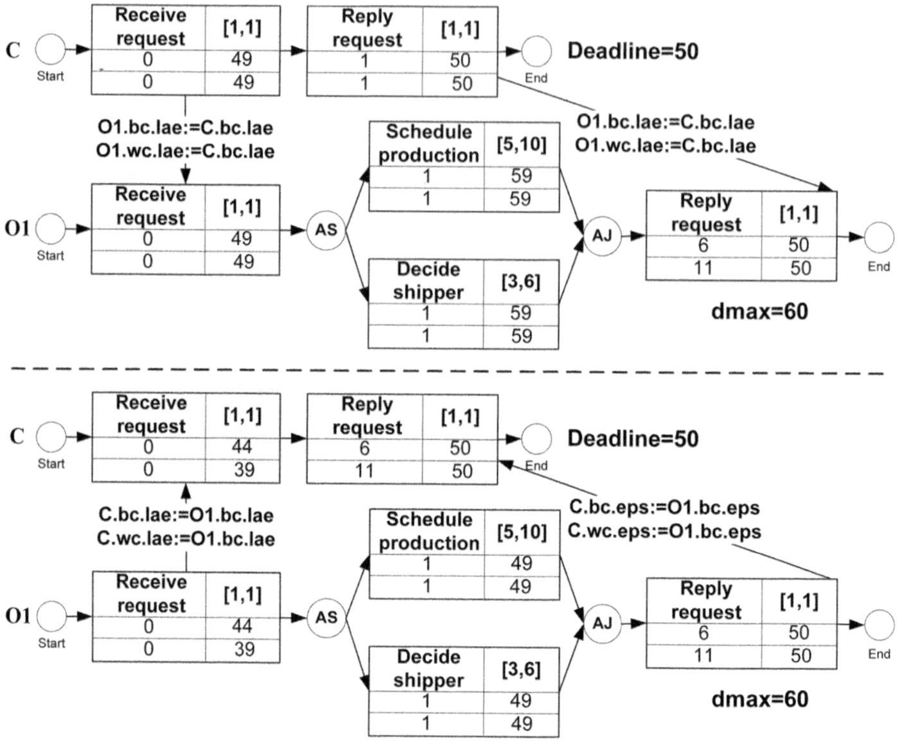

Fig. 8. Propagation of values for the same activity in different graphs

not empty. This can be an executable process or another abstract process. The combo box beneath allows for choosing processes that support this process. Dependencies can be added or removed. The result is written in an XML-file called dependencies.xml.

Temporal constraints can be set under *Constraints* (see fig. 10). It is possible to set minimum and maximum duration of activities and the deadline for the process. Further it is possible to add and remove optional lower and upper bound constraints between activities. The right part of the fig. 10 shows the temporal values of each activity after calculation.

Certainty allows the definition of probabilistic values: durations of activities and their probabilities as well as the deadline of the whole process. The probabilistic temporal values can be calculated by the *Calculate* button.

4.2 Run Time Component

The run time component is implemented in Apache ODE 1.3.4. It monitors the process execution and checks if activities are executed within their valid temporal interval. At process instantiation time, an actual calendar is used in order to transform all time information which was computed relative to the start of the flow to absolute time points [17]. For every instantiated activity, the calendar e-value is compared with the start date

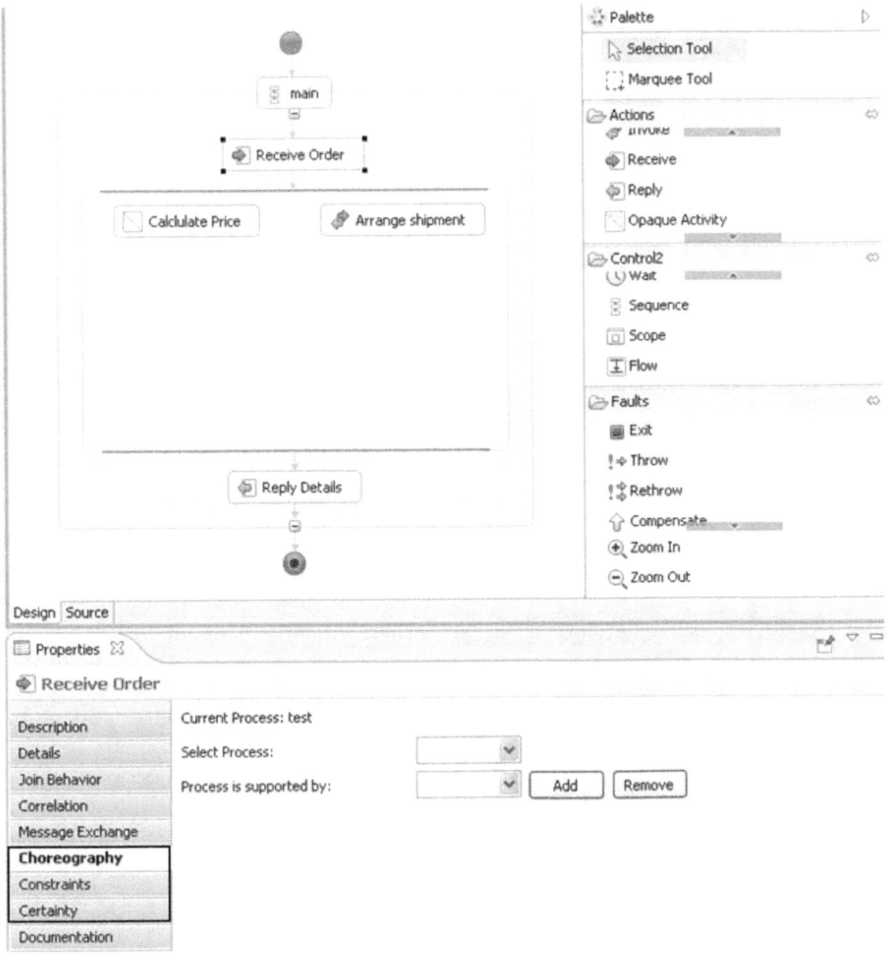

Fig. 9. Definition of dependencies between processes

of the instantiated activity. In the same way, the mapped calendar l-value is also compared with the end date of the instantiated activity. The traffic light model [5] provides an overview for process manager. If activities execute within their calculated interval at design time it is guaranteed that all processes remain temporally compliant. If some activities are delayed and deviate from their valid temporal window, it is possible that a deadline be violated. In this case the traffic light turns to yellow indicating that some activities are delayed but it is still possible to finish the execution in time. The process manager may decide to force the process to execute the shortest path in order to guarantee the temporal compliance. If activities are delayed to the extent that future execution in any case leads to temporal violation, the traffic light turns to red. In this case, the process manager may want to cancel execution prematurely in order to reduce the process execution costs. Fig. 12 shows a screen shot of the run time component.

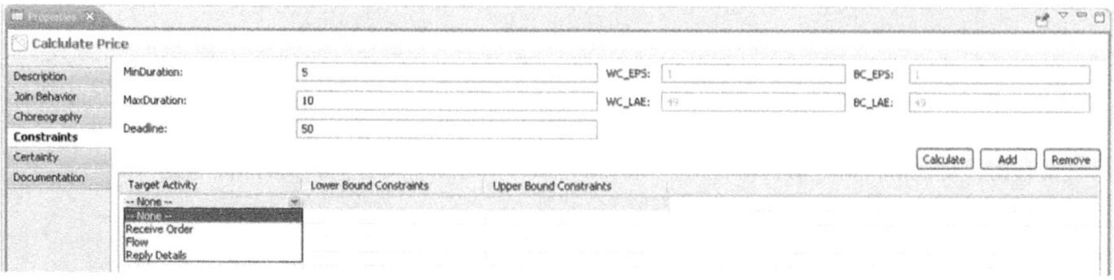

Fig. 10. Definition and calculation of interval-based temporal values

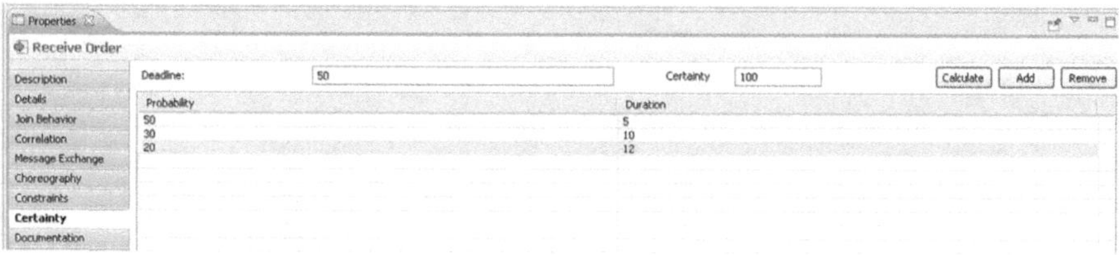

Fig. 11. Definition and calculation of probabilistic temporal values

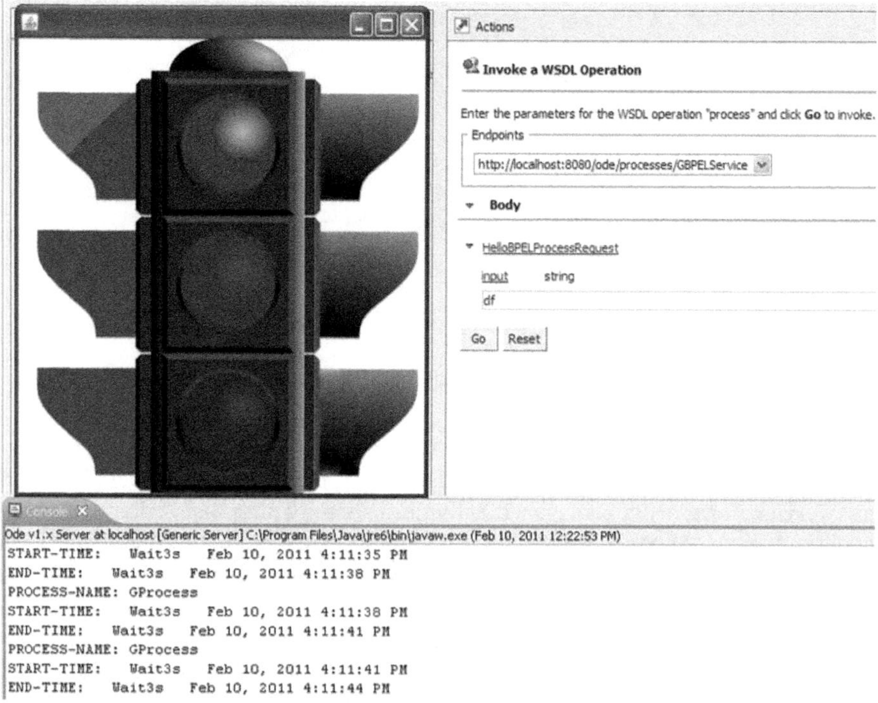

Fig. 12. The run time component monitors the execution

5 Conclusions

Temporal management and consistency are important quality criteria for business processes. They improve QoS and reduce costs. WS-BPEL lacks sufficient time management capabilities. In this work we introduced an extension of WS-BPEL that makes business processes time aware and overcomes this shortcoming. The user can define different temporal constraints, check temporal feasibility and monitor the execution. The two considered techniques, interval-based and probabilistic, caters for different needs of the users in different scenarios. We have described how we handle temporal management of a set of cooperating abstract and executable processes.

References

1. Tahamtan, A.: Modeling and Verification of Web Service Composition Based Interorganizational Workflows. PhD thesis, University of Vienna (2009)
2. Alves, A., et al.: Web services business process execution language version 2.0. Technical report, OASIS (2007)
3. Tahamtan, A., Oesterle, C., Tjoa, A., Hameurlain, A.: Bpel-time: Ws-bpel time management extension. In: Proc. of ICEIS 2011 (2011)
4. Workflow process definition interface - xml process definition language. Technical Report WFMC-TC-1025, The Workflow Management Coalition (2002)
5. Eder, J., Panagos, E.: Managing Time in Workflow Systems. In: WfMC WorkFlow Handbook 2001. J. Wiley & Sons (2001)
6. Eder, J., Tahamtan, A.: Temporal Conformance of Federated Choreographies. In: Bhowmick, S.S., Küng, J., Wagner, R. (eds.) DEXA 2008. LNCS, vol. 5181, pp. 668–675. Springer, Heidelberg (2008)
7. Eder, J., Pichler, H., Tahamtan, A.: Probabilistic time management of choreographies. In: Proc. of QSWS 2008 (2008)
8. Pichler, H.: Time Management for Workflow Systems. A probabilistic Approach for Basic and Advanced Control Flow Structures. PhD thesis, Alpen-Adria-Universitaet Klagenfurt (2006)
9. Eder, J., Pichler, H.: Duration histograms for workflow systems. In: Proc. of the IFIP TC8 / WG8.1 Working Conference on Engineering Information Systems in the Internet Context (2002)
10. Eder, J., Lehmann, M., Tahamtan, A.: Choreographies as federations of choreographies and orchestrations. In: Proc. of CoSS 2006 (2006)
11. Tahamtan, A., Eder, J.: View driven federation of choreographies. In: Proc. of ACiiDS 2010 (2010)
12. Tahamtan, A., Eder, J.: View driven interorganizational workflows. Int. J. Intelligent Information and Database Systems (to appear)
13. Decker, G., Overdick, H., Zaha, J.M.: On the suitability of ws-cdl for choreography modeling. In: Proc. of EMISA 2006 (2006)
14. Dijkman, R.M., Dumas, M.: Service-oriented design: A multi-viewpoint approach. Int. J. Cooperative Inf. Syst. 13(4), 337–368 (2004)
15. Eder, J., Lehmann, M., Tahamtan, A.: Conformance test of federated choreographies. In: Proc. of I-ESA 2007 (2007)
16. `http://www.ifs.tuwien.ac.at/`
17. Eder, J., Panagos, E., Rabinovich, M.I.: Time Constraints in Workflow Systems. In: Jarke, M., Oberweis, A. (eds.) CAiSE 1999. LNCS, vol. 1626, pp. 286–300. Springer, Heidelberg (1999)

Model Based Testing in Software Product Lines

Pedro Reales[1], Macario Polo[1], and Danilo Caivano[2]

[1] University of Castilla-La Mancha, Ciudad Real, Spain
[2] University of Study, Bari, Italy
{pedro.reales,macario.polo}@uclm.es, caivano@di.uniba.it

Abstract. This article describes an approach for test case generation in Software Product Lines, using Model Driven. Our proposal defines a set of metamodels, models and algorithms, all of them organized and managed in a 5-step process, which are implemented in a tool specifically developed for this goal, Pralíntool.

Keywords: Model-based, Test generation, Software product lines, Metamodel, Transformation.

1 Introduction

Over the last few years, the construction of software based on the principles of product lines has emerged as a new development paradigm. According to Clements and Northrop [1], a software product line (SPL) is "a set of software-intensive systems sharing a common, managed set of features which satisfy the specific needs of a particular market segment or mission and which are developed from a common set of core assets in a prescribed way". In SPL development, organizations work on two levels: (1) Domain Engineering, where both the common characteristics of all the products, as well as their variation points, are described and (2) Product Engineering, where specific products are built, transferring the common characteristics (described on the top level) to them and appropriately applying variability. Thus, variability management plays a central role in SPL and constitutes a new challenge when compared to classic software engineering. Due to the nature of SPL (the complexity inherent to variability management, need for the future reuse of design artefacts, etc.), most works dealing with SPL require an intensive use of models [2], which must be appropriately annotated with variability labels. At some time, some kind of transformation must be applied, both to deal with artefacts on the domain engineering level (translating, for example, a design model into test models), as well as to obtain product engineering artefacts from the domain engineering ones. This article describes an approach for SPL design and test case generation. It is made up of:

- a set of models and metamodels that were built almost from scratch;
- a 5-step process that guides the Product Line Engineer in SPL modelling and test case generation;
- a tool, PralínTool, that automises the process execution.

The goal is to automate the derivation of test cases in SPL contexts. This approach offers agility due to the complete control of metamodels and algorithms, which can be quickly

R. Zhang et al. (Eds.): ICEIS 2011, LNBIP 102, pp. 270–283, 2012.

adapted or modified to incorporate the implementation of new ideas. One important obstacle in testing research is oracle automation. In order to solve the oracle problem, the approach supports the use of states and special notations, which would allow the partially automatic generation of oracles. Since SPL requires some effort to guarantee reuse, traceability, the adoption of tools and the application of other good practices, the context is excellent to investigate the possibilities of model-driven techniques to achieve its automation, since these techniques implicity assure characteristics such as traceability, reuse, automation and other good chracteristics for the engineering process.

The following section analyses the most significant works relating to testing in SPL and the oracle problem. Section 3 presents an example, which will be used to illustrate the proposal. After that, the approach is presented in Section 4. Finally, we draw our conclusions and present future lines of work.

2 Related Work

Testing in the context of SPL includes the derivation of test cases for the line and for each specific product, exploiting the possibilities of variability to reduce the cost of creating both the test model and the line test cases. This includes their instantiation to test each product. In general, testing artefacts are derived at domain engineering level, and they are transformed for specific products afterwards. Almost all the proposals to generate tests for SPLs define their own models to represent the testing artefacts and variability in the test model.

The next paragraph summarises the most important works.

Nebut et al. [3] propose a pragmatic strategy in which test cases for each of the different products of an SPL are generated from the same SPL functional requirements. Source artefacts are parameterised use cases annotated with contracts (written in 1st-order logic) that represent pre- and post-conditions. Bertolino et al. [4] propose a methodology based on the category-partition method named PLUTO (Product Line Use Case Test Optimisation), which uses PLUCs (Product Line Use Cases). A PLUC is a traditional use case with additional elements to describe variability. For each PLUC, a set of categories (input parameters and environment description) and test data is generated. Kang et al. [5] use an extended sequence diagram notation to represent use case scenarios and variability. The sequence diagram is used as the basis for the formal derivation of the test scenario given a test architecture. Reuys et al. [6] present ScenTED (Scenario-based Test case Derivation), where activity diagrams are used as test models from which test case scenarios are derived. Olimpiew and Gomma [7] describe a parametric method, PLUS (Product Line UML-based Software engineering). Here, customisable test models are created during software product line engineering in phases.

Whether in the context of software products lines or in the traditional context, one of the most important tasks in software testing is the definition of the oracle, which is the mechanism provided for a test case to determine whether it has found a fault. According to Baresi and Young [8], all the methods for generating tests depend on the availability of oracles, since they are always required to determine the success or failure of the test. For Bertolino [9], an "ideal oracle" realistically is an engine/heuristic that can emit a pass/fail verdict over the observed test outputs. Thus, the automation of the oracle is one the most important difficulties in testing research [10], since there is no a known method for its generic description and, in practice, it must always be manually described. The work by Baresi and Young [8](published in 2001) is a complete analysis of the state–of-the-art about the oracle problem. Most of the proposals they analyse refer to the insertion of assert-like instructions in the source code. Later, other works have made proposals to solve this problem using other techniques such as artificial neural networks [11] or metamorphism [12]. The automation of the oracle has special significance in SPL, since meaningful portions of the system are analysed and developed at the domain engineering level, which includes the definition of their tests. Therefore, it is quite interesting to apply reusing and traceability not only to develop artefacts, but also to test them, including oracle descriptions.

In summary, software engineering communities have everything ready to work intensively with model driven approaches in SPL, but none of existing proposals for testing in SPL automate their transformations. Also, the problem of oracle automation still remains and it is important to propose ideas for its resolution. The SPL context offers an excellent opportunity to improve classic software engineering practices, development methods and techniques for testing. The joint use of SPL and model-based testing is very propitious for improving test and oracle automation. In the approach presented in this document, a set of metamodels and a process of seven steps have been developed with three goals: 1) generate test artefacts automatically at domain level with variability, 2) remove variability and generate automatically executable tests for specific products, and 3) support the generation of oracles through states and special notations in the models. The main advantage of this technique is that a complete framework is presented (from the design of the line to the execution of tests) and this framework supports the automatic generation of oracles, thanks to special notations.

3 Proposed Approach

The proposed approach is made up of:

- a **metamodel** that was built almost from scratch.
- a 5-step **process** that guides the Product Line Engineer in PL modelling and test case generation.
- a **tool**, called PralínTool, that automates the process execution.

It uses class and sequence diagrams as the main element for representing SPL and, later, for generating test cases. In order to enable the automation (and the future extension) of both the process and the supporting tool, these elements were represented by means of metamodels.

3.1 SPL Metamodels

Figure 1 shows the defined metamodels. Here, Variability is provided by the *Variation Points* Metamodel package, with the element *VariableElement* and its specialisations.

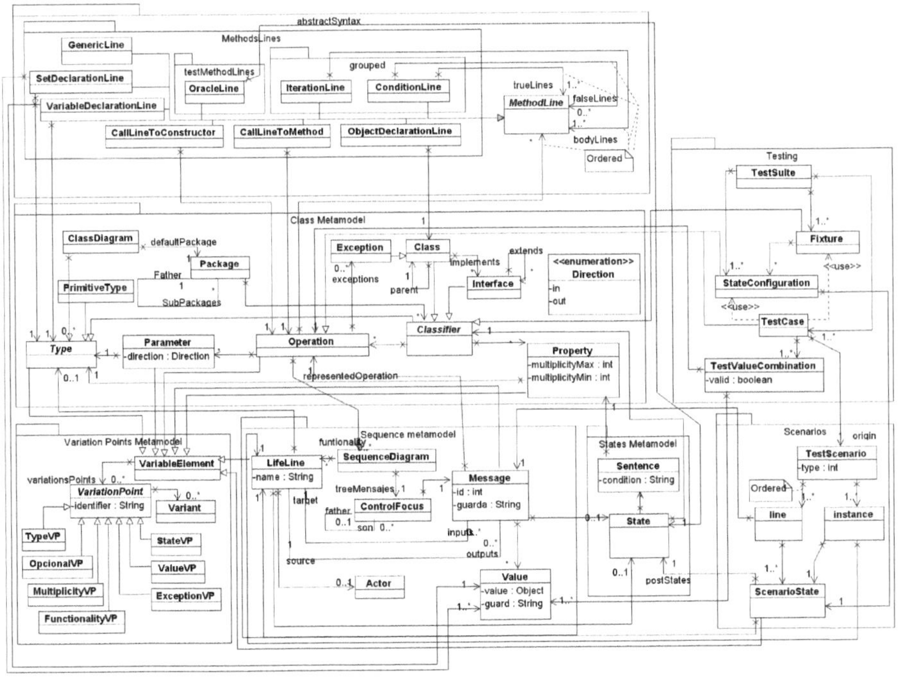

Fig. 1. Metamodel for designing software product lines

A *VariableElement* has a collection of *VariationPoint*, which defines the type of variability and the range of possibilities through its *Variant*.

This metamodel makes it possible to represent all the elements required to design a product line according to our principles, removing the complexity inherent to the UML 2.0 standard metamodel (OMG, 2007), although also losing part of its expressiveness. Currently, the metamodel only supports one type of event in sequence diagrams, instead of the wide variety of messages allowed by UML 2.0 (call, creation, signals, etc.). In fact, our metamodel was built from scratch and, thus, it is not completely based on the UML specification. This can be a thread in a real context, but due to the flexibility of our metamodels, they can be adapted to new modelling requirements.

3.2 The Process

The process guides the Product Line Engineer in PL modelling and test case generation. Its general structure is shown in figure 2 and it is implemented in PralínTool (Section 3.3).

It is made up of 5 different steps:

1. Step 1: Product Line modelling;
2. Step 2: Sequence diagram enrichment;
3. Step 3: domain-level test scenario generation;
4. Step 4: domain level test case generation;
5. Step 5: product level test case generation and automation.

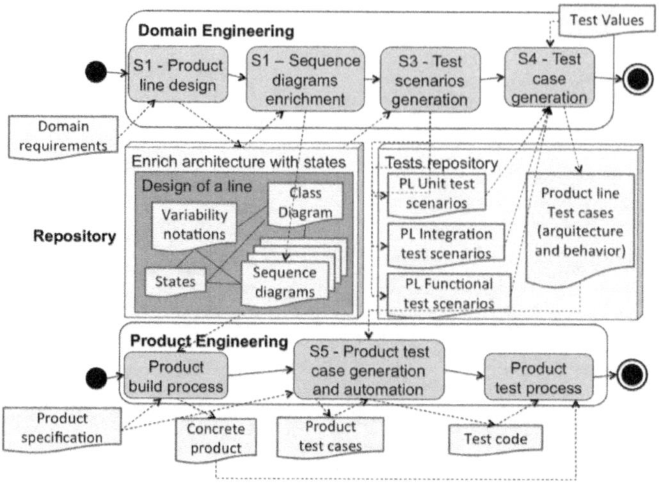

Fig. 2. General description of the process

Step 1: Product Line Modelling. At the domain engineering level, the software engineer models the software product line, which includes class structure and sequence diagrams. These models also contain variability specification. In order to illustrate this and the following steps, a product line consisting of a distributed, client-server system for playing board games has been developed. These kind of games share a broad set of characteristics, such as the existence of a board, one or more players, possibly the use of dice, the possibility of taking pieces, the presence or absence of cards, policies related to the assignment of turns to the next player, etc. Currently, this SPL works with four types of board games: Chess, Checkers, Ludo and Trivial. Since it is impossible to show the whole system in this paper, it instead shows some of the variation points and variants identified for this SPL, which are described according to the Orthogonal Variability Model (OVM) graphical notation [13]. This notation identifies each variation point with a triangle and each variant with a rectangle. Arrows are used to include restrictions.

Figure 3 shows four variation points: Game, corresponding to one of the possible games supported (Chess, Checkers, Ludo or Trivial); Opponent indicating whether the player is playing against the computer or another online human player; Players where the minimum number of players is 2, but some games have the option of being played by more players; and Type, which depends on whether the games use dice or quiz the player.

In this system, one of the clearly variable use cases is "Piece movement", which is executed on the server when a client sends a message corresponding to the movement of a piece. Figure 4 shows the sequence diagram that describes the functionality of "Piece movement". This sequence diagram has special notations, which are explained in the following section, which describes the treatment given to the modelling, development and generation of test cases given to this SPL with our approach, which is illustrated using the functionality "Piece Movement".

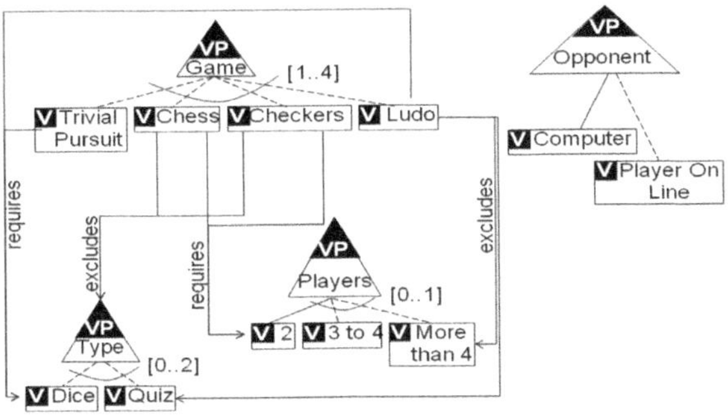

Fig. 3. Variation points and variants

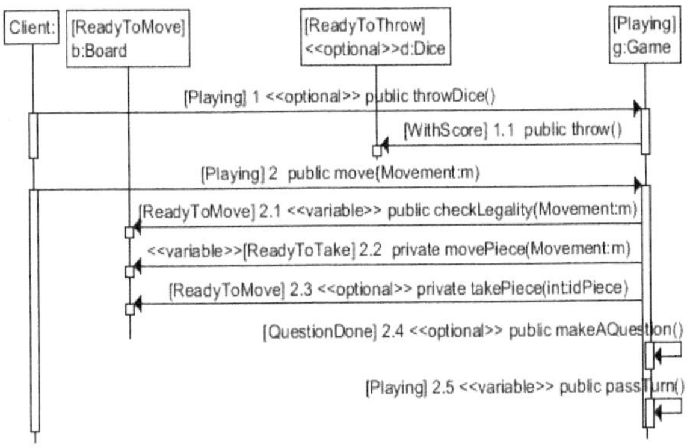

Fig. 4. Normal event flow of Piece movement for the line, draw with PralínTool

Step 2: Sequence Diagram Enrichment. In this proposal, a test scenario is a sequence of method calls, which must be executed to perform a test. Test scenarios are generic, in the sense that they belong to the domain engineering level of the SPL design. Since an interesting aspect is the generic description of oracles (for later inclusion in specific products, in the form of specific oracles), test scenarios must include the state of the different objects involved in the scenario before and after each method call. For this, both the messages and the objects are annotated with information about the states.

Figure 4 shows the sequence diagram corresponding to the normal flow of events of the Piece movement use case. It includes information about the expected states of each object (within square brackets) as well as variability labels (as stereotypes). For example, before entering this scenario, the d:Board instance must be ReadyToMove (see the annotation between the square brackets in the instance). These annotations are supported by the *States Metamodel* package.

States are described by means of Boolean expressions, written as a function of the fields and methods in the corresponding class. Since some of these expressions will affect some products but not others, states can be variable too, which will require different types of processing when specific test cases must be produced (this transformation is presented in Section 4.4). Table 1 shows an example of a state for the *Game* class: when

Table 1. Description of a state in the Game class

Playing	this. clients.size() > 0
	this.pWithTurn != null
	this.clients.contains(this.pWithTurn) == true
	this.winner == null
	this.dice !=null <<*Optional*>>

the game is in *Playing*, the instance must have a board, the number of clients must be greater than zero, a player must have the turn, there is no still winner and, depending on the product, dice may exist.

Step 3: Domain-Level Test Scenario Generation. The elements to model test scenarios are provided by the *Scenarios* package. The main element is *TestScenario*, which has an ordered set of *lines* that represents a sequence of *messages* that will be executed and a set of *instances* that represents the elements that will execute each message. All these elements include states for the future generation of oracles.

For generating scenarios, three transformations have been developed (see section 3.4): 1) for unit testing, where the scenarios are focused in concrete units; 2) for integration testing, where the scenarios are focused in interactions between to units; and 3) for system testing, where the scenarios are focused in complete functionalities designed in the sequence diagrams.

Table 2 groups the elements of the functional test scenario generated with the third transformation corresponding to the sequence diagram of figure 4; it holds all the instances involved in the execution of the functionality. Note that, in this example, since it is a functional scenario, only the messages arriving from an actor client appear in the message sequence (in the sequence diagram, only *throwDice* and move come from an actor). As can be seen, pre- and post-states are also saved. Note that this kind of description is supported by the metamodel.

Table 2. Functional test scenario of *Piece movement*

LifeLines (instances)	**Pre-State**
g:Game	Playing
d:Dice <<*Optional*>>	ReadyToThrow
b:Board	ReadyToMove
Messages	**Post-State**
1:throwDice <<*Optional*>>	gGame Paying d:Dice WithScore
6:move	g:Game Playing b:Board ReadyToMove <<*Variable*>>

Up to now, the process has produced test scenarios (representations of interesting test situations at the domain-engineering level). Now, these scenarios must be translated into specific test cases for the line and for the specific products of the line. This requires two steps: (1) still on the domain level, a test architecture must be generated, which takes into account variability, and the behaviour of each test case must be obtained; and (2) on the product-engineering level, variability must be resolved for each product, and the test architecture and behaviour must be translated into specific product test cases.

Step 4: Domain Level Test Case Generation. In this step, specific test cases are obtained from the previously obtained test scenarios. The main difference between test scenarios and test cases is that the latter describe specific execution situations and, therefore, have specific test data and oracles. Moreover, the test suite is part of the test architecture of the system. Since the package Scenarios of the metamodel supports the three types of scenarios described, only a single transformation is required to obtain specific test cases from the three types of scenarios.

The architecture of the tests (supported by the package Testing) has a *TestSuite* as its basic element, which contains all the required elements to compose the tests: it has a set of *Fixture* elements (representing types under test or required types), a set of *TestCase* elements and a set of configuration methods (*StateConfiguration*, which is used to put the objects in the required state).

An instance of the test architecture stores the information required to generate specific test cases. A transformation for generating the test architecture has been developed. The transformation takes the set of test scenarios and the class diagram as inputs and produces a *TestSuite*. It adds the required fixtures to represent the lifelines, as well as the *StateConfiguration* elements required to put each Fixture into the specific required state.

Finally, it obtains the specific test cases corresponding to each test scenario passed as a parameter, also combining the test data, and generates methods to check if the post-states of the fixtures are correct after the test executions. This transformation makes use of the combination algorithms implemented in *testooj* (*All combinations, Each choice* and several kinds of *Pair wise* [14]). Figure 5 shows the architecture generated from the sequence diagram in the figure 4.

Once the test architecture has been instantiated, a further step obtains the functionality of each test case. As other authors have shown (i.e., [15,16]), our metamodel contains a package for object-oriented source code (package *AbstractSyntax*), which actually represents the abstract syntax tree of the test cases. Thus, a new transformation

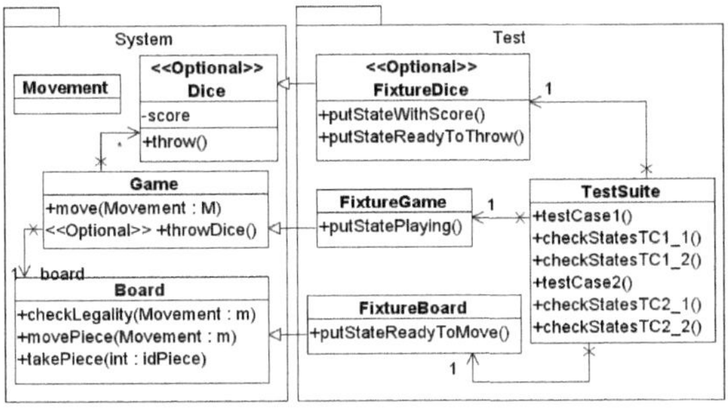

Fig. 5. Test classes generated from the test scenario

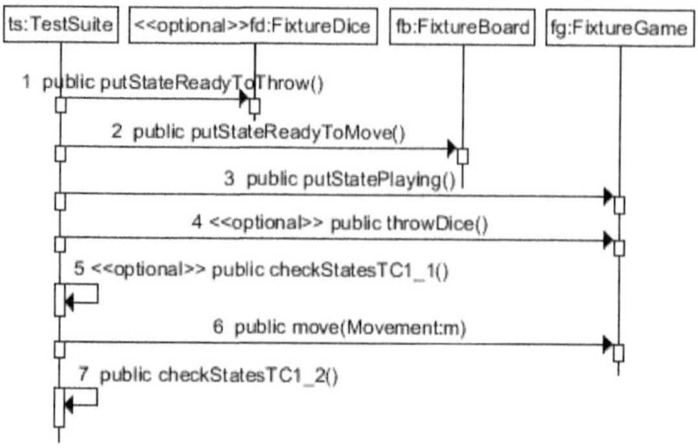

Fig. 6. Functionality of test case 1

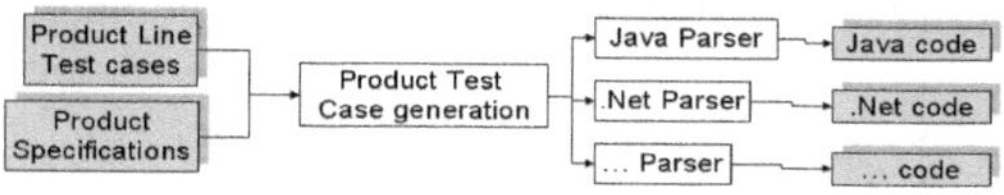

Fig. 7. Schematic view of executable test case generation

has been developed to translate the ordered sequence of method of each test scenario into an abstract syntax tree for each test case.

This transformation analyses the generated scenario and, for each test case, includes in the abstract syntax tree a message to put each fixture in the correct pre-state. Then, the transformation adds the sequence of messages of the scenario with a concrete combination of test values, and after each message of the sequence, a message to check the post-states is added (these messages are considered the oracles of the test). Figure 6 shows the generated functionality of a test case (Note that the argument of message 6 is a concrete value. The metamodel supports this but it cannot be represented graphically yet).

Step 5: Product Level Test Case Generation and Automation. In this step, executable test cases are obtained from their respective models (actually, instances of the metamodel), and executed in two substeps (figure 7): (1) generation of cases for a specific product, which involves the removal of variability; (2) generation of executable code for the desired technology.

In the first substep, variability is removed from domain specifications, proceeding in the same way as the variability is removed for generating a product (not a test case) from the line design. These specifications are made up of the different selected variants

Table 3. Selected variants for the *Chess* product

Variation point	*Selected variant*
Game	chess
Players	2
Opponent	Player
Type	(*excluded*)

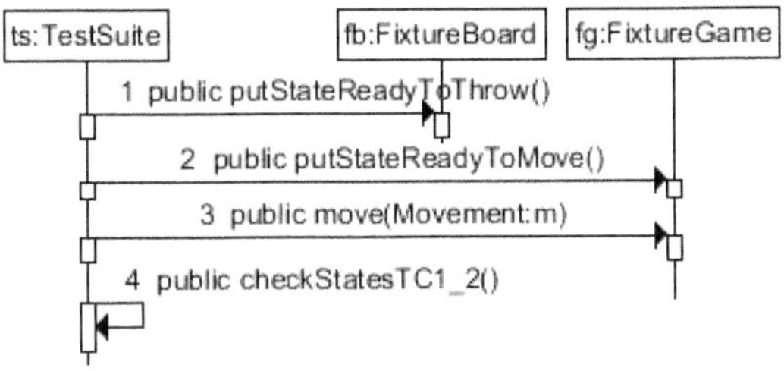

Fig. 8. Test case without variability

for each variation point in the line. As an example, table 3 shows all the variation points for the board games product line (left column), together with the selected variants for the specific product of *Chess*.

Figure 8 shows the functionality of the generated test case in Figure 6 after removing the variability. It can be seen that the features related to Dice have been removed because there are no dice in chess.

Finally, the executable code of the test cases is obtained from the transformation of the abstract syntax tree instances (package *abstractSyntax* of the metamodel), but now taking into account the specific characteristics of the selected technology, which can be either Java (figure 9) or .NET.

```
public class TestSuite{
    private FixtureGame fg;
    private FixtureBoard fb;
    public void testCase2(){
        Object v1 = new Movement(14,18);
        fg.putStateTC1();
        fb.putStateTC1();
        fg.move(v1);
        this.chackStatesTC1_2();
    }
    public void checkStatesTC1_2(){
        assertTrue(fg.clients.size()>0 &&
          fg.pWithTurn!=null &&
          fg.clients.contains(fg.pWithTurn)==true &&
          fg.winner==null); assertTrue(fd.pieces.size() >0);
    }
    public void testCase2(){...}
    public void checkStatesTC2_2(){...}
}
```

Fig. 9. Source code of a Java executable test case

3.3 A Short Overview of PralínTool

Figure 10 shows an aspect of PralínTool, the tool we developed to support test case generation in SPL. With the tool, it is possible to include capabilities for describing use cases with a structured template, which makes the almost automatic transformation of

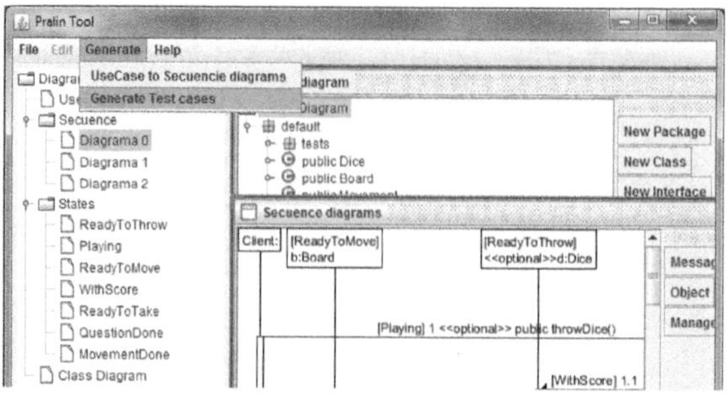

Fig. 10. A view of PralínTool

scenarios to sequence diagrams easy. States can be also defined for each class in the system, which are also specified in a hierarchical tree. The sequence diagram editor enables the annotation of the event flows with variability labels. The generation of test scenarios and test cases is supported by the implementation of the previously described algorithms.

3.4 Transformation Algorithm Implementation

The next sub-sections show the pseudocode of the transformation algorithms used to generate test scenarios (see section 3.2). There are three different algorithm to generate test scenarios 1) for unit testing, 2) for integration testing and 3) for system testing (Note that the pseudocode of the auxiliary functions is not show because lack of space).

Unit Test Scenarios Generation Algorithm. Unit test scenarios consider the messages producing a single object in the sequence diagram. The scenarios only keep a method,

Algorithm 1. Unit test scenario generation algorithm

```
generateUnitTestScenarios(SequenceDiagram ds) :Vector<TestSecenario> {
    scenarios = new Vector<TestScenarios>
    For all ll of ds.lifelines {
        For all m of ll.inputs {
            t = new TestScenario
            cf = ds.getControlFocus(m)
            lifeLines = getTargetLifeLines (cf)
            For all lli of lifeLines {
                ScenarioState s = getPreStateOfTheExecution(cf,ds,lli)
                Instance i = new Instance (lli,s) t.addInstance(i) }
            ScenarioState sm = new ScenarioState(m,m.postState)
            If(m.hasStateVariationPoint()){
                sm.addStateVP(m.getStateVP) }
            Line l = new Line(m,sm)
            t.addLinea(l)
            scenarios.add(t) } }
    return scenarios }
```

Algorithm 2. Integration test scenario generation algorithm

```
generateIntegrationTestScenarios(SequenceDiagram ds):Vector<TestSecenario> {
    scenarios = new Vector<TestScenarios>
    messages = ds.getMessages()
    For all m of messages {
        If(m.source.type != null and m.target.type != null){
            t = new TestScenario
            nm = ds.getNodoMessage(m).father
            lifeLines = getTargetLifeLines (nm)
            For all lli of lifeLines {
                ScenarioState s = getPreStateOfTheExecution(nm,ds,lli)
                Instance i = new Instance(lli,s) t.addInstance(i) }
            ScenarioState s1 = new ScenarioState(nm.message.postState)
            If(nm.message.hasStateVariationPoint()){
                s1.addStateVP(nm.message.getStateVP()) }
            ScenarioState s2 = getPostStateOfTheExecution(nm,ds,m.receiver)
            Linea i = new Linea(m)
            i.addScenarioState(s1)
            i.addScenarioState(s2)
            t.addLinea(i)
            scenarios.add(t) }}
    return scenarios }
```

Algorithm 3. Functional test scenario generation algorithm

```
generateFunctionalTestScenarios(SequenceDiagram ds):TestSecenario {
    scenario = new TestScenarios
    For all ll of ds.lifelines {
        ScenarioState s =new ScenarioState(ll.preState)
        Instance i = new Instance(ll,s)
        secenario.addInstance(i) }
    For all cf of ds.treeMensajes {
        If(cf.father == null){
            Linea i = new Linea(cf.message)
            For all ll of lifeLines {
                ScenarioState s = getPostStateOfTheExecution(cf,ds,ll)
                i.addScenarioState(s) }
            scenario.addLinea(i) } }
    return scenarios }
```

together with the states which annotate the instance (pre-state) and the message (post-state). With the goal of having all the objects in the correct state, the test scenario also knows the pre-state of all the objects involved in the method execution.

Integration Test Scenarios Generation Algorithm. Integration test scenarios test the interactions between any two connected objects (i.e., one instance sends a message to the other). The scenario saves: (1) the method of the first instance whose execution produces its interaction with the second one; (2) the post-states of both instances. As with the unit test algorithm, the pre-states of all instances involved in the scenario must be taken into account to ensure that the scenario is, in fact, reproducible.

System Test Scenario Generation Algorithm. Functional test scenarios test the system from an actor's point of view. Thus, the scenario executes the messages arriving from an actor to the system, which is considered as a black box. In addition to these messages, the scenario must also hold the corresponding state annotations, both in the instances and in the events.

4 Conclusions and Future Work

This paper has presented an approach for automating the generation of test cases in SPL. A set of metamodels to design class and sequence diagrams has been developed. These metamodels allow variability and can include special notations to generate oracles for the tests. The approach is a complete framework that makes it possible to design an SPL and to generate test models and executable tests. The entire process takes the oracle problem into account. To solve this, the developers can define states and relate them to sequence diagram messages. These relations (represented as special notations in brackets) are used to generate oracles for the tests.

However, the approach has some disadvantages, because only sequence and class diagrams (similar to UML) can be defined, which results in a loss of expressiveness. But, due to the flexibility of the metamodels and transformation algorithms, they can easily be modified and extended, so they can be adapted to new expressive necessities with no difficulties.

The strict practices in SPL software development make it possible to obtain new and additional knowledge for software engineering. In particular, the intensive use of models and tools can enrich knowledge about MDA. In the case of testing, it is relatively easy to experiment with algorithms and ideas with self-metamodels, before passing them on to a standardised approach, whose elements and tools will likely be adopted by the industry soon. In our opinion, the solution to this problem, which has been the subject of research for many years, is now closer to being resolved, especially today, when significant effort is being devoted to the model-driven discipline. In general, our future work will continue to incorporate new techniques for model transformation and test automation in SPL, since it is easy to extrapolate the results obtained here to other contexts.

Acknowledgements. This work is partially supported by the ORIGIN *(Organizaciones Inteligentes Globales Innovadoras), DIMITRI (Desarrollo e implantación de metodologías Tecnologías de Testing) and PEGASO/MAGO (Mejora avanzada de procesos software globales) projects* and FPU grant AP2009-3058.

References

1. Clements, P., Northrop, L.: Salion, inc.: A software product line case study. Technical report, DTIC Research Report ADA412311 (2002)
2. Czarnecki, K., Antkiewicz, M., Kim, C.H.P., Lau, S., Pietroszek, K.: Model-driven software product lines. In: Conference on Object Oriented Programming Systems Languages and Applications, pp. 126–127. ACM, New York (2005)

3. Nebut, C., Pickin, S., Le Traon, Y., Jezequel, J.: Automated requirements-based generation of test cases for product families. In: Proceedings of the 18th IEEE International Conference on Automated Software Engineering, pp. 263–266 (2003)
4. Bertolino, A., Gnesi, S., di Pisa, A.: PLUTO: A Test Methodology for Product Families. In: van der Linden, F.J. (ed.) PFE 2003. LNCS, vol. 3014, pp. 181–197. Springer, Heidelberg (2004)
5. Kang, S., Lee, J., Kim, M., Lee, W.: Towards a formal framework for product line test development. In: 7th IEEE International Conference on Computer and Information Technology, CIT 2007, pp. 921–926 (2007)
6. Reuys, A., Kamsties, E., Pohl, K., Reis, S.: Model-Based System Testing of Software Product Families. In: Pastor, Ó., Falcão e Cunha, J. (eds.) CAiSE 2005. LNCS, vol. 3520, pp. 519–534. Springer, Heidelberg (2005)
7. Olimpiew, E., Gomaa, H.: Customizable requirements-based test models for software product lines. In: International Workshop on Software Product Line Testing (2006)
8. Baresi, L., Young, M.: Test oracles. Technical Report Technical Report CIS-TR01 -02, Dept. of Computer and Information Science, Univ. of Oregon (2001)
9. Bertolino, A.: Software testing research: Achievements, challenges, dreams. In: International Conference on Software Engineering, pp. 85–103. IEEE Computer Society, Washington, DC (2007)
10. Offutt, A.J., Liu, S., Abdurazik, A., Amman, P.: Generating test data from state-based specifications. Software Testing, Verification and Reliability, 25–53 (2003)
11. Jin, H., Wang, Y., Chen, N., Gou, Z., Wang, S.: Artificial neural network for automatic test oracles generation. In: International Conference on Computer Science and Software Engineering, vol. 2 (2008)
12. Mayer, J., Guderlei, R.: An empirical study on the selection of good metamorphic relations. In: Proceedings of the 30th Annual International Computer Software and Applications Conference (COMPSAC 2006), vol. 01, pp. 475–484. IEEE Computer Society, Washington, DC (2006)
13. Pohl, K., Backle, G., Van Der Linden, F.: Software Product Line Engineering: Foundations, Principles, and Techniques. Springer (2005)
14. Polo, M., Piattini, M., Tendero, S.: Integrating techniques and tools for testing automation. Software Testing, Verification and Reliability 17, 3–39 (2007)
15. Baxter, I.D., Yahin, A., Moura, L., Sant'Anna, M., Bier, L.: Clone detection using abstract syntax trees. In: International Conference on Software Maintenance, pp. 368–377 (1998)
16. Khatchadourian, R., Sawin, J., Rountev, A.: Automated refactoring of legacy java software to enumerated types. In: International Conference on Software Maintenance (ICSM 2007), Paris, France, pp. 224–233 (2007)

A Set of Well-Formedness Rules to Checking the Consistency of the Software Processes Based on SPEM 2.0

Eliana B. Pereira[1,2], Ricardo M. Bastos[1], Toacy C. Oliveira[2], and Michael C. Móra[1]

[1] Faculty of Informatics,
Pontifical University Catholic of Rio Grande do Sul Porto Alegre, Brazil
{eliana.pereira,bastos,michael}@pucrs.br
[2] COPPE Department, Federal University of Rio de Janeiro, Rio de Janeiro, Brazil
toacy@cos.ufrj.br

Abstract. Considering the need to avoid errors in a software process, this paper proposes checking it before enactment. Process checking is the activity of verifying the correctness and the consistency of a process. In this paper, process checking is made from a set of well-formedness rules specified from the SPEM 2.0 metamodel. The well-formedness rules are described using the Unified Modeling Language - UML multiplicity and First-Order Predicate Logic – FOLP and their use and evaluation are made using a part of the OpenUP process.

Keywords: Software process, Consistency, Process checking, SPEM, Well-formedness rule.

1 Introduction

Software processes prescribe the activities that must be carried on when creating software products. They recommend a set of roles, documents and workflows to facilitate and organize transforming user requirements into actual software applications [1]. Although developers can find off-the-shelf software process specifications such as *Rational Unified Process* - RUP [2] and *Object-Oriented Process, Environment and Notation* - OPEN [3], there is no "one size fits all" process, which means a process must be defined to meet each project's needs [4].

To define a software process it is necessary to consider project's constraints such as team, resources, technology and time-to-market, to create the fabric of interconnected process elements that will guide software development [1]. Typically, software process engineers combine elements from "off-the-shelf" processes, since they represent best practices in the software engineering discipline. Software process engineers are also assisted by *Situational Method Engineering* - SME. SME recommends creating a set of method fragments or method chunks (pieces of processes) where each one of these fragments or chunks describes one part of the overall method (in this paper called software process). Each software project starts with a process definition phase where the method fragments or chunks are selected and organized to attend the specific needs related to the project [5].

R. Zhang et al. (Eds.): ICEIS 2011, LNBIP 102, pp. 284–299, 2012.

Regardless the strategy used to define a software process specification, it is important to understand the associated complexity of interconnecting the process elements that will be used to maximize the outcome of a software project. Typically a process specification interconnects dozens, sometimes hundreds, of process elements and any inconsistency in the process will negatively impact on how developers perform. Inconsistent processes have several forms. For example, inconsistency may appear when a task requires information that is not produced by any other task; when two or more work products duplicate information; or even when tasks are sequenced in cycles. These problems are hard to identify if no automated approach is adopted.

According to Hug *et al.* in [6], as software processes are based on process models, which are directed by concepts, rules and relationships, a metamodel becomes necessary for instantiating these process models. Meta-modeling is a practice in software engineering where a general model (metamodel) organizes a set of concepts that will be later instantiated and preserved by specific models (instances). In this scenario, a software process metamodel could represent basic interconnection constraints that should hold after the metamodel is instantiated [7], thus minimizing inconsistencies. An evidence of the importance of metamodels for software processes is the existence of metamodels such as *Software & Systems Process Engineering Meta-Model Specification* - SPEM 1.1 [8], *OPEN Process Framework* - OPF [3], among others. Recently the *Object Managements Group* – OMG issued a new version of its standard for Process Modeling, namely SPEM 2.0, which offers the minimal elements necessary to define any software process [9].

Although the SPEM 2.0 metamodel represents a great advance in software process specification and consistency, its use is not straightforward. SPEM 2.0 defines several concepts using the UML class diagram notation and represents several constraints with natural language. For example, SPEM 2.0 allows the specification of a *Task* that does not consume, produce and/or modify any *Work Product*. This is clearly an inconsistency once a *Task* has a purpose, expressed in terms of creating or updating *Artifacts* (*Work Products*) [2].

In order to improve the consistency of the software processes instantiated from SPEM 2.0 this paper proposes a set of well-formedness to the activities, roles, work products, tasks and their relationships in a software process. Each well-formedness rule expresses a condition that must be true in all software process instances. To create the well-formedness rules we have started our work by redefining some relationships in the SPEM 2.0. For those more elaborated well-formedness rules we have used FOLP. The focus of this paper is extending the content presented in [10] by presenting new well-formedness rules and evaluating a new well-formedness rule.

The paper is organized as follows: Section 2 presents the related works. Section 3 describes the SPEM 2.0. Section 4 presents some packages of SPEM 2.0. In Section 5, the consistency well-formedness rules are shown. Section 6 evaluates some well-formedness followed by the conclusions.

2 Related Work

Several papers have focused on defining software process from a process metamodel. Some approaches [11], [12], [13], [14] propose solutions using well known metamodels such as OPF or SPEM, while others define their own process metamodels [15], [16],[17].

In [11], [13], [15] and [17] the authors consider metamodels to define method fragments, method chunks or method components. Although they differ in terminology, fragments, chunks or components, represent small elements of a software process. This approach is known as *Situational Method Engineering* - SME, which is a subset of the *Method Engineering* - ME discipline. According to [5], SME provides a solid basis for creating software process. Chunks, fragments or components are typically gleaned from best practice, theory and/or abstracted from other processes. Once identified and documented, they are stored in a repository, usually called method base [7].

In [14], the authors propose an extension to SPEM 2.0 to address the lack of the "executability" of this metamodel. The objective of the extended metamodel is to include a set of concepts and behavioural semantics. In [12], the authors present a process metamodel that embodies attributes to facilitate the automated analysis of the process, revealing possible failures and associated risks. The metamodel allows associating risks to the activities and mitigates them before they are propagated into software product. Gnatz *et al.* in [16] also propose a metamodel to define software process. The authors are mainly interested in performing process improvement together with static and dynamic tailoring (adjustment) of process models.

Though process metamodels are used by many research groups, the software process consistency issue is not widely explored. Most works lack rules to check the consistency of the created software processes. Specifically related to the software process consistency some few works might be found in the literature. Bajec *et al.* in [18] describe an approach to process configuration and present some constraint rules in their work to constrain some aspects of the software process construction. The authors decompose their rules in four subgroups: *process flow rules*, *structure rules*, *completeness rules* and *consistency rules*. The *completeness rules* and *consistency rules* are related to this work since these rules are derived from a process metamodel. According to Bajec *et al.*, the completeness rules help to check whether a software process includes all required components. To the authors these rules can be specified in a simple manner using attributes in the metalink class, which is equivalent to multiplicities in the association relation in UML. An example of the completeness rule in [18] is that *each activity must be linked with exactly one role.* The consistency rules are considered by the authors similar to completeness rules. Their goal is to assure that the selection of the elements to a process is consistent. While completeness rules only apply to elements that are linked together, consistency rules deal with interdependency between any two elements. An example of the consistency rule is *each artifact depends on at least one production activity.*

Hsueh *et al.* in [19] propose an UML-based approach to define, verify and validate software processes. The authors consider UML as the modeling language to define the processes and work with class diagram to model the process static structure, the state diagram to model the process element's behavior and the activity diagram to model the process sequence. For the process structure they describe a process metamodel based on UML 2.0 and present some rules in *Object Constraint Language* - OCL. Conceptually, that work is related to this one as it considers a process metamodel and some formalized rules to help model verification. However, there are some important differences. In [19], the correctness, completeness and consistency of a process are verified by only checking the class multiplicities. All their OCL rules are CMMI-related rules and are used to verify if the software process meet the requirements of CMMI.

Atkinson *et al.* in [20] propose using an existing *Process Modeling Language* - PML to define process. Although the authors do not consider a metamodel they present a set of rules related to the process consistency. They also present a tool, *pmlcheck*, used to check a process before performing it. Basically, the consistency rules implemented in *pmlcheck* are related to the actions (the tasks of SPEM 2.0) and resources (the work products of SPEM 2.0). Rules to check errors related to action requirements are implemented. These types of rules check four errors: actions consuming and producing no resources, actions only consuming resources, actions only producing resources and actions modifying a resource that they were not consuming. There are also rules to trace dependencies through a process. These rules are: checking if resources required by an action are produced in an earlier action and checking if produced resources are consumed by at least one action.

Besides the studies above, we consider our work similar to the works about UML model consistency. Although, usually, these works are interested in consistency issues between the various diagrams of an UML specification they also consider the UML language and the consistency aspect. Additionally, in their majority, they describe formal approach [21], what we have also been done.

3 SPEM 2.0

The SPEM 2.0 metamodel is structured into seven packages. The structure divides the model into logical units. Each unit extends the units it depends upon, providing additional structures and capabilities to the elements defined below. The first package is Core that introduces classes and abstractions that build the foundation for all others metamodel packages. The second package, the Process Structure, defines the base for all process models. Its core data structure is a breakdown or decomposition of nested Activities that maintain lists of references to perform *Role* classes as well as input and output *Work Product* classes for each *Activity*. The Managed Content package introduces concepts for managing the textual content of a software process. The Process Behaviour package allows extending the structures defined in the Process Structure package with behavioural models. However, SPEM 2.0 does not define its own behaviour modelling approach. The Method Content package provides the concepts to build up a development knowledge base that is independent of any specific processes. The Process with Methods package specifies the needed concepts to integrate the Process Structure package and Method Content package. Finally, the Method Plugin package allows managing libraries and processes.

SPEM 2.0 is expressed using *MetaObject Facility* - MOF 2.0 meta-modeling language. Figure 1 shows the use of MOF 2.0 and UML 2.0 for modelling and defining SPEM 2.0. The Figure shows different instantiation layers of the formalism used for the SPEM 2.0 specification. MOF is the universal language that can be used on any layer, but in our case MOF is instantiated from the M3 layer by SPEM 2.0 on the M2 layer. The UML 2 meta-model itself, as depicted on the right-hand side of the M2 layer, instantiates MOF defined on M3 layer in the same way. Finally, process models can be instantiated using the M1 layer. In Figure 1, "Method Library" is shown as an example of a concrete instance of SPEM 2.0. In that sense, SPEM 2.0 defines process elements such as *Tasks* and *WorkProducts* as well as relationships among them whereas Method Library provides the concrete instance to these elements.

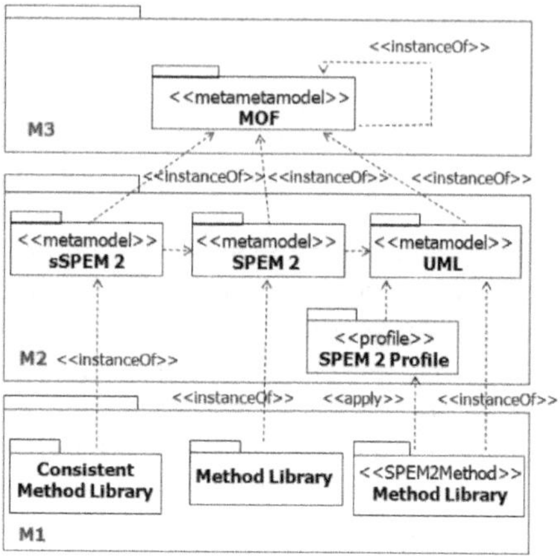

Fig. 1. Specification Levels

The consistency well-formedness rules proposed were defined in the M2 layer. They are based on the elements and relationships of the Process Structure and Process with Methods packages. In Figure 1 we have also represented how our proposal is located in the instantiation layers. In the left-hand side of the M2 layer, the sSPEM 2.0, which stands for *conSistent SPEM 2.0*, has all content of SPEM 2.0 more our consistency well-formedness rules. The sSPEM 2.0 is also an instance of MOF and it may be instantiated using the M1 layer. In Figure 1 the "Consistent Method Library" is shown as an instance of the sSPEM 2.0. It means that the "Consistent Method Library" has concrete instances of the elements and relationships of the SPEM 2.0 which were checked using the consistency well-formedness rules of the sSPEM 2.0.

4 Process Definition

This section explores the main SPEM 2.0 packages and introduces our proposal for process checking.

4.1 Process Structure in the SPEM 2.0

In SPEM 2.0 the main structural elements for defining software processes are in the Process Structure package. In this package, processes are represented with a breakdown structure mechanism that defines a breakdown of *Activities*, which are comprised of other *Activities* or leaf Breakdown Elements such as *WorkProductUses* or *RoleUses*. Figure 2 presents the Process Structure metamodel.

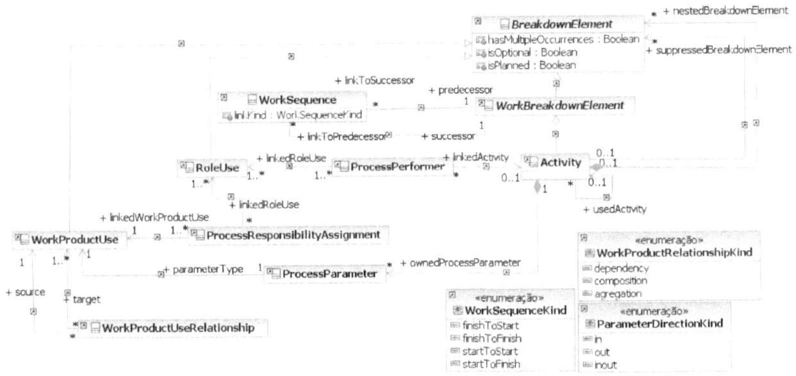

Fig. 2. Process Structure Metamodel

The *ProcessPerformer*, *ProcessParameter*. *ProcessResponsabilityAssignment* and *WorkProductUseRelationship* classes are used to express relationships among the elements in a software process. The *WorkSequence* class also represents a relationship class. It is used to represents a relationship between two *WorkBreakdownElements* in which one *WorkBreakdownElement* depends on the start or finish of another *WorkBreakdownElement* in order to begin or end. Another important process element which is not defined in the Process Structure package is the *Task*. This element is defined in the Process with Methods package which merges the Process Structure package. A task describes an assignable unit of work. In the *Process with Methods* package the class that represents the task element is the *TaskUse* class which is a subclass of the *WorkBreakdownElement* class of the Process Structure package. Figure 3 shows the relationships for the *TaskUse* class which are defined in the Process with Methods package.

Basically, the *TaskUse* class has relationships with the same elements as the *Activity* class. Figure 3 also shows that both the *TaskUse* class as well the *RoleUse* and *WorkProductUse* classes have, respectively, relationships with *TaskDefinition*, *RoleDefinition* and *WorkProductDefinition* classes. These classes are defined in the Method Content package and are used in the Process with Method Package by the merge mechanism.

All software process may use the concepts defined in the Method Content by creating a subclass of *Method Content Use* class and reference it with a subclass of *Method Content Element* class. The *Method Content Element* and *Method Content Use* classes are defined, respectively, in the Method Content package and Process with Methods package. All software process may use the concepts defined in the Method Content by creating a subclass of *Method Content Use* class and reference it with a subclass of *Method Content Element* class. *RoleUse, WorkProductUse* and *TaskUse* are subclasses to the *Method Content Use* class and *RoleDefinition*, *WorkProductDefinition* and *TaskDefinition* are subclasses to the *Method Content Element* class.

It is important to consider that both models presented in Figure 2 and Figure 3 had some multiplicities modified from the SPEM original metamodel. This is so because these models already represent models of sSPEM 2.0 and include some well-formedness rules proposed in this paper (which will be explained in Section 5).

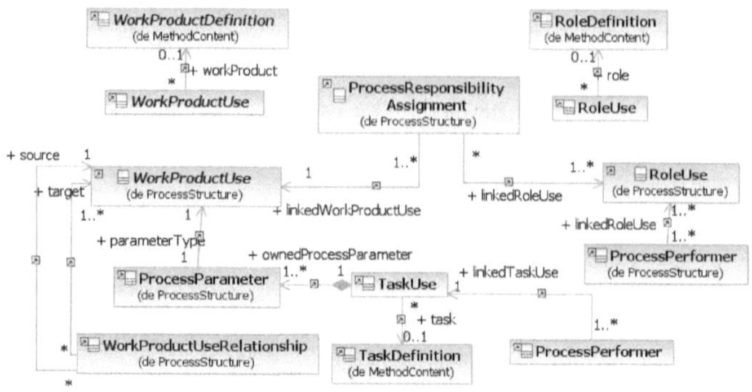

Fig. 3. Relationships of the TaskUse Class

4.2 Errors in a Software Process

We consider that errors in a process are motivated mainly by the following two reasons: (1) process metamodels are typically specified with UML class diagrams, which are only capable of representing simple multiplicity constraints. As a result they need an external language such OCL or Natural Language to represent complex restrictions. As with SPEM 2.0, most constraints are represented in Natural Language, which can lead to interpretation errors; and (2) software process metamodels are usually composed by several elements as they must represent activity workflows, information flows and role allocations. As a result, using a process metamodel can be cumbersome as the user must deal with several concepts to represent a process. According to Atkinson *et al.* in [20], the errors in a software process are most often introduced by a modeller and related to syntax or typographical mistakes that affect the process consistency. A modeller might, for example, make a simple error by connecting a work product that still was not produced in the software process as an input in a task. It would break a dependency because the task was expecting an unavailable work product.

To avoid errors in a process we propose checking it before enactment. Process checking is the activity of verifying the correctness and the consistency of a process. In this paper, process checking is made from a set of well-formedness rules specified from the SPEM 2.0 metamodel. The well-formedness rules are associated with the metamodel classes and relationships which represent the process elements and their relations. Every instance of process elements and relationships that have one or more associated well-formedness rules is checked. If violated, error messages appear. In the next section, we explain our well-formedness rules. Some rules are expressed using UML multiplicity and others, which involve more elements and/or express more elaborated rules, are described in FOLP.

5 Process Checking

In this section we describe a set of well-formedness rules related to software process correctness and consistency. We propose using these rules for process checking.

The well-formedness rules from this research were defined considering the concepts defined in the Process Structure and Process with Methods packages of SPEM 2.0 metamodel. Although the Method Content package has also important concepts for software process it only defines reusable content which is used through the classes of the Process with Methods package.

5.1 Well-Formedness Rules

As the SPEM metamodel is represented by UML class diagrams we consider that many constraints already exist in this metamodel through the multiplicity used between the classes. The following rule is one that is already defined in the SPEM 2.0 metamodel and constraints process multiplicity: a *Process Performer* must be associated to exactly one *TaskUse*. There is a "*linkedTaskUse*" relationship between *TaskUse* and *Process Performer* classes. The multiplicity is constrained to have only one relationship.

Considering all multiplicities defined between the classes of the Process Structure and Process with Methods packages we have noted that inconsistencies may be introduced into a software process. For example, it is possible create tasks that are not performed by anybody because a *TaskUse* can be associated to 0..* *ProcessPerformers*. This type of error could be introduced by an oversight that may hinder enactment since every task must be performed by at least one agent (human or automated agent).

To solve the problem above and others similar to it, we have started our work by redefining some relationships in the SPEM 2.0 metamodel. The modified relationships define rules as the rules shown in Table 1, which contain a numeration to ease its identification.

Table 1. Example of Relationship modified in SPEM 2.0

A *ProcessParameter* must be associated to exactly one *WorkProductUse*	*(Rule #1)*
A *TaskUse* must have at least one *ProcessParameter*	*(Rule #2)*

The classes and relationships that represent the rules above are depicted in Figure 2 and Figure 3. Basically, the rules presented define: **1)** Tasks must have input and/or outputs in terms of work products. Due to space constraints, the other modified relationships are not detailed here. They can be found in [10].

Since not all well-formedness rules could be expressed through UML diagrammatic notation we introduced first-order predicate logic (FOLP). To write the rules, we first translate the classes, relationships and attributes of SPEM 2.0 metamodel into predicates and logical axioms. Due to space constraints, the translation is not detailed here. We assume that each class and attribute of the metamodel represents a predicate. For example, the *ProcessPerformer* class and its attributes *linkedRoleUse* and *linkedTaskUse* are expressed using the following predicates:

processPerformer(x) where x is a instance of a *ProcessPerformer* (P1)

linkedRoleUse(x, y) where x is a instance of a *ProcessPerformer* and y is a instance *of RoleUse.* (P2) *linkedTaskUse(x, y)* where *x* is a instânce of a *ProcessPerformer* and *y* is a instance *of TaskUse* (P3)

The composition relationship which is a special type of UML association used to model a "whole to its parts" relationship is represented in FOLP with the predicate *part-of(x,y)*. In this predicate, x is an instance of *part* and y represents its *whole*. Considering the properties defined in UML for this type of association the following logic axioms are defined:

$$\forall x \ \neg part\text{-}of(x,x) \tag{A1}$$

$$\forall x,y \ (part\text{-}of(x,y) \rightarrow \neg part\text{-}of(y,x)) \tag{A2}$$

$$\forall x,y,z \ (part\text{-}of(x,y) \wedge part\text{-}of(y,z) \rightarrow part\text{-}of(x,z)) \tag{A3}$$

$$\forall x,y,z \ (part\text{-}of(x,y) \rightarrow \neg part\text{-}of(x,z)) \tag{A4}$$

Some additional predicates that express usual relations in a software process were also created. Such predicates are needed as they are reused for many different well-formedness rules. For example, the following predicates represent, respectively, a work product that is produced by a task and the dependency relationship between two work products. Dependency relationships are used to express that one work product depends on another work product to be produced in a software process.

$$\forall x,y,z((taskUse(x) \wedge workProductUse(z) \wedge processParameter(y) \wedge direction(y,\text{'out'}) \wedge parameterType(y,z) \wedge part\text{-}of(y,x)) \rightarrow taskProduce(x,z)) \tag{P4}$$

$$\forall z,x,y((workProductUse(x) \wedge workProductUse(y) \wedge (workProductUseRelationship(z) \wedge kind(z,\text{'dependency'}) \wedge source(z,x) \wedge target(z,y))) \rightarrow dependency(x,y)) \tag{P5}$$

Similar predicates also exist for the modification and consumption relations of the work products by the tasks in a software process. Such relations are obtained just replacing the value of the constant *'out'* of the *direction* predicate by *'in'* or *'inout'*. When the *'in'* value is used we have the predicate *taskConsume(x, z)* **(P6)** and when the *'inout'* value is used we have the predicate *taskModify(x, z)* **(P7)**. Activities have the same relations of input and output (production, consumption and modification) with work products, so we have considered similar predicates to these elements (**P8**, **P9** and **P10**).

Work products also may assume other types of relationships, in addition to the dependency relationship. In the SPEM 2.0 metamodel these types of relationships are *'composition'* and *'aggregation'*. Both relationships express that a work product instance is part of another work product instance. However, in the composition relationship the parts lifecycle (child work products) are dependent on the parent lifecycle (parent work product). The composition and aggregation predicates just replace the value of the constant *'dependency'* of the *kind* predicate by *'composition'* or *'aggregation'* (**P11**, **P12** and **P13**).

The *composition*, *aggregation* and *dependency* relationships between work products are transitive relations. The logical axioms bellow formalizing this property:

$$\forall x,y,z(composition(x,y) \wedge composition(y,z) \rightarrow composition(x,z)) \tag{A5}$$

$$\forall x,y,z(aggregation(x,y) \wedge aggregation(y,z) \rightarrow aggregation(x,z)) \tag{A6}$$

$$\forall x,y,z(dependency(x,y) \wedge dependency(y,z) \rightarrow dependency(x,z)) \tag{A7}$$

Considering the predicate and logical axioms above the first consistency well-formedness rules to *WorkProductUse* were expressed in FOLP. They are presented in the Table 2 and define: **1)** A work product may not be the *whole* in a relationship (composition, aggregation or dependency) if one of its *parts* represent its *whole* in another relationship or represent its *whole* by the relation transitivity. (*Rule #3, #4and #5*); **2)** A work product may not represent the *whole* and the *part* in the same relationship (composition, aggregation or dependency). (*Rules #6, #7 and #8*) and **3)** A work product that represents the *part* in a composition relationship may not represent *part* in another relationship of this type. (*Rule #9*)

Note that the well-formedness rules above define the same properties that logical axioms of the *part-of* predicate. However, the well-formedness rules are necessary once the relationships between the work products are not expressed using the UML association represented by the *part-of* predicate. These relationships are expressed using UML classes and attributes and consequently, need to be represented by other predicates and constrained by new rules.

Table 2. First Well-formedness Rules to WorkProducts

$\forall x,y\ (composition(x,y) \rightarrow \neg\, composition(y,x))$	*(Rule # 3)*
$\forall x,y\ (aggregation(x,y) \rightarrow \neg\, aggregation(y,x))$	*(Rule # 4)*
$\forall x,y\ (dependency(x,y) \rightarrow \neg\, dependency(y,x))$	*(Rule #5)*
$\forall x\ \neg\, composition(x,x)$	*(Rule # 6)*
$\forall x\ \neg\, aggregation(x,x)$	*(Rule #7)*
$\forall x\ \neg\, dependency(x,x)$	*(Rule # 8*
$\forall x,y,z\ (composition(x,y) \rightarrow \neg\, composition(x,z))$	*(Rule # 9)*

A second important group of consistency well-formedness rules to the *WorkProductUse* written in FOLP are shown in Table 3.

Table 3. Second Group of Well-formedness Rules to WorkProducts

$\forall x\ (workProductUse(x) \rightarrow \exists y\ (processParameter(y) \wedge direction(y, \text{'out'}) \wedge parameterType(y, x)))$	*(Rule #10)*
$\forall x,y(taskProduce(x,y) \rightarrow \exists r,w,z(roleUse(r) \wedge processPerfomer(z) \wedge linkedTaskUse(z,x) \wedge linkedRoleUse(z,r)) \wedge processResponsabilityAssignment(w) \wedge linkedRoleUse(w,r) \wedge linkedWorkProductUse(w,y))))$	*(Rule #11)*
$\forall x,y,t\ (workProductUse(x) \wedge dependency(x,y) \wedge taskProduce(t,x) \rightarrow taskConsume(t,y))$	*(Rule #12)*

The well-formedness rules above establish: **1)** Work products must be produced by at least one task in a software process. (*Rule #10*); **2)** At least one responsible role by the work product must be associated in its production tasks. (*Rule #11*); and **3)** If a work product has dependencies in terms of other work products these dependencies must be input in its production tasks. (*Rule #12*)

Consistency well-formedness rules related to the optionality of the process elements were also defined. Related to this aspect the well-formedness rules are important once the SPEM 2.0 metamodel defines that *Activities*, *TaskUses*,

WorkProductUses and *RoleUses* may be optional in a software process. This means, for example, that if an *Activity* is optional it does not need be performed and could be deleted. However, it is essential to guarantee that an optional *Activity* has not mandatory elements, which could not be deleted. The formalization to the consistency well-formedness rules that constrain the optionality aspect are shown in Table 4. In this Table, a specific well-formedness rule to the Activity element also is presented. Basically, the presented rules define: **1)** Mandatory activities must have at least one mandatory task and optional activities must not have any mandatory element (roles, work products and tasks). (*Rule #13 and #14*); **2)** Mandatory tasks must have at least one process parameter associated with a mandatory work product and must be associated through a process performer to at least one mandatory role. (*Rule #15*); **3)** Mandatory roles must be associated through a process performer to at least one mandatory task. (*Rule #16*); **4)** Mandatory work products must be produced by at least one task mandatory and must be associated through a process responsibility assignment to at least one mandatory role. Additionally, the mandatory role responsible for the mandatory work product must be associated to its production task. (*Rule #17*); and **5)** When activities establish parameters in terms of work products they must be compatible with the parameters of their tasks. *(Rule #18)*

Table 4. Well-formedness Rules to Optionality and the Activity Element

∀x((activity(x) ∧ isOptional(x, 'false'))→ ∃y (taskUse(y) ∧ isOptional(y, 'false')))	*(Rule #13)*
∀x((activity(x) ∧ isOptional(x, 'true'))→¬∃y,z,w((taskUse(y) ∧ isOptional(y, 'false'))∧ (w orkProductUse(z) ∧ isOptional(z, 'false')) ∧ (roleUse(w) ∧ isOptional(w, 'false'))))	*(Rule #14)*
∀x((taskUse(x) ∧ isOptional(x, 'false')) → ∃y,z,w,r ((workProductUse(y) ∧ isOptional(y, 'false')) ∧ (processParameter(z) ∧ parameterType(z,y)) ∧ part-of(z,x) ∧ (roleUse(w)∧ isOptional(w, 'false'))∧ (processPerformer(r) ∧ linkedRoleUse(r, w) ∧ linkedTaskUse(r,x))))	*(Rule #15)*
∀x((roleUse(x)∧ isOptional(x, 'false'))→ ∃y (taskUse(y) ∧ isOptional(y, 'false')))	*(Rule #16)*
∀x((WorkProductUse(x) ∧ isOptional(x, 'false')) → ∃y,z,w,r,p ((taskUse(y) ∧ isOptional(y, 'false')) ∧ (processParameter(z) ∧ direction(z,'out') ∧ parameterType(z,x)) ∧ part-of(z,y) ∧ (roleUse(w) ∧ isOptional(w, 'false')) ∧ (processResponsabilityAssignment(r)∧ linkedRoleUse(r,w)∧ (linkedWorkProductUse(r,x)) ∧ (processPerformer(p)∧ linkedRole Use(p, w) linkedTaskUse(p,y)))))	*(Rule #17)*
∀x,y (activityConsume(x,y) → ∃t (part-of(t,x) ∧ taskConsume(t,y))) *∀x,y (activityModify(x,y) → ∃t (part-of(t,x) ∧ taskModify(t,y)))* *∀x,y (activityProduce(x,y) → ∃t (part-of (t,x) ∧ taskProduce(t,y)))*	*(Rule #18)*

The last group of well-formedness rules are related to *TaskUses* sequencing. To establish the tasks sequence from SPEM 2.0 metamodel the *WorkSequence* class and its *linkKind* attribute are used. It is possible using the following values in sequencing between *TaskUses*: *finishToStart*, *finishToFinish*, *startToStart* and *startToFinish*.

Some predicates and logical axioms related to precedence between the tasks were created. Initially, to capture the concept of successor and predecessor task we have defined the predicates *pre-task*(t_1, t_2) and *pos-task*(t_2, t_1), where t_1 and t_2 are *TaskUse* instances and indicate, respectively, t_1 as predecessor task of t_2, or, inversely, t_2 as successor task of t_1. The predicates *pre* and *pos-task* are transitive and asymmetric relations. The following logical axioms establish these properties to these relations:

$$\forall (t_1, t_2)\ (pre\text{-}task(t_1, t_2) \leftrightarrow pos\text{-}task(t_2, t_1)) \quad \text{(A8)}$$

$$\forall (t_1, t_2, t_3)\ (pre\text{-}task(t_1, t_2) \wedge pre\text{-}task(t_2, t_3) \rightarrow pre\text{-}task(t_1, t_3)) \quad \text{(A9)}$$

$$\forall (t_1, t_2)\ (pre\text{-}task(t_1, t_2) \rightarrow \neg pre\text{-}task(t_2, t_1)) \quad \text{(A10)}$$

$$\forall t_1\ \neg pre\text{-}task(t_1, t_1) \quad \text{(A11)}$$

Based on the predicates and logical axioms related to precedence between tasks we have defined new consistency well-formedness rules. These rules, shown in Table 5, define: 1) The tasks sequencing must not have duplicated sequences. (*Rule #19*) **2)** Work Products must be produced before they are consumed. (*Rule #20*) and **3)** The dependencies of a work product must be produced before it in a software process. (*Rule #21*)

The well-formedness rule *#19* shown in the Table 5 is only to *startToFinish* transition. Consider the same rule to the following transitions: *startToStart*, *finishToFinish* and *startToFinish*.

Table 5. Well-formedness Rules to Process Sequence

$\forall x,x1,x2((taskUse(x1) \wedge taskUse(x2) \wedge (workSequence(x) \wedge predecessor(x, x1) \wedge sucessor(x, x2) \wedge linkKind(x, startToFinish'))) \rightarrow \neg\exists y(workSequence(y) \wedge predecessor(x,x1) \wedge sucessor(x,x2) \wedge linkKind(x, \text{'startToFinish'})))$	(*Rule #19*)
$\forall x, y\ (taskConsume(x, y) \rightarrow \exists x2\ (taskProduce(x2, y) \wedge pre\text{-}task(x2, x)))$	(*Rule #20*)
$\forall x,y\ (dependency(x,y) \rightarrow \exists t1, t2\ (taskProduce(t1, x) \wedge taskProduce(t2, y) \wedge pre\text{-}task(t2,t1)))$	(*Rule #21*)

6 Evaluation of the Well-Formedness Rules

This section presents a process checking example using a part of the OpenUP process. The section also evaluates one of the well-formedness rules proposed in this paper. The main goal is demonstrate that the predicates and logical axioms used in the well-formedness rules really express the intended meaning.

6.1 Process Checking Example

To present a process checking example we have considered the *Inception Iteration* of the OpenUP process, which is shown in Figure 4. In this Figure, above the dash line, the activities and tasks of the iteration are represented. Additionally, some information about activities sequence is also shown. Below the dash line, the tasks of the *Initiate Project* activity are detailed in terms of roles and work products (inputs and outputs). All information shown in the Figure 4 is based on the OpenUP process except the *Rule Test* which was introduced by us only for this evaluation. Originally, in OpenUP, the *Analyst* is also responsible for the *Vision* work product.

One of the tasks of Figure 4 (*Plan Project*) is also represented with a UML object diagram, which is shown in Figure 5. The object diagram show the class instances of the SPEM 2.0 used to create tasks, work products, roles and their relationships in a software process. In Figure 5 letters are used to facilitate its understanding. The *letter A* indicates the *WorkProductUse* classes. The *letter B* represents the objects that are instances of the *ProcessParameter* class. These kinds of objects represent the inputs and outputs to the task objects. In Figure 5, the object that represents a task is represented by the *PP* (*Plan Project*) identifier. This object is an instance of *TaskUse* class and is indicated in the Figure 5 by the *letter C*. The objects representing instances of the *RoleUse* class are indicated in Figure 5 by the *letter D*. Finally, the *letters E* and *F* represent, respectively, objects of the *ProcessResponsabilityAssignment* and *ProcessPerformer* classes. The instances of the *ProcessResponsabilityAssignment* are used to define roles as responsible for work products and the instances of the ProcessPerformer are used to link roles as performer to the tasks.

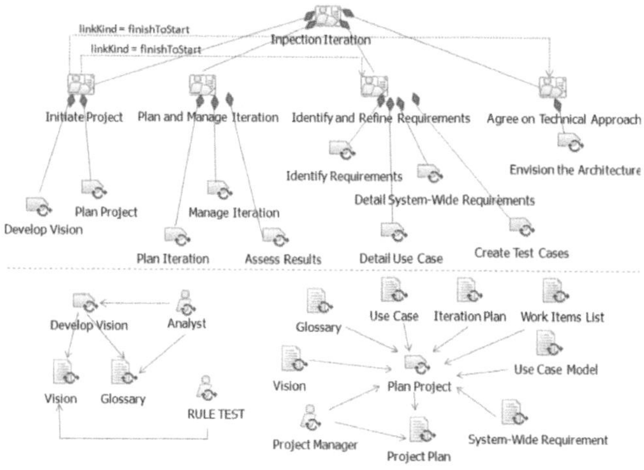

Fig. 4. Inception Iteration of the OpenUp

As seen, all process information of this example may be represented using classes and relationships of the SPEM 2.0. It means that the used process is compliance with the SPEM 2.0 metamodel. Another fact that shows the consistency of the used process is the validation result of the object diagram found in the *case* tools like *Rational Software Modeler*. This validation result is error free.

However, as mentioned in Section 4, not all need information in a software process can be expressed using only the UML language. Thus, when we carry out the checking in the same process using our well-formedness rules it presented errors indicating some inconsistencies. The first inconsistency of the software process used in this example is in the task *Develop Vision*. As seen in Figure 4, the task *Develop Vision* produces the work product *Vision* which has as responsible role the role *Rule Test*. This role does not perform the task *Develop Vision* and this fact violates the *Rule #11* which defines that at least on responsible role of a work product must participate of their production tasks. Another problem can be seen in the task *Plan Project*. Note that this task has as mandatory inputs the work products *Use Case, Use Case Model* and *System-Wide Requirements* which are not yet produced in the software process when this task is performed. This inconsistency violates the *Rule #20*.

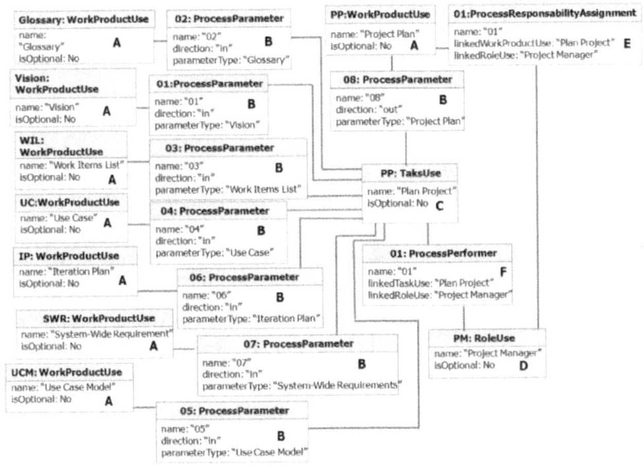

Fig. 5. Object Diagram to the *Plan Project* Task

6.2 Evaluation of the Well-Formedness Rules

We have evaluated our well-formedness rules expressed in FOLP to check their correctness. Since the amount of rules presented in this paper is vast and due the space constraints, we present only the evaluation of rule *Rule #20*. It will be described the evaluation to the work product *Use Case* which is input to the task *Plan Project*. The evaluation of the rule *Rule #11* can be found in [10].

To start the evaluation we have created some variables and assigned values for them. Each variable represents an object of the object diagrams shown in Figure 5. Table 6 lists the variables and values used to this evaluation.

Table 6. Variables used in the Evaluation

x::= 'PP'	x represents the 'Plan Project' *TaskUse*
y::= 'UC'	w4 represents the 'Use Case' *WorkProductUse*
t::= '04'	t represents the '04' *Process Parameter* with *direction* equal to 'In' and *parameterType* equal to 'Use Case'

The *Rule #20* in FOLP is: $\forall x,y\ (taskConsume(x,\ y) \rightarrow \exists x2\ (taskProduce(x2,\ y) \wedge pre\text{-}task(x2,x)))$. Note that the predicates *taskConsume(x, y)* and *taskProduce(x2, y)* need to be evaluated first. Considering the predicates *taskConsume(PP,UC)* and *taskProduce(IR, UC),* the result of these evaluations will return *Truth* and *Truth*, respectively. Note that the variable *IR* does not exist as a variable value in Table 6 and does not represent an object in above object diagram. Consider that it represents the task *Identify Requirements* task which produces the work product *Use Case*.

Below, we show the details to the evaluation of the predicate *taskConsume(PP,UC)*. Since we are already showed one evaluation to the predicate *taskProduces(x,y)* in [10] and due the space restrictions, we will not detail it here.

$$\forall x,y,t((taskUse(x)\wedge workProductUse(y)\wedge(processParameter(t) \wedge direction(t, \text{'in'})\wedge parameterType(t,y))\wedge part\text{-}of(t, x)) \rightarrow taskConsume(x, y))$$

taskUse(PP)::= T
workProductUse(UC)::= T
processParameter(04)::= T
taskConsume(PP, UC)::= T
parameterType(04, UC)::= T
direction(04, 'in')::= T
part-of(04, PP)::= T

Then:

$$\forall x,y,t\ ((T \wedge T \wedge (T \wedge T \wedge T) \wedge T) \rightarrow T)$$

$$\forall x,y,t\ (T \rightarrow T)::= T$$

To evaluate the *Rule #20* it is also necessary evaluate the predicate *pre-task(IR, PP)*. The result *Truth* indicates the task *Identify Requirements* as predecessor to the task *Plan Project* and *False* indicates the opposite. Considering the sequence established in Figure 4 among the activities it is possible note that the predicate *pre-task(IR, PP)* is *False*. It because the *Initiate Project* activity is linked with the *Identify and Refine Requirements* activity through the linkKind *finishToStart.* Thus, it is established that all tasks of the *Initiate Project* activity must be finished before the tasks of the *Identify and Refine Requirements* activity started. Considering the results and the *Rule #20* we have:

$$\forall x,y(taskConsume(x,y) \rightarrow \exists x2(taskProduce(x2,y)\wedge pre\text{-}task(x2,x))$$

Then:

$$\forall x,\ y\ (T \rightarrow \exists x2\ (V \wedge F))$$

$$\forall x,\ y(T \rightarrow \exists x2\ (F))$$

$$\forall x,\ y\ (T \rightarrow F)::= F$$

The value to the *Rule #20* is *False*. This value was expected once the values assigned to the variables generate one inconsistency in the software process as already shown in the Subsection 6.1. It suggests that the theory of the *Rule #20* is valid.

7 Conclusions

In this paper, we have proposed well-formedness rules that allow finding errors in a software process before it is enacted. By noting inconsistencies, we believe it is possible for modellers to refine a process model until it is free of inconsistencies.

The proposed well-formedness rules were based on SPEM 2.0 metamodel. To define them we have modified multiplicity constraints and for the more elaborated rules which could not be expressed only with UML, we have used FOLP.

Several research directions, which we are working on, have been left open during this paper, and here we emphasize two of them. First, more well-formedness rules considering others process elements and consistency aspects need to be provided. Related to this, preliminary studies suggest two important facts: (1) other process elements and relationships must be included in the SPEM 2.0 metamodel and (2) the OCL language does not support the definition of all well-formedness rules needed to guarantee consistency. For example, the well-formedness rules to check cycles in a software process, which involve temporary aspects, may not be expressed using OCL. This fact has been the motivation to use FOLP in this paper. Secondly, with regard to automatic support, the prototype of a tool prototype is being developed. This will support the definition and tailoring of SPEM-based software processes. Furthermore, a process checking, which implements the well-formedness rules, will be provided.

References

1. Jacobson, I., Booch, G., Rumbaugh, J.: The Unified Software Development Process (2001)
2. Kruchten, P.: The Rational Unified Process: An Introduction. Addison Wesley, NJ (2000)
3. Open (2006), `http://www.open.org.au`
4. Xu, P., Ramesh, B.: A Tool for the Capture and Use of Process Knowledge in Process Tailoring. In: Proc. of Hawaii Int. Conference on System Sciences (2003)
5. Henderson-Sellers, B., Gonzalez-Perez, C., Ralyté, J.: Comparison of Method Chunks and Method Fragments for Situational Method Engineering. In: 19th Australian Conference on Software Engineering (2008)
6. Hug, C., Front, A., Rieu, D., Henderson-Sellers, B.: A Method to Build Information Systems Engineering Process Metamodels. The Journal of Systems and Software (2009)
7. Henderson-Sellers, B., Gonzalez-Perez, C.: A Work Product Pool Approach to Methodology Specification and Enactment. Journal of Systems and Software (2007)
8. OMG, SPEM 1.1 (2002), `http://www.omg.org/`
9. OMG: SPEM 2.0 (2007), `http://www.omg.org/`
10. Pereira, E.B., Bastos, R.M., Oliveira, T.C., Móra, M.C.: Improving the Consistency of SPEM-Based Software Processes. In: 13th International Conference on Enterprise Information Systems - ICEIS 2011, Beijing, China (2011)
11. Puviani, M., Serugendo, G.D.M., Frei, R., Cabri, G.: Methodologies for Self-organising Systems: a SPEM Approach. In: International Conference on Web Intelligence and Intelligent Agent Technology (2009)
12. Habli, I., Kelly, T.: A Model-Driven Approach to Assuring Process Reliability. In: 19th International Symposium on Software Reliability Engineering (2008)
13. Serour, M.K., Henderson-Sellers, B.: Introducing Agility – A Case Study of SME Using the OPEN. In: 28th Computer Sof. and Applications Conf. (2004)
14. Bendraou, R., Combemale, B., Cregut, X., Gervais, M.P.: Definition of an Executable SPEM 2.0. In: 14th Asia-Pacific Software Engineering Conference (2007)
15. Wistrand, K., Karlsson, F.: Method Components – Rationale Revealed. In: Persson, A., Stirna, J. (eds.) CAiSE 2004. LNCS, vol. 3084, pp. 189–201. Springer, Heidelberg (2004)
16. Gnatz, M., Marschall, F., Popp, G., Rausch, A., Schwerin, W.: The Living Software Development Process (2003), `http://citeseerx.ist.psu.edu/viewdoc/summary?doi=10.1.1.60.3371`
17. Ralyté, J., Backlund, P., Kuhn, H., Jeusfeld, M.A.: Method Chunks for Interoperability. In: 25th Int. Conference on Conceptual Modelling (2006)
18. Bajec, M., Vavpotic, D., Krisper, M.: Practice-Driven Approach for Creating Project-Specific Software Development Methods. Information and Software Technology (2007)
19. Hsueh, N.L., Shen, W.H., Yang, Z.W., Yang, D.L.: Applying UML and Software Simulation for Process Definition, Verification and Validation. Information and Software Technology, 897–911 (2008)
20. Atkinson, D.C., Weeks, D.C., Noll, J.: Tool Support for Iterative Software Process Modeling. Information and Software Technology, 493–514 (2007)
21. Lucas, F.J., Molina, F., Toval, A.: A Systematic Review of UML Model Consistency Management. Information and Software Technology, 1631–1645 (2009)

A Multiobjective Optimization Approach to the Software Release Planning with Undefined Number of Releases and Interdependent Requirements

Marcia Maria Albuquerque Brasil, Thiago Gomes Nepomuceno da Silva, Fabricio Gomes de Freitas, Jerffeson Teixeira de Souza, and Mariela Inés Cortés

Optimization in Software Engineering Group (GOES.UECE),
State University of Ceara (UECE),
Av. Paranjana 1700, Fortaleza, Ceara, 60740-903, Brazil
{marcia.abrasil,thi.nepo,fabriciogf.uece}@gmail.com,
{jeff,mariela}@larces.uece.br

Abstract. In software development, release planning is a complex activity which involves several aspects related to which requirements are going to be developed in each release of the system. The planning must meet the customers' needs and comply with existing constraints. This paper presents an approach based on multiobjective optimization for release planning. The approach tackles formulations when the number of releases is not known a priori and also when the stakeholders have a desired number of releases (target). The optimization model is based on stakeholders' satisfaction, business value and risk management. Requirements interdependencies are also considered. In order to validate the approach, experiments are carried out and the results indicates the validity of the proposed approach.

Keywords: Software release planning, Multiobjective optimization, Search based software engineering, Requirements engineering, Genetic algorithms.

1 Introduction

Software Release Planning is an important activity which concerns on scheduling the set of system's requirements in releases, in order to meet customers' needs and to attend the related constraints. When the development process is based upon small deliveries, the software itself is not fully developed at once, rather the work being focused on frequent releases, when by each release a subset of functionality is delivered. This way, customers can receive software features sooner rather than waiting a long time to get the complete system. This development model has several positive aspects, such as: earlier feedback from stakeholders, better risk management, and it also allows incremental tests execution [1].

An important aspect in Release Planning is to decide how many releases will be necessary to deliver the functionalities. Also, the clients and stakeholders may ask for a number of releases, and then this issue has also to be considered. In addition, to decide which requirements should be developed in each release is not an easy task

R. Zhang et al. (Eds.): ICEIS 2011, LNBIP 102, pp. 300–314, 2012.

and involves several conflicting aspects. These aspects regard mainly on balancing the customer satisfaction, business value, priority, involved risks, delivery time, available resources, and requirements interdependencies, among others.

This work addresses the Software Release Planning and presents an approach based on multiobjective optimization to assist project managers in an effective planning, including to aim to determine the ideal number of releases.

Search techniques have been successfully applied for solving complex Software Engineering problems, strategy which belongs to the research field called Search-Based Software Engineering – SBSE [2]. As shown in [3], SBSE can be effective in providing better solutions, in comparison to human generated solutions.

This paper's contributions are:

- A multiobjective formulation for the Software Release Planning when the number of releases is not determined in advance or it is an expectation among stakeholders. The aspects customer satisfaction, business value, risk management, available resources and requirements interdependencies (technical precedence, coupling and business precedence) are considered;
- Resolution of the problem by multiobjective metaheuristics algorithms;
- Results from experiments in order to indicate feasibility of the formulation.

This paper is organized as follows. Section 2 discusses related works in the Requirements Prioritization and in the Software Release Planning. Section 3 presents important aspects and definitions considered in the problem, including requirements interdependencies. In Section 4, the proposed approach is explained and formally defined. Section 5 is devoted to explain concepts of multiobjective optimization and the algorithms used in the experiments. Section 6 regards the experiments and provides a discussion on the results. Section 7 concludes and outlines future research.

2 Related Work

The authors in [4] develop an approach based on cost/value to prioritize requirements using the Analytic Hierarchy Process [5] method to compare requirements pair wise based on their value and implementation cost. A variant of the 0-1 knapsack problem to reduce the complexity in the cost/value approach is proposed in [6].

The requirements selection was initially addressed in [7], the "The Next Release Problem" (NRP), which consists on the selection of which customers will be met in the next release. The approach prioritizes the most important customers and complies with the available resources and requirements precedence. Several techniques were employed, including Integer Programming, GRASP, Hill Climbing and Simulated Annealing. In this mono-objective formulation, the release planning is defined only for the next release and does not consider requirement value for customers.

Later, [8] presents an iterative approach based on genetic algorithms to the Software Release Planning. The method is called EVOLVE and provides decision support in a changing environment. The objective function is a linear combination of two functions, aimed to maximize the total benefit and minimize the total penalties. The number of releases is not decided *a priori* and re-planning releases is allowed.

In [9], a hybrid method that combines computational algorithms with human knowledge and experience is proposed. The objective function determines the value for the weighted average satisfaction according stakeholders priorities for all features. They solved the problem using Integer Linear Programming and the approach was implemented as part of a intelligent decision-support tool. [10] presents some technical and nontechnical factors affecting release planning, and evaluate methods based on these aspects. They also propose a framework considering the impact of existing systems characteristics to make decisions about release planning.

A multiobjective formulation for NRP was presented by [11]. Customer satisfaction and project cost were the objectives to be optimized, when selecting the optimal requirements set. Four different multiobjective optimization techniques were used, including NSGA-II. However, their formulation does not include any requirement interdependence, which is uncommon in the context of real projects, since one requirement may depend on another in different ways [12].

The authors in [13] present a technique for detecting coupling between features from the implementation perspective. The work focuses in the evaluation of the release plans from business perspective and based on relationships between the components that would realize the features.

A multiobjective approach to the Software Release Planning is proposed in [1]. The formulation tries to be complete and aims to maximize customer satisfaction and minimize project risks, by selecting the requirements to be developed in a fixed number of releases. Customer satisfaction is achieved by implementing earlier the highest priority requirements and the project risks are minimized by implementing the requirements with higher risk first. NSGA-II is applied to solve the problem and the human-competitiveness of the approach is also studied.

An overview on requirements optimization is available in [14].

3 Problem Definition

This section describes aspects related to the proposed approach. Numeric scales are used as a way to evaluate values for risk, importance, priority, time and cost to enable the mathematical modeling of the problem. Other scales can be used in other contexts.

3.1 Requirements

Let be $R = \{r_i |\, i = 1, 2, \ldots, N\}$ the set of functionalities to be developed and assigned to releases. System requirements include features, functions and attributes in the software system [4]. The implementation of each requirement r_i demands a certain amount of cost and time denoted by $cost_i$ and $time_i$, respectively. Each requirement r_i has an associated risk $risk_i$, ranging on a scale of 1 (lower risk) to 5 (higher risk).

3.2 Stakeholders

Let be $C = \{c_m |\, m = 1, 2, \ldots, M\}$ the set of stakeholders involved in the process. They may include customers and users, a software engineer, developers and so on. For each stakeholder c_m there is a weight based on their relative importance to the company. Thus, w_m defines the importance of a stakeholder to the software organization and is quantified on a scale from 1 (lower importance) to 10 (higher importance).

3.3 Releases

Let be $S = \{s_k | \; k = 1, 2, \ldots\}$ the set of releases. The number of releases is not initially defined, which will be determined by the approach. For each release s_k, bounds are given for budget ($budgetReleaseMin_k$ and $budgetReleaseMax_k$) and duration ($timeReleaseMin_k$ and $timeReleaseMax_k$).

3.4 Project

The whole project consists of all the releases that should be planned. Thus, the project has a maximum schedule ($timeProject$) and a total budget ($budgetProject$) that should not be exceeded. These values are used to select, during the prioritization, the requirements to be implemented.

3.5 Requirements versus Stakeholders

Different stakeholders may have different interests in the implementation of each requirement. Just as in [8] and in [9], the concepts of priority, in terms of urgency, and value, in terms of business value-added, are used in this work. These concepts are analyzed from the stakeholders' perspective. Thus, $value(m, i)$ quantifies the perceived importance that a stakeholder c_m associates to a requirement r_i by assigning a value ranging from 0 (no importance) to 10 (highest importance), and $priority(m, i)$ denotes the urgency that a stakeholder c_m has for the implementation of requirement r_i, ranging from 0 (no urgency) to 10 (highest urgency).

3.6 Requirements Interdependencies

According to a study [12], 75% of interdependencies come from roughly 20% of the requirements. The set of requirements interdependencies addressed in this work are:

- Coupling (T1) – It is DESIRABLE that a requirement r_i be implemented together with a requirement r_j, i.e. in the same release.
- Business Precedence (T2) – It is DESIRABLE that requirement r_i be implemented before r_j. In this case, r_i can be implemented in a previous or the same release of requirement r_j.
- Technical Precedence (T3) – A requirement r_i MUST BE implemented before a r_j. The requirement r_i must be implemented in a previous or the same release of requirement r_j.

For example, when two requirements have a Technical Precedence relationship to each other, the interdependence between r_i and r_j is denoted by $Dr_i, r_j = T3$. The same applies to the other forms. T1 and T2 relationships are objectives to be optimized in the proposed approach. Reducing or minimizing the coupling between releases means implementing requirements with similar characteristics in the same release. In fact, the detection of coupling and implementation of requirements with similar characteristics bring benefits, as reuse and resources saving (time and effort) [13]. T2 expresses relationships from the business viewpoint according to stakeholders' perspectives.

4 Mathematical Formulation

The approach proposed in this paper for release planning is divided into two methods. The first one is used when the number of releases is not initially defined and the approach will try to determine this number. In the second one, the number of releases is also undetermined *a priori*, but there exist a consensual value expected by the stakeholders and the approach will try to reach this value. Each of these methods is performed in two phases, where the first phase is common for both.

4.1 Release Planning with Undefined Number of Releases

First Phase: Requirements Prioritization. In this phase, the requirements will be prioritized according to the goals of value, priority and risk, while respecting technical precedence and available resources (overall time and budget). Due to constraints of budget and time of the project, it is possible that not all requirements from the initial set of requirements are selected.

Therefore, the first phase for software release planning can be mathematically formulated with the following objective and constraint functions:

$$Max\ f_{VALUE}(y) = \sum_{i=1}^{N} score_i . y_i \ . \tag{1}$$

$$Max\ f_{PRIORITY}(x^{Prio}, y) = \sum_{i=1}^{N} prior_i . (N - {x^{Prio}}_i) . y_i \ . \tag{2}$$

$$Min\ f_{RISK}(x^{Prio}) = \sum_{i=1}^{N} risk_i . {x^{Prio}}_i \ . \tag{3}$$

Subject to:

$$\sum_{i=1}^{N} cost_i . y_i \leq budgetProject \ . \tag{4}$$

$$\sum_{i=1}^{N} time_i . y_i \leq timeProject \ . \tag{5}$$

$${x^{Prio}}_i < {x^{Prio}}_j, if\ Dr_i, r_j = T3\ (Technical\ Precedence) \ . \tag{6}$$

The variable ${x^{Prio}}_i$ indicates the position of the requirement r_i in the established prioritization. It is a value in $\{0, 1, 2, \ldots N\}$ for $i = 1, 2, \ldots N$. The variable y_i indicates if the requirement r_i will be implemented ($y_i = 1$) or not ($y_i = 0$), for $i = 1, 2, \ldots N$. If ${x^{Prio}}_i > 0$, $y_i = 1$; $y_i = 0$, otherwise.

Function 1 – This objective function expresses the stakeholders' satisfaction by implementing the most important requirements, where $score_i = \sum_{m=1}^{M} w_m . value(m, i)$ means the weighted business-value added by the development of requirement r_i.

Function 2 – This objective function expresses, in a weighted way, the customer satisfaction for the early implementation of the highest priority requirements ($prior_i = \sum_{m=1}^{M} w_m . priority(m, i)$).

Function 3 – This objective function expresses the project risk management as a whole. Requirements with a high risk associated are more likely to give problems in development [15]. Thus, in the same way that [1], requirements at higher risk should be implemented earlier.

The constraints of this phase are expressed in 4, 5 and 6. Thus, (4) is the restriction that limits the cost of implementing to the overall project budget. And (5) is the restriction that limits the time necessary of implementation to the overall project duration. The constraint (6) expresses technical precedence between requirements. If a requirement r_i technically precedes a requirement r_j, then r_i should be implemented before r_j $({x^{Prio}}_i < {x^{Prio}}_j)$.

Second Phase: Scheduling in Releases. The second phase will allocate the requirements (selected and prioritized in the first phase) in releases. The approach tries to put in the same release the requirements with a coupling interdependency. It also tries to maintain the established prioritization and respect the existing business precedence. The mathematical formulation follows:

$$Min\ f_{COUPLING}(x^{Rel}) = C_{Rel}(x^{Rel})\ . \tag{7}$$

$$Min\ f_{PRIORITIZATION\_ORDERING}\ (x^{Prio}, x^{Rel}) = PO(x^{Prio}, x^{Rel})\ . \tag{8}$$

$$Min\ f_{BUSINESS\_PRECEDENCE}(x^{Rel}) = \sum_{i=1}^{N}\sum_{j=1}^{N} BP({x^{Rel}}_i, {x^{Rel}}_j)\ . \tag{9}$$

Subject to:

$$budgetReleaseMin_k \leq \sum_{i=1}^{N} cost_i . v_{i,k} \leq budgetReleaseMax_k\ , \forall k \in \{1,2,\ldots\}. \tag{10}$$

$$timeReleaseMin_k \leq \sum_{i=1}^{N} time_i . v_{i,k} \leq timeReleaseMax_k\ , \forall k \in \{1,2,\ldots\}\ . \tag{11}$$

$${x^{Rel}}_i \leq {x^{Rel}}_j, if\ Dr_i, r_j = T3\ (Technical\ Precedence)\ . \tag{12}$$

The variable ${x^{Prio}}_i$ indicates the position of r_i in the prioritization. The variable ${x^{Rel}}_i$ denotes the release for implementation of the requirement r_i, and is a value in $\{1,2,\ldots\}$ for $i = 1,2,\ldots N$. The variable $v_{i,k}$ indicates if the requirement r_i is implemented in the release s_k $(v_{i,k} = 1)$ or not $(v_{i,k} = 0)$.

Function 1 – This objective function aims to minimize the coupling between releases, according to the strategy presented in [12].

$$C_{Rel}(x^{Rel}) = \left[\frac{1}{2} . \sum_{i=1}^{N}\sum_{j=1}^{N} C\left({x^{Rel}}_i, {x^{Rel}}_j\right)\right] / I\ . \tag{13}$$

$$C\left({x^{Rel}}_i, {x^{Rel}}_j\right) = \begin{cases} 1, & if\ Dr_i, r_j = T1\ and\ {x^{Rel}}_i \neq {x^{Rel}}_j \\ 0, & otherwise \end{cases} . \tag{14}$$

$$I = \frac{1}{2} . \sum_{i=1}^{N}\sum_{j=1}^{N} C_{Req}\left(r_i, r_j\right)\ . \tag{15}$$

$$C_{Req}\left(r_i, r_j\right) = \begin{cases} 1, & if\ Dr_i, r_j = T1 \\ 0, & if\ Dr_i, r_j \neq T1 \end{cases} . \tag{16}$$

Function 2 – This function tries to maintain the prioritization ordering obtained in the phase 1 and counts negatively when this sequence is broken:

$$PO\left(x^{Prio}, x^{Rel}\right) = \sum_{i=2}^{N}\sum_{j=1}^{i-1} Violation(z[i], z[j])\ . \tag{17}$$

$$Violation(z[i], z[j]) = \begin{cases} 1, if\ x^{Rel}[z[i]] < x^{Rel}[z[j]] \\ 0, \quad otherwise \end{cases}. \tag{18}$$

$$\begin{aligned} z[i] &= A, for\ each\ x^{Prio}[A] = i \\ z[j] &= A, for\ each\ x^{Prio}[A] = j\,. \end{aligned} \tag{19}$$

The vector z is an auxiliary vector to sort the requirements according to the prioritization and to compare their elements with the release implementation of each requirement to verify if the ordering obtained in the phase 1 was not followed.

Function 3 – This function tries to minimize the amount of Business Precedence that was not fulfilled. This situation occurs when a requirement r_i is prerequisite, from the business perspective, for a requirement r_j but is allocated in a later release.

$$BP(x^{Rel}{}_i, x^{Rel}{}_j) = \begin{cases} 1, if\ Dr_i, r_j = T2\ and\ x^{Rel}{}_i > x^{Rel}{}_j \\ 0, \quad otherwise \end{cases}. \tag{20}$$

Equations 10, 11 and 12 are the constraints. Restriction (10) limits the implementation cost in a release to the interval of budget available for this release. Restriction (11) limits the implementation time in a release to the interval of schedule available for this release. Restriction (12) is the same as in phase 1. But in this case if r_i technically precedes r_j, then r_i should be implemented in a release prior to the release of r_j, or both should be implemented in the same release $(x^{Rel}{}_i \le x^{Rel}{}_j)$.

4.2 Release Planning with Expected Number of Releases

This approach is very similar to the first one. The overall formulation remains the same (it is executed in two phases and has the same objectives and constraints) and one more objective function is added, as below:

$$Min\ f_{TARGET\_DISTANCE}(K) = |K - TR|\,. \tag{21}$$

Function 7 – This function tries to reach the number of releases wanted by the stakeholders (the target release). K is the number of releases obtained by the approach and $target_m$ is the number of releases expected by the stakeholder c_m. The expected number of releases is obtained in a weighted form, according to:

$$TR = \sum_{m=1}^{M} (w_m . target_m) / \sum_{m=1}^{M} w_m\,. \tag{22}$$

5 Multiobjective Optimization

Since the problem addressed in this paper is modeled as a multiobjective optimization problem, we present some concepts related to multiobjective optimization and describes the algorithms, NSGA-II [16] and MOCell [17], used in the experiments.

5.1 Pareto Front

In multiobjective optimization problems, two or more functions must be optimized, the solutions are partially ordered and the search is done by a set of solutions. Often, many real world optimization problems have conflicting goals and involve the minimization and/or maximization of more than one function. When trying to optimize multiple objectives simultaneously, the search space becomes partially ordered and is based on the concept of dominance. The search is not restricted to find a single solution. Instead, it returns a set of solutions called non-dominated solutions (solutions that are not dominated by any other solution). A solution S_1 dominates a solution S_2 if S_1 is better or equal to S_2 in all objectives and strictly better in at least one of them. Each solution in the set of non-dominated solutions is said to be Pareto optimal. The collective representation of all these solutions is called Pareto front.

5.2 NSGA-II – Non-dominated Sorting Genetic Algorithm II

NSGA-II [16] is a metaheuristic based on genetic algorithms for multiobjective optimization. It is implemented in two phases, using the mechanisms Non-dominated Sorting Algorithm (that performs a search for solutions near the Pareto front) and Crowding Distance Sorting (that performs a search for solutions with a good distribution in space). The operation begins with an initial population randomly created, of size N. Next, a second population, also of size N is generated based on the first using genetic operations as crossover and mutation. These two populations are then combined into a new population of size 2N. Next, the individuals are classified in fronts, according to their non-dominance degree. Thus, in the first front will be ranked the best individuals and in the last front, the worst. This process continues until all individuals are classified into a front. After this process, a new population, of size N, should be generated. As the number of individuals is 2N, all fronts cannot be included in the new population. It is also possible that in the inclusion of individuals from the last allowed front, there is not enough space to include all its elements. The procedure for selecting which individuals from the last front will compose the new population is called Crowding Distance and aims to sort and choose the best elements scattered within this front, using a diversity metric, which calculates the distance between an individual and its neighbors taking into account all the objectives.

5.3 MOCell

MOCell [17] is an adaptation of a cellular model of genetic algorithm (cGA - cellular genetic algorithm) canonical for multiobjective optimization. The algorithm uses an external file to store non-dominated solutions found during the search and applies a feedback mechanism in which the solutions in this file replace, randomly, existing individuals in population after each iteration. To manage the insertion of solutions in the Pareto front, for a diverse set, a density estimator (based on crowding distance method) is used. This mechanism is also used to remove solutions from the archive when it becomes full (the external file has a maximum size). The algorithm starts by creating an empty Pareto front. Individuals are organized into a two-dimensional grid and genetic operators are successively applied to them until a stop condition is reached. For each individual, the algorithm selects two parents from their neighborhood, makes a recombination between them in order to obtain a descendant, executes a mutation and evaluates the resulting individual. This individual is inserted both in helping population (if not dominated by the current individual) as in the Pareto front. After each iteration, the old population is replaced by an assistant and a feedback procedure is triggered to replace a fixed number of individuals in the population, randomly selected, for solutions from the file. It is an elitist algorithm useful for obtaining competitive results in terms of both convergence and diversity of solutions along the *Pareto front*.

5.4 Metrics for Comparison

At least two performance metrics must be used when comparing algorithms for multiobjective optimization: one to evaluate the spread of solutions and another to assess the progress toward the Pareto-optimal front [18]. In this work, the metrics *Spread* and *Hypervolume* were used for comparing the performance of algorithms.

Spread [18] is used for evaluating diversity among non-dominated solutions. An ideal distribution has zero value for this metric. The first condition for this is there exists the true extreme Pareto-optimal solutions in the obtained set of non-dominated solutions. And the second is that the intermediate solutions are uniformly distributed. The closer to zero, better the distribution. An algorithm that achieves a smaller value for *Spread* can get a better diverse set of non-dominated solutions.

Hypervolume [18] provides a qualitative measure of convergence and diversity. In problems of minimization (all objectives must be minimized), it calculates the volume covered by members of the set of non-dominated solutions in the objective space. An algorithm finding a large value of this metric is desirable.

5.5 Representation of Results

In a multiobjective problem with two objectives, a two-dimensional objective space plot is used to show the performance achieved by the metaheuristics by illustrating the obtained non-dominated solutions. In the multiobjective problem modeled in this work, there are more than two objectives, for each approach, for each phase.

In a situation like that, when number of objectives is greater than two, a representation in a two-dimensional space is difficult and the obtained non-dominated solutions can be represented through several illustration techniques [18]. In this work, the scatter-plot matrix method [18] was applied.

6 Experiments, Results and Analysis

6.1 Experiments

Three different instances of problems were randomly generated and used to analyze the proposed approach in different contexts. The datasets are used as a mean of simulating a generic context. Therefore, without loss of generality, the instances represent a practical application scenario, and its use with the aiming of analysis of the proposed approach is valid.

The values for $risk_i$,$value(m,i)$, $priority(m,i)$ were generated according to the scales defined. The values for $cost_i$, $time_i$ and w_m were randomly generated using scales from 10 to 20, 10 to 20 and 1 to 10, respectively. The values for $timeProject$ and $budgetProject$ were considered as 70% of the necessary resources to implement all requirements. The other values (range of resources necessary for each release) were also randomly obtained. Matrices of interdependencies were randomly generated according to the kinds of relationships defined in subsection 3.2, with 10% of interdependencies. Table 1 shows the attributes of each instance.

Table 1. Description of the instances

Instance Name	Requirements	Stakeholders	Releases (consensual value)
InstanceA	30	3	5
InstanceB	50	5	10
InstanceC	80	8	6

To solve the problem formulated, the metaheuristics NSGA-II and MOCell were applied. The parameters used for each method were set from execution of preliminary tests and are showed in table 2 below.

Table 2. Parameter Settings

Parameter / Metaheuristic	NSGA-II	MOCell
Population Size	250	256
Stopping Criteria (number of evaluations)	32,000	32,768
Crossover Rate	0,9	0,9
Mutation Rate (N – number of requirements)	$^1/_N$	$^1/_N$

The implementation for the proposed approach was performed using a known framework, called *jMetal* [19], which provides metaheuristics for multiobjective optimization, including NSGA-II and MOCell.

6.2 Results

In this work, the average and the standard deviation of two executions of the algorithms in each instance and in each approach were calculated. In addition to the *Spread* and *Hypervolume* metrics, the execution time was also computed (in milliseconds).

The results obtained in each instance for each approach are presented below. Because of space limitations, only some important graphics are presented.

Results for Release Planning with Undefined Number of Releases. The tables 3, 4 and 5 show the results for performance of the two algorithms for each instance using the metrics.

Table 3. Results for *Spread*

Instance Name	NSGA-II	MOCell
Instance A	1.875096	0.261888
Instance B	1.027938	0.275178
Instance C	0.488216	0.337055

Table 4. Results for *Hypervolume*

Instance Name	NSGA-II	MOCell
Instance A	0.320515	0.288779
Instance B	0.335314	0.291431
Instance C	0.407802	0.400079

Table 5. Results for Execution Time (in milliseconds)

Instance Name	NSGA-II	MOCell
Instance A	6247.755725	1415.790476
Instance B	4463.549180	3264.715517
Instance C	8721.25	6798.402515

The graphs below show the results for the execution of the two algorithms in the instances. Figure 1 shows results for the instance A, where the two algorithms have found diverse solutions. This has also happened in the instances B and C, which have their results for this approach respectively shown in Figure 2 and Figure 3.

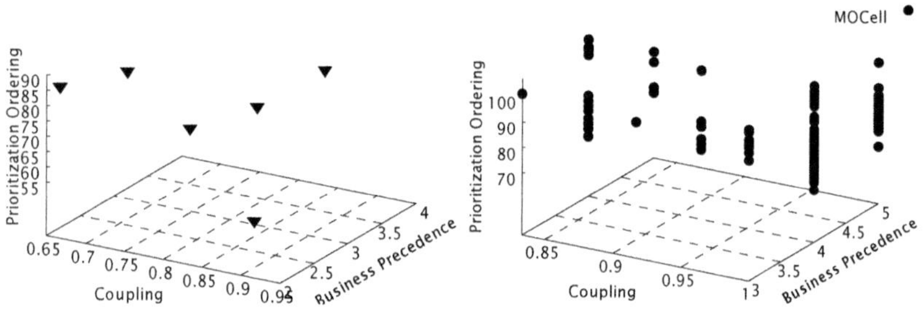

Fig. 1. Results for Instance A in the first approach

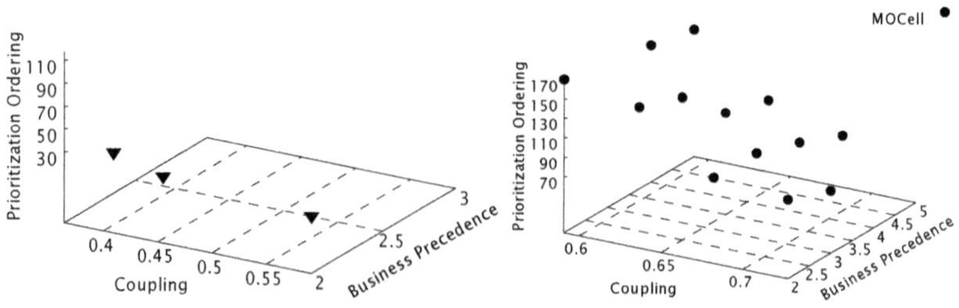

Fig. 2. Results for Instance B in the first approach

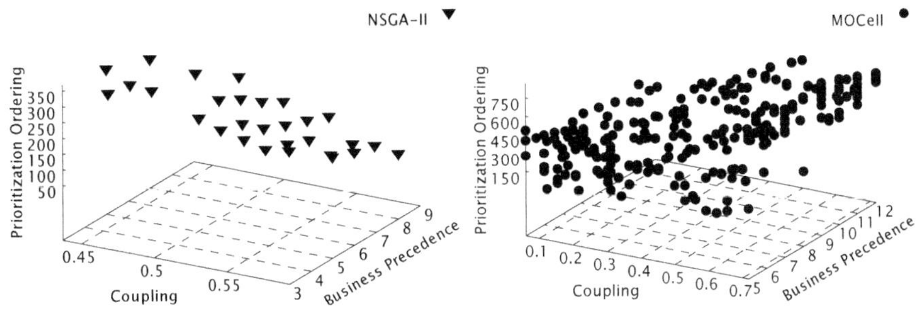

Fig. 3. Results for Instance C in the first approach

Results for Release Planning with Expected Number of Releases. Tables 6, 7 and 8 show the results for performance metrics of the algorithms in each instance.

Table 6. Results for *Spread*

Instance Name	NSGA-II	MOCell
Instance A	1.876102	0.243523
Instance B	1.695456	0.441614
Instance C	1.612609	0.432743

Table 7. Results for *Hypervolume*

Instance Name	NSGA-II	MOCell
Instance A	0.224599	0.248997
Instance B	0.339315	0.535095
Instance C	0.302255	0.381188

Table 8. Results for Execution Time (in milliseconds)

Instance Name	NSGA-II	MOCell
Instance A	2893.175438	1473.625
Instance B	4539.538461	3933.222543
Instance C	6524.685393	6729.600798

Figures 4 and 5 show the results for both algorithms for instances B and C.

For this approach, few solutions were found, which demonstrates the complexity of the problem and thus an indication that your resolution manually would be inappropriate and inefficient. The results from the metrics in the metaheuristics indicate that both MOCell and NSGA-II have good results. This is confirmed by the better spread value in all instances for the MOCell, and the better value of hypervolume for NSGA-II. The execution time of MOCell has been show generally better.

6.3 Analysis

The figures 1, 2 and 3 show the solutions generated by the NSGA-II and MOCell metaheuristics in the instances A, B and C, respectively, for the first approach. As a result from the experiments, we can indicate that the use of both techniques is desired for this problem since the algorithms have found solutions in different areas. The plots also indicate that it is possible to choose a solution taking in account, for instance, the business-precedence wanted for the decision maker. By each possible value in this objective, there is a set of solutions optimized to the others objectives.

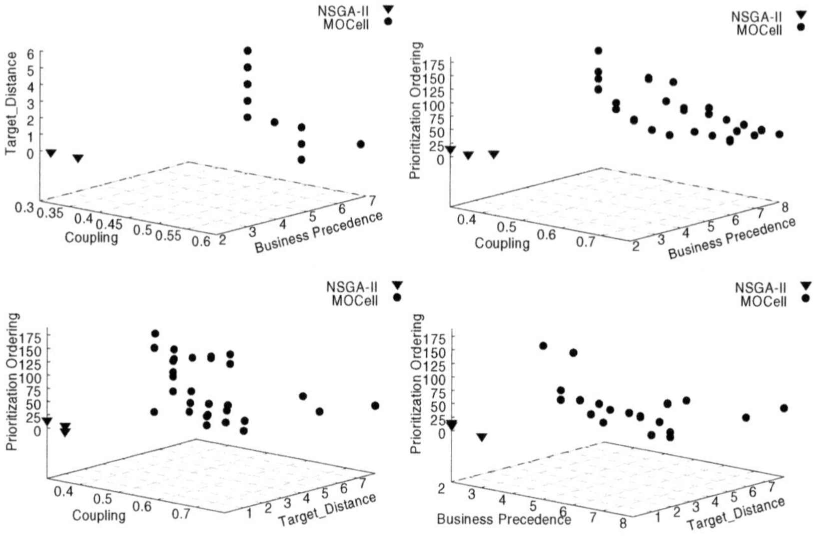

Fig. 4. Results for Instance B in the second approach

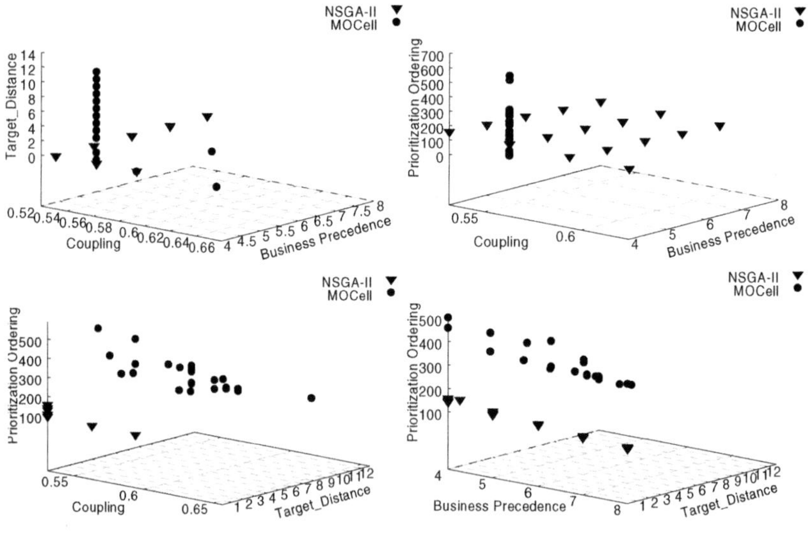

Fig. 5. Results for Instance C in the second approach

Additionally, we show next, in figures 4 and 5 the solutions to the second approach, which deals with expected number of releases. The formulation to this approach has four objectives. In order to be able to show the results in an effective way, we have decomposed the four-dimensional solution space in four tridimensional graphics. These graphics allow a better visualization of the solutions, regarding different combinations of the objectives. In addition, information in the graphs is combined referent to the original solutions.

7 Conclusions

According to [8], three things must be taken into consideration when planning releases: the technical precedence intrinsic to requirements, the conflicting priorities established by the most important stakeholders and the balance between the necessary and available resources.

In this study, the Software Release Planning problem was addressed as completely as possible, considering different aspects in a way closer to real practice environment. Thus, the proposed approach has a broader applicability.

The problem was solved using elitist multiobjective evolutionary algorithms on artificial data. Since search techniques have been successfully applied to solve problems in Software Engineering, the alternative release plans generated provide better support for decision making.

One negative aspect of this work was the amount and size of the instances used. Although the approach has proved feasible in the context used, more experiments are necessary in order to generalize it. Thus, future work includes further analysis of these preliminary results and definition and evaluation of other instances and studies using real-world data sets.

References

1. Colares, F., Souza, J., Carmo, R., Padua, C., Mateus, G.R.: A New Approach to the Software Release Planning. In: Proceedings of the XXIII Brazilian Symposium on Software Engineering (SBES 2009), pp. 207–215. IEEE Computer Society, Fortaleza (2009)
2. Harman, M., Jones, B.F.: Search-Based Software Engineering. Information & Software Technology 43(14), 833–839 (2001)
3. Souza, J.T., Maia, C.L., Freitas, F.G., Coutinho, D.P.: The Human Competitiveness of Search Based Software Engineering. In: Proceedings of the 2nd International Symposium on Search Based Software Engineering (SSBSE 2010), pp. 143–152. IEEE, Benevento (2010)
4. Karlsson, J., Ryan, K.: A Cost-Value Approach for Prioritizing Requirements. IEEE Software 14(5), 67–74 (1997)
5. Saaty, T.L.: The Analytic Hierarchy Process. McGraw-Hill (1980)
6. Jung, H.-W.: Optimizing Value and Cost in Requirements Analysis. IEEE Software 15(4), 74–78 (1998)
7. Bagnall, A.J., Rayward-Smith, V.J., Whittley, I.M.: The Next Release Problem. Information and Software Technology 43(14), 883–890 (2001)

8. Greer, D., Ruhe, G.: Software Release Planning: An Evolutionary and Iterative Approach. Information & Software Technology 46(4), 243–253 (2004)
9. Ruhe, G., Saliu, M.O.: The Art and Science of Software Release Planning. IEEE Software 22(6), 47–53 (2005)
10. Saliu, O., Ruhe, G.: Supporting Software Release Planning Decisions for Evolving Systems. In: Proceedings of 29th Annual IEEE/NASA on Software Engineering Workshop (SEW 2005), pp. 14–26. IEEE Computer Society (2005)
11. Zhang, Y., Harman, M., Mansouri, S.A.: The Multi-Objective Next Release Problem. In: Proceedings of the 9th Annual Conference on Genetic and Evolutionary Computation (GECCO 2007), pp. 1129–1137. ACM, London (2007)
12. Carlshamre, P., Sandahl, K., Lindvall, M., Regnell, B., Dag, J.N.: An Industrial Survey of Requirements Interdependencies in Software Product Release Planning. In: Proceedings of the Fifth IEEE International Symposium on Requirements Engineering, pp. 84–91. IEEE Computer Society, Toronto (2001)
13. Saliu, M.O., Ruhe, G.: Bi-Objective Release Planning for Evolving Software Systems. In: Proceedings of the 6th Joint Meeting of the European Software Engineering Conference and the ACM SIGSOFT Symposium on the Foundations of Software Engineering, pp. 105–114. ACM, Dubrovnik (2007)
14. Zhang, Y.-Y., Finkelstein, A., Harman, M.: Search Based Requirements Optimisation: Existing Work and Challenges. In: Rolland, C. (ed.) REFSQ 2008. LNCS, vol. 5025, pp. 88–94. Springer, Heidelberg (2008)
15. Sommerville, I., Sawyer, P.: Requirements Engineering: A Good Practice Guide. John Wiley & Sons (1997)
16. Deb, K., Pratap, A., Agarwal, S., Meyarivan, T.: A fast and elitist multiobjective genetic algorithm: NSGA-II. IEEE Transactions on Evolutionary Computation 6(2), 182–197 (2002)
17. Nebro, A.J., Durillo, J.J., Luna, F., Dorronsoro, B., Alba, E.: MOCell: A Cellular Genetic Algorithm for Multiobjective Optimization. International Journal of Intelligent Systems 24, 726–746 (2009)
18. Deb, K.: Multi-Objective Optimization Using Evolutionary Algorithms. Wiley (2009)
19. Durillo, J.J., Nebro, A.J., Luna, F., Dorronsoro, B., Alba, E.: jMetal: a Java Framework for Developing Multi-Objective Optimization Metaheuristics. Technical Report: ITI 2006-10, University of Málaga (2006)

Cost Estimation of Web Applications through Knowledge Elicitation

Emilia Mendes

College of Information Technology, Zayed University
P.O. Box 19282, Dubai, U.A.E.
emilia_mendes@yahoo.com

Abstract. Objective – The objective of this paper is detail the use of tacit knowledge elicited from domain experts in the domain of Web effort estimation to build an expert-based Web effort model for a medium-size Web company In Auckland (New Zealand). Method – A single-company Web effort estimation model was built using Bayesian Networks (BN), using knowledge solely elicited from two domain experts who were experienced Web project managers. The model was validated using data from eleven past finished Web projects. Results – The BN model has to date been successfully used to estimate effort for numerous Web projects developed by this Company. Conclusions – Our results suggest that, at least for the Web Company that participated in the case study, the use of models that allow the representation of uncertainty, inherent in effort estimation, can outperform expert-based estimates. Thus far, another nine companies in New Zealand, and on in Brazil have also benefited from using Bayesian Networks, with very promising results.

Keywords: Web engineering, Web effort estimation, Expert-based effort models, Knowledge elicitation, Case studies.

1 Introduction

A cornerstone of Web project management is effort estimation, the process by which effort is forecasted and used as basis to predict costs and allocate resources effectively, so enabling projects to be delivered on time and within budget. Effort estimation is a very complex domain where the relationship between factors is non-deterministic and has an inherently uncertain nature. E.g. assuming there is a relationship between development effort and an application's size (e.g. number of Web pages, functionality), it is not necessarily true that increased effort will lead to larger size. However, as effort increases so does the probability of larger size. Effort estimation is a complex domain where corresponding decisions and predictions require reasoning with uncertainty.

Within the context of Web effort estimation, numerous studies investigated the use of effort prediction techniques. However, to date, only Mendes [7,8,9,10,11,12] investigated the explicit inclusion, and use, of uncertainty, inherent to effort estimation, into models for Web effort estimation. Mendes [7,8,9] built a Hybrid Bayesian Network (BN) model (structure expert-driven and probabilities data-driven), which presented significantly superior predictions than the mean- and median-based

R. Zhang et al. (Eds.): ICEIS 2011, LNBIP 102, pp. 315–329, 2012.

effort [8], multivariate regression [7,8,9], case-based reasoning and classification and regression trees [9]. Mendes [10], and Mendes and Mosley [12] extended their previous work by building respectively four and eight BN models (combinations of Hybrid and data-driven). These models were not optimised, as previously done in Mendes [7, 8, 9], which might have been the reason why they presented significantly worse accuracy than regression-based models. Finally, Mendes et al. [15], and Mendes [11] detail two case studies where expert-based Web effort estimation BN models were successfully used to estimate effort for projects developed by small Web companies in Auckland, New Zealand. This paper extends [11] by detailing further the process that was used to build the expert-based BN model, and its validation.

A BN is a model that supports reasoning with uncertainty due to the way in which it incorporates existing complex domain knowledge [5]. Herein, knowledge is represented using two parts. The first, the qualitative part, represents the structure of a BN as depicted by a directed acyclic graph (digraph) (see Fig. 1). The digraph's nodes represent the relevant variables (factors) in the domain being modelled, which can be of different types (e.g. observable or latent, categorical). The digraph's arcs represent the causal relationships between variables, where relationships are quantified probabilistically. The second, the quantitative part, associates a node conditional probability table (CPT) to each node, its probability distribution. A parent node's CPT describes the relative probability of each state (value); a child node's CPT describes the relative probability of each state conditional on every combination of states of its parents (e.g. in Fig. 1, the relative probability of Total effort (TE) being 'Low' conditional on Size (new Web pages) (SNWP) being 'Low' is 0.8). Each column in a CPT represents a conditional probability distribution and therefore its values sum up to 1 [5].

Once a BN is specified, evidence (e.g. values) can be entered into any node, and probabilities for the remaining nodes automatically calculated using Bayes' rule [17]. Therefore BNs can be used for different types of reasoning, such as predictive and "what-if" analyses to investigate the impact that changes on some nodes have on others [4].

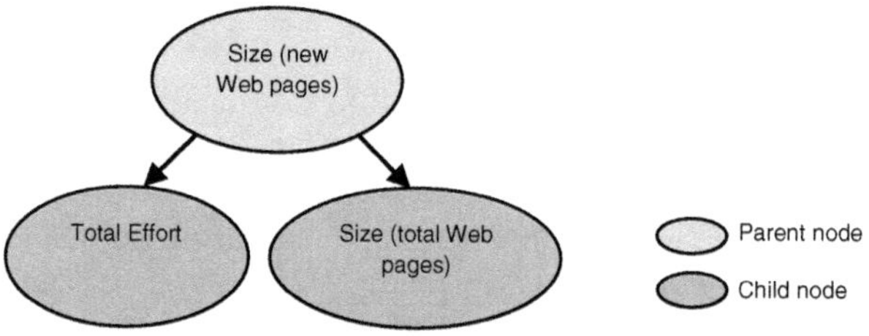

CPT for node Size (new Web pages)	
Low	0.2
Medium	0.3
High	0.5

CPT for node Total Effort (TE)			
Size (new Web pages)	*Low*	*Medium*	*High*
Low	0.8	0.2	0.1
Medium	0.1	0.6	0.2
High	0.1	0.2	0.7

Fig. 1. A small BN model and two CPTs

Within the context of Web effort estimation there are issues with building data-driven or hybrid Bayesian models, as follows:

1. Any dataset used to build a BN model should be large enough to provide sufficient data capturing all (or most) relevant combinations of states amongst variables such that probabilities can be learnt from data, rather than elicited manually. Under such circumstance, it is very unlikely that the dataset would contain project data volunteered by only a single company (single-company dataset). As far as we know, the largest dataset of Web projects available is the Tukutuku dataset (195 projects) [14]. This dataset has been used to build data-driven and hybrid BN models; however results have not been encouraging overall, and we believe one of the reasons is due to the small size of this dataset.

2. Even when a large dataset is available, the next issue relates to the set of variables part of the dataset. It is unlikely that the variables identified, represent all the factors within a given domain (e.g. Web effort estimation) that are important for companies that are to use the data-driven or hybrid model created using this dataset. This was the case with the Tukutuku dataset, even though the selection of which variables to use had been informed by two surveys [14]. However, one could argue that if the model being created is hybrid, then new variables (factors) can be added to, and existing variables can be removed from the model. The problem is that every new variable added to the model represents a set of probabilities that need to be elicited from scratch, which may be a hugely time consuming task.

3. Different structure and probability learning algorithms can lead to different prediction accuracy [12]; therefore one may need to use different models and compare their accuracy, which may also be a very time consuming task.

4. When using a hybrid model, the BN's structure should ideally be jointly elicited by more than one domain expert, preferably from more than one company, otherwise the model built may not be general enough to cater for a wide range of companies [12]. There are situations, however, where it is not feasible to have several experts from different companies cooperatively working on a single BN structure. One such situation is when the companies involved are all consulting companies potentially sharing the same market. This was the case within the context of this research.

5. Ideally the probabilities used by the data-driven or hybrid models should be revisited by at least one domain expert, once they have been automatically learnt using the learning algorithms available in BN tools. However, depending on the complexity of the BN model, this may represent having to check thousands of probabilities, which may not be feasible. One way to alleviate this problem is to add additional factors to the BN model in order to reduce the number of causal relationships reaching child nodes; however, all probabilities for the additional factors would still need to be elicited from domain experts.

6. The choice of variable discretisation, structure learning algorithms, parameter estimation algorithms, and the number of categories used in the discretisation all affect the accuracy of the results and there are no clear-cut guidelines on what would be the best choice to employ. It may simply be dependent on the dataset being used, the amount of data available, and trial and error to find the best solution [12].

Therefore, given the abovementioned constraints, as part of a NZ-government-funded project on using Bayesian Networks to Web effort estimation, we decided to develop several expert-based company-specific Web effort BN models, with the participation of numerous local Web companies in the Auckland region, New Zealand. The development and successful deployment of one of these models is the subject and contribution of this paper. The model detailed herein, as will be described later on, is a large model containing 37 factors and over 40 causal relationships. This model is much more complex than the one presented in [15], where an expert-based Web effort estimation model is described, comprising 15 factors and 14 causal relationships. This is the first time that a study in either Web or Software Engineering describes the creation and use of a large expert-based BN model. In addition, we also believe that our contribution goes beyond the area of Web engineering given that the process presented herein can also be used to build BN models for non-Web companies.

Note that we are not suggesting that data-driven and hybrid BN models should not be used. On the contrary, they have been successfully employed in numerous domains [21]; however the specific domain context of this paper – that of Web effort estimation, provides other challenges (described above) that lead to the development of solely expert-driven BN models.

We would also like to point out that in our view Web and software development differ in a number of areas, such as: Application Characteristics, Primary Technologies Used, Approach to Quality Delivered, Development Process Drivers, Availability of the Application, Customers (Stakeholders), Update Rate (Maintenance Cycles), People Involved in Development, Architecture and Network, Disciplines Involved, Legal, Social, and Ethical Issues, and Information Structuring and Design. A detailed discussion on this issue is provided in [13].

The remainder of the paper is organised as follows: Section 2 provides a description of the overall process used to build and validate BNs; Section 3 details this process, focusing on the expert-based Web Effort BN focus of this paper. Finally, conclusions and comments on future work are given in Section 4.

2 General Process Used to Build BNs

The BN presented in this paper was built and validated using an adaptation of the Knowledge Engineering of Bayesian Networks (KEBN) process proposed in [21] (see Fig. 2). Within the context of this paper the author was the KE, and two Web project managers from a well-established Web company in Auckland were the DEs.

The three main steps within the adapted KEBN process are the Structural Development, Parameter Estimation, and Model Validation. This process iterates over these steps until a complete BN is built and validated. Each of these three steps is detailed below, and presented in Fig. 2.

Structural Development: This step represents the qualitative component of a BN, which results in a graphical structure comprised of, in our case, the factors (nodes, variables) and causal relationships identified as fundamental for effort estimation of Web projects. In addition to identifying variables, their types (e.g. query variable, evidence variable) and causal relationships, this step also comprises the identification of the states (values) that each variable should take, and if they are discrete or continuous. In practice, currently available BN tools require that continuous variables be discretised by converting them into multinomial variables, also the case with the

BN software used in this study. The BN's structure is refined through an iterative process. This structure construction process has been validated in previous studies [3, 4, 6, 16, 21] and uses the principles of problem solving employed in data modelling and software development [19]. As will be detailed later, existing literature in Web effort estimation, and knowledge from the domain expert were employed to elicit the Web effort BN's structure. Throughout this step the knowledge engineer(s) also evaluate(s) the structure of the BN, done in two stages. The first entails checking whether: variables and their values have a clear meaning; all relevant variables have been included; variables are named conveniently; all states are appropriate (exhaustive and exclusive); a check for any states that can be combined. The second stage entails reviewing the BN's graph structure (causal structure) to ensure that any identified d-separation dependencies comply with the types of variables used and causality assumptions. D-separation dependencies are used to identify variables influenced by evidence coming from other variables in the BN [5, 17]. Once the BN structure is assumed to be close to final knowledge engineers may still need to optimise this structure to reduce the number of probabilities that need to be elicited or learnt for the network. If optimisation is needed, techniques that change the causal structure (e.g. divorcing [5]) are employed.

Parameter Estimation: This step represents the quantitative component of a BN, where conditional probabilities corresponding to the quantification of the relationships between variables [5, 17] are obtained. Such probabilities can be attained via Expert Elicitation, automatically from data, from existing literature, or using a combination of these. When probabilities are elicited from scratch, or even if they only need to be revisited, this step can be very time consuming. In order to minimise the number of probabilities to be elicited some techniques have been proposed in the literature [2, 3, 20]; however, as far as we are aware, there is no empirical evidence to date comparing their effectiveness for prediction, compared to probabilities elicited from scratch, using large and realistic BNs. This is one of the topics of our future work.

Model Validation: This step validates the BN that results from the two previous steps, and determines whether it is necessary to re-visit any of those steps. Two different validation methods are generally used - Model Walkthrough and Predictive Accuracy. Model walkthrough represents the use of real case scenarios that are prepared and used by domain experts to assess if the predictions provided by a BN correspond to the predictions experts would have chosen based on their own expertise. Success is measured as the frequency with which the BN's predicted value for a target variable (e.g. quality, effort) that has the highest probability corresponds to the experts' own assessment.

Predictive Accuracy uses past data (e.g. past project data), rather than scenarios, to obtain predictions. Data (evidence) is entered on the BN model, and success is measured as the frequency with which the BN's predicted value for a target variable (e.g. quality, effort) that has the highest probability corresponds to the actual past data. However, previous literature also documents a different measure of success, proposed by Pendharkar et al. [18], and later used by Mendes [7,9], and Mendes and Mosley [12]. This was the measure employed herein.

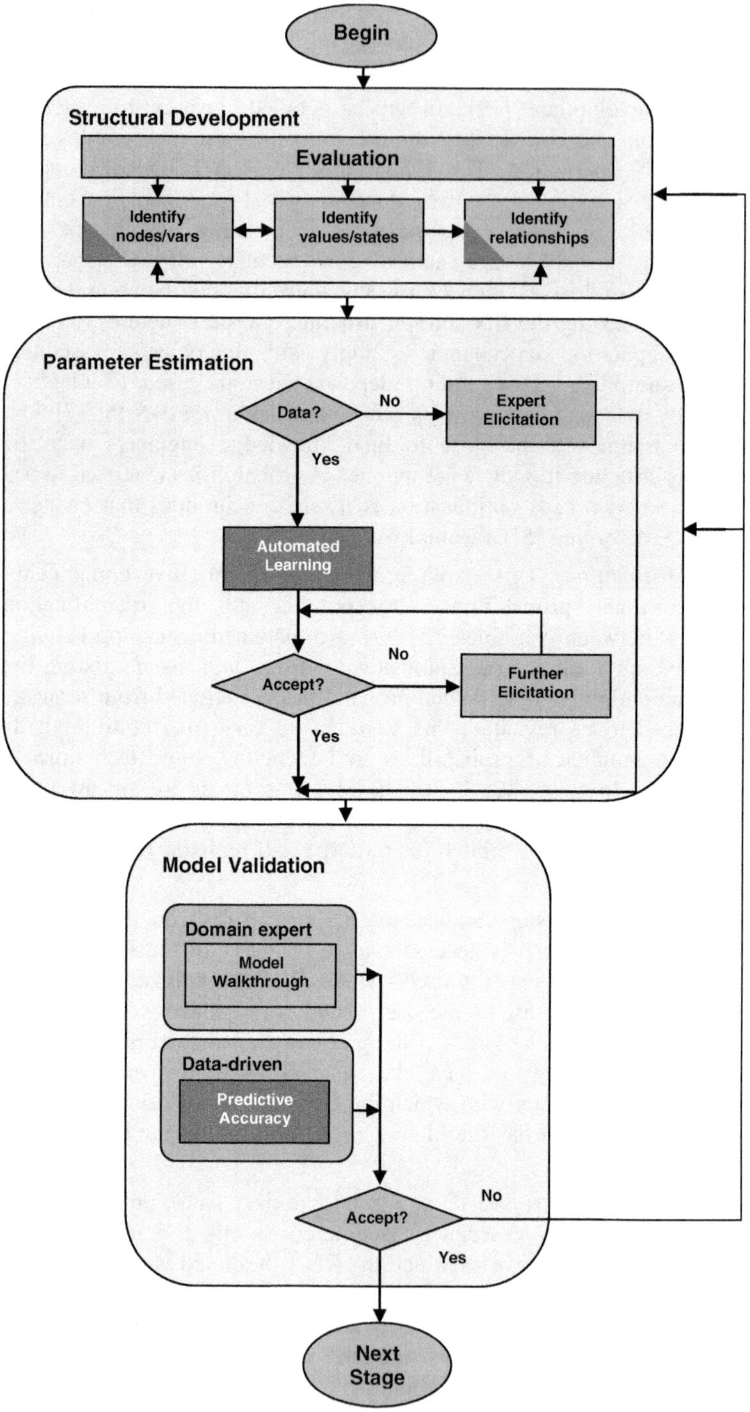

Fig. 2. KEBN, adapted from [21]

3 Process Used to Build the Expert-Based BNs

This Section revisits the adapted KEBN process, detailing the tasks carried out for each of the three main steps that form part of that process. Before starting the elicitation of the Web effort BN model, the Domain Experts (DEs) participating were presented with an overview of Bayesian Network models, and examples of "what-if" scenarios using a made-up BN. This, we believe, facilitated the entire process as the use of an example, and the brief explanation of each of the steps in the KEBN process, provided a concrete understanding of what to expect. We also made it clear that the knowledge Engineers were facilitators of the process, and that the Web company's commitment was paramount for the success of the process. The entire process took 54 person hours to be completed, corresponding to nine 3-hour slots.

The DEs who took part in this case study were project managers of a well-established Web company in Auckland (New Zealand). The company had ~20 employees, and branches overseas. The project managers had each worked in Web development for more than 10 years. In addition, this company developed a wide range of Web applications, from static & multimedia-like to very large e-commerce solutions. They also used a wide range of Web technologies, thus enabling the development of Web 2.0 applications. Previous to using the BN model created, the effort estimates provided to clients would deviate from actual effort within the range of 20% to 60%.

Detailed Structural Development and Parameter Estimation: In order to identify the fundamental factors that the DEs took into account when preparing a project quote we used the set of variables from the Tukutuku dataset [14] as a starting point (see Table 1). We first sketched them out on a white board, each one inside an oval shape, and then explained what each one meant within the context of the Tukutuku project. Our previous experience eliciting BNs in other domains (e.g. ecology) suggested that it was best to start with a few factors (even if they were not to be reused by the DE), rather than to use a "blank canvas" as a starting point. Once the Tukutuku variables had been sketched out and explained, the next step was to remove all variables that were not relevant for the DEs, followed by adding to the white board any additional variables (factors) suggested by them. We also documented descriptions for each of the factors suggested. Next, we identified the states that each factor would take. All states were discrete. Whenever a factor represented a measure of effort (e.g. Total effort), we also documented the effort range corresponding to each state, to avoid any future ambiguity. For example, 'very low' Total effort corresponded to 4+ to 10 person hours, etc.

Within the context of the Tukutuku project, a new high-effort feature/function requires at least 15 hours to be developed by one experienced developer, and a high-effort adapted feature/function requires at least 4 hours to be adapted by one experienced developer. These values are based on collected data.

Once all states were identified and documented, it was time to elicit the cause and effect relationships. As a starting point to this task we used a simple medical example from [5] (see Fig. 3). This example clearly introduces one of the most important points to consider when identifying cause and effect relationships – timeline of events. If smoking is to be a cause of lung cancer, it is important that the cause precedes the effect. This may sound obvious with regard to the example used; however, it is our view that the use of this simple example significantly helped the DEs understand the notion of cause and effect, and how this related to Web effort estimation and the BN being elicited.

Table 1. Tukutuku variables

	Variable Name	Description
Project Data	*TypeProj*	Type of project (new or enhancement).
	nLang	Number of different development languages used
	DocProc	If project followed defined and documented process.
	ProImpr	If project team involved in a process improvement programme.
	Metrics	If project team part of a software metrics programme.
	DevTeam	Size of a project's development team.
	TeamExp	Average team experience with the development language(s) employed.
Web application	*TotWP*	Total number of Web pages (new and reused).
	NewWP	Total number of new Web pages.
	TotImg	Total number of images (new and reused).
	NewImg	Total number of new images created.
	Num_Fots	Number of features reused without any adaptation.
	HFotsA	Number of reused high-effort features/functions adapted.
	Hnew	Number of new high-effort features/functions.
	TotHigh	Total number of high-effort features/functions
	Num_FotsA	Number of reused low-effort features adapted.
	New	Number of new low-effort features/functions.
	TotNHigh	Total number of low-effort features/functions

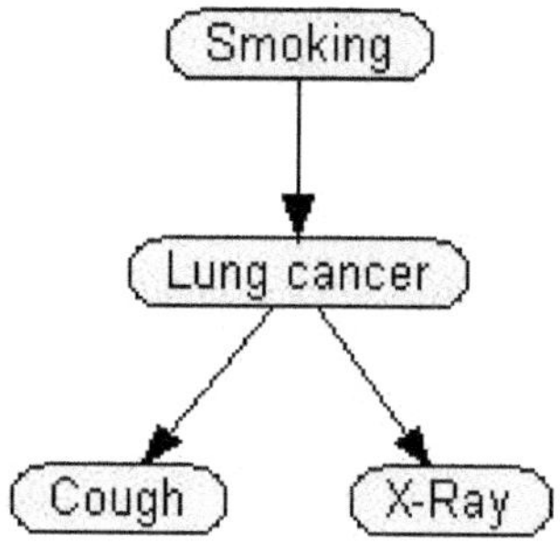

Fig. 3. A small example of a cause & effect relationship

Once the cause and effect relationships were identified, the original BN structure needed to be simplified in order to reduce the number of probabilities to be elicited. New nodes were suggested by the KE (names ending in '_O'), and validated by the Des (see Fig. 4). The DEs also made a few more changes to some of the relationships. At this point the DEs seemed happy with the BN's causal structure and the work on eliciting the probabilities was initiated. All probabilities were created from scratch, and the probabilities elicitation took ~24 hours. While entering the probabilities, the DEs decided to re-visit the BN's causal structure after revisiting their effort estimation process; therefore a new iteration of the Structural Development step took place. The final BN causal structure is shown in Fig. 4. Here we present the BN using belief bars rather than labelled factors, so readers can see the probabilities that were elicited. Note that this BN corresponds to the current model being used by the Web company (also validated, to be detailed next).

Detailed Model Validation: Both Model walkthrough and Predictive accuracy were used to validate the Web Effort BN model, where the former was the first type of validation to be employed. The DEs used four different scenarios to check whether the node Total_effort would provide the highest probability to the effort state that corresponded to the DEs' own suggestions. All scenarios were run successfully; however it was also necessary to use data from past projects, for which total effort was known, in order to check the model's calibration. A validation set containing data on 11 projects was used. The DEs selected a range of projects presenting different sizes and levels of complexity, where all 11 projects were representative of the types of projects developed by the Web company: five were small projects; two were medium, two large, and one very large.

For each project, evidence was entered in the BN model, and the effort range corresponding to the highest probability provided for 'Total Effort' was compared to that project's actual effort (see an example in Fig. 5). The company had also defined the range of effort values associated with each of the categories used to measure 'Total Effort'. In the case of the company described herein, Medium effort corresponds to 25 to 40 person hours. Whenever actual effort did not fall within the effort range associated with the category with the highest probability, there was a mismatch; this meant that some probabilities needed to be adjusted. In order to know which nodes to target first we used a Sensitivity Analysis report, which provided the effect of each parent node upon a given query node. Within our context, the query node was 'Total Effort'.

Whenever probabilities were adjusted, we re-entered the evidence for each of the projects in the validation set that had already been used in the validation step to ensure that the calibration already carried out had not affected. This was done to ensure that each calibration would always be an improved upon the previous one. Within the scope of the model presented herein, of the 11 projects used for validation, only one required the model to be re-calibrated. This means that for all the 10 projects remaining, the BN model presented the highest probability to the effort range that contained the actual effort for the project being used for validation. Once all 11 projects were used to validate the model the DEs assumed that the Validation step was complete.

The description of the factors that were part of the final expert-based BN model are shown in Table 2.

The BN model was completed in September 2009, and has been successfully used to estimate effort for new projects developed by the company. In addition, the two DEs changed their approach to estimating effort as follows: prior to using the BN model, these DEs had to elicit requirements using very short meetings with clients, given that these clients assumed that short meetings were enough in order to understand what the applications needed to provide once delivered. The DEs were also not fully aware of the factors that they subjectively took into account when preparing an effort estimate; therefore many times they ended up providing unrealistic estimates to clients.

Once the BN model was validated, the DEs started to use the model not only for obtaining better estimates than the ones previously prepared by subjective means, but also as means to guide their requirements elicitation meetings with prospective clients. They focused their questions targeting at obtaining evidence to be entered in the model as the requirements meetings took place; by doing so they basically had effort estimates that were practically ready to use for costing the projects, even when meeting with clients had short durations. Such change in approach provided extremely beneficial to the company given that all estimates provided using the model turned out to be more accurate on average than the ones previously obtained by subjective means.

Table 2. Factors, their Description and measures

Factor	Description	Measure
Number of Languages used in the content	Number of languages (e.g. English, Portuguese) in which content has been written	1, 2, 3+
Client's personality	Whether the client´s personality suggests someone with strong ideas, controlling, or unfocused –	good (have done part of the planning even before the project starts, willing to listen to alternatives), normal (average, no real effect, not proactive but also doesn't hinder), bad (totally unfocused, inconsistent)
Client's knowledge of the application domain	Whether a client has a clear idea of what they want to achieve, what the application needs to do	low, medium, high
Number of stakeholders involved	number of companies/people (client-side) involved in the process	single (1 person), low (2 to 3), high (4+)
Similarity to previous projects	Similarity between this and previous projects in relation to domain/functionality/design	high, medium, low
Quality of existing code being adapted/integrated	applies to code developed in house or by third party	known, unknown
Number of Features off the shelf being used	Features apply to features developed in house and also by third-party. Here each feature requires a very low/low effort to be adapted (30 minutes up to 6 features, then 1 hour total up to 9 features; 10+ would take 1 ½ hours, average of 5 minutes per feature).	(4-6) (7-9) (10+)
Number of Features[1] off the shelf being used that require adaptation	here each feature requires medium effort (~2 hours) to be adapted.	none,1,2,3,4,5
Number of High effort New Features[1] that need developing	Each feature takes ~15+ to 20 person/hours.	None,1,2,3,4,5
Number of Medium effort New Features[1] that need developing	Each feature takes between ~10 to 15 person/hours.	None,1,2,3,4,5
Number of Low effort New Features that need developing	Each feature takes around ~5 person/hours.	None,1,2,3,4,5

[1] Features within this context mean functionality (here they include the testing to work on each feature, but not the integration testing looking at the coupling between features).

Table 2. (*Continued*)

Deployment environment	if the application is being hosted by their company, or by a third party	us, others
Existing online presence	existing domain names, email addresses, websites that the client already has.	none, small, extensive
Number of different page types	Number of different Web page layouts.	(1-2) (3-6) (7+)
Amount of interaction in the application	Represents interaction in the application (to give immediate feedback on forms, how to present google maps etc)	none, low, medium, high
Level of Integration	relates to the level of coupling (interaction) bt. features, and how much will this impact on testing	none, low, medium, high
Deployment time	How quickly a client wants the site to be deployed. If they want it deployed quickly, it will generally result in more post-deployment work to optimise it.	short, normal
Quality of project management	Degree of involvement of the Project Manager, and also their skills (inexperience)	abysmal, low, normal, high
Team inexperience	Team's average experience with designing websites, with the languages used, with using the Web (browsing and awareness of what's possible)	none, low, medium, high
Number of third parties involved	Third parties can be sub-contractors, printing, SMS gateways, hosting providers, domain registration, payment providers, etc.	none, 1, 2, 3+
Third party inexperience		none, low, medium, high
Total Inexperience (O)		none, low, medium, high
Proposal Scoping effort	Effort needed to identify what the site is going to do - (technical requirements, marketing requirements (what the site owner will get out of it), user requirements (what the visitors will get out of it); should be a scope that complies with the available budget. No specification is generated, the scope is worked out by the project manager(s).	low (0+ - 1), medium (1+ to 2), high (2+ to 5), very high (5+).
Technical scoping effort	Effort to identify how the site is going to do what it has to do - (technical requirements); should be a scope that complies with the available budget. A specification should be generated	none, low (2-5%), medium (5%+to7%), high (7%+ to 10% of implementation effort).
Level of Technical scoping	level of project planning, technical requirements	low, normal, high

Table 2. (*Continued*)

Legacy browser support	If there is a need to ensure back compatibility with IE6 etc	yes, no (if Yes then it's 50% of presentation code effort)
Presentation code effort	Amount of effort to write html and javascript and css	easy (4 to 6 hours), normal (6+ to 10 hours), above average (10+ to 15), complex (15+ to 20), highly complex (20+ to 30 hours), very highly complex (30+ hours)
Compliance effort	Effort to make an application comply with what is needed.	none, normal (0+ to 7.5 person/hours), high (7.5+ to 20), very high (20+)
Compliance	For example, government websites have to comply with standard accessibility guidelines/etc, accessibility.	none, 1 (50% of presentation code effort), 2 (75% of presentation code effort)
Risk Factor	risk of increasing effort compared to the ideal effort.	None, low, medium, high, very high
Total effort		very low (4+ - 10), low (10+ - 25), medium (25+ - 40), high (40+ - 80), very high (80+ - 150), extremely high (150+)
Implementation effort		very low (4+ - 7), low (7+ - 15), medium (15+ - 30), high (30+ - 60), very high (60+ - 120), extremely high (120+)
Project management factor	This effort also includes the planning of the application.	low (10-15% of implementation effort), medium (15+to20% of implementation effort), high (20% to 25% of implementation effort), very high (25+% of implementation effort). PM also includes any training that needs to be done so staff get up to speed.
Integration effort		none, low (0+ - 2), medium (2+ - 8), high (8+)
Feature code effort		very low (0+-1 hour), low (1+-4), medium (4+-12), high (12+-30), very high (30+-80), extremely high (80+)
Total New Features Effort (O)		none, low (5+ - 12), medium (12+ - 25), high (25+ - 80), very high (80+)
Communication Overhead (O)		low overhead, normal, high overhead, very high overhead (not quantified as #hours)

Clients were not presented the model due to its complexity; however by entering evidence while a requirements elicitation meeting took place enabled the DEs to optimize their elicitation process by being focused and factor-driven.

We believe that the successful development of this Web effort BN model was greatly influenced by the commitment of the company, and also by the DEs' experience estimating effort.

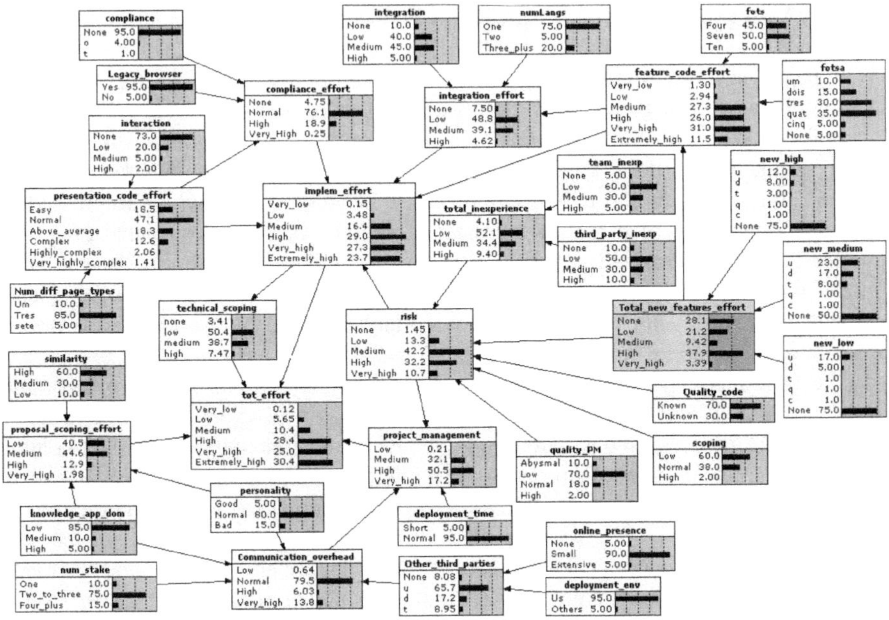

Fig. 4. Final expert-based Web effort BN model

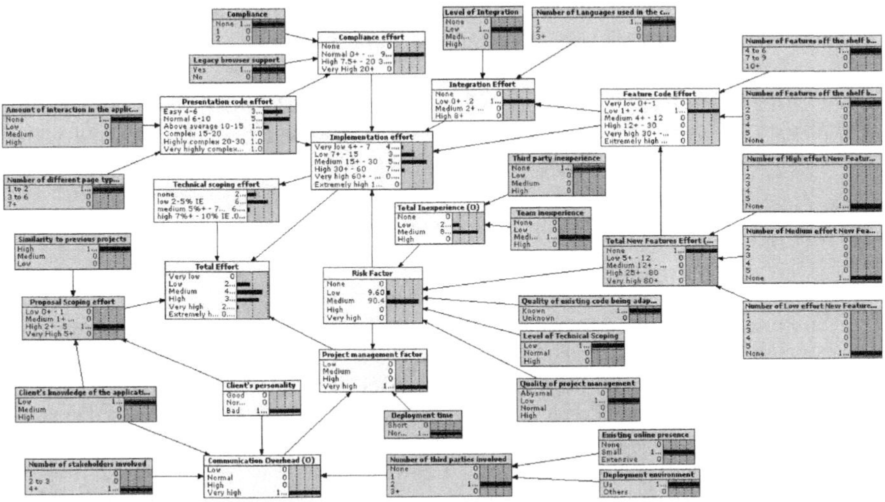

Fig. 5. Example of evidence being entered in the Web effort BN model

4 Conclusions

This paper has presented a case study where a Bayesian Model for Web effort estimation was built using solely knowledge of two Domain Experts from a well-established Web company in Auckland, New Zealand. This model was developed using an adaptation of the knowledge engineering for Bayesian Networks process. Its causal structure went through three versions, because as the work progressed the experts' views on which factors were fundamental when they estimated effort also matured. Each session with the DEs lasted for no longer than 3 hours. The final BN model was calibrated using data on eleven past projects. These projects represented typical projects developed by the company, and believed by the experts to provide enough data for model calibration.

Since the model's adoption, it has been successfully used to provide effort quotes for the new Web projects managed by the company.

The entire process used to build and validate the BN model took 54 person hours, where the largest amount of time was spent eliciting the probabilities. This is an issue to those building BN models from domain expertise only, and is currently the focus of our future work.

The elicitation process enables experts to think deeply about their effort estimation process and the factors taken into account during that process, which in itself is already advantageous to a company. This has been pointed out to us not only by the domain experts whose model is presented herein, but also by other companies with which we worked on model elicitations.

To date we have completed the elicitation of six expert-driven Bayesian Models for Web effort estimation and have merged their causal structures in order to identify common Web effort predictors, and causal relationships (Baker and Mendes, 2010).

Acknowledgements. We thank the Web company who participated in this case study, and also all the participating companies in this research. This work was sponsored by the Royal Society of New Zealand (Marsden research grant 06-UOA-201).

References

1. Baker, S., Mendes, E.: Aggregating Expert-driven causal maps for Web Effort Estimation. In: Proceedings of the International Conference on Advanced Software Engineering & Its Applications (2010) (accepted for publication)
2. Das, B.: Generating Conditional Probabilities for Bayesian Networks: Easing the Knowledge Acquisition Problem (2004), arxiv.org/pdf/cs/0411034v1 (accessed in 2008)
3. Druzdzel, M.J., van der Gaag, L.C.: Building Probabilistic Networks: Where Do the Numbers Come From? IEEE Trans. on Knowledge and Data Engineering 12(4), 481–486 (2000)
4. Fenton, N., Marsh, W., Neil, M., Cates, P., Forey, S., Tailor, M.: Making Resource Decisions for Software Projects. In: Proc. ICSE 2004, pp. 397–406 (2004)
5. Jensen, F.V.: An introduction to Bayesian networks. UCL Press, London (1996)
6. Mahoney, S.M., Laskey, K.B.: Network Engineering for Complex Belief Networks. In: Proc. Twelfth Annual Conference on Uncertainty in Artificial Intelligence, pp. 389–396 (1996)

7. Mendes, E.: Predicting Web Development Effort Using a Bayesian Network. In: Proceedings of EASE 2007, pp. 83–93 (2007)
8. Mendes, E.: The Use of a Bayesian Network for Web Effort Estimation. In: Baresi, L., Fraternali, P., Houben, G.-J. (eds.) ICWE 2007. LNCS, vol. 4607, pp. 90–104. Springer, Heidelberg (2007)
9. Mendes, E.: A Comparison of Techniques for Web Effort Estimation. In: Proceedings of the ACM/IEEE International Symposium on Empirical Software Engineering, pp. 334–343 (2007)
10. Mendes, E.: The Use of Bayesian Networks for Web Effort Estimation: Further Investigation. In: Proceedings of ICWE 2008, pp. 203–216 (2008)
11. Mendes, E.: Building a Web Effort Estimation model through Knowledge Elicitation. In: Proceedings of the 13th International Conference on Enterprise Information Systems, pp. 128–135 (2011)
12. Mendes, E., Mosley, N.: Bayesian Network Models for Web Effort Prediction: a Comparative Study. Transactions on Software Engineering 34(6), 723–737 (2008)
13. Mendes, E., Mosley, N., Counsell, S.: The Need for Web Engineering: An Introduction, Web Engineering, pp. 1–28. Springer (2005); Mendes, E., Mosley, N. (Eds.) ISBN: 3-540-28196-7
14. Mendes, E., Mosley, N., Counsell, S.: Investigating Web Size Metrics for Early Web Cost Estimation. Journal of Systems and Software 77(2), 157–172 (2005)
15. Mendes, E., Pollino, C., Mosley, N.: Building an Expert-based Web Effort Estimation Model using Bayesian Networks. In: Proceedings of the EASE Conference, pp. 1–10 (2009)
16. Neil, M., Fenton, N., Nielsen, L.: Building Large-scale bayesian networks. The Knowledge Engineering Review, KER 15(3), 257–284 (2000)
17. Pearl, J.: Probabilistic Reasoning in Intelligent Systems. Morgan Kaufmann, San Mateo (1988)
18. Pendharkar, P.C., Subramanian, G.H., Rodger, J.A.: A Probabilistic Model for Predicting Software Development Effort. IEEE Trans. Software Eng. 31(7), 615–624 (2005)
19. Studer, R., Benjamins, V.R., Fensel, D.: Knowledge engineering: principles and methods. Data & Knowledge Engineering 25, 161–197 (1998)
20. Tang, Z., McCabe, B.: Developing Complete Conditional Probability Tables from Fractional Data for Bayesian Belief Networks. Journal of Computing in Civil Engineering 21(4), 265–276 (2007)
21. Woodberry, O., Nicholson, A., Korb, K., Pollino, C.: Parameterising Bayesian Networks. In: Proc. Australian Conference on Artificial Intelligence, pp. 1101–1107 (2004)

PART IV

Software Agents and Internet Computing

Applying Conflict Management Process to Wiki Communities

Juliana de Melo Bezerra and Celso Massaki Hirata

Computer Science Department, Instituto Tecnologico de Aeronautica, S.J. Campos, Brazil
{juliana,hirata}@ita.br

Abstract. Conflicts are disagreements among members and imply incompatible goals, whishes and interests. Unhandled conflicts can negatively impact group performance and members' satisfaction. In virtual communities, members discuss when performing collaboratively online tasks so that conflicts can arise. Wiki communities are popular virtual communities that involve an expressive number of members for the online production of articles. Conflicts in wiki context are then critical, being responsible for damaging articles' quality and even wiki credibility. We propose a management process that includes activities for identification, analysis, response, and monitoring and control of conflicts for wiki communities. In order to explain the activities and evaluate the process, we use Wikipedia.

Keywords: Conflict analysis, Wiki community, Conflict management process, Conflict response mechanisms, Wikipedia, Wikis.

1 Introduction

Conflict is a disagreement, both manifest and latent, among members and implies incompatible goals and interests [28]. A conflict can have positive and negative impacts, which are in general concerned to group performance and members' satisfaction. Performance is mostly related to task quality and effectiveness. The positive effects of conflicts are related to the stimulation of members' creativity and innovation, and also to the quality improvement in decisions taken in group. The negative effects of conflicts occur when they produce tension and distract members from performing the task [3,10,19,22].

Conflicts are intrinsic to the life and dynamics of groups [22]. According to Preece [26], virtual community is a group of people, who come together for a purpose online, and who are governed by norms. In order to accomplish the online tasks collaboratively in virtual communities, members are in general involved in discussions, where conflicts can arise. The misunderstandings and divergences in discussion can be amplified in virtual communities, since they are likely to experience greater coordination and communication restrictions, due to the missing of context and social cues on online environments [8].

As conflicts are beneficial to virtual communities, the participation of members in discussions has to be stimulated. One way to do that is acting on members' motivation

R. Zhang et al. (Eds.): ICEIS 2011, LNBIP 102, pp. 333–348, 2012.

by designing appropriated motivation mechanisms, as described in literature [5,29]. If conflicts are managed properly, the virtual community can take advantage of the benefits of conflicts and reduce the negative impacts. So, a process of management conflicts in virtual communities is of interest.

A conflict can have one or more causes and, if happens, one or more impacts. Liu et al. [18] discuss about the human factors that contribute to conflicts in work groups, such as group diversity and conflict resolution styles. Conflict resolution styles refer to individual negotiation approaches that a member can have during a conflict [12]. Paul et al. [23] study the use of distinct conflict resolution styles during the decision-making processes in virtual teams. Kankanhalli et al. [15] propose that, besides the human factors, task characteristics also contribute to conflicts. The related work is mainly concerned about the factors that contribute to conflicts, which are useful for the identification of potential conflicts and their related causes in virtual communities in a complete conflict management perspective.

Wiki communities are virtual communities of online production groups, which generate, share, and make sense of information collaboratively in a distributed manner [16]. Wikis are used in distinct contexts, such as enterprise [9], education [20,34], collaborative software projects (eg. Second Life Wiki, and Eclipse Wiki), and e-government (eg. Intellipedia, and dKospedia). Depending on the context, there can be adaptations in using the wikis. Some wikis are private, particularly within enterprises and e-government. Others wikis are public, based on volunteering, and can allow registered users and unregistered users. The most prominent example of wiki communities is Wikipedia. Wikipedia is a free online encyclopedia driven by volunteer contributions, and it has been studied by many researchers due to its popularity.

The study of conflicts in wiki communities has attracted attention. Kittur and Kraut [16] suggest that conflicts in wikis communities depend not only on the number of contributors involved, but also on the density of members in an information space. Their measure for conflicts are the number of reverts in a wiki. A revert is to return the article to a previous version, and implicitly indicates task conflict. Viégas et al. [31] use a visualization method to study cooperation and conflict between authors of articles, by analyzing reverts in articles, which represent how competing perspectives negotiate their differences. We are particularly interested on the conflicts, including task and relationship conflicts [14] that arise during the discussions among members in wiki communities, and how the community manages them.

We propose a conflict management process for wiki communities, based on the risk management process designed for projects and described in PMBoK [27]. We argue that the process can be applied to wiki communities, in order to advance the quality of discussions, by considering an early recognition of conflicts and their causes, and an appropriate level of intervention. We believe that the proposed process is useful for designing new wiki communities and re-evaluating existent ones, in order to define and improve mechanisms of conflict response. This article extends the conflict management process for virtual communities proposed by Bezerra and Hirata [6] by both emphasizing the inputs, techniques and outputs of each activity in the process, and customizing to wiki communities.

The article is organized as follows. Section 2 presents the conflict management process for wiki communities. In Section 3, we apply the proposed process to

Wikipedia. Section 4 discusses the application of the process to Wikipedia and potential other wiki communities. Section 5 concludes our work and indicates future work.

2 Conflict Management Process for Wiki Communities

We conjecture that risk management processes as described in PMBoK [27] are a sound basis to the conflict management proposal. The reason is that conflict as well as risk is a situation that has to be planned before occur, in order to be correctly addressed. However, there are some differences. For instance, identifying conflicts depends on considering human factors, such as culture, experience, and members' behavior, which are essentially abstract factors. We conjecture that the activities of risk management are not that different for conflict management, and also that similar inputs, tools, techniques, and outputs can be used. We elaborate the customization on the descriptions of the conflict management activities.

The proposed activities for the conflict management process are: Identification of Conflicts and Causes, Analysis of Conflicts, Conflict Response Planning, and Monitoring and Control of Conflicts. The three first activities are concerned to planning; and the last activity is related to manifested conflicts that occur in community and they are generally handled according to the planning made before.

These activities interact among themselves and with other areas, for example the process that regulates the development and implantation of new technological features in community. Each activity can be assigned to a one or more members or groups inside the community. The activities are presented here as distinct entities; however they may overlap in practice. In the next sections, we explain each activity in the conflict management process.

2.1 Identification of Conflicts and Causes

The Identification of Conflicts and Causes activity determines which conflicts are likely to occur in a wiki community, and their potential causes. It is an interactive activity, because as the community evolves, new kinds of tasks and interactions among members can appear, which can lead to conflict situations. The participants of this activity can be community administrators, expert members on performing community activities, members already involved on handling conflicts in the community or with experience in other communities or contexts, and even a group of general members to share their particular perspective.

According Preece [26], four aspects build a virtual community, namely purpose, system, norms, and members. The four aspects are essential to identify conflicts in a wiki community. The inputs of the Identification of Conflicts and Causes activity are community goals, community type, community norms and procedures, community system, self-organization feature, learned lessons, and human and task factors that contribute to conflicts.

To be familiar to the community goals it is essential to understand the community culture and the context where conflicts may arise. The community type is a rich source of information regarding both the kind of membership and the motivations for members participate in community. Porter [25] proposes a typology for virtual communities, which applies to wiki communities, considering the establishment and relationship orientation. The establishment can be member-initiated or organization-sponsored. The relationship orientation includes social or professional for member-initiated communities; and commercial, nonprofit or government for organization-sponsored. Other typologies for virtual communities can be useful too, for example the one proposed by Markus [21] that takes into account distinct community orientations, such as relationship building, entertainment, and learning.

Norms regulate the people relationships and activities, and procedures detail the operational participation of members in order to guide the norms' accomplishment. So, community norms and procedures constitute other input for the identification of conflicts and related causes, because they allow the recognition of activities performed collaboratively in community, where members are involved in discussions and conflicts can happen. The community system is also useful in the identification of conflicts, because the system dictates how the activities are performed, so that they can amplify or mitigate possible cause of conflicts.

In self-organizing virtual communities [4,13], members are expected to participate not only in the execution of the community operational activities, but also in the definition of norms and in the execution of related procedures. So, there are other activities performed by members, wherein they are involved in discussions and conflicts can happen. Learned lessons are other input for the identification of conflicts and related causes. Ideally, the lessons are documents of the community itself about previous initiatives regarding conflict management, and they can also be results of conflict management in similar communities.

The last relevant input for the identification of conflicts and their related causes is to inquiry the human and task factors that contribute to conflicts. Human factors are characterized by group diversity and individual conflict behavior. Group diversity is defined as any attribute that people use to tell themselves that another person is different [24]. For example, demographic characteristics (such as age, sex, ethnicity, and education), differences in beliefs and preferences, psychological perceptions of interpersonal relationship [18]. Group diversity is intrinsic to virtual communities, because members can be from different countries or regions, and have distinct interests and experiences.

Other human factors are the individual behaviors under conflicts. It means the distinct forms of behavior that members involved in discussions can perform individually. The behavior aims, for instance, to avoid conflicts, find a compromised solution, and enforce one's own view on others. It is also known as conflict resolution styles [23, 30] or conflict management behaviors [18]. Due to group diversity and the chosen behavior, the way that members express themselves can lead to misunderstandings and aggravate the conflict.

Task factors include three main aspects: timing, subject and level. Timing is the timeline of the task being developed by members. There are some moments that are critical to the task accomplishment, requiring the involvement of members in discussions of important issues and decisions, so conflicts can happen. Depending on the subject being debated, conflicts are more likely to occur, for instance, polemic themes can easily generate controversy. Operational, procedural and normative are examples of task levels. Task level analysis is particularly interesting for the self-organizing virtual communities.

The techniques for Identification of Conflicts activity include the documentation analysis, and information gathering techniques. The documentation analysis refers to the study of the assets provided as inputs. Some information gathering techniques are to execute brainstorming with the participants of the activity, in order to capture a list of conflicts, which can the detailed later. Other technique to gather information is the interviews, using questionnaires previously designed by experts. Although the interaction in a wiki community is essentially online, the interviews can also be performed outside the community, for example using telephone calls and face meetings.

The main outputs of the Identification of Conflicts and Causes activity are a list with identified conflicts and a list of potential causes of these conflicts. There can also be generated a list with potential responses for the conflicts; although it is performed in detail later during the Conflict Response Planning activity.

2.2 Analysis of Conflicts

The Analysis of Conflicts evaluates the priority of the identified conflicts, considering both the probability of the conflict occurrence and the impact on community if the conflict occurs. It is a suitable approach for establishing focus for next activity, the Conflict Response Planning. There can be the need of reexamine the Analysis of Conflicts activity during the community's life cycle, because some conflicts can become less relevant due to maturity of the community and its members.

The inputs of the Analysis of Conflicts activity comprise the list of identified conflicts and related causes, and also learned lessons about the community itself and other communities. Other input can be the definition of probability and negative impact of a conflict. The conflict probability is related to the probability of occurrence of its causes. The negative impacts of a conflict in a wiki community can include the following: the quality reduction of community assets, the exposition of community credibility, the disturbance of members' trust on community, the reduction of members' participation, and even the loss of members.

Some techniques are used during the Analysis of Conflicts activity, for example the evaluation of probability and impact, and the matrix of probability and impact. The conflict evaluation through the probability and impact perspectives can be performed through interviews with expert members in community. In order to facilitate this evaluation, some levels for of probability and impact can be defined. There can be defined a relative scale of probability, including for example the levels *not probable*, *probable* and *high probable*. It is also possible to use numeric probabilities. The scale about impact has to reflect its importance, and it can also be relative or numeric. The matrix of probability and impact is useful to combine the scales of these two factors with the priority classification of the conflict (for example, low, medium and high priorities). PMBoK [27] suggests a matrix of probability and impact that can be adopted for prioritizing conflicts.

The output of this activity is classification of the conflicts according to their priority. Conflicts with high and medium priorities are addressed during the next activity of the Conflict Management Process, aiming to identify some suitable responses. Conflicts with low priority can be registered to be revised later.

2.3 Conflict Response Planning

The Conflict Response Planning activity refers to the development of options and the determination of actions to handle conflicts. It deals with conflicts considering their priority. In general it is necessary to choose some suitable responses among all the possible ones. In case of wiki communities, it is expected that the mechanisms required some technological implementation, so the choice of the mechanism should also consider aspects regarding the implementation feasibility, such as time and cost of development. As a technological analysis has to be made, the group of participants in this activity can also be composed by system managers and developers.

The input of the Conflict Response Planning activity is essentially the prioritized list of conflicts with their causes. The output of this activity is to define suitable response mechanisms for the conflicts. In order to guide this definition, one technique is to reason about three approaches for conflict response, namely avoidance, transference and mitigation. Our proposal is based on the strategies for risk response in project management proposed in PMBoK [27].

The avoidance approach refers to the impediment of the emergence of conflicts. The transference approach is to assign to an entity, outside the wiki community, the negative impact of a conflict as well as the right to give to it a proper response. To mitigate a conflict, it is possible to act on the reduction of its probability and/or its impact. The reduction of the conflict probability is related to the reduction of the probabilities of the causes of the conflict. Mechanisms related to the reduction of conflict impact are associated to the assistance to members in conflicts to reach a conclusion, for instance there can be used facilitation, mediation, arbitration [17], and voting systems.

Depending on the severity of a conflict, a mechanism cannot be sufficient, so it is necessary to use other mechanisms. In this case it is important to make an analysis of coverage of the mechanisms with respect to conflicts as well as define an order of mechanisms in the community, in order to trigger the correct one for a particular situation.

2.4 Monitoring and Control of Conflicts

The Monitoring and Control of Conflicts activity deals with real instances of conflicts that occur in the wiki community. Monitoring refers to the detection of conflicts, and control consists in addressing the correct response to conflicts.

As inputs, the Monitoring and Control of Conflicts activity requires the list of potential conflicts and the planning made for their correct response. The response planning can be used faithfully or only as a reference in case of unexpected situations. Other inputs are the response mechanisms already implemented in community. The technique includes the tracking of manifested conflicts, in order to know their status and all the mechanisms used during its life cycle. Members have to be aware about the conflict mechanisms provided in community, in order to use them accordingly. The mechanisms have to work properly and to handle conflicts in an acceptable deadline. Not addressing conflicts properly and promptly can damage the members' trust in the community mechanisms. So, a desirable output of the Monitoring and Control of Conflicts activity is to provide a feedback about the mechanisms' effectiveness. Ineffective mechanisms should be improved, replaced, or even eliminated of the community.

3 Application of the Conflict Management Process to Wikipedia

In this section we apply the Conflict Management Process previously discussed to a wiki community, the Wikipedia. Wikipedia is a free online encyclopedia available in distinct languages. We used the English Wikipedia [32], the largest one, which contains more than 3.6 millions of articles.

3.1 Identification of Conflicts and Causes in Wikipedia

We identify conflict and causes in Wikipedia by analyzing the inputs suggested for this activity, namely, community goals, community type, community norms and procedures, community system, self-organization feature, and human and task factors that contribute to conflicts. Conflicts are known as disputes in Wikipedia.

The Wikipedia goal is to make a publicly editable encyclopedia, by allowing anyone to add or change content at any time on Internet. It is supported by a free and open software platform called MediaWiki. Wikipedia articles are written collaboratively by a large number of volunteers, who can be registered or not in the system. In order to assure the edit accountability, the IP address of the connected computer is always logged in the system. In case of a contribution of an unregistered member, it is signed with the respective IP address. The registered member has a username, which is used to sign his contributions. Members can choose usernames as real identity, or as pseudonyms to keep their anonymity. Wikipedia is a self-organizing community [4]. The fundamental principles by which Wikipedia operates are the *Five Pillars*. The Wikipedia community has developed many *policies* and *guidelines* to improve the encyclopedia, which constitute its norms and procedures.

We identify three main levels wherein conflicts may happen in Wikipedia: operational, normative, and procedural. The operational level is characterized by the articles' edition. During the articles' edition, there can be some discussions among members, which are held in the talk pages associated to the content pages. The talk page is a kind of discussion board, where members can debate aspects of the article, and determine which content is appropriate. The normative level is characterized by the discussion regarding the edition of norms. As norms are also implemented as wiki pages, the related discussions are held in the associated talk pages. The procedural level is characterized by the discussions of members when executing procedures, where there can be difficult cases to handle and consequently critical decisions to make.

In order to identify conflicts and related causes in Wikipedia in the operational level, we gather some cases reported in a mechanism called *Editor Assistance* [11]. It is mechanism to request feedback or advice from another editor with more experienced in community. It is also used to help in solving conflict cases. We select ten cases from November, 2010, and analyze the discussion that originates the conflict in the article's talk page. The eight studied conflict cases about the definition and maintenance of norms, we retrieve from the discussions about the *Civility* norm [7], which is an important standard of conduct that sets out that members should interact with consideration and respect. It is also one of the components of the *Five Pillars*.

The conflicts regarding the execution of procedures in Wikipedia are analyzed trough the discussions held in two boards: *Articles for Deletion* [2], which discusses if a page has to be deleted; and *Administrators' Noticeboard/Incidents* [1], which discusses cases about incorrect conduct of members, such as vandalism and uncivil behavior.

Table 1. Conflicts in Wikipedia

Id	Conflict
C1	Divergence between editors about the content of an article
C2	Divergence between editors about the presentation of an article
C3	Divergence between editor and administrator about the content of an article
C4	Divergence between editor and administrator about the presentation of an article
C5	Divergence regarding the decision to be taken during the execution of a procedure
C6	Divergence about the content of a norm
C7	Divergence about the presentation of a norm

Through the investigation of conflict cases in Wikipedia, we identified seven main conflicts, which are shown in Table 1. In the operational level, conflicts can occur frequently, because the members diverge about the content of the article being edited (C1). This kind of misunderstandings can happen between general members, but can also involve members in administrative positions (C3). We call administrator a member with any administrative function, which include the following roles in Wikipedia: *administrators*, *bureaucrats*, *stewards*, *checkusers*, *reviewers*, *account creators*, *oversighters*, and *rollbackers*. There can be also divergences in discussions in the procedure level, which characterize conflicts (C5). In the normative level, discussions about changes in the content of norms (C6) can generate conflicts, because norms affect substantially the community. For instance, one case reports divergences about a change of the way the blocking for incivility is performed. Other example of an inflamed conflict happens due to a criticism regarding the Civility norm. The conflicts C1, C3, and C6 comprise of divergences regarding content, however there are also divergences about the presentation of articles (C2 and C4) and norms (C7). The presentation includes text comprehension, text formatting, and organization of subsections.

Table 2. Causes of conflicts in Wikipedia

Id	Cause of conflicts
CA1	Missing of explanation about taken actions
CA2	Distinct interpretations about contents
CA3	Distinct interpretations about norms
CA4	Difficult to explain the issue to be discussed
CA5	Lack of context
CA6	Persistence when expressing opinion
CA7	Difficult to express an opinion
CA8	Missing explanation about an opinion
CA9	Missing member identification
CA10	Incorrect use of emphasis
CA11	Personal attacks and judgments
CA12	Critical timing of task accomplishment
CA13	Polemic subjects

The investigation of the conflict cases in Wikipedia leads us to identify also causes of conflicts in Wikipedia, which are listed in Table 2. For this identification we use the background regarding the human and task factors that can contribute to conflicts. Discussions about the identified causes are provided below.

Members often complain when someone else reverts or changes what they have made without making clear the reason (CA1). Conflict can happen due to differences in interpretation of the issue (CA2). It can be explained by the group diversity factor that impacts the understanding of contents, due to ambiguities in text, cultural singularities in language, and differences of members' experiences. In Wikipedia, it can also be verified regarding the interpretation of norms (CA3). Other causes of conflicts are related to problems to specify an adequate name for the topic under discussion (CA4) to reflect the real issue to be handled, and also to provide context (CA5) about the issue, such as initial proposal and its benefits.

To express persistently the same opinion (CA6) can be perceived by other members as a competing behavior and negative reactions can occur, which generates conflicts. It can be difficult to understand ones' opinion (CA7) without reading all the conversation, especially if the sentence mentions some particular point of the conversation. So, some misunderstandings can occur, consequently contributing to conflicts. Besides a member correctly expresses an opinion during a discussion, it is desired that he explains his point of view (CA8). The explanation of opinion can enrich the discussion, by giving additional information. It can help to reduce conflicts, because an opinion without a reason can be interpreted as a tentative to impose someone's view in a competing behavior.

Conflicts occur among members. It is important for members to know the contributions of each participant of the conflict, in order to be able to analyze the distinct views and form an opinion. So, the correct identification of the contributions is desired (CA9). The heated discussions, characterized by personal attacks and judgments (CA11), are particularly related to conflicts, because they are used to criticize, offend and expose members. The use of emphasis, such as capital letters, italic format and quotation marks, in written language can contribute to conflicts, when they are used to express negative feelings (CA10). For example, a sentence in capital letter can be understood as a scream, and the italic format can express angry. The use of emphasis is not always harmful, for example capital letters can be used to write an abbreviation, and quotation marks can be used to identify the name of an article section.

To reason about the timing factor (CA12) in Wikipedia conflicts, it is possible to investigate the number of archived discussions regarding an article according its life cycle. The high number of discussions and comments in discussions indicates possible conflicts during a period. Other possibility is to observe the number of visualizations of a page [33]. Peaks in visualization can inform critical moments when the article content has to be well elaborated, so there can be associated discussions during this intense elaboration. In Wikipedia, the task subject factor is represented by the article subject. There can be conflicts when members discuss about any subject, for example the analyzed conflict cases are about distinct topics, such as games, politics, music, and place. However, there can be a high number of conflicts about specific subjects, in general polemic subjects (CA13) as politics, religion, and war.

With the conflicts and causes identified, we can proceed to the next activity of the Conflict Management Process.

3.2 Analysis of Conflicts in Wikipedia

The objective of this activity is to evaluate the probability and impact of each conflict, identified in Table 1, in order to define its priority in Wikipedia. To evaluate the probability of a conflict in Wikipedia, we can evaluate the probability of its causes. It is a possible technique, since a conflict can have many causes with distinct criticality. However, it is not a trivial task due to the correlation among the causes. To evaluate the impact of a conflict, we firstly identify the following impacts in Wikipedia context: the reduction of article quality, the decrease of community credibility, the decrement of new members' entrance, the reduction of confidence and admiration of members on community, the reduction and even cessation of members' participation, and the loss of members.

We adopt the matrix of probability and impact proposed by PMBOK, because it already includes the scales for both aspects and the priority classification. The result is shown in Table 3. For each conflict, the probability is indicated according to the horizontal scale, the impact is assigned according to the vertical scale, and priority is given by the colored zones: high priority (hard gray), medium priority (light gray) and low priority (medium gray).

Table 3. Analysis of conflicts in Wikipedia

Probability	**0.90**				C1	
	0.70					
	0.50		C2	C3, C5		
	0.30		C4, C7		C6	
	0.10					
		0.05	**0.10**	**0.20**	**0.40**	**0.80**
	Impact					

The conflict C1 is very probable considering the number of contributors, because many members are involved in the edition of contents, which is the main activity in Wikipedia. C1 has a considerable impact, due to the direct relation with the quality of articles, and consequently with the credibility of the community. Besides, C1 can impact members' motivation to contribute.

The conflict C3, although similar to C1, has an important difference that is the involvement of an administrator in the conflict. This kind of conflict occurs mainly because a general member does not agree with the attitude or guidance of the administrator. The impact of C3 is the decrease of confidence of members on the community, because general members see administrators as community representatives.

In discussions of the procedure level, it is common for the members to express an opinion in a clear way using statements, as *oppose* and *support*, for the initial proposal. This practice helps to reduce the probability of the conflict C5. The impact of C5 is related to the confidence of members on the decisions made during the procedure execution.

We consider a low probability for conflict C6 due to the high maturity of the community, which already has established its norms. However, the associated impact is very high, because modification of norms can configure a significant change in the way the community operates, so conflicts regarding this topic are critical. The conflicts C2, C4, and C7, regarding the presentation of articles and norms can occur, however they have low impact to the task quality. The low impact contributes to the low priority of these conflicts.

The next section details the forms to respond to conflicts in Wikipedia.

3.3 Conflict Response Planning in Wikipedia

In this activity, we identify the existent mechanisms of conflict response in Wikipedia, according to the three possible approaches: avoidance, transference and mitigation. It is important to explain that in Wikipedia the mechanisms can be applied for any kind of conflict.

Regarding the avoidance approach, we identify a mechanism called *Page Protection*. It restricts the editing of a page. There are many kinds of protection; one of them is regarding the content disputes. By eliminating new editions in articles, the mechanism prevents disagreements among members and consequently avoids conflicts. Protection can be indefinite, or expire after a specified time. It is important to note that an adopted mechanism may have other consequences on the community. For instance, in the *Page Protection* case, other members who are not involved in the conflict may not agree with the adopted mechanism, because they desire to contribute to the article while the editions are blocked.

No mechanism is identified about the transference approach in Wikipedia. However, we believe that, if a conflict involves serious threats, such as death threats, some justice entity outside the wiki community can be called to investigate the case.

The mitigation approach includes the mitigation of conflict probability and the mitigation of conflict impact. In Wikipedia some actions are perceived aiming to decrease the probability of conflicts by addressing the causes of conflicts. One example is the existence of specialized boards, called *WikiProjects*, to discuss critical themes (CA13). Other example is that some expert members help general members with the article edition, trying to improve content and assure quality. These expert members have more experience in Wikipedia and can contribute to the interpretation of general contents (CA2) and norms (CA3).

Regarding the mitigation of conflict impact, one example of mechanism is to inform the community the status of a task that is under conflict using *Templates*, in a way to indicate its reliability. The templates have associated symbols and notes. Some examples are: *POV* (Symbol: balance. Note: *The neutrality of this article is disputed*), and *Pp-dispute* (Symbol: lock. Note: *This page is currently protected from editing until disputes have been resolved*). Other mechanisms that address the conflict impact include: *Editor Assistance*, *Third Opinion*, *Request Comments*, *Mediation Cabal*, *Mediation Committee* and *Arbitration*. Each mechanism has its own characteristics, which defines how cases are accepted and dealt. Depending on the severity of the conflict, multiple mechanisms can be applied in an ordered way. For example, *Third Opinion* mechanism is indicated to disputes between two editors with observance of good faith and civility. Other example is *Arbitration* mechanism, which is the last step of dispute resolution on Wikipedia, and has the authority to impose binding solutions to disputes between editors.

3.4 Monitoring and Control of Conflicts in Wikipedia

In this section, we discuss how conflicts can be monitored and controlled in Wikipedia, using the mechanisms presented in the previous section.

When a conflict arises in Wikipedia and cannot be handled by the involved members, some member requests the use of a mechanism. So, there is no automatic detection in the monitoring phase in Wikipedia.

Regarding the control of conflicts in Wikipedia, frequently the own members are aware of the adequate mechanism to help them during conflicts. There is a page called *Dispute Resolution* that explains how to avoid conflicts during discussions and also presents the mechanisms of negotiation, mediation and arbitration. One concern is that sometimes members are really confused about which is the suitable mechanism to manage the current conflict, which may lead to more discontentment for them. It is a concern especially for new members, who can have doubts about how to resolve a conflict and can trigger the wrong mechanism.

Conflicts can lead to a deadlocked situation where members of same level are not able to break it. In this situation, if a higher instance response mechanism exists, it should be employed. For this, members should agree on resorting to higher level mechanism to resolve their dispute. In general, an administrator informs the members involved in conflict that a higher mechanism is necessary. The involved members may have to submit the case again to the new mechanism. The problem is that it may require extra discussion and can generate new conflicts.

The tracking of a conflict refers to be aware about the mechanisms applied to the conflict and also how the mechanisms addressed them. This tracking may be difficult in Wikipedia, in the way that mechanism assistants may have doubts about the real situation of conflicts.

4 Conflict Management Process Applied to Wikipedia: An Evaluation

The Identification of Conflicts and Causes activity was performed by retrieving the perspective of Wikipedia members through the conflict cases reported in community. The direct participation of the community members in this activity would enhance the identified topics, especially regarding the causes of conflicts, because members would provide their particular view about the conflicts' motivations.

It is desired, as output of the Identification of Conflicts and Causes activity, the association between conflicts and causes, in a way to recognize the particular causes of each conflict. For Wikipedia, we provide a list of causes without this association, due to the fact that all identified causes can lead to all conflicts, however with distinct importance. We believe that it is a particularity of wiki communities, because the tasks performed in the community are mainly related to the collaborative online edition.

Although the identified conflicts and causes are for a particular community, the Wikipedia, we believe that they are quite general and can be used as suggestions for the conflict management of other wiki communities. Many wikis communities, especially the ones driven by volunteers, are influenced by the norms and conventions developed in Wikipedia [16], in this case, the list of conflicts and causes can be convenient. Depending on the wiki community goal, the subjects of the produced articles may not include polemic themes, so the cause CA13 may not be applied. The self-organization feature is not observed in some wiki communities, for example the private ones sponsored by enterprises or e-government, so the conflicts C5, C6 and C7 may not be applied, and conflicts C3 and C4 may have their priority reduced.

The Analysis of Conflicts activity is not a trivial activity, because it needs a considerable understanding of the members' roles, community work, and experience of the responsible to perform this activity with conflict management. So, it may require the assistance of experts in community. The provided analysis is limited for Wikipedia since it reflects our interpretation about the conflicts in this community.

The Conflict Response Planning activity helps the identification of the existent mechanisms in Wikipedia. It was expected to find mechanisms specific for each kind of conflict; however we found that the Wikipedia mechanisms can actually address all the identified conflicts in an indistinct way. The application of the mechanisms varies according the conflict priority, and it is important is that the mechanisms cover all kinds of relevant conflicts that were identified.

We argue that some mechanisms can be proposed to mitigate the identified conflicts in Wikipedia by addressing the probability of the related causes. For instance, the explanation of a change performed by a member in a page could be required. Other mechanism can aim to regulate the use of personal pronouns and language emphasis, in order to detect and avoid cases of incivility, personal attacks and judgment. One concern about the last proposal is related to the natural language parsing, which is dependent of the idiom used in community, and also of group cultural aspects, for instance the use of regional expressions and abbreviations.

The investigation about the Monitoring and Control of Conflicts activity in Wikipedia leads to some findings. There can be designed mechanisms to facilitate the automatic detection of conflicts in Wikipedia, considering metrics as number of comments in discussions and usage history of members. The tracking of a conflict during its life cycle in Wikipedia can also be improved. It is expected that the conflict response mechanisms in wikis be more automatic; however, as conflict resolution is dependent of human analysis, the analysis of the manifested conflicts and the effect of the related mechanisms should be necessarily performed by humans.

The adoption of mechanisms can raise some problems in wiki communities. One concern is related to the availability of members to develop and maintain the mechanisms. It may be difficult especially in communities composed by volunteers. Other problem is related to the mechanism technological performance, since the new implementation should not impact negatively the operation of the current tasks in the wiki community.

Considering the existing wiki communities, we believe that Wikipedia is mature in terms of conflict management. The community has designed many mechanisms to address conflicts and there are several volunteers administrating such mechanisms. It perhaps explains partially the Wikipedia success.

5 Conclusions

During discussions in wiki communities, conflicts can arise due to divergences among members. Conflicts are part of communities' life and are more likely to occur in wiki communities, due to the communication restrictions and the expressive number of members involved. As unhandled conflicts can impact negatively, we proposed a conflict management process for wiki communities. The process is composed by activities considering the identification and prioritization of conflicts, the response planning for the critical conflicts, and the monitoring and control of conflicts when they occur in community. As new situations can occur due to the community evolution, generating new kinds of conflicts not already identified, it can be necessary to review the planning and adapt response mechanisms along the community life cycle.

The proposed process was then applied to Wikipedia. We believe that wiki communities may benefit themselves by applying the proposed process, especially the communities driven by volunteers, where unhandled conflict may contribute to the reduction of members' motivation and lead to their leaving of the community. As future work, we intent to apply the proposed process to other communities, such as Wikipedia in other languages, private wikis, and even virtual communities not based on wikis.

The investigation about Wikipedia leads us to some future work, which includes the study of automatic mechanisms to both reduce the probability of occurrence of conflicts and detect conflicts during the monitoring activity. Other work is related to the evaluation of the efficiency of the existent conflict response mechanisms in Wikipedia. We are interested in understanding the members' concerns about the mechanisms in order to propose improvements.

The reputation conquered in a wiki community can impact on the reduction of conflicts, because a member in general respects the position of other reputed member and does not contest his opinion. The reputation is assigned to members as result of motivation mechanisms in community. So, an interesting research topic is to study the relation between the motivation mechanisms and the conflict response mechanism. Other aspect to study is when the reputation is not conquered inside the wiki community, but it is inherent from the real life, in the case that members know each other physically, but also interact online using the wiki community.

References

1. "Administrators' Noticeboard/Incidents" procedure. Wikipedia, `http://en.wikipedia.org/wiki/Wikipedia:ANI`
2. "Articles for deletion" procedure. Wikipedia, `http://en.wikipedia.org/wiki/Articles_for_deletion`
3. Amason, A.C.: Distinguishing the effect of functional and dysfunctional conflict on strategic decision making: resolving a paradox for top management teams. Academy of Management Journal 39, 123–148 (1996)
4. Bezerra, J.M., Hirata, C.M.: Self-Organization of Virtual Communities: Need and Members' participation. In: 7th International Conference on Web Information Systems - WEBIST (2011)
5. Bezerra, J.M., Hirata, C.M.: Motivation and Its Mechanisms in Virtual Communities. In: Vivacqua, A.S., Gutwin, C., Borges, M.R.S. (eds.) CRIWG 2011. LNCS, vol. 6969, pp. 57–72. Springer, Heidelberg (2011)

6. Bezerra, J.M., Hirata, C.M.: Conflict Management Process for Virtual Communities. In: 13th International Conference on Enterprise Information Systems - ICEIS (2011)
7. Civility norm. Talk page. Wikipedia, http://en.wikipedia.org/wiki/Wikipedia_talk:Civility
8. Cramton, C.D.: The mutual knowledge problem and its consequences for dispersed collaboration. Organization Science 12(3), 346–371 (2001)
9. Cunha, D.A.F.G., et al.: Organizational Wikipedia. In: IADIS International Conference WWW/Internet (2010)
10. De Dreu, C.K.W., Weingart, L.R.: Task versus relationship conflict, team performance and team satisfaction: a meta-analysis. Journal of Applied Psychology 88, 741–749 (2003)
11. Editor Assistance Request. Wikipedia, http://en.wikipedia.org/wiki/Wikipedia:Editor_assistance/Requests
12. Foundation Coalition: Understanding Conflict and Conflict Management (2010), http://www.foundationcoalition.org
13. Fuchs, C.: The Self-Organization of Virtual Communities. Journal of New Communications Research 1(1) (2006)
14. Jehn, K.A.: A multimethod examination of the benefits and detriments of intragroup conflict. Administrative Science Quartely 40, 256–282 (1995)
15. Kankanhalli, A., Tan, B.C.Y., Bao, Y.: Conflict and performance in global virtual teams. Journal of Management Information Systems 23, 237–274 (2006)
16. Kittur, A., Kraut, R.E.: Beyond Wikipedia: coordination and conflict in online production groups. In: Computer Supported Cooperative Work (CSCW). ACM (2010)
17. Lewicki, R., Weiss, S., Lewin, D.: Models of conflict, negotiation and third party interventions: A review and synthesis. Journal of Organizational Behavior 13, 209–252 (1992)
18. Liu, Y., et al.: An Integrated Model of Group Diversity, Conflict and Outcomes: A Process-based Perspective. In: International Conference of Wireless Communications, Networking and Mobile Computing. IEEE (2008)
19. Mannix, E.A., Grifith, T., Neale, M.A.: The Phenomenology of Conflict in Distributed Work Teams. In: Hinds, P., Kiester, S. (eds.) Distributed Works. The MIT Press (2002)
20. Marks, A.: Students' Acceptance of E-group Collaboration Learning. In: 13th International Conference on Enterprise Information Systems - ICEIS (2011)
21. Markus, U.: Characterizing the virtual community, 5th edn. SAP Design Guild (2002)
22. Medina, F.J., Munduate, L., Dorado, M.A., Martínez, I., Guerra, J.M.: Types of intragroup conflict ad affective reactions. Journal of Managerial Psychology 20, 219–230 (2005)
23. Paul, S., et al.: Understanding Conflict in Virtual Teams: An Experimental Investigation using Content Analysis. In: 38th Hawaii International Conference on System Sciences. IEEE (2005)
24. Pelled, L.H.: Demographic diversity, conflict, and work group outcomes: an intervening process theory. Organization Science 16, 615–631 (1996)
25. Porter, C.E.: A Typology of Virtual Communities: A Multi-Disciplinary Foundation for Future Research. Journal of Computer-Mediated Communication - JCMC 10(1), article 3 (2004)
26. Preece, J.: Online Communities: Designing Usability, Supporting Sociability. Wiley, Chichester (2000)
27. PMBoK. Project Management Body of Knowledge. Project Management Institute (PMI). ANSI/PMI 99-001-2004 (2004)
28. Robbins, S.P.: Managing Organizational Conflict. Prentice Hall, Englewood Cliffs (1974)

29. Tedjamulia, S.J.J., et al.: Motivating Content Contributions to Online Communities: Toward a More Comprehensive Theory. In: 38th Hawaii International Conference on System Sciences. IEEE Press (2005)
30. Thomas, K.W., Kilmann, R.H.: Thomas-Kilmann Conflict Mode Instrument. Xicom, Tuxeco (1974)
31. Viégas, F.B., Wattenberg, M., Dave, K.: Studying cooperation and conflict between authors with history flow visualizations. In: Conference on Human Factors in Computing Systems (CHI). ACM (2004)
32. Wikipedia (English version), http://en.wikipedia.org
33. Wikipedia article traffic statistics, http://stats.grok.se/
34. Xu, W., Frezza, S.: A Case Study: Integrating a Game Application-driven Approach and Social Collaborations into Software Engineering Education. In: 13th International Conference on Enterprise Information Systems - ICEIS (2011)

Research on Grid-Based Mobile Business Process and Analysis on Process Simulation

Dan Chang and Li Si

School of Economics and Management,
Beijing Jiaotong University Beijing, 100044, P.R. China

Abstract. Since the emergence of mobile commerce, there have been much research and practice on how to improve wireless communication technology and safety technology, however, the research which integrated wireless technology and business processes of the original e-commerce is still in its early stage, lacking of systematic analysis and theoretical support regarding the information sharing, business collaboration, and effectively access of mobile devices in practice. In this paper, mobile business processes is the research object. On the basis of combing and analyzing the current mobile business process, utilizing the grid management theory construct mobile business process based on grid. Furthermore, a quantitative simulation will be made on non-grid and grid-based mobile business processes in order to prove the superiority of mobile business processes based on grid.

Keywords: Grid management, Mobile grid, Mobile business process.

1 Introduction

Mobile business, currently, is receiving more and more attention with the features of flexibility, convenience. With further research, it was discovered that the business process can reflect the integrated features of wireless information technology and traditional business. In the research of mobile business theory and method, mobile business process is the backbone throughout. Utilizing the modern theory of process reengineering and internal logic of mobile business to optimize mobile business process, in order to enhance the capacity of mobile commerce services, and resource utilization levels has become the focal point of current mobile business research.

The research of mobile business research is still scattered on this stage, lacking an overall research and modeling approach. The lack of theory will delay the development process of mobile business processes and increase the cost of development [1]. Based on recent research, grid-based management is an effective method to solve the problems of resource sharing, collaborative work in the whole system, meanwhile, the latest finding-mobile grid is the expansion of traditional grid in the wireless computing environment, it can also effectively solve problems of mobile devices access, offering a solution for overall optimization, resource sharing, efficient management, wireless access and other issues in the mobile business process [2]. As it has a quantitative mathematical description, so the logistics flow,

R. Zhang et al. (Eds.): ICEIS 2011, LNBIP 102, pp. 349–361, 2012.

information flow and operation flow in the grid management system can be quantitatively calculated, achieving a transmission of qualitative analysis to quantitative analysis. Besides, this mode can also use simulation for quantitative analysis, which reflects the superiority of grid management methods.

In this paper, with mobile business process as the research object and grid management as the research theory, combing the computer simulation, conduct a research of mobile business process based on grid management. Following is the research ideas. Firstly, analyze the existing mobile business process, finding the problems. Then construct a grid-based mobile business process in the support of grid management theory. Finally, conduct a simulation comparison between grid-based and non-grid based mobile business process.

2 Theory

2.1 Grid Management

Grid management is the integration of a variety of distributed resources of the community to achieve the goal of efficient, economical, fast and convenient management for the purpose of efficient transmission of information to save materials and energy and enhance the efficiency of resources.

Huanchen Wang proposed grid management as an emerging management mode to deal with the current complex management issues; this idea is based on the grid boundaries in the chosen system to achieve information integration, operational synergies, and combined slice of modern style of a management network system. In the view of system structure, grid management should have the features of grid layout. In the view of resource association, it should have the feature of resource sharing. In the view of the operation of the system, it should have the feature of operate cooperatively and presses orderly [3]. In the structure and operation grid management, it involves at least five essential factors, namely material, energy, information, space and time, referred to as MEIST.

Fig. 1 illustrates the basic process of grid management that can be abstracted into the following aspects.

- Business acceptance: Accept all classified business within the network.
- Business dispatch: Standardized assessment and operational coordination, after the approval of the command center, the segmentation of tasks will go to the corresponding functional department.
- Business process: Functional department accept business task, organizing work tasks to meet demand.
- Service delivery: The completed task will turned back to the reception center, by passing to the users.
- Supervision and inspection: Monitoring center compared the completion of verification of service and user demand.
- Disclosure of Information: During the entire business process, users can query the real-time business process [4].

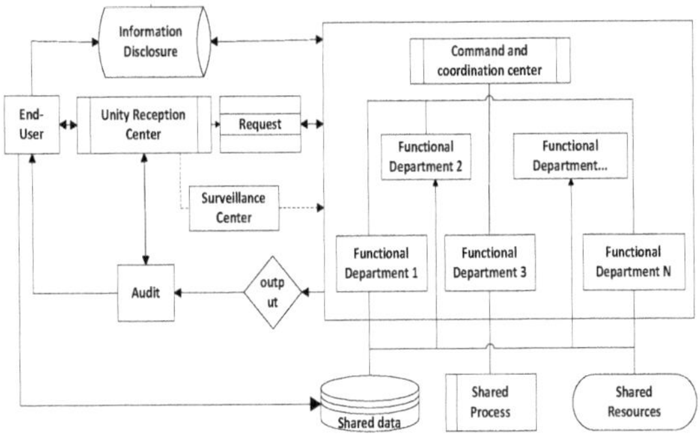

Fig. 1. Basic process of grid management

2.2 Theory of Mobile Grid

With the rapid development of mobile wireless network system, the user can access to global network resources at any place and any time, which means grid system should also take mobile nodes into consideration, and this combination leads to mobile grid computing. It supports mobile users and resources in a seamless, transparent, safe and effective way; it is an integration of wireless technology and girds computing. Mobile grid integrates mobile devices into grid, becoming a new type of resource sharing network [5].

Currently, most grid structures and algorithms do not take mobile devices into account as mobile devices have not been considered as a legitimate grid computing resources or interfaces. There two methods to locate mobile devices in the grid computing environment. The first one: as the as the interface to interact with the grid system, the user can require service via mobile devices from grid system to complete tasks, you can perform remote monitoring and obtain required results from the grid system. The other one: as the computing resources of grid system, mobile devices involves in grid computing task, not just the recipient of grid service. Therefore, effectively embedded into the grid, the mobile device can not only work as a recipient of the grid service but also can be used as grid service providers. Fig.2 is the designed mobile grid computing system structure.

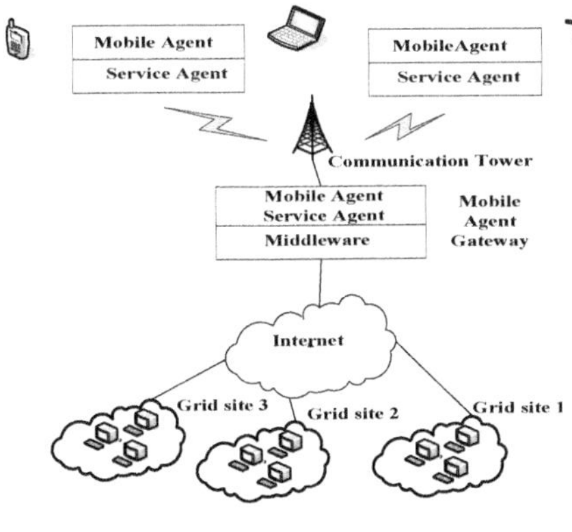

Fig. 2. Mobile grid system structure

The grid system is divided into three parts: static grid sites, mobile devices group and the gateway which connects static and mobile resources. Mobile devices can be connected to Internet via WLAN or remote cellular network. On the side of mobile devices and gateways, mobile agents and service agents are required. When a mobile user submits a task to obtain the service of grid computing service, it interacted by the mobile agents in the mobile device and gateway first and then submitted to grid system by mobile agent in the gateway [6].

2.3 Arena Simulation Software

Arena was an visualized interactive integration simulation software developed by System Modelling Company; it provides a good organic integration of computer simulation and visualization. The theoretical basis of Arena is discrete event simulation theory, using the event scheduling method. The basic idea is to use the view of events to analyze the real system, by defining the events and the change to the system when events occur. The mobile business process is a need arrived, processed and finished process, in line with the principle f discrete event simulation; accordingly, Arena can be used for quantitative simulation research [7].

3 Current Mobile Business Process Analysis

3.1 Current Mobile Business Process

Mobile business works in the Internet open network environment, based on the application of mobile communication devices, realizing the B2B and B2C transactions, a new business operation mode of mobile payment[8]. As a new economic form, mobile business is co-created by network economy and modern logistics. Fig. 3 illustrates the main dynamic transaction flow.

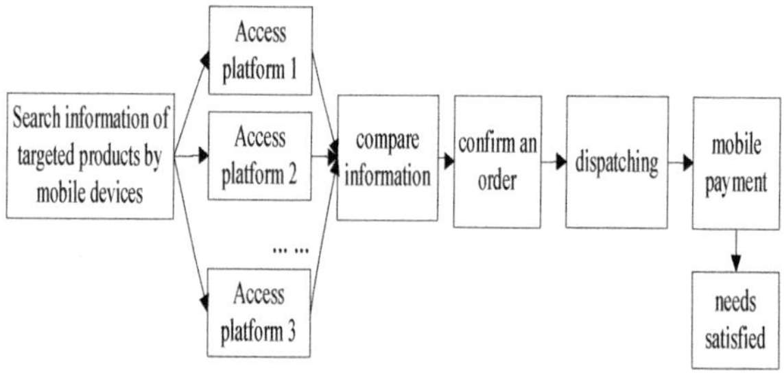

Fig. 3. The main process of mobile business

1. Once the user has needs, he can use mobile devices to login on mobile business information platform to search for information of targeted products. However, as each platform assigns different access rights to different users, so resource and information cannot be shared in a certain format.

2. After obtaining the required information of targeted products, users still need to login on different platforms to compare the product information, in order to find the satisfied product and fill orders.

3. Business confirms the order with customer, informing the payment, preparing the product and organizing the logistic delivery.

4. Customer receives the product, after acceptance, paying the payment via mobile devices, transaction finished.

3.2 The Drawbacks of Current Mobile Business Process

The application of information technology greatly contributed to the development of mobile business; however, information technology alone cannot achieve a holistic approach to mobile business reorganization of the participants. The shortcomings of existing mobile business process are as follows:

- Mobile operators do not fully play his role as a bond. Compared with other market participants, the mobile operator takes a control role and dominant position by holding the network resource and customer base; it can affect the development trend in depth. However, its advantages do not play an effective role in a series of cooperation [9].
- Inadequate cooperation among mobile business participants. As a new business operating model, the greatest strength of mobile business lies in its integration of a range of social resources using latest mobile communication technology and tools, serving for end users and realizing the maximization of social benefits. However, the lack of cooperation within mobile business participants inevitably leads to information asymmetry and low efficiency in transaction.
- Within the mobile business domain resources distributed unevenly. In some small enterprises, the lack of resources hindered the development of mobile business, whereas, some large enterprises have vacancy resources which results in a great waste.
- Internal and external information Island phenomenon exists. Due to the unsuccessful integration of enterprise e-commerce systems, a great sum of resources on the network cannot be fully shared.
- The whole mobile business field is not well integrated, so that members cannot update information dynamically and efficiently.

3.3 Feasibility Analysis

Grid management provides effective solutions for the problems in mobile business. Grid broke the previous technical limitations, so that people can use a new, freer and more convenient way to utilize resources, which brings following benefits:

- The emergence of mobile grid technology makes the application of grid management into the research of mobile business process possible. It supports mobile users and resources in a seamless, transparent, safe and effective way, an integration of wireless technology and grid computing.

- Grid management integrates varied application systems together into a unified platform, enables enterprises to fully share resources and business process, breaking the bottleneck of information exchange between enterprises.
- Grid management breaks the restriction that sharing and collaboration is only limited to data transmission, it enables resources sharing can reach a remote operate and control level.

4 Modeling of Grid-Based Mobile Business Process

4.1 Basic Ideas of Modeling of Grid-Based Mobile Business Process

The general concept based on the problem analysis of mobile business process, fully using the existing grid management and mobile grid research results to construct a grid-based mobile business process, achieving the goals of good service, efficient management and effective regulatory of mobile business process.

This paper will utilize the research result of grid management, redefining the job roles of participants, responsibility and right norms, and business process within the current mobile business system, in order to build a basic mobile business process based on grid management, to form a unified operation of business process, and to provide grid end-user an integrated service platform.

4.2 Basic Model of Grid-Based Mobile Business Process

Grid-based mobile business process is based on the principles of "unified service, resources sharing, and business collaboration" of grid management to determine process links, basic data and service port sharing mode. Accepting the demand in a unified way for task decomposition, and then distribute it into various department foe processing. The grid-based mobile business process can be abstracted into a unified mode: demand starts→ order accepted→ goods delivery→ mobile payment→ evaluation and feedback see as the Fig. 4 demonstrate.

Further refinement of the steps:

1. Login on the unified platform. End-users login on the unified platform, sending requirements through the business platform, the requirements will be sent to the grid computing service end through the mobile agents in the mobile device and gateway. After the unified processing in the grid computing site, end-users can get useful information through the interaction between mobile agents in the mobile device and gateway.
2. Analyze product information. By comparing the goods information offered and communicating with businessman online, customer gets a good understanding of goods.
3. Place an order. End-user fills the order bill, including price, quantity, delivery address and contact information.
4. End-user pays for the goods to a third party payment platform. End-user should pay for the goods within a certain period of time, or the order will be cancelled. The third party payment system ensures the security of transaction by transferring the payment to businessman only after the customer has received the goods.

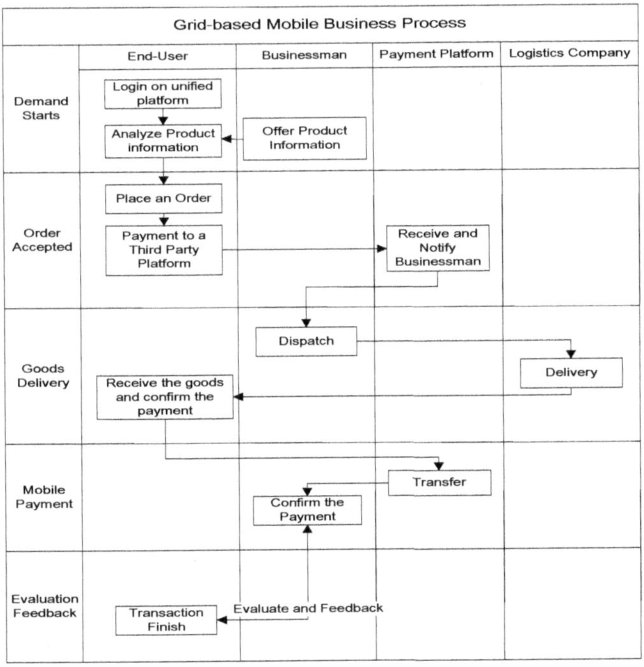

Fig. 4. Grid-based Mobile Business Process

5. Receive payment and notify businessman. The third party payment system will automatically send a notification to businessman after receiving the payment from customer.
6. Dispatch. Businessman prepares the goods and chooses a logistics company for delivery.
7. Delivery. The third party logistics company delivers the goods to customer.
8. Receive the goods and confirm the payment. Customer checks and receives the goods, confirming to transfer the payment to businessman.
9. Transfer. The third party payment system transfers the payment to businessman after receiving the confirmation from customer.
10. Businessman receives the payment.
11. Evaluation and feedback. Customer evaluates the goods, service quality and logistics quality or gives suggestion for improvement.

5 Simulation Comparison of Grid-Based and Non-grid Mobile Business Process

5.1 Model I of Non-grid Process Simulation

Fig. 3 illustrates the existing mobile business process, namely the non-grid mobile business process. The specific description of the process: Suppose a mobile business platform provides X (x=1,..., X) categories of service for the public, each kind of resource is available 8 hours a day, 5 days a week and users can access and submit requirement to the 24-hour system. When the mobile user needs to get the No. x business service, it is required to login on n (i=1, ..., n) business websites to search for useful information. As to users, it means they have to login on many distinct platforms until they get the wanted information. For simplicity, in this paper, we assume that users give up searching for information if they cannot find the required information after three times of attempt.

For the convenience of description, in this paper non-grid mobile business process will be abbreviated as MBP (Mobile Business Process). In process model I, users need to search for distinct mobile business platforms, login on and submit requirement for several time to get the required information. Fig. 5 demonstrates the model.

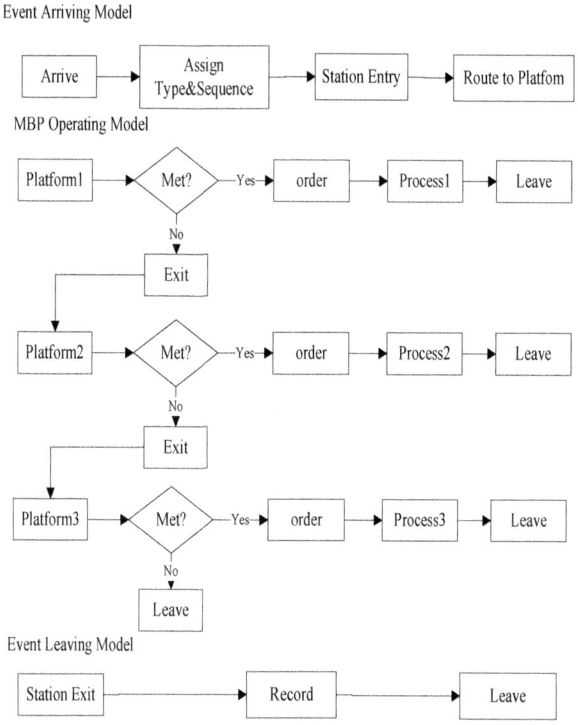

Fig. 5. Model I Simulation Logic Model

Table 1[10] illustrates the model unit, function and distillation function of Model I.

Table 1. Model Unit of Simulation Logic Model

Model unit	Function of model unit	Distillation function
Arrive	User arrives or service needs occur	Generation time is subject to a random distribution
Route	Transfer path between sites	Transfer time is subject to a random distribution
Process	Specific service provided by institutions.	Service time is subject to a random distribution
Decide	Service judgment	/
Record	Record related events and indicators	/
Leave	Service finished; leave	/
Dispose	Leave system	/

5.2 Model II of Grid-Based Process Simulation

Fig. 4 illustrates the grid-based mobile business process model. Each time user login on the platform, the requirement submitted and the service department will transact the service by rules and regulations. Users can access and submit requirement to the 24-hour system. For simplicity, in this paper, one resource servers one requirement, not considering a need having two or more resources.

Grid-based mobile business process focuses on requirement service. Users can submit their requirement through unified processing window directly and the order will be sent to various providers for implement. The response cycle of grid-based process includes landing process, unified information service and service waiting time. For simplicity, the mobile business center will be abbreviated as MBC (Mobile Business Center), as Fig. 6 illustrated.

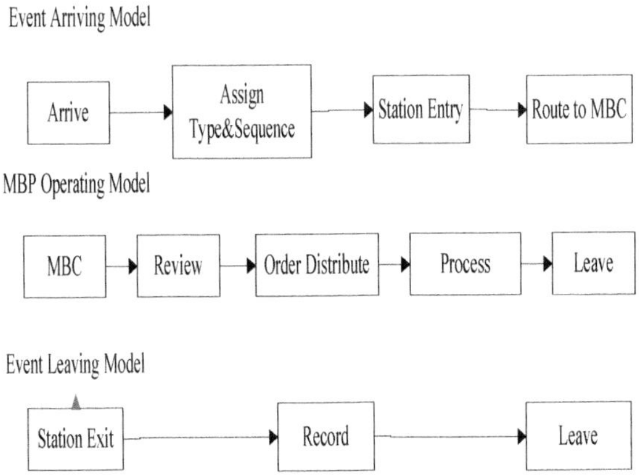

Fig. 6. Model II Simulation Logic Model

5.3 Simulation Results Analysis of Grid-Based Process and Non-grid Process

5.3.1 Index of Simulation Evaluation

According to the grid-based mobile business process's goal of serving for the public, in this paper, some common service quality evaluation indicators [11] are selected to evaluate the service of grid-based mobile business process.

1. Average queue length L_q

L_q ——Average waiting queue length, expectation value of the number of customers waiting for service in a steady-state system.

$$L_q = \lim_{T\to\infty} \int_0^T \frac{L_q(t)dt}{T} \tag{1}$$

$L_q(t)$ is the waiting queue length at the time of t, T is the operation time. Average waiting queue length means the number of customers waiting for service in the mobile business process.

2. Average queue length

L ——Average queue length, expectation value of the number of all customers.

$$L = \lim_{T\to\infty} \int_0^T \frac{(L_q(t) + S(t))dt}{T} \tag{2}$$

$S(t)$ means the customers receiving the service, queue length at t means $L_q(t)$ plus $S(t)$. The sum of average customer number marked as WIP .Average queue length in a real mobile business processes means the total number of customers in the system (the number of customers waiting in line plus the number of customers who are receiving service and).

3. Average waiting time

W_q ——Average waiting time, the expectation value of waiting time.

$$W_q = \lim_{K\to\infty} \sum_{i=1}^{K} \frac{Z_i}{K} \tag{3}$$

Z_i indicates the time customer i spends waiting for, K indicates the total customer service number .Waiting time in the real business processes indicates the period of time from the requirement is submitted to the time the requirement is processed.

4. Resource utilization

In terms of each resource, Arena will report two kinds of utilization statistics, namely Instantaneous Utilization and Scheduled Utilization.

- Instantaneous Utilization is the resource utilization at a certain point of time. If $B(t)$ is the number of resource at a t in a busy state, $M(t)$ is the number of available resource at t. Suppose $U(t) = B(t)/M(t)$, $M(t) > 0$. If $M(t) = 0$, and define $U(t) = 0$. If the simulation starts from 0 to T, then the Instantaneous Utilization is:

$$\int_0^T U(t)dt/T \tag{4}$$

That is the average time of function $U(t)$.

- Scheduled Utilization is the ratio of the average number of resources in the busy state with the average number of available resources. The Scheduled Utilization is:

$$\frac{\int_0^T B(t)dt/T}{\int_0^T M(t)dt/T} = \frac{\int_0^T B(t)dt}{\int_0^T M(t)dt} \tag{5}$$

In summary, the first three indicators are commonly used to evaluate the steady-state capability, the services responsiveness and service congestion can be evaluated from the view of user and process service.

5.3.2 Simulation Hypothesis

It is assumed that non-grid and grid-based service model have the same business, namely user submit requirement in the same way, arrival time has the same distribution and the arrival time follows TRIA(1,3,5)triangle distribution, making the simulation comparable.

Assuming the service cycle is 8 hours a day and grid-base model users can submit requirement in 24 hour. Besides, we also assume the arrival of system events and the processing time of each node follow exponential distribution; the delay of internal operation process follows triangular distribution. The basic statistical unit of simulation is minutes; the length of simulation is one week.

5.3.3 Simulation Results Analysis

According to the simulation model and inputted data, using the Arena software for simulation operation. The system works 8 hours a day and 7 days each time, a .txt file will be generated after the simulation with all the statistic results in a report form. Finally, a serious of simulation results is obtained, as Fig.7 stated.

(1) Comparison of Average Waiting Time

Waiting time indicates the period of time from the requirement is submitted to the time the requirement is processed. The services responsiveness and service congestion can be evaluated from the point of view of user and process service. In Fig.7.a, the average waiting time in non-grid mobile business process is more than 4 minutes, and there is almost no waiting time in the grid-based mobile business process model. It is obvious that grid-based mobile business process has faster response capability.

(2) Comparison of WIP

Average queue length means the total number of customers in the system (the number of customers waiting in line plus the number of customers who are receiving service and). The Fig.7.b demonstrates that the average queue of non-grid process is about three time of that of gird-based process.

(3) Comparison of Resource Utilization

The resource utilization includes Instantaneous Utilization and Scheduled Utilization. In the simulation result, they have the same indicators which referred to here as resource utilization. It can be seen from the Fig.7.c that grid-based process has higher resource utilization than non-grid based process.

In conclusion, grid-based model has great advantage over the non-gird model.

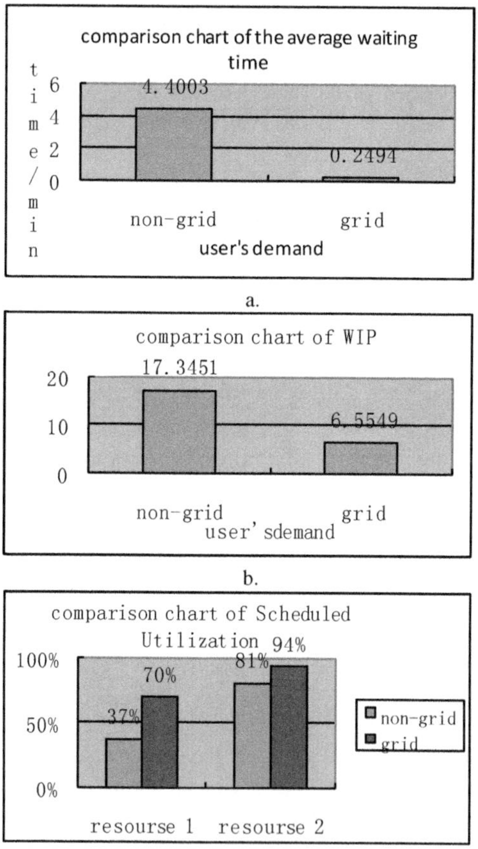

Fig. 7. Simulation results

6 Conclusions

With the development of information technology, mobile business has entered into a service –oriented and process optimization focused stage. The main difficulties are information sharing, business collaboration and business process reengineering. There is no in-depth systematic analysis on this issue but only some ideas in theory. In this paper, combing the research result of grid management theory, mobile grid and Arena simulation technology, in the view point of system engineering, a grid-based mobile business process is built, paving the way for the research on mobile business process.

References

1. Taudes, A., Feurstein, M., Mild, A.: Options analysis of software platform decisions: A case study. MIS Quarterly 24(2), 227–243 (2000)
2. Varshney, U., Vetter, R.J., Kalakota, R.: Mobile commerce: a new frontier. Computer 33, 32–38 (2000)
3. Wan, T., Wang, H., Ma, D.: Principles of Grid Management and research on grid model structure. Information Science 25(03), 456–461 (2007)
4. Zhen, S., Xv, H., Wang, H.: Summary of grid and grid management System Engineering, vol. 3, pp. 1–7 (2005)
5. Gao, H., Wang, S.: Modeling and Verifying of Grid Computing Based on FSM. JCIT: Journal of Convergence Information Technology 6(1), 170–181 (2011)
6. Wang, D., Wang, H.: Thinking the terms on the Grid Management. Grid Management Seminar Papers 24, 109–115 (2003)
7. Deng, C., Zou, K.: Analysis of E-Commerce based on grid technology. Information Science 11 (2006)
8. Ahmadi, K.D., Charkari, N.M., Enami, N.: e-Negotiation System Based on Intelligent Agents in B2C E-Commerce. AISS: Advances in Information Sciences and Service Sciences 3(2), 60–70 (2011)
9. Ma, C.: The application research of OGSA based grid service. Hehai University (2008)
10. Hem, K., Zhao, Y.: Grid Resource Management and Scheduling Review. Wuhan University of Technology (Information & Management Engineering) 27(4), 1–5 (2007)
11. Chi, Z.: Research of Urban E-Government based on grid management and Information Distance Theory. PhD thesis, Shanghai Jiao Tong University (2008)

PART V

Human-Computer Interaction

Understanding User's Acceptance of Social Shopping Websites: Effects of Social Comparison and Trust

Jia Shen

College of Business Administration,
Rider University, 2083 Lawrenceville Rd., Lawrencevill, NJ, U.S.A.
jiashen@rider.edu

Abstract. Social shopping websites are among the latest developments in E-commerce to combine the power of social networking with Internet shopping to provide a unique online experience. While the adoption of information technology is well studied, new theoretical development is needed to account for the specific characteristics of social shopping websites. This study augments the TAM (Technology Acceptance Model) with social factors including an online shopper's tendency to social comparison, and trust in information privacy and data security. Results provide significant support of the extended model. Directions for future research are discussed.

Keywords: Social shopping, Social comparison, Trust, Privacy, Technology acceptance.

1 Introduction

Online social networking and social media technologies continue to gain recognition in the popular press [1]. Seeking to tap into the potentials of these technologies for E-commerce, businesses are exploring ways to combine the power of social networking with online shopping for better service and new business opportunities. For example, there is an upward trend of merchants creating ads and retails pages on Facebook and Myspace, with the intention of attracting online social network users and their friends [2]. Additionally, a new wave of start-up firms are developing text mining algorithms to track "social relationship data" between online users, that can be used to target behavior-oriented ads. However the evidence is still inconclusive that these are the best online platforms to increase sales using social networking.

Social shopping sites have emerged as another platform to combine online social networking with online shopping. Gathering people in an online place to exchange shopping ideas, social shopping sites offer features similar to social networking sites such as personal blog and profile webpage, with the addition of E-commerce tools and software to allow users to easily copy product pictures and post them on their web pages. Users can also post product recommendations, create wish lists, comment on items, and make purchases. The result is the creation of online social shopping communities. Examples of social shopping sites include Kaboodle.com, ShopStyle.com, ThisNext.com, and Wists.com, all launched between 2006 and 2007.

R. Zhang et al. (Eds.): ICEIS 2011, LNBIP 102, pp. 365–373, 2012.

Social shopping aims at addressing the fundamental nature of shopping as a social experience. Despite tremendous business interest and anticipated potential benefits, some central questions remain. Will consumers adopt social shopping technology? What are the factors that lead to the adoption? Although technology adoption in general and e-commerce adoption in particular are both well studied, the specificity of social commerce clearly calls for further theoretical development. Such understanding will also better inform business managers who make strategic decisions regarding the integration of social networking and online commerce. Additionally, system designers will have important insight that may lead to improved functionality, design, and use of such systems.

2 Conceptual Background

To answer these questions, this research utilizes the Technology Acceptance Model (TAM) [3]. TAM has been recognized as one of the most powerful models in examining the acceptance of new IT. Adapted from the Theory of Reasoned Action (TRA) model, TAM posits that two beliefs – perceived ease of use (PEOU) and perceived usefulness (PU) - determine one's behavioral intention to use a technology. While the parsimony of TAM makes it easy to apply to a variety of situations, the leanness of the model is also considered as its key limitation. The model lacks the ability to help business managers or system designers to understand the factors that contribute to the adoption or abandonment of new IT. As a result, a number of studies have been conducted to examine additional antecedents to IT use (e.g., cultural dimensions [4]).

This study proposes two additional constructs as key antecedents to the adoption of social shopping sites: tendency to social comparison (TSC) and trust. Social comparison is an essential social phenomenon where human beings compare themselves with others for self-evaluation and information seeking. Rooted in social science, the original theory of social comparison treated social comparison as a secondary choice when objective information to evaluate oneself is not available [5]. Subsequent research suggests that social comparison is a central feature of human social life [6]. In this study, tendency to social comparison is defined as the degree to which an individual tends to compare his or her opinions with others, and be influenced by others. Recent studies have found that individuals differ quite a bit in their tendency to compare themselves with others [6]. A related yet different construct that has been examined in extended TAM research is social influence [7], which is defined as the degree to which an individual perceives that it is important that others believe he or she should use the new system. While social influence measures an individual's compliance with social norms under pressure, the tendency to social comparison factor operates through an individual feeling bond with likable sources, and accepting information from outside sources.

The second construct, trust, is important in business transactions and the adoption of new technologies. Studies have shown that trust is particularly important in E-commerce because of the limited human interactions between the shopper and the vendor [8]. In online shopping, previous studies have found that factors contributing to consumers' trust in online stores are related to personal information privacy and data security. Research suggest that privacy is the number one consumer issue facing Internet use, and continues to be the main concern affecting online behavior such as website personalization [9] and online trading [10]. Data security concerns such like security breaches of online vendor's information systems and interception of transactional data are also important in customer trust. Prior studies suggest that when privacy and data security are perceived to be low, consumers are reluctant to give out personal information over the web [11].

3 Research Model and Hypotheses

Based on TAM and the two additional variables described above, a research model is proposed with five variables: Perceived Ease of Use (PEOU), Perceived Usefulness (PU), Tendency to Social Comparison Online (TSCO), Trust, and Behavioral Intention to use social shopping sites (BI). Figure 1 shows the research model.

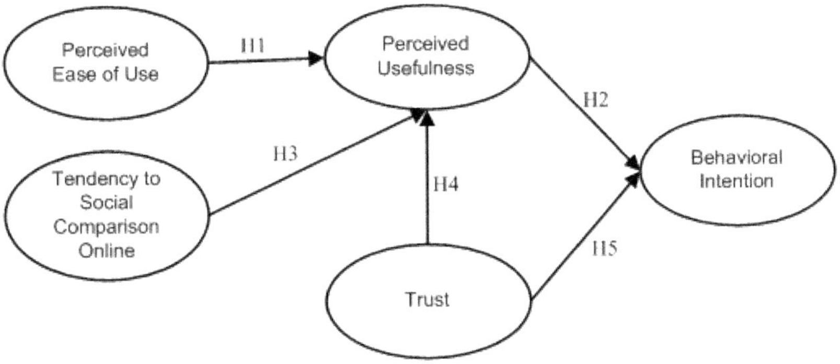

Fig. 1. Research Model

According to TAM, the hypothesized relationship among PEOU, PU, and BI are specified below:

H1: Perceived Ease of Use will positively affect Perceived Usefulness of social shopping websites.

H2: Perceived Usefulness will positively affect Behavioral Intention to use social shopping websites.

Given the social nature of shopping, tendency to social comparison is postulated to have an impact in user's adoption of social shopping sites. Empirical studies of online shopping suggest that the provision of recommendations and consumer reviews increase the perceived usefulness of the website [12]. These findings are consistent with marketing research indicating that consumers are influenced by other consumers in their decision making process, such as information seeking, alternative evaluation, and choice [13]. Given the social nature of shopping and the features specific to social shopping websites, it is postulated that people who are more likely to compare and be influenced by others are more likely to find the social shopping sites useful (H3). Thus the hypothesis is:

H3: Tendency to Social Comparison Online will positively affect Perceived Usefulness of Social Shopping Websites.

Many studies have shown that trust is crucial in business and social interactions that are characterized by a dependency on another party combined with a lack of control over that party. Empirical studies have demonstrated that trust significantly affect perceived usefulness of information systems such as E-commerce and ERP systems [14]. In particular, research indicates that consumers' trust is determined by their concerns about information privacy and security measures of online stores [11]. In this study, we measure trust in terms of privacy concerns and security measures in social shopping sites, and hypothesize that increased level of trust with the social shopping site will be associated with increased level of perceived usefulness of the website and intended use of the website.

H4: Trust in the sites will positively affect Perceived Usefulness of social shopping websites.

H5: Trust in the sites will positively affect Behavioral Intention to use social shopping websites.

4 Data Collection

Data were collected through a survey conducted in spring 2008 and spring 2009. The survey was given to undergraduate business students at a university in the northeastern region of United States. Subjects were instructed to use a specific social shopping site, Kaboodle.com, and to explore its various features. Kaboodle.com was chosen for this study given it is the leading social shopping site at the time of the research, with about 2.5 million visitors each month as of spring 2009 [15] and presently over 14 million monthly visitors as of April 2011 (www.kaboodle.com/zm.about). The site provides many features supporting social shopping activities. The features subjects were instructed to explore include unique features on social shopping sites such as shopping soul mates and compatibility tests, shopping groups, and featured shoppers, as well as traditional E-commerce functions such as browsing by brands and searching. Subjects were then asked to write up and submit a short essay reflecting on the features provided on the website. Extra course credits were awarded for subjects' participation in the survey. The precise purpose of the study and the research model were not discussed with the subjects.

After completing the assignment, students were given the URL to participate in the online survey. In constructing the questionnaire, the PEOU, PU, and BI items were adapted from Davis [3]. Items for the Tendency to Social Comparison scale were adapted from Gibbons and Buunk [16] study. The trust scale was adapted from Chen et al. [11] on perceived trust of virtual stores in terms of information privacy and data security. All items were measured on a seven-point scale ranging from strongly disagree (1) to strongly agree (7).

5 Data Analysis and Results

This section provides the results of respondents' demographics and the research model.

5.1 Demographic Statistics

Among a total of 157 students, 117 valid responses were collected, resulting in the response rate of 74.5%. 54% were male (n=63) and 46% were female (n=54). The majority of the respondents were between 20-24 years old (n=92, 79%). The respondents reported being very experienced in using a PC (Mean=6.06, SD=1.06), and very experienced in using the Internet (Mean=6.66, SD=.80).

When asked about their online shopping frequency, the majority (69.2%) reported that they shop online from time to time (every few months), followed by 23.9% who shop online regularly (every month). Only 6.8% reported never shopping online before. In terms of their use of social networking sites, the top site subjects reporting having an account and using regularly is Facebook. Table 1 lists respondents' use of social networking sites.

Table 1. Use of social media sites

Social media sites	Number of subjects use the site daily or weekly	Percent (%)
Facebook	81	69.2
MySpace	31	26.5
LinkedIn	2	1.7
Flickr	3	2.6

Respondents were also asked about their use of the social shopping site Kaboodle before the study. The great majority had never heard about Kaboodle before (82.9%), or had heard about Kaboodle but do not have an account (13.7%).

5.2 Hypotheses Testing

To examine the hypotheses and research model, the data were analyzed using Structural Equation Modeling (SEM) and SmartPLS software [17]. This approach allows simultaneous analysis of the measurement model (factors), and the structural model (path analysis), and has been widely used. In the measurement model, the reliability of the constructs as measured in the AVE and composite reliabilities of the different measures all exceed the recommended 0.70 level, indicating that the measures are robust. Tests on convergent validity and discriminant validity were conducted, and the results supported the measurement model. Analysis on the mean and standard deviation (SD) for each of the main constructs in the model reveal that subjects reported overall positive attitude towards the social shopping site, and found it easy to use, useful, trustworthy, and are likely to use it in their shopping tasks in the future (mean varies between 4.20 and 4.99 and SD varies between 1.15 and 1.57).

Figure 2 shows the results of the structural model. The test yields results of path coefficients (β), which indicates the positive and negative relationships between the constructs, the strength of the relationships, and their statistical significance. The test also yields squared multiple correlations (R^2) values, which indicate the amount of variance of the dependent construct that can be explained by the independent constructs.

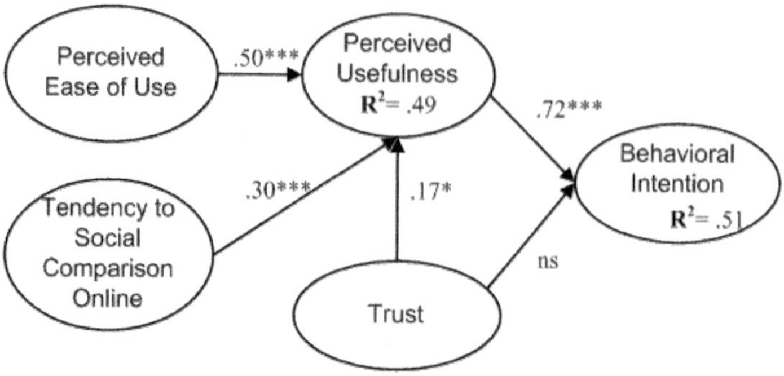

Note: Path Coefficients
*** path is significant at .001 level; * path is significant at .05 level;
ns: not significant

Fig. 2. Research Model Results

Overall the model accounts for 51% of variance in behavioral intention and 49% in PU. PEOU is a strong antecedent to PU (β= .50, $p<.001$), and PU has a strong effect on BI (β= .72, $p<.001$). Tendency to Social Comparison Online has a significant effect on PU (β= .30, $p<.001$). Trust affects PU (β= .17, $p<.05$), but not BI directly.

Thus hypotheses H1-H4 were supported. H5 was not supported.

6 Discussions

This study examined factors associated with one's intention to use social shopping websites. The significant relationship between perceived usefulness and the intention to use these kinds of site for online shopping has important practical considerations. As the use of social media continues to grow among Internet users and consumers, our results strongly suggest that businesses should consider the potential power associated with integrating online social networking technologies with their e-commerce strategies.

The study revealed that trust affects PU (with a coefficient of .17), suggesting the importance of protecting user's privacy and strengthening data security to build trust. Individual user's tendency to social comparison affected how much they perceived the website as useful (with a coefficient of .30), pointing to importance of designing features that support easy comparison with other online shoppers.

One interesting result is that trust did not affect BI directly. The effect was through PU. This result indicates that in the context of social shopping, trust does not lead directly to the acceptance of such websites, although it does lead to perceived usefulness of the sites. An explanation for this may be that the online consumer may already have a certain level of trust associated with the usefulness of online shopping activities, therefore the difference between an online storefront and a social shopping site is not a differentiating factor.

In the open-ended questions, study participants reported that one of the main reasons they would adopt the website in future shopping activities is because of the social interactions with other shoppers online: "I would use Kaboodle over other online shopping sites because it has a more personable feel and the recommendations for other products come from people instead of computer generated outputs." "What I liked best is the ability to meet people. It allows for a more personal connection and a more trusted opinion." "Amazon is also more of an individual experience while shopping online. Kaboodle being a social shopping website makes shopping a little bit more fun."

The social features of the website not only enable social interactions among web users, but can also serve other purposes such as making new discoveries of products online. "I find the people functions of Kaboodle the most useful. The shopping soulmates and compatibility test really helped me discover new gift ideas and it was neat to see other people's profile lists and similar tastes that they had to me." "I would (use the website in the future) because it would allow me to see what people with shopping habits similar to mine to see what they like and purchase, and can help me decide on gifts and purchases in the future."

When asked about concerns that prevent them from using the site in the future, privacy concerns topped the list. "I may have privacy issues because it is very interactive with others, which I believe could create easier access for other to hack into my account and learn about my information." "I am not able to limit what others see on my profile." Another issue that was pointed out was the trust in other shoppers. "For me, shopping has always been a social activity. I go with my family or my friends to get their input on certain items. I found it difficult to trust the opinions of the other online shoppers at Kaboodle.com simply because I did not know them." This suggests that for social shopping sites to be truly useful, the credibility of the website and its users are critical.

7 Contributions and Future Research

This research is among the first to empirically examine the merging of social networking with E-commerce technologies for consumer online purchasing. Theoretically, this research contributes by extending the Technology Acceptance Model with factors extracted from social comparison theory and trust theory. The two additional factors: tendency to social comparison and trust were significant in the model in addition to PEOU and PU. A new scale, tendency to social comparison, was developed and empirically tested as reliable.

Understanding consumer perceptions and intentions to use a social shopping website have direct management implications. A recent study empirically confirmed the economic value associated with online user reviews and product sales through an investigation that used text mining algorithms [18]. In the study, a clear relationship emerged between user-generated product information and reviews and online product sales. The combined empirical evidence from their study with this one, which shows overall favorable attitudes towards the adoption of web sites that go beyond consumer reviews and enables consumers to enjoy the social aspects of shopping online, demonstrates that the strategic integration of online products sales with online social networking is very important.

From a practical perspective, the current research model suggests that in addition to focusing on ease of use and usefulness, the site should allow users to easily compare their shopping experiences and opinions with others, while also fostering a sense of trust by protecting privacy with strong data security. The result can produce a greater likelihood that consumers will find the site useful, use the site, and increase product sales. Regarding trust on privacy and data privacy, firms that experiment with ways to combine social networking with E-commerce may face information privacy violations if they are not transparent in their data collection activities [19]. Some companies are addressing the privacy concerns by providing users with more information and controls on the data that being tracked [20]. The potential value of the social shopping website is that users voluntarily create shopping profiles to aid in their own shopping. Because the profile data is not personally identifiable, the relevant value of the content can be shared and integrated with other users without violating personal information privacy.

One possible direction for future research is to examine the type of online shopping tasks that are most suitable for social shopping websites. Will users prefer using social shopping sites than traditional E-commerce site for certain shopping activities, such as browsing or searching [21]? Will they prefer the site when they are more involved with the product, i.e., when the product is more relevant to them? Also, will the strength of the social ties affect users' trust of such shopping sites, such as family and friends vs. other online shoppers? With the growing popularity of social media and e-commerce technology integration, research in this area is timely and important.

References

1. Vascellaro, J.E., et al.: The Year Ahead for Media: Digital or Die. Wall Street Journal, B1 (January 4, 2011)
2. Needleman, S.E.: Merchants Push Sales Through Social Media - Early Adopters Add Shopping-Cart Apps to Fan Pages to Sell Items. Wall Street Journal, B6 (June 1, 2010)
3. Davis, F.D.: Perceived Usefulness, Perceived Ease of Use and User Acceptance of Information Technology. MIS Quarterly 13(3), 319–340 (1989)
4. Mao, E., Palvia, P.: Testing an Extended Model of IT Acceptance in the Chinese Cultural Context. ACM SIGMIS Database 37(2-3), 20–32 (2006)
5. Festinger, L.: A Theory of Social Comparison Processes. Human Relations 7, 117–140 (1954)
6. Buunk, A.P., Gibbons, F.X.: Social Comparison: The End of a Theory and the Emergence of a Field. Organizational Behavior and Human Decision Processes 102(1), 3–21 (2007)
7. Hsu, C.-L., Lu, H.-P.: Why Do People Play On-line Games? An Extended TAM with Social Influences and Flow Experience. Information & Management 41(7), 853–868 (2004)
8. Palvia, P.: The Role of Trust in E-commerce Relational Exchange: A Unified Model. Information & Management 46, 213–220 (2009)
9. Chellappa, R.K., Sin, R.G.: Personalization versus Privacy: An Empirical Examination of the Online Consumer's Dilemma. Information Technology and Management 6(2-3), 181–202 (2005)
10. Lee, M.-C.: Predicting and Explaining the Adoption of Online Trading: An Empirical Study in Taiwan. Decision Support Systems 47(2), 133–142 (2009)

11. de Chen, L., Gillenson, M.L., Sherrell, D.L.: Consumer Acceptance of Virtual Stores: A Theoretical Model and Critical Success Factors For Virtual Stores. Databse for Advances in Information Systems 35(2), 8–31 (2004)
12. Kumar, N., Benbasat, I.: The Influence of Recommendations and Consumer Reviews on Evaluations of Websites. Information Systems Research 17(4), 425–439 (2006)
13. Friedman, H.H., Fireworker, R.B.: The Susceptibility of Consumers to Unseen Group Influence. Journal of Social Psychology 102(1), 155–156 (1977)
14. Gefen, D.: What Makes an ERP Implementation Relationship Worthwhile: Linking Trust Mechanisms and ERP Usefulness. Journal of Management Information Systems 21(1), 263–288 (2004)
15. Kasteler, J.: Why You Should Get Involved With Social Shopping: E-comerce 2.0. Online Report (2009), `http://searchengineland.com/`
16. Gibbons, F.X., Buunk, B.P.: Individual Differences in Social Comparison: Development of a Scale of Social Comparison Orientation. Journal of Personality and Social Psychology 76(1), 129–142 (1999)
17. Ringle, C.M., Wende, S., Will, A.: SmartPLS 2005. University of Hamburg Hamburg, Germany (2005)
18. Ghose, A., Ipeirotis, P.: The EconoMining project at NYU: Studying the Economic Value of User-generated Content on the Internet. Journal of Revenue and Pricing Management: Special Issue: Distribution and Revenue Management 8(2-3), 241–246 (2009)
19. Steel, E.: Marketers Watch as Friends Interact Online. Wall Street Journal, B5 (April 15, 2010)
20. Valentino-Devries, J.: What They Know About You. Wall Street Journal, B1 (July 31, 2010)
21. Hong, W., Thong, J.Y.L., Tam, K.Y.: The Effects of Information Format and Shopping Task on Consumers' Online Shopping Behavior: A Cognitive Fit Perspective. Journal of Management Information Systems 21(3), 149–184 (2004)

Seeing Social Software Analysis and Evaluation through the Lenses of Culture

Roberto Pereira and M. Cecília C. Baranauskas

Institute of Computing, University of Campinas (UNICAMP)
Av. Albert Einstein N1251, Campinas – SP, CEP 13083-852, Brazil
{rpereira,cecilia}@ic.unicamp.br

Abstract. Social software is a growing reality worldwide, while the analysis and evaluation of this kind of system still is a quite unexplored challenge. The complex scenario of social software has been marked by the diversity of users, their limitations, preferences, cultural aspects such as values, beliefs, customs and so on. This paper sheds light on this scenario proposing a culturally aware artifact to support designers in the task of analyzing and evaluating social software, taking values and other cultural issues into account in an explicit way. The artifact, named VF4SS, was used by a group of designers to evaluate five different prototypes of systems for supporting cross-cultural collaboration. The results obtained from this activity demonstrate that the artifact can bring effective contributions to the evaluation as well as to the design of social software.

Keywords: Cultural aspects, Values, Organizational semiotics, Valuation framing for social software.

1 Introduction

Social software has triggered transformations that are changing the way people relate, use and are affected by technology. Systems such as *Twitter*, *Facebook* and *Youtube* are well-known examples of how technology has left the workplace context to pervade every aspect of people's personal and social life, causing not only technical impacts but also formal and informal ones in the way people interact and live [1]. In this scenario, as Boyd [2] highlights, social software is all about the new, but in this case, the new has more to do with the way people behave than with the technology itself.

Although current increase in its popularity, number of users and of systems available on the web, the success of social software is an exception rather than a rule and the concern with human values such as privacy, reputation, autonomy, among other cultural aspects (e.g., beliefs, behavioral patterns), is almost absent of its design. An evidence of the negligence with the social aspects of these applications is that users have been inadvertently serving as testers of beta applications as well as subjects of implicit behavioral experiments to identify the viability of a resource or product, instead of being involved through recognized practices, such as the

R. Zhang et al. (Eds.): ICEIS 2011, LNBIP 102, pp. 374–387, 2012.

Participatory Design [3]. Privacy policies and agreement terms are constantly changed and updated, many times without users' awareness, under the same justification that is used to remove/discontinue products that were not approved in their beta tests.

Furthermore, as shown in [1], traditional concepts and practices in the Human-Computer Interaction (HCI) area, such as accessibility, are not often prioritized in the design of social software and need to be put into perspective and understood as technical values crucial for the project of any technological artifact.

Some authors [e.g. 4, 5, 6] mention that traditional approaches for software development based on Software Engineering's best practices (specification, design, development, testing etc.) and agile methods created for developing Web 2.0 applications need to be rethought in order to produce effective systems. Other authors [e.g. 7, 8, 9] draw attention to the inability of traditional inspection methods, such as the Heuristic Evaluation, to consider and deal with subjective and contextualized issues (e.g., emotional and affective aspects) as well as characteristics of Web 2.0 applications (e.g., collaboration, user-produced content). These discussions highlight the need for developing new methods, or extending the existing ones, in order to understand and deal with cultural and contextualized subjects in the social software landscape.

Hendler *et al.* [10] recognize the challenges of developing systems in such a complex scenario and advocate that a Web application should be understood as a "social machine" which includes an underlying technology, but also rules, strategies and organizational structures used to manage the technology. In this sense, the authors argue that designers of technologies have a responsibility to ensure that the products and services they develop on the Web do not produce side effects that harm society. Considering people's culture and values is a basic condition for the design of social software in the context of the third HCI paradigm.

According to Harrison *et al.* [11], while the first and second HCI paradigms are oriented to issues of ergonomics and cognitive factors, respectively, the third must deal with the establishment and multiplicity of meaning. In this paradigm, artifacts and their contexts are mutually defining and being subject of different interpretations. The interaction of people with computers has assumed new dimensions and cannot be addressed only as task-oriented; concepts we previously mentioned, such as human values, motivational and pragmatic aspects, emotion and affection, that were traditionally left on the margin of HCI approaches are moved to the centre, playing a key role. Differently from the two previous paradigms, which have substantial work and knowledge produced in the last three decades, the third one still remains quite unexplored by the HCI academy, requiring collaboration with other areas (e.g., anthropology, sociology) and the development of theories, approaches, methods and tools for understanding and dealing with its complex nature.

In this paper, we highlight the importance of taking into account cultural aspects of the different stakeholders in the project of social software; we propose, evaluate and discuss a culturally aware artifact, the Valuation Framing for Social Software (VF4SS), for supporting designers in their task. Our proposal is inspired by the Socially Aware Computing approach [6] and grounded on the building blocks of culture [12] and Organizational Semiotics [13].

The paper is organized as follows: section 2 presents the main theoretical and methodological bases of our research; section 3 proposes the VF4SS as an artifact for analyzing social software, taking into account people's cultural aspects and making values an explicit issue; section 4 describes our main findings when using the artifact to analyze five different projects during their design phase; finally, section 5 presents our conclusions and directions for further research.

2 Methodological and Theoretical Bases

According to Hall [12], humans operate on three different levels: informal, formal and technical. Each level is present in any situation, but one will always dominate in a given moment. Sometimes, the shifts (and boundaries) between these levels are subtle and rapid, but understanding these shifts is the basic requirement to understand the process of change.

In the Organizational Semiotics (OS) theory [13], an organization and its information system are considered a social system in which human behaviors are organized by a system of norms. This theory structures the informal, formal and technical levels in a scheme similar to an onion in order to represent the idea that any technological artifact is embedded in a formal system, which in turn, exists in the context of an informal one. The Semiotic Onion is an artifact of the OS that represents this scheme (see Fig. 1). Social software can be understood as a **technical** system situated in the core of the Semiotic Onion. This technical system exists within a **formal** system in which there are rules, procedures and norms; this formal system exists in the context of an **informal** one, where cultural aspects, such as customs, values, beliefs, habits and even individual behavior patterns, exist and influence the construction of meaning and the raising of intentions.

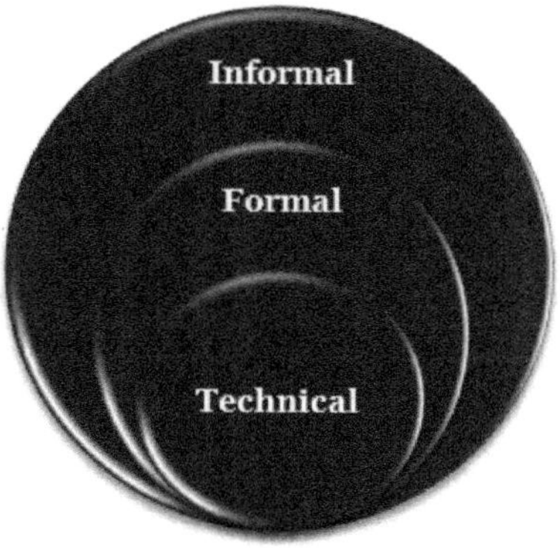

Fig. 1. The Semiotic Onion

Our previous work on social software and its elements [1], argued that they should be approached as values of different nature and with different relationships. Indeed, if we could take a picture of the social software context, these values would be predominantly manifested in one of these three levels, e.g., informal, although they exist simultaneously in the other two. For instance, consider the value of "privacy" that, according to Schwartz's circular model of values [14], is related to aspects of safety, harmony and stability of the self, which are usually treated as informal concepts. When we talk about privacy, we are talking about a subjective concept that is culturally built: everyone has his/her own informal understanding of what privacy is and what it means. However, there are social protocols, conventions, rules and laws that are formally established to define the meaning, limits and guarantees of an individual's privacy. Finally, there are also some facets of privacy that are so formally accepted that can be technically supported, such as a curtain to cover a window, the keys of a house/car, or the resources provided by internet banking systems in order to protect customers' data.

In this sense, the structure represented by the Semiotic Onion draws attention to the need of considering values that are manifested in each level, but that at the same time exist in the other two. Consequently, when designing or evaluating any technological artifact, designers must be aware that neglecting one or two levels of a given value can prevent the fully understanding of its meaning, scope and impact; completely neglecting the existence of values manifested in a given level may lead to the development of solutions that do not make sense to users and do not meet their needs.

Besides the Semiotic Onion, the OS theory provides methods and artifacts, such as the Stakeholders Identification Diagram, Semiotic Ladder and Ontology Charts [13] that allow considering the social world from the articulation of problems stage to the modeling of computer systems. Following we present the Valuation Framing, an artifact of OS created for assisting in the identification and understanding of the cultural (and social) dimensions of a product, technological or not, and its impact on people and their culture.

2.1 Valuation Framing

The Valuation Framing (VF) is an artifact of OS [13] created on the grounds of the ten building blocks of culture [12] (see Fig. 2). Within a culture, many patterns of behavior relate to each other in complex ways. In this context, each stakeholder group has a cultural system that governs how it will value an innovation: different stakeholders may react differently to the proposed innovation [13]. For instance, consider the introduction of electronic payment systems through credit card: the stores, customers, employees, banks, card management agencies, insurance companies and IT professionals are direct or indirectly interested and/or affected by that innovation and, consequently, are groups of stakeholders. These stakeholders may belong to quite distinct subcultures with different set of values so that the innovation tends to have rather different impacts on their lives.

Understanding the potential impact of the introduction of an innovation requires awareness of designers about the reactions of these groups of stakeholders. Kolkman [15] argues that if an innovation is inserted in each group accordingly, probably no serious problems will occur. Nevertheless, sometimes there may be conflicts and designers will be able to anticipate the reactions of stakeholders only if they could see the world through the lenses of these stakeholders. The VF helps in carrying out this kind of analysis by supporting the identification and understanding of the cultural dimensions of a product.

The basic principles of the VF are: all the stakeholders involved in a project are accustomed to have, in their cultural settings, a range of behavior patterns divided into 10 areas, or the building blocks that Hall [12] calls Primary Message Systems (PMS) — see the column "PMS" in Fig. 2. The analyst's work consists of questioning, predicting and hypothesizing how the innovation may affect/is affecting these stakeholders regarding these areas. From the original areas, Kolkman [14] renamed "Defense" to "Protection" and "Bisexuality" to "Classification".

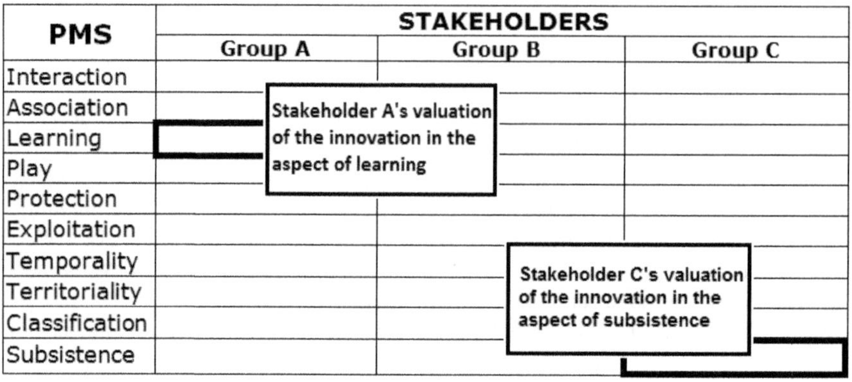

Fig. 2. The Valuation Framing, adapted from [13]

Considering the case of credit card systems, the stores' employees (stakeholders) could see the innovation as a threat because they do not know how to operate the new machines introduced in their environment (learning). On the other hand, the manager could perceive this innovation as an unnecessary operational cost, once it requires firing and hiring more employees and/or training them (subsistence). The other groups will also value the innovation from a different perspective. In this sense, understanding and dealing with values and cultural systems of each group of stakeholders could determine how they would react to such an innovation and, ultimately, whether that innovation would be appropriated or rejected by them.

According to the exposed, the VF can be seen as a powerful artifact for enabling designers to anticipate and deal with cultural issues in the context of the project of any innovation. However, using this artifact is not a trivial activity because it requires knowledge in anthropology and social sciences. This knowledge is necessary so that designers are able to understand the areas that compose a culture and recognize the values related to each one.

As Sellen *et al.* [16] point out, the curricula in Computer Science do not traditionally dispend much effort in enabling its students to deal with social issues. Multidisciplinary teams could contribute with different visions to a project; however, although a desirable scenario, multidisciplinary teams are not always possible or viable. In the example of credit card systems the problem space is, at least in parts, well known to them. However, in the project of social software it is even more complicated to know exactly what must be taken into account. For instance, what are the values related to the aspects of temporality, territoriality or association? What values come into play when the innovation is not a tangible device but a computer system usable through different devices?

Indeed, regarding social software there are neither knowledge nor ways (or experience) for anticipating stakeholders' reactions, so that dealing with a so diverse range of stakeholders with quite different cultural systems become a very costly and complex task. In this case, the need for lightweight and principled methods that support designers in seeing through the lenses of each stakeholder group is emphasized. In the next sections, we present our research and its preliminary results as a further step towards the construction of such methods.

3 Valuation Framing for Social Software

Several authors, such as Harrison *et al.* [11] and Sellen *et al.* [16], highlight the need for developing and publishing studies to support designers and evaluators to deal with the complexity and different requirements that current technologies have. In this section, we present the Valuation Framing for Social Software (VF4SS): a VF specially adapted to guide designers in dealing with cultural aspects, mainly values, involved in the context of social software.

When discussing the ten areas and the way they could map culture, Hall [12] affirms that each culture develops values in regard to these areas. For instance, values in classification center on preferred style of dressing, jobs, sports, and so on, of men and women. Values in learning can be related to valued kind of abilities, knowledge and professions; the relative importance of experience, expertise, meritocracy, and others.

In the context of social software, we developed a discussion regarding the elements that compose this kind of system approaching them in terms of values, and presented a set of values identified through technical analysis and an extensive literature review [5]. This set encompasses technical as well as formal and informal aspects, and draws attention to their differences and interactive nature. The main idea is that depending on which values are prioritized, how these values are combined and technically supported, quite different environments which promote certain values while inhibit others will be produced. Because values are culturally built, established and modified, the viability of approaching the social software elements as values was verified when classifying them into the culture area more suitable to each one.

Therefore, the VF4SS includes an additional column, named “Value”, that suggests at least one value for each one of the ten anthropological areas (see Fig. 3). Besides being classified into the culture’s areas, each value was also classified through the Semiotic Onion according to the level that represents its predominant state. As a result, values were classified at the **informal** (mostly values of personal and ethical nature), **formal** (collective or social values where there is some rule or system of norms), or **technical** level (values that can be understood as attributes of quality or special features of technology). In an alternative classification [5], we referred to these levels as Personal, Social and Technical, respectively.

Although this value distribution is not complete for some areas, the spaces corresponding to the three levels remain explicit in the artifact in order to encourage designers to identify new values and think on possible manifestations of each area as well as their values at the three levels.

The main goal in creating an adapted version of the VF for the context of social software is to support designers in the understanding, analysis and evaluation of such systems. As previously mentioned, traditional methods and techniques for software evaluation and analysis do not draw attention to cultural aspects, and the original VF is not an easy to use artifact for those who do not have experience with social (cultural) issues in design. In this sense, embedded in the original VF, these values favor designers, evaluators and analysts to keep values in mind, helping them to learn how to use the artifact itself and situate themselves with respect to what they must investigate and consider in each area. To situate our discussions in a practical context, in the next section we present an experiment in which the VF4SS was applied to the evaluation of five different projects.

PMS	Value			STAKEHOLDERS		
	I	F	T	Group A	Group B	Group C
Interaction	Identity	Norms				
Association	Conversation, Trust	Relationship, Groups				
Learning			Meta-communication			
Play	Emotion and Affection		Aesthetic			
Protection	Informed consent, Reputation		Security			
Exploitation		Object, Ownership	Accessibility, Usability			
Temporality	Presence		Availability, Awareness			
Territoriality	Privacy, Visibility		Portability, Scalability			
Classification			Adaptability			
Subsistence	Autonomy, Reciprocity	Collaboration, Sharing				

Fig. 3. The Valuation Framing for Social Software

4 The Case Study

Aiming at verifying the acceptance and applicability of the VF4SS, the artifact was used in the evaluation of five different projects related to the prototyping of systems for supporting cross-cultural collaboration. This context was an ideal setting for assessing our artifact due to the explicit need for dealing with cultural aspects and, consequently, with values. These projects were developed in a graduate course called "Topics in User Interfaces: Semiotics of Human-Digital Artifact Interaction" in which the Organizational Semiotics [13] theory was used as an approach for the development of information systems. The group of participants was formed by 16 designers divided into five groups: G1 (formed by designers: D1, D2 and D3), G2 (D4, D5, D6), G3 (D7, D8, D9), G4 (D10, D11, D12) and G5 (D13, D14, D15, D16).

The five projects for supporting cross-cultural collaboration involved different subjects; the Project of G1 was related to international sporting events; the Project of G2 and G3 were related to gastronomy and culinary practices; the Project of G4 was related to musical tastes and compositions and the Project of G5 to residential tourism. This variety was useful because it favored the diversity in terms of stakeholder groups, cultures, values, including system's requirements and features.

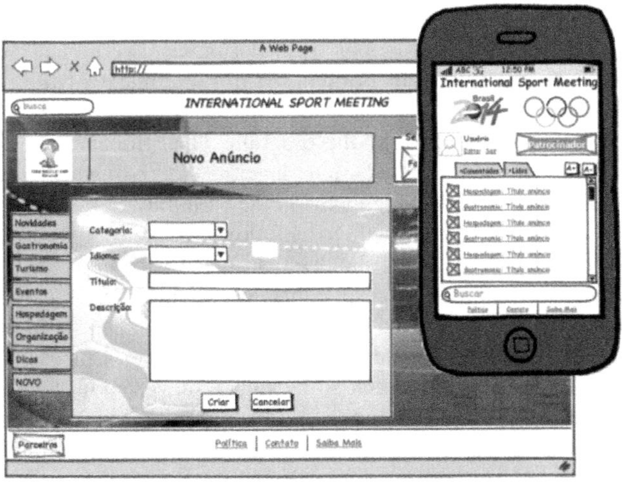

Fig. 4. Prototypes produced in the Project 1 (G1)

When the evaluation activity started, each group had completed the documentation and had finished the prototyping of the first increment of their systems — see Fig. 4 for an example. The main goals in evaluating the prototype from the designers' point of view were to identify: i) the impact the produced system could cause in its different groups of stakeholders; ii) the possible conflicts between these groups; and iii) the values involved in the system and the way these values were being technically supported or promoted. On the other hand, the two main goals of this activity from our point of view were: 1. to identify if the VF4SS would support designers in evaluating social software; and 2. to verify whether the values suggested would make sense to designers, and what other values should be included or removed.

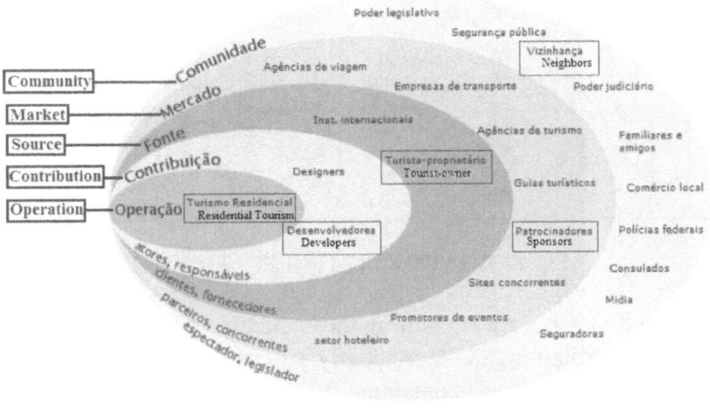

Fig. 5. The Stakeholders Identification Diagram filled in the Project 5 (G5)

When the evaluation activity took place, the identification of all stakeholder groups involved in each project was already carried using another artifact of OS: the Stakeholders Identification diagram [13]. This artifact distributes the stakeholders in different categories ranging from the actors directly involved in the project to the community who may not use the system but can be affected by it. In the diagram illustrated by Fig. 5 (some translations from Portuguese were made by the authors), designers identified the stakeholders involved in the context of the project G5. For instance, in the "Residential Tourism" case, the focus of their project was placed in the Operation layer — the core of the diagram; "Developers" was identified as a stakeholder group in the Contribution layer; "Tourist-owner" in the Source; "Sponsors" in the Market and "Neighbors" in the Community.

The evaluation activity was carried out as follows: in the **first** step, designers should select three different groups of stakeholders and place each group in a column of the VF4SS (see Fig. 6). In order to ensure that the system's cross-cultural nature was explicit, the groups should be from different layers of the Stakeholders Identification Diagram and from different national cultures (e.g., Brazilian, Chinese and Russian). In the **second** step, designers should look at the values suggested in the VF4SS and mark those they were already considering in their project. In the **third** step, designers should analyze and discuss the importance of each value and the impact it could cause on each stakeholder group. In the corresponding cell of the artifact, designers should indicate how that value was being technically supported in the project. Finally, in the **fourth** step designers should analyze if there would be any conflict in the way each value was being supported in the system according to the different groups of stakeholders. If any, they should indicate how the conflict could be treated.

Area (PMS)	Value (Personal / Social / Technical)	STAKEHOLDER: Translator (Brazilian)	Amateur Cook (Japanese)	Culinary School (French)
1. Interaction	Identity Norms	Translator's profile informing the languages he is fluent, the content he has translated and his/her ranking compared to other translators.	Cook's profile, including his/her tastes, culture, published recipes, followed recipes and comments on them.	School's profile, including its gastronomy style, its website, courses, published recipes, followed recipes and their evaluation.
		System's use and copyright terms. It is possible to translate recipes and evaluate the translation accomplished by others.	Copyright terms; usage policy; This stakeholder can publish and evaluate recipes.	Copyright terms; usage policy; This stakeholder can publish and evaluate recipes and divulgate gastronomy courses.

Fig. 6. The VF4SS filled in the Project 2 (G2)

As background material for supporting the evaluation task, designers were supplied with: i) guidelines explaining the four activity's steps; ii) the VF4SS both in press and digital format; iii) a document containing a simplified explanation of each area of culture; and iv) a table containing a description and an example for each value suggested in the artifact. As activity outcomes, each group should fulfill the VF4SS, answer a survey related to its applicability, redesign the system according to their discussions and share their findings with the other groups.

4.1 Activity Main Findings

In general, the evaluation of the projects through the VF4SS provided us data, insights and evidences that show the viability of using this artifact for social software evaluation as well as social software requirements clarification and design. Following, we present some findings and highlight some results regarding the case study.

From designers' point of view, the activity outcomes confirmed our expectations regarding (i) the VF4SS's usefulness for identifying the impact caused by the system on its different stakeholders. All groups reported that the artifact was determinant in the process of discussing the challenges, difficulties and even opportunities for each stakeholder group regarding the system being prototyped. The VF4SS and its areas enabled designers seeing (or at least, trying to see) the system through the lenses of different stakeholders who would be affected by the system in different ways. For instance, D10 reported: "*the Valuation Framing brought us* [G4] *a better understanding about the impacts that the introduction of our system could bring to musicians, producers and fans*". In this project, questions related to copyright, property and privacy that could be affected by the system usage were put into the scene by the VF4SS.

Another point covered by the VF4SS was (ii) the identification of possible conflicts between the groups of stakeholders. In some cases the solution to conflicts was achieved through the specification and design of additional features in the system, while in other situations it was understood as a new norm, rule, or even as a system limitation. Some interesting examples are: "*Sponsors want a greater emphasis on their advertisements, while readers want a clean interface; Advertisers want to post any content, while the moderator have to supervise them*" (G1). "*A negative rating for a recipe by the users can bother the system's sponsor*" (G3). "*When musicians are composing a song in a private mode, their fans should not be able to view it. The system must offer features that enable users to manage the visibility of their productions*" (G4).

Finally, the VF4SS was also able to support designers (iii) to identify the values involved in their projects and the way these values were being technically supported. For instance, in the Project 2, the VF4SS led designers to think about the differences in the profile feature according to the stakeholder group and to redesign the system to reflect these differences. In the same project, designers identified the need for mechanisms to encourage the participation of users as a way of technically implementing the value of "Emotion and Affection". They proposed features that took into account the different needs and expectations of stakeholders. For instance, the feature for encouraging the participation of the "Translator" (of recipes) stakeholder was prototyped as a scheme of credits (cash prizes were cited as an alternative) while the feature for the "Culinary School" stakeholder was prototyped as the possibility for free announcements in the system. These aspects were not being addressed before the evaluation through the VF4SS.

According to designers' feedback and our own observations during the execution of the projects, we could perceive the VF4SS as an artifact capable of generating fruitful discussions among designers, allowing them to exercise a critical thinking regarding the whole impact of the solutions they were designing. This artifact effectively contributes to the development of products compatible with the values of the people they are intended for, instead of the values of their designers. In doing so, it also contributes to a proper deployment of the product in the target environment: if a product reflects an understanding and respect to the values of its different stakeholders, then, it has better chances of being appropriated by these stakeholders. These findings are naturally extended to the original VF.

From the point of view of our research, we confirmed our hypothesis regarding (1) the utility of the VF4SS for assisting designers to analyze and evaluate social software, and also regarding (2) the relevance and benefits of the values suggested (i.e., whether the values suggested would make sense to them).

According to the survey designers answered after the evaluation activity, 60% found the values very useful for the system evaluation; 40% found them useful; and none answered they are neutral, unhelpful or useless. According to D4, the suggested values assisted the group (G2) in carrying out the evaluation task because they served as a starting point of several considerations. Since they had no previous experience with cultural issues, if no values were suggested they could get lost without knowing what to do or how to proceed. Designers would hardly know what values or aspects they should consider when discussing each area. Therefore, the values suggested in the VF4SS are important not only to support designers in carrying out the evaluation of their projects, but also in learning how to use the artifact itself.

Moreover, in the survey, designers suggested no additional values to the 28 presented in the VF4SS. Using designer's words: "*we identified no values to be included in the framework*" (G1); "*the table* [with a description and example for each value] *is generic enough for fitting any value into the available options*" (G3); "*the suggested values were capable of expressing in a complete way what we seek and discovered*" (G2).

Other evidence that the values suggested into the VF4SS made sense to designers was the percentage of values that were effectively considered or discussed (pointed out as important) in the Projects — see Table 1. Designers from G1 identified, or at least discussed, values related to the suggested by the VF4SS during the second step in the evaluation activity, indicating that these values were being considered in their project; in the same way, designers from G3 marked 82% of the values. Although no additional values were considered, they reviewed and complemented their discussions, looking for possible conflicts and specifying technical features to support those values. On the other hand, in the G2, G4 and G5 groups, designers were explicitly considering 39%, 57% and 79% of the values, respectively, when the evaluation took place. However, while filling the VF4SS they recognized the importance of paying attention to new values and discussed how these additional values could be technically supported in their systems. When the activity finished, these groups were considering 61%, 61% and 100% of the values, respectively.

Table 1. Values considered and discussed in each project

Group	G1	G2	G3	G4	G5
Values considered	100%	39%	82%	57%	79%
Values discussed	100%	61%	82%	61%	100%

We should highlight, however, that considering more or less values is not just a question of designers' choice but also of the project context and scope. Also, it does not mean that designers implemented all the marked values in their prototypes: some of them were considered as limitations, constraints, future work and ideas. However, they were useful in generating critical discussions and in keeping in mind the concern of stakeholders' culture. Consequently, these data do not suggest the values as a definitive and exhaustive set but that they made sense to designers, were useful in promoting critical discussions and met their needs in the context of their projects.

An interesting example from G2 is related to the "meta-communication" value, which was not considered by designers during the prototyping of the system's first increment. However, because the VF4SS suggested this value in the cultural aspect of "Learning", designers started discussing how their system could technically support it. After some discussions, they identified that each group of stakeholders had different views and different needs regarding the value of meta-communication. For instance, the "Translator" stakeholder would need support to understand how the process of collaborative translation would work and to learn how to use the functionalities related to it; the "Gastronomy school" stakeholder, in turn, would need support to learn how to use the system: to publish, search and evaluate recipes; and the "Amateur cook" stakeholder would need support, through a resource other than text, for teaching him/her how to run the recipe. Thus, designers decided to offer support to the value of meta-communication through the use of tutorials and videos placed in the system's interface; e.g., each recipe should have a subtitled video showing a step-by-step of how to cook it. After these specifications, the project documentation was updated and the prototype was redesigned in order to include the new system's features.

In fact, the VF4SS not only supported designers in the task of analyzing and evaluating the system they were projecting, but also made they think on new requirements and features that were missing or could be included in their systems. By suggesting values, the VF4SS incited designers to discuss and consider aspects that were being neglected. Therefore, it showed to be a useful artifact also for clarifying and eliciting requirements. The explicit feedback from designers can confirm this assertion:

D2: "*I would find it very interesting to apply this artifact* [VF4SS] *for requirements elicitation. The reason is quite simple: it enables those involved in the development process to see, or try to see, through the eyes of other stakeholders involved in the project they are proposing. As a developer, I feel that a lot of rework is caused by developing systems without thinking of people who will actually use it*";

D3: "*The VF4SS is very interesting because it forces us to imagine the system through the views of different stakeholders, making designers think whether the values are being addressed in the proposed project according to these different stakeholders. This activity resulted in new requirements identified. So, in my opinion, it is a very important activity to be performed at different times within a project, from requirements elicitation to the system evaluation*";

D5: "*The VF4SS is, in my opinion, a great tool not only for evaluating the design of a system, but also to identify important requirements*";

D9: "*The VF4SS was the tool that I found most interesting in the whole process. It allows checking for any conflicting requirements between the various stakeholders and makes it possible to deal with this information so that such conflicts do not hinder the development of the project*";

D14: "*Hardly in the development of a system we think of all the users who can use it. The way we had to think, as users from other nationalities and with different profiles, since a single user until the government of a country, made us see the points that initially were not being covered. So, we could evolve our system and consider other points to the elaboration of the final prototype*".

Grounded on the results briefly discussed in this section, we are convinced of the viability of using the VF for the evaluation as well as for the requirements elicitation of any technological artifact in order to make cultural aspects an explicit issue. Specifically in the context of social software, the VF4SS showed to be a promising artifact for supporting designers in dealing with the complexity imposed by the social context of these systems. Indeed, this artifact can be used in research projects as well as industrial settings favoring discussions around cultural aspects while guiding and capacitating designers regarding social subjects. Finally, this study also contributes to validate the relevance of the values we identified and discussed in [5], in the context of social software.

5 Conclusions

The design of social software still demands approaches, artifacts, methods and tools for reflecting and dealing with the social nature that characterizes it. In fact, there is even a lack of theoretically grounded approaches for investigating this kind of system. Moreover, although clearly recognized as important, there are few initiatives in literature related to values in technology; even fewer are those concerned with the development of solutions to guide researchers and practitioners in dealing with cultural issues.

In the present paper, we shed light on this scenario proposing the VF4SS, a culturally aware artifact specially adapted to the context of social software design. This artifact is a result of previous discussions that articulate key concepts and theories, such as the three levels in which humans operate, the ten basic building blocks of culture and the Organizational Semiotics theory with some of its artifacts.

The results obtained from the evaluation of five prototypes of systems situated in the context of cross-cultural collaboration indicate the benefits of using the VF4SS for evaluating as well as clarifying requirements for social software design. However, although this research is focused on the social software subject, we believe the artifact itself, the way it was used, the theories that ground it and the arguments we present here, are timeless and can be used in the analysis of any technological artifact.

Nevertheless, some important points still remain quite unexplored and can be seen as a research agenda in the area. For instance, it is necessary to investigate how the artifact could be applied in a practical context of requirements clarification and interaction design. What kind of results would it provide? How can designers move from its unstructured discussions to formal requirements? What methods and tools can be developed in order to support the use of the artifact?

Finally, although a key artifact, the VF4SS alone is not enough to guarantee an effective consideration of values in social software design. Indeed, as the experiment described in this paper showed, other artifacts, methods and tools are needed in order to allow the articulation and involvement of cultural aspects during the different stages of a system development (e.g., the Stakeholders Identification diagram). We are naming culturally-informed approach (CIA) such set of tools, methods and artifacts we are investigating in ongoing and further research.

Acknowledgements. This research is partially funded by FAPESP (#2009/11888-7), and by CNPq through the EcoWeb Project (#560044/2010-0). The authors specially thank the designers who collaborated with the evaluation activity and authorized the use of the documentation of their projects in this paper, and the anonymous reviewers that contributed through their comments and evaluations.

References

1. Pereira, R., Baranauskas, M.C.C., Silva, S.R.P.: A Discussion on Social Software: Concept, Building Blocks and Challenges. International Journal for Infonomics 3(4), 382–391 (2010)
2. Boyd, D.: The Significance of Social Software. In: BlogTalks Reloaded: Social Software Research & Cases, Norderstedt, pp. 15–30 (2007)
3. Schuler, D., Namioka, A.: Participatory design: principles and practices. Lawrence Erlbaum Associates Inc., Hillsdale (1993)
4. Friedman, B.: Value-Sensitive Design. Interactions, 16–23 (1996)
5. Pereira, R., Baranauskas, M.C.C., Silva, S.R.P.: Softwares Sociais: Uma Visao Orientada a Valores. In: IX Brazilian Symposium on Human Factors in Computer Systems (IHC 2010), pp. 149–158. ACM Press, Belo Horizonte (2010)
6. Baranauskas, M.C.C.: Socially Aware Computing. In: ICECE 2009 – VI International Conference on Engineering and Computer Education, Buenos Aires, pp. 1–4 (2009)
7. Hart, J., Ridley, C., Taher, F., Sas, C., Dix, A.: Exploring the Facebook Experience: A New Approach to Usability. In: NordiCHI 2008, pp. 471–474. ACM Press, Lund (2008)
8. Thompson, A.-J., Kemp, E.A.: Web 2.0: extending the framework for heuristic evaluation. In: ACM CHINZ 2009, pp. 29–36. ACM Press, Auckland (2009)
9. Silva, P.A., Dix, A.: Usability – Not as we know it! In: 21st BCS Conference on Human-Computer Interaction, Lanchester, pp. 103–106 (2007)
10. Hendler, J., Shadbolt, N., Hall, W., Berners-Lee, T., Weitzner, D.: Web science: an interdisciplinary approach to understanding the web. Communications of the ACM 51, 60–69 (2008)
11. Harrison, S., Tatar, D., Sengers, P.: The three paradigms of HCI. In: Alt CHI – Proceedings of CHI 2007, pp. 1–21. ACM Press, San Jose (2007)
12. Hall, E.T.: The Silent Language. Anchoor Books, New York (1959)
13. Liu, K.: Semiotics in Information Systems Engineering. Cambridge University Press, New York (2000)
14. Schwartz, S.H.: Basic human values: Their content and structure across countries. In: Values and Behaviors in Organizations, Vozes, Rio de Janeiro, pp. 21–55 (2005)
15. Kolkman, M.: Problem articulation methodology. PhD thesis, University of Twente, Enschede (1993)
16. Sellen, A., Rogers, Y., Harper, R., Rodden, T.: Reflecting Human Values in the Digital Age. Communications of the ACM 52, 58–66 (2009)

Electronic Government in Brazil: Evaluating Brazilian Initiative and How to Improve It

Giovanni Bogéa Viana and Maria Beatriz Felgar de Toledo

Universidade Estadual de Campinas, Instituto de Computação, Campinas, Brazil

Abstract. This article presents an overview of a major e-government site in Brazil, the Transparency Portal, and makes a comparison with electronic government of some other countries, in order to assess the degree of accessibility of each site. To obtain the results, the validation tools ASES, DaSilva and Total-Validator have been used to evaluate the sites based on e-MAG and WCAG. A survey with entities, such as NGOs and ordinary users is also presented, aiming at evaluating the Transparency Portal according to criteria such as navigation and ease of use. These assessments and a proposed architecture will be used as suggestions for improving the Brazilian site and make it easier to use and accessible to a greater number of citizens, regardless of educational level and specific needs.

Keywords: e-Government, e-Society, Accessibility, Usability, Interfaces.

1 Introduction

The Electronic Government (or e-gov) is a new form of government that can be understood from three different viewpoints: the government itself, which brings advantages such as greater ease in dissemination of laws, decisions, regulations and more efficient service provisioning; to the entrepreneur, enabling fast and simple access to the offered services, agility and transparency in the negotiations with the government; and to the individual citizen, who also has easier access to services in a convenient, fast and cheap way [1].

To achieve its objectives, the e-government has principles such as to allow access to databases of the government and to deliver services truly transparent, efficient and convenient. These services can be offered through the use of information technologies and communication technologies (ICTs) [1], which can reach a large number of people including groups like elderly, young, people with special needs and others distant from government centers. Restrictions of each group must be identified, and applications and infrastructure tailored so that all groups can finally participate of the government.

The aim of this paper is to compare e-government sites according to accessibility standards recommended by the World Wide Web Consortium (W3C), to evaluate the usability of the Transparency Portal (www.portaldatransparencia.gov.br), a leading e-government site in Brazil, and to propose an architecture for government spending portals. The paper is divided as follows: in the "Related Work", some works that try to ensure the usability for all are presented. In "Accessibility and Usability" the respective terms are conceptualized. Next, the section "The Transparency Portal in Brazil" provides assessments of accessibility and usability of a leading e-government site in Brazil

R. Zhang et al. (Eds.): ICEIS 2011, LNBIP 102, pp. 388–402, 2012.

and proposes a new architecture for it. In the section "Comparison to Other Portals", the Brazilian site is compared with other e-government sites around the world. Finally, we present the "Conclusions".

2 Related Work

The use of Organizational Semiotics is proposed by Neris [2] to understand the different interactions with the various potential public of the interfaces and then use the concept of customization to tailor the interface for each. The work proposes a framework called PLuRal which is based on three pillars: the identification of user needs, definition of features that will be offered, and determination of the possibilities of adaptation based on the former pillars.

Fortuna et al. [3] propose a framework for building interfaces based on Ajax and Norms. The framework does not require reloading pages, it infers user behavior and allows users to have a better experience with the application. The framework contains a perception module, which captures the user interactions, a SOAP client for loading the rules, and an action module, responsible for making the change in the system according to a plan of action drawn from the Norms. Finally there is a storage module of the events generated by users (for future reference) and modules for storage of Inferences, Norms and creation of action plans. Sites like the Transparency Portal (in Portuguese "Portal da Transparência") does not require registration, making inferences based on previous experiences difficult.

Diirr et al. [4] believe that one way to encourage the participation of citizens in the political movement is through conversations related to areas of public interest. They define a process as "a sequence of inter-dependent actions that consume one or more resources to convert inputs into outputs", and the discussions around the process. The work focuses on the first levels of democratic participation (where the initial levels represent the population's access to information and the upper levels represent the public participation in decision making, as a direct democracy). Based on the responses, the services offered can then be improved.

Veenstra and Zuurmond [5] reinforce the idea that e-government is not just offering online services but should include personalized services to citizens. Accordingly, departments of one or more organizations should cooperate to offer services as a unique view to citizens, no matter which number of departments would be involved. Consultants, government officials and specialized sites were used as sources to identify the relationship between variables related to the factors of organizational change (e.g. aligning IT to business, vertical or horizontal organization, internal/external management, non-duplication of activities, technology deployment and systems, among others) and quality of service offered. The results showed that yes, there is a relationship between some factors of organizational change and quality of service, and the factors related to information technology in large part impact the measures of the quality of service.

3 Accessibility and Usability

E-government aims at the development of applications with good usability and accessibility, here understood as the requirement that applications can easily be accessed and understood by the entire population. Whereas accessibility allows information to be obtained even by those with special needs, a good usability ensures that the path to obtain the information will be found in an objective and easy way. Usability testing should be made to identify the interface more suitable, especially when considering the needs of different users.

Accessibility is a requirement in applications developed by the Brazilian Government since December 2004 and a standard called Accessibility Model for Electronic Government (e-MAG, in Portuguese "Modelo de Acessibilidade de Governo Eletrônico") [6] is the reference to be followed. The current version 2.0 was released in December 2005 and is based on the Web Content Accessibility Guidelines (WCAG) standard. Usability, in turn, does not have a legal obligation in Brazil. However, it involves fundamental principles such as effectiveness and efficiency in information search, satisfaction of use, frequency of errors and memories of previous experience [7]. Accessibility is still a keyword to W3C, which in its specification for HyperText Markup Language (HTML) 5 [8] mentions the creation of accessible pages as part of its scope.

Accessible applications and appropriate usability lead to a greater participation in government by all and make communication with authorities about local issues easier. An example is the site "FixMyStreet" [9], in which citizens of Great Britain report problems about cleaning and lighting, among others. Electronic Government challenges to the population also exist: the site "Apps for Democracy" [10] stimulates a contest with prizes for the identification and resolution of the main types of problems that can be treated by ICTs.

4 The Transparency Portal in Brazil

The website Transparency Portal is an official project released in November 2004 by the Brazilian Inspectorate-General office (In Portuguese, "Controladoria-Geral da União") in order to expose all the expenses of the executive branch of the Brazilian government in one place. The initiative intended to strengthen the defense of the public patrimony and to increase the transparency of public management, roles performed by this office, through the so called "Popular Control" of federal spending. A view of the current interface of the portal can be seen in Fig. 1 and the site requires no registration for information to be queried in order to encourage its use by the entire population.

4.1 Difficulties

Although there are tips and instructions for accessing the data, it is hard for the average citizen to know where to start searching ("direct expenditures" or "transfer of funds"?) or even understand the classification of displayed expenditures ("function", "subfunction", "program", "action", among other things). This difficulty is mainly caused by the lack of technical knowledge of citizens about the terms of budget execution. Moreover, some segments with greater technical knowledge, as control offices and organizations, can find information easily and even prefer the division of expenses in the way they are detailed in the budget. The current approach can not be totally discarded, but there should be a complement to allow customization of the information to the regular user.

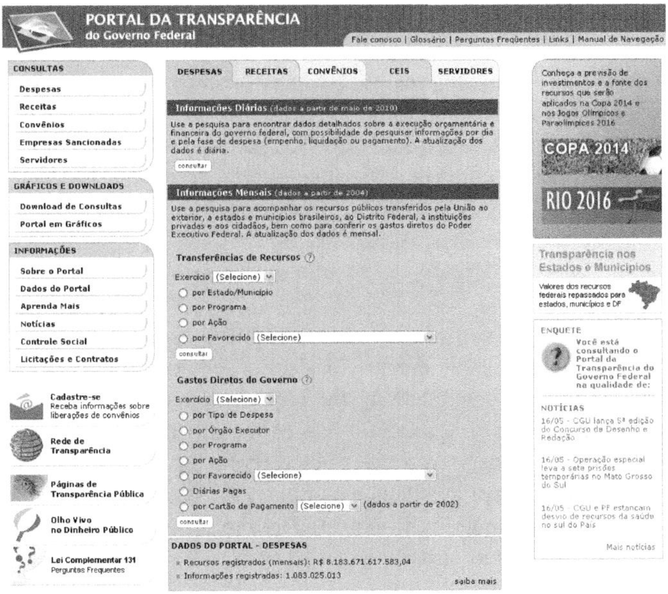

Fig. 1. Current interface of the Transparency Portal

4.2 NGOs Evaluations

Aiming at getting different views on the Transparency Portal, a survey was made with entities/non-governmental organizations (NGOs) which work in the areas of transparency, corruption combat and engagement of citizens in government actions. The objective of research was to evaluate the adequacy of the portal interface and its use by such entities. The result showed that these entities have no navigation problems and even feel there is a lack of more technical details. The questions are listed below:

I Does the entity use the Transparency Portal in any way in encouraging the fight against Corruption?

All surveyed organizations answered they use the site, in proportions ranging from consultation only the spending on payment cards (official credit cards, information not available in other sites) to congratulations for its completeness. When partially used, other sites like Follow Brazil (In Portuguese "Siga Brasil" - www9.senado.gov.br/portal/page/portal/orcamento_senado/SigaBrasil) (with details of expenses of the branches Judiciary and Legislative) are used to complement the information.

II - On the Transparency Portal being an official tool for the dissemination of public spending, does the organization miss any data or facility not available?

There were considerations of no exposure of expenditures of State Companies, the means used to acquire the products and (more specifically related to credit cards) the description of the goods purchased. One factor raised more than once was the difficulty in making crosses of expenditures. This reason has even been a cause to the use of other sites.

III - Is it difficult to use / find the data on the Transparency Portal? Is it slow? Is navigation user friendly?

The usability of the site has been praised and navigation classified as even very easy. These evaluations were complemented with accessibility tests made with specific tools and are discussed in the following section (section "Comparison with other Websites"). Finding the data was considered a simple task and the navigation of the portal quick.

As NGOs showed satisfaction with the portal usability, they were not asked to participate in the next experiment. The experiment uses two developed prototypes and is described as follows.

4.3 Evaluations by Common Users

Aiming at obtaining views of ordinary users about the usability of the Transparency Portal, two prototypes have been created, one proposed according to the technique of card sorting [7] and the other reflecting the current structure of the site. In the first prototype, using the card sorting, twenty-five of the most common queries available at the site were listed and users were instructed to gather the information in the way they considered most appropriate. This experience showed that if to NGOs users the data were easily found, ordinary users expected to find the information on a completely different place. The generated prototype can be seen in Fig. 2. It is a simplification of the official version.

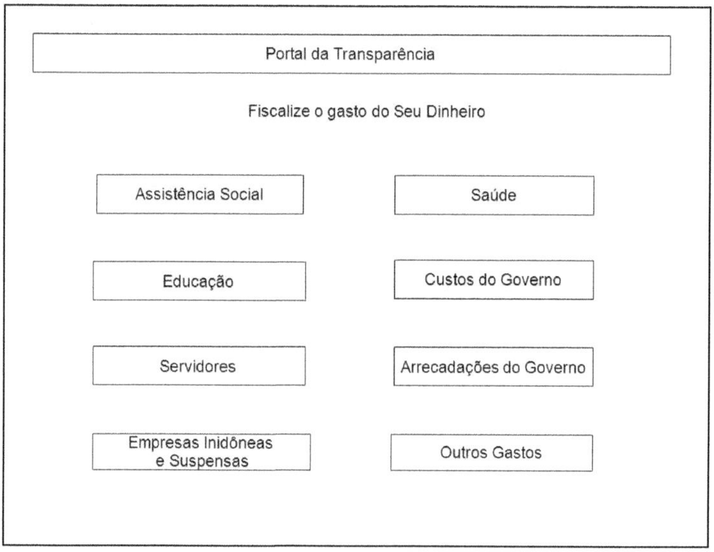

Fig. 2. Prototype based on card sorting

In the second prototype, shown in Fig. 3, the intention was to obtain a mirror of the current interface of the Transparency Portal. This prototype resembles the one generated by card sorting. The official site, available on the Internet since 2004, was not used so that a fair comparison could be achieved with the experiment. Selected users do not previously know the official website of the Brazilian Government. This requirement was important as prior knowledge of the site would lead to a false easy navigation in the model representing the current interface. The order of evaluation of the two prototypes

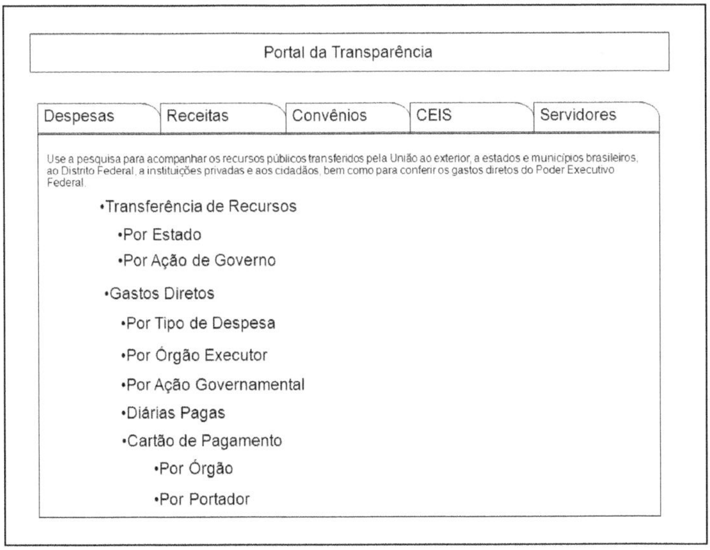

Fig. 3. Prototype of the current Transparency Portal

was also alternated between the prototype of proposed model (card sorting) and the prototype of the current interface.

Participants received instructions about what was the objective of the test and also what was the Transparency Portal. Each participant should find in the two prototypes specific information about government spending but not in the government portal itself. Difficulties in obtaining the answers would be faults on the organization of information. There was no time limit, the counting would start individually for each question until the user found the answer.

A total of five questions were asked and should be answered for the two prototypes. No significant differences in response time related to the order of evaluation of prototypes were found. Among the selected users, including the ones involved in the development of card sorting, there were students, lawyers, a language teacher, a police investigator, civil servants and retirees. The test reinforced the idea that tabs (as the ones in browsers) need to be used with caution because in some cases much of the time spent in searching was used in recognizing the tab. Another factor that has been proven is that although the availability of various search options (ways to reach the information) may facilitate queries to the advanced user, the average user is penalized for not knowing which option to choose.

The questions are presented below and demonstrate information that can actually be obtained from the Transparency Portal:

I - What are the beneficiaries of the social program called Family Grant (in Portuguese "Bolsa Família") in the city of Castanheiras? (fictional town)

II - How much and for whom it was the spending on maintenance of health centers at the "Hospital das Clínicas" hospital?

III - What are the public servants of the Ministry of Education?

IV - How much was the incoming of the government with Taxes and Fees?

V - How much was spent by the Federal Government with the public agreement for implementation of Digital Inclusion Centers?

Each of the five questions was assessed against four criteria, listed below, and the test results can be found in tables 1 and 2. With the exception of Public Agreement consultation, for which there is a specific section in the current model of the Portal and the card sorting technique grouped according to the area of the agreement operation, all other consultations showed significant improvements in the proposed model. This model was considered more appropriate for all users of the test, and the improvements were obtained due to the simplified view of the prototype.

Each of the previous questions were analyzed according to the following aspects with results presented in tables 1 and 2:

I - Success in obtaining the data (regardless of what navigation path followed).

II - Total time spent on the question.

III - Ease of navigation (grades 1-4 assigned by the user, with 1 being very difficult and 4 very easy).

IV - Navigation paths traversed until the user says that information has been found.

Table 1. Average success, spent time in seconds, facility and paths taken by users to obtain the requested information - the original model

Question	Success	Time (s)	Facility	Paths
"Bolsa Família" social program	100%	126,4	2,6	4
"Hospital das Clínicas" maintence	0%	82,2	2,6	3,8
Servants of the Ministry of Education	20%	72,4	3	2,8
Taxes and Fees	100%	25,8	3	1,2
Digital Inclusion Centers agreement	100%	17,8	3,4	1,2

Table 2. Average success, spent time in seconds, facility and paths taken by users to obtain the requested information - proposed model

Question	Success	Time (s)	Facility	Paths
"Bolsa Família" social program	100%	19,8	3,6	1,2
"Hospital das Clínicas" maintence	100%	14,6	3,8	1,2
Servants of the Ministry of Education	100%	8,2	3,8	1,2
Taxes and Fees	100%	4,6	4	1
Digital Inclusion Centers agreement	80%	31,8	2,8	3,2

4.4 Proposed Improvements

The Transparency Portal falls short of its goal with the current interface, as demonstrated in the evaluation with regular users and even organs and entities that have technical knowledge about the budget. Whereas the former may have a difficult navigation, due to technical terms, the latter have difficulties especially related to cross-checks and the lack of information on the expenses of other powers. The cross-checks limitation, linking of data, could be circumvented by the availability of the so-called "raw data" such that data of the consultations would be available in its original form (without treatment). Although there is an option to download spreadsheets with some of the display data in the Portal, the information is not complete.

Aligned with the considerations of Veenstra and Zuurmond [5], the Transparency Portal should show the data of the three powers (legislative, judicial and executive). The fact that the Brazilian Inspectorate-General is an office of the executive should not be a hindrance to the development of a portal vision of a single-service consulting for government spending. Regarding the difficulties of using the interface (common user), customizable user interfaces with the use of Norms would lead to an easier use by citizens and especially to a greater identification of irregularities in public spending. This would also ease the process of discussion about public policy because the public would know better how their money is being spent. At the same time, advanced users would not be harmed because the interface would also be adjustable to their skill levels.

With the increasing prevalence of smart phones, the mobile government should also be considered in the Transparency Portal. Queries to their databases should be available in a manner optimized for these mobile devices. Moreover, modern features like GPS could and should be available to consult expenses wherever the citizen is. Only this function would be a great facility and citizens could oversight the funds invested in his city or even his neighbourhood and street only with basis in the GPS position. There would be no more need of budget expertise to find information. Another possibility would be realization of online denounces with the dispatch of proofs by the device itself.

Coupled with the possibility to adapt the site so that more frequent consultations are more easily available, voting could be used so that the citizen feels part in building a more dynamic portal, sending their positions to changes that could effectively be seen in the portal. Regarding the definition of public policy, beyond votes on approval or disapproval of expenditures that may direct the government on how to invest its funds, platforms for identification of trends of opinion [11] could be used to assess the predominate trends about contrasting actions/policies.

4.5 Proposed Architecture

The proposed architecture presented in Fig. 4 shows the complexity of dealing with a wide range of information and the different views of data presentation that takes into account physical constraints of the target audience and limitations of their understanding of written language (functional illiteracy). There is also a special concern that the views turned to nontechnical citizen should reproduce the technical data in a friendly way so that the Transparency Portal can more tightly control public spending in Brazil.

At the top of Fig. 4, it is shown the various sources of information concerning all expenses of the legislative, executive and judiciary and also the expenses of the autonomous units of federation (states and municipalities). These are macro sources of information in a common country based on a Federal State of Law. To integrate the government information into a single point of view, all these expenditures are grouped into a staging area from which several extractions (aligned with the concept of Data-Mart) are created to meet the different needs of data visualization.

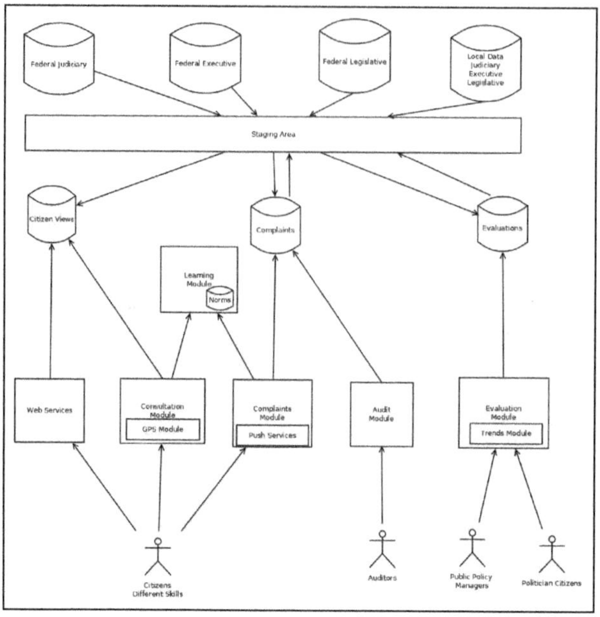

Fig. 4. Proposed Architecture

The DataMart CitizenView then represents the different views of the stored information (e.g. grouping of data) in the database. As these views are stored in magnetic media, and the amount of information to be registered is great, they are not normalized. To present a simple view for non-technical citizens, each of these views should be carefully designed to allow their understanding. To avoid citizen auditors being affected by a change in the Transparency Portal, two DataMart were initially defined by keeping the current technical view and a new view, based on the survey conducted with card sorting. Data stored on Complaints and Evaluations are stored in a relational manner, as they suffer from their respective access modules updates in data (see below).

The Consultation module is responsible for the access to data in the CitizenView and still responds to inform the Learning module interactions made by the user (local clicks, the time for decision making, selected font, etc.). It is important to note that the definition of Norms is contained in the Learning module and the latter returns to the Consultation module the user profile indicated of the current user. After receiving the profile, Consultation selects the appropriate data view to be presented to the user as well as it provides the adaptations needed for objects appearance on the screen. Simplified language can be achieved with contextualized hyperdocuments [12]. The GPS component inside Consultation is responsible for allowing access to information based on location reference received from mobile clients. Web Services enables the automatic sharing of information.

Complaints can be made by citizens located where source was applied and are managed by the Complaints module that can also receive files to documentation/prove of irregularities. Aligned with the concept of Web 2.0, the Consultation module is affected by Complaints, Audit and Evaluation (below) as they return data to Staging. With the returned data, views (Citizen Views) presented to users can explore the irregularities identified by the public, the treatment received and consequently, for example, the amount of irregular public spending avoided. Complaints are also responsible for mapping the complaints, detecting priority areas (a lot of complaints in the same area have priority for evaluation). To follow the situation of a complaint, PUSH services are offered.

The Audit module is exclusively accessed by control offices and seeks to manage the consistency of complaints received. It accesses the same database of Complaints, but with unrestricted access to all the complaints received and is responsible for the control of their consistency. They also can access the expenditures through the citizen view.

The Evaluation module receives evaluations from the public of the various federal and local government programs in order not to identify irregularities but to get a response about the quality of spending. There are two profiles provided, registered citizens and policy makers. Based on opinions obtained, the Trends module similar to the work in Tavares et al. [11] can identify trends of opinion that should be taken into account by government when formulating policy on public spending.

5 Comparison with Other Sites

The Transparency Portal can be considered the main site of the Brazil Federal Government for the disclosure of their expenses. However, by its own characteristic, there is no concentration of all the features of electronic government. The e-government portal in Brazil (http:// www.governoeletronico.gov.br), Brazil's Government Portal (http://www.brasil.gov.br) and also sites of the various bodies that comprise the Federal Administration have other services. To compare the state of the evolution of electronic government in Brazil, a review of other sites in Brazil and abroad will be made, taking into consideration the provision of services and means of access.

The e-government portal of Singapura (http://www.ecitizen.gov.sg) is shown in Fig. 5 and is distinguished for offering a wide range of services for day-to-day citizen needs. Services such as issuing passports and accident reports, medical appointments and payment of taxes are available online. Payment is simple and even credit cards can be used. Additionally, there is information for services that can not be made electronically and the option for mobile devices. Brazil has some of the services offered (e.g. police report), but not the same facility for transactions involving payments.

The South Africa site (http://www.services.gov.za, Fig. 6) provides integrated services for citizens, organizations and foreigners, and works as a means of official communication for documents, events, laws and general information (you can, for example, refer to the country constitution, understand its organizational structure or obtain a study about the prison system). The services part of the portal allows queries using SMS, but most services do not allow the online resolution but gives guidance on how people should proceed to get what they want, usually including a visit to a physical position of the government. The Brazilian government page offers an official means of communication more updated. African documents, on the other hand, seems more simple, facilitating the involvement of the population.

The government of Dubai provides a site (http://dubai.ae/en.portal) with nearly four hundred online services to the public and entrepreneurs, ranging from permission to

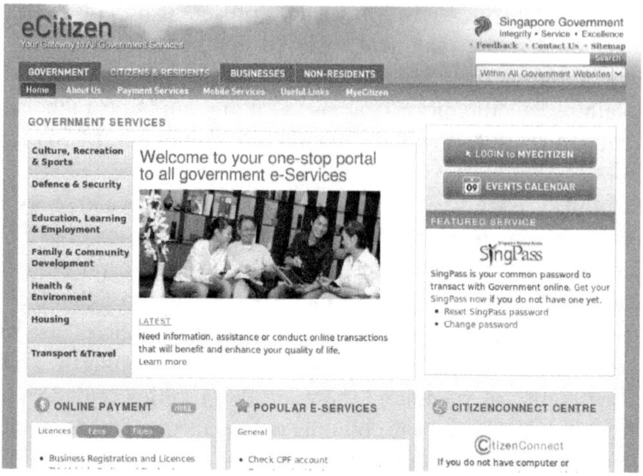

Fig. 5. Interface of the Singapore Portal

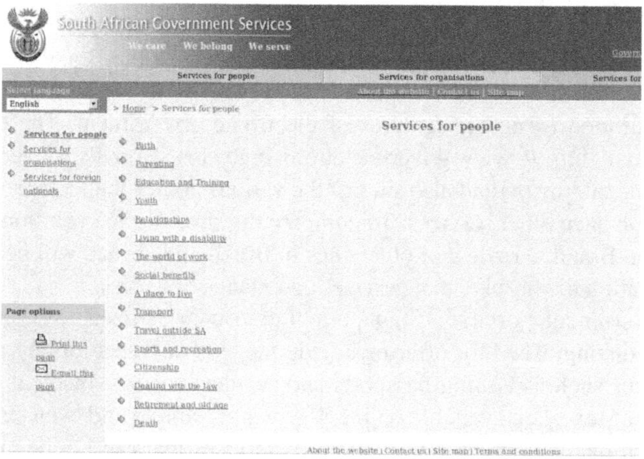

Fig. 6. Interface of the South Africa Portal

visit shrines to recruiting services. The site, shown in Fig. 7, has as objective the strengthening of local economy (providing better services for organizations) and lower costs of public administration (reducing the need for staff and physical posts). Alternative means of access such as SMS and email facilities are provided and include payment by credit card. The number of online transactions executed passes 2 million [13], for an estimated population of 1.5 million. In comparison, the Transparency Portal in Brazil recorded in its release about 1.8 million visits to their pages, to the estimated population of 180 million.

A site that deserves mention as a government initiative is the Chile site (http://www.gobiernodechile.cl). The Chilean government has as principle that it is responsible for creating the need for e-gov services [14]. Online processing of documents, fees payment and buying needs are some of the facilities provided.

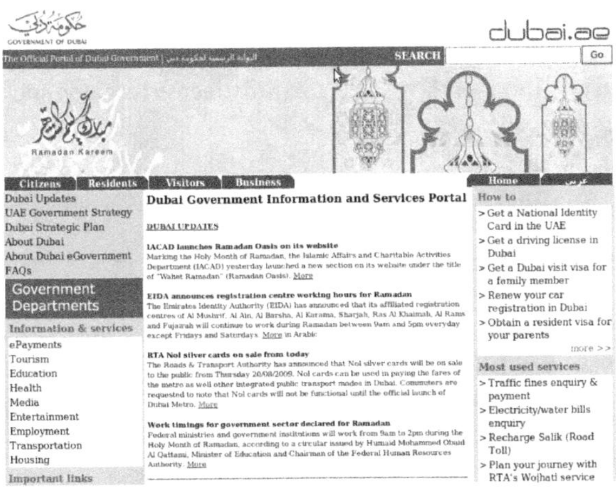

Fig. 7. Interface of the Dubai Portal

5.1 Comparison of Accessibility by ASES and DaSilva

ASES, Evaluator and Simulator for Accessibility Sites (In Portuguese, "Avaliador e Simulador de Acessibilidade de Sítios"), is an official tool released by the Federal Government of Brazil on its electronic government home page for verification of compliance with the standard e-MAG. The e-MAG standard is based on the W3C WCAG v1 [15] and specifies the obligations and recommendations to be observed by all government sites regarding accessibility. Three priority levels are defined: in level 1, the failure to implement a requirement prevents the accessibility of the site for at least one group of users; level 2, obligations not observed are significant obstacles to accessibility; level 3, obligations not implemented may create difficulties [6]. The recommendations generally require a certain subjective judgment by the developer and are not evaluated in this article. ASES found some false errors such as no identification of labels for certain HTML tags, that were not considered. The site DaSilva is an updated version of the ASES, available for use on the Web and, as ASES, identifies the same types of errors.

The Transparency Portal was the chosen site for accessibility comparison with other official government sites as it has greater visibility in the country. It showed good compatibility with the requirements assessed by the ASES. For the pages evaluated, only one flaw (easily resolved) of priority level 1 was found. It was an image that showed no textual equivalent description (e-MAG Recommendation 1.11). For priority 3 flaws, there was the use of outdated tags (e-MAG Recommendation 3.1). There were no failures of priority 2. Because of the legal obligations for e-MAG accessibility in Brazil, it can be concluded that care has been taken in the development of the site.

The site of Singapore, in turn, presented a series of problems regarding the requirements set by e-MAG. Besides several figures without corresponding description, dimensions were specified with absolute values (e-MAG Recommendation 2.2 violation), inaccessible frames (e-MAG 1.16 Recommendation violation), lack of language definition (e-MAG Recommendation 1.1 violation), among many others. The portals of South Africa and Dubai have shown similar problems as Singapore's, and, therefore, low accessibility with respect to e-MAG. As these sites are from other countries and not governed by Brazilian laws and obligations, failures to conform with e-MAG standard were expected. Table 3 shows the total distinct errors per site evaluated for an average of 5 different pages each.

Table 3. Distinct accessibility errors by e-MAG/ASES (evaluation of five pages for each site)

Site	Priority 1	Priority 2	Priority 3
Transparency Portal (Brazil)	1	0	1
Singapore Portal	6	4	2
South Africa Portal	3	4	2
Dubai Portal	5	4	2

5.2 Comparing Accessibility with TotalValidator

The online tool TotalValidator (http://www.totalvalidator.com) was used to check compliance of the websites with the standard WCAG v2 AAA [16] and identified a greater number of errors in all evaluations. This difference occurred both in the number of different errors identified as in the reduction of false errors raised by ASES. Instead of priorities levels, TotalValidator, following the rules of the W3C, has three levels of "success criteria". For Level A accessibility, tools can be used to make the site accessible. In the AA level, there is greater support for assistive technology and also facilities for those who do not have such technology. The AAA level improves the support for assistive technologies and also to the common access.

The Transparency Portal had a lower performance in this new analysis. As examples of issues not previously considered are duplicate identifiers and lack of possibility of explicit change context (submit button). Error as the lack of textual description of figure was again identified. A total of seven distinct errors were found, all of level A "success criteria". The other sites once again underperformed the Transparency Portal. Taking into account that this time all countries assessed were not obligated to comply with WCAG recommendations, the tool may be considered fairer to evaluate the sites mentioned. Table 4 shows the individual versus total number of errors found for each site examined.

Table 4. Distinct errors // total errors of accessibility by TotalValidator (evaluation of five pages for each site)

Site	Criteria A	Criteria AA	Criteria AAA
Transparency Portal (Brazil)	7//37	0//0	0//0
Singapore Portal	9//168	1//136	1//1
South Africa Portal	8//160	1//43	0//0
Dubai Portal	17//455	2//109	1//2

6 Conclusions

The article presented a comparison of accessibility of international e-government sites. Different countries without tradition in the area were chosen in order to achieve a fair comparison of current e-government evolution. The results showed that among the sites evaluated, the Brazilian site has the highest compliance with W3C standards, which represents a good result especially when considering the order of absolute errors found.

A questionnaire was also presented with answers of entities / NGOs regarding the use of the Transparency Portal (Brazil). The purpose of this research was to find out whether there was recognition by organizations about the e-government effort, any difficulties not yet identified, and especially getting responses from opinion leaders about the accessibility and ease of navigation of the site.

Another evaluation, now with ordinary users of different profiles, was performed and aimed at obtaining insight about the Transparency Portal by people who have no technical knowledge of public budget. Two prototypes were created and the evaluation showed that one of the prototypes, developed in accordance with the technique of card sorting, had performance far superior than the other. To match both ordinary users and NGOs / Offices, the Portal should then allow alternative views of information through the use of customization. One fact raised was that even using the card sorting, one consultation was better accessed in a different path than the one suggested by the technique.

Taking into account this previous evaluation, an architecture was proposed to overcome the difficulties found and to allow a stronger participation of society in the control of public spending and public policies. To match both ordinary users and NGOs / Agencies, the architecture allows alternative views of information through the use of customization. These assessments will be used as suggestions for improving the Transparency Portal site, in order to make it easier to use and accessible for all.

Acknowledgements. The authors wish to thank the site "Contas Abertas", the "Transparency International", the "Instituto de Fiscalização e Controle" and the "United Nations Office on Drugs and Crime" for participation in the evaluation of Transparency Portal.

References

1. Satyanarayana: E-government principles, `http://siteresources.worldbank.org/INTEGOVERNMENT/Resources/eGovPrinciplesJS5Nov06.ppt` (page accessed on September 23, 2010)
2. Neris, V.: Estudo e Proposta de um Framework para Design de Interfaces de Usuário Ajustáveis. PhD thesis, Universidade Estadual de Campinas (UNICAMP), Brazil (2010)
3. Fortuna, F.J., Bonacin, R., Baranauskas, M.C.C.: A framework for flexibility at the interface - joining ajax technology and semiotics. In: 12th International Conference on Enterprise Information Systems (ICEIS), Portugal (2010)
4. Diirr, B., Araujo, R., Cappelli, C.: Conversas sobre processos públicos. In: 7th Brazilian Symposium of Collaborative Systems (SBSC), Belo Horizonte, Brazil (2010)
5. van Veenstra, A.F., Zuurmond, A.: Opening the Black Box: Exploring the Effect of Transformation on Online Service Delivery in Local Governments. In: Wimmer, M.A., Scholl, H.J., Janssen, M., Traunmüller, R. (eds.) EGOV 2009. LNCS, vol. 5693, pp. 234–244. Springer, Heidelberg (2009)

6. Departamento de Governo Eletrônico: e-mag, acessibilidade de governo eletrônico. Reference document, Secretaria de Logística e Tecnologia da Informação, Ministério do Planejamento, Orçamento e Gestão (2005)
7. U.S. Department of Health & Human Services (DHHS): Usability.gov., http://www.usability.gov (page accessed on September 23, 2010)
8. Hyatt, D., Hickson, I.: HTML 5. W3C working draft, W3C (2009), http://www.w3.org/TR/2009/WD-html5-20090825/
9. MySociety.Org: Fixmystreet, http://www.fixmystreet.com/ (page accessed on September 23, 2010)
10. iStrategyLabs: Appsfordemocracy, http://www.appsfordemocracy.org/ (page accessed on September 23, 2010)
11. Tavares, R.L., Pimentel, M., Araujo, R.M., Cappelli, C.: Percepção de tendências em discussões democráticas. In: VII Simpósio Brasileiro de Sistemas Colaborativos, Brazil (2010)
12. de Magalhães, V.M.A., Silva, M.A.R., Anacleto, J.C., de Magalhães Jr., W.C.P., Torres, T.Z.: Processo de construção de hiperdocumentos contextualizados culturamente de acordo com o nível de letramento do aprendiz. In: Conferência IADIS Ibero Americana WWW/Internet (CIAWI), Algarve, Portugal (2010)
13. Lootah, H.N.: Dubai municipality's e-government initiative (June 2006), www.dm.gov.ae (page accessed on September 23, 2010)
14. Budge, E.C.: Chile e-gov experiences and lessons. Digital Opportunities for Development (2003)
15. Jacobs, I., Vanderheiden, G., Chisholm, W.: Web content accessibility guidelines 1.0. W3C Recommendation, W3C (1999), http://www.w3.org/TR/1999/WAI-WEBCONTENT-19990505/
16. Reid, L.G., Vanderheiden, G., Cooper, M., Caldwell, B.: Web content accessibility guidelines (WCAG) 2.0. W3C Recommendation, W3C (2008), http://www.w3.org/TR/2008/REC-WCAG20-20081211/

PART VI

Enterprise Architecture

A Service-Oriented Framework for Distributed Collaborative Knowledge Work

Jonas Schulte

University of Paderborn, 33102 Paderborn, Germany
schulte@uni-paderborn.de

Abstract. Business data of a company, latest research results of an university or learning content in education – these are just some of many possible examples to illustrate that knowledge is the key factor in modern society. However, the information flood and the growing complexity of data made it more difficult to manage relevant data and distinguish between irrelevant information. Furthermore, there is now a challenge not only store data in an information system but also to remove them if desired. In this article WasabiBeans, a service-oriented framework for distributed collaborative knowledge work, is presented. WasabiBeans provides virtual knowledge spaces that are self-administrated by the users. This article outlines the framework's powerful authentication and authorization infrastructure as well as a flexible user-driven repository integration – WasabiPipes – to build up complex knowledge networks.

Keywords: Cooperation, Framework, Integration, Knowledge management, Distributed, WasabiBeans.

1 Introduction

Albert Einstein, a German physicist borne in 1879, said: *"Progress requires exchange of knowledge"*. This sentence is more relevant than ever, since projects in economy and research become increasingly complex. Business data of a company, latest research results of an university or learning content in education – these are just some of many possible examples to illustrate that knowledge is the key factor in modern society. Knowledge is created by people, managed and shared. One contribution of computer science to support these knowledge processes is the research on *Computer-Supported Cooperative Work (CSCW)* and *knowledge management (KM)*. Both, CSCW and KM are very interdisciplinary and novel fields of research. CSCW has been substantially shaped by Paul Cashman and Irene Greif through the first conference on CSCW in 1986 [1]. In the same year the term knowledge management was mentioned for the first time by Karl Wiig [2].

Collaborative work environments are supposed to support the coordination as well as the teamwork of people in different places. This is mandatory to work efficient on common projects in spatially divided teams. In [3] basic (media) functions for collaborative work environments are given. Furthermore, the author presents a basic structure to establish work environments in the digital media: the *virtual knowledge spaces (VKS)*. Using the metaphor of a space in which knowledge is stored, structured, and cooperatively generated, virtual knowledge spaces are not only an implementation of the basic

R. Zhang et al. (Eds.): ICEIS 2011, LNBIP 102, pp. 405–419, 2012.

functions, but also an intuitive understanding and use of the collaborative work environment by the user. Hence, virtual knowledge spaces are a central concept for building collaborative work environments for everyday use.

The concept of virtual knowledge spaces is most helpful to the organization of knowledge in distributed environments and whenever knowledge exchange takes place in asynchronous work processes. Since, asynchronous work processes can effectively be supported by a CSCW system, it is important to design flexible cooperation support systems that address both collaboration among people and knowledge management. When considering these two research fields, it is important to distinguish between data and knowledge. Data does not make any statement about its interpretation, but knowledge is the ability to interpret the data correct [4]. Justin Hibbard gave the following definition of KM in 1997: *"Knowledge Management is the process of capturing a company's collective expertise wherever it resides – in databases, on paper, or in people's heads – and distributing it to wherever it can help produce the biggest payoff."* [5].

However, classic CSCW focus on working with data instead of knowledge. The intention of the *WasaibBeans* framework, presented in this article, is to support collaborative knowledge and information organization in distributed environments. This is relevant to the fact that people are knowledge carriers and new knowledge is mainly produced in team work. WasabiBeans is an implementation of the concept of virtual knowledge spaces and bases on latest Java EE[1] technologies. Furthermore, the framework considers the deep influences of the Web 2.0 on CSCW. WasabiBeans does not offer a complete cooperative work environment, instead it provides functions to work with virtual knowledge spaces. As a *service-oriented architecture (SOA)* with a microkernel, WasabiBeans is highly expendable and can be customized to different fields of application. Thereby, knowledge processes and especially the externalization of knowledge (see Figure 1) can be facilitated. Problematic is the transformation of explicit to tacit knowledge, since tacit knowledge can not be digitalized and made persistent.

To prevent this transformation of knowledge computer science particularly develops solutions to support the externalization of knowledge. Externalization means that the knowledge is extracted from the peoples' head and permanently stored in databases, knowledge management systems or the like. The "destruction" of explicit knowledge occurs when automatizing (work) processes. For example step-by-step instructions may be unnecessary after an automatization. The intention of the WasabiBeans framework is to integrate various systems and applications to embed efficient KM into existing workflows.

In practice, there are numerous systems for knowledge management. Often these systems are monolithic and require a fundamentally restructuring of the business processes and they are not optimized for collaboration and team work. The WasabiBeans framework tries to fill the gap between cooperation support and knowledge organization by providing functions for cooperation support as well as solutions for flexible integration of "arbitrary" (knowledge) databases and repositories.

[1] Java Enterprise Edition, a widely used platform for server programming in the Java programming language. Online available: `http://www.oracle.com/technetwork/java/javaee/overview/ index.html`

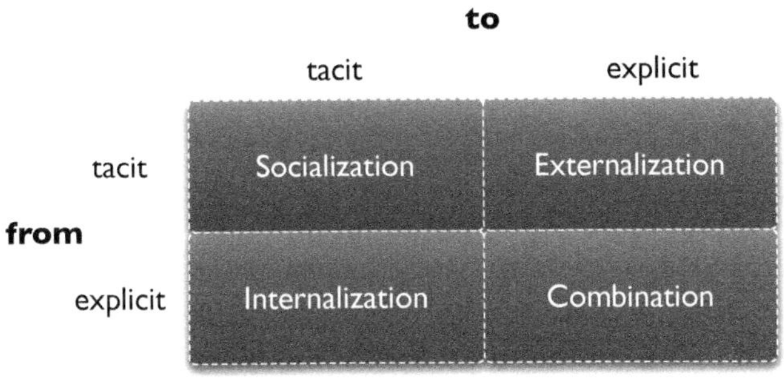

Fig. 1. Knowledge Processes by Nonaka and Takeuchi

This article is structures as follows. In Section 2 the concept of virtual knowledge spaces is introduced. Based on this concept the architecture of the WasabiBeans framework is described in section 3. To discuss the framework more detailed section 4 will focus on the authentication and authorization infrastructure of WasabiBeans and section 5 explains WasabiPipes. WasabiPipes is a *pipes and filter (PaF)* architecture to connect different repositories and web applications with the framework. This is very important for cooperative work, since it allows the integration of all necessary knowledge and data repositories. Finally, the results are summarized and discussed in section 6.

2 Knowledge Spaces

Virtual knowledge spaces are a key concept to create dynamic and flexible cooperative work and learning environments. It allows to structure the data unrestrictedly and provides means for generating multiple views on the same data collection (see section 2.2). Thus, it is possible to adjust the environment exactly to the users' needs, without having redundancy of the underlying data. The concept of virtual knowledge spaces has been proven for several years and in various fields of application [6]. The following section 2.1 describes the class hierarchy for setting up virtual knowledge spaces. After that we show how to create different views of a data collection (section 2.2).

2.1 Data Model of Knowledge Spaces

Knowledge spaces are our concept for the representation and the structuring of information within a cooperative work process. This the concept has been applied to various fields of application and is well-proven due to almost ten years experience of software development in the scope of CSCW.[7]

The basic object structure of virtual knowledge spaces is quite easy. We distinguish between the following objects: `Room`[2], `Container`, `Document`, `Attribute`, `Link`, `Group` and `User`. A `Room` is the representation of a real room, whereas `Container` can be compared with a folder. The intention behind the `Room`-object is having an object, that stands for a place where uses can meet each other and cooperate with each other.

[2] In the object model a `Room` stands for a virtual knowledge space.

Furthermore spaces are intended to assure awareness. Awareness is indispensable for successful CSCW applications [8,9]. Besides, the `Container`-object is a lightweight construct to organize information and correlate data. Objects of the type `Document` are used as a wrapper around the real content (e.g. a picture, a PDF file, ...). There is a fundamental difference between on the one hand storing content and linking it with additional information and on the other hand *combined data object* that wrap content, annotations, comments, access rights, and further information. The first option links different data to each other, whereas the second and preferred option builds up a *common space of action*. Working with combined data object might have different advantages. For instance, when creating versions of an object it is a lot easier to generate a coherent version object of a combined data object instead of creating equivalent versions of all related objects that match the combined data object. The data model of WasabiBeans allows free attributes at any type of object, thus the model is highly customizable to the requirements of the current application area. `Group`-, `User`- and `Link`-objects are self-explanatory. It is mentionable, that we use `Group`-objects not only for grouping users, but also to describe roles. The concept of virtual knowledge spaces allows to group and structure combined data objects on a higher level. Our model allows free attributes at any type of object; in this way users keep track of their information. The WasabiBeans framework is a modern service-oriented architecture implementing the concept of virtual knowledge spaces.

2.2 Multiple Views on a Data Collection

Different applications require different types of data representation. Often each application comes with its own repository containing the related data. In this article the understanding of handling information in cooperative work environments is different. An ideal concept would be to work with one data repository and make these data available in different field of application. Several reasons argue for the use of one data collection instead of creating data redundancies. In order to avoid problems as updating different data collections or the distribution of changes among various repositories, the use of a common data space is essential. When setting up an uniform data collection, it is important to provide different interfaces. Therefore, the concept of virtual knowledge spaces is complemented with free attributes. Free attributes may be used to store application specific values, e.g. the objects' positions for a shared whiteboard application.

Unique and creative concepts, e.g. the pyramid discussion for decision-making processes desire totally different views and representation types [10]. But even the presentation of miscellaneous file formats benefit from different views. Image files might be displayed as a picture gallery, whereas documents are listed alphabetically. There are boundless possibilities to display a data collection or a set of a data collection. It is obvious, that different views are meaningful. Making one data collection available in different applications requires a sophisticated rights management (see section 4).

WasabiBeans, as an implementation of the concept of VKS, intends to be a flexible and adjustable framework. In addition, it provides various interfaces as *Remote Method Invocation (RMI)* or Web services to access the data. In the following these interfaces and the famework's architecture are discussed.

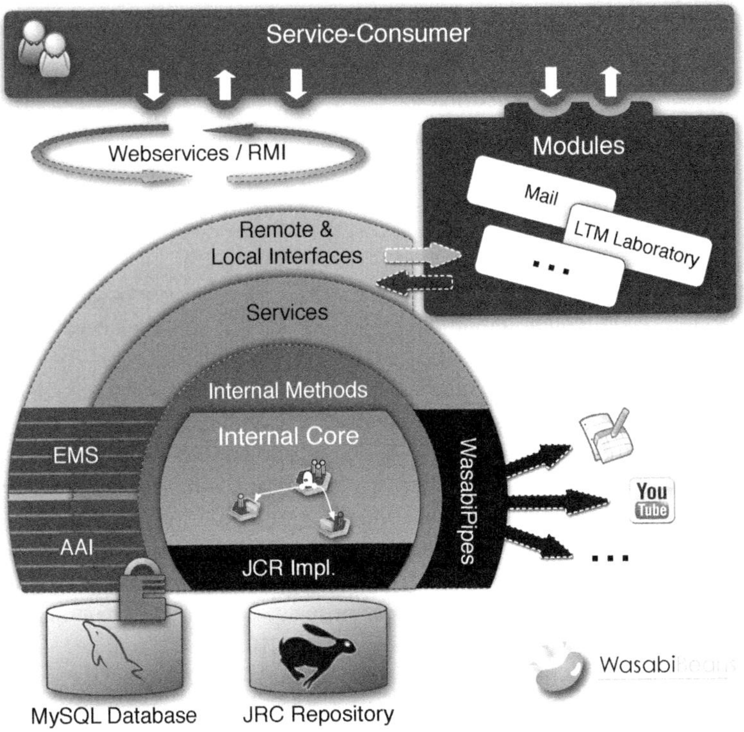

Fig. 2. Overview of WasabiBeans' Architecture

3 Architectural Concept

In this section the framework's architecture is described in general. Afterwards, section 4 describes the authentication and authorization infrastructure and section 5 describes WasabiBeans' extension WasabiPipes to integrate multiple repositories.

Figure 2 gives an overview of WasabiBeans' architecture, which consists of four consecutive layers: internal core, internal methods, services, and the remote and local interfaces.

1. The **internal core** consists of an implementation of the *Java Content Repository (JCR)*[3]. Accordingly, the core provides all functions specified by JCR and is responsible for data storage. Each Wasabi object is represented by a specific JCR node (compare section 2.1).
2. The **internal methods** are implemented as static methods have two tasks. For one thing they are responsible for basic manipulation of the Wasabi objects, and for another thing for the integration of alternative data sources. More specifically, internal methods work on JCR nodes of the internal core. In addition to the internal methods for retrieval, creation, deletion, and modification of Wasabi objects, there

[3] `http://jcp.org/en/jsr/detail?id=283`

are methods for the transaction management, (section 3.2), the event management (section 3.3) and the version control.
3. The **services** layer consist of stateless session beans. Methods of these stateless session beans supply functions for clients to work with Wasabi objects. For that purpose they use and combine internal methods.
4. The fourth layer **remote & local interfaces** provides interfaces of stateless session beans of the service layer. Thereby, the distinction between local clients[4] and remote clients can be made.

The WasabiBeans framework is an implementation of the concept of virtual knowledge spaces, hence a hierarchical data model is necessary. In consequence of this requirement WasabiBeans uses a JCR implementation rather than the *Java Persistence API (JPA)*[5]. In this implementation Apache Jackrabbit[6] was the first choice, since it is an open source implementation and fully support the JCR standard.

The technology used for managing distributed systems with the WasabiBeans framework server is the *JBoss Application Server (JBoss AS)*[7], which is an open-source technology for building, deploying, and hosting enterprise Java applications and services. Since the JBoss AS provides extended enterprise services including clustering, caching, and persistence, it forms a good base for managing distributed systems. In particular the clustering enables to use multiple WasabiBeans framework for one collaborative system and accordingly to perform load-balancing. JBoss AS is founded on a service-oriented micro-kernel architecture that ensures all services are accessed, managed, and integrated in a unified and consistent manner. This functionality is essential for the WasabiBeans framework in order to fulfill the design paradigm of service-oriented architectures and thus being adaptable for various field of application.

3.1 Main Service Methods

The main service methods provide all functions for clients to operate on the data model. More precisely, these methods allow to work with *Data Transfer Objects (DTOs)*. WasabiBeans has four types of DTOs: object, value, version, and pipeline DTOs. Object DTOs represent Wasabi objects. Value DTOs represent the attributes as well as links. These DTOs are also important for optimistic locking (see section 3.2). Version DTOs stand for a version of a version-able Wasabi object. Pipeline DTOs represent WasabiPipelines (see section 5). Roughly, main service methods can be divided into read and write methods. The structure of write methods is more complex, since they have to consider locks, events, and concurrent writing operations that may lead to failures. The following method invocation of the `create` method of the `AttributeService` shows exemplary how to generate a DTO.

---

[4] Local clients are deployed together with the the WasabiBeans framework in one runtime environment.
[5] `http://www.jcp.org/en/jsr/detail?id=317`
[6] `http://jackrabbit.apache.org/`
[7] `http://www.jboss.org/jbossas`

```
WasabiAttributeDTO attributeDTO =
  attributeProxy.create(<"name">, <"value">,
  <dtoOfAffiliation>);
```

A main service method (in this example `create`) can be invoked via a proxy object of the actual service. In the sample above the proxy object is *attributeProxy* of the `AttributeService`. This proxy object can be created by means of a JNDI[8] lookup.

3.2 Transactions

Transactions are absolutely necessary for multi-user systems. Thus, each service method is executed by default within a *Container Managed Transaction (CMT)*. To avoid excessive transaction handling, WasabiBeans can re-use transactions when calling a service method within an already existing transaction. Thereby, existing transactions can be re-used and several service methods may be combined to a single transaction. The following code sample illustrates how a user can combine three method invocations to a single transaction.

```
UserTransaction utx = (UserTransaction)
    jndiContext.lookup("UserTransaction");
utx.begin();
try {
  documentService.create("doc1", roomDTO);
  documentService.create("doc2", roomDTO);
  documentService.create("doc3", roomDTO);
  utx.commit();
} catch (Exception e) {
  utx.rollback();
}
```

The object to control the transactions has to be requested from the Java EE server via a JNDI lookup. By means of this object the Java EE server can be instructed to begin, commit, or rollback a transaction. All invocations of service methods are performed as part of a single transaction. It should be mentioned that WasabiBeans supports both optimistic and pessimistic locking mechanisms. By default it uses optimistic locking.

3.3 Events

Another key feature of WasabiBeans is the event system. A flexible event system is very important for collaboration and cooperative knowledge management. Users may request a notification if a team member changes a certain file or creates a new document. To create, send, and receive events WasabiBeans uses an *Enterprise Message Service (EMS)*. The current implementation allows the following events:

- *REMOVED:* A Wasabi object was deleted.
- *CREATED:* A Wasabi object was created.

[8] Java Naming and Directory Interface (JNDI).

- *MOVED:* An existing Wasabi object was moved within the hierarchical structure.
- *PROPERTY_CHANGED:* An attribute was changed.
- *ROOM_ENTERED:* An user entered a room.
- *ROOM_LEFT:* An user left a room.
- *MEMBER_ADDED:* An user joined a group.
- *MEMBER_REMOVED:* An user left a group.

WasabiBeans uses JBoss HornetQ[9] as EMS respectively as *Message-oriented Middleware (MoM)*. The main challenge was to ensure data privacy for the event system. JMS lack in possibilities to define user specific filters on global JMS queues or topics, yet this is mandatory to prevent users from reading events of others. The obvious solution might be the definition of individual queues for each user. Actually, this would be a secure option, but when specifying event queues for all users (even though they are not logged in), the application server has to manage too many queues. This will definitely lead to performance problems. Instead of defining individual queues for each user, there is a *MessageDispatcher* in WasabiBeans, which divides the messages from a global queue to temporal queues (TempDest). To receive change notifications of an object three logical steps are necessary. Firstly, a temporal JMS destination has to be created. Secondly, the new JMS destination has to be registered in the WasabiBeans framework. Thirdly, the user has to be registered as receiver of events for a given Wasabi object. The second and third step are done by means of a stateless session bean.

The advantage of this implementation is that the number of JMS queues can be reduced to a minimum without loosing security. Temporal queues are created if a user logs in and subscribes to events of at least one Wasabi object.

4 AAI-Infrastructure

Especially for applications in the area of Computer-Supported Cooperative Work it is essential to ensure data security. This aspect becomes even more important if the CSCW application is used for safety critical business areas, e.g. knowledge management.

4.1 The Seven Access Rights in WasabiBeans

There exist seven different kinds of permissions in WasabiBeans:

1. VIEW,
2. READ,
3. EXECUTE,
4. COMMENT,
5. INSERT,
6. WRITE, and
7. GRANT.

[9] `http://www.jboss.org/hornetq`

As shown in figure 2 these access rights are stored in an own mySQL database and are linked to the corresponding object. The current set of seven access rights may be extended to specific field of application.

Furthermore, there are several determinations to define a hierarchy of access rights. Thus, it is possible accelerate the authorization functions and solve conflicts when different access rights are set for one specific object and user/group. Each access right may be specified as unlimited right or time-based right. Section 4.5 explains the consequences to the authorization infrastructure that are accompanied by temporal access rights. In the following, different criteria that have to be interpreted for the validation of an access right are discusses.

4.2 User Access Rights

An access right always refers to a specific WasabiUser object. It assesses an operation for which the user is authorised on the specific data object or for which he is forbidden. Because of the fact that a WasabiBeans environment may contain plenty of different users, it is not practicable to allocate each conceivable right as a user right. To simplify the right allocation, WasabiBeans offers to specify group rights (see section 4.3).

4.3 Group Access Rights

Within its function, a group right is similar to a user right, with the difference that it is not granted to a specific user, but a whole group of users. Because of this fact, it is sufficient to be a member of the specific group or the corresponding subgroups to gain all associated allowances and forbiddances. Furthermore, there must be a mechanism or rules, that specify which access right is prioritized. This problem may happen in various situations, e.g. if a user is member of two different groups. As a member of group A the user may get an allowance for a certain document, but as member of group B the user may get a forbiddance for the same document. To solve this problem there is a hierarchy (or rules) that specify which right type has to be prioritized. Figure 3 illustrated the eight different right types in WasabiBeans.

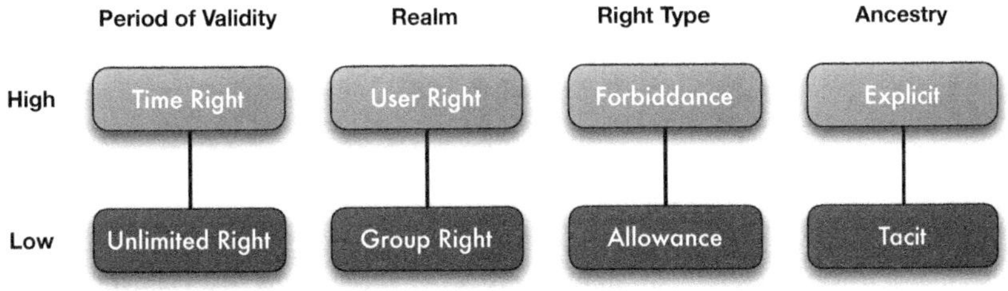

Fig. 3. Hierarchy of Access Rights

By the concept of group rights it is possible to define special fields of responsibility. For example, a group can be created whose members may access on special parts of the object tree to perform well defined operations there. If we want to allocate some users for this field of responsibility, we only need to assign them to this group. A declaration of additional user rights is not necessary.

4.4 Inherited Access Rights

The adjustment of data inside a tree structure suggests that access rights may be passed from a high into a junior instance, which can be considered as inheritance. If we abstain from this possibility, it is necessary to grant explicit rights for each single data object which increases the administrative effort. In addition to this, on ordinary scenarios we often have got the case, that all objects inside a junior structure have the same or at least very similar rights. The possibility of inheritance should support this.

Basically, we have got the principle that with two or more relevant rights within the same triple relationship (subject, permission, object), always the right which is nearer to the target object has got priority. This means, if there are for example two containers above a WasabiDocument, in which is in each case indicated a right for the same user, the right of the lower container is preferred. If there is even a collision of an inherited right with an explicit right, the inheritance may not occur. For time rights, there again is the principle that the rights with the shorter distance to the specific object may shorten, occlude or divide the intervals of the rights with the larger distance.

The concept of inheritance together with hierarchy for access rights allows to modify rights without high administrative effort.

4.5 Time-Based Access Rights

As a difference to the common infinite rights, a time based right is only valid for a certain interval. As a consequence, we generate two different layers for the differentiation of time rights and clearly unlimited rights. Figure 4 illustrates this concept of the two different layers. Another advantage is the fact that we always have the possibility of a clearly abdication from time-based rights.

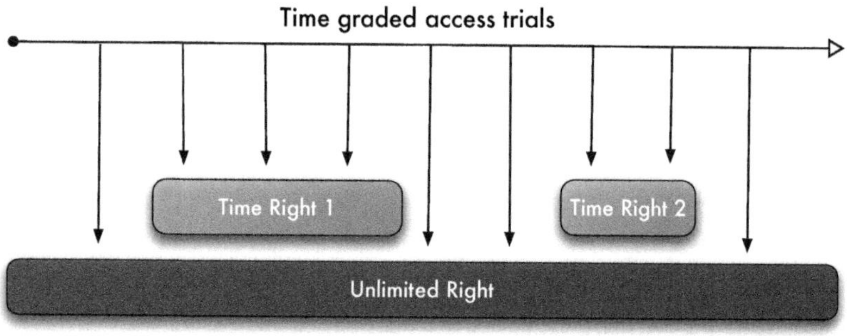

Fig. 4. Time-Based Access Rights

This means, it is similar to a common right which is expanded by a starting point and an ending point. These two points in time are expressed in the number of milliseconds, which are elapsed since the first January 1970. Referring to this, a time-based right gets in use if the actual computer time is within this interval. Conflicts with other time-based rights are automatically avoided by the system. This means, if a new time right is granted, whose interval overlaps at least one of another relevant time right, this interval may be shortened. In an extreme case, it may also be split in two other time rights or totally annulled.

If we abstain from the concept of time rights, a temporary allowance or forbiddance must always be initiated by the administrator to the designated point of time and annulled at another point of time. Thereby, the administrative effort would be elevated and the flexibility of the system would be decreased.

Overlapping Access Rights. As it was already mentioned in this section 4.5, by the initiation of new time rights, there may occur inconsistencies to other time rights which already exist. These inconsistencies are dissolved by preferring the new time right. This means, it may overlap existing rights. To ensure this, before the initiation the system must check every available time right which contains the same user or group name and the same allocated object. Now the interval of the new right becomes compared with the one of the old right. It is $N = (N_1, N_2)$ the interval of the new time right and $O = (O_1, O_2)$ the interval of the old time right. There is the condition $N_1 \leq N_2$ and $O_1 \leq O_2$. Now we can divide between the following cases (the above cases exclude the below cases, the system works in sequence during the check):

1. $N_2 < O_1$ or $N_1 > O_2 \rightarrow$ There are no difficulties because the two intervals do not interfere.
2. $N_1 \leq O_1$ and $N_2 \geq O_2 \rightarrow$ The old time right becomes replaced by the new one.
3. $N_1 \leq O_1$ and $N_2 < O_2 \rightarrow$ The old time right is shortened on $(N_2 + 1, O_2)$.
4. $N_1 > O_1$ and $N_2 < O_2 \rightarrow$ The old time right has to be split in two sub-rights with the intervals $(O_1, N_1 - 1)$ and $(N_2 + 1, O_2)$.
5. $N_1 > O_1$ and $N_2 \geq O_2 \rightarrow$ The old time right becomes shortened on $(O_1, N_1 - 1)$.

5 WasabiPipes: A Pipeline Editor for WasabiBeans

This section describes *WasabiPipes*, a dynamic and adjustable solution to integrate various repositories. WasabiPipes bases an the *Pipes and Filter (PaF)* architectural pattern that divides the tasks of a system into several sequential processing steps. A common definition for this pattern is given by Buschmann et al. *"The Pipes and Filter architectural pattern provides a structure for systems that process a stream of data. Each processing step is encapsulated in a filter component. Data is passed through pipes between adjacent filters. Recombining filters allows you to build families of related systems."* [11].

Inspired by *Yahoo Pipes*, a service that is normally used to assemble RSS[10] feeds, WasabiPipes is implemented as an extension of the WasabiBeans framework. Nevertheless, this concept to integrate different repositories is not limited to WasabiBeans and can easily be adapted to other purposes and infrastructures. Yahoo Pipes allows to handle (information) sources, mix them up, and modify the data using filters. It does not only support the connection of filter modules but also the connection of single fields of filter modules. Therefore, very complex and flexible pipelines can be assembled. Thus, Yahoo Pipes is a powerful composition tool to aggregate, manipulate, and mashup content from around the web [12]. Exactly this understanding of aggregating and connecting information goes along with the intention to integrate different repositories in a

[10] RSS 2.0 Specification: `http://www.rssboard.org/rss-specification`

complex IT infrastructure to set up a powerful cooperative work and learning environment. Similar to the Web 2.0 mashup concept[11], the intention is to aggregate various repositories to a new high-level collection of information.

The current implementation of WasabiPipes includes the binding of seven different repository types. So far Apache Jackrabbit, Amazon web services™, Google Docs, Flickr, YouTube, common file systems, and databases can be connected using via the PaF architecture. Basically, filters are mapped in WasabiPipes through the abstract class *Filter*, the interfaces *Source*, *Sink*, *ContentStore*, and the classes *Wire*, *Sink.Input*, *Source.Output*.

- **Source.** All filters that deliver data have to implement the Source interface, which procures the method void connect (Source.Output output, Sink.Input input).
- **Sink.** All classes that define inputs; have to implement the Sink interface. The method filter will be invoked by the previous filter and is responsible for the processing logic.
- **ContentStore.** A ContentStore offers a method to retrieve stored data.
- **Sink.Input.** An input of a filter is defined by the Sink.Input class. This class contains a reference to both, the filter and the name of the input.
- **Source.Output.** Analog to the class Sink.Input, the class Source.Output procures an output.
- **Wire.** The class Wire connects an output with an input.
- **Filter.** The abstract class Filter includes basic functions. The method forward can be invoked by any subclass. Afterwards it invokes all dependent filters that are connected with the output specified via the parameter. This class is also checks whether the execution is synchronous or asynchronous.
- **ConcreteSource.** This class has an output and invokes the method fillPipeline, thus the pipeline can be filled data. After completion this method invokes the forward method of the superclass to forward the data within the pipeline.
- **ConcreteFilter.** This class defines two inputs and two outputs. Within the filter method data are forwarded from input1 to output2 and from input2 to output1. The inputs and outputs are crossover connected.
- **ConcreteSink.** Finally, this class dumps the data of both inputs. Additionally, it reports which input passed the data.

For the implementation of WasabiPipes the JavaScript library WireIt[12] was used. WireIt allows to store the wiring states in the *JavaScript Object Notation (JSON)*[13] format.

5.1 Concrete Filter Implementations

To create a better understanding of filter implementations, the *MimeFilter* and the *YouTubeSink* are discussed exemplarily below.

---

[11] A Web 2.0 mashup is a (re-)combination of existing services to an aggregated new service that provides additional functions by combining the functionalities of the original services.

[12] `http://javascript.neyric.com/wireit`

[13] JSON is a lightweight data-interchange format. Online available: `http://www.json.org/`

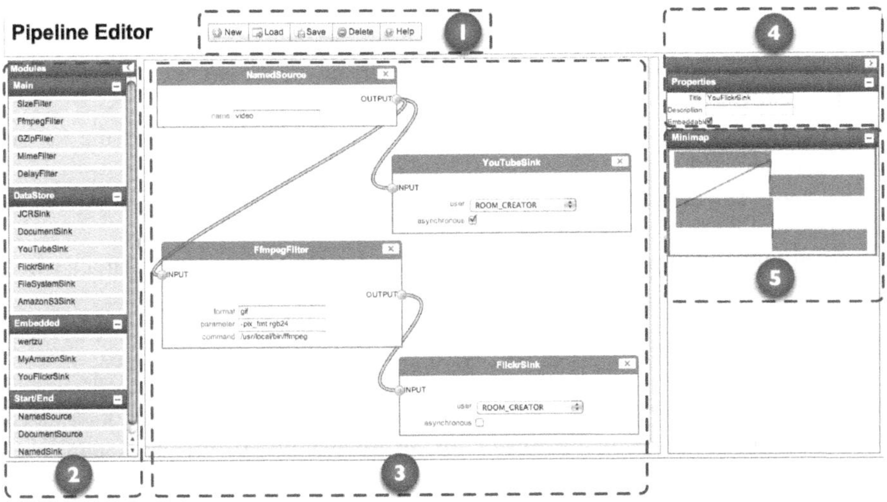

Fig. 5. The Pipeline-Editor

The *MimeFilter* consists of one input, two outputs (MATCH and NOMATCH), and a field to specify the MIME type. The method *filter* compares the MIME type of the document and the one defined as filter parameter. In case of a matching MIME type the data are forwarded to the MATCH output, otherwise to the NOMATCH output. Afterwards, the method *forward* of the super class *Filter* is invoked to notify all dependent filters about the result.

The *YouTubeSink* allows uploading videos directly from WasabiBeans to YouTube. However, the upload isn't straightforward and needs some special parameters. For authentication purpose YouTube requires a *developerKey*, a *consumerKey*, and a corresponding *consumerSecret* (a private key). The keys can be requested on the Google website. In addition an *accessToken* with a matching *accessTokenSecret* for the user is mandatory. YouTube provides an OAuth service to afford this token. Unfortunately, YouTube offers read access only; hence the content is not directly accessible through WasabiBeans. Accordingly, the *getContent* method is not implemented yet. Other repositories, such as the Amazon web services^{TM}, don't lack of a method to retrieve the content. In that case we can request the data directly from the integrated repository and show it within WasabiBeans' GUI.

5.2 A Graphical User Interface to Connect Repositories

WasabiPipes is accessible via the WasabiBeans administration GUI. Figure 5 shows the editor, that allows creating and managing pipes for specifying the data flow. The WasabiPipes editor consists of five main parts.

1. A toolbar to create, load, save, and delete pipes. Additionally the interface supports a help button for unpracticed users.
2. In the left area the modules are available. Modules are filters, data storages, embedded, and start/end components. Users can reuse these modules via simple

drag-and-drop action. It should be mentioned, that it is possible to save pre-defined pipes as embedded modules and use them in more complex configurations. Thereby, different pipes can be nested and a clear overview of the entire configuration can be guaranteed.

3. This is the main working area to arrange the components and specify the sources, filters, and sinks.
4. In this area users can add some additional meta data, e.g. title and description to the designed pipe.
5. To ensure a clear overview of large pipes we also offer a mini map, marked with 5.

6 Conclusions and Outlook

Since collaborative activities are very similar in various fields of application, a CSCW system should be flexible and adaptable for the usage in different fields of application. Although there are common CSCW tools (e.g. Blackboard[14] and Moodle[15]) there is a demand for integrating existing applications to achieve system convergences [13]. WasabiBeans is a flexible framework to maintain the implementation of cooperation support environments by integrating existing applicaitons. In addition, WasabiBeans provides functions to work efficient in virtual knowledge spaces. Due to the flexible SOA, WasabiBeans is ready for the next generation of CSCW applications. The object model with free annotations is optimized for adjustable knowledge management.

Web 2.0 evolutions have placed a new focus on current CSCW developments. New technologies (e.g. RSS feeds, tagging, etc.) have to be integrated in an existing the architecture to serve the demands of semantic knowledge structuring. The presented WasabiBeans framework is able to adapt multiple Web 2.0 services and systems in flexible and scalable manner. Beyond, the extension WasabiPipes, a pipes and filter architecture, allows the integration of heterogeneous repositories. By means of encapsulated functionality and isolated filters it was possible to provide highly parallel operations and data transfer. In particular, when integrating external services this is beneficial. Thereby, the execution of further filters is enabled, even if the system is waiting for the completion of an upload. During the Web 2.0 era more and more services were offered and APIs are ubiquitous in the Internet. The most prominent sample is Google with its services (YouTube, Google Docs, ...), which can interact by way of using the common interface gdata. Cooperation and knowledge management supporting systems have to meet the challenge of integrating this wide range of different repositories, since knowledge management bases on information sharing and a common persistent data repository.

References

1. Greif, I.: Computer-Supported Cooperative Work: A Book of Readings. Morgan Kaufmann Publishers, Inc., Santa Mateo (1988)
2. Liebowitz, J. (ed.): Knowledge Management Handbook, Boca Raton, Adelphi, USA (1999)

[14] `http://www.blackboard.com/`

[15] Moodle is a Learning Management System (LMS), `http://moodle.org/`

3. Hampel, T.: Virtuelle Wissensräume - Ein Ansatz für die kooperative Wissensorganisation. Dissertation, Universität Paderborn (2001)
4. Dengel, A.: Künstliche Intelligenz - Allgemeine Prinzipien und Modelle. BI-Taschenbuchverlag, Mannheim (1994)
5. Hibbard, J.: Knowing What We Know. InformationWeek - The Business Value of Technology (1997)
6. Eßmann, B., Hampel, T., Goetz, F., Elsner, A.: Embedding collaborative visualizations into virtual knowledge spaces. In: 7th International Conference on the Design of Cooperative Systems, France, Provence, pp. 33–40 (May 2006)
7. Hampel, T., Keil-Slawik, R.: sTeam - designing an integrative infrastructure for web-based computer-supported cooperative learning. In: Proceedings of the 10th International Conference on World Wide Web, pp. 76–85 (2001)
8. Licht, T., Schmidt, L., Luczak, H.: Goal awareness in distributed cooperative work settings. In: Luczak, H., Zink, K.J. (eds.) Human Factors in Organizational Design and Management VII (Aachen 2003), pp. 329–334. IEA Press, Santa Monica (2003)
9. Prinz, W., Gross, T.: Ubiquitous awareness of cooperative activities in a theatre of work. In: Bode, A., Karl, W. (eds.) Fachtagung Arbeitsplatzcomputer: Pervasive Ubiquitous Computing, APC, pp. 135–144 (October 2001)
10. Hampel, T., Heckmann, P.: Deliberative handling of knowledge diversity the pyramid discussion and position-comentary-response methods as specific views of collaborative virtual knowledge spaces. In: 16th International Conference Annual Proceedings of Society for Information Technology and Teacher Education, SITE 2005, Arizona, USA (2005)
11. Buschmann, F., Meunier, R., Rohnert, H., Sommerlad, P., Stal, M.: Pattern-oriented Software Architecture - A System of Patterns. John Wiley & Sons, Chichester (1996)
12. Yahoo!: Yahoo! pipes (April 2010), `http://pipes.yahoo.com/pipes`
13. Papazoglou, M.P., van den Heuvel, W.J.: Service oriented architectures: Approaches, technologies and research issues. Very Large Data Bases 16(3), 389–415 (2007)

IS/IT Resources and Business Value: Operationalization of an Information Oriented Framework

Alexander Borek[1], Markus Helfert[2], Mouzhi Ge[3], and Ajith Kumar Parlikad[1]

[1] Institute for Manufacturing, Department of Engineering, University of Cambridge
17 Charles Babbage Road, Cambridge, CB3 0FS, U.K.
{ab865,aknp2}@cam.ac.uk
[2] School of Computing, Dublin City University, Glasnevin, Dublin 9, Ireland
markus.helfert@computing.dcu.ie
[3] Fakultät für Informatik, Technische Universität Dortmund
Baroper Str. 301, 44227, Dortmund, Germany
mouzhi.ge@tu-dortmund.de

Abstract. Several studies have highlighted the importance of information and information quality in organisations and thus information is regarded as key determinant for the success and organisational performance. In this paper, we review selected contributions and introduce a model that shows how IS/IT resources and capabilities could be interlinked with IS/IT utilization, organizational performance and business value. Complementing other models and frameworks, we explicitly consider information from a management maturity, quality and risk perspective and show how the new framework can be operationalized with existing assessment approaches by using empirical data from four industrial case studies.

Keywords: IS/IT business value, IS/IT resources, IS/IT impact, Information management maturity, Information quality, Information risk.

1 Introduction

Organisations invest substantial capital into the development and maintenance of information technologies (IT) and information systems (IS), in the following denoted as IS/IT as both terms are overlapping and difficult to differentiate in practice. IS/IT play an increasingly important role for the support of management activities on all organisational layers, and spending for IS/IT therefore increases year after year [1].

However, the question how and to what extend IS/IT enhances organisational performance has been a major focus of interests and dispute over decades of IS/IT research [2]. Some research pointed out that there might be even no positive relationship between IS/IT and business success, a phenomenon labelled as the IT productivity paradox [3]. Brynjolfsson and Yang argue that a positive connection exists, although it can be diminished by miss-measurement, lags, redistribution, or miss-management [4]. Factors that influence the relationship have been identified, which include the type of IS/IT, management practices, organisational structure, and

R. Zhang et al. (Eds.): ICEIS 2011, LNBIP 102, pp. 420–434, 2012.

the competitive and macro environment [5-7]. Furthermore several studies have shown a significant impact of information and its quality on the performance of an organization [8, 9].

So far, frameworks that attempt to explain the IS/IT business value relationship range from focusing either on IS/IT resources and capabilities, utilization/usage and behavioural aspects of IS/IT, impact on business process and decisions, or IS/IT performance measurements [2, 10-12]. Delone & McLean's models indicate the importance of information and information quality to understand the IS/IT business impact, but do not specify its role further [11, 13].

In this paper, we show how these frameworks could be combined to a coherent model that relates the discussed aspects. Moreover, we argue that a framework that aims to explain the business value of IS/IT has to be centred around information as a resource, since IT is the primary technology that is used to manage information [14]. In order to explicitly represent informational aspects, we propose therefore to extend current frameworks by adding an information perspective that puts a stronger emphasis on information quality and information-quality related risks. Objective of this work is to link previous work on the business impact of IS/IT with the extensive body of knowledge of the information quality discipline, e.g. [15-17], which, as far as we know, has been mostly ignored in the previous attempts by the IS community to explain the IS/IT business value. This new extended framework can serve as a bridge between existing frameworks by adding information management, information quality and information risks (caused by poor information quality) as the elements that link IS/IT resources with organizational performance. The results can hence be helpful to explain the actual business value of IS/IT from an information perspective and provide a reference point for further research.

The paper is structured as followed: First, we give an extensive review of related work that provides the components to build and explain the IS/IT business value chain, but also uncovers its limitations. Then, we propose and describe a new framework and show how it can be operationalized using material from four in-depth case studies previously conducted. Eventually, we discuss the framework regarding its validity, but also outline research directions for the future.

2 Literature Review

Gustafsson et al. have presented a comprehensive model that aims to explain the business impact of IS/IT, which has three generic elements: IT, organizational impact, and business value [18], as shown in Figure 1. Other related frameworks have been presented in the literature aiming to refine this generic model. We use this framework as orientation to relate other frameworks.

Fig. 1. A generic model of IS/IT business value [18]

We present related frameworks by classifying them into four categories depending on their primary focus: frameworks that focus on resources and IS/IT capabilities (section 2.1), frameworks that concentrate on IS/IT utilisation and behavioural aspects (sections 2.2), frameworks that centre on processes and decisions (section 2.3), frameworks that have a focus on IS/IT performance and impact measurement (section 2.4.).

2.1 Resources and IS/IT Capabilities

Nevo and Wade [10] suggest a path that links IS/IT assets to sustainable competitive advantage. Their model describes how IS/IT assets and organizational resources such as departments or teams are combined in order to create IS/IT-enabled resources, which can provide sustainable competitive advantage for a company. The model is based on systems theory and conducts a resource-based view on the strategic potential of an organizational resource. This potential reflects the ability of implementing strategies to improve firms' efficiency and effectiveness. It directly indicates a firm's sustainable competitive advantage. The work provides a path to explore the business value from IS/IT assets. In the presence of compatibility and integration effort, sustainable competitive advantage can be attained by IS/IT-enabled resources, which is a result of interactions between IS/IT assets and organizational resources. Moreover Melville et al. [2] conduct an extensive review on the literature that studies the relationship between IS/IT resources and organizational performance. Based on the review, they propose an integrative model of IS/IT business value that connects IS/IT resources (in form of technology and humans) and complementary organisational resources to organisational performance. They conclude that IS/IT resource is confirmed to be valuable and that it can provide various potential benefits such as quality improvement and cost reduction.

Relating IS/IT resources to IS/IT capability, Ravichandran and Lertwongsatien [19] consider IS/IT capability as the ability to deploy IS/IT resources. They further point out that IS/IT resources are the raw materials in the development of IS/IT capabilities. Their findings confirm that IS/IT resources are positively associated with IS/IT capabilities, which in turn affect Firm's Performance. Bharadwaj [20] conducts an empirical research to study the relationship between IS/IT capability and firm performance. The paper defines IS/IT capability as the "ability to mobilize and deploy IS/IT-based resources in combination or copresent with other resources and capabilities" (p.171). IS/IT-based resources can be classified into IS/IT infrastructure, human IS/IT skills, and IS/IT-enabled intangibles. Bharadwaj discusses the three resource-based views of IS/IT and develops the notion of IS/IT as an organizational capability. With an empirical test, this work concludes that increasing IS/IT capability can result in increasing organizational performance. It also indicates the importance of creating a firm-wide IS/IT capability rather than merely investing in IS/IT.

2.2 IS/IT Utilization

Apart from the resource-based view above, some researchers investigate the organizational impact from the view of IS/IT utilization by recognising the behavioural aspects and individual task performance. For instance, Goodhue and

Thompson [21] propose a model that focuses on association between information systems and individual performance, i.e. the task technology fitness (TTF). Their work emphasizes the fit between IS/IT and users' tasks and provides an evaluation approach to test whether IS/IT meets the user needs. They conclude their work by showing how IS/IT add value to individual performance and arguing the effects of task-technology fit and utilization on IS/IT success, diagnostics for IS/IT problems, and related user involvement. In addition, they also point out that data quality is one of the key constructs to identify the research gaps between systems capabilities and user needs. Furthermore, Goodhue [22] propose the user evaluation of TTF as a measure of IS/IT success. He defines TTF as "the extent that technology functionality matches task requirements and individual abilities" (p.1829). From this definition, three factors can be found relating to TTF, which are task, technology and individual. Thus users evaluate TTF based on the extent to which systems meet their needs and abilities. By using a survey, Goodhue provides both theoretical and empirical basis of user evaluations of TTF as a measure of IS/IT success. Connecting TTF to utilisation, Goodhue considers utilization as a performance indicator besides TTF. Furthermore, utilization can be affected by TTF. This means if a technology is useful, a higher TTF of the technology will result in a better performance.

Based on a systematic review, Delone and McLean [13] propose a comprehensive IS/IT success model that stresses the effects of use and user satisfaction on individual and organizational impact. System quality and information quality are considered as the influencing factors to use and user satisfaction. Importantly, this model brought the attention of information quality to the IS/IT research community and can be considered as one of the pioneering contributions in information quality research. Ten years later, Delone and McLean [11] proposed a revised model that directly focusses on the net benefit instead of organisational impact. As the net benefit can be considered as one form of business value, Delone and McLean' model is not only in line with the model from Gustafsson et al. [18], but also emphasizes the importance of information quality and service quality to business value.

2.3 Process and Decision Impact

A substantial contribution to understand IS/IT business value has been studies showing how IS/IT impacts on business processes and/or decision making. A business process can be defined "a specific ordering of work activities across time and place, with a beginning, an end, and clearly identified inputs and outputs: a structure for action" (p.5) [23]. Porter and Millar argue that activities that create value consist of a physical and an information-processing component and each value activity uses information [24]. Information technology has therefore a strategic significance in every company as it can transform the value chain of a product or service. In their integrative model of IS/IT business value, Mooney et al. propose a process framework for assessing the IS/IT business value [25]. They present a typology of processes that subdivides business processes into operational and management processes and argue that IS/IT creates business value as it has automational, informational, and transformational effects on the processes. Similarly, Melville et al. see business processes and business process performance as the key steps that link IS/IT resources and complementary organizational resources to organizational performance [2].

Other researchers gathered evidence that information quality has a considerable effect on decision quality. Keller and Staelin investigated the effects of quality and quantity of information on decision effectiveness of consumers [26]. Their results indicate that increasing information quantity impairs decision effectiveness and, in contrast, increasing information quality improves decision effectiveness. Jung et al. made a study to explore the impact of representational information quality, (which comprises the IQ dimensions interpretability, easy to understand, and concise and consistent representation), on decision effectiveness in a laboratory experiment with two tasks, which have different levels of complexity [27]. The results strongly support the hypothesis that a higher representational data quality improves the decision-making performance regarding problem-solving accuracy and time. Furthermore, Ge and Helfert's work [16] shows that the improvement of information quality in the intrinsic category (e.g. accuracy) and in the contextual category (e.g. completeness) of Wang and Strong's information quality framework enhance decision quality [15]. Overall, there is enough evidence to conclude that IS/IT has a significant impact on decision making and business processes.

2.4 IS/IT Performance and Impact Measurement

In addition to measuring IS/IT performance and its impact to organizations, organizational performance has always been of consideration to IS/IT researchers and practitioners, resulting in a plethora of performance related contributions. Earlier approaches focused, for example, on the economic value of information systems (e.g. [28]). They were more recently detailed, as outlined above, to frameworks for assigning the impact of IS/IT to businesses [2, 25]. Irani [12] provides a review of literature in the area of IS/IT evaluation. In addition to these IS/IT oriented frameworks, research related to performance measurement (PM) have resulted in an abundance of recommendations, frameworks and approaches for PM systems [29]. PM recommendations provide some indications for performance measures, whereas frameworks provide more information about the process or PM system. PM systems aim to provide a detailed PM process together with PM indicators.

However, in comparison to the variety of PM frameworks, there are only very few comprehensive PM systems in existence. As these contributions are mostly based on organizational best practice and experiences, the comparison of various performances measures between different organisations is difficult or not possible, and thus prevents thorough examination between IS/IT and organisational performance.

Folan and Browne [29] outline major PM recommendations, frameworks and systems. In relation to our work we selected four approaches as most indicative. Fitzgerald et al. [30] examine the result and determinants related to performance, and distinguish explicitly in their framework competitiveness and performance as results in contrast to the determinants such as quality, flexibility, resource utilization and innovation. The relationship between quality and performance was more recently examined by Angel and Chandra [31] and is seen as essential in order to understand the different elements influencing organizational performance. The balanced scorecard represents a prominent PM system as an approach to describe various views on organizational performance together with a management and measurement approach [32]. As described above, Mooney et al. [25] describe a process oriented framework for assessing the business value of IS/IT, and include the value perspective. Neely et al. [33] describe a structured methodology for the design of performance measurement system. Explicit performance indicators are provided for example in [34] and in practitioners oriented reference models such as SCOR [35].

2.5 Summary

Based on the literature review, the IS/IT business value can be explained using the four relationships:

1) IS/IT resources and complementary organizational resources influence IS/IT capabilities.
2) IS/IT capabilities further have an impact on IS/IT utilization.
3) IS/IT utilization affects business processes and decision-making.
4) These effects are visible in the short-term in the form of financials and other performance measures; in the long-term it has an impact on competitive advantage.

Table 1. IS/IT business value literature overview

Literature	Resources and IS/IT capabilities	IS/IT usage and behavioural aspects	Processes and decisions	IS/IT performance and impact measurement
Resources and IS/IT Capabilities				
Nevo and Wade [10]	●	○	◖	○
Melville et al. [2]	●	○	◖	◖
Ravichandran & Lertwongsatien [19]	●	○	○	◖
Bharadwaj [20]	●	○	○	◖
IS/IT Utilization				
Delone & McLean [13]*	○	●	◖	◖
Delone & McLean [11]*	○	●	◖	○
Goodhue and Thompson [21]	○	●	○	◖
Goodhue [22]	○	●	○	◖
Process and Decision Impact Frameworks				
Porter & Millar [24]	○	○	●	●
Mooney et al. [25]	○	○	●	●
Melville et al. [2]	●	○	●	◖
Keller & Staelin [26]*	○	○	●	○
Jung et al. [27]*	○	○	●	○
Ge & Helfert [16]*	○	○	●	○
IS/IT Performance & Impact Measurement				
Fitzgerald et al. [30]	○	○	○	◖
Kaplan & Norton [32]	○	○	○	●
Neely et al. [33]	○	○	○	◖
Medori and Steeple [34]	○	○	○	●

* Information quality is explicitly mentioned.
● fully covered ◖ partially covered ○ not covered

As shown in Table 1, existing work focuses only at one or two aspect of the IS/IT business value chain. The role of information as a resource is not explicitly mentioned in most of the frameworks. The reviewed literature has thus so far ignored or undervalued the role of information in the IS/IT business value chain. The functionality of IS/IT is limited to select, acquire, describe, organise, store, process, integrate, search, retrieve and manage information resources [36]. The input and output of IS/IT is therefore always information and can be compared to the physical in- and output in a traditional manufacturing system [37]. As a consequence, a framework that tries to explain the relationship between IS/IT and business value should be centred on information as a resource and describe how IS/IT is interlinked to information management, quality, and risks. We therefore propose a new IS/IT business value framework that integrates the current work on resources and IS/IT capabilities, IS/IT utilization, process and decision impact, and performance and impact measurement and adds an information oriented perspective.

3 An Information Oriented Framework

Figure 2 shows a framework that integrates the components from (a) to (d) in Table 1 and its underlying relationships. Moreover, related concepts are connected to each component in the figure.

The inventor of the resource-based view of the firm has defined resources as "those (tangible and intangible) assets which are tied semi-permanently to the firm" (p. 172) [38]. IS/IT resources comprise therefore everything from hard- and software, IS/IT personnel and managers, to technological knowledge that is available in the given organisation. Complementary organisational resources are all other resources in the company that interplay with the IS/IT resources. In addition, information resources, which have been not mentioned in previous frameworks, are an important type of resource that should be considered in particular. Information resources are generated and modified in the process of utilization of IS/IT and therefore create an enforcing feedback loop, enabling the continuous enhancement of IS/IT capabilities.

Capabilities can be viewed as superior business processes [39]. All resources taken together need to be coordinated in order to form IS/IT capabilities. The coordination of the resources itself requires special capabilities, i.e. coordination capabilities, which again take use of a part of the defined resources, e.g. management personnel, information resources [40]. Moreover, Mills et al. suggest that capabilities can be coordinated in order to get higher level capabilities. Coordinating all IS/IT capabilities can therefore be seen as a higher level capability, i.e. the information manufacturing or information management capability. The maturity of the IS/IT capabilities can be measured using an information management maturity assessment model like, for instance, IQM-CMM [41]. Altogether, the IS/IT capabilities have a major influence on the fitness for use of information, i.e. information quality [15], which can be measured with various assessment methods when IS/IT is utilized to access information in a business process or for decision making.

For instance, if a server that contains customer data has constantly downtimes, it will affect the accessibility of the customer data, which is one of the frequently used information quality dimensions (e.g. [15]). If the customer data is used, for example, by an online shop to send out products to the customers, the unavailability of the customer data can have a major impact on some of the business processes that are related to logistics. These information-quality related risks, which are referred as 'information risks' in the following, eventually have an influence on the financial performance and the competitiveness of an organisation, or other targets depending on the mission and goals of the particular organisation [8]. Measures can be both financial and non financial and are strongly context-dependent.

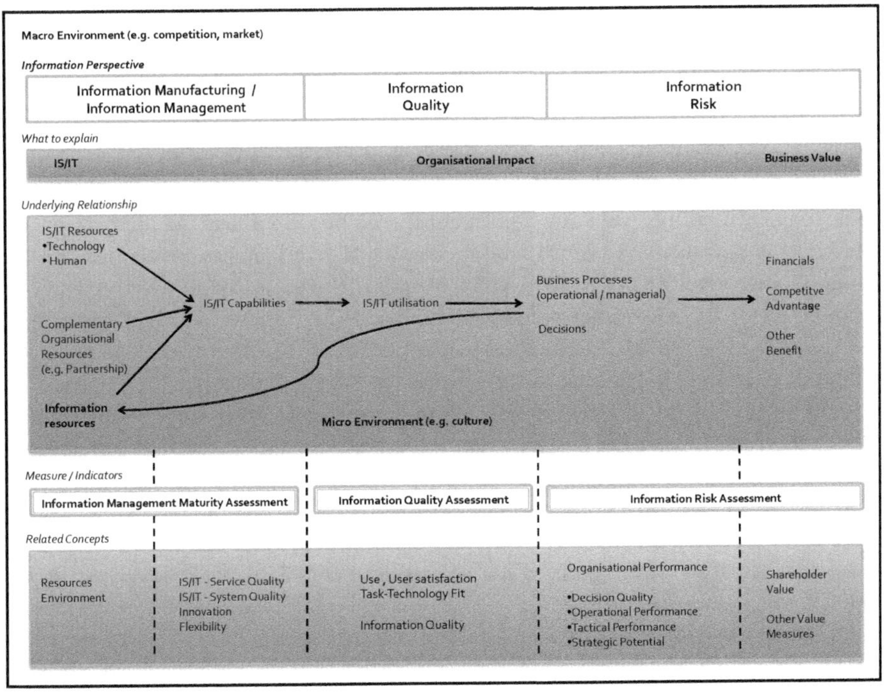

Fig. 2. An integrated framework for IS/IT business value from an information perspective

The entire IS/IT business value chain takes place in (1) a macro environment, which is strongly dependent on a number of external factors like industry, market situation, competition, etc., and in (2) a micro environment, which summarizes the soft factors within an organisation that are difficult to change in the short-term, e.g. the company culture and employee satisfaction.

In summary, information is manufactured and managed with the help of IS/IT capabilities that use a variety of IS/IT resources, complementary organisational resources, and already existing information resources. The quality of the resulting information products/resources is defined in the context of its use, i.e. depending on the IS/IT utilization. If information quality is poor, the IS/IT utilization cannot meet its purpose and might have a negative influence on business processes, decision making and eventually on organisational performance. These effects might be even observable in highly aggregated measures like, for instance, changes of the share prices of a company in the stock market.

4 Operationalization of the Framework

Each component in the information-oriented framework can be measured by using existing methods. The assessment of each component in our model is important to ensure usability and to validate the information-oriented model. In the next sections, we hence describe the assessment approaches in further detail and show how the framework can be operationalized by applying the assessment approaches in four independent case studies.

4.1 Information Management Maturity Assessment

This work stream is mostly based on the capability maturity models proposed in the software engineering discipline [42], which have their roots in Crosby's maturity model introduced in the quality management area [43]. A maturity model is used to assess capabilities by evaluating the maturity of processes and to identify priority areas for improvement. A typical model consists of five maturity levels: initial (level 1), repeatable (level 2), defined (level 3), managed (level 4), and optimizing (level 5), although levels are sometimes named differently. Within these models, each maturity level is based on a comprehensive set of criteria of information management comprising concept, function, behavioural aspects, requirements to be met, and measurement [42]. In order to assess maturity, for each level and criteria data are collected for analysis, reflection and synthesis. Measurement of both quantitative and qualitative factors is used that includes: a defined process for building the outcomes from each level to monitor progress, and to take corrective actions at each level when necessary. Increased maturity evolves then, through a progression of levels or stages with transformations over time. Both, the assessment of maturity levels as well as understanding the transformation to higher maturity levels are important to increase maturity of an organisation. An example of a maturity model for IS/IT Management is the IT-Capability Maturity Framework (IT-CMF) [44]. Based on capabilities and categories along 32 critical processes, this framework is designed as a systematic framework that enables senior chief executives to interrogate, understand and improve an organisation's maturity, ensuring realisation of IS/IT capabilities and optimal delivery of business value from IS/IT investments. Moreover, information quality management maturity frameworks specifically focus on evaluating capabilities for information quality management [17, 41]. Ryu et al. [45] show in an empirical study with 119 participants that a company that moves up in the information quality management maturity ladder is likely to improve information quality.

4.2 Information Quality Assessment

Information quality assessments can be classified into objective and subjective assessment [46]. Objective information quality assessments reveal information quality problems in the database whilst subjective information quality assessments reflect the needs and experiences of data consumers. Objective information quality assessment is used to measure the extent to which information conforms to quality specifications and references. This type of assessment accords with the data perspective and focuses on the quality of the data in the database. Savchenko [47], for example, developed item frequency rules and regular expression patterns to facilitate automated intrinsic information quality assessment. Furthermore, objective information quality assessment can also follow an ontological perspective and focuses on information quality deficiencies that can take place during the system design and data production, for instance, Wand and Wang [48] identified data mapping deficiencies between the real world state and information system representation. Subjective information quality assessment is used to measure the extent to which information is fit for use for information consumers [46]. Information consumers evaluate the quality of information according to their demands and expectations. Subjective information quality assessment follows the user perspective and focuses on any discrepancy between the current quality of information and the user's expectation. Woodall and Parlikad have created a hybrid approach that enables to combine existing IQ assessment methodologies according to the requirements of an organisation [49].

4.3 Information Risk Assessment

Many studies have shown that information quality can have a negative impact on organizational performance [8, 9]. These information risks that arise from poor information quality need to be assessed and managed. So far, there are only a handful approaches to assess the business impact of information quality and its risk. Most approaches are part of an overall methodology for information quality assessment and improvement (e.g. [17, 50]). Loshin's COLDQ methodology [50] is an approach that connects an information quality problem with its position in the information chain, the activities in which information is used and it's cost and impact in a Data Quality Score Card. McGilvray [51] has proposed eight different techniques for information quality business impact assessment that differ in their degree of complexity and required effort and which can be used and combined freely. Borek et al. [52] present a process for Total Information Risk Management (TIRM) that enables the assessment and treatment of risks that arise from information resources and their quality. The TIRM process, thus, takes the probabilistic nature of information risks into account.

4.4 Operationalization in Case Studies

We have shown that the information oriented framework presented in this paper can be operationalized using three core elements: (1) information management maturity assessment, (2) information quality assessment and (3) information risk assessment. We have applied the framework by executing the all three assessments in four case studies in medium-sized to large production and energy companies. We have used Baškarada's model for the assessment of maturity [41], a subjective questionnaire using a qualitative scale for information quality assessment [46] and information risk assessment based on the process for Total Information Risk Management [52]. The assessments have focused on different core processes of the particular organization, as for example, sales & marketing, maintenance, customer service, production, purchasing, planning, logistics etc. The results from the information management assessment are shown in Table 2. The following results are not generalizable as they come from qualitative observation in the in-depth case studies (and are not quantitative results).

Table 2. Information Management Maturity Results

Case Study	Information Management Maturity Results
1	Level 4 (69%)
2	Level 2 (56%)
3	Level 2 (46%)
4	Level 2 (56%)

Table 3. Examples of information quality problems and related information risks

Information Quality Problem	Information Risk	Impact on Business Objectives
The selection decision is sometimes based on inaccurate information about physical asset, which comes from the vendors.	Equipment design and vendor are selected sub-optimally or simply wrong	Investment costs, Equipment availability, Environmental incident frequency
There is no unified terminology for materials, which makes it hard to find out which material is actually used. Moreover, the ERP system does not allow to enter details about materials (incomplete and inaccessible information).	It becomes very difficult and time consuming to find a cheaper supplier for a material.	Production costs
Maintenance engineers find it often hard to use the system. System is not easy to use and the user interfaces are not standardized (information accessibility).	Maintenance engineers waste time using the system or even stop using it.	Maintenance costs, Failure rate per asset, Product quality
It is difficult to find information in the system. It can take some time or entry cannot be found at all if the wrong search keywords are entered (information accessibility).	When the expert for a specific manufacturing IT system is not available, it takes longer to mitigate an incident	Maintenance costs, Failure rate per asset, Lost time incident frequency
Pricing of materials sometimes fall into the hands of the customer (information security).	Customer is unhappy about pricing.	Customer satisfaction
People do not follow procedures and do not update notes regularly or forget to create a note, which leads to lack of detail concerning the job (incomplete information).	Changes to job are not implemented, which leads to lowered quality of work and more resources spent.	Quality of service Customer satisfaction Service costs

However, we perceived that there had been some tendency in our case studies that companies with a higher level of information management maturity had a lower amount of IS/IT related information quality problems and fewer information risks resulting from IS/IT. Some less surprising observations were that that we could see some positive correlations between the size of the company, the level of maturity and the financial impact of information risks, which can be simply explained: Larger companies spend more money to have more sophisticated management processes. But equally, when there is more at stake, there is also more to loose. Furthermore, we could clearly observe in over a hundred of cases in the four in-depth case studies that information quality problems caused information risks that had a significant impact on one or more business objectives in the organisations. Some examples are presented in Table 3.

5 Discussion

In the above section we proposed a framework for IS/IT business value. The framework is developed based on reviewing relevant literature. In the following, we discuss its validity based on the following four questions: (1) Is the model complete and accurate? Is there a linkage missing? (2) Which relationships in the model have a large amount of empirical evidence, and where is evidence lacking? (3) Which research methods have been used and what are their limitations? (4) How does the proposed model differ from other models?.

This paper has reviewed a part of the existing literature and uses the concepts and conclusions from the literature to build the new model. There are no major contradictions that might indicate inaccuracy in the model. Furthermore, the review has taken previous literature reviews into account. Although specific terms might have not been mentioned, major concepts and relationships from the literature in the IS/IT business value chain should be therefore covered. The relationship between IS/IT capabilities and IS/IT utilization (e.g. [21, 22]) and the relationship between information use and decision performance (e.g. [26, 27]) have been demonstrated in major studies. It is further clear that business process performance and decision performance have an impact on organisational performance, which can be reflected by financial performance and shareholder value (e.g. [23]). However, the creation of IS/IT capabilities from IS/IT and complementary organisational resources and information resources is an underexplored area. Similarly, the impact of IS/IT utilisation on business processes needs to be further investigated. Finally, a problem with research that tries to link a concept to a performance measurement is that performance is very context-dependent and that there are different layers of performance, e.g. business process performance, financial performance, shareholder value etc. Additionally, many external variables can influence performance like, for example, country characteristics, industry characteristics and trading partner resources. The variety of approaches proposed (and used) is therefore nearly infinite. In the literature so far, predominant research methods have been conceptual work and literature reviews, case study research, experimental research and survey research. A more explorative qualitative research method like design science [53] would be suitable to get more in-depth insights into the investigated relationships. Moreover, a better combination of technical computer science and IS/IT management social science research might provide better results. The framework proposed in this paper has a higher granularity and links performance closer to IS/IT by using an information perspective, integrating the body of knowledge from the IS/IT and the information quality discipline. It can provide a useful research framework for researchers, who can focus on different sections of the whole model.

6 Concluding Remarks

The question if and how IT and IS enhances organisational performance has been a major point of focus in the IS communities in the last decades. Connected to this discussion has been the IS/IT business value chain that aims to explain the different steps and relationships that lead from IS/IT resources to business value. We have proposed an integrated framework for IS/IT business value and discussed its validity. Reviewing prominent frameworks one key observation demonstrated the lack of information focus in these frameworks. The proposed framework aims to address this limitation, and includes explicitly an information lens to the IS/IT-Business value discussion. This will help, so we believe, researchers to explain some of the important observations and give practitioners indications to improve the IS/IT capabilities. As indicated in the discussion, rather than replacing existing frameworks, it complements existing approaches. Our framework can thus bridge the often isolated research works addressing the complex relationship between IS/IT and business value. We discussed assessment for information management, information quality and information risks in this context and showed how the framework can be operationalized using materials from four different in-depth case studies in the industry. In future research, the relationships between information and the IS/IT business value chain need to be examined in further detail in empirical settings.

Acknowledgements. This research has been partly funded by EPSRC project "Information Quality in Asset Management", reference number EP/G038171/1.

References

1. Eastwood, G.: The Technology Investment and Outsourcing Outlook - Spend forecasts by vertical market. Business Insights Ltd. (2008)
2. Melville, N., Kraemer, K., Gurbaxani, V.: Review: Information technology and organizational performance: An integrative model of IT business value. MIS Quarterly, 283–322 (2004)
3. Brynjolfsson, E.: The productivity paradox of information technology. Communications of the ACM 36, 77 (1993)
4. Brynjolfsson, E., Yang, S.: Information Technology and Productivity: A Review of the Literature. Advances in Computers 43, 179–214 (1996)
5. Brynjolfsson, E., Hitt, L.M., Yang, S.: Intangible assets: Computers and organizational capital. Brookings Papers on Economic Activity, 137–181 (2002)
6. Cooper, B.L., Watson, H.J., Wixom, B.H., Goodhue, D.L.: Data warehousing supports corporate strategy at First American Corporation. Mis Quarterly 24, 547–567 (2000)
7. Dewan, S., Kraemer, K.L.: Information technology and productivity: evidence from country-level data. Management Science, 548–562 (2000)
8. Redman, T.C.: The impact of poor data quality on the typical enterprise. Communications of the ACM 41, 79–82 (1998)
9. Slone, J.P.: Information quality strategy: An empirical investigation of the relationship between information quality improvements and organizational outcomes (2006)
10. Nevo, S., Wade, M.R.: The Formation and Value of IT-Enabled Resources: Antecedents and Consequences of Synergistic Relationships. MIS Quarterly 34, 163–183 (2010)

11. Delone, W.H., McLean, E.R.: The DeLone and McLean model of information systems success: A ten-year update. Journal of Management Information Systems 19, 9–30 (2003)
12. Irani, Z.: Information systems evaluation: navigating through the problem domain. Information & Management 40, 11–24 (2002)
13. DeLone, W.H., McLean, E.R.: Information systems success: the quest for the dependent variable. Information Systems Research 3, 60–95 (1992)
14. Eaton, J., Smithers, J., Curran, S.: This is IT: A Manager's Guide to Information Technology. Philip Allan (1988)
15. Wang, R.Y., Strong, D.M.: Beyond accuracy: What data quality means to data consumers. Journal of Management Information Systems 12, 33 (1996)
16. Ge, M., Helfert, M.: Effects of information quality on inventory management. International Journal of Information Quality 2, 177–191 (2008)
17. English, L.P.: Improving data warehouse and business information quality: methods for reducing costs and increasing profits. John Wiley & Sons (1999)
18. Gustafsson, P., Franke, U., Höök, D., Johnson, P.: Quantifying IT impacts on organizational structure and business value with Extended Influence Diagrams. The Practice of Enterprise Modeling, 138–152 (2009)
19. Ravichandran, T., Lertwongsatien, C.: Effect of information systems resources and capabilities on firm performance: A resource-based perspective. Journal of Management Information Systems 21, 237–276 (2005)
20. Bharadwaj, A.S.: A resource-based perspective on information technology capability and firm performance: an empirical investigation. Mis Quarterly 24, 169–196 (2000)
21. Goodhue, D.L., Thompson, R.L.: Task-technology fit and individual performance. Mis Quarterly 19, 213–236 (1995)
22. Goodhue, D.L.: Understanding user evaluations of information systems. Management Science, 1827–1844 (1995)
23. Davenport, T.H.: Process innovation: reengineering work through information technology. Harvard Business Press (1993)
24. Porter, M.E., Millar, V.: How information gives you competitive advantage. Harvard Business Review 63, 149–160 (1985)
25. Mooney, J.G., Gurbaxani, V., Kraemer, K.L.: A process oriented framework for assessing the business value of information technology. ACM SIGMIS Database 27, 68–81 (1996)
26. Keller, K.L., Staelin, R.: Effects of Quality and Quantity of Information on Decision Effectiveness. The Journal of Consumer Research 14, 200–213 (1987)
27. Jung, W., Olfman, L., Ryan, T., Park, Y.T.: An Experimental Study of the Effects of Representational Data Quality on Decision Performance. In: AMCIS 2005 Proceedings, p. 298 (2005)
28. Van Wegen, B., De Hoog, R.: Measuring the economic value of information systems. Journal of Information Technology 11, 247–260 (1996)
29. Folan, P., Browne, J.: A review of performance measurement: Towards performance management. Computers in Industry 56, 663–680 (2005)
30. Fitzgerald, L., Johnston, R., Brignall, S.: Performance measurement in service businesses (1991)
31. Angel, L.C., Chandra, M.J.: Performance implications of investments in continuous quality improvement. International Journal of Operations & Production Management 21, 108–125 (2001)
32. Kaplan, R.S., Norton, D.P.: The balanced scorecard–measures that drive performance. Harvard Business Review 70, 71–79 (1992)

33. Neely, A., Mills, J., Platts, K., Richards, H., Gregory, M., Bourne, M., Kennerley, M.: Performance measurement system design: developing and testing a process-based approach. International Journal of Operations and Production Management 20, 1119–1145 (2000)
34. Medori, D., Steeple, D.: A framework for auditing and enhancing performance measurement systems. International Journal of Operations & Production Management 20, 520–533 (2000)
35. Huan, S.H., Sheoran, S.K., Wang, G.: A review and analysis of supply chain operations reference (SCOR) model. Supply Chain Management: An International Journal 9, 23–29 (2004)
36. Fattahi, R., Afshar, E.: Added value of information and information systems: a conceptual approach. Library Review 55, 132–147 (2006)
37. Ballou, D., Wang, R., Pazer, H., Kumar, G.: Modeling information manufacturing systems to determine information product quality. Management Science 44, 462–484 (1998)
38. Wemerfelt, B.: A resource-based view of the firm. Strategic Management Journal 5, 171–180 (1984)
39. Stalk, G., Evans, P., Shulman, L.E.: Competing on capabilities: The new rules of corporate strategy. Harvard Business Review, 57–69 (1992)
40. Mills, J., Platts, K., Bourne, M.: Competence and resource architectures. International Journal of Operations & Production Management 23, 977–994 (2003)
41. Baskarada, S.: IQM-CMM: Information Quality Management Capability Maturity Model (2008)
42. Humphrey, W.S.: Characterizing the software process: a maturity framework. IEEE Software 5, 73–79 (1988)
43. Crosby, P.B.: Quality is free. McGraw-Hill (1979)
44. Curley, M.: Introducing an IT Capability Maturity Framework. Enterprise Information Systems, 63–78 (2008)
45. Ryu, K.S., Park, J.S., Park, J.H.: A data quality management maturity model. ETRI Journal 28, 191–204 (2006)
46. Pipino, L.L., Lee, Y.W., Wang, R.Y.: Data quality assessment. Communications of the ACM 45, 211–218 (2002)
47. Savchenko, S.: Automating objective data quality assessment. In: Eppler, M., Helfert, M., Pipino, L., Segev, A. (eds.) Proceedings of the 8th International Conference on Information Quality. MIT, Cambridge (2003)
48. Wand, Y., Wang, R.Y.: Anchoring data quality dimensions in ontological foundations. Communications of the ACM 39, 95 (1996)
49. Woodall, P., Parlikad, A.K.N.: A hybrid approach to assessing data quality. In: Proceedings of the 15th International Conference on Information Quality (ICIQ 2010), Little Rock, AR, USA (2010)
50. Loshin, D.: Enterprise knowledge management: The data quality approach. Morgan Kaufmann (2001)
51. McGilvray, D.: Executing Data Quality Projects: Ten Steps to Quality Data and Trusted Information. Morgan Kaufmann (2008)
52. Borek, A., Woodall, P., Parlikad, A.K.: A Risk Management Approach to Improving Information Quality for Operational and Strategic Management. In: Proceedings of the 18th EUROMA Conference: Exploring Interfaces, Cambridge, UK (2011)
53. Hevner, A.R., March, S.T., Park, J., Ram, S.: Design science in information systems research. MIS Quarterly 28, 75–105 (2004)

Author Index